THE SHAPING OF AMERICA

THE SHAPING OF AMERICA

THE
SHAPING
OF
AMERICA

A GEOGRAPHICAL
PERSPECTIVE
ON 500 YEARS
OF HISTORY

Volume 4
Global America
1915–2000

D. W. MEINIG

Yale University Press
New Haven and London

Set in Goudy Old Style type by The Composing Room of Michigan, Inc. Printed in the United States of America by Vail-Ballou Press.

The Library of Congress has catalogued the hardcover edition as follows:
[Revised for vol. 4]

Meinig, D. W. (Donald William), 1924–
    The shaping of America
    Includes indexes
    Includes bibliographies
        Contents: v. 1. Atlantic America, 1492–1800.—v. 2. Continental America, 1800–1867.—v. 3. Transcontinental America, 1850–1915. v. 4. Global America, 1915–2000.
    1. United States—History. 2. United States—Historical geography.
E178.M57   1986   973   85-17962
ISBN 0-300-03548-9 (v. 1 : cloth)
        0-300-03882-8 (v. 1 : paper)
        0-300-05658-3 (v. 2 : cloth)
        0-300-06290-7 (v. 2. : paper)
        0-300-07592-8 (v. 3 : cloth)
        0-300-08290-8 (v. 3 : paper)
        0-300-10432-4 (v. 4 : cloth)

A catalogue record for this book is available from the British Library.

ISBN-13: 978-0-300-11528-4 (v. 4: pbk)
ISBN-10: 0-300-11528-8 (v. 4: pbk)

10 9 8 7 6 5 4 3 2 1

for
Lee

Think of the past as space expanding infinitely beyond our vision. . . . Then we choose a prospect. The higher it is, the wider and hazier our view. Now we map what we see, marking some features, ignoring others, altering an unknown territory . . . into a finite collection of landmarks made meaningful through their connections. History is not the past, but a map of the past drawn from a particular point of view to be useful to the modern traveler.

Henry Glassie

CONTENTS

PART THREE
MISSION:
ASSERTIONS AND IMPOSITIONS

ILLUSTRATIONS

PREFACE

Like each volume in this series, *Global America* stands on its own as a discrete, co-herent account of selected themes, in this case of a revolutionary era beginning with the emergence of the automobile age and geopolitical participation in a world war, and concluding with the high-tech, single superpower so broadly involved with the world at the end of the twentieth century. Of course it can be more fully appreciated and assessed as the concluding phase of this special perspective on 500 years of the Euro-American creation and changing geographical formation and character of the United States.

Given the date of publication I want to make clear that this half-millennium coverage ends in the 1990s. Nearly all of Parts One and Two were written before the end of the century, with no attempt to have each of the many topics conclude on the same year; in such a long perspective the most recent details are likely the least important. Population figures from the 2000 census were incorporated as they became available. More important, I wish to emphasize that the whole character and tone of Part Three had been set long before the attacks of 9–11–01. I have lived through most of the era under study and have been teaching, learning, and re-flecting upon the United States, its relations with its neighbors, and recurrent wider involvements for a long time, and none of my commentary on America and the World has been shaped by twenty-first-century events (I write this on the day the United States invaded Iraq)—and no attempt is made to project the shape of the future.

In the Preface of *Atlantic America* I noted that although I believed that geogra-phy and history, by their very nature, were analogous, complementary, and interde-pendent fields there had as yet been little evidence of significant interaction and convergence between them in common American practice. Although a subse-quent exhaustive bibliographic search has turned up a plethora of individual stud-ies that might be assigned to these borderlands (Conzen, Rumney, and Wynn), that generalization still holds true. Geography, like history, provides strategies for thinking about large and complex topics, and *The Shaping of America* offers the first detailed panoramic geographic view and assessment across the entire span of space and time relevant to the development of the United States. I work alone, and my selective focus is synthetic and idiosyncratic, as any such interpretation must be. It is not a celebration of American virtues and achievements, nor is it a polemic against American vices and failures. It is the distillation set forth as thoughtfully and lucidly as I can of a professional lifetime immersion in study and in the field of the geography and history of this country.

Beyond all parochial academic considerations much of my writing has been motivated by the search for better self-understanding of my own locales and regions, of how they came to have the shape and character I could see all around me. I began in home districts and worked outward to larger areas, and all the while I have hoped to share something of my historical geographic perceptions with other residents of those areas. I am not so brazen or naive as to suggest that I have influenced very many, but letters and reports of one kind or another over many years assure me that I have helped some in just such ways in the Columbia Interior, Mormon Country, Texas, and the Southwest (as well as in South Australia). Obviously few people will read a four-volume set on anything, but I already know that some who have read only parts of it have come to understand America in fresh ways—just as I have by writing it.

D. W. Meinig
Syracuse, New York

ACKNOWLEDGMENTS

The completion of this long project brings even more forcefully to mind how very fortunate I have been in having the unstinted support of two institutions critical to it all: Yale University Press and Syracuse University.

Works on this scale tend to take on a life of their own, expanding beyond original proposals, defeating initial schedules, and sometimes delaying completion beyond the official presence of primary sponsors. Such has been the case at Yale, where before I was able to complete the manuscript of this final volume, my editor, Judy Metro, left to become editor-in-chief at the National Gallery of Art, and John Ryden, director of Yale University Press, retired. I am deeply indebted to them both. Judy Metro accepted this project on the basis of a short proposal, responded to the first manuscript with enthusiasm, and remained strongly committed to it; John Ryden endorsed a multivolume work, accepted its expansion from three books to four, and provided extra money for illustrations. I was fortunate to have Assistant Editor Michelle Komie take over and see *Global America* into print, to have Nancy Ovedovitz imprint her design upon all four volumes, and again to have Laura Jones Dooley's appreciative copy-editorial touch upon every word of this manuscript. My thanks to all at Yale whose expertise and care have produced these handsome books.

At Syracuse University administrators at every level have been supportive in many ways over many years. Especially—perhaps decisively—important was the creation midway through this project by Robert G. Jensen, then chairman of the Geography Department, and John L. Palmer, dean of the Maxwell School, of a Maxwell Research Professorship to allow me to devote full time to its completion. All research, manuscript preparation, and most of the cartographic and other illustration expense for this final volume has been fully covered by that generous appointment. Once again, Kay Steinmetz not only has translated my handwriting into print but has filtered every word and sentence through her keen editorial eye to good effect, and has provided indispensable help with the index. I was fortunate that although Michael Kirchoff took early retirement from the Syracuse University Cartographic Laboratory he continued to translate my often messy sketches into clear, attractive maps from his new home in Tennessee. Joseph W. Stoll, his successor as manager of the laboratory, has also been a joy to work with, eagerly applying his talents to the search for and preparation of all other illustrations.

In addition to those acknowledged in the captions, the following persons also helped in the search for illustrations or information related to their use: Dawn L. Aiu, San Jose Redevelopment Agency; Scott W. Anderson, SUNY Cortland; Samuel Elliott, Charles E. Young Research Library, UCLA; Christopher Miller, University of Iowa Libraries Map Collection; Jovanka R. Ristic, The American Geographical Collection at the University of Wisconsin–Milwaukee Library; Seymour Sacks, emeritus professor of economics, Syracuse University; Richard H. Smith, Cartographic and Architectural Branch, National Archives; LCDR Lee Meinig Tate, USN, Ret.; Richard F. Weingroff, Federal Highway Administration; Geoffrey A. White, Hawaii State Archives; Hank Zalatel, librarian, Iowa Department of Transportation.

I have looked forward to the opportunity occasioned by the conclusion of this more-than-twenty-year project to recognize a special debt to a fellow historical geographer. Cole Harris is considerably younger in years, but he has long been well ahead of me in the ability to express with depth and clarity the philosophies, relations, modes, and values of our common field. Furthermore, he has done so in both definitional and substantive terms; his recent studies of his native British Columbia are superb examples of a highly skilled, sensitive, humane geographer at work. Although I have expressed my appreciation for his succession of penetrating, contextual commentaries, public and private, on *The Shaping of America*, he cannot really know just how much his support has meant to me over these many years.

Like all the others, this book is dedicated with deepest thanks to the one who has lived it with me day by day—and shared a life for a great many other days as well.

PART ONE
TECHNOLOGY: MOBILIZATION AND ACCELERATION

Changes within the transportation system have engendered a mobility of the population that is unprecedented. . . . There has been a constant extension of the range of mobility. . . . Popular conceptions of speed and distance have been completely revised. . . . The tempo of life is speeded. . . . An interconnecting, interconnected web of communication has been woven about the individual. . . . The web has developed largely without plan or aim. The integration has been in consequence of competitive forces, not social desirability.

Recent Social Trends in the United States, Report of the President's Research Committee, 1933

Prologue

Movement has long been central to characterizations of the American scene and society: "a people in motion," "a civilization on wheels," "Moving. Always moving." The term of course has many connotations and our present concern is rather narrow, a focus not directly on people, but on some of the instruments and networks that actually channel movement and communication between places, on various ligatures that bind together the American space. Herein that space has been confined to the forty-eight contiguous states, leaving connections with outlying areas, domestic as well as foreign, for later consideration.

We begin with that most radical and engaging of tools, the automobile, and follow through a remarkable set of technologies that diversified and accelerated the circulation of people and goods, of energy, information, and messages, until we reach those most amazing and mysterious of tools, the computer and the Internet.

All of these implements are utterly familiar and ordinary at the end of the twentieth century, but each has its particular history and geography, and the formation of this elaborating national infrastructure bears careful study if we are to make sense of the shaping of America in our time.

1. Mobilization: The Automotive Revolution

ROADS TO RUN ON

NATIONAL HIGHWAYS VS PANAMA CANAL. You own the second. Do you want to own the first? They cost the same. How many rural people does the second serve? The first will serve 99 per cent of our people! This includes 98.3 per cent of our rural (country) population.

So proclaimed the heading on a 1915 map of the United States "showing one hundred thousand miles" of roads proposed by the National Highways Association. Just how the association figured the cost to be the same is not clear. It had taken ten years to build the canal; we now know that it would take considerably longer to build such a highway system, but 1915 was a pivotal moment in our national transportation history because the completion of the one great task was followed by the initiation of the other even greater one.

During the previous two years congressional hearings had been held, the status of roads and highway systems had been collected from the states and from major foreign countries (with embarrassing results: "roads in the United States are said to be the worst of any civilized country in the world"), the many bills introduced had been narrowed to a single one in each house, and these were resolved into "Federal Aid in the Construction of Rural Post Roads," which became law in 1916.

Pressures for national action had been mounting for twenty years. Since 1895, when the first American automobiles were offered for sale and a new magazine, *The Horseless Age*, had declared the motor vehicle "already established" in "the necessary sequence of methods of locomotion" ("the growing needs of civilization demand it, the public believe in it"), exuberant American inventiveness had rapidly improved the design and quality of vehicles, hundreds of companies had entered the field (most survived only briefly), and demands for their products had constantly outrun the supply. In 1914 annual production had passed half a million units (surpassing for the first time the output of wagons and carriages) and two years later was more than a million and a half. By that time American cities were rapidly approaching the horseless age. There had been strong public support for such a change ("a horseless city" would be a "flyless city . . . a clean, quiet, odorless city"), and taxis, buses, delivery trucks, motorized fire engines, and ambulances were now regarded as essential, thereby setting a standard for smaller centers as well: "The motor vehicle had definitely been accepted as an integral part of American life."

Yet beyond the solid streets of city and suburb, the automobile, though well known and eagerly desired, was a severely limited vehicle, and a motor truck was rarely to be seen. There were few country roads of reliable quality, as yet only bare semblances of statewide networks, and in spite of ever-stronger campaigns by various interests (such as the National Highways Association) no formal program whatever for a national system. Thus, as a 1915 government report concluded: "the problem of good roads is not surpassed in importance by any other subject now before the American people."

Why this should have been so was itself peculiarly American. The methods of building good roads were well known among engineers, new industrial tools (rock crushers, steam shovels, steamrollers, specialized graders) had been available for some years, there were plenty of examples in and around urban areas, and several European countries already had extensive and in some cases highly regarded national highway systems (most notably France). The scale of the task was of course far greater in the United States, but Americans had never faltered in the face of such challenges (hence the telling example of the Panama Canal).

One factor was the presence of a comprehensive, high-capacity transportation system fully in place. In every city and town and thousands of villages the depot was the focal point of commerce. Therefore, as a powerful member of Congress put it: "for practical purposes, the railway station is the terminus of roads; . . . neither freight nor passengers will ever be carried long distances over roads as cheaply as they could be over railways; . . . the proper function of roads is . . . to make easy communication between the farms on one hand and the towns and railway stations on the other." Not everyone agreed with that, of course, but even so limited a role for roads posed practical and legal problems.

For nearly a century, following an early flurry of turnpikes (toll roads), public highways had been dependent on local poll or property taxes, which in rural areas were commonly met by contributions of labor: by small groups of neighbors (able-bodied males) working a few days a year on their local roads. Use of convicts was also common practice in many counties and states. "This 'corvée,' or forced-labor system," this "remnant of feudalism" that "has led our people to look upon road-building as a nuisance," was becoming obviously inadequate even before much impact of the automobile was apparent. With the new craze of bicycling in the 1890s the League of American Wheelmen began a loud campaign for radical improvement, and this was readily supported and soon surpassed by various automobile interests. Good Roads movements sprouted up, national associations were formed, congresses held, and in cooperation with several railroads Good Roads Trains, moving from town to town featuring road-making equipment, methods, and lectures from experts, became popular attractions. Rural Free Delivery, initiated by the Post Office experimentally in the 1890s and rapidly expanded in the new century, was strongly supported by the farm population and directed attention to the need for all-weather roads even for the horse-drawn postal carriage: "Today, in the rich state of Iowa," said a prominent highway advocate in 1916, "not a wheel turns outside the paved streets of her cities during or sometime after the frequent heavy rains. Every farm is isolated. Social intercourse ceases. School attendance impossible. Transportation is at a standstill" (fig. 1).

Yet resistance to higher taxes remained strong and was magnified when local people thought they might have to pay for roads serving traffic that was merely passing through their district—and especially when that traffic seemed to be rich

1. The "Good Roads" Imperative.
A Model T on a main highway in central Iowa, c. 1919, the home territory of Thomas H. MacDonald, first head of the federal Bureau of Public Roads. (Courtesy Iowa Department of Transportation)

tourists enjoying their expensive machines. New Jersey and Massachusetts were the first states to break from old patterns and form highway departments and provide state aid directly for road construction (and Harvard began the first program in highway engineering); others, primarily in the Northeast, soon followed. Initially such funds were spent on short demonstration roads to show county officials what a good road was and how to build one. Sharing the costs of important county roads became a common practice, but the more important step was the construction of major highways solely at state expense, under the supervision of state engineers. Thus in many states (but far from all—most Southern states remained strongly county and rural centered) a system of improved highways was slowly and sporadically taking shape.

The national government was actually formally involved throughout this new era of concern, but in a typically hesitant, carefully circumscribed way. In 1893 an Office of Road Inquiry (ORI) was established to conduct investigations and disseminate knowledge about road construction. Placed in the Department of Agriculture, its activities were educational, akin to the agricultural experiment stations of this same era. The ORI built demonstration roads, tested materials and created standards, undertook cost-benefit analyses, set up model county systems, and advised on road management. As Bruce E. Seely notes, its existence and programs were a typical expression of the Progressive reforms of the day, characterized by "an attempt to replace political corruption with honest efficient administration, a rational desire to base action on information, a reliance on voluntary cooperation, and a sense of social justice." As the head of the office stated in 1911: "My whole object . . . is to get the state highway department out of politics . . . and . . . put it in charge of engineers." By that date public pressures for a major effort at road improvement were becoming intense, the need for federal aid more generally accepted, and bills to provide it multiplying in Congress. A reconstituted Office of Public Roads (successor to the ORI) was now given greater authority over selected post roads and was influential in shaping the decisive act of 1916: "To provide that in order to promote agriculture, afford better facilities for rural transportation and marketing farm products, and encourage the development of a general system of improved highways, the Secretary of Agriculture . . . shall in certain cases aid the States in the construction, improvement, and maintenance of roads which may be used in the transportation of interstate commerce, military supplies, or postal matter."

That combination of objectives displayed both the marked variety of interests in good roads and the cautious congressional approval of national power over state prerogatives in the working of this federal republic. Furthermore, the formula adopted for apportioning aid to each state was based on a combination of area, population, and miles of postal routes, thereby taking into account, so it was argued, the special interests, respectively, of the West, the East, and the federal government. Selection and ranking of roads to be improved were to be done by "the highway department of each State, representing both county and State interests, acting in co-operation with the Federal Government representatives."

It was assumed that the linking of through routes as trunk lines might be needed in some sections, and the social and political benefits of facilitating ever-broader intersectional contacts were proclaimed by various interests (including President Woodrow Wilson, who stated succinctly to an Indianapolis audience in 1916 that his interest in good roads derived from his chief interest "in the nationalization of America"). Nevertheless, the rural bias of this legislation was explicit: the primary purpose of federal aid was to improve country roads and, more specifically, "rural post roads." Roads and streets within places of 2,500 or more population were excluded (except those "along which the houses average more than two hundred feet apart"—a provision well adapted to deal with the New England concept of town). The rationale for this emphasis involved much more than postal services and farm-to-market economies; it looked to the ease of farm-to-town travel as a means of erasing the notorious social disparity between rural and urban life: good roads

2. Caravan of Trucks.
From Detroit to Atlantic ports, winter 1917–18. (Courtesy Federal Highway Administration)

would allow country people to partake of the same schooling, churches, shopping, and social affairs. Furthermore, larger fears of the time were brought into play:

> the growth of the city population is far outstripping the growth of the country population. Congestion of people in cities will ultimately produce the most unsatisfactory economic conditions, and it may even lower the moral stamina of our race. It is therefore of really vital as well as economic importance that the country be opened up and made accessible, attractive, and profitable so that this alarming drift of population may be checked, and certainly an adequate system of public roads will go far toward producing the desired result.

Thus the central government stepped gingerly into the highway movement, moving from advisory to supervisory and on to direct aid to the states—but with a national system nowhere in the official view.

Before the 1916 act could have any real impact, it was suddenly overtaken by dramatically new conditions. In his annual message to Congress in December 1915, President Wilson had warned that "the transportation problem is exceedingly serious and pressing in this country. There has from time to time of late been reason to fear that our railroads would not much longer be able to cope with it successfully, as at present equipped and coördinated." The American railroad network was essentially completed, but a sixth of it was in receivership and many more com-

panies were in trouble. Gross overextension, ruinous competition, and scandalous financial manipulations lay at the root of the problem (the railroads blamed recent government regulation of rates). The Great War in Europe brought a surge in traffic and income but placed heavy pressures on operations; U.S. entry into that war compounded the difficulties. The railroads became choked with traffic, shortages of cars and locomotives were severe, shipments piled up in East Coast ports (in part because of a shortage of ships), congestion spread inland, and a creeping paralysis began to affect the system. In December 1917 the federal government assumed emergency control of all major railroads in an effort to resolve the crisis by "bettering the conditions under which the railroads are operated and . . . making them more useful servants of the country as a whole" (to use Wilson's words of two years earlier when urging Congress to study the problem).

The railroad crisis forced a search for alternatives. Shippers began to send city delivery trucks on short runs to nearby cities and sources, and soon longer runs were being tested; rubber tires, for example, were hauled from Akron to Boston. Most spectacularly, having placed orders for huge numbers of heavy army trucks, officials began to have them driven in convoys from Toledo, Detroit, and other Midwestern factories to Baltimore, Philadelphia, and New York Harbor; eventually 18,000 were so delivered (fig. 2). The theaters of war were also a great testing ground of motorized transport: in supply trains, weapons carriers, mobile field kitchens, ambulances, and various other equipment. At the end of the war, in November 1918, a leading American engineering journal declared: "the four years of conflict have put us in a new era." The limitations of the national railroad system had been exposed, the versatility of the motor vehicle compellingly demonstrated, and the need for radical improvement of roads made appallingly apparent: the great exhibit being the "sudden" and "complete" failure of "hundreds of miles of road" under those army convoys and other heavy traffic. Moreover, it was clear that domestic peacetime pressures would be relentless. Registration of autos and trucks had soared from 1.8 million in 1914 to more than 6 million in 1918. As Thomas H. MacDonald, the new head of the Bureau of Public Roads (as the Office of Public Roads was now called), said in 1920 (when the number of registrations was nearly 10 million): "present day traffic descended upon the highways like an avalanche."

In December 1918 a highway congress in Chicago sponsored by the association of state highway officials and various industries called for "a national system of highways to be built, maintained and controlled by the Federal Government" and administered by a national highway commission. There followed a new flurry of public campaigns and professional lobbying, congressional hearings and legislative proposals, culminating in the Federal Highway Act of 1921. It was a major step forward in American highway development, but it did not create the national system many proponents had envisioned.

The war had been the "crystallizing element" for much wider public support for such a system, but the idea was nearly as old as the automobile. A good deal of the early publicity for national action had focused on building a transcontinental highway as an initial great step toward a more comprehensive network. Reviving the rhetoric of half a century earlier, such a grand highway, like the first Pacific Railroad, would be another great phase in the conquest of the continent, the building of a nation, the display of national character. The first actual crossing of the continent by automobile (sixty-five days, including three weeks of stops for rest and repairs) was made by a Vermont physician in 1903, and he was soon followed by others in well-publicized challenges to better the time and prove the ability and durability of particular makes of automobiles (in 1916 the best time was reduced to six days, ten hours, fifty-nine minutes). In 1912 Carl Graham Fisher, wealthy owner of another favorite proving ground, the Indianapolis Speedway, began to promote the idea of a "Coast-to-Coast Rock Highway" to be "finished in time for twenty-five thousand cars to cross the continent for the Panama-Pacific Exposition" in San Francisco in 1915. Henry B. Joy, president of the Packard Motor Company and supporter of Fisher's program, had suggested that such a road could be "the most enduring memorial to the greatest name in history," and within a year Joy became president of the newly formed Lincoln Highway Association and successor to Fisher as the most vigorous promoter of the "establishment of a continuous improved highway from the Atlantic to the Pacific, open to lawful traffic of all description without toll charges."

The exact route of this first New York to San Francisco axis, a matter of keen anticipation, was revealed at an annual conference of state governors meeting in Colorado Springs in 1913 (fig. 3). The Lincoln Highway Association never raised enough money to build more than a few demonstration miles of concrete roadway (it assumed that states and counties and the motor industry would supply the means), but its *Official Road Guide,* published in 1915, did help several thousand motorists find their way to San Francisco for the fair. The association was much the most famous in a great proliferation of promotions that "blossomed into a dense and unruly matting of named roads" across the map of the United States, east and west (such as the Yellowstone Trail from Boston to Seattle, the Portland to Portland Theodore Roosevelt Highway, and the Old Spanish Trail from St. Augustine to San Diego), and north and south (the Meridian Highway from Winnipeg to Galveston, Dixie Highway from Michigan to Florida, and many others). Every city and state became involved in this tangle of a hundred or more competitive, overlapping schemes, and it was such groups along with many older Good Roads associations that banded together under the National Highways Association to prepare tentative maps of a comprehensive network and pressure the federal government toward the creation of a truly national system.

Both the cause in general and the Lincoln Highway in particular received a boost in 1919 when the army selected the highway for a training mission and testing of vehicles. The struggles of this convoy and its impact on the roadway (100 bridges were broken) dramatically publicized the need for a much upgraded highway system. In subsequent congressional hearings, the War Department testified that a general system of good roads for commerce, rather than a special set of strategic superhighways, would be sufficient for its needs. Despite some strong lobbying to transform the Bureau of Public Roads (BPR) from a small subordinate office in the Department of Agriculture to "the dignity of a separate major arm of government," Congress refused to set up a national highway commission. With the South protective of states' rights and the Midwest of the entrenched rural emphasis, the Federal Highway Act of 1921 authorized an enlarged program for federal aid to the states to create systems of improved roads, under the general supervision of the bureau as constituted. Earlier that year President-elect Warren G. Harding had ridden to his inaugural in a motorcar (a Packard) instead of a carriage, and that change might be taken as official confirmation of the arrival of the Automobile Age.

A FEDERAL SYSTEM

Amid the clamor of competing interests legislators increasingly turned to the BPR for what they considered to be less-partisan advice. As a native Iowan and former director of that state's highway commission, Thomas MacDonald was thoroughly attuned to rural conditions, but he was also the one who had referred to the

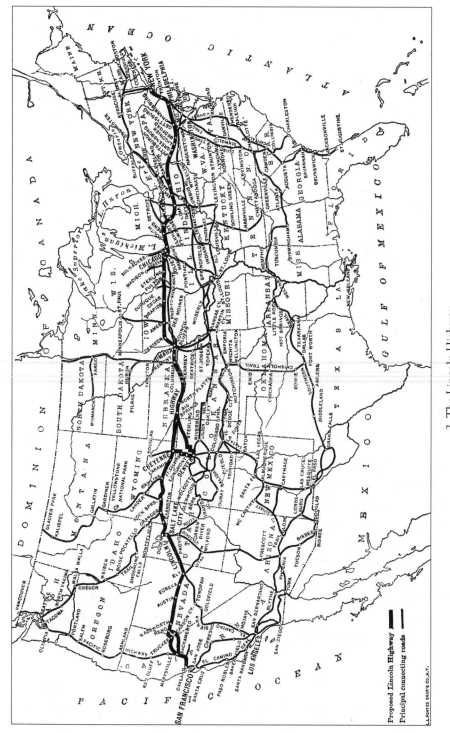

Proposed Lincoln Highway
Principal connecting roads

L.L.PATES ENGR'G CO.,N.Y.

3. The Lincoln Highway.

As proposed by Henry B. Joy, who said "it might be called . . . the Vertebra Route of America, the backbone of travel," "the best road serving the greatest population." This map from *Scribner's Magazine* shows a dogleg to Denver added in response to local protests when the transcontinental route was first revealed at a conference of state governors in Colorado Springs.

"avalanche" of traffic that now clogged the roads, and the new act directly addressed both needs. Each state was required to classify its roads and then designate a system of highways not exceeding 7 percent of that total mileage upon which all federal aid must be spent. Although the act specifically sought to "expedite the completion of an adequate and interconnected system of highways, interstate in character," it allowed no more than 60 percent of this federal aid to be applied to such "primary" roads; the remainder was to be spent on "secondary or intercounty roads."

The selection of particular roads for improvement was obviously a critical and politically charged action within each state. Cities were logical foci, but legislators, ever keenly aware of their constituencies, tended toward more comprehensive networks. For example, Pennsylvania had defined a system consisting of "the main travelled roads between county seats and principal cities, boroughs, and towns, and the main travelled routes leading to the State line." An early California statute was somewhat more geographically explicit, authorizing a set of roads to be acquired by the department of engineering and "so laid out and constructed as to constitute a continuous and connected State highway system running north and south through the State traversing the Sacramento and San Joaquin Valleys and along the Pacific coast by the most direct and practical routes connecting the county seats . . . and joining the centers of population" (fig. 4). The federal government (formally the secretary of agriculture) was empowered to review and require changes to ensure selection of the best interstate and intercity routes. While awaiting the highway system maps required from each state, the BPR undertook its own massive cartographical compilations. An index based on population and economic productions applied to each county produced a national map of varying densities revealing the major centers "through which diagrammatic routes could be laid out." Negotiating the numerous connections between the dense state systems in the East and selection of the few long traverses across low-traffic Western states posed the main problems.

The future of truck traffic was a major uncertainty. Studies by the BPR had indicated that "100 mi. seemed to have marked the limit of such hauls" and that it would likely be largely confined to links between large centers close enough to allow at least daily one-way trips. More immediate was the conflict over weight regulations. State highway officials had reacted strongly over the destruction caused by heavy trucks and sought to prohibit their sale and use, whereas truck manufacturers were adamant against restrictions and demanded that states should "build the roads to carry the loads." The BPR began road tests of the problem, while the states remained free to establish their own limits.

In 1921 MacDonald asked the War Plans Division of the Army General Staff to designate the most important roads for national defense. In the following year

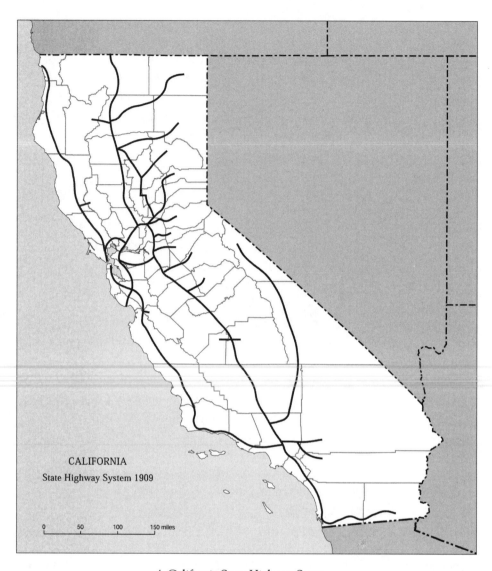

4. California State Highway System.
Designed by the new Highway Commission in 1909 to include every county. The one exception was Alpine, a nearly empty area (population 309) high on the headwaters of the Carson River and much more accessible from Nevada. Note that the only interstate connection was with Oregon. (*The State Highways of California*. Report by California State Automobile Association and the Automobile Club of California, 1921)

General John J. Pershing presented a map of recommended national highways, subdivided into three levels of priority for development (fig. 5). As Pershing had already testified that a network of good commercial roads would serve the military as well, his map provided a useful reference for the general task and most of his recommended routes were incorporated into the 1921 federal aid program. However,

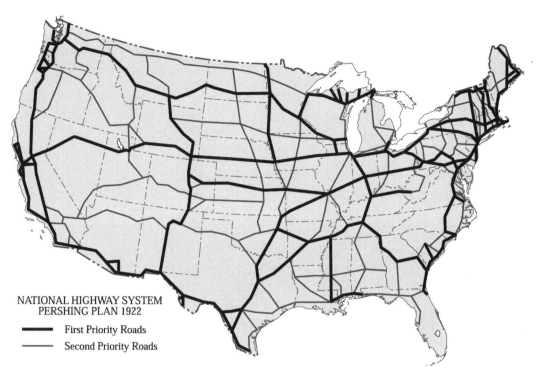

NATIONAL HIGHWAY SYSTEM
PERSHING PLAN 1922

━━━━ First Priority Roads
──── Second Priority Roads

5. The Pershing Plan, 1922.
Only the first two of the three-level priority of roads are shown. (Adapted from the original in the National Archives)

no such national plan was actually imposed at this time by the central government. Rather, the subsequent system of "federal highways" was a patchwork of forty-eight state selections linked under minimal supervision of the central government; it was, therefore, literally an "inter-state" network (as distinct from the later "Interstate System," which would be a nationwide network of standardized superhighways). This new 50,000-mile system (fig. 6) began to emerge into public consciousness and the landscape after the adoption in 1925 of an orderly numbering system displayed on a standard shield specifically designed "to give them a conspicuous place among the highways of the country as roads of interstate and national significance." These numbers and a uniform set of symbols and shapes for all official highway signs replaced (by law) all the various emblems of the many privately promoted named highways. (The Lincoln Highway was granted an exception as a worthy memorial, but failing to get its route across the country designated by a single number, the association soon disbanded and the name gradually faded from use.)

The limited and localized character of this system was displayed in the actual pace and priorities of road improvement. States tended to seek "ubiquity," to bring some modest improvement to every county, and, under federal law and guidance,

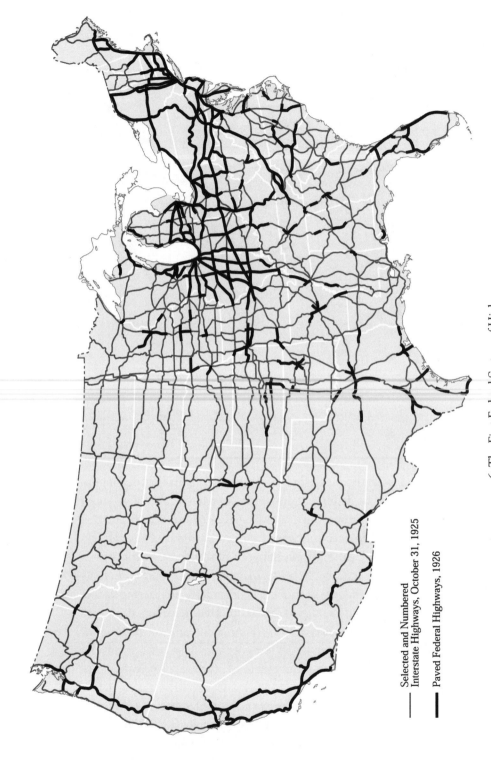

6. The First Federal System of Highways.

(Adapted from the original in the National Archives.) Paved federal highways based on *Rand McNally Auto Road Atlas of the United States*, 1926. The actual density of paved roads on state rather than federal highways was much greater in New York and New England.

Selected and Numbered
Interstate Highways, October 31, 1925

Paved Federal Highways, 1926

to focus major upgrading on existing traffic needs. Because road conditions heavily influenced the volume of movement, extensions of the improved system tended to be incremental, piecemeal, and not to a uniform standard (in part because urban roads were excluded from federal aid). Even as trucking and bus services were rapidly expanding in volume and reach, the BPR gave little attention to long-distance traffic potentials and continued to regard "cross-country highways as economically and socially unnecessary." Thus the expansion of first-class paved roads commonly began as a radial fan of short stretches out of major cities, followed by connections between nearby cities, then two or three selected traverses east and west and north and south across the state (often punctuated for some years by sections of unpaved road in costly stretches), and the formation of larger interstate networks. Regionally, the national system of paved highways emerged in the densely populated, urbanized Northeast, spread westward, and connected with thickening patterns in the industrial Middle West, with several long tentacles into the South and Southwest. Meanwhile lesser regional patterns were forming in Florida and Texas, and a border-to-border longitudinal line (Route 99) linked the expanding metropolitan and regional systems of Southern California, San Francisco, the Willamette Valley, and Puget Sound. The first paved transcontinental link was completed in the mid-1930s. Large sections of the Far West and the South were the last to become knit into the national network.

In his great 1925 regional geography, *North America*, J. Russell Smith noted: "It has been well said that the railroads decided where there should be villages, what villages should become towns, what towns should become cities, and what cities should become markets, and what markets should become metropolises." Although an exaggeration (important patterns of places were established during the preceding waterways era), such a statement underscores the powerful impact of the railway upon much of the American settlement system. Eventually almost-universal auto ownership, ease of travel, the lure of larger commercial centers, and the counterlure of suburb and country home to urban workers would also lead to significant changes in that pattern, but the impact during this formative highway era was comparatively modest. The system was designed to serve all established places; villages and towns did not have to move to the highway to survive—the roads came to them.

In spite of vigorous construction programs following World War I (aided by large transfers of "surplus motor-propelled vehicles," pipe, explosives, and other material from the War Department to state highway uses), extensions of improved roads could not keep up with the traffic. The number of registered vehicles more than doubled between 1920 and 1925 ("the whole population of the United States in 1925 could have been put into automobiles at the same time, for there was one motor car for every five and eight-tenths persons") and reached 26.5 million in 1930 before leveling off in the first years of the Great Depression. New Deal public works programs seeking to get the farmer out of the mud, relieve urban congestion (exclusion of such areas from federal funds was suspended and later eliminated), and speed up intercity movements, provided greater federal aid for all classes of roads (creating jobs being the main impetus). Nevertheless, by the mid-1930s traffic problems seemed to be greater than ever and fueled a renewed cry for a new level of national highways. "Our main roads," said the editor of a leading trade journal, "are merely connected neighborhood roads. Even though some main roads follow the course of early long distance trails, most of our highway trunks are patchworks of roads built originally to serve local purposes alone"—as indeed they were; in the Middle West federal highways still followed many a square corner around section-line boundaries.

To see a modern national system one had to go to Europe ("Germany has the roads while we have the traffic"). Thomas MacDonald was one of many who made the trip to examine "tomorrow's roads," but he did not regard the German program as an appropriate model for the United States. The *Autobahnen* were meant to encourage greater use of cars and to serve military needs, whereas in America there was no pressing need for either; therefore, he said: "We are proceeding on the principle that the utilization of the highways must directly produce the revenues with which to finance their construction. So long as we adhere to this method of financing [from taxes on gasoline and vehicles] the building of super-highways must be limited to those areas where the present and prospective traffic will justify. . . . Their location will be carefully integrated with the population centers and the layout will not be on the transcontinental basis." Unfortunately, in America the principle that there must be heavy traffic before one can afford to build roads adequate to handle such traffic simply engendered congestion and showed little evidence of ever solving the problem.

In 1937 Franklin D. Roosevelt asked MacDonald to study the feasibility of a national superhighway network, and at some point the president took a map of the United States and drew a set of bold lines to suggest the sort of thing he had in mind (fig. 7). The following year the BPR produced the first comprehensive traffic survey map, which MacDonald used to confirm his focus on metropolitan regions (including perhaps one superhighway between Washington and Boston) and to ignore transcontinental—or even "semicontinental"—routes (fig. 8).

Meanwhile several states began to revive the idea of toll ("self-liquidating") roads, and a bill in Congress proposed a national system of them. Automobile and trucking interests and many state highway officials were strongly opposed (such a solution was "not the reasoned thought of engineers and transport managers"), and the BPR insisted that few routes (perhaps Philadelphia–New Haven) would ever pay for themselves. Nevertheless, Pennsylvania took the lead, and when its turn-

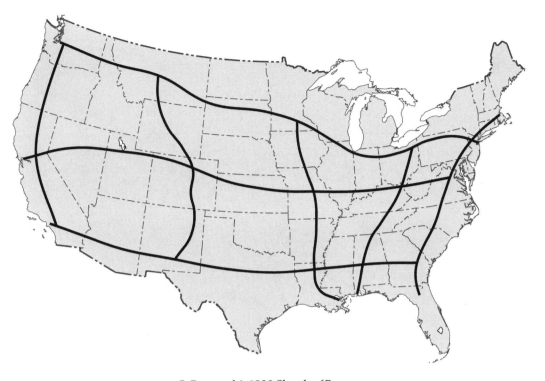

7. Roosevelt's 1938 Sketch of Routes.
The original, in the National Archives, is drawn on the standard base map of the federal highway system (fig. 6).

pike across the mountains (making use of the tunnels and roadbed of an uncompleted super-railroad) opened in 1940 and saved truckers several hours between Philadelphia and Pittsburgh, it was an immediate success.

During the summer of 1939, 5 million people were offered "a visual dramatization of a solution" to America's traffic problems. "In long queues that often stretched more than a mile, from 5,000 to 15,000 men, women and children at a time, stood, all day long for their turn to get a sixteen minute glimpse at the motorways of the world of tomorrow" at the General Motors Highways and Horizons Exhibit at the New York World's Fair. This "Futurama" featured a pattern of superhighways and urban trafficways superimposed on an elaborate geographical mosaic modeled on a variety of actual terrain and selected American cities as these might appear twenty years hence with roads designed "to perform their function properly." As presented in book form, it was envisioned by its chief designer, Norman Bel Geddes, as a "National Motorway System . . . organized and built . . . by full and central authority."

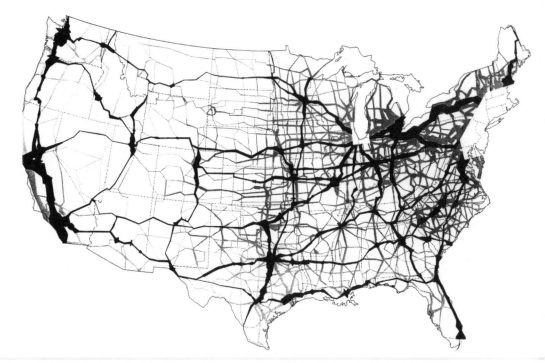

8. Highway Traffic, 1937.

Width of lines represents average daily number of passenger cars. Black lines are "principal routes serving interregional traffic"; gray lines, "other important routes." The Washington-Boston corridor was shown separately at a different scale. (U.S. Congress, *Toll Roads and Free Roads*, H. Doc. 272, 1939)

By this time the influence of the BPR (which MacDonald had headed for twenty years and whose programs never seemed to catch up with the traffic) was waning, military needs were pressing, and soon full mobilization showed "in a startling way how dependent the United States had become on its highways for its very existence." In 1941 President Roosevelt had initiated yet another assessment of the problem. After very extensive study, in 1944 that committee proposed a "National System of Interstate and Defense Highways" totaling nearly 34,000 miles. Lengthy negotiations with the states brought agreement in 1947 on a slightly larger system of interstate roads (fig. 9) conforming to the basic objective: "so located as to connect by routes, as direct as practicable, the principal metropolitan areas, cities, and industrial centers, to serve the national defense, and to connect at suitable border points with routes of continental importance in the Dominion of Canada and the Republic of Mexico." It was not, however, a national system of superhighways: "there was no thought of requiring that every mile of the system be built according to a rigid pattern," controlled access was recommended but not required, and only

9. National System of Interstate Highways, 1947.
"Selected by joint action of the several state highway departments as modified and approved by the Administrator, Federal Works Agency." (*Highway Needs of National Defense*, H. Doc. 249, 1949)

the most congested routes would have multiple lanes. High-capacity roads were recommended for major intercity links within the industrial belt, but especially for major metropolitan centers. Surveys had shown that urban centers were the greatest generators of traffic and suggested a general correlation between city size and radius of traffic influence (from six miles for cities of 10,000–25,000, up to thirty-five miles for those over 3 million). The overall result, therefore, was (as the original report was entitled) a complex, composite set of "interregional highways."

It was generally understood that a major road construction program must be undertaken after the war, but, as was the case following World War I, before much could be done the existing system was overwhelmed by a new avalanche of traffic: between 1945 and 1950 the number of registered vehicles increased from 31 million to 49 million (including 8.6 million trucks). American life was now thoroughly permeated with this maturing motorized age, but that great transforming force had also created powerful sets of interests that deeply disagreed over *where* to build, *what* to build, and, especially, *who would pay* for such an essential system. It took ten years of political agitation to reach a resolution and begin a new program on a new scale. During this long deadlock the notable financial and traffic-moving success of some toll roads lured many states into such undertakings. The longest project was the New York Thruway, following the famous water-level route across the state. Toll roads were especially attractive to states with much cross-state traffic serving external areas, such as New Jersey, Connecticut, and Indiana, but even a few relatively isolated states, such as Kentucky and Oklahoma, built extensive sections. By 1955, 1,239 miles of toll roads had been completed and many more were planned.

The impasse in Congress was resolved only by the steadfast support of President Dwight D. Eisenhower and General Lucius D. Clay, his appointed head of a National Highway Advisory Committee, and, finally, by giving something important to every highway interest. Thus the Interstate Highway Act of 1956 provided lavish federal funds for several classes of roads—farm-to-market, urban, intercity trunk, and a nationwide network (incorporating into this last category several state-constructed toll roads); it created a Highway Trust Fund to receive all taxes and income generated by users and prohibited diversions to other purposes; and it kept taxes on heavy trucks relatively low. The principal feature was a nationwide system of 41,000 miles of superhighway to be built to uniform standards for the fast and safe movement of large volumes of vehicular traffic (see fig. 21).

The geographical lineage of this system is readily traceable back through the 1947 network and the Pershing Map of 1922: differing in details, but a basic pattern of four or five east-west routes, nine or ten north-south, together with various shorter intercity and access links; thicker in the eastern half of the country, thinner in the western half. Such continuity confirmed that even in 1956 the highway system was fitted to the settlement system, following general routes already fixed in the railroad age. The close conformity of these several highway networks was also a reflection of forty years of incremental selection and upgrading of major routes state by state under advice and pressure from federal highway authorities. The 1956 legislation directed use of existing routes wherever feasible (in practice this would result mostly in parallel roads), and the new system was given its own distinctive shield and numbering system (high numbers beginning in the east and north, reversing the geographic sequences in the older, separate federal network).

This great new geographical impress upon the American landscape would be powerfully national in appearance and consequence, and 90 percent of its cost was borne by the central government. Yet, as students of the political battles involved have shown, it was not, in effect, a radically new national system imposed upon the states. The states, together with the truckers and other interests, had reluctantly turned to the federal government because it was the only adequate source of funds to undertake such a prodigious program (worthy indeed of comparison with the Panama Canal), but they defeated any idea of creating a separate central authority to build and operate this nationwide system (as some officials had sought). They preserved the concept of cooperation between federal supervision (by a staff largely drawn from state highway departments) and the states. As Mark N. Rose concluded, "what they managed to secure . . . was federal funding for localistic and largely impermeable commercial and professional subcultures," leaving engineers and transportation managers to build roads "largely as they wished"—a triumph of *federation* over *nation*.

COMMERCIAL SYSTEMS

The ubiquity and power of motor transportation in American life at the end of the twentieth century is so obvious and impressive as to obscure the fact that early in the century it was briefly outdistanced by another new form. Emerging from its experimental phase at about the same time as the automobile, the electric railway surged into prominence. Its superiority over horsecars for street service was so obvious that cities made the change as rapidly as possible. Extension of suburban lines through the countryside to nearby towns and, in many cases, on to the next city quickly followed. By 1910 nearly 10,000 miles of electric interurbans were in service; by 1917 more miles were being abandoned than built: "few industries have arisen so rapidly or declined so quickly, and no industry of its size has had a worse financial record."

As "a transitional step from almost sole reliance upon the steam railroad to an almost equally complete dependence on the automobile," the electric interurban represented a transition between the *paleotechnic* and *neotechnic* eras of industrialization. Employing a radical new form of energy to propel its lightweight cars quickly, frequently, and cheaply over lightly built railbeds, such lines could attract most of the local passenger traffic from parallel steam roads. Yet they were also rigid in route, a form of mass transportation but drawing primarily upon rural areas and small towns and cities, and rarely conceived as effective freight lines. Many companies were obvious speculations (the most grandiose being the highly touted Chicago–New York Air Line proposal for a 750-mile high-speed double-track railroad, 150 miles shorter than any existing connection), but others saw themselves as (profitable) instruments of social and economic change, bringing a more effective urban link to outlying towns and fostering rural diversification and intensification (frequent stops for milk and light produce were a common feature). Such themes were the same as those of contemporary good roads promoters, but railroad entrepreneurs (in some cases leaders of very profitable electric power companies) were able to build for a decade or more while public highway programs were barely getting under way. Their networks radiating from cities and towns anticipated the patterns of paved roads twenty years later. But if we superimpose the bus routes of 1928

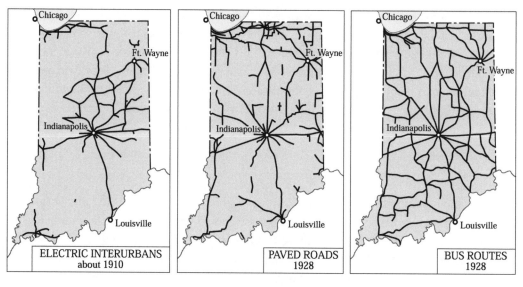

10. Statewide Spread of Services.
(Sources: electric interurbans, Hilton and Due, *Electric Interurban;* paved roads, *Official Paved Road and Commercial Survey of the United States;* bus routes, American Automobile Association, *Established Bus Routes in the United States* [American Geographical Society Library])

(fig. 10), ranging well beyond the fragmented lines of those pavements, the triumph of road transport over light rail becomes already apparent (though it was a victory owing more to the automobile than to the motor bus). During the ensuing Great Depression the electric interurban, burdened with debt, essentially disappeared from the American scene after only thirty years of service.

Running on public highways, free of the financial and regulatory restrictions encumbering the railroads, bus services multiplied and expanded prodigiously in the 1920s. The Greyhound system provides a common illustration: beginning in 1914 as a one-man jitney between two towns in the Mesabi iron range, extended to Duluth a year later, thence (under new ownership) to Minneapolis, forming a holding company to buy other small regional systems and, by 1933, operating 40,000 miles of scheduled service. By that date some steam railroads were substituting buses for unprofitable passenger trains, more than 9,000 miles of interurban electric lines had been abandoned, and streetcar systems had been replaced by buses in many cities (a change aided and accelerated by a well-financed, and later exposed, conspiracy of General Motors, Firestone, Standard Oil, and other motor interests). As regional networks of paved highways were extended, bus companies competed for longer-distance service; by 1940 intercity buses rivaled the steam railroads in the number of passenger miles. The railroads responded by upgrading their luxurious fast passenger trains, such as the 20th Century Limited and Broadway Limited, which averaged eighty miles per hour over long portions of their runs between New York City and Chicago. In the mid-1930s several Western roads introduced entirely new diesel-powered "streamliners" (carrying such names as Zephyr and Rocket), which offered even faster service between Chicago and Minneapolis, Kansas City, and Denver. On the longer runs to the Pacific Coast the railroads remained supreme until challenged by the airlines in the 1950s.

During these same years, and for the same basic reasons, trucking "grew like a field of weeds": it was cheap, flexible, unregulated, and instantly expandable; anyone could start a service, of any kind, on any route, charging any rate. The most immediate growth was in cities and in farm-to-market deliveries. At first railroads welcomed such services as useful adjuncts; the Interstate Commerce Commission (ICC) agreed and allowed railroads to use their own trucks to handle local freight between points along their own lines, and in 1929 the railroads as an association began operating the nationwide Railway Express Agency, offering pickup and delivery service by truck. However, adjuncts quickly turned into adversaries. As pavements were extended vehicles improved, and shipping systems developed (a set of regional return-load bureaus was a crucial innovation), trucks took over much of the less-than-carload traffic, offered overnight deliveries within 200 miles of major cities, and were challenging the sluggish railroads on longer runs. In the 1930s, as the Great Depression was bankrupting the American railroad system, trucking continued to expand. Yet such growth was not entirely a sign of success, for within itself the new mode was intensely competitive, individualistic, and unstable. Furthermore, as hauls got longer the lack of standardization of weights, sizes, taxes, and licensing (and the policing of these) among the states became more and more vexing. In 1935 pressures from various interests resulted in the first federal regulation of this burgeoning industry. This Motor Carrier Act imposed some controls over common carriers and contract carriers (specialized service for selected customers) operating in interstate commerce; haulage of agricultural commodities was exempt, as were private trucks.

The ICC might regard this act as another step toward a new ideal of "coordination of all existing transportation agencies on land, water, and air"; a delegate at a 1930 convention of transportation officials offered a more realistic view: "I believe that there is a place in our transportation system for both the railroad and the truck, but that it will take years of economic strife to outline the respective places of each and that the comparative utility of each system, not being constant, the relationship to each other will never be definitely defined." The inroads of trucking on rail transport were widely apparent but difficult to measure. By 1940 trucks accounted for only 14 percent of the ton-miles in intercity freight handled by the two modes, but the average rail haul was more than twice that of trucks, and railroads were far superior in the handling of heavy bulk commodities, such as coal and grain. The re-

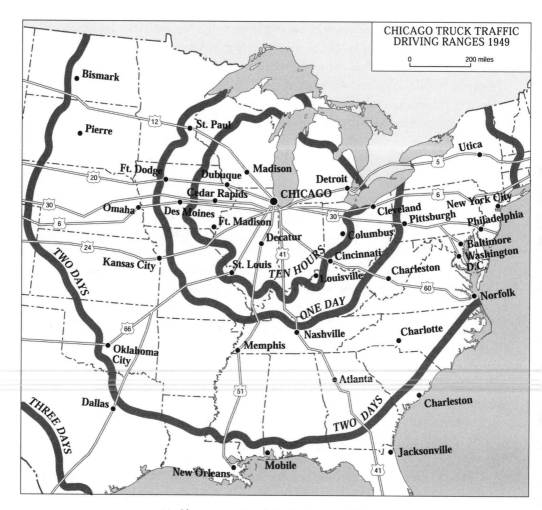

11. Chicago as a Truck Traffic Center, 1940s.

As with railroads, Chicago was the leading center, with some 700 intercity common or contract carriers. Unlike railroad traffic, however, more than 80 percent of this movement originated or terminated in Chicago, and much of it was less-than-truckload freight. ICC regulations limited a driver to ten hours of work. (Adapted from Fellmann, *Truck Transportation Patterns*)

ally important change was truck dominance of all kinds of merchandise and produce in distances up to 200 miles or so (fig. 11). In a telling observation of the time, "the tide of heavy trucks rolling northward . . . day and night" past Wilmington, Delaware, looked "like freight trains of boxcars loosely coupled." By that date there were dense regional networks of paved highways, and steam railroads had abandoned more than 25,000 miles of line.

During World War II all transportation facilities were used to the utmost. The government asserted certain controls over priorities of shipment but did not take over the operation of any private systems. Whereas World War I had been a great proving ground for motorized land transport, World War II greatly accelerated the use and capacities of air transport, thereby further complicating major adjustments among the several competing forms of national transportation services that would take place during the latter half of the century.

IMPACTS

"It is probable that no invention of such far reaching importance was ever diffused with such rapidity or so quickly exerted influences that ramified through the national culture." That conclusion of a Hoover-appointed commission on *Recent Social Trends in the United States*, published in 1933, has been repeatedly endorsed by authoritative studies of the history of the automobile in American life. The American love affair with the car is a major characterizing feature of the twentieth century, and there were geographical as well as deep cultural reasons for this avid affectionate response.

The automobile has touched our "national soul" or "some controlling springs and gears in our national life," noted *Motor* magazine in 1923. As for the first, the automobile made direct, exhilarating connection with powerful American ideals of individualism, freedom, and progress. It was also a radically democratic machine, undermining social distinctions, for the highways were open equally to anyone and the possibilities for ostentatious displays of wealth far more limited in cars than in houses and estates. Geography was more a matter of "springs and gears"—the practical dimensions of the topic. America was not just vast in area; its population was spread thinly over most of that space. With few exceptions, rural families lived isolated on farms rather than clustered in villages, and unlike European villages, America's meager hamlets were also relatively far apart rather than within walking distance of one another. The whole hierarchy of central places was spacious, with the distribution of lower-level commercial towns controlled by the spacing of railroad stations and by the general scale of counties and their seats.

The impact of the automobile ramified through the whole settlement system, but this decentralized pattern helps account for the rapid adoption of cars by much of the rural population, once durable and affordable vehicles were available. By the mid-1920s, 93 percent of Iowa farmers owned a car, and nationally 40 percent of all automobiles were owned by those living in rural areas or towns of less than 2,500. Thus even before most of the rural roads were at all good, a major objective of Good Roads advocates was attained: the monthly shopping trip to town had become weekly or even more often; the school bus was putting an end to one-room country schools, and the central school, with its sports and music, plays and debates, became a focus of a larger community life, augmented by ready rural access to churches, lodges, social clubs, the cinema, and various professional services. Sociologists began to refer to "rurban" communities, a fusion of rural and urban, and to predict the many benefits, local and national, that would ensue.

It must be emphasized, however, that the automobile was not the only instrument in this rural transformation. Tractors and trucks and powered machinery were revolutionizing farming tasks, electricity and water systems easing domestic drudgery, telephones and radios reducing isolation. Such improvements were also accompanied by higher costs, often resulting in heavy debt, consolidation of farms, fewer laborers, and an accelerated exodus of young adults from the rural scene. The smaller towns began to feel the competition of larger ones nearby; preachers and rural sociologists began to warn of a loss of "community" from the changing "*structure* of rural social life."

Although a broad selection of larger towns benefited from this intensification of rural trade and traffic, many of these same places came under competition from the next level. These small cities of 20,000 to 100,000 had readily embraced and accommodated the automobile. In "Middletown" (Muncie) the car had become "an accepted essential of normal living" by the early 1920s for "business class people," and mortgaging a home to buy a car was not uncommon among those aspiring to such status. Livery stables and feed barns, carriage works and harness makers, hitching posts and water troughs gave way to the motor car and its special needs, and the grid plan and broad streets of many of these cities were quickly adapted to the new mode. In residential areas the car was lodged in a former stable at the back of the yard or in a new small boxlike garage on the alley. On the outskirts the automobile began to shape its own environment. The American propensity for separation and privacy, for the single-family house on its own spacious lot, had been feeding suburban expansion along radiating streetcar and interurban lines for twenty years, providing country living for relatively affluent commuters. In the economic boom of the mid-1920s developers began to fill the intervening open sectors with housing tracts for a broader automotive public, changing linear extension into suburban sprawl (and, in the 1930s, bringing the garage forward to a corner of the house, and soon an integral part of it). The Great Depression quelled such expansion but only momentarily dampened the rise in automobile ownership. Traffic lights, parking meters, and parking lots failed to cope with the congestion, but the central business district remained the focus of traffic in cities of this size until after World War II.

In the greater urban centers problems arose more rapidly and severely, even though the proportion of car owners was smaller and streetcar service usually superior. The sheer volume of cars, taxis, and trucks confined between solid miles of multistoried commercial blocks and apartments posed new challenges to businesses, developers, architects, city officials, and a new profession of traffic engineers. The problems were compounded by the paradox of the 1920s as a booming period of centralized urban development featuring private competition and public pride in taller skyscrapers, larger office blocks, and bigger department stores, thereby increasingly paralyzing city administrations by the "stupendous difficulties and expense" of widening streets, providing parking, or building new access roads to relieve the choking traffic.

The most important geographic response, therefore, was suburbanization on a grand scale: not merely new residential tracts as in smaller cities but more nearly complete communities of homes, convenience shops, and services designed with curving streets and spacious plazas for a fully automotive society. The most famous early example was the Country Club District on the edge of Kansas City, created and elaborately controlled and landscaped by a local developer who had traveled in Europe and been influenced by current Garden City concepts. Suburbs similar in general type if not usually in planning and elegance emerged on selected fringes of every American metropolis during the 1920s. However, these new suburbs were not really complete communities because most heads of households continued to work in the city. Thus decentralization of residence added to the already heavy traffic along major access roads, magnifying the very problems it was in part designed to avoid. In the late 1920s Sears, Roebuck and Company initiated an important commercial change by building large multistoried department stores surrounded by ample parking lots on a main artery near the edge of many cities, convenient to town and country alike—the famous catalogue company thereby responding to and enhancing the fusion made possible by the automotive revolution (and posing the first threat to downtown businesses from the changing structure of urban life).

As was the case with highway financing, the creation of trafficways sufficient for this new era had to overcome established laws and practices. Attempts to restrict access from every bordering property "ran counter to the most deeply ingrained tradition of English common law and also most American statute law." Not until 1937 did New York and Rhode Island pass legislation supporting limited access, and by 1945 only fifteen more states had followed their lead. Thus the most common and immediate impact of automobility on the American landscape was the commercial strip, the uncontrolled opportunistic rise of individual businesses along every major route in and near every city and larger town, and, indeed, at attractive new locations in the countryside. As John A. Jakle and Keith A. Sculle have well documented, "gasoline stations were in the vanguard" of this development, they were the "invaders" of residential neighborhoods, the "pioneers" colonizing the "frontier" of unsettled land along the roadside. They were also leaders in the rapid emergence of a new "commercial vernacular" (to use J. B. Jackson's term). From a solitary curbside pump outside a shop or house, to a separate canopied station, to a standardized design emblematic of a particular company, the gasoline station per-

fectly exhibited the ever-changing landscape of an ever-expanding complex of facilities, driven by ever-intensifying competition to lure trade from the ever-greater
traffic: tourist home to tourist cabins to auto courts to motels; roadside lunch coun-
ters to substantial cafés (sometimes in bizarre eye-catching forms of tepees, wind-
mills, or coffee cups) to streamlined diners to drive-ins; barnside slogans to billboards to flashing neon script—and much else, now decaying along older bypassed
roadways, still familiar to every American traveler. The acceleration of this new dimension of urban growth in the midst of the Great Depression attested to the
power of the automotive impact. In a period of massive business failure the roadside
strip became a frontier of opportunity for individuals and families of modest means
to provide some simple service—gas station, used tires, radiator repairs, coffee
shop, ice cream stand, or various forms of cheap entertainment—to a growing
clientele. An "automobile row" of car dealers and major services was also a routine
part of the scene, but, for example, until after World War II, 98 percent of roadside
lodging was family owned and operated.

The spread of this new automobile landscape was, of course, uneven in timing
and magnitude, its tentacles radiating most rapidly from the larger commercial
cities of the East, Middle West, and California and most slowly in the South, where
the lagging impact would prove all the greater on society, urban as well as rural:
"Detroit automobile makers set off the most effective Yankee invasion that ever
disturbed Southern complacency." But the spread was relentless, by 1940 it was nationwide, and the wonderful mobility conferred by the automobile was becoming
more and more constrained, the pleasures of driving and the joy of travel more and
more sporadic and episodic—and dangerous (40,000 killed in auto accidents in
1941). Insofar as such problems arose from relationships between road and roadside, in making ready connection with basic American ideals of freedom, individualism, privacy, and progress the automobile empowered an ambivalent feature inherent in such aspirations: the tensions between public highways and private
property, between unimpeded passage and the unrestrained search for profit—a dynamic that would ramify through the whole related geographic system and defy stable resolution.

That the volume of cars on the road, even beyond urban environs, repeatedly
surpassed the most careful and generous predictions was surely because "motoring,"
as George R. Stewart observed, "must be for most people, an end in itself, not a
means of getting somewhere." The continued extension of good roads served both
purposes. As the government report *Recent Social Trends* noted: "Travel for necessity and travel for the sake of travel (pleasure travel) alike are involved in the new
mobility. The trip of a few hours duration (the drive) and the longer pleasure trip
(touring) have become accepted parts of modern life. It is the general extension of
a touring habit that is particularly impressive." Automobile touring was especially

well developed in New England and other scenic areas of the Northeast (permits to enter Canada from the United States for periods of two to thirty days soared from 59,000 in 1919 to almost 1.3 million in 1930), and it was an especially important feature of the new mobility in the Far West. Long journeys over only moderately improved roads to visit national parks and other natural attractions became very popular. Special roads to local vistas (such as the one to the top of Pikes Peak, even though the cog railway had long been in place) were constructed, and all manner of rodeos, frontier days, and festivals sprang up to lure more traffic and bolster local economies.

California was not only a great source of tourists, it was a premier destination for those from elsewhere, even from great distances and before one could get there on paved roads. In 1930, 25 percent of the cars entering the state were from east of the Mississippi. An unknown portion of these visitors were not merely sightseers, they were site appraisers sizing up the prospects for relocation to the most auto-centered region in America. Even before one could conveniently arrive there by car, Los Angeles County had the highest ratio of cars to population in the United States. Such leadership continued and was of course rooted in the special character of Southern Californian settlement since the boom of the 1880s (see *Transcontinental America*, 59–64). A visitor of 1913 noted the hotels filled with prosperous Eastern urbanites and "young bloods, without hats and in white flannels, talking golf, polo, and motor cars." By that date the Automobile Club of Southern California (formed in 1900) was already a powerful voice of the motoring public, lobbying on its behalf and supplying excellent road maps and other travel services. The 1920s brought another surge of newcomers to the Los Angeles region and the shaping of hundreds of new subdivisions for the new mobility (while Downtown was becoming famous as the most congested in the United States). Climate was not only a great lure, it made roads easy to make and maintain and had made the car a year-round convenience even before the advent of enclosed bodies. In such an environment and under such growth the bungalow and pseudo-mission styles of houses were soon joined by those of simpler façades featuring a garage half as broad as the house and domestic life focused rearward on patio, pool, and garden. By 1930 Los Angeles was notable as having the highest proportion of single-family dwellings of any city in America (93.7 percent compared with barely 50 percent in big Eastern cities), and its vast "sprawl" across the plains and foothills had become a cliché in visitors' commentary.

Similarly, in urban commercial design "the first real monument of the Motor Age" was the "Miracle Mile on Wilshire Boulevard," created in 1927 (fig. 12). Located six miles west of Downtown, halfway to Santa Monica and the sea, adjacent to the new fashionable suburb of Beverly Hills, it featured solid rows of high-quality shops fronting on the street ("the Fifth Avenue of the West"), with public park-

12. Wilshire Boulevard, Los Angeles.
Reproduced from a brightly colored postcard, c. 1930.

ing immediately behind each shop and attractive residential areas behind this narrow commercial swath. As Reyner Banham noted, it was in effect "the first linear
downtown" carefully designed to accommodate the automobile in an attractive
shopping environment. It was a compelling exhibit of the aspirations of a forward-
looking civic leadership. As a prominent local city planner said to a national convention in 1924, Los Angeles had a "chance . . . of showing the right way of doing
things. It will not be the west looking back to the east to learn how to do it, but the
east looking to the west to see how it should be done. This is our regional ambition
for Southern California"—and it was soon famous for the latest concepts in super-
markets, shopping centers, drive-ins, and all kinds of designs and services catering
to a society on wheels. Not every such item made its first appearance in this corner
of the nation, but taken as a whole this new automotive landscape, this new way of
life, took shape more rapidly and fully here than anywhere else in the world.

Moreover, the image of this new lifestyle was rapidly and powerfully diffused to
all the world by another revolutionary instrument that took root in this same remarkable region during these same years. Coeval with the automobile and also first
nurtured elsewhere, the American film industry converged upon and flourished in
those same special attractions of Southern California: the mild sunny climate, ample space, varied landscapes, and an unconstrained business and social environment. Here an altogether new group of aggressive, creative, competitive entrepre-

neurs developed a medium of enormous public influence. Much of their product, as well as the glamour of "Hollywood," featured in some degree actual or idealized images of a Southern California landscape and way of life in which the automobile was an integral and essential part: "as it flickered before Middle America in darkened movie halls . . . Los Angeles was being announced subliminally . . . as a new American place with its own ambience and visual signature." Thus one may say that in the 1920s and for a generation thereafter, "Detroit made the cars, but Los Angeles taught us how to live with them"—that here, for better or for worse, was the clearest glimpse of what the automotive future of the nation might be like.

The 1940s, war and aftermath, brought new millions to California and generated enormous demands for new housing and services, new tracts and trafficways. In 1939 the state legislature had paved the way for limited-access highways, and in 1947 (nine years ahead of the national government) California adopted a ten-year master plan for 14,000 miles of freeway—the first segments and interchanges of which would become instantly famous as the latest "essential expression of the automotive culture of Los Angeles."

George R. Stewart, one of the most engaging and perceptive interpreters of the American highway landscape, noted in his famous traverse *U.S. 40* (1953) that having been born in 1895 his was the only generation that "will ever have grown up along with the automobile and have experienced the miraculous unfolding." That he and his generation were indeed witnesses to an astounding transformation of American life is undoubted, but it was not entirely unprecedented. A person born sixty years earlier and reflecting in 1895 on his or her own experience might well have said the same about the railroad. Each of these radical innovations worked enormous unforeseen changes in the shaping of American life and landscape, and each took about the same time to do so: twenty years to become accepted as a routine necessity (autos replacing horses in cities; railroads putting an end to the canal boom); forty years to span the continent (first paved road across, 1935; the Golden Spike, 1869); sixty years to define a truly national system (Interstate System, 1956; railroad network of 1890), and twenty-five more years to complete it.

These similar phases of development are less important, however, than the actual historical interrelations of the two modes. For half of their overlap in time Lewis Mumford's early generalizations held true: "the new machines [automobiles] followed not their own pattern, but the pattern laid down by previous economic and technical structures"; thus the *neotechnic* followed the imprint of the *paleotechnic*, and in terms of actual routes even earlier patterns: "this private locomotive was set running on the old-fashioned dirt roads or macadam highways that had been designed for the horse and wagon"—the *eotechnic*. Furthermore, in each case once the power of this revolutionary instrument became apparent, every town sought it as essential for survival, anchoring its commercial and broadened cultural life on the depot in the one case and insisting that the highway pass through Main Street in the other, and maintaining those patterns in the face of mounting physical problems of intrusion and congestion. After midcentury, however, a marked divergence in power and direction of these two modes in the shaping of America was becoming apparent. The role of the railroad, a set of private corporations now under comprehensive government regulation, seemed to be waning; the role of the highway, a government-provided trafficway open to unrestricted private use, was breaking loose from older conformist patterns to extend the "miraculous unfolding" of the automobile into that freedom of movement in "safety, comfort, speed, and economy" envisioned by its most avid promoters.

Historians looking back upon this Automotive Age have sometimes said that the great achievement of the automobile "was to free the common man from the limitations of his geography." While that seems an apt phrasing of the radical, discretionary mobility conferred, our special perspective reminds us that we are never really "free" of geography and suggests that we also note that what the automobile did was to free—and force—the society as a whole to reshape its geography to a broader scale.

2. Mobilization: Neotechnic Evolution

Just as the railroad seemed the embodiment of the coal-iron-steam age, of paleotechnic industrialism, so the automobile stands as the prime exhibit of the new sources of power, materials, and mobility characteristic of the neotechnic. Although we tend to think of the one as emblematic of the nineteenth century and the other as a wholly twentieth-century product, in the broader view of industrial eras the two complexes are not sharply separated in time and content but, as earlier noted, overlap and interpenetrate. For example, the electric telegraph was almost as old as the railroad and became essential to its operation long before the widespread impact of electricity, and the steam-powered locomotive was the dominant freight hauler on American railroads for half of the twentieth century before giving way to diesel; coal, the supreme power source of the paleotechnic, was slowly replaced in one use after another but developed a major market in electric generating plants.

So, too, with our more general concern, the geography of American industry. Much of the new evolved within the areal framework of the old, reinforcing for a while established regional concentrations; yet as new resources and technologies came to the fore and population and market patterns changed, important alterations in economic locations followed and neotechnic industrialism became a powerful dynamic in the reshaping of America.

AUTOMOBILE INDUSTRY

The impact of the automobile was nearly as dramatic and far-reaching on American industry as it was on American life in general. In less than a generation the automobile industry rose from nothing to become the nation's largest manufacturing enterprise. Moreover, it was a prodigious economic multiplier, demanding an ever-wider range of specialized products and becoming a huge consumer of malleable iron, steel sheets, plate glass, rubber, copper, lead, aluminum, cotton, leather, paints, plastics, and much else—to say nothing of gasoline and lubricants.

Automobile manufacturing began as a sideline to other industrial operations, it was from the first dependent upon parts obtained from other companies, and it developed into a massive complex whose huge factories were in large part assembly centers of hundreds of products manufactured by specialized companies. Such interdependence was an important factor in the historical geography of the industry.

Bicycle manufacturers were a ready source of interest, experience, and production. The nation's largest, the Pope Company of Hartford, experimented with electric automobiles and eventually reorganized as an automobile company with branch plants in Toledo, Indianapolis, and Hagerstown, Maryland. Other prominent bicycle companies that switched to automobiles were located in Buffalo, Cleveland, and Kenosha, Wisconsin. Carriage and wagon makers were another obvious nurturing ground. Studebaker of South Bend, Indiana, the largest and the most successful in this transition, after dabbling in self-propelled carriages reorganized in 1910 to concentrate on them (but continued to make horse-drawn vehicles until 1920). Flint, Detroit, Racine, and St. Louis were the homes of other major carriage companies that became important in the early auto industry. However, as John B. Rae notes, many of the great names in the new industry were men whose approach "was from the engine to the vehicle rather than from the vehicle to the engine" (as had been the case with bicycle and carriage manufacturers). Duryea, Stanley, Olds, Ford, Packard, White, Marmon, and Maxwell were among a diversified group of engineers, mechanics, and technicians working in various industries who became fascinated with the development of lightweight engines for this new need, whether electric (early favored for urban use), steam (the famous Stanley Steamers were manufactured for more than twenty years), or gasoline (soon much the most common mode).

Other famous names, such as Durant, Willys, Nash, and Chrysler, were skillful managers and promoters during a chaotically competitive time. During the early stages of the industry more than a thousand companies were formed, and a large number of these actually produced at least a few automobiles for sale. Charles W. Boas's map of the 327 such companies of 1900 shows their factories sprinkled unevenly across the United States in more than a hundred cities and towns. The vast majority were within what was by that time widely recognized as the American Manufacturing Belt, with the greatest number in New York City, many in other industrial centers of the northeastern seaboard, and Buffalo, Cleveland, and Chicago showing up as prominent clusters within a thick scattering to the west (only two of the 327 were in the South). As a few larger companies began to emerge from the mass, a few locations emerged as anchors of a new industrial pattern. Within ten years the Midwest far surpassed the East, a shift commonly attributed to ineffective business leadership in particular New England companies, but an almost certain eventual change because of the differential in costs for nationwide marketing (the leading New York City firm had expanded production by opening factories in Michigan and Indiana). Indianapolis and St. Louis became additional important centers, but by 1910 Detroit was the largest and well on its way to becoming the world-famous focus and symbol of the American automobile industry.

Detroit had been a vigorously growing city, prospering on its waterway and isthmian location, Michigan lumbering and woodworking; it had bicycle factories, carriage works, and companies working on engines for marine service or agricultural use. But it held no obvious great advantage over a number of other places, such as Cleveland, Toledo, or Chicago. All of these were diversified manufacturing cities in the midst of an industrial region whose many specialized factories could readily supply or quickly create all the parts necessary for automobile production, and all were served by a dense railroad network giving ready access to those materials and to markets anywhere in the nation. Detroit emerged as primary because of a group of men who combined mechanical and managerial talent to an unusual degree and (backed in some cases at a critical early stage by local capitalists) became leaders of successful companies—and, of course, especially because of one man who transformed the whole scale and character of automobile manufacturing and marketing.

On January 1, 1910, Henry Ford began volume production of his Model T at his new Highland Park plant. Ford was not the first to envision or to offer a low-cost, lightweight "motor car for the great multitude" (as he would later claim and be commonly credited with); his great achievement was to offer a superior car on an unprecedented scale. The Model T was user-friendly and readily affordable; easy to drive, maintain, and repair; durable, flexible, designed to cope with the poor roads most Americans were faced with; standardized and simplified, mass-produced and efficiently marketed, the price lowered year by year as more and more were sold. In 1915 Ford's new moving assembly line turned out half a million cars. This mass production in one place was linked with further assembly in a widely dispersed set of places. From Detroit carloads of "semi-knocked-down" units were sent to regional branch plants for final assembly into vehicles for sale, saving the cost of shipping bulky complete automobiles by boxcar. Similarly, a nationwide system of company-owned regional sales headquarters closely supervised and supported Ford dealers.

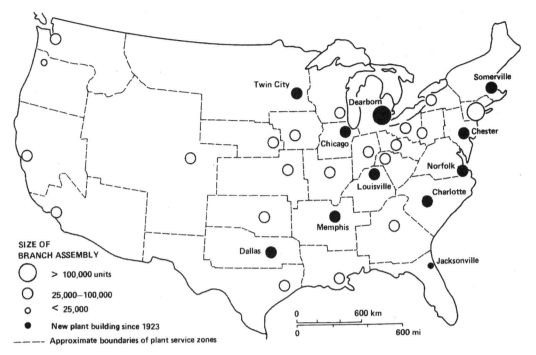

13. Ford Branch Assembly Plants, 1929.
From Gerald T. Bloomfield, "Coils of the Commercial Serpent," in *Roadside America*, ed. J. Jennings. (Courtesy Iowa State University Press)

Branch plants and sales territories were not a new concept in American business, but the Ford system was first and foremost in the automobile industry (fig. 13). By 1920 half of the world's cars were Model Ts; by May 1927, when its production was finally halted, 15 million had been sold, making it, by a large margin, "the world's most widely used single piece of large mechanical equipment."

There were important ramifications and ironies of this astounding success. Ford had led the way in a great and rapid broadening of car ownership, confirming the automobile as a necessity of modern life in America. But the Ford Company commanded no more than half of that market, and it offered only a single simple model, leaving the way open for expanding sales of a variety of higher-grade cars to an expanding middle-class market (as ownership became more widespread, make and model of car became a more common measure of social rank, leaving the unadorned, practical "Tin Lizzie" near the bottom of the scale). Yet the enormous capital costs of mass production and nationwide marketing severely limited the number of companies that could afford to compete with Ford. By the late 1920s only General Motors (a composite of several early companies, with Buick and Chevrolet as featured products) and Chrysler (a lesser company augmented by recent acquisition of Dodge) were really mass producers, commanding, with Ford, 80 percent of the U.S. market. By that time, however, Ford was seriously overextended and underrepresented, a costly system supporting a fading product; by 1930 it had lost its leadership (to Chevrolet) and soon reduced its thirty-one American regional assembly plants to eight.

The Great Depression demonstrated that, although the demand for new cars was elastic, the demand for cars was not: production was quickly cut in half, and then almost in half again, before beginning a slow recovery, but the total number of cars in use (registered) was only slightly and briefly depressed before growing again each year; by 1940 production was still well under that of 1929, while the number registered was more than 4 million greater. World War II brought a complete cessation of civilian sales and a shift to military vehicles and other equipment. After this interruption, Henry J. Kaiser, famed for his vast shipbuilding success during the war, purchased Willow Run, a huge aircraft plant west of Detroit, and converted it to automobile production. This bold entry lasted only a few years, however, for once the pent-up demand for cars had eased, Kaiser's lack of an attractive car and of an efficient national sales system doomed the enterprise; he hung on awhile by purchasing the Willys Corporation of Toledo, which had survived on production of a civilian version of the famous wartime jeep. In 1954 other small producers, all of long lineage, merged into two (Nash and Hudson, Studebaker and Packard) in a desperate effort to continue in the shadow of the Big Three. By 1955 both the number of cars produced and the number in use had doubled the eve-of-war figures, and the more than 50 million crowding America's roads and streets gave powerful evidence of the need for a truly national system of mass-capacity highways to cope with this mass production of cars (and trucks).

Despite these huge ups and downs from the 1920s into the 1950s, the geography of this volatile industry remained relatively stable. Detroit was the unchallenged capital of the nation's largest industry: headquarters of the Big Three (and of Packard and Hudson), the decision-making center, seat of research, design, and planning. The metropolitan area contained the greatest factories (fig. 14) and a close hinterland reaching to Flint, Saginaw, Lansing, Jackson, and Toledo was thick with others producing cars and parts. Viewed comprehensively, nearly every state in the Union contributed some material or part to the many thousands needed for each vehicle, but the heaviest concentration of automobile-related factories lay within a 250–300-mile radius, reaching from Cleveland on the east, through Akron, Columbus, Dayton, and Cincinnati, thence northwestly to Indianapolis, South Bend (Studebaker), Chicago, and a short extension to Kenosha (Nash), all within a day's drive of, and direct railroad links with, Detroit. The Canadian industry (largely initiated and eventually completely controlled by U.S. firms), concentrated in Windsor across the river from Detroit and in the Toronto

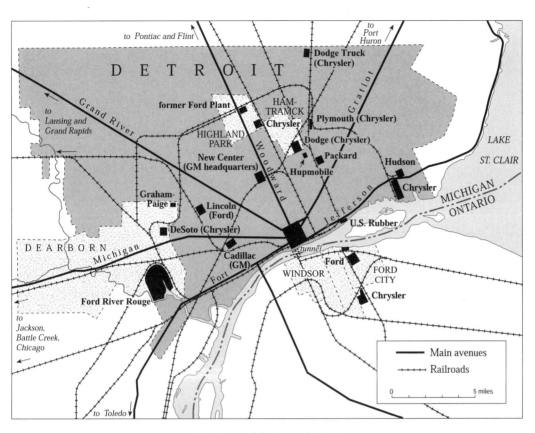

14. Automobile Capital, 1940.

The avenues radiating from the remnant of Judge Woodward's abortive plan for an elaborate metropolis suggest the focal nature of this old strategic site on the narrow passage between the upper and lower Great Lakes. The railroad lines connecting the broad fan of automobile plants indicate how completely America's fourth largest city was devoted to automobile manufacture: there was no concentrated industrial district; factories and worker residences were spread over much of the urban pattern. Highland Park, Hamtramk, and Dearborn were separate municipalities. Ford had had production on the Canadian side since 1904; Chrysler since 1924. (Principal sources: *Michigan*, American Guide Series, 1941; Kerr and Holdsworth, *Historical Atlas of Canada*, vol. 3, 1990)

area, completed the circle of this broader pattern. Assembly plants were of course spaced throughout the national market, and the largest single concentration was in the Los Angeles area (which was also second only to Akron in the production of tires and tubes).

The Big Three along with another giant, International Harvester of Chicago, became dominant in trucks as well, but the market for these was much more diversified, and a larger number of small companies were able to survive as specialized producers in a wider scattering of original locations, such as Mack of Allentown and White of Cleveland, both of whose trucks became famed for sturdy service in World War I, Brockway in Cortland, New York, Kenworth in Seattle, and several others.

RELATED INDUSTRIES

Henry Ford was obsessed with controlling all aspects of automobile manufacturing. After the transforming success of mass production at Highland Park he began the gigantic River Rouge complex, "which almost literally converted coal, iron ore, and other materials into a finished automobile by a consecutive and continuous series of processes centered at a single site" (fig. 15). The coal was transported by his own railroad from his own coal mines in Kentucky to coke ovens on the premises,

15. River Rouge, 1930.
Ford's enormous complex on a dredged ship canal included coke ovens, blast furnaces, foundry, open-hearth furnaces, rolling mills, pressed steel shop, tool and die shops, tire factory (supplying half of Ford's needs), glass plant, soybean mill (meal used in foundry, oil for enamels), paper mill, and box factory (containers for parts). Working at capacity 81,000 employees could produce 5,000 automobiles in sixteen hours. (From the collections of Henry Ford Museum and Greenfield Village, P.833.55282.A)

the ore in his own vessels from his Lake Superior mines and the iron smelted there-from to the foundries, steel furnaces, rolling mills, and pressed steel plants; a glass factory, tire factory, and various other works completed the local system, all pow-ered by Ford's own giant coal-fired electric plant. (The most extreme, and least suc-cessful, part of the program was the attempt to produce enough rubber on new Ford plantations in the Amazon Basin, a project begun in 1927 and finally given up after World War II.) In curious conjunction with this massive concentration was a set of Ford-established "village industries" in the near hinterland of Detroit, using local waterpower to produce lamps, gauges, valves, tools, and other small parts, a pro-gram expressing Ford's nostalgic concern to foster improvements in rural life and economy (today's Greenfield Village in Dearborn stands as a monument to such in-terest).

Ford alone made Detroit an important iron and steel center. No other automo-bile manufacturer sought that kind of vertical integration and concentration. (General Motors moved in the opposite direction of decentralized automobile manufacturing, and by horizontal diversification into other durable consumer goods, such as refrigerators and washing machines, as a means of offsetting the fluc-tuations of the car market.) A number of small steel works and specialty mills soon appeared in the area, but major steel companies served this enormous market from expanded plants in the established Pittsburgh-Youngstown-Cleveland and Chi-cago districts. So, too, despite the River Rouge and other tire plants, the rubber in-dustry remained anchored in Akron, which in 1940 produced more than 70 per-cent of the nation's tires and consumed nearly 40 percent of the world's rubber (as an economic geographer noted, it would "be difficult to find a city more highly spe-cialized in the manufacture of a single type of product").

The petroleum industry, forty years old and still concentrating on kerosene at the turn of the century, was, like rubber, utterly transformed by the automobile rev-olution. However, whereas rubber was entirely dependent on imports (very largely from Southeast Asia), nothing better illustrates the prodigious domestic riches un-dergirding the American economy than the fact that for more than fifty years pe-troleum production expanded sufficiently to serve the astonishing increases in the number of motor vehicles. A series of oil discoveries in the early years of the new century greatly broadened the base of the industry from its Appalachian beginnings and made it well poised to meet heavy new demands. Thus as the number of vehi-cle registrations soared from 2.5 million to nearly 10 million between 1915 and 1920 and from that postwar baseline increased another threefold by 1940 and to nearly 50 million ten years later, so annual American oil production increased from just under half a billion barrels in 1920 to nearly three times that by 1940 and nearly 2 billion barrels in 1950 (oil imports were negligible through all these years). Such growth came from typically erratic, sporadic booms in dozens of fields, especially in Texas, Oklahoma, Kansas, Louisiana, and California, with significant amounts from new or rejuvenated fields in half a dozen other states. Most of the enormous output of the Mid-Continent and Gulf regions (and even that of such distant producers as Wyoming) was sent by pipeline or tanker to the Manufacturing Belt. However, an increasing amount was refined before shipment and the establishment of large refineries on the Gulf Coast and emergence there of a petrochemical industry (based upon new methods of catalytic cracking) was an important diversification of the region and a modification of the industrial geography of the nation. California was self-sufficient in crude oil and refined products, served much of the Far West, and exported a small surplus.

Natural gas generally accompanies petroleum underground, is basic to the extraction of oil, and is itself a valuable by-product (although for years much of it was simply flared—burned off). This excellent fuel was early piped from northern Appalachian fields to nearby cities, but extensive national exploitation awaited the development in the 1920s of high-pressure pipelines for long-distance transport from major Mid-Continent oil fields and from distinct natural gas fields in the Texas Panhandle, northern Louisiana, and southwestern Kansas. In 1930 a large, nearly thousand-mile pipeline was being built from Texas to Chicago, with branches to fifty cities en route. Twenty years later total production had tripled, and New England, the Pacific Northwest, and most of Florida were the only major regions as yet unserved by the national network. Beyond that consumed in the fields themselves, two-thirds of this rapidly expanding volume was used directly by industry, and most of the remainder found a ready market as a clean and efficient residential fuel.

No other country enjoyed such a bounty. At midcentury the United States produced more than half of the world's crude oil and nearly 90 percent of the world's natural gas. Just as massive resources of coal had been fundamental to America's rise to industrial leadership, so the superb domestic availability of oil and gas empowered it in the neotechnic twentieth century. Cheap gasoline (far cheaper than in Europe, which was nearly devoid of local petroleum until well after World War II) was fundamental to the rapid spread of automobile use, and that foundational experience, as well as the never-ending growth in the number of vehicles, has made keeping fuel cheap one of the most powerful pressures on American domestic policies.

Rural Americans eagerly took to the automobile, well before they were served by good roads, but adoption of its logical automotive companion, the gasoline-powered tractor, was less easy even though it was a longer-awaited revolution in farming life. For nearly a century after McCormick's reaper American farmers had been served by an ever-greater variety of machinery, but they had been unable to partake of the really transforming impact of paleotechnic industrialism because steam power was generally unsuited for mobile fieldwork. Such ponderous expensive machines might be put to use on great corporation estates in the Dakotas or the San Joaquin, but for the rest horses or mules provided the motive power—more than 20 million of them in 1915. By that date the gasoline-powered caterpillar tractor had made its appearance and was proving its worth in the mucklands of the Sacramento and the rolling hills of the Columbia wheatlands, but there were as yet only 25,000 tractors in total on America's 6.5 million farms. Henry Ford, characteristically, now gave the matter attention, produced his Fordson tractor in 1917, and by 1921 about two-thirds of the 343,000 tractors by then in use were from his factory. Other companies, especially such big implement manufacturers as John Deere and J. I. Case, were soon competing for this expanding market. By 1931 a million farm tractors were in use, by 1940, a million and a half and small gasoline engines were harnessed to many other farm tasks, such as shelling corn, pumping water, and sawing wood.

Tractors are more like trucks than like automobiles: many kinds, adapted to specialized work, in conjunction with an array of complementary machinery. Thus the patterns of adoption were related to the various kinds of farming: most rapid in the simple economies of the great Wheat Belts, where the radical efficiencies of tractors and combines fostered major westward expansions of cultivation all along the western margins of the High Plains from Texas to Montana; more slowly in the diversified family farms of the Corn Belt and northern dairy lands; and hardly at all in the minutely subdivided tenant-farmed Cotton Belt. This uneven spread of tractors ramified through the structure of American agriculture. By 1940, 9 million horses and mules had been displaced and 30 million acres formerly devoted to their feed had been released for commercial cropping. Furthermore, the land newly put under cultivation by means of the tractor was far more productive than that being taken out of cropping (thin-soiled hilly margins all across the Appalachians and Ozarks, cutover lands in the Upper Lakes, deeply depleted soils in the Piedmont). Together these changes greatly increased agricultural productions—and further depressed agricultural prices, which had been declining ever since the end of the war. These new machines were expensive as well as efficient, driving the desire for larger farms to cover the costs; mortgages and tenancy increased, the need for farm labor reduced, rural-to-urban migration accelerated. By the 1930s farmers were deeply involved in both the neotechnic benefits and capitalistic problems of American life.

ELECTRIFICATION

Automobiles and electricity were not so obviously interdependent, but there were important connections (beyond the internal power provided by car batteries). Their industrial expansion in America was almost exactly concurrent, and together they became the greatest agencies and symbols of the transforming power of the new technology of the twentieth century. Furthermore, Henry Ford, who had worked as a power plant engineer for Detroit Edison, had a direct role in binding the two.

The United States was not an early leader in the development of electric power. Alpine Europe, short of coal but rich in waterpower, pioneered and thereby provided in the 1890s some of the leading engineers and scientists who joined with Americans in "the brilliant execution of the great Niagara project[, which] was a turning point in the history of the electric power industry. . . . It demonstrated to the world the possibilities of large-scale production and long-distance transmission of electrical energy." The Niagara project was designed to serve the varied needs of a small region, but generally "electrification was fragmented and individualized" during its early phases, with each industry, each institution, each municipality having its own plants to serve only its own needs.

Various industries, such as textile plants, full of light machinery and poised at waterpower sites, began to turn to this new source of power, but the full potential of this radical new form of energy required a new kind of factory—the kind Henry Ford first created at Highland Park. Instead of the usual vertical building of several floors stacked over a single plant powering a maze of shafts and belts, his concept of continuous, sequential manufacture was made possible by providing each tool at each task along the moving assembly line with its own electric motor, all in a well-lighted, air-filtered factory spread out on a spacious lot. As Ford went on to apply the same concepts at a greater scale at River Rouge, so industrial America became rapidly more electrified and redesigned. By 1920 about half (by value) of the nation's manufacturing output was being produced with electricity; by 1940 over 85 percent, and the manufacture of electrical equipment and appliances had become a major industry.

In the cities the big hotels, theaters, department stores, and residences of the rich were among the first to make the change, soon followed by extravagant illumination of downtown commercial centers—the "Great White Way"—and more general street lighting from central municipal power stations. Such things provided brilliant visual announcement of the new age, but the full impact came only with comprehensive residential service and the adoption of an array of household appliances. Between 1915 and 1932 the proportion of the population enjoying residential electrification rose from 20 to 70 percent (about a third of these had lights only, no appliances). Such figures, however, tend to mask the stark contrast between bright cities and dark countrysides, for the 70 percent included only 10 percent of the Americans living on farms, and this lag in rural electrification had become a national political issue.

By the early 1920s expansion of demand and the feasibility of much longer-distance transmission pointed toward larger systems and goals. "The time is ripe for a great national program," said Secretary of Commerce Herbert Hoover: "to 'electrify America' is not only a great economic purpose, but it is also a great human purpose." Nationwide electrification must take the form of an interlocking set of regional systems each served by large plants providing low-cost power for distribution to the many lesser systems in a large territory ("somewhat comparable to the relation of the Federal Reserve District banks to the local banks," noted one prominent planner). The great issue was over the control and objectives of such a comprehensive network, a debate that became publicized as "Super Power" versus "Giant Power." The first term originated with a plan by private power companies to create an integrated network covering the cities from Washington, D.C., to Boston during World War I and was now applied to their larger schemes for the nation. Giant Power was a concept first promoted by Gifford Pinchot, famous Progressive and now governor of Pennsylvania, for concerted development of the cheapest sources of power and transmission lines to serve every point of use, the whole operated as a single efficient system. As a "natural monopoly" that "cannot by regulated by competition," it must be placed under public control or close regulation.

Rural electrification became the main theater of combat because so much remained to be done: whole regions of the country were as yet only spottily electrified. Both camps conducted studies and test cases of the problem. Private industry concluded that only certain kinds of intensive farming, such as dairying and irrigation agriculture, could be profitably served; thus, the field officer in charge of a sponsored project in Alabama concluded that the Cotton South would need to adopt "a more balanced program of agriculture that will make possible continuous use of electric power throughout the different seasons of the year." Such a stance ensured powerful Southern political support for some sort of government program for rural electrification.

Public power advocates pointed to other countries (such as Germany, Sweden, New Zealand) that had already achieved extensive rural electrification, and especially to the attractive nearby example of Ontario Hydro, established as a government agency in 1906 by a province eager to reduce its heavy dependence on imported Appalachian coal. A common complaint was that private power companies "skimmed the cream" by angling lines across the countryside to pick up only the best customers, leaving others stranded. As the eventual federal program argued, such "unsocial practices must give way to the policy of considering the electrification of an entire area at one time," so that for each area the agency "spots on a map the location of every farm, store, school, rural home, small industry, power line and other pertinent features within the established boundaries," then prepares load estimates and "designs a power system to provide service for every establishment." By building cheaply, keeping rates low, one could be confident of increased use as farming and local industries became more efficient and profitable.

In the 1920s Super Power won the main battles. A few rural electric cooperatives were formed (they were prohibited by some states), and a few states (such as Washington and New York) moved toward some encouragement of public power, but the resolute opposition of private electric companies generally prevailed at state and federal levels. Such opposition was only broken by the Great Depression and the New Deal response. By 1932 the bright lights of the city showed closed factories and breadlines, the countrysides were more deeply darkened by rural poverty, and the provision of electricity for all became a compelling program for social and economic betterment. During his campaign for the presidency, Franklin D. Roosevelt had called for "four great government power developments, . . . the St. Lawrence River in the Northeast, Muscle Shoals in the Southeast, the Boulder Dam in the Southwest, and . . . the Columbia River in the Northwest" (Boulder Dam on the Colorado was already under construction but did not include electric distribution by the government). Once Roosevelt was in office, the Tennessee Valley Authority was quickly enacted, an experimental comprehensive electrification of a county adjacent to that area was pronounced a great success, and in 1935 the Rural Electrification Administration (REA) was created (and placed under the direction of Morris L. Cooke, who, under Pinchot, had been the primary designer and advocate of Giant Power). The REA defined "rural" as areas "not included within the boundaries of any city, village, or borough having a population in excess of fifteen hundred inhabitants"; its primary instrument was low-cost loans for construction and operation of electrical systems, with priority given to local governments, people's utility districts, and cooperative associations.

The Tennessee Valley Authority (TVA), a radical multipurpose federal development project, which was given "full responsibility for meeting all power supply requirements in . . . [its] sizeable area of operations," was the only grand exhibit of Giant Power, but the federal government undertook other massive hydroelectric projects (completing them in three of the quarters of the country—plans for the St. Lawrence were delayed by the need for a treaty with Canada), as well as eventually assisting nearly a thousand local cooperatives and many municipal and state systems. The private power industry, spurred by such competition, also moved much more vigorously into rural electrification, selecting, as before, the better districts (private lines averaged more than twenty consumers per mile, co-ops three). By the mid-1950s "for all practical purposes American agriculture was electrified." And so, of course, was all of America. Consumption of electricity, like automobile registrations, was one of the anomalous growths during the Great Depression, and expansions of public power continued well after, increasing from 5 percent in 1930 to more than 20 percent of the total production of utility systems by the early 1950s.

That the distribution of electricity, one of the really vital spatial systems of the modern world, began and remained dominantly a realm of private enterprise in the United States was of course wholly in keeping with powerful American predilections already on display in other systems, such as the railroad, the telegraph, and the telephone. Electricity was "a commodity in the marketplace rather than a service." Like railroad strategists fifty years earlier, power companies, working under intensive competition, sought domination of the major markets of a particular territory. Although in this as in other forms of commerce, the central government only slowly asserted its regulatory power over interstate transmissions, it did eventually intervene selectively but massively into electric power production and distribution at an early enough stage to shape some important parts of the national network. One state, Nebraska, and a number of cities, including several large ones, such as Cleveland, Los Angeles, and Seattle, also developed their own public power. Thus in actual operation, the American network was a complex patchwork.

The general sequential patterns of electrification were not unlike those of paved streets and roads: appearing first within cities, then links to nearby towns and cities, followed by long main lines (in this case between major sources of power and major centers of use), with many branch lines, then forming mutually advantageous connections between major systems (rather like the first interstate trunk lines) (fig. 16), and eventually, through rural electrification, providing service to all places, just as states and counties gradually extended good roads to every community and most residences (aided by federal funding in each case). Although the effective distance of electric power transmission was markedly increased and very high voltage lines were the superhighways of the network, the most efficient scale remained regional rather than national and the overall system functioned as a set of major power supply territories, interlocked so that power could be shunted between them to meet special needs. (As early envisioned by its planners, these regional systems were rather like "the successful railways that have emerged out of the maze of the railway-construction period," achieving an efficient scale of management and articulated with other systems at a few border points.)

The specific historical geography of electrification was shaped by major sources of power as well as by the demands of industries and cities. America made ready use of its riches of both waterpower and coal in the early stages (as it later would of natural gas and fuel oil—and, eventually, atomic energy). New England and Upstate New York, the Carolina Piedmont and Southern Appalachians, and the rougher parts of the Upper Midwest were early leaders in hydroelectric development, as was the Pacific Northwest. California, however, was the first to create an extensive re-

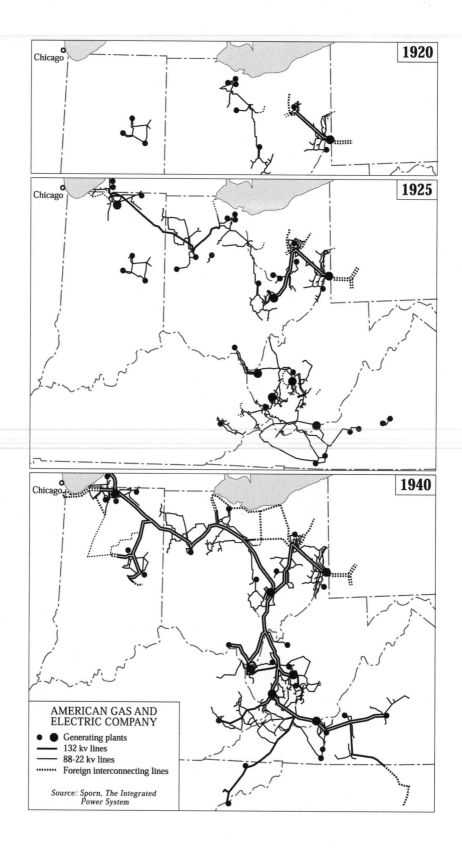

1920

1925

1940

Chicago

AMERICAN GAS AND
ELECTRIC COMPANY

● ● Generating plants
——— 132 kv lines
——— 88-22 kv lines
·········· Foreign interconnecting lines

*Source: Sporn, The Integrated
Power System*

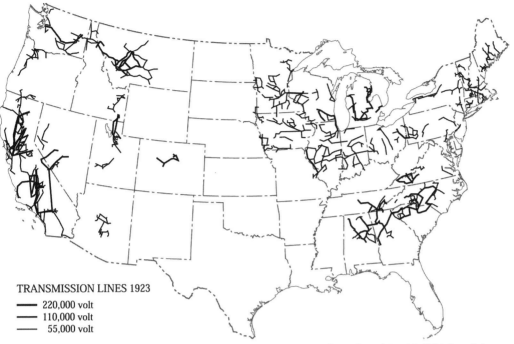

Source: Baum, Atlas of the U.S.A. Power Industry

17. Early Regional Electrifications.
The California system displays great densities in the Central Valley irrigation areas as well as long lines to Nevada mining operations. The surprisingly extensive network in Montana is largely that of the Anaconda Copper Company and of the Milwaukee Railroad, which had electrified its lines across the Rocky Mountains (and across the Cascade Range in Washington).

gional system (fig. 17). Such leadership was impelled not only by considerable waterpower potential (and lack of coal) and plenty of opportunistic entrepreneurs but by the close association of electricity and irrigation. The hydropotential of dams, the revolutionary efficiency of electric pumps, and the rapid expansion of irrigation in the Central Valley and Los Angeles Lowland meant a rapid expansion of farm (but not necessarily comprehensive rural) electrification. Connections among many such agricultural, mining, industrial, municipal, and interurban railway sys-

16. Development of a Private Electric System.
The first large generating plant was a mouth-of-mine location with abundant cooling-water supply just north of Wheeling on the Ohio River. By 1925 local systems in southern West Virginia had been acquired in preparation for major expansion based on excellent coal resources. By 1940 the enlarged system was bound together by double-circuit high-voltage lines.

tems resulted in much the most dense and extensive network through all the early phases of national electrification (in 1923 it claimed "the largest interconnected system in the world and the highest percentage of residences lighted by electricity"). Other irrigation areas in the Far West enjoyed somewhat similar if less intensive development. Power production became a major feature of later large dam-building projects by the federal government, especially on the Columbia River at Bonneville and Grand Coulee.

From New Jersey and Pennsylvania westward across the Manufacturing Belt coal was the greatest source of power, and improvements in long-distance transmission resulted in larger numbers of mine-mouth generating plants, reducing costs from rail shipment. Expanding industrial and municipal demands led to ever-more intricate and extensive networks, but the eventual density of later rural cooperatives across much of the Corn Belt displayed the lag in rural electrification. The thick spread of such co-ops across the whole of the South similarly attested that earlier systems in that region of high hydroelectric potential had been created to serve industries rather than farms and small settlements.

The automobile and electricity were contemporary instruments in the "miraculous unfolding" of the new age. Conquerors of distance and drudgery, together their radical mobility and flexibility ("where mankind wishes to go, copper wires can go too") promised a reshaping of America. Sketches of that future included an emphasis on decentralizing industry and healing the social differentials between rural and urban life. In 1921, Henry Ford, already a famous force in accelerating such changes, made a dramatic bid to assume a major role in the electrification of America. His was the only significant response to the government's invitation to private industry to lease and operate a great federal power and industrial installation at Muscle Shoals, on the middle Tennessee River in northwestern Alabama, an emergency wartime project to manufacture nitrates for munitions and now lying idle and incomplete. The magic of Ford's name, along with his visit to Muscle Shoals accompanied by his aged friend Thomas A. Edison, generated enormous public interest in his bid. Although the focus was at first on producing nitrate for cheap fertilizer, far greater implications emerged to fuel discussions and debates. Ford fostered these with talk of demonstrating "what can be done with water power" to initiate "a new epoch in American agriculture and industry," and such statements as "there is enough water power on this continent to run railroads, factories, homes—everything and cheap," and "we could make a new Eden of our Mississippi Valley, turning it into a great garden and powerhouse of the country." Nothing caused greater excitement in the South than his talk about creating a "great city," a "new Detroit," a new *kind* of city seventy-five miles long bordering this entire power-potential stretch of the Tennessee. Furthermore, Muscle Shoals was to be "only the first of a whole series of such projects Ford planned eventually to build in various sections of the country." The famous man insisted that his proposal was offered as "an industrial philanthropy . . . based on a desire for great public service," but his formal bid contained nothing of these larger plans, or anything about distribution of power to the region (he later spoke of running "power lines 200 miles in every direction from Muscle Shoals"), and it generated alarmed opposition from both private power interests and public power advocates. After two years of intense public and congressional controversy an embittered bigoted Ford (blaming Wall Street and International Jewry) withdrew his offer. These years of impassioned debate and the several more that followed illustrated the great ideological issues and structural complexities built into the American electric power system—and in this case would lead directly into America's largest and most controversial example of regional planning: the TVA.

"The instruments of a neotechnic civilization are now at hand," declared Lewis Mumford in 1934, and he foretold important geographic changes: "By means of the motor car the upland areas, where electric power can be cheaply produced, and where the railroad enters at a considerable disadvantage can be thrown open to commerce, industry, and population. These upland areas are likewise the most salubrious seat of living. . . . Here is, I must emphasize, the special habitat of the neotechnic civilization, as . . . the valley bottoms and coal beds were for the palaeotechnic period." He was realistic enough, however, to know that there were powerful structural and social resistances to fundamental changes and that "palaeotechnic purposes with neotechnic means . . . is the most obvious characteristic of the present order" (a Henry Ford talking about rural utopias—"why should the factory stay in the city?"—while building the largest concentrated industrial complex in America). Even as Mumford was writing, the first in a sequence of unprecedented crises, the decade-long Great Depression to be followed by the massive upheaval of a truly World War, was under way, and together these would so shake the established system that they would accelerate the reshaping of America, though not exactly as envisioned.

RADIO BROADCASTING

"The dramatic evolution of the radio within one decade from a mysterious curiosity to a widely diffused and universally accepted instrument of entertainment, business, learning and mass communication, has few if any counterparts in social history." Thus, at the end of that decade, did the massive government report *Recent Social Trends* record the amazing emergence of yet another technological marvel. In 1920 one station in the United States began broadcasting regular scheduled daily programs; in 1929, 12 million American families could tune in to one or more of 623 licensed stations.

Guglielmo Marconi received his first patent in 1897, in Britain, and initiated a twenty-year prelude to that dramatic decade during which a great variety of inventors, amateurs, government agencies, institutions, and corporations on both sides of the Atlantic experimented with, rapidly improved the technologies of, and enlarged perceptions of the possibilities for "wireless communication." Wireless telephony (transmission of articulate speech rather than Morse code) was especially important to maritime operations. Successful transmission between San Francisco and Honolulu in 1912 spurred the U.S. Navy to establish networks across the Pacific and the Caribbean, just as Britain was constructing its own, far more extensive, imperial wireless system. During the World War all amateur radios were shut down, the U.S. Navy took charge of all ship-to-shore facilities, and the U.S. Army took over many inland stations; immediately after the war the military strongly endorsed proposals for government control of radio, "to give Uncle Sam the same relation to wireless messages that he possessed as to mail," as the secretary of the Navy put it. But the war had accelerated experiments with small radios, and the development of the vacuum tube had provided the technical basis for the broadcasting industry, and a political decision against government monopoly opened the way for aggressive commercial expansion by big corporations.

Thus a "national mania" for broadcasting swept over the country in the early 1920s. Colleges, churches, municipalities, department stores, newspapers, telephone companies, electric companies, and a host of others large and small sought to make use of this magical instrument. These mushrooming stations varied greatly in broadcasting power and purpose, leadership and resources, but the whole scene seethed with "the feeling that broadcasting was a key to influence and power"— and, for many, profits. The early simple transmission of messages had given way to the airing of talks, concerts, and other local events. Experimental broadcasts of major events (such as presidential speeches and prizefights) *simultaneously* in several cities by the use of telegraph or telephone lines was a major advance and pointed toward the obvious possibility of some sort of nationwide system.

In 1920 Westinghouse, seeking to recover from the loss of wartime Navy business, began to offer scheduled daily programming from KDKA, its Pittsburgh station, and also to market improved inexpensive radio receivers. KDKA was much the most powerful station in the nation, and Westinghouse asserted that fifteen such stations "could serve the whole country adequately." The government, however, was faced with imposing some sort of order on a chaotic broadcasting scene. In 1922 Secretary of Commerce Herbert Hoover, working in this new realm with uncertain formal authority, convened a National Radio Conference, set up a classification of stations, allocated frequency bands to various categories of service, issued licenses, and proposed recognition of a set of "clear channel" stations (that is, no other stations allowed to broadcast on that particular frequency within a specified distance) to be spaced across the country. By 1926 so many stations were jammed into a narrow spectrum that the issuance of new licenses was temporarily suspended.

Meanwhile, further experience with linking a set of stations for simultaneous programming—"chain broadcasting" was the current term—led to the formation of the National Broadcasting Company (NBC) by the most powerful combination in the business: Radio Corporation of America (RCA), General Electric (GE), and Westinghouse, using long-distance lines leased from American Telephone & Telegraph (AT&T). Two networks, the Red and the Blue, were formed (the names derived from the pencils used to sketch the scheme on a blank map), each based on a powerful company-owned New York station and providing a particular set of programs to formally affiliated stations across the nation. The system was launched in November 1926, with thirty-nine stations in the two networks. During this same season a much smaller and weaker system of thirteen stations across the Northeast began service as the Columbia Broadcasting System (CBS) (fig. 18).

In 1927 Congress finally passed a comprehensive Radio Act "to maintain control of the United States over all the channels of interstate and foreign radio transmission; and to provide for the use of such channels, but not the ownership thereof, by individuals, firms, or corporations, for limited periods of time, under licenses granted by federal authority." The country was divided into five "zones" and a Federal Radio Commission (FRC) composed of one member from each zone was empowered to classify stations, prescribe the nature of service for each class, assign broadcasting frequencies, power, and times of service, and undertake an equitable allocation of stations for each zone. Twenty-five stations were licensed for national clear-channel broadcasting (all but three of which were within the newly formed networks), and another thirty-one designated as regional clear-channel stations.

There were still many stations operated by educational or other philanthropic institutions, but Hoover's notion of 1922 that "it is inconceivable that we should allow so great a possibility for service to be drowned in advertising chatter" was already very conceivable indeed. NBC and CBS were "deluged with requests for admission to their 'chains.'" Since these networks were designed on the basis of "population and purchasing power," "the natural tendency was to admit the stations with the greatest audiences and the greatest ranges, since this would guarantee the advertiser the largest permanent national 'circulation'" (affiliated stations broadcast network programs and received a share of the advertising income). The map of these networks in the opening phase clearly displays the results of this search for profits and how far they were from providing comprehensive national coverage. More than two-thirds of the network stations were in the Northeastern core area, and none in the Gulf South, Texas, or Mountain West. The FRC wanted regional clear-channel stations to be spaced more than 300 miles apart but delayed such a

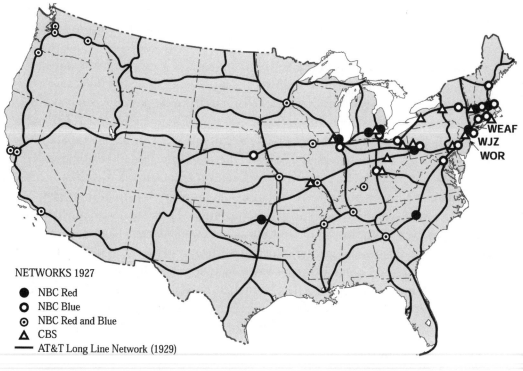

NETWORKS 1927

● NBC Red
○ NBC Blue
◉ NBC Red and Blue
△ CBS
▬ AT&T Long Line Network (1929)

WEAF
WJZ
WOR

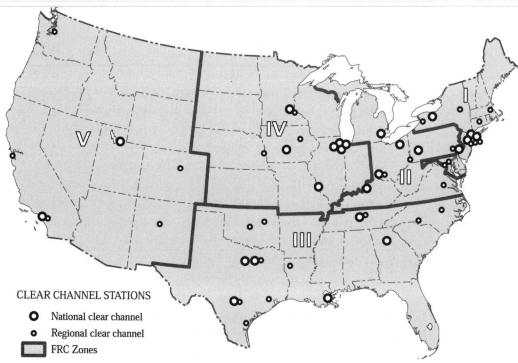

CLEAR CHANNEL STATIONS

◯ National clear channel
○ Regional clear channel
▭ FRC Zones

18. Early Radio Networks and Clear-Channel Stations.
(Sources: Archer, *Big Business*; Hugill, *Global Communications*; White, *American Radio*)

requirement. Maximum power was set at 50,000 watts, but the only one operating at that level was the GE station at their Schenectady headquarters. Only a dozen other stations operated at 10,000 watts or more, 5,000 was considered relatively strong, and a few of the original NBC stations broadcast with as little as 500 watts of power.

Although at the end of this dramatic decade 40 percent of American households had a radio, the distribution was starkly uneven. The highest levels were in the suburbs of major cities, the lowest in poor rural areas without electricity: New Jersey with 63 percent, Mississippi with 5.4 percent, representing the extremes by statewide measurement. Such a pattern generated congressional pressure from the South and West for "equality of radio broadcasting service," but continued rapid expansion of the industry—stations and networks, broadcasting power and quality of transmissions, programming and availability of cheap reliable radio sets—(and of electrification) rapidly solved the problem. By 1940 more than 90 percent of American homes had a radio (only 63 percent had a telephone), network broadcasting covered the country, and this first of the "mass media" had become a commonplace of American life.

The sudden appearance of this revolutionary instrument posed a challenge to sociologists and others to assess its impact on society. The committee in charge of the topic for *Recent Social Trends* (after what must have been some rather tedious sessions) came up with a list of 150 "social effects" of the radio. Many of these were trite ("a new form of advertising" had been created), and not all were of equal significance ("the contralto favored over sopranos through better transmission"), but the list did include several that might be presumed to have some bearing on the shaping of the national society: "Homogeneity of peoples increased because of like stimuli"; "Regional differences in cultures become less pronounced"; "Distinctions between social classes and economic groups lessened"; "Isolated regions are brought into contact with world events"; "Favoring of the widely spread languages"; "Standardization of diction and discouragement of dialects." Just what was—and ought to be—the role of the mass media in American society was now an enduring and controversial topic, and one that gathered even greater interest and concern toward midcentury, when radio was becoming supplemented, and in part supplanted, by an even more powerful medium of wireless communication.

AIR SERVICE

Still another miraculous unfolding was taking place during this same span of years, one perhaps more dramatic even if it did not seem likely at first to transform the lives of ordinary citizens. The Air Age in America parallels the Automobile Age in many ways, with only a slight lag in time. By 1908 Orville and Wilbur Wright were demonstrating their remarkable machine to a fascinated Europe, and five years later the world's first scheduled passenger service was begun, connecting St. Petersburg with Tampa twenty-two miles across the bay. The World War was a famous proving ground for aircraft as well as for land vehicles, and in 1918 the Army Air Service began flying the first scheduled airmail route, between Washington, Philadelphia, and New York. Three months later the Post Office Department took over that operation but soon faced the problem of justifying such expenditure to a skeptical Congress.

For years American railroads had provided excellent mail service between major cities. The obvious niche for airmail was on those routes where greater speed and directness might offer practical advantages to banking and business. The Post Office therefore focused on transcontinental service. Beginning in 1919 with a Cleveland-Chicago segment, the full New York to San Francisco route was completed in the following year, and the initial westbound crossing was twenty-two hours faster than regular surface mail. Intensive efforts to improve facilities and operations and extend service along other routes followed. Really major advantage over railroads required night flying and, therefore, the lighting of airfields and spacing of beacons along the flight paths (this latter task was assigned to the Lighthouse Service). More powerful planes allowed higher and more direct flight, rather than skimming along railroad routes ("by keeping the Wabash Railroad in sight for the next 125 miles you will come in sight of Lake Michigan"—assured the "Pilots' Log of Distances, Landmarks, and Flying Directions" for the first transcontinental mail), keeping an eye alert for notable features ("A white fire tower may be seen on the crest of the last mountain to the north") and a way out of trouble ("excellent emergency landing field is located one-half mile south of Wahoo; a smooth barley field approximately 1 mile long and a quarter of a mile wide"). By 1925 a saving of three days over transcontinental surface mail, including "a complete working day between the two biggest business centres" (New York and Chicago), was achieved and the value of airmail convincingly demonstrated (at a considerable cost: 157 crashes and forty pilots killed during the Post Office operations).

In 1926 the Post Office got out of the flying business and contracted with private airlines to carry the mail (Henry Ford, already operating express services from Detroit to Cleveland and Chicago, got one of the first contracts). In that same year the Air Commerce Act assigned the secretary of Commerce "to designate and establish airways, to organize air navigation, arrange for research and development of such aids, license pilots and aircraft, and to investigate accidents." Local governments and communities were already involved in the competition for air service by providing airfields, hangars, and other facilities (in setting up the initial transcontinental route the Post Office's own agent had calculatingly pitted one city against another: Cheyenne versus Laramie, Salt Lake City versus Ogden, Reno versus

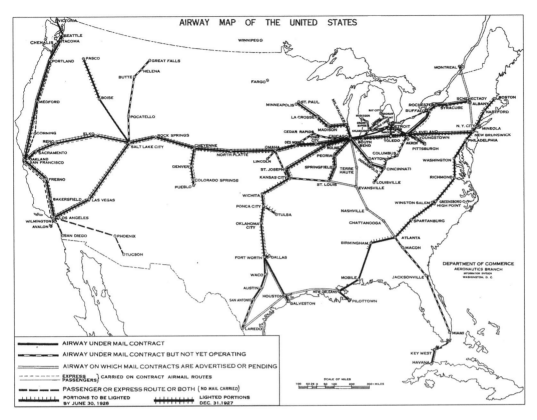

19. Airway Map, 1928.

Showing air mail service in operation and pending, and the progress of lighting such routes. The density of service in the Chicago-Detroit area reflects the early development of express services. Pasco, the small town at the terminus of the Salt Lake City–Pacific Northwest route, was a major railroad center offering frequent service to Portland, Seattle, and Spokane. (Print from Aeronautics Bulletin No. 8, U.S. Department of Commerce)

Carson City). Entrepreneurs eagerly responded to mail subsidies and the general prospects for rapid growth, and the airmail system was soon extending over all regions of the country by means of some forty companies (fig. 19).

Many kinds of planes, American-built and foreign, were used in this pioneering service, and some had a few seats for passengers. By the late 1920s "the Lindbergh euphoria" and the advent of larger and safer planes, especially the well-tested Ford Tri-Motor (modeled extensively on European prototypes) broadened public acceptance of air travel. Nevertheless, the first scheduled transcontinental service, initiated in 1929, reflected important hesitancies about this exciting new mode. Assuming that passengers would be uneasy about the safety and comfort of night flying, a combination railroad-airline service was offered: passengers traveled by

Pullman sleepers from New York to Columbus, thence by air to Waynoka, Oklahoma, again by Pullman overnight to Clovis, New Mexico, and by air on to Los Angeles. The Ford planes averaged 110 miles per hour, twice the speed of trains, and this touted "Lindbergh Line" (he was a consultant on the plan) reduced the usual 100-hour crossing to 48. Three other such rail-plane combinations were soon established, but late the next year United Air Lines offered an all-air schedule (with stewardesses and meal service in the ten-passenger cabins) of 33 hours between New York and San Francisco, including an overnight stop in Chicago, and the race to create bigger and better planes and foster nationwide air travel was under way. In 1933 Boeing produced what has usually been called "the first modern airliner," the B247, and United Air Lines soon had these in service on a coast-to-coast schedule of just under 20 hours; other airlines turned to Douglas Aircraft Company, and in the next year its DC-2 allowed a New York–Los Angeles run of 18 hours; but the real breakthrough came two years later with the Douglas DC-3, larger (twenty-one passengers) and faster (170 mph), comfortable, reliable, and efficient—the first plane to make passenger service by itself profitable. By 1938, 95 percent of U.S. air traffic was carried by DC-3s.

In 1930 an amendment to the Air Commerce Act had enlarged and altered mail subsidies so as to encourage greater attention to express service and passengers, and it gave the postmaster general great power over the selection of routes and companies for such contracts. As a result, President Hoover's appointee, Walter Folger Brown, became "the architect of the major U.S. airline route networks. . . . Using his almost dictatorial authority he rationalized the unco-ordinated system of dozens of small companies into the nucleus of the Domestic Trunk airlines." Brown was especially influential in the establishment of transcontinental routes and interregional trunk lines as the framework for a national airways system (fig. 20). His role was abruptly ended (and subjected to lengthy investigation for collusion) by the Roosevelt administration, and airline passenger service was opened to more companies and competition, yet this enlarged pattern was soon placed under comprehensive regulation by a Civil Aeronautics Board (CAB) empowered to regulate the entry of companies, interstate routes, competition, fares, and much else. Established in 1938, this powerful agency remained in place for forty years and "from the outset, . . . controlled roughly half of the world's airline activity."

In spite of the unstable complexity of specific company operations over this twenty-year formative period, the general pattern of a national airways system can be discerned, with passenger service built upon the framework established by airmail. Major segments and stages were:

1. *Axis of the American Core Area: New York–Chicago.* The first link to provide major time advantage for banking and business, and the first to generate sufficient pas-

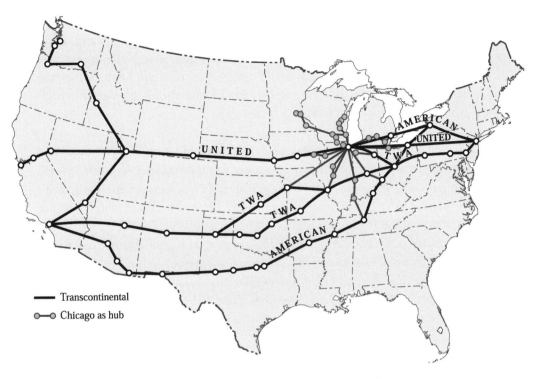

20. Transcontinental Passenger Service, 1933.
(Source: *Official Guide*, November 1933)

senger demand to sustain extensive competitive service. In 1933 United Air Lines offered eleven round-trips daily (with a stop in Cleveland); a few years later three airlines were offering multiple nonstop flights.

2. *Transcontinental Axis: New York–California.* Initially along the central route directly to San Francisco; soon with branches to Los Angeles and to the Pacific Northwest (by United Air Lines, shaped to the pattern of the Union Pacific–Central Pacific); next, competitive service to Los Angeles on more direct southwestern routes. Los Angeles became the main western focus as the airlines partook of the glamour of Hollywood while providing a vital link between New York finance and Southern California cinema, broadcasting, and other new industries.

3. *Chicago Hub.* Early development of radial connections with all major Middle West cities and many local lesser ones. Begun for mail and express, passenger service soon followed (as with railroads, "bridge lines" to bypass Chicago were also early in place, such as Kohler Aviation, offering six-passenger amphibious planes from Milwaukee directly across Lake Michigan to Detroit).

4. *Interregional Trunk Lines.* Among the most important were New York City and Washington, D.C., to Atlanta and New Orleans, and by way of the Carolinas to Florida; Chicago to Nashville, Atlanta, and Florida, Chicago to New Orleans, and Chicago to Texas; the Pacific Coast line linking cities from San Diego to Seattle; and, belatedly (not until the mid-1930s), the old northern "transcontinental" route between Minneapolis–St. Paul and Seattle.

5. *Local Service.* A surprising number of small cities and towns enjoyed air service from an early date. Much of this was the result of mail subsidies supporting small planes that required frequent stops; even as planes became larger, refueling and rest stops were spaced along trunk routes. For example, in 1933 scheduled stops west of Kansas City on Transcontinental and Western Air's (TWA's) "shortest route coast-to-coast" included Wichita, Amarillo, Albuquerque, and Winslow, en route to Los Angeles, and American Airways' transcontinental service west of Fort Worth included Abilene, Big Spring, El Paso, Douglas, Tucson, and Phoenix. Larger and faster planes would make most of these stops optional, but some service was usually maintained (and after 1938 could not be dropped without governmental approval).

In the summer of 1940 TWA "took air transport another step forward by introducing the thirty-three-passenger Boeing 307 Stratoliner on its transcontinental routes," a more powerful and high-flying plane (four engines and pressurized cabins) that cut two hours off the usual schedule; a year and a half later all were transferred to war service (the plane itself was a modification from the B-17 bomber). Once again, war greatly accelerated the developing Air Age. Mass production and use (military and civilian, freight and passenger) vastly expanded experience and technology, perceptions and possibilities, and when thousands of planes suddenly became surplus, with hundreds of entrepreneurs eager to put them to use, an "air transport explosion" followed. It was, however, a controlled explosion, managed by the CAB. By 1940 the board had decided that air service had become big enough to warrant distinct levels of companies. In 1944 it created a new classification, "Feeder Airline," specializing in "the shorter, sparser traffic routes between minor cities," and with a new aim of "providing air service to every citizen of the United States," it soon certified more than a dozen new companies. These new short-haul carriers (aided by heavier subsidies) together with expansion of service by trunk-line companies put about 200 new cities and towns on the airline map of the United States—a highly popular political cause that tended to stabilize the points of service (even if not the actual frequencies and patterns of connections).

The CAB also helped lesser trunk-line carriers to compete more directly with the Big Four (American, United, TWA, Eastern), allowing them access to busy intercity routes and creating new direct connections (such as Minneapolis–Los Angeles); it also authorized reduced coach fares to broaden the market (and in 1949 the first scheduled all-cargo service). By midcentury these expansions together with much larger and faster planes on the main routes (DC-6s, Lockheed Constellations, Boeing Stratocruisers) had made air travel a far more common experience, with the millions of passenger miles by air now approaching the declining number by train.

Thus the American system was created under conditions of direct government influence and market competition working on a continental scale. Airmail was driven by the imperatives of conducting business thousands of miles across four time zones, air passenger service by similar advantages in business management together with the glamour of the latest form of elite travel. Incentives to build larger and better planes and to improve the efficiencies of airline operations were empowered by the heady prospects of expanding the market for air travel to include a large proportion of a large population spread across a continent.

To return to our parallels with the Automobile Age, the transcontinental air passenger service of the early 1930s coincided with the completion of the first paved highways across the country (and along the same routes); the great expansions of the air network after World War II were comparable to the completion of the first full federal highway system, while a supersystem of the air awaited the jet plane, first placed in service in 1958, two years after authorization of the Interstate System of superhighways.

3. Acceleration: On the Surface

INTERSTATE HIGHWAY SYSTEM

"The largest public works project in the history of the world"—as it became commonly touted—made its public debut on November 14, 1956, with the formal dedication of an eight-mile stretch of I-70 west from Topeka, just four and a half months after President Dwight D. Eisenhower had signed the Interstate Highway Act (a piece of I-70 that would soon reach his hometown of Abilene). That act had set in motion "a great tidal wave of federal money breaking over every sector of the American economy and influencing every aspect of American life." This $130 billion, 42,500-mile national system was generally in place by its scheduled completion date of 1972, although many short sections remained to be finished over the next several years, and it was soon carrying more than 20 percent of all vehicular traffic more quickly and safely than ever before. If, as Tom Lewis put it, "the automobile was the passport to the postwar American dream," this new Interstate roadway marked the arrival a quarter century later of that fully auto-centered world.

This set of standardized superhighways was in effect a comprehensive network

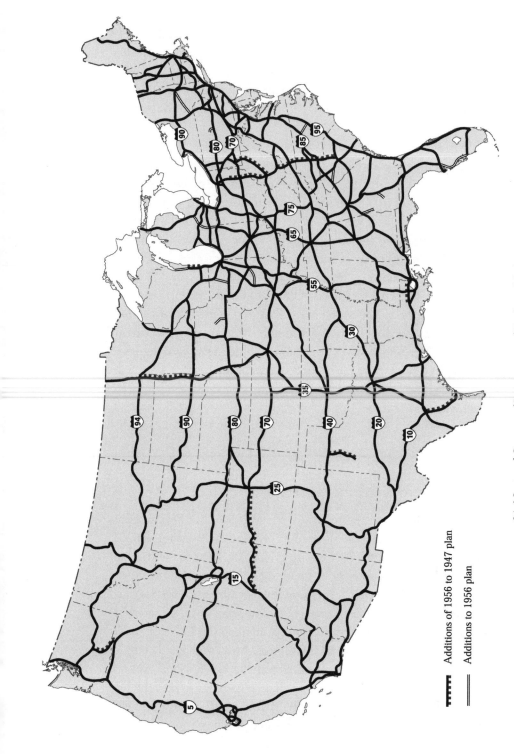

21. National System of Interstate and Defense Highways.

The identifications shown are selected simply to provide a sense of the numbering system. A comparison with the 1947 system shows that I-80 was shifted southward to give a more direct route west from New York City, forming what had been locally promoted as the "Keystone Shortway," rather than along U.S. 6 across the northern tier of Pennsylvania counties.

▰▰▰ Additions of 1956 to 1947 plan

▬▬▬ Additions to 1956 plan

superimposed simultaneously upon all parts of the nation (fig. 21). Unlike canals, railroads, and even the preceding federal highway system, it was not an incremental, piecemeal creation expanding out of particular areas to form larger networks by accretion. Excepting only the earlier completion of a few toll roads incorporated into the Interstate, no region, no particular linkage of major cities, had a head start in reaping the benefits of this superior transportation facility. In pattern it was a giant grid of trunk lines fitted to the national expanse, coast-to-coast and border-to-border, thicker in the East, thinner in the West, with numerous shorter laterals and angled connections to provide more direct flow from one segment to another, and necessitating very few stubs to bind an otherwise isolated city into the network (such as the tap lines to Lubbock, Cedar Rapids and Waterloo, and Columbus, Georgia). A thinner grid than the earlier federal system, the Interstate tended to channel traffic along fewer paths.

Although it was a single *national* program, it was also, as earlier noted, a distinctly *federal* pattern that reflected forty years of participation of the forty-eight states in planning highway networks. Thus the overall design was shaped for continental connectivity, linking all the states, rather than capacity appropriate to anticipated traffic. There were long stretches of high-capacity highway across very sparsely inhabited country, connecting a wide spacing of towns and small cities. The continuation of political influence is reflected in the general density of routes in the South (greater than the predicted traffic might warrant) and in such specific additions to the basic 1947 consensus plan (see fig. 9) as I-79 and I-77 in West Virginia, and I-70 west of Denver, which, at the insistence of influential Coloradans, was extended at enormous expense directly across the Rockies (by parallel tunnels at elevations of more than 11,000 feet), down the narrow Glenwood Canyon, and, veering from the established route, on across the San Rafael Swell (where no road of any kind had ever gone) to join I-15 and form a new direct route between Denver and Los Angeles.

Wherever they appeared Interstate highways became a massive new presence, on a different scale and detached from previous roadways and facilities. Design standards for widths of right-of-way, roadbed, shoulders, medians, and (after 1966) at least four lanes of traffic, together with severe limits on gradients and curvature, large clearances, no at-grade crossings, limited access, and the general objective of providing the most direct path along a designated route, resulted in huge new cuttings, fills, embankments, bridges, and tunnels; even in level terrain it was an altogether formidable imprint on the landscape, bypassing settlements and cutting a wide swath through the country, leaving fragments of properties on either side. From the local standpoint it was clearly a national presence, a continental system shaped by distance, speed, and uninterrupted movement rather than service to adjacent communities. Whereas formerly the roads came to the towns and cities, and federal highways ran down Main Street, this new mode—like the railroad—allowed access only at selected points spaced along the route. Selection of these privileged locations was made by state highway officials; at least the offer of local hearings was mandated, but the public had no formal power over this vital geographical decision making, and highway departments commonly preferred working quietly with local chambers of commerce "as their chief clientele."

Thus within the span of a few years the Interstate interchange, "the node joining national, regional, and local worlds in the country's daily circulation," emerged as a powerful new feature in the American landscape. These great entry- and exitways, cloverleaf or diamond in pattern, "divided the land into four quadrants, each ready for developers to transform into cash-producing real estate." Manuals on the principles of site selection at these new crossroads soon appeared, defining levels of traffic, exact positioning, design, and local contexts for business success; geographers began to classify a whole new set of settlement types and sequences, ranging from those offering the simplest set of food, fuel, and lodging—"the triple pillars of American roadside commerce"—to various larger complexes of such facilities ("new players in the exit game favor and enlarge well-developed clusters, and erect a forest of on-premise signs as clue to security and choice"). Truckstops, with their enormous expanses of asphalt, outsized facilities, and specialized services, became a giant variant of the same type. Spaced along every Interstate, such clusters of franchised businesses have created "at least five thousand new but nameless 'places' in the American landscape." These new nodes may draw some trade from the surrounding countryside; those near established towns tend to have a more powerful effect, reshaping the town and shifting its business focus to new shopping plazas and a commercial strip connecting the old local Main Street to this new national main street (fig. 22).

The impact on large cities was more complex. The Interstate Highway Act authorized 2,300 miles of urban construction. Most of this was for perimeter roads that would intersect existing streets radiating from the Central Business District. In the early stages of fragmented Interstate construction the main effect was to shorten the time and lengthen the distance of suburban commuting, thereby accelerating the exodus of urban residents and suburban expansion. Soon, however, office parks and shopping malls sprouted up at the most strategic interchanges, and as circumferential roads were completed into "beltways" ("a rim connecting the spokes of the radial expressways [creating] a giant urban wheel") major new patterns of urban life rapidly formed, featuring what Joel Garreau has vividly described and definitively named "Edge Cities." These huge clusters of office buildings and malls became in effect the new "downtowns" (with plenty of parking) for wide suburban, exurban, and, indeed, urban hinterlands, for most of the major department stores, quality shops, hotels, and other services have been drained out of most historic centers.

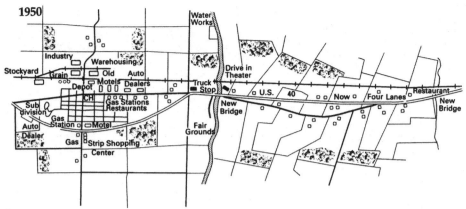

Stage 6

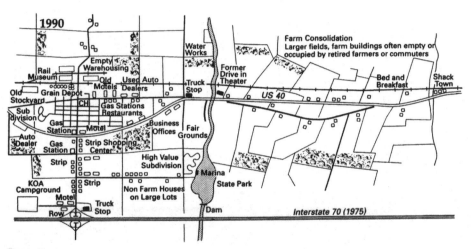

Stage 7

22. Interstate as Reshaper.

Karl Raitz's great work on the history of *The National Road* includes this generalization of forty years of change in small towns along U.S. 40 following the arrival of I-70. The 1950 pattern shows a new bypass of Main Street, the first rerouting to cope with post–World War II traffic; by 1990 commercial life has been almost entirely reoriented toward the interchange. (Source: Karl B. Raitz, ed., *The National Road*, 369. © 1996. Reprinted with permission of the Johns Hopkins Univ. Press)

The scale and power of this accelerated dispersal and restructuring of metropolitan form was one of the unintended consequences of the Interstate, and it was exaggerated by another dimension of this highway revolution: the thrust of these massive trafficways directly into and often through the heart of the city (fig. 23). The first stage of this assault required the destruction of all buildings and streets in its path; the second was in effect the creation of a great wall formed by a set of road-

23. Interstate Intrusion.
This 1962 view of the construction of an interchange between the heavily used Harbor Freeway and the new Santa Monica Freeway (the westernmost portion of I-10) in Los Angeles well displays the massive disruptive power of such superhighways.

ways far wider than any urban street, often elevated or depressed and with few points of access, resulting in the perceptual and actual separation of one part of the city from the other. Highway planners, seeking the cheapest as well as the shortest routes, were drawn to areas of low-grade housing and marginal commercial districts; city officials eager to bind Downtown to this vital new system of circulation regarded the destruction of such neighborhoods as opening up opportunities for "urban renewal" (thereby tapping another great inflow of federal funds). Such attitudes of the 1950s and 1960s were strongly analogous with those of a century earlier. As we noted in the case of railroads: "no civic authority in America could or wanted to resist the intrusion of this radical space-conqueror; in the open competitive environment of that critical formative geographic era, growth and prosperity did in fact depend upon superior railway connections. And so every city avidly enticed railroads and readily ceded to them streets, public squares, waterfront, and large acreages, all with deeply disturbing and long lasting effects upon the pattern of urban life."

Before the final vote on the Interstate Highway Act every congressman received a small book of maps showing the routes planned for every metropolitan area. As Tom Lewis noted, "as two-dimensional abstractions the lines looked harmless" (only one congressman from such a district voted against the bill), yet they displayed "the future urban battlegrounds," for when these lines became "three-dimensional structures of concrete and steel they became great creatures that threatened the life of the city." By the late 1960s it had become clear that the superimposition of this enormous linear structure upon already densely developed areas could have enormous unwanted ramifications. In the larger cities thousands of persons uprooted by this invasion, unable to move to the suburbs, became themselves invaders of other neighborhoods, often generating severe racial, ethnic, and class confrontations; others were shifted into new high-rise public housing projects (financed by urban renewal funds). Such people were generally powerless, but there were others who also became deeply disturbed about what was happening to their city even if they themselves were not directly in the path of destruction. Thus public opposition to further extensions of urban superhighways welled up in many cities. Rarely could anything halt the powerful momentum of this nationally endorsed self-financing juggernaut, but there were a few famous victories, such as halting construction along the historic waterfronts of the Embarcadero in San Francisco and Jackson Square in New Orleans, and canceling an eight-lane Inner Belt projected through a dozen Boston neighborhoods.

Such attacks were a shock to federal and state highway officials and to most congressmen and mayors, who assumed that Americans would always welcome better roads and localities welcome the jobs and development potentials their construction would bring. Under such pressures the Interstate program was periodically modified by legislative acts and policies requiring greater concern for "beautification" (primarily the control of billboards), historic sites, environmental impacts, and, in 1976, neighborhoods: "those particularly vulnerable to freeway disruption and therefore to be avoided are high density pedestrian-dependent neighborhoods with few autos available and strong racial or ethnic ties." Such changes were of course prompted by the widespread evidence of disruptions already experienced. The most important change came in 1975, when the Highway Trust Fund was for the first time modified to allow cities to use some portion for other forms of transportation: subways, light rail, bikeways, pedestrian paths.

"Over the full span of American history," said Peirce Lewis, one of our most discerning students of the American scene, "one is hard-put to find a single legislative act that so profoundly altered the face of the American landscape, did it so quickly, and yielded so many unexpected and unintended results." That the Interstate Highway Act yielded unintended results was surely because since the days of Thomas MacDonald highway planners in America proceeded with only one basic intention: to keep the traffic moving; that many results were unexpected was surely because such people lived in a specialized professional and political world isolated from other societal concerns and were left to build roads "largely as they wished." Even though by intent the Interstate was to be fitted to portions of the general geographic framework of the federal highway network, such a separate massive structure and superior traffic-moving system was bound to have far-reaching geographic consequences. When "in 1986, an informal group of academics, federal and state transportation officials, and representatives of the private sector, began to discuss the future of the surface transportation system in the United States," major unpredicted results of the Interstate System were starkly apparent, including the development of edge cities and "a fundamentally new kind of urban structure"; "a 'stop the highway' backlash and a political polarization between the build vs. no-build factions [that] became a fact of political life in U.S. transportation"; and a heavy impact on the railroads, which suffered "a financial blow" as they "lost substantial market in high-value freight" to a massive increase in trucking. Well before the great task was completed, the builders of the Interstate were facing failure in a critical part of their one intended objective: although traffic between cities was moving faster, heavier, and safer than ever before, congestion on the beltway and crosstown freeways seemed to be getting worse day by day—"rush-hour conditions in many metropolitan areas often extended through the day." As most Americans lived in metropolitan areas, the Interstate solution for mobile America was seriously compromised.

In 1991 Congress passed the Intermodal Surface Transportation Efficiency Act (ISTEA); the title might suggest a new era in national planning, but the contents revealed much continuity with previous programs, with most of the funds supporting highway construction and maintenance. There was a substantial allocation to mass transit and other kinds of urban trafficways, but no major emphasis on nationwide intermodal development. Nevertheless, various specialists had concluded that the transportation problems of the United States "would have to be addressed by means other than simply constructing additional conventional highways." In 1992 the Department of Transportation began funding a Strategic Plan for Intelligent Vehicle Highway Systems, initiating a twenty-year plan "to create something wholly new in the world of transportation." The program involves using computers, the newest communication system, and sensors to predict potential congestions, continuously provide drivers with strategic data, and eventually create vehicles and roadways with automatic controls over guidance, spacing, and movement. Such systems would first be applied to metropolitan traffic problems, but sketches of a continental grid of "multimodal service corridors" with segments accommodating surface movement at minimum speeds of 150–200 miles per hour on special roadways, moving platforms, intermodal trains, or other devices were being offered, with "Coast-to-Coast in One Day" a suggested goal and slogan (and the simple map of the proposed grid recalling the bold design Franklin Roosevelt sketched for Thomas MacDonald in 1938).

The Interstate Highway System had provided a superb continentwide intercity network, but with nearly 200 million vehicles on the road the automotive revolution was, as usual, in need of help. "As we enter a new century," lamented Jane Holtz Kay, "our vaunted mobility is, in fact, obstructed by a car culture in which every attempt to move is fraught with wasted motion, wasted time, wasted surroundings, wasted money." Her indictment is obviously broad in target, but her *Asphalt Nation* is representative of a now-large polemical literature assessing life in Interstate America. Yet, since "the fast, individually controlled vehicle that can carry its occupants door-to-door in comfort and privacy is as close to the ancient flying carpet ideal as anybody can expect," transportation planners feel they must perforce continue to try to envision "Good Roads" for tomorrow.

RAILROAD RESPONSE

"In 1917, American road and rail entered the modern era," said Stephen B. Goddard in his report on the ensuing "epic struggle" between the two. The contestants were at the time markedly uneven in status, stature, and prospect: the one an infant struggling to gain firm footing to sustain its amazing early growth; the other a mature and dominating presence, strong in work but rigid in attitude and displaying weaknesses from its chronic indulgences. As already noted, the Great War was a great proving ground for motor vehicles, thereby underscoring the imperative need for highway development, whereas the railroads failed the test of coping with a massive emergency traffic. Government intervention was applied in both cases.

Federal assumption of control over the railroads in March 1918 aimed at "the prompt merger without friction of all carriers' lines, facilities, and organizations into a continental and unified system." Although there was no serious political interest in transforming this emergency measure into a permanent nationalization, the demonstrated advantages of such imposed coordination and centralized management were such that shortly after returning the railroads to their owners Congress attempted to achieve such gains by guiding and pressuring the major companies to create a more efficient network. The central feature of the Transportation Act of 1920 was *consolidation*: the Interstate Commerce Commission was directed to "prepare and adopt a plan for the consolidation of the railroad properties of the continental United States into a limited number of systems." In the Senate version of the bill, companies might be compelled to join if they did not do so voluntarily, but the House blocked that provision. (It is worth noting that Great Britain was dealing with the same problem at this same time, and in 1921 Parliament forced the consolidation of 129 separate railway companies into four big systems.)

Such a directive was a complete reversal of thirty years of firm governmental opposition to major railroad mergers as being antithetical to the public interest. A whole sequence of anti-trust and related laws had been passed to halt ever-larger combinations of various kinds of companies, break up great concentrations of power (notably Standard Oil), and curb freedoms to charge and discriminate as managements might wish. Thus, in this 1920 act, the railroads "became the first major industry in which large combinations were looked upon with favor and in which systematic integration of properties was promoted as part of national policy." However, fear of monopoly still ruled, and Congress stipulated that in the creation of these new systems "competition shall be preserved as fully as possible and wherever practicable the existing routes and channels of trade and commerce shall be maintained." In 1921 the specialist assigned the task presented a plan to consolidate all American railroads into nineteen regional systems (the Ripley Plan). A storm of protests from a variety of interests followed. Even though each regional system was designed to preserve some competition between major points in the network, greater efficiencies would require reductions in duplicate services and consolidation would create many more single-company places, and, as Senator Albert B. Cummins of Iowa, a major author of the bill, had earlier acknowledged: "from the unguided, uncontrolled right of owners to build railroads wherever they may see fit to build them. . . . We are now under the disadvantage of having developed a system which must be maintained because communities have been built up along the railways and their interests cannot be disregarded."

Every student of the railroad problem knew that thousands of miles of line would have to be downgraded and some of it abandoned to form an efficient national network, but the very design of the act showed that Congress was unwilling to venture far into such geographic modifications. An unprecedented "recapture" clause that empowered the federal government to take over "excess" profits from strong companies and use such funds to shore up weak companies demonstrated further support for the existing network. The ICC was also given greater power over abandonments and new construction of lines, assessing each proposal in terms of "present or future public convenience and necessity," and mandatory public hearings likely delayed many abandonments of line or service. As for new extensions, wording of the act invited at least one radical proposal: business interests in southwestern Oregon convinced the ICC to *compel* the Union Pacific to build a 187-mile connection across the unproductive High Desert so as to provide a much more direct line to the East (a saving of up to 400 miles over the existing route via Portland). The Supreme Court overruled the ICC in this case, but three dissenting judges supported such compulsion as appropriate to the congressional intent of creating a more effective national transportation system. All of these provisions were a reaffirmation of what the ICC had asserted from its beginning (1887): that the railroads ought to be regarded and regulated as a public utility.

The railroad crisis was so serious that high conservative Republic leaders (including Harding, Coolidge, and Hoover) endorsed the concept of compulsory consolidation if the railroads failed to act within a stipulated number of years. Yet nothing came of it. The big companies defied any such compulsion, Congress showed little desire for further involvement in such a controversial corporate and geographical matter, and even the ICC could not agree internally to adopt formally either of its proposed consolidation plans (an alternative had been presented in 1929).

In the 1930s the context changed dramatically. The inherent high fixed costs of railroads (solely responsible—and taxable—for every mile of their own roadbeds) made them especially vulnerable to business depressions; drastic reductions in forest, mine, and heavy industrial productions, together with rapid increases in competition from trucks, buses, and private autos, cut deeply into all categories of traffic; the number of cars of revenue freight declined by nearly a half, passenger traffic and overall net income by more than 70 percent, and the situation of the railroads of the United States, "collectively the greatest and most important industry in our country," became "a matter of grave concern." Therefore, the National Transportation Committee (a private group sponsored by major financial institutions and chaired by Calvin Coolidge) concluded: "regional consolidations should be hastened and, where necessary enforced, looking eventually to a single national system with regional divisions and the elimination of all excess and obsolete lines and equipment." A new plan, consolidating the railroads into seven systems (and the legal rationale for doing so) was set forth (the Prince Plan). However, the Emergency Transportation Act of 1933 did not include any such compulsions. The railroads remained adamantly opposed, labor unions (and politicians) feared a great loss of jobs, communities were alarmed over widespread reductions in competition, the constitutionality of any such action was seriously in question, and it was all much too drastic to muster any breadth of support (the financial institutions were obviously looking toward an eventual government buy-out of these many perilous companies). The 1933 act repealed the complicated ineffective recapture clause and began a program of heavy government subsidies to secure the national network (nearly a third of which was bankrupt). By 1940 the ICC had authorized abandonment of about 26,000 miles of line, but most of this related to shortlines and branches built to tap some now-exhausted resource or a local service readily taken over by trucks; no major segment of the national network was eliminated.

On the eve of World War II the railroads handled about half of the total ton-miles of freight in the United States and nearly 80 percent of the total land traffic (that is, leaving aside coastal and Great Lakes movements). With the onset of war their inherent capacity for mass movements of freight and passengers was well demonstrated, company prosperity temporarily restored, and official pressures for consolidation withdrawn. After the war major companies made a strong effort to retain a commanding position in both passenger and freight. Heavy investment in more multiple track and centralized or automatic traffic control systems allowed high density and speed on main lines. The revolutionary shift from more than a century of dependence on steam to diesel locomotives was essentially completed by the mid-1950s (the first freight diesels were sold to the Santa Fe in 1941; the last big steam locomotives were those built in 1953 by the great coal-hauling Norfolk & Western) and brought a great increase in efficiency and a vast alteration of the railroad landscape, along with a marked decrease in the number of locomotive service centers spaced along the line (steam locomotives needed water and fuel every hundred miles or so and further servicing after a few hours of operation). New sets of fast streamliners competed for intercity and long-distance traffic. Yet the number of passengers rapidly dwindled; by 1959 the total was the lowest since the depths of the Depression, passenger miles by air exceeded those by rail, the number by bus nearly equaled those by train, and the U.S. Post Office, ever under public and political pressure to improve service and reduce costs, began a major new distribution program, shifting from trains to trucks and planes. As passenger deficits rose, railroad companies moved to get out of the business as soon as possible (because of ICC constraints, driving the remaining customers away through poor service was the fastest means). By 1956 the total freight traffic also began to decline and a general business recession began to take another heavy toll. Thus as the railroads entered the 1960s, a new era of jet planes, Interstate Highways, and 74 million motor vehicles on the roads (up from 50 million only ten years earlier), this old basic national system was again in trouble and old familiar symptoms and solutions reappeared.

"General consolidation of railroads in the near future is . . . the most important measure to restore the railroad industry to the health and vigorous status of over 30 years ago and as a necessary basis for a coordinated transportation system for the Nation," concluded a lengthy report on National Transportation Policy prepared for the U.S. Senate and published in January 1961 (the Doyle Report). It repeated a recent ICC examiner's conclusion that intercity passenger service by rail "meets no important needs that cannot be provided by other carriers and possesses no uniquely service advantages. It serves no locations that cannot be served by air or highway." However, "in the foreseeable future, there is no means of transportation that offers the combination of economy and dependable service to handle the mass movement of freight between the major centers of our Nation." Thus an effective nationwide network must be saved, and consolidation (initiated by the companies, with government aid) should begin in "the northeast area where conditions of the industry are acute."

That such attention should focus on "the northeast area" was especially note-worthy—and alarming. In geographic characterizations this was the historic Man-ufacturing Belt, the American Core; in railroad terminology this was Trunk Line Territory, with much the most elaborate network and heaviest traffic, the primary focus of the national system. Trouble in certain portions of this complex area were readily understandable. The precipitous decline in domestic and industrial use of coal, and especially anthracite, crippled a whole set of companies that had special-ized in shipments from Pennsylvania mines (in 1957, the weakest of these, the al-ways redundant 541-mile New York, Ontario & Western, became the first com-plete abandonment of a large railroad). New England, a special subsystem of this Territory, had been suffering a long decline in industrial freight (especially tex-tiles), and its short hauls between regional centers were highly vulnerable to truck competition. But the big systems, the New York Central, Pennsylvania, and Balti-more & Ohio, with their high-capacity trunk lines linking New York Harbor with Chicago and St. Louis and all the big industrial and commercial centers in be-tween, had been among the most famously successful railroads in America. The Pennsylvania's four-track main line across the Allegheny Front connecting New York City and Philadelphia with Pittsburgh and Cleveland had long carried the heaviest industrial and merchandise traffic on the nation's railroad system, and the New York Central's famous water-level route via Albany, Buffalo, and Lake Erie shores was another heavy trafficway (fig. 24). There were many reasons for the cur-rent weaknesses of these once-powerful companies (including their own manage-ments as well as inexorable shifts in the character and locations of industries), but one new feature seemed vividly apparent: the Interstate Highway System, epito-

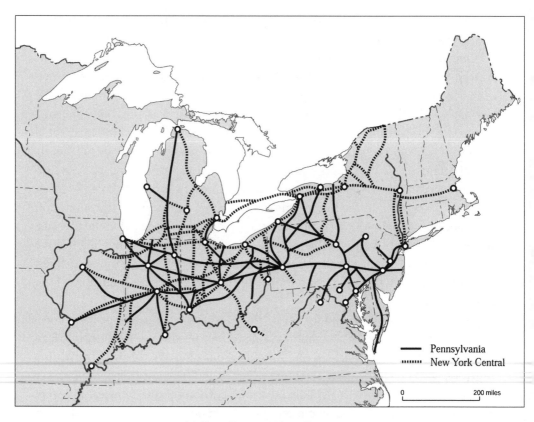

24. From Dominance to Disaster.
For seventy years these two great rivals were among the most prosperous and powerful railroads in America. Their desperate merger into Penn Central led to the government's emergency creation of Conrail.

mized in this case at this time by those early superhighway toll roads across Pennsylvania and New York. When, in November 1957, leaders of the Pennsylvania and the New York Central announced their intent to study a possible merger, "it was a thunderclap that shook all railroading."

The reverberations from that radical proposal destabilized long-existing patterns of companies and service in the East and initiated a tumultuous sequence of changes that eventually revolutionized railroading in that critical region and helped open the way nationally for consolidation on a massive scale. We shall note only a few major actors and events in this complicated history.

That this merger talk was initiated by the Pennsylvania, the haughty, self-styled "Standard Railroad of the World" that had blocked every attempt since 1920 to reduce the many trunk-line railroads to a few viable systems, bespoke a desperation not yet widely apparent in these two principals. Assuming that such a combination

would powerfully dominate the East, lesser roads scrambled to find any sort of suc-
cor (including mergers among themselves, such as Erie-Lackawanna). But it took
more than ten years for the new Penn Central to begin operating, and it was soon
clear that "merger, rather than a panacea, was the catalyst for collapse." The management systems of the two companies—computers, accounting, marketing, traffic
control, employee practices, maintenance, or whatever—were incompatible; programs for concentrating traffic on a few trunk lines and terminals created enormous
congestions and, eventually, chaos (lost cars, misdirected trains, shipments lost or
delayed weeks, even months). Thus this supposedly formidable creation became
"the *Titanic* of the railroad merger era," its bankruptcy in 1970 "the most miserable
fiasco in American business," and nearly every other company in the region was
carried down with it. (Coincidentally, the almost solid lines of huge trucks barrel-
ing along at seventy miles an hour on I-80, the newly completed direct New York–
Chicago route drawn boldly across the Appalachians, seemed to announce a new
shorter, faster primary axis of the national transportation system.)

   "The East was a railroad graveyard," but "the ICC insisted it was not possible to
dismantle vast sections of the eastern railroads without doing violence to the industrial fabric of the nation"; therefore in 1973 Congress arranged a resurrection. It
took the form of the Consolidated Rail Corporation—"Conrail"—an amalgamation of nearly all these bankrupt railroads into a single system. Although designed
to be run as a profit-making corporation, Congress had to pump in billions of dollars to keep the trains running, and there seemed little prospect of any such return;
"in the late Seventies it seemed inevitable in Washington that the [entire] industry
would have to be nationalized." (Britain had done so in 1948, as much from ideological as from financial pressures.) Yet ten years later Conrail was in the black. The
key to this surprising financial success was the Staggers Act of 1980, which deregulated American railroads, leaving them largely free to run themselves as businesses
rather than as quasi-public utilities; and the immediate key to this fundamental
change was the dismal prospect facing Congress of having to subsidize Conrail forever. (Deregulation—of trucks as well—became a campaign promise of both parties and President Jimmy Carter signed this act just before his defeat in November).

   Thus Conrail, like other railroads, became essentially free to abandon or sell unwanted lines, trim labor costs, try new modes of shipment, set its own rates, and operate almost as it pleased. The Reagan administration, eager to get out of the railroad business, transformed it into a private company in 1987, and soon this
resurrected and radically reformed system, holding a virtual rail monopoly over a
vital part of the national network, was being sought by two powerful railroad companies: CSX and Norfolk Southern (NS). These two systems had themselves been
formed from a recent sequence of major mergers. The nucleus of each was a railroad
long prospering on the massive movement of Appalachian coal (much of it for ex-

port or for electrical generation in the Middle West and therefore less vulnerable to decline). The CSX Corporation was formed when the Chesapeake & Ohio purchased the Baltimore & Ohio, thereby greatly enlarging its presence in Trunk Line Territory; in 1986 it added the Seaboard System, one of two giant new networks in the South. Norfolk Southern was created when the Norfolk & Western, which had recently acquired lines extending its reach to Buffalo, Cleveland, Detroit, Chicago, and west to St. Louis, Kansas City, and Omaha, added the large Southern Railway system. The rapid formation of these two huge systems was a major step toward reducing the entire American main-line network to—at most—a handful of companies. After an intense bidding war, CSX and NS agreed to divide Conrail between them. When the various segments were absorbed by their new owners, the famous competitive main lines of the New York Central and Pennsylvania largely reappeared in new guise as rival trunk lines of CSX and NS, respectively (fig. 25).

Meanwhile, west of Chicago and St. Louis a sequence of mergers also resulted in two gigantic rival systems. These amalgamations began with the creation of the Burlington Northern (BN) in 1970 (the ICC thereby approving the same combination of Great Northern, Northern Pacific, and Burlington that the Supreme Court had blocked in 1904 in a famous anti-trust ruling that had ended big railroad

25. Trunk-Line Railroads, Late 1990s.

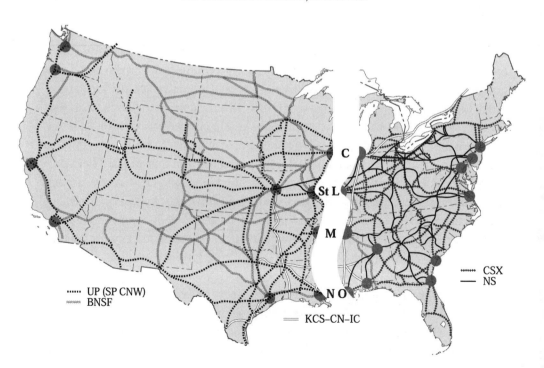

mergers for nearly sixty years). In 1995 the BN took over the Atchison, Topeka & Santa Fe and became the Burlington Northern Santa Fe (BNSF). The Union Pacific built its rival system by absorbing such major companies as the Missouri Pacific and Chicago & North Western, and capping these with purchase of the Rio Grande and Southern Pacific.

By the end of the century about 85 percent of the American railroad network was being operated by these four giant systems, forming two vast territories linked at Chicago, St. Louis, Memphis, and New Orleans, thus preserving the historic structural break between East and West (and preserving as well two anomalies: the now NS route west to Kansas City and the BNSF line from Kansas City to Birmingham). Two much lesser but important companies, the Illinois Central and the Kansas City Southern, survived by providing north-south service along that structural divide. As with the Interstate Highway network, railroad traffic was now channeled along fewer routes, but competition was maintained in every major port and in most large metropolitan areas (Boston was a marginal case, with competition provided only by a regional company). Each of these big systems was primarily a set of high-capacity interregional trunk lines. Whereas earlier railroad strategies had favored branch-line development seeking to dominate all parts of a territory, these companies sought to get rid of thousands of miles of low-traffic lines. That shift in strategy, begun under the severe economic pressures of the 1960s, resulted in much abandonment (more than 80,000 miles since 1950), but spreading fear of such irreversible loss caused many local interests or states to take over various portions of such unwanted trackage. With deregulation, operation of many of these lesser lines became far more flexible and financially attractive and brought on "The Great Railway Bazaar," in which more than a hundred new companies purchased or leased former pieces of these big systems. Thus, consolidation and disintegration were complementary processes in the transformation of the overall American railroad network into a set of giants and pygmies, with little left in between. Total mileage had been reduced by more than 40 percent from its 1915 peak.

The four dominant companies were unprecedented not only in size (24,000 to 36,500 miles of line—several times larger than most pre-merger roads) but also in capacity and types of service. Heavy investment in track, locomotives, cars, traffic control, and much else created super-railroads designed to compete with superhighway and water-borne commerce. The inherent railroad superiority in overland mass movement of heavy bulk commodities has been much enhanced, most strikingly apparent in the enormous volumes of Powder River coal shipped in long unit trains from Wyoming to as far east as Georgia. But the greatest changes have come from the development of larger and specialized cars and systems of cargo shipment, together with much faster freight service. Double-stack container trains, intermodal trailer haulage (piggyback), and special automobile cars have made the railroads far more efficient carriers; consolidation has reduced the number of time-consuming terminal interchanges, and the railroads are once again keen competitors in long-distance merchandise traffic. Intermodal operations are expected to continue to grow with increasing highway congestion. An important incentive for gaining control of Conrail by CSX and NS was to capture a far greater share of north-south shipments from trucks, a market Conrail had neglected because of the short haul within its territory. The eighty-year-old "epic struggle" between road and rail is far from over, but the relative status, stature, and prospect of the contestants has gone through a sequence of radical changes, and a mutual interest in cooperation is becoming more apparent.

American railroad companies had escaped nationalization (the British reformed their system into a new set of private companies in the early 1990s) and regained a major role in freight, but passenger service was an altogether different situation. Although such service was dismissed at midcentury as nonessential to the transport needs of the nation, the bankruptcy of the Penn Central (which carried about a quarter of all such traffic) created a crisis Congress could not ignore, and, along with Conrail, Congress established the National Railroad Passenger Corporation to sustain some measure of intercity service (states and municipalities had assumed—or soon would—major responsibility for metropolitan commuter services). Railroad companies were allowed to get out of the passenger business entirely (after 130 years of service) if they cooperated with *Amtrak*, the new government-sponsored operation. Although the Washington-Boston corridor and other relatively short intermetropolitan hauls, such as Chicago-Detroit or New York City–Buffalo, appeared to have the greatest potential for competitive service, the residual passenger network of the 1960s still "served every major region . . . [and] preservation of the passenger train had wide geographic" and political support. Thus the initial Amtrak system was a lean interregional and transcontinental network and soon expanded under congressional pressure (such as adding service to West Virginia and a second route across Montana) (fig. 26).

In 1976 Amtrak acquired from Conrail its own separate line from Washington to Boston, and Congress began supporting the upgrading of that track to provide competition to the popular air shuttles. That Northeast Corridor continues to be much the most successful operation; elsewhere Amtrak has been generally unable to provide the kind of service to lure sufficient traffic to operate without subsidy. Part of the problem obviously lies with the uncertainties of recurrent congressional support, but a major difficulty arises from having to operate on the tracks of private companies. Although Congress instructed "that Amtrak trains be given priority over freight trains" (unless formal exception was granted), such a privilege has not proven easy to manage—or enforce—and has become increasingly difficult in the face of much greater density and urgency of freight movements. Accommodation

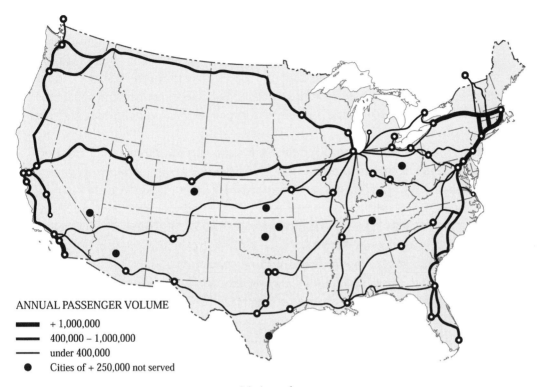

ANNUAL PASSENGER VOLUME

▬▬ + 1,000,000
▬ 400,000 – 1,000,000
— under 400,000
● Cities of + 250,000 not served

26. Amtrak.

Service as of 1996; passenger volumes as of 1993. (Source: U.S. Congress, *Amtrak's Current Situation*)

of passenger trains is obviously an unwanted complication in the operations of America's super-railroads. Thus Amtrak service has been generally unreliable as well as very limited in frequency and extent, its most admired trains being those traveling a few days a week leisurely across the Mountain West—a subsidized scenic service—rather than an accelerated mass movement between major metropolitan centers.

The success of superfast and frequent passenger trains in Japan and Europe has underscored the paucity and poverty of the American situation. Congress has funded investigations and demonstrations of these new technologies, and various proposals by private interests and states have been made (notably in Florida, Texas, California, and New York). But the American context is different: the great expanse of the country—trains cannot compete with planes over long distances; the dispersal of population among many cities—reducing the demand for travel between many particular pairs of places; the superhighway network and comprehensive vehicle ownership; and, not least, a super-railroad network owned by companies that have no interest whatever in passenger service. Americans have readily subsidized radically new transport systems—railroads in the nineteenth century, highways and airways in the twentieth—but super-passenger trains (requiring exclusive new roadbeds) represent an enormously expensive upgrading of an old form, and aside from rather modest but costly initiatives in the Northeast Corridor there seems little likelihood that anything comparable to the Shinkansen or the French TGV (Train à Grande Vitesse) will appear in the United States anytime soon.

Thus the American railroad system underwent a series of tumultuous transformations in the twentieth century: from being the one great instrument of movement for passengers and freight, to a rapid erosion of that monopoly by new modes of transport, to a condition so precarious as to induce radical government intervention, followed by withdrawal of long-existing restraints, and thereby empowering railroads to redevelop an intrinsic specialized role in the nation's transportation complex. Since 1920 a major theme of those concerned with "the railroad problem" has been the need for major geographic change, in the form of consolidation. Yet it took nearly half a century even to begin such a process. Why it took so long was primarily the result of the special character of railroads in the United States wherein each major company was a militantly distinct capitalistic corporation developed out of a century of intensely competitive territorial warfare. As earlier noted in our coverage of the nineteenth-century formation of the American network (quoting the historian Maury Klein): "Every road was a sovereign state whose officials ruled their domain with possessive zeal, . . . regarding outsiders with suspicion. Relations between companies were a form of diplomacy of which war was, as always, a last extension." As Klein later reemphasized, at all levels of management and operations "railroaders inhabited a closed world of their own making"—that is, *each company* was a closed world (hence the debilitating operational problems that commonly followed upon actual mergers: not just the notorious example of the desperate Penn Central case; the Union Pacific takeover of the Southern Pacific in 1996 caused such an immense breakdown in the Houston area that it took embargoes on shipments and federal intervention to untangle the mess). Government regulations obviously played an important role in merger delay, but the more basic factor was this special inward allegiance and separateness—each company a separate cultural geographic system.

The pattern of the American network at the end of the twentieth century is the result of recent company initiatives rather than of any government design for a national system. Holding true to historic character, every merger was a strategic geographical move by a company seeking to strengthen itself, and every such move was challenged by other railroads; many other proposals and attempts failed. It is commonly assumed that the pattern remains unstable; as an industry analyst observed: "railroads are in a transitional phase—a Darwinian evolution. The configuration is not settled." Perhaps the next likely step will be an East-West merger creating at last a truly transcontinental system—which would surely be followed by a defensive merger of the remaining big pair. Will "survival of the fittest" eventually lead to a single national system under one vast company?

WATERWAYS

During the first decades of the twentieth century inland waterways, which had provided the foundational transport network of national life, had so faded from use that there was "no common carriage of consequence on the Mississippi" system. Such a characterization leaves aside the heavy traffic on the Great Lakes, which was essentially an oceanlike harbor-to-harbor activity, and the coal barges on the upper Ohio, but elsewhere the railroads were in command.

That very domination by the railroads, however, generated interest in the revival of water-borne service. At first the focus was on providing effective competition, for "wherever a navigable river runs beside railroads the problem of regulating rates on the railroads becomes far easier" (a 1912 act disallowed most railroad ownership of waterway services, including their Great Lakes fleets), but it was more the prodigious growth of the national economy that pushed the matter to a new level. As President Theodore Roosevelt stated: "It is common knowledge that the railroads of the United States are no longer able to move crops and manufactures rapidly enough to secure the prompt transaction of the business of the nation, and there is small prospect of immediate relief. . . . There appears to be but one complete remedy—the development of a complementary system of transportation by water." Various studies were initiated, and war soon confirmed the need. In 1918, under the stress of the wartime emergency, the federal director of railroads also commandeered all available vessels on the lower Mississippi and Warrior rivers (the latter linked Birmingham with the Gulf of Mexico) and began construction of a new fleet. After the war these facilities were transferred to a federal Inland Waterways Corporation, and the government continued to operate barge lines until 1953.

In 1920 Congress passed a Rivers and Harbors Act to reinvigorate work on waterway improvements. It was an old form of governmental activity, dating from 1824, but in spite of many good works it had also been an old favorite pork barrel of local projects authorized to satisfy particular members of Congress. As a result, said Herbert Hoover, "we have wasted vast sums of money in interrupted execution and sporadic and irresolute policies, until today we find ourselves with a mass of disconnected segments of a transportation system." As secretary of Commerce, Hoover became a strong advocate of a "great integrated system." As he described to an audience in St. Louis (in his final address of the 1928 presidential campaign):

We have an opportunity to create three great trunk lines of water transportation—
one north and south fifteen hundred miles from New Orleans through St. Louis to
Chicago, and thus by the Lakes to the northern boundaries of our country. Another
east and west sixteen hundred miles from Pittsburgh through St. Louis to Kansas City.
And the third a shipway through the St. Lawrence connecting Duluth and all the
lake ports with the sea. Vital to this system is the improvement of the laterals such as
the upper Mississippi connecting Minneapolis and St. Paul, the upper Missouri connecting Sioux City and beyond, as well as the Cumberland, the Tennessee, the
Arkansas, and the Red rivers, and lesser streams. When completed, including the St.
Lawrence waterway, this entire system will comprise twelve thousand miles of most
essential transportation connecting twenty states with the Gulf on one hand and
with the North Atlantic on the other.

It was the most comprehensive program since the Gallatin Plan of 1808—and
like that great vision for Potamic America it was never authorized as a whole, but
major segments were undertaken by a succession of administrations (fig. 27). Work
on the Ohio, Mississippi, and Missouri was initiated in the 1920s. The Tennessee
Valley Authority well displayed the now-advantageous combination of dams and
locks for electric power as well as navigation. By World War II the main portions of
Hoover's Mississippi plan were completed. The critical link was the Illinois–Lake
Michigan connection. The original canal of 1848 had long since fallen into disuse;
the next stage had been the Chicago Sanitary and Ship Canal, completed in 1900,
designed primarily, as its name suggests, to deepen and reverse the flow of the
Chicago River so as to divert urban sewage toward the Mississippi; further improvements of channels and locks on this entire Illinois waterway were finished in
1933.

"I know of nothing that should so appeal to the imagination of the people of
North America as the final consummation of the struggle of generations to open
these Great Lakes as part of the 'Seven Seas,'" said Hoover on another occasion,
and his advocacy did help stimulate another upwelling of popular and political interest in that idea. The concept was not quite as simple as the map of the natural
outlet of these inland waters might indicate, for there were two great Atlantic-
bound waterways and two great empires sharing these Great Lakes. Rivalry over
the project dates from the State of New York's bold initiative of the Erie Canal; by
the time the first enlargement of that hugely successful Lake Erie–Hudson River
link was completed, Canada had opened several short canals around the most severe rapids on the St. Lawrence. Railroad expansion soon dampened further interest in such facilities until the later popular support for government-assisted waterway competition. In 1903 New York began another enlargement and realignment,
completing this new State Barge Canal in 1918. In Canada the huge grain harvests
in the new Prairie Provinces were reviving support for a seaway and rivalry over

27. Major Waterways.

routes between a Laurentian one or a Georgian Bay–Ottawa River passageway (a much shorter, all-Canadian route between Lakehead and Montreal). Meanwhile, international waterway commissions had been formed (the boundary follows the St. Lawrence for 115 miles), and the prospect of electric power generation had heightened interest in the great river.

In 1912 Canada decided to build a new twenty-five-foot-depth Welland Canal

between Lake Erie and Lake Ontario (bypassing Niagara Falls); completion was delayed by the war and other matters until 1932, but many on both sides of the border
came to regard this link as the first step in creation of a seaway. However, Ottawa
was not ready to proceed with or join in the huge expense of the overall project.
Only Ontario (and especially Ontario Hydro) was much interested; the Prairie
Provinces were pinning their hopes on the railway to Hudson Bay (completed in
1929); Quebec feared loss of business at Montreal and preferred the Ottawa River
route if any seaway were to be built. Most of the agitation for a St. Lawrence Seaway therefore took place in the United States, where it generated a major regional
confrontation. The prospect of turning the Great Lakes into an American Mediterranean with ocean vessels traveling 2,000 miles into the heart of the continent—"every Lakeport a Seaport"—was a powerful lure to Midwestern farmers,
shippers, and chambers of commerce, and a Tidewater Association under the direction of an energetic promoter from Duluth gathered endorsements from many
governors and legislatures, and general support from national administrations. But
of course such a radical physical geographic alteration threatened to destabilize the
regional industrial and commercial structure of the nation. New York and other
Atlantic ports, the powerful Trunk Line railroads, and many other Eastern interests
mounted strong opposition, deriding this "magnificent conception" as "the Great
Delusion," the Seaway as "the Iceway" (frozen shut several months of every year),
and the cost as an enormous government subsidy of an unneeded facility. (The
State of New York's promotion of an Erie-Hudson seaway as an all-American alternative found little support—although endorsed by some military spokesmen—
because of even greater cost.) This regional division was readily apparent but
somewhat deceptive: some big Eastern companies were attracted by the power
potentials of a St. Lawrence Seaway; some Chicago interests were closely bound to
those Eastern railroads and other opposing corporations.

In 1931 renewed interest by Canada (the new prime minister pointing with
pride to the new Welland Canal—and with warning to a similar deepening of the
Hudson River to Albany by the United States) led to detailed negotiations and the
signing of a treaty for joint construction of the Seaway. However, this document
did not come to a vote in the U.S. Senate until early 1934, and although passed
(46–42), it was far short of the two-thirds majority needed for treaty ratification.
The Great Depression ended all momentum for this grand scheme, but the outbreak of war soon brought a revival. In December 1940 Franklin Roosevelt declared that "the United States needs the St. Lawrence Seaway for defense. The
United States needs this great landlocked sea as a secure haven in which it will always be able to build ships and more ships in order to protect our trade and our
shores." Furthermore, the United States needed St. Lawrence power "to produce
aluminum and more aluminum for the airplane program which will assure com-

mand of the air." Canada, of course, was already in the war, and in March 1941 the two countries signed an "executive agreement" (not a treaty) to build the Seaway. Such a document needed only a majority in both houses of Congress but became stalled by opponents and the exigencies of war.

Nevertheless, the war not only helped sustain attention to the topic, it changed the context of the controversy in its aftermath. There was the prospect of severe power shortage in the expanding economies of both countries, causing New York State to shift from opposition to support for a St. Lawrence Seaway. Far more ominous, the depletion of Lake Superior iron ores was so severe that much greater dependence on imported ore seemed inevitable (taconite beneficiation of lower-grade ores was not yet in view), yet massive relocation of much of the North American steel industry to the seaboard would be enormously expensive and disruptive ("the economic consequences to the Midwest could be tragic"). Fortunately for Seaway supporters, immense and rich iron deposits had just been discovered in Labrador and were under development by a major consortium of Midwestern steel companies. Thus a deepened St. Lawrence would become an expanded "lakeway" for the specialized carriers already bringing ore to coal for the steel centers of the Interior. These new factors enhanced the national defense argument for the project (although U.S. Air Force generals pointed to the vulnerability of canals and dams). The issue of cost had also undergone important change. Although states and private corporations had usually charged fees for the use of canals and locks, the federal government had treated the Great Lakes and major rivers, whatever their improvements, as "free highways," a concept, referring to their "natural state," dating from the first years of the Republic. Waterway interests had, of course, always resisted the idea of tolls, but now important congressional support for charging for use of such a seaway (as with the Panama Canal) altered all cost-benefit calculations.

It remained for a new (and aptly named) prime minister of Canada, Louis St. Laurent, to find "the key to the completion of the Seaway": Canada would proceed to build the entire project, with or without American participation—a decision Parliament endorsed unanimously in 1951. Many Americans were skeptical that their neighbor would actually undertake such an enormous program alone, but Canada had undergone major growth in national sentiment and self-confidence, as well as in population and industry, since 1939 (and was prospering from the current war in Korea), and it was no longer willing to await American initiative on a project so deeply impacting on Canadian interests. St. Laurent had a willing ally in Harry S. Truman, who had voted for the Seaway as a Missouri senator and now urged the United States to "join as a full partner . . . [and] not be content to be merely a customer of Canada's for the use of the Seaway after it is built." But the American president and his party were increasingly beleaguered by a Republican ascendancy, and his successor was deterred by the project's cost and "geographical" controversy. Finally, in 1953 Eisenhower, on advice of the National Security Council, declared his support, and a year later both houses of Congress gave their approval. The Seaway was completed in 1959 and officially opened by Queen Elizabeth II and President Eisenhower at the Montreal entrance, whereafter the royal yacht *Britannica*, carrying the queen and Prince Philip, led a procession of fifty vessels to Chicago.

Two other large postwar additions to the inland waterways system were authorized in 1946, but each was delayed by further congressional and court battles over such notorious pork barrel projects. In 1971 completion of a nine-foot channel up the Arkansas and Verdigris rivers made Tulsa a port on the Mississippi system. A year later construction finally began on the Tenn-Tom Waterway to connect the Tennessee River to the south-flowing Tombigbee and provide a nine-foot channel to the Black Warrior River (which had earlier been developed to provide barge traffic from the Birmingham coalfields). This long-proposed and oft-studied link between the Tennessee Valley and the Gulf at Mobile seemed on the map a major shortcut (of more than 500 miles) but had been repeatedly rejected as far too costly for any anticipated traffic and was never part of Hoover's grand scheme.

This extensive midcontinent river and canal network was complemented and intersected by the peripheral Intracoastal Waterway lacing through lagoons and swamps behind barrier beaches and shortcuttings between bays to form a twelve-foot channel along the Atlantic and Gulf coasts, the two segments still separated by the as yet unbuilt Cross Florida Barge Canal. Elsewhere, in the Pacific Northwest, a series of dams on the lower Snake River extended Columbia barge traffic to Lewiston, Idaho.

Commerce on all these waterways has been almost entirely bulk cargo (ores, coal, stone, grain, petroleum, chemicals) moving by barge systems on the rivers and canals and in specialized carriers on the Great Lakes. Such traffic has provided added competition to railroads along this limited pattern of routes, but the volume on nearly all segments has been less, and often much less, than proponents had predicted, not only because their estimates were often unrealistic politically driven projections, but because of changes in industrial demands and major improvements in other modes of shipment. The St. Lawrence Seaway is a notable example of divergence between expectations and reality. At first Labrador ore did move to Midwestern steel mills, but the development of taconite greatly extended the reserves of Lake Superior ores and in the 1970s the American steel industry underwent a major decline followed by extensive restructuring and dispersal into new, smaller, and more efficient specialized plants. Small ocean vessels did arrive in Cleveland, Toledo, Detroit, and Chicago, but from the time the Seaway opened, world shipping was moving rapidly into much larger specialized vessels and intermodal systems beyond the capacity of this long-awaited new oceanway.

All of these extensions and enlargements of inland waterways added traffic and potential to the overall North American transportation complex, but the really significant *acceleration* involving water-borne movement was the recent and radical change in ocean-overland delivery services. Containerization was invented by U.S. ocean carriers as a means of moving cargo on and off far more efficiently and with less damage and pilferage. Experiments in the use of such steel boxes as a means of providing return-haul on empty tankers led to the development of special vessels and dock facilities, and these to specialized railroad stack-trains and truck delivery services, and, in the 1980s, to international standards of sizes and weights and automatic tracking of containers. Thus, by the early 1990s a great majority of ocean traffic to and from the United States was containerized (including about 90 percent of the rapidly growing trans-Pacific trade) and concentrated on a few big ports: Long Beach–Los Angeles (with by far the largest volume), Seattle and Tacoma, and Oakland on the Pacific Coast; New York Harbor, Miami–Port Everglades, Charleston, and Norfolk on the Atlantic; and Houston-Galveston on the Gulf. Moreover, the efficiency of the railroads in handling this new form plus the new timing demands of industrial and distribution operations now favor the quickest and shortest transport links (rather than the cheapest), and at least half of the surface shipments between East Asia and New York now arrive by long unit-trains on the "land bridge" across America in half the time of movement by way of Panama or Suez.

Thus by the end of the century unprecedented forms of intermodal movement along with specializations in types of commodities and services provided by each mode have given the United States a transportation system that has handled an immensely expanded and dispersed national economy with remarkable efficiency. And by that time more revolutionary quickenings of the connections between places had also become critical parts of the system.

4. Acceleration: In the Air

By midcentury the national government was playing an unprecedented role in the geographic shaping of a major new transportation service. Whereas the Interstate Commerce Commission had been imposed upon a largely completed nationwide railroad network with routeways already fixed in place by enormous investments of the carriers themselves, the Civil Aeronautics Board was presiding over a revolutionary kind of carrier undergoing rapid improvements in speed, distance, capacity, and safety amid intense public demands for additions to and improvements of the links between places. Cities and counties built most of the airports, the federal government provided critical routeway facilities and other subsidies, and airline companies were eager to provide whatever connections might seem advantageous for any particular time and place (we shall confine our attention here as earlier to the domestic system in the forty-eight contiguous states).

Even as air traffic was soaring past the declining billions of passenger miles by train, the CAB tried to maintain a degree of stability over the basic hierarchy and route systems of this radically flexible mode of transport. In spite of the great postwar boom there had been no additions to the general complement of Trunk Line carriers, and that category itself remained subdivided into two groups: the Big Four and the eight lesser companies. The former, regarded in the industry as "the Establishment" and by the government as "a national asset," consisted of American, United, TWA (the initials now standing for Trans World Airlines), and Eastern, which together accounted for more than half of the national total of seat miles in service. The first three were structured around their well-established transcontinental routes, while Eastern held a dense pattern in the eastern third of the country, including very popular links to Florida. The lesser trunks were interregional airlines usually anchored on some primary axis with intermediate services, such as Chicago and Detroit-Atlanta (Delta), Chicago-Dallas (Braniff), Minneapolis-Seattle (Northwest), and Los Angeles–San Francisco–Seattle (Western).

The CAB followed a policy of responding to the growth of air travel in part by extending the reach of lesser trunks to other large cities as a means of strengthening such companies and providing more competition with the Big Four at major traffic points. For example, in the late 1950s Delta and Braniff were allowed to serve New York City, National Airlines was granted a New York–Miami route to break Eastern's monopoly, and Denver-based Continental's network was extended west to Los Angeles and east to Chicago.

Below these dozen Trunk lines were thirteen survivors of the flurry of postwar formations, expansions, and mergers of feeder lines that were granted permanent authorizations as Local Service carriers in 1955. As most of their names suggested, each was a distinct regional network connecting many small cities with one or more major centers (fig. 28). These companies, offering the only links to more than 250 points in the national system, were basic to the declared goal of providing reasonable access to air service to every American. (Even below these were a growing number of much smaller, less regulated companies providing "commuter," or what was in effect scheduled air taxi, service in very small aircraft, in many cases for specialized traffic, such as Boston-Provincetown, Denver-Aspen, Dallas-Killeen.) By the late 1950s the ever-increasing subsidies to sustain short-haul, low-volume regional carriers led to a modification of this geographic ideal when the CAB announced a "Use It or Lose It" policy for points generating fewer than five passengers per day (or 1,800 annually). However, relatively few places were dropped before this hierarchy of companies and air travel in general were altered by the advent of jets.

The jet engine, "the greatest single advance in technology in aviation history,"

28. Regional Airlines.
"Local Service" companies, early 1960s. (Source: Davies, *Airlines of the United States*)

transformed long-distance air travel. First placed in passenger service in 1952 by Great Britain but interrupted two years later by disastrous flaws in that pioneer model (*Comet I*), the first sustained service was begun in 1956 in the Soviet Union on the Moscow-Irkutsk route. The jet age arrived in America in late 1958 when National Airlines introduced a Boeing 707 on its New York–Miami run (the design derived from Boeing's famous B-47 bomber, just as the Russians had adapted their first passenger jet from a military plane). The great strategic advantage of jets was *speed*; the first *Comet* had been assigned to the long London-Johannesburg run, and transcontinental travel in the United States could be suddenly reduced from nine hours to five. Even beyond such dramatic time-saving, to the public "the term jet conveyed an image of progress and sophistication," all other planes were suddenly old-fashioned, therefore "matching equipment now became mandatory" and the major companies became locked into "their own armaments race." Within two years all Trunk lines had some jet service, and such planes (either B-707s or Douglas DC-8s) concentrated on long-haul routes, accounted for at least half of all passenger miles flown. (A very brief interlude of new turbine-propeller planes, also first developed in Britain, had only minor impact in the United States.)

The jet revolution quickly ramified and destabilized the whole corporate and geographic structure of the American airline system. The major companies, faced with the enormous costs of replacing their fleets and the great superiority of jets in high-altitude, long-haul routes, sought to concentrate on their main metropolitan connections and to get rid of much of the rest; Local Service companies, seeing the opportunity to pick up larger surplus propeller planes cheaply, were eager to take over any unwanted routes and expand their networks. The CAB was thus suddenly faced with a mass of petitions for changes in the patterns of service. The shift of many short routes to lesser companies meant increases in subsidies, and the CAB therefore began to favor them with nonstop routes between major cities on the edge of, and even well beyond, their local regions in the hope of increasing their income and reducing the need for government aid (fig. 29). Similar moves were made to help the weaker trunk lines through this costly imperative transition into the new air age. Thus regionals became interregionals, interregionals underwent further expansion, even into nonstop transcontinentals (Northwest: Seattle-New York; National: Miami-Los Angeles). Although the national market was rapidly expanding, competition had increased, the hierarchy of companies became blurred, and the map of services was very extensively redrawn.

This general turbulence in the industry was extended and compounded in the 1970s by a sudden great increase in fuel costs (the world oil crisis), general economic depression, and recent heavy investment in huge, wide-bodied jets (B-747, DC-10, Lockheed 1011). During this prolonged crisis the CAB put a temporary hold on new route awards, approved several big mergers to save companies from bankruptcy (for example, Capital Airlines disappeared into Eastern; Frontier absorbed Central; Allegheny took over Lake Central, then Mohawk, and in 1979 became USAIR), and tried closer management over fares and competition, which only intensified pressures from the companies for greater freedom to manage their survival. Although there was no great public demand for change, and the airlines themselves only sought some easing of controls, the government (as it soon would with the railroads) turned toward full deregulation. By an act of 1978 control of route entry was to be phased out by 1981, of passenger fares the following year, and the CAB itself by 1984. A massive scramble followed (in its *Annual Report,* American Airlines declared 1980 "the worst in aviation history for the trunk line industry"). Over the next decade famous companies became bankrupt and disappeared (Eastern, Braniff, Pan American—which had belatedly entered domestic service by absorbing National Airlines), new ones appeared at every level and mostly soon disappeared, and more than a dozen regional or larger companies were absorbed into one of the eight major systems: American, United, TWA, Delta, Northwest, Continental, USAIR, and Southwest (this last an expansion from an internal Texas service begun in 1971). Thus "what remains is a rather small number of very

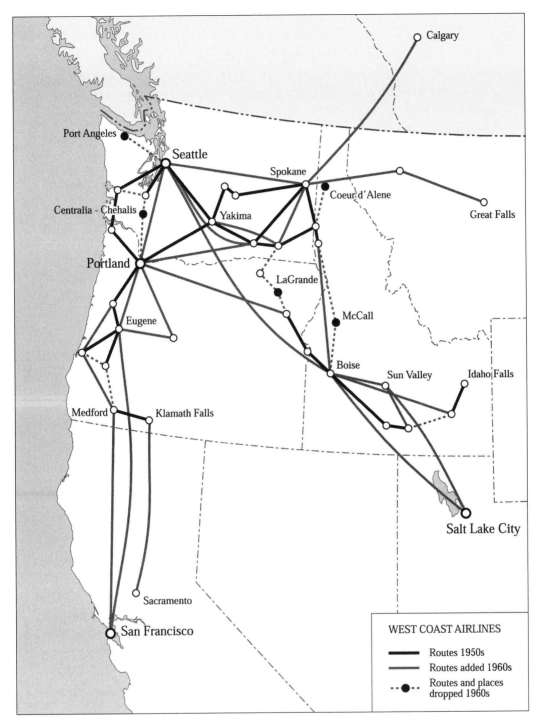

29. A Regional Airline.

Showing changes authorized by the CAB to drop local low-traffic points and to add nonstop within and well beyond the original region.

large airlines, of great geographical reach, handling a great deal of business." More-over, by the 1990s many short-haul services to medium-sized cities and nearly all local links with smaller ones were being handled by "commuter airlines" (the term now expanded to include use of aircraft of up to sixty seats), which were themselves subsidiaries of the big companies.

A familiar kind of map in any monthly airline magazine will show the points and links of service of that particular company, but as Douglas Fleming, geographic spe-cialist on the industry, notes, "the flow of passengers through these complex net-works is a dynamic phenomenon to which no map does full justice." Nevertheless, as in our treatment of the formative period, we can at least identify several impor-tant geographic features of the recent national air service system.

1. *Transcontinental Nonstop Service*. This fast, smooth overflying of all intervening cities and regions was much the most important segment and expression of the new age in domestic air travel. Initiated by American Airlines on its New York–Los Angeles run, it immediately generated intense pressure on competing carriers and from other major coastal cities for similar service (fig. 30). Since deregulation all major airlines provide some transcontinental service, and the number of coastal cities enjoying such connections has considerably expanded, although the original link continues to have the heaviest traffic.

2. *Hub and Spoke Networks*. Underneath those overarching transcontinental flights, the national domestic system operates through a set of major connection points. Pioneered by Delta funneling most of its regional passengers through At-lanta, each nationwide company has formed its own particular spatial network to channel passengers to one or more hubs and transfer them for continuation on its own planes and routes (spokes) to their destinations (or as near to as possible). All these big airlines serve Chicago, long the greatest hub of the domestic system, but each company has selected one or more other cities as a focus for such captive traf-fic. Viewed as a whole, in addition to Chicago there are three main sets of these piv-otal points: Pittsburgh, Cleveland, Detroit, and Cincinnati in the East; Atlanta, Charlotte, and Memphis in the South; and Minneapolis, St. Louis, Dallas–Fort Worth, and Houston as gateways to and from the West. Within the West, Denver and Salt Lake City are important hubs, just as Newark and Philadelphia are for traf-fic to and from the Northeast. If plotted on a map, some connecting routes through these hubs may seem far from a direct line between origin and destination, but with the great reduction in modern jet travel time they may not be significantly longer.

3. *Metropolitan Corridors*. In 1961 Eastern Airlines, making use of propeller planes made surplus by jets, began its Air Shuttle connecting New York with Washington

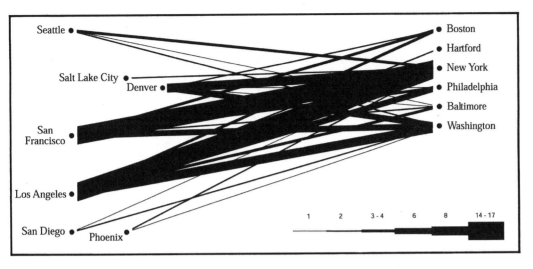

30. Early Nonstop Jet Service.
Showing only connections between cities of the West and the Northeast seaboard.

and Boston. This famous initiative guaranteed a seat without reservations for hourly departures on this heavily traveled Northeast Corridor (the CAB did not usually assert control over the number of flights on authorized routes); successive carriers have continued such service. In California low-cost, no-frills intrastate companies (therefore never under CAB regulations) have been the main instruments in developing links between the San Francisco and Los Angeles metropolitan areas into the heaviest air traffic in the United States.

4. *Resort Traffic.* The appearance of jet planes first on the New York–Miami run attested to the established strength and great potential of such traffic, and there has been a massive expansion of nonstop service from all the larger Northern cities to half a dozen Florida points, with Miami and Orlando now among the nation's leading traffic generators. On the other side of the country Las Vegas has a prominence on the air service map far out of proportion to its population and hinterland; Phoenix, Tucson, and San Diego show sharp winter upturns, and traffic to Denver and Salt Lake City increases in both winter and summer seasons.

5. *Traffic Shadow.* Aside from hubs and resorts and other specialized traffic, we might assume that the number of passengers emplaned at any particular city would be reasonably proportionate to its population. However, as air transport, even more than surface forms, is far more efficient on long hauls than short, the spacing of cities can distort such relationships. Thus "the tendency of the largest city in any

cluster of cities to act as the receiving point for the entire cluster" has led to what Edward Taaffe years ago called "the traffic shadow effect." Writing before the jet age, he pointed to Philadelphia and Baltimore as notable examples "because of their position between the two great passenger-generating centers of New York and Washington." The close spacing of many cities in the East and Midwest gave rise to marked differences in the frequency and character of air service, and the CAB held hearings on complaints in some important cases, such as those of Toledo (in the shadow of Detroit) and Milwaukee (Chicago), as well as a notorious standoff between Fort Worth and Dallas, which was only resolved later with the building of a gigantic airport between them. In a few cases, an airline has been attracted by one of these underused airports in a broadly strategic region as a place to develop a hub, such as Dayton (in the shadow of Cincinnati) selected by an expansive Piedmont (only to be downgraded again when that company was taken over by USAIR with its main hub at Pittsburgh).

6. *Air Express.* Although carrying packages (as distinct from letters) was about as old as airlines, and all-cargo air service was initiated by the big companies in the 1940s and expanded by freight-only airline companies after the war, "the U.S. air express industry went from infancy to adulthood between 1970 and 1990." This rapid breakthrough came with deregulation, the end of the U.S. Post Office monopoly on letters (1979), and overnight, door-to-door delivery from shipper to receiver by a single company. While the passenger airlines continue to handle cargo, working in conjunction with freight forwarders, this new service was developed by specialized intermodal companies, the largest being Federal Express and United Parcel Service (UPS). The first, begun as a documents delivery service in 1973, had seventy-six planes by 1982, and in 1989 absorbed Flying Tiger, the largest all-cargo carrier; UPS was already the largest surface operator when it entered overnight air service in 1982. These and a few lesser companies offer what is now a routine and highly valued form of shipment over the whole country, making unprecedented nighttime use of uncongested midcontinent airports, such as Memphis and Louisville.

7. *Airports.* The enormous growth and change in air travel has put great strains on support systems and necessitated recurrent enlargements, replacements, or multiplication of airports. Different types of traffic and local geographic situations tend to be served by different patterns of airport location. Large metropolises generating most of their traffic may have a main airport plus several satellite airports in different sectors of the metropolitan area, as in the case of Los Angeles, with outlying Ontario, Orange County, and Burbank; San Francisco, Oakland, and San Jose; or New York City with three large airports (Kennedy, LaGuardia, Newark) and sev-

eral lesser ones (Islip, White Plains). Where city centers remain primary in business or government, as in New York City and Washington, there is pressure to keep as much service as possible in the most convenient airport (LaGuardia and National) even when less congested alternatives are available.

Large hubs, where most of the flow is connecting traffic, require huge airports (like the great Union Stations of the railroad age), such as those at Atlanta (where nearly three-quarters of all boardings are change-of-plane), Pittsburgh, Detroit, and Dallas–Fort Worth. O'Hare has long been the nation's busiest, but Chicago also generates much traffic, which helps keep Midway Airport (O'Hare's predecessor and closer to downtown) in use as well. The immense scale of wholly new airports, such as Dallas–Fort Worth and Denver, requires a location well beyond the edge of the city—and the lure of such a place becomes a powerful incentive for the emergence of a new edge city on the nearest outer beltway (such as the famous example of Tysons Corner, "halfway between Dulles Airport and the Pentagon"), as well as making the airport itself a shopping mall (as at Pittsburgh). Every city wants a busy airport of the latest style to serve as its gateway, and the air age has added its massive mobilization and acceleration to the reshaping of metropolitan America.

8. *An Unstable and Uneven System.* Even during the forty years that the federal government attempted to manage the expansion of air travel the relentless swelling of consumer demand and dramatic improvements in aircraft forced many unsettling changes in the overall system; deregulation brought greater instabilities and differentiations in the character of air service. As an early study anticipated, with the advent of jet travel "civic pride, if nothing else, will prompt cities to demand service comparable to that received by jet-serviced neighbors." Over the next twenty years most cities did obtain some degree of such service, yet the high cost of new small jets left many places with a high proportion of less-desirable propeller service. Far more important was the sharp differentiations in fares imposed upon selected routes. The incidence of such discrimination has been very uneven, but not uncommon: "there are not a few pockets of pain; there are problems in many places in America." Most long-haul routes between major cities operate under keen competition, and average fares have been kept low. But single companies monopolize many lesser direct routes, dominate one or more hubs ("fortress hubs"), and can charge as much as they please.

High fares impinge most heavily on short-term round-trip travel, therefore especially on businesses and thereby affecting city and regional economies. Such conditions naturally generate protests from community leaders ("Sky-High Fares Hurting Local Business") and pressures on states and Congress to intervene. Upstate New York provides a good example of the problem and the difficulties such movements face. Saddled with some of the highest fares in the nation, its civic, business, and government representatives have tried to lure another major airline, foster the creation of a new regional carrier, and get federal officials to ease restrictions on entry into critical hubs (the number of flights at LaGuardia, Kennedy, National, and O'Hare airports has been controlled to limit further congestion and pollution). So far little has been achieved, and here, as elsewhere, the most notorious feature of air travel in America remains the fact that it can cost more to fly 200 miles than to fly across the continent.

During the decades following World War II, travel by air has undergone amazing expansion: domestic passenger miles rose from 6 billion toward 600 billion annually and the number of passengers emplaned exceeds 600 million. Even with the loss of service by some places, nearly all Americans are within an hour or so of a commercial airport (thanks in part to the Interstate and other highway improvements), and from that point "it is possible to reach almost anywhere within continental North America within a working day, usually within half a day." Even though "some passengers get bargains while other passengers subsidize those bargains," such has been the case in some degree with any extensive transportation system.

This late twentieth-century airline system was not unlike the American railroad system of the late nineteenth century: comprehensive in scope, unrivaled in its kind of transport service, essential to the established routines of the national economy and society, and therefore vital to individual cities and towns. And like the railroads of that day, it is a system dominated by a set of large private corporations that are free to monopolize routes, dominate key points, and provide whatever level and price of service they wish—their only fear being invasion of their territories by a rival company. There were important differences, however, in their historical phases of development. As we have noted, the federal government had a strong role in shaping the actual network of airline routes and fares, seeking to provide a national service through regulation of private companies; whereas the government intervened at a much later stage in railroad history, seeking consolidation of companies as a means of improving service on an established network. Both systems underwent periods of turbulent change, which the government attempted to ease and then withdrew to let the surviving companies manage themselves.

As with the current railroad pattern, we may assume that the existing airline network is unstable and that change will be shaped by the territorial strategies of companies seeking "to build up market share" rather than by public pleas for equitable service. As Fleming has observed, "there is very little in American law . . . to prevent development of geographical monopolies." Nevertheless, although there seems little prospect of any general reregulation, pressures for selective governmental intervention will very likely increase, not only because of ever-greater congestion on the nation's airways, but because of a growing public feeling that, as the attorney general of Iowa put it: "this industry should not choose the winners and losers of economic development."

5. Acceleration: Invisible and Instantaneous

TELEPHONE AND TELEVISION

In July 1918 the federal government took possession of "each and every telegraph and telephone system, and every part thereof, within the jurisdiction of the United States." A year later all was returned to their former owners, who numbered more than 200 telegraph and over 1,000 telephone companies. Military leaders and the Post Office Department had argued in favor of a permanent government-operated national system (as existed in virtually every other modern nation), yet there was, in effect, already a national system rapidly expanding in extent and efficiency. What the government had taken over was a vast array of local companies operating in connection with AT&T to form a national network; what the government chose to do was to sustain private ownership, with AT&T as "network manager" and the telephone industry as a whole regulated as a public utility (with most local companies under the jurisdiction of individual state commissions).

AT&T and its subsidiaries had already controlled virtually all long-distance lines, the key switching stations, and the design and manufacture of telephone equipment. In seeking government support of a complete monopoly, under regulation, it was committed "to continue expansion into uneconomic, sparsely settled and difficult-to-reach territories" so as to provide "universal service so that everyone who desired a telephone could have one and could communicate with everyone else." Thus in the 1920s AT&T undertook a vigorous program to create a completely "wired America." A first, feeble transcontinental link had been formed in 1915, but a full national system required far more extension and improvement. Bell Laboratories, the first great research and development center in the United States, provided the technology (and the critical patents) to keep up with rapidly expanding demands for service, such as supplanting open wires with cables in the 1920s, then far more capacious coaxial cables in the 1930s, and microwave transmission in the 1950s. In each case the first major trunk line completed was New York–Chicago, with transcontinental connections a few years later. In the 1960s AT&T had the first satellite in orbit and became a leader in the complex private and public, national and international, program of telecommunications soon formed (Comsat). By 1980 every major American city was being served by all of these forms, and thus "much of our telephone transmission network is a splicing of different types of technologies" and its "infrastructure is largely invisible to users."

These newer wireless technologies also undermined the long-standing government support of AT&T as a necessary monopoly. In 1969 the Federal Communications Commission (FCC) approved an experimental rival microwave connection between Chicago and St. Louis. Within a few years satellite operations were opened to domestic competition, and in 1984, after lengthy hearings, court cases, and negotiations, the AT&T system was radically reconstituted (in that same year the British government privatized its national telephone system). AT&T was forced to relinquish control of and reorganize its regional networks (the Bell companies) into a set of independent systems through which other long-distance suppliers might compete for service to customers. AT&T was allowed to continue operation of its own comprehensive long-distance network, as well as Bell Laboratories and manufacturing facilities.

Thus the telephone provides still another pattern in the shaping of American national networks. Like electricity, this new invisible current quickly became regarded as an essential service (for businesses more than homes). As always, the government preferred that it be provided by private companies, but, as with electricity, there was also a strong pressure to see that such service was universal, reaching into every locality. Differences in response and pattern arose from differences in technology. Whereas because of spatial transmission costs the electrical network remained a set of regional power supply and distribution systems interlocked for neighboring support when needed, the telephone system required massive nationwide connections every day and therefore some sort of highly efficient national network manager, a role AT&T had achieved (as had Western Union for the telegraph system) well before it became the government's chosen instrument.

As earlier noted, the national telephone network allowed the rapid development of national radio networks, and the same kind of service was fundamental to radio's powerful successor and dominator. The concept of television was almost as old as radio but far more difficult to perfect. Experimental stations were authorized in the 1930s, the first public demonstration, at the 1939 World's Fair in New York, stirred public interest, and World War II brought further technical advances (such as those related to radar). In 1945 major companies were eager to get a head start at commercial broadcasting, and the FCC drew up a program for allocation and supervision of stations. Neither initiative was an immediate success. The start-up costs were high, programming was limited, and home sets were expensive; moreover, extensive trials showed that the FCC plan needed spatial revision. From the outset the commission had declared that its "first priority was to provide at least one television service to all parts of the United States," reserving some channels for broad rural areas that might not be able to sustain a station economically. This rural bias (so contradictory of American marketing principles) was compounded by the need to increase the spacing of channels broadcasting on the same frequency so as to minimize interference. As a result, the revised standards of 1951 (varying regionally between 170 and 220 miles) forced a reduction in the number of stations already allocated in thirty-seven of the fifty largest metropolitan markets. All of these problems were soon resolved, AT&T had expanded its coaxial and microwave systems to serve nationwide network broadcasting, and by 1960 more than 400 stations were reaching into 60 million homes and radio was becoming reduced to little more than music and news.

Seeking simplified standards for an intensely competitive industry, the FCC had explicitly barred consideration of "terrain features . . . as a basis for reduced spacing" of channels. As a result in some small cities in the Appalachian East and the Far West local cable systems connected to an antenna on some high intervening ground were created to provide reliable reception (Mahanoy City, Pennsylvania, and Astoria, Oregon, were apparently the first to do so). On the other hand, the use of cable simply to provide additional, specialized channels for a fee on a metropolitan scale was considered commercially risky—would there be enough customers to cover the expense? First tried in San Diego in 1962, its general success awaited the vast increases in capacity and reductions in cost provided by fiber-optic cables and satellite transmission in the 1980s. By that time this selective rewiring of America and this new splicing of technologies seemed a routine expansion amid far more revolutionary changes.

INFORMATION AND INTERNET

Toward the end of the twentieth century, nearing the threshold of the much-anticipated new millennium, entry into a new, revolutionary era was widely proclaimed and increasingly assumed: the "Information Age," the "Knowledge Revolution," "a fundamental change in the technological basis of society"—an even more "miraculous unfolding" than any in the rapid sequence of remarkable developments that had already transformed daily life and the national economy—or so it seemed to many Americans.

Certainly a technical revolution in the gathering and transmission of incredible amounts of data at incredible speed for general business, public, and individual use took place—an acceleration so great as to require a new vocabulary: megabytes, nanoseconds, and so on. Skeptics cautioned that "information must not be confused with meaning," and whether far greater ease of access and interaction constitutes or will bring about a "Knowledge Revolution" remains controversial. All of this was a product of what had become known as "high-tech" industries, a rather loose term referring to heavy investment in research and use of scientific and technical expertise in the development of new highly sophisticated products and processes. Such activity was of course apparent in some degree all through the century, as in the fields of electricity, telephone, and radio (Bell Laboratories, established in New Jersey in 1925, was a premier example of a high-tech center). Our focus here, as with these others, is not so much on the industries as on the infrastructure, on nodes and networks and movements, insofar as these can be generally described or envisioned.

However great the power of this movement, there were important connections and parallels, as well as contrasts, with earlier neotechnic transformations. If we date this development from the invention of the transistor in 1947 through its early applications and the succession of minicomputers, microprocessors, and Internet to the opening of the World Wide Web to public access in 1993, the span of time between early invention and nationwide impact is at least as long as that between the first gasoline-powered buggy and a nationwide network of paved highways, or as that between Marconi and a radio in every home. And, to an even greater degree than with most of its neotechnic predecessors, wars and military interest were a great spur to invention and improvement. The first modern computers were employed in World War II to crack enemy codes (in Britain) and to calculate gunnery trajectories (in the United States), and for thirty years thereafter military and aerospace demands provided most of the research momentum that carried development from these crude and cumbersome wartime machines to those in routine office use ("the computer survived the Second World War *in utero* to be born as a child of the nuclear age"); the first long-distance computer network, forerunner of the Internet, was a Cold War Defense Department project.

The bulk of such government contracts were with major corporations already involved in electronics and related activities. Although these companies had research facilities in many locales, two concentrations became unusually important and soon emerged as the "culture hearths" of the new age. One of these became commonly known simply as Route 128. This early outer beltway around Boston provided attractive open space for physical expansion along with ready access to the rich scientific, intellectual, corporate, and financial resources of the city (fig. 31). Route 128 became famous as an American "technopolis" where the concept and dynamic of the new high-tech complex featuring a concentration of science-based companies (many of them newly born) focused on innovations in information processing, applications, and diffusion first appeared. The most creative among numerous advances was the development of more efficient mainframe computers and their application through minicomputers to routine office work. Meanwhile, on the other side of the country the Santa Clara Valley, south of San Francisco, an agricultural area ("an almost endless orchard of apricot and prune trees") was being so transformed through a similar combination of resources, facilities, and

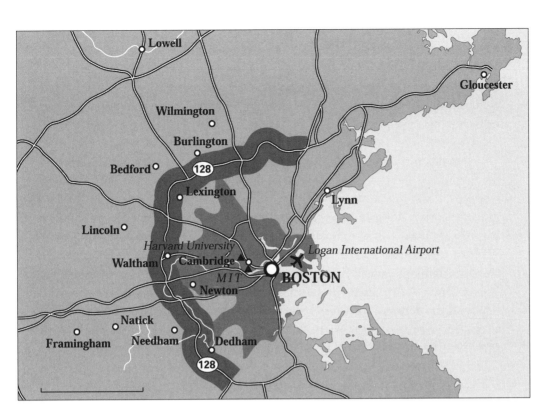

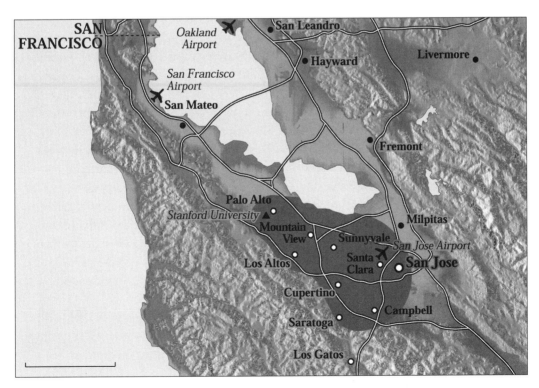

31. Primary Technopolises.
Route 128 and Silicon Valley.

innovations that it surpassed its East Coast counterpart and "gained fame as Silicon Valley, the capital of the semiconductor industry and the densest concentration of 'high technology' enterprises in the world." The revolutionary innovation here was the development of integrated circuits on silicon chips, leading to microprocessors (1971) and personal computers of ever-greater power and versatility.

The emergence of these two technopolises has been so unusual in kind, so powerful in impact, and productive of so much wealth for many of their inventors, entrepreneurs, and investors that it has prompted many studies of the decisive features of their impetus and growth. Most of these have focused on Silicon Valley as the more spectacular and characterizing exhibit (and one that flourished in some degree at the expense of the Massachusetts complex, as the microprocessor surpassed the minicomputer), but the two areas shared several fundamental features. Our concern is with a few basic geographic features of this formative period, rather than with the details of this new technology (which quickly reached into realms beyond geographical imagination: "in the mid-1960s the complexity of a chip was comparable to the network of streets in a small town"; by 1980 a chip was "comparable to the streets of greater Los Angeles. And an ultimate complexity . . . of the quarter-micron chip is similar to a street map covering the entire North American continent").

Robert W. Preer has defined "technopolis" as "a region that generates sustained and propulsive economic activity through the creation and commercialization of new knowledge." The unusual feature in each of these two regions was the very active role of an educational institution in creating such links with industry. At the Massachusetts Institute of Technology (MIT), a Division of Industrial Cooperation and Research was established after World War I, in 1932 MIT researchers were allowed to share in the royalties from patents, and after World War II its president helped found a corporation to raise capital in support of new companies. Similarly, at the premier private university in the West, Frederick Terman created Stanford Industrial Park as a means of fostering new companies drawing directly upon university research. Such initiatives were unprecedented; indeed, the very idea of fostering such interlocking relationships between creation and commercialization was commonly opposed by major universities (such as neighboring Harvard and the University of California at Berkeley). Thus Terman would refer to his science park as "Stanford's secret weapon," and it "became the nucleus for Silicon Valley" and "a model for scores of other high-technology parks in the United States and around the world."

In the early stages the links were with well-established firms, such as IBM, GE, and Lockheed, that were already in the area or were drawn there by the rapidly growing cluster of related industries, all sustained in large part by government contracts that allowed intensive focus on innovation with little concern for the mar-

ket. The really "propulsive" economic activity came from "spin-offs," new companies formed to promote some new marketable feature, and successions of other
companies, each specializing on some new notion or niche (Fairchild Semiconductor, the first to work exclusively in silicon, was the source of fifty new companies in
twenty years). The astounding profits from some early initiatives lured a flood of
venture capital, fueling the process and freeing development from government
funding. Such creativity and propulsive expansion was both a product and a rein-
forcement of these geographic concentrations, wherein "inventive and entrepreneurial talent thrived in a milieu which was highly conducive to interfirm communication, information transfer and personal mobility." Such talent also thrived in
the larger geographic settings of these remarkable clusters. The historic cosmopolitan urban environments of Boston and San Francisco, each within broader landscapes of great natural attractions, have long drawn creative people from across the
nation, and such "quality of life" considerations have become increasingly important in an ever-more mobile and increasingly affluent America undergoing widespread restructuring of its economic geography.

As Preer summarized, "the formula for creating a technopolis is a world-class
university, an affiliated science park where research can be commercialized, an ample supply of venture capital, a pleasant physical environment and a stimulating social milieu." Such a prescription has generated a proliferation of science parks by
universities, municipalities, and states, and intense competition for branches, spin-
offs, or imitators of those notoriously successful companies. The results of such promotions vary from negligible to substantial, but none have approached the intensity and creativity of the original clusters. Among the most notable examples are
the North Carolina Research Triangle established by 1960 by the state government
in an attractive area anchored by three universities and, much later, Austin, fueled
by ample Texas money and state aid, early high-tech initiatives in oil-related industries elsewhere in the state, and a location on the margins of the Hill Country,
which many would consider the most attractive physical setting between Atlanta
and Albuquerque. In the 1990s Austin became the largest microchip producer outside Silicon Valley. Perhaps the most important and distinctive cluster has emerged
along the Capital Beltway skirting the District of Columbia. Long the site of major
national research institutes and attractive to companies dependent on defense
contracts, it more recently became the headquarters of major telecommunications
companies. Although close contacts with federal agencies and Congress are surely
an important location factor (issues of taxes and regulation loom large), much
more than lobbying is involved because these high-tech industries now employ
more people locally than does the federal government—and more than Silicon
Valley or Route 128.

Preer's formula for technopolis, which seems such a departure from long-standing basics of industrial location (raw materials, power, labor, transportation, market), can be misleading as to the actual labor requirements of the new industry, even though much of this is performed elsewhere. Initially the Boston and San Francisco areas had ample supplies of all levels of skills, but especially with the development of silicon chips the demands for large numbers of reliable workers for meticulous, monotonous, semiskilled tasks soon led American companies abroad. Thus a large share of the silicon wafers manufactured in the United States became shipped daily to branch plants in East Asia (Taiwan, Malaysia, Singapore, Manila, South Korea) for installation of circuits, then airfreighted back for final inspection and marketing. More recently many semiconductor plants have been built in the United States, mostly in the Southwest and California (and employing much Hispanic and Asian labor).

There are of course many high-tech centers in the United States, varying in size and specialties, and essential to all of them is the other great dimension of the information-processing revolution: the networks of transmission from one place to another.

Long-distance transmission of data between computer centers was initiated by the Department of Defense in 1969 in a trial link between the Stanford Research Institute and the University of California–Los Angeles, quickly followed by two other connections, all designed to provide alternative bases and links ("decentralization" and "redundancy") in case of enemy attack. This ARPA (Advanced Research Projects Agency) Net was soon followed by other specialized networks by the National Aeronautics and Space Administration (NASA) and other agencies. In the 1970s the National Science Foundation (NSF) began providing a much more extensive system to serve many universities and other research centers, forming a transcontinental axis of supercomputer centers to which regional and local networks could be linked. Development was so rapid that by 1990 this NSF system bound a thousand networks serving hundreds of points within the United States and managed links with networks in many other countries; what had become collectively known as the Internet had become a routine focus for more than a million users (fig. 32).

In spite of amazing improvements in speed, capacity, and utility, traffic on this vast system had increased so rapidly and relentlessly that there was much talk in Congress and elsewhere about the need for a national "data superhighway" to relieve congestion and delays and to accelerate movement between points on the network. More familiar trafficways provided the obvious analogy. As Albert Gore, leading advocate of a massive federal government program, put it, the need was for "a network of highways, much like the interstates of the 1950s . . . highways carrying information rather than people or goods." The overall system would not be "just one eight-lane turnpike, but a collection of interstates and feeder roads made

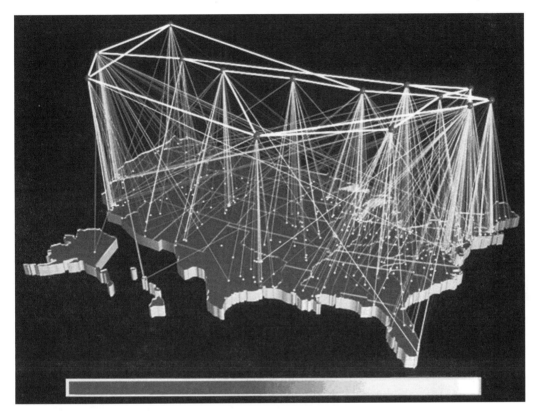

32. NSFNET.
An attempt to visualize the NSF "backbone" and links with universities and research centers at an early stage of the Internet, September 1991. (Courtesy National Center for Supercomputing Applications; Donna Cox and Robert Patterson, principal investigators and visualization. Copy supplied by Paul F. Starrs, editor, *Geographical Review*)

of different materials in the same way that highways are concrete or macadam or gravel. Some highways will be made of fiberoptics, others of coaxial cable, others will be wireless." Furthermore, like the Interstate, this highway must be "a public right-of-way" and provide for "two-way" traffic, "so that each person will be able to send information in video form as well as just words, as well as receiving information."

The NSF Net already provided the "backbone" of such a supersystem, and commercial networks were fast developing other links. The emergence of the World Wide Web (from 1989 onward) and invention of the first browser (in 1993 at the federal government's supercomputer center at the University of Illinois) made general public access to the Internet feasible and compelling, and the government began to shift funding and operation of the NSF Net to the private sector, to be managed from four regional hubs spaced across the country: Pennsauken, New Jersey (across the Delaware from Philadelphia), Washington, Chicago, and San Francisco.

Analogies with other spatial networks and the familiar geographic vocabulary of routes and places can offer some sense of a highly generalized skeletal framework and some of the main stations in this newest transmission system (it is interesting to find out that a large share of the world's e-mail "makes at least a quick stop . . . in Schaumburg," Illinois, a few miles from O'Hare Airport, or that nearly all automatic bank deposit and payment transactions in the United States are handled by a cluster of computers in and near Secaucus, New Jersey, alongside the Meadowlands across the Hudson from New York City), but the Internet "ranks among the most complex and organized entities on earth" and no ordinary map—or imagination—can provide much sense of the actual patterns of movement through such a maze. In its earliest stages of development the idea of alternative routes was adopted to ensure against a failure in any one segment (in terms of the familiar analogy: "like the network of back roads weaving together every municipality in the country. Each point is connected to its nearest neighbor by several redundant paths"). But the radical difference came with the realization that any "message from one computer to another" could be "chopped up into many little packets, which would be sent swarming through the network to find their way. Some would take this route, some would take that. Each would carry a destination label along with instructions for where the packet fit inside the overall message. No matter in what sequence the pieces arrived, they could be reassembled." Nevertheless, as we have noted, even this revolutionary form of transmission is dependent upon the vast infrastructure of its neotechnic predecessors, on the lines of electricity, telephone, and cable television and the right-of-ways of railroads and highways; so far it is one more historical stage in the elaboration of a wired America: "The growing use of fibre optic systems thus tends to strengthen the major existing telecommunication concentrations and therefore the existing hierarchies."

As daily use of the automobile by the general public had to await a network of good roads to run on, so general use of the computer had to await the formation of links for data to travel on; however, unlike with the auto the public also had to await general individual access to those networks. When it did gain that privilege (by way of further new technology as well as government permission), it was suddenly involved in a new realm, in "cyberspace," wherein the movement was by information data in a hitherto unimaginable compression of space and time and expansion of source and volume. In spite of our opening reference to nearly half a century of development of this new media, it was this abrupt breakthrough of public access that was revolutionary. As Paul Starrs observed: "I cannot think of a comparable change so rapidly adopted; it blows by the adoption and diffusion of the telephone like an airplane past a passenger pigeon." Such an amazing change makes one further use of our common analogy worth quoting: the geographer John Pickles' reminder that "like all highways, the information highway requires points of access, capital investment, navigation skills, and spatial and cultural proximity for effective use. Like the automobile highway, the information highway fosters new rounds of creative destruction and differentiates among users and between users and nonusers. It brings regions of difference under a common logic and technology, and through differential access and use exacerbates old and creates new patterns of social and economic differentiation."

As might be expected, it is widely assumed—even more than was the case with the automobile—that this radical compression, marvelous versatility, and open discretionary use of this new instrument will "free the common man from the limitations of his geography." But, without belittling the great power of the instrument, we may again remind ourselves that we are never "free" of geography; we are simply moving into yet another stage in adapting our human geography—altering its limitations—to realities and potentialities of new technologies.

In general those realities are too evident in daily life to need mention. By the end of the century it was clear that the new powers of data processing had revolutionized the form and facility of many tasks, and information access and communication had vastly enlarged levels of interaction, but it was not at all clear that the human geography of the United States had as yet been significantly changed directly by the computer and the Internet. At most there had been some acceleration of trends already under way and dependent on many factors, such as the decline of many older industries and the expansion of newer ones, regional shifts in population and economy, selective metropolitan growth and spread. Even though that new emblematic and mercurial activity, the creation of software, seems like "a system for producing something valuable from virtually nothing," it all must be done somewhere; home and office are becoming increasingly combined for many workers, but homes and offices have specific locations; shopping on the Internet is increasingly routine, but that is not fundamentally different from shopping from a Sears & Roebuck catalogue, and the goods still have to be produced and delivered (the soaring popularity of Amazon.com of Seattle led to the construction of six huge warehouses spaced across the country to house and ship the books). Geographic changes were surely under way, but American life at the end of the century was still daily and firmly dependent upon or infused with automobiles, airplanes, electricity, radio, television, telephones, and the networks these had created.

That at the beginning of the twentieth century none of these instruments existed—or at least had as yet much effect upon national life—directs attention to America's rapid adoption of these transforming technologies. They did not, of course, all originate in the United States. Our focus on American formations obscures important work of European inventors and scientists and the spreading networks across European countries and elsewhere (the World Wide Web was initiated by a British physicist working in Geneva). Yet the scale and dynamism of American development soon gave it world leadership in every case. The sheer size of the country, a nation of 3,000 miles and four time zones across, gave it a special interest in space-conquering instruments. The railroad, the nineteenth century's radical creation, had ensured the feasibility of a transcontinental republic and rapidly bound all parts of the nation together. The subsequent growth in population and economy of all its regions made efficient nationwide networks an obvious goal of every new system. The rapid rise of California to national prominence made links between New York City and Los Angeles–San Francisco the primary axes of national networks.

The federal government obviously had an interest in the provision of nationwide access to these important utilities, but its role varied greatly: from direct construction, as with Interstate highways, or operation, as in early air mail service; to regional assistance, as with TVA and rural electrification, or subsidies to feeder airlines; to comprehensive regulation, as under the CAB, to minimal supervision, as with the FCC and recent airline operations. Military needs provided many crucial technical developments and involvement with some of these spatial systems, varying from the brief emergency takeovers of World War I, to ostensible needs, as with the National System of Defense Highways (better known as the Interstate), to full and exclusive creation of the first long-distance computer network. However, unlike most industrial nations of this era, the general bias and pressure in the United States was always toward private ownership and operation of these vital systems. Advocates of public power were a political minority that won only a few victories; nationalization of an existing system was never more than a dire prescription to prevent collapse of an essential service. That bias, so deeply embedded in the American system and psyche, was surely heavily responsible for the vigorous, intensive expansion of all these services. Although a higher degree of government supervision was apparent in the twentieth century than in the nineteenth, the formative context for many of these new technologies remained much like that of the railroad era, which, as we have earlier noted, provided a great opportunity "for an unlimited number of capitalists to carve up a continent, parcelling out large territories, creating intercity axes and interregional connections, . . . setting the basic network and controlling the pulse of circulation for the internal body of the nation" (*Transcontinental America*, 245). When, atypically, the government built the network and opened it to public use, expansion was especially intense: the Internet and World Wide Web, like trucking, "grew like a field of weeds"—"cheap, flexible, unregulated, and instantly expandable"; and the whole Silicon Valley phenomenon, "resting on continuous technological innovation, entrepreneurial fever, and vigorous economic competition" has been called "a special kind of supercapitalism" quite beyond anything elsewhere in the world.

Referring to the automobile, the airplane, the motion picture, and the radio, the government-sponsored report *Recent Social Trends* observed that "each new communication agency bids for public favor and its ultimate acceptance adds to the complexity of our civilization"; from our perspective sixty years later, we may well emphasize that each of the new systems under review soon found public favor, each new instrument soon shifted from being a luxury to a necessity (as that 1933 report noted, "to be without a telephone or a telephone listing is to suffer a curious social isolation in a telephonic age"), and thereby each not merely added to the "complexity of our civilization," it became one of the American *measures* of "civilization" itself. The spread of these modern services has of course been widely welcomed around the globe, but Americans, imbued with the cult of progress and assertive leaders of "modern" living, have long had "an untroubled zeal for technology" as "a liberating force."

Looking back over this century of the neotechnic, one is reminded of Lewis Mumford's comments in 1934 following his assessment of the telephone and the radio (and in anticipation of television) that "one is faced here with a magnified form of a danger common to all inventions: a tendency to use them whether or not the occasion demands. . . . *As with all instruments of multiplication* [of contact between persons] *the critical question is as to the function and quality of the object one is multiplying.* There is no satisfactory answer to this on the basis of technics alone: certainly nothing to indicate, as the early exponents of instantaneous communication seem uniformly to have thought, that the results will automatically be favorable to the community."

PART TWO
MORPHOLOGY: MIGRATIONS
AND FORMATIONS

Geographers study space and map spatial location, adding system to the structure that humans give to space. Less frequently do we think of the other two dimensions of location—time and culture. In truth, both are as integral to location as is space. . . . Taken separately, each of the three dimensions has its own dynamic, but a different pattern emerges when all are taken together.

Daniel J. Elazar

Prologue

The remarkable sequence of new transport and communications instruments inevitably had a great impact on the shaping of the nation, but such changes could be very uneven in pace and place. The years under consideration are again subdivided into two distinct eras. The thirty-five-year period spanning two world wars was marked by extremes of prosperity, depression, and wartime stimulus and featured unprecedented efforts to manage the dynamics and patterns of regional development and the growth and character of American society. Nevertheless, the shape of the country at midcentury was still generally congruent with local, regional, and national formations of fifty years earlier.

During the next fifty years, however, the United States underwent an increasingly comprehensive restructuring into an ever-more efficiently integrated and broadly balanced geographical entity. Furthermore, partly through changes in official policies and partly through quite unexpected and unmanaged growth and changes, it became an ever-more dispersed, loosened, diversified, and, in critical ways, segmented and segregated society.

Thus the shape of America at the end of the twentieth century was significantly different from its shape at the beginning. As usual, our concern is to map and assess selected changes through that past rather than attempt an overview of the present or a projection into the future.

1. Populations and Policies, 1915–1950s

Growth and movement, the continuous reshaping of the size and distribution of the American population, are two of the great dynamics of American life, each at once a reflection of and an influence upon other basic changes. The first forty years of the era under study was a period of unprecedented fluctuations in population growth. The 100 million of 1915 had become 165 million by 1955, but that sizable addition represented a marked slowing in the rate of growth, for the nation had always at least doubled in population over such a span of time.

The irruption of war in Europe and curtailment of transatlantic immigration produced a sharp, brief change (compounded by a sharp, brief rise in the American death rate from the worldwide influenza epidemic of 1918); the revival of such movement was potentially strong but the United States itself imposed severe reductions on that great invigorating source (which had accounted for 20 percent of the nation's population increase in 1900–1910). A marked reduction in birth rates during the Great Depression and a near-cessation of immigration (even a small net *outflow* in the early 1930s) resulted in a deep dip in the rate of growth. However, World War II brought another sudden change, and a new surge of population on past midcentury carried the possibility of soon dwarfing "any previous growth the nation has known." And although by 1915 the United States had become a fully transcontinental nation, the peopling of the continent has never stilled. As a demographer in the 1950s noted: "the annual volume of movement and migration involves many millions of persons. Over a period of only a few years mobility involves a majority of the population; over a period of a lifetime it involves almost everybody." Our concern at this point is with broad regional and national patterns of such differential growth and residential flux, with generalized movements and volumes rather than with their impacts upon the social geography of regions and localities.

INTERNAL PATTERNS AND MIGRATIONS

The year 1915 contained an interesting moment in the shaping of America: for the first time, rural and urban populations in balance—50 million rural dwellers, 50 million urban. It was, of course, an arbitrary as well as momentary equality, a census calculation based on its standard definition of 2,500 as the base line of urban places. The trend toward greater urbanization had long been relentless but continued to be uneven in pace, slowing nearly to a halt in the 1930s, then quickly accelerating during the war and after, so that by the early 1950s, 60 percent of Americans were urban dwellers (by the same definition).

Not all rural Americans were farmers, and the farm population was declining more rapidly than these figures may suggest. In 1915 an estimated one-third of the total population lived on farms, by 1955 only 13.5 percent, about 10 million fewer than forty years earlier. Other rural dwellers were distributed among a variety of settlement types, with some of them bunched together in unincorporated locales just outside city limits. How to fit enumerations to the actual geographies of settlement, to the areal frameworks of daily life, had become an increasingly difficult problem in census reporting. In 1910 the populations of "metropolitan districts," encompassing the entire built-up area rather than just that within the legal bounds of a city, were reported for the larger centers. By 1950 similar measures of "urbanized areas" were offered for all cities of 50,000 or more. Also from that census onward the definition of *urban* was changed from a threshold of 2,500 to 8,000. By midcentury a quarter of Americans lived in the twelve urbanized areas of more than a million, but more than half of the urban population was in cities and towns of fewer than 50,000.

The impact of the automobile on suburbanization and the radiating reach of urban life prompted the Census Bureau to create a set of larger "standard metropolitan areas" (SMAs) consisting of a central city and closely associated counties as a further measure of the functional clustering of the population (figs. 33, 34). By this

33. Urban Settlement and Enumeration Frameworks.
This schematic diagram illustrates a central city (defined by its legal boundaries), satellite cities (separate incorporations), the actual continuous urbanized area, a census-defined "metropolitan district," and a two-county "standard metropolitan area" (SMA). (From Bogue, *Population Growth in Standard Metropolitan Areas, 1900–1950*)

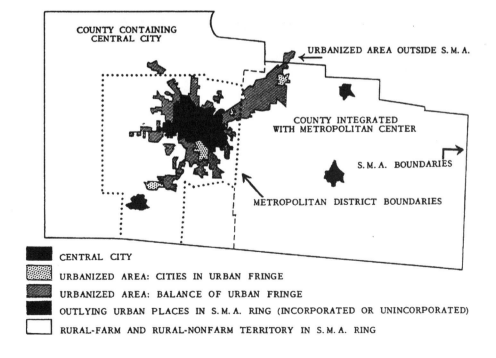

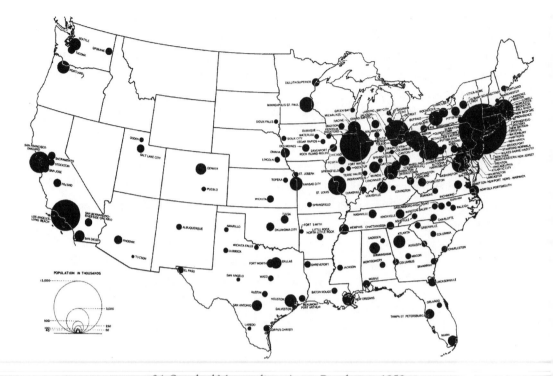

34. Standard Metropolitan Areas, Population, 1950.
(Source: Taeuber and Taeuber, *The Changing Population of the United States*. Reprinted with permission of the Social Science Research Council)

alternative definition (the specific areas determined on the basis of traffic surveys, commuting patterns, telephone flows, and other indicators), 57 percent of the American people lived within such metropolitan areas. An estimated 25 million lived in suburbs (but there was no standard definition of that term).

In the 1940s special surveys began to offer better measures of American mobility. The 1930s and the 1940s were both exceptional, the one for considerably less, the other for considerably more than what came to be seen as a more normal amount of moves. Between 1940 and 1945, 12 million persons served in the American armed forces and more than 15 million civilians changed residence, half of them moving to another state. In the later 1950s about 20 percent of Americans changed residence in any one year, but such shifts were "primarily a phenomenon of late adolescence and early maturity": young people leaving home, seeking jobs, setting up family households, moving to larger or better quarters, much of it taking place within the same community. More important to the geography of the country was the 5 to 7 percent who moved from one county to another, and especially those who moved to another state or region. We need to identify the major streams of migrations and important patterns of loss and gain resulting from these longer-distance movements.

"In recent years the most spectacular movement of the population within the United States," noted the 1929–32 government-sponsored study of *Recent Social Trends*, "has been the shift of hundreds of thousands of Negroes from south to north, introducing into industry a new type of labor and changing the environment of the migrants from the most rural to the most metropolitan." That movement was spectacular not just for its volume and composition but for its direction—the first of its kind, an anomaly in the historical patterns of American migration (fig. 35). Blacks had long been seeping northward from Virginia and across the Ohio to various borderland cities, but these trickles suddenly became a torrent rising far deeper within the South and flowing strongly into major Northern cities. Industries stim-

35. Migration Streams.

This map by C. W. Thornthwaite catches the important movements under review, even though it was compiled midway through our selected period. By design it of course includes earlier migrations, such as the inrush to Oklahoma and long-continuing migrations into Texas, but it offers appropriate emphasis on the great westward flows to California and the northward movement of Blacks. Note that no eastward migrations were of sufficient volume to be shown. Omission of the foreign-born has little effect on such interstate depictions as immigrants tend to stay in place for a generation or more. (Adapted from Goodrich et al., *Migration and Economic Opportunity*)

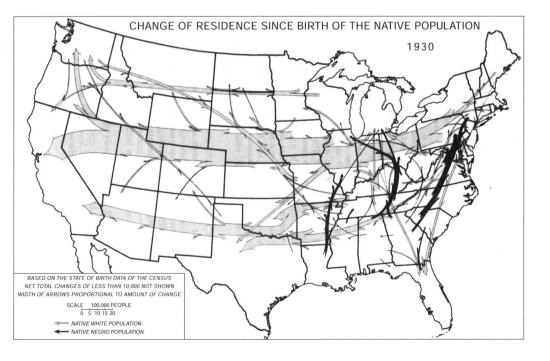

ulated by war but cut off from their usual supply of new immigrants sent labor agents fanning out across the Deep South promising free transportation and good wages to long-exploited Blacks in a Cotton Belt now ravaged by the boll weevil and heavy floods. The response quickly swelled into a great exodus; between 1916 and 1920 an estimated 400,000 departed their land of lamentations for a new "Promised Land" in the industrial North. After a brief slackening, it was soon clear that this wartime episode was only the first phase of what became widely known among Blacks as "the Great Migration"; by 1930 over 700,000 more had joined in this movement, and the census recorded that 21 percent of American Blacks now lived in the North (compared to just over 10 percent in 1910). Even the Great Depression could not halt the Great Migration; although some Blacks returned South as industrial jobs disappeared, more came North to join family members now settled there (many of them, as with millions of Whites, sustained by government relief programs), and with the onset of war the great tide surged again, bringing a million more Blacks out of the South by 1950, making a total movement of 3 million in thirty-five years.

This influx came in two great streams of equal volume: an Atlantic Coast branch from Georgia and the Carolinas to Baltimore, Philadelphia, New York City, with limited dispersals to lesser cities, and a Mississippi Valley route from Alabama and the Mississippi Floodplains to St. Louis, Chicago, Detroit, and other industrial centers. Much of the actual travel was by train, using the several Southern lines connecting to the Pennsylvania Railroad (itself an important early recruiter of Black labor) on the East Coast, and the Illinois Central, offering a straight line from the heart of the Cotton Belt to Chicago.

A much lesser South-to-North migration involved rural Whites from the Appalachians to nearby industrial cities. During World War I and the 1920s it was shallow and small because expanding coal mining and lumbering in many of the mountain counties absorbed much of the rural increase (and the expansion of textile and tobacco manufacturing made North Carolina the only state of the older South to have net in-migration). In the 1930s there was a net return southward as families reassembled to eke out survival on hardscrabble farms. World War II initiated the first big surge, pulling more than a million out of the hills to factories all across the western half of the Manufacturing Belt and forming distinct Appalachian sectors in Cincinnati, Hamilton, Columbus, Detroit, Akron, and other cities. Continued expansion of Northern industries, modernization and its accentuation of the marginality and privations of hill country farming, plus the evergreater ease of travel between the two regions undergirded a continuing migration in the 1950s.

There was also an episodic and selective migration from North to South during these years. It was not really a countermovement, for it bypassed the traditional

South to reach the more tropical lures of Florida. The land boom of the 1920s became infamous for its many speculative and fraudulent schemes, but it lured millions of visitors and added 300,000 residents to the state. This great surge subsided abruptly in 1926 (with the collapse of banks, followed by a succession of devastating hurricanes), but the winter climate and ease of getting there by automobile over the spreading network of good roads continued to attract migrants from a broad band of Northern states. World War II with its many military bases in and near Florida constituted another massive visitation, and postwar prosperity plus broader retirement benefits and the general popularity of a leisure lifestyle ensured an ever-enlarging influx. By the mid-1950s Florida's population was fourfold greater than it had been in the mid-1920s and Miami was one of the fastest-growing cities in America.

As ever the case in American migration, much the largest flow during all these years was from East to West. In the broadest view, between 1915 and 1955 about 7 million people moved from all the East to all the Far West (the eleven Pacific and Mountain states), the volume fluctuating in some degree with the national economy, but heavy in every decade (more than a million during the 1930s), swelling hugely with World War II, and running at more than a million every three years in the early 1950s.

This vast westward movement was channeled into several major streams. One was truly transcontinental, rising lightly in New England, gathering strength in New York and Pennsylvania, and heavily augmented state by state from Ohio westward across the Plains, but bifurcating in the mid-Midwest, one branch carrying some portion directly on to Northern California, the other veering across Kansas to the Southwest and across the desert to Southern California. This southwestern flow was joined and swollen by heavy outpourings from another major source region: the western Appalachians, Ozarks, and other marginal lands of Arkansas, Oklahoma, and parts of Texas. During the 1920s the Middle West and other Northern states were much the largest source of migrants to California, continuing a pattern established in the 1880s (and augmented, as always, by net inflows from all the other Far Western states). The 1930s brought a strong upsurge from the western South and Southern Plains, migrations made famous by the plight of the "Okies" and Dust Bowl refugees but actually considerably broader in source and status than suggested by such vivid publicity. Some other states received locally important deposits from these long-distance moves, especially Arizona, where the citrus and cotton, recreation, ranching, and sprawling towns in the Salt River oasis made it seem like an attractive anteroom of California. A much smaller but growing stream led out of Illinois, the Upper Midwest, and Northern Plains to Washington and Oregon (helping to offset the flow from those states to California). The total number moving west in the depressed 1930s was only a little less than that of the booming 1920s, and World War II brought a massive expansion of all these streams, as well as an important addition drawing upon broader sectors of the Lower South in Louisiana, Arkansas, and Texas. Between 1940 and 1955 about 4.7 million Americans moved to the Far Western states, most of them to California.

The cumulative effects of these interregional migrations magnify their impacts upon local natural increases in both source and destination areas. As noted, the nation as a whole grew by 65 million during this forty-year period. Almost a quarter of this increase, 15 million, took place in the Far West, and two-thirds of that in California. Yet the states of the American Core increased by double that amount and that northeastern quarter of the country was hardly diminished in its proportionate dominance, still containing almost half of the nation's people. In addition to the northward migrations already noted (especially important in the growth of New York and Michigan), European immigration, though much curtailed, also flowed almost entirely into this region.

As a great source of migrations to the North and West, the South was markedly slower in growth (despite relatively high rates of natural increase) and declining in its proportion of population. Florida and Texas were important exceptions to this broad generalization, the only Southern states to more than double in population during these forty years. We have already noted the case of Florida, where the spectacular influx headed for areas beyond the southern margins of the Traditional South (thirteen new counties were formed during the brief boom of the 1920s). During that same decade Texas was still an expanding frontier of that South. The high platform of the South Plains became a major and rejuvenating extension of the Cotton Belt, and together with new oil discoveries, this cotton-grain-livestock complex was spread on across the political boundary to impress a strong Texas imprint on southeastern New Mexico (Little Texas). Most of this expansion was by Texans themselves, but neighboring areas contributed to the overall growth of the state. Thus, while 57,000 Texans moved to California in the 1920s, almost twice that many moved into Texas from Oklahoma, Arkansas, and Louisiana. Even during the Depression and Dust Bowl years more people shifted to than departed from Texas, and the war magnified that gain (which was further augmented by immigration from Mexico).

Leaving aside Florida and Texas, the South added only about 10 million people over this forty-year span and declined to 18.3 percent of the national population. The heaviest losses in the South were from the hill country and older Cotton Belt. By the 1920s the farming population began to decline almost everywhere in the country (new irrigation areas being the major exception), but those regions most heavily dependent on grain farming lost the most (more through mechanization and enlargement of properties than from actual abandonment of land). Three million people left the Western Prairies and High Plains. The western tier of those states, from North Dakota through Oklahoma (and the eastern halves of Montana and Colorado as well), all lost population in the 1920s and most of the 1930s, and held few if any more people by 1950. The region as a whole dropped from about 12 percent to less than 9 percent of the nation's population, and half of these were urban dwellers.

Demographers commonly referred to all such migrations as "spontaneous," vast folk movements of individuals and families motivated by some perceived personal advantage in shifting from one area to another, undirected by any formal governmental policy on internal migration. With the onset of the Great Depression, however, "Americans were finding the problem of where to go more perplexing than in the past," and the topic of "misplaced populations" and "what part, if any, the Government should take in encouraging or guiding" migration became a prominent social and political issue. Much attention was given to "stranded populations" in regions where local resources appeared to be seriously inadequate to support current or future populations at an acceptable "plane of living," such as the Southern Appalachian Coal Plateaus, the Old Cotton Belt, the Great Lakes Cutover Region, and the Great Plains. How to induce some people to move from or industries to decentralize into such areas was studied and debated, and a great scattering of New Deal programs more or less pertinent to the problem were initiated (such as the TVA, rural electrification, irrigation, reforestation, soil conservation, and various housing and community projects). However, the number of people directly assisted to move was very small and longer-term prospects were uncertain (the hasty relocation of 202 families from the Great Lakes Cutover Lands to a government-sponsored farm colony in the Matanuska Valley in Alaska was the "most conspicuous current case"—and would become an example of the small scale and marginal results of such efforts). While recognizing that spontaneous migration must continue to be the main vehicle of population redistribution, the need for "social policy to encourage mobility and give it a surer purpose and direction" was widely assumed by students of the topic. In the end, of course, such public and government concern suddenly disappeared when World War II unleashed the greatest spontaneous migrations in American history, which reverberated on past midcentury: "never before in the history of our country has there been so great a shuffling and redistribution of population in so short a time."

IMMIGRATION: NARROWING THE FRONT DOOR

"The essential characteristic of the post-war period in the United States," said André Siegfried in the opening of his 1927 book *America Comes of Age*, "is the nervous reaction of the original American stock against an insidious subjugation by foreign blood." A "latent uneasiness was crystallized by the War," and "the change in the atmosphere . . . has been startling for there has been a complete reversal of ethnic, social, and political thought." Siegfried (a geopolitical essayist, latest in a long line of keen French observers of the American scene and system) was referring especially to "the immigration laws of 1917, 1921, and 1924," which he called "the most significant occurrence in their [U.S.] history since the Civil War."

Concern over the volume and character of European immigration had been rising since the 1890s. Amid ominous warnings by influential groups about the "immigrant invasion," Congress began lengthy hearings and its voluminous Dillingham Report of 1911 endorsed restriction. Mildly restrictive laws had actually been passed several times only to be vetoed by successive presidents as being against America's best traditions and interests. However, in 1914 the guns of August reverberated across the Atlantic with startling effect. Siegfried, who was in New York City at the time, noted the "processions of the various nationalities in the chief avenues of the city," the abandonment of hotel kitchens by their French chefs, and the besieging of consulates and shipping companies by various nationalities for passage back "home" to serve the mother country. New York of course was the great portal, hundreds of thousands of its immigrants had been in America only a short while and a good many never intended to stay permanently, but such actions, along with the shrill partisanship expressed in the local foreign-language press, cast suspicion on all "hyphenated Americans" ("Germany seems to have lost all her foreign possessions with the exception of Milwaukee, St. Louis, and Cincinnati," complained a Houston newspaper in 1915; in 1916 more than 170,000 Milwaukeeans attended a Charity War Bazaar and raised $150,000 "for war relief—for Germany"). Once the United States entered the war all things German—language, music, foods, personal names, even place names—came under heavy and often hysterical attack (despite President Wilson's insistence that the war was against the kaiser and German militarism rather than the German people or culture).

In 1917 Congress passed (over Wilson's veto) the first law aimed at a general restriction of European immigration, in the form of a literacy test to exclude illiterate adult heads of household and their families—the exclusion of large numbers from Southern and Eastern Europe being the primary aim of its sponsors. When the war ended there was widespread fear that "millions of war-torn Europeans were about to descend on the United States—a veritable flood which would completely subvert the traditional way of life." The Republican party platform of 1920 called for admitting only those "whose standards are similar to ours" and who "can be assimilated with reasonable rapidity." After their election triumph the House voted to suspend immigration entirely; the Senate refused that extreme and negotiated an emergency bill (shaped by William Dillingham of Vermont) limiting the annual number to about 350,000, apportioned according to the 1910 census of foreign-born residents in the United States. This temporary measure was replaced by the

Immigration Act of 1924, which programmed a reduction to 150,000 (with immigrant visas to be issued only by American consuls in Europe, thereby ending the unselected flood pouring into Ellis Island). This act, which was passed by large majorities (323–71 in the House, 52–6 in the Senate) and remained in force until 1952, temporarily changed the basis of apportionment to the 1890 census, thereby allocating 80 percent of the annual intake to Northwestern Europe, but stated that final quotas "were to be computed on the basis of the national composition of the total American population in 1920"—excluding descendants of "involuntary immigrants." Application of this deceptively simple formula was delegated to a panel of statistical experts who were thereby faced with the impossible task of determining such "national origins." Leaving aside the preposterous "eugenics" analysis sought by advocates of this program to determine what "percentage of the white blood in the population of the United States was derived from each country," no data on simple country of origin were available for the long formative period of the American population, and only indirect and flawed numbers for all of the remainder. This Quota Board therefore worked with inferences, basing its concept of the early Euro-American "native stock" on a 1909 census study that had classified the 1790 census population on the basis of surnames, and calculated the subsequent "immigrant stock" by estimates and probabilities applied to standard census data. Its initial report, allocating nearly half of the total quota to Great Britain, generated a storm of protest from other groups (especially Irish, German, and Scandinavian) and caused Congress to postpone its application. Recalculations (modified partly on the basis of a separate study of the 1790 data sponsored by the American Council of Learned Societies) altered these proportions somewhat, and after further protests and postponements a final annual quota of 154,000 (including a minimum of 100 for each country) was signed into law in 1929.

"Since the passage of the Immigration Act of 1924 . . . interest in the subject has rapidly subsided, since the issue has been considered permanently settled," wrote Maurice Davie in his 1936 study of *World Immigration;* "the Atlantic no longer provides the setting for the drama of migration on a large scale," it is "the end of an epoch." Writing in the midst of the Great Depression, when more people were leaving the United States than arriving, Davie's conclusions seemed obvious at the time. Those particular domestic circumstances of the moment would, of course, soon change, and the topic of immigration would reappear with dramatic force, yet some fundamentals of American policy established in the 1920s would endure: restriction and selectivity remained unchallenged as objectives, however controversial in numbers and basis, and even the bitterly controversial "national origins" plan would remain essentially in place for forty years.

Proposals to modify immigration policies to provide asylum for political refugees date from the early Nazi persecutions but received little public or congressional support as long as there were "10,000,000 . . . American refugees who have been walking the streets of our city in vain" (as one congressman put it in 1939). The president favored some such help and through various administrative directives about 250,000 political refugees had been granted resident visas by the end of the war. The Europe of 1945–46, with cities and economies in shambles, horrors revealed, armies in occupation, boundaries redrawn, new regimes implanted, and millions of "displaced persons" in temporary camps, created great pressures for a far more liberal response. The Western Allies found themselves custodians of more than a million persons who steadfastly refused to return to lands now under Soviet domination. About 40,000 were admitted to the United States by presidential directive, but it took more than two years of bitter wrangling before a special Displaced Persons Act was passed by Congress. Under this law of June 1948, and later amendments, about 415,000 visas were made available to specified categories of people (those whose countries had been annexed by the Soviet Union, and Germans expelled from Eastern Europe, received the largest allocations). So as not to warp the national origins formula, most of these visas were to be charged against future national quotas.

In the meantime, a "full and complete investigation of our entire immigration system" had been initiated in the Senate. Before considering the results of this action it will be useful to bring other sources and entryways into view.

THE BACK DOOR

Well before the United States decided to narrow its front door, it had used various means to keep the back door, facing Asia, pretty firmly closed. The Chinese Exclusion Act of 1882, a federal response to insistent pressures from and unilateral actions by California, was the first in a sequence that by 1904 had essentially locked the door against direct entry from China and denied resident Chinese the right to naturalization (the first nationality specified for such treatment). In 1907 President Roosevelt had gotten a reluctant Japan to voluntarily reduce emigration of its citizens to the United States. Thousands had been recruited for labor in Hawaii and many had moved on to the mainland, prompting a resurgence of cries for restriction or removal. The 1917 Immigration Act added an "Asiatic Barred Zone" that included the islands of Southeast Asia and much of Melanesia and Micronesia, and most of South and Central Asia (east of the Caspian and Iran). The 1924 act excluded immigration of all persons ineligible for citizenship, which became interpreted to include "non-White" Asians. (The original naturalization law of 1790 specified only "free white" persons as eligible for citizenship; in 1870 a Reconstructionist Congress added aliens of African nativity or African descent as eligible.)

Filipinos constituted a special case. They were, by court decision, American "nationals" but not citizens of the United States; in effect, they were wards of the American government, free to emigrate to the United States but not eligible for naturalization (except those who had served at least three years in the U.S. Navy— where they were valued as stewards and housekeepers). By 1930 there were 64,000 Filipinos in Hawaii and 45,000 on the mainland. Demands for their exclusion as "non-whites" generated a strong response from them against any such categorization. In Congress this embarrassing matter became linked with the larger question of how to dissolve this imperial relationship, and when the 1934 bill specifying a grant of independence to the Philippines ten years hence was passed, it included a provision that after that anticipated date Filipinos would be treated as Asiatic aliens ineligible for citizenship; in the meantime they would be restricted to an annual quota of fifty immigrants (with more allowed to go to Hawaii if needed there for labor but not entitled to emigrate to the continental United States).

None of these Asiatic exclusions was absolute; laws and interpretations varied; wives and children were usually admitted, as were various other special cases (though often interned on Angel Island in San Francisco Bay for weeks awaiting a decision); some came after residing for several years in an unrestricted country, such as Canada. Although averaging only 3,000–4,000 annually, even such small additions were important to the vitality of Asian-American communities.

The attack on Pearl Harbor and World War II changed all these relationships. The loyalty of the resident Japanese in Hawaii upon any outbreak of hostilities had long been of concern to the American military. Under the shock of the attack the senior Army officer declared himself military governor and placed the islands under martial law (and so they remained until late 1944). Panicky cries for rounding up and shipping all 150,000 Japanese to the mainland for internment were soon quelled by the impracticalities of expelling so large a portion of the population and workforce, the opposition of important leaders, and the lack of any evidence of sabotage or subversion. Military rulers closed down some Japanese schools and newspapers, but local Japanese leaders worked assiduously to demonstrate the firm loyalty of their people to the American government and war effort.

The contrasting outcome on the mainland is now considered one of the most serious embarrassments in the history of American ethnic and racial relations. Yielding to the outcry of other residents and military fears of spies and coastal attacks, the War Department was authorized to uproot all of the 112,000 people of Japanese ancestry in California and western Oregon and Washington (nearly two-thirds of whom were American citizens) and ship them to ten primitive detention camps in the dry wastelands of the interior West, where most were held for most of the war. (The Japanese of coastal British Columbia endured a similar fate.) The fervent, unifying nationalism and anti-Japanese hatred provoked by the Pearl Harbor attack was so strong that the Supreme Court upheld this drastic treatment of innocent American citizens as legitimate under wartime emergency. Upon their release a few moved on to Chicago and other eastern cities, but the great majority saw no alternative but to return to their home areas to try to reestablish themselves. Years later the U.S. Congress appropriated $38 million recompense—a small fraction of their actual losses of property.

Meanwhile, as a gesture of friendship and support for a beleaguered ally, the Chinese Exclusion Act was repealed in 1943 (and China granted an annual quota of 105, and persons of Chinese descent became eligible for citizenship). With the Philippines under Japanese control on the scheduled independence date, the change of immigrant status was deferred until 1946.

THE SIDE DOORS

It was often remarked during this new era of restriction that "we have locked the front door but left the side door open"—there being no limitation on immigration from other countries in the Western Hemisphere. There were, of course, two side doors, but little concern was expressed about the opening to the north even though Canada was contributing more than 60 percent of the total from the Americas during these years. French Canadians followed long-established paths to New England mill towns, and Anglophone Canadians continued to move into the American scene "with scarcely a ripple," as they had for more than a century. The only rationale offered in a 1930 proposal to intervene on this open situation was the need "to complete the established policy of immigrant restriction" by extending controls over all entryways. Although Canada was to be given the largest quota of any country so that no actual reduction would be imposed, opponents stressed the needless irritation of any such policy: why "alienate our friendly sister nation, with ties of blood and sympathy that have united us for upward of 100 years." The proposed restriction on Canada was removed from pending legislation.

The real concern, of course, was over the doors opening to the south. It was an issue that came into national prominence only in the 1920s. Before World War I immigration from Mexico had been small and marginal in impact, regarded as a practical, unregulated regional matter, but labor shortages during the war (and refugees from the revolutionary upheaval in Mexico) brought a sudden increase. In the 1920s various American industries began to recruit Mexican laborers, especially to fill the jobs formerly dependent on immigrants fresh from Europe. These new distinct people began to show up in the steel mills of Bethlehem and Gary, in Midwestern packinghouses, cement plants, and railroad track gangs; sugar beet growers in Colorado, Nebraska, and Michigan shifted almost wholly to Mexican labor as the inflow of Slavic immigrants was curtailed; many subtropical specialty

crops in Texas, Arizona, and Southern California became dependent on their labor, and all along the western reaches of the Cotton Belt, Texas landowners shifted
from tenant sharecropping to the use of seasonal Mexican workers. As a congressional report put it, these "lower classes of the Mexican population"—this "peon
type"—became "sucked into the United States in large numbers" and spread into
areas "far removed from the southern border." During the 1920s nearly half a million, ten times the prewar rate, had entered the United States.

Such a rising inflow through this side door inevitably drew increasing attention
during this decade of immigration polemics, national selection, and racial fears.
Congressional hearings on the topic "turned into a bitter contest between the
forces of bigotry and greed," that is, between those who warned that the "infiltration and differential fecundity" (high birth rates) of these newcomers "will in a
comparatively short time change the complexion of the population . . . and bring
about a hyphenated, politically unstabilized, Latinized majority throughout the
Southwest," and those on the other side of the debate, who regarded keeping the
door open "as a necessary evil" to ensure a supply of cheap and docile labor for basic regional economies. Obviously neither side regarded Mexican workers as desirable residents or citizens. Restrictive legislation imposing a small quota on Mexico
was passed in the Senate in 1930 but tabled in the House under pressure from the
Hoover administration, which, not wanting to embarrass and further complicate
relations with a neighbor, decided to use existing regulatory devices (such as liabil-
ity of becoming a public charge) to reduce the inflow. With the full onset of the Depression jobs disappeared, many people voluntarily returned to Mexico, and even
larger numbers (some of whom were U.S. citizens) were expelled (often by actions
of state or local authorities seeking to reduce public assistance costs). The 1940
census recorded an almost 60 percent reduction from the size of the 1930 Mexican-
born population.

World War II transformed this situation. In 1942 the United States and Mexico
agreed on a "bracero" program for the regulated annual admittance of several
hundred thousand seasonal workers. However, as demands for low-cost labor
expanded, the lure of jobs, ease of entry, and familiarity of migratory paths and
networks, together with the connivance of employers and labor agents, resulted in
far more "undocumented" entrants, leading to a chronic issue of "illegal immigrants"—"wetbacks"—and fear of "losing control of our borders." In the early
1950s the Border Patrol (created in 1924) was annually apprehending several hundred thousand illegal immigrants. The 1950 census recorded 450,000 Mexican-
born residents and 1,343,000 of Mexican stock, but such figures are routinely considered to be far short of the actual numbers. (The U.S. Census has long been
bedeviled by deep-rooted American problems with other categorizations: until

1937 Mexican immigrants were racially classified as "other than white," or simply as "other"; thereafter all Mexican-born residents "who were not definitely Indian or of other nonwhite race" were classified as "white.")

Other doors opened to the south, but sustained immigration from the West Indies and the rest of the Americas remained small and of relatively little concern. Cubans had long moved back and forth between island and mainland, and small numbers of seasonal laborers from the Bahamas, Jamaica, and Barbados were common along the East Coast. (Proponents of Mexican restriction tended to argue for limits on West Indians as well in order to close out an alternative source of cheap and "colored" labor.) Blacks and Hispanics from the Caribbean found niches in Harlem and elsewhere in New York City. Puerto Ricans were the special case in this sector. Like Filipinos they enjoyed unrestricted access to the continental United States, but unlike Filipinos they had been granted American citizenship in 1917. A modest trickle of migrants resulted in about 60,000 in New York City by 1940, a nucleus quickly enlarged to 250,000 after the war when surplus planes and cheap fares resulted in the first great "airborne immigration"—or so this sudden insurge of Latin Americans was popularly viewed; technically, of course, it was an overseas migration of American citizens.

REASSESSMENT

Debate on the formal reassessment of immigration policy began in 1950. Critics of the national origins concept sought a different basis for selection and a greater flexibility for special situations, such as shifting unused quotas to other countries to accommodate pressing needs. Many of these voices were keenly aware of the difficulties of responding to the plight of "displaced persons," especially Jewish refugees, even though since 1924 less than half of the total quota allocations had actually been used by immigrants. They regarded the whole basis of this selective formula as now tainted by Nazi racial theories and horrifying practices. Defenders of the national origins concept argued that even if not perfect it has "provided a fixed and easily determined method for controlling immigration which is not subject to the whims and caprices of administrative interpretation. The formula is automatically resistant to pressures for special treatment." Furthermore, they insisted, that "without giving credence to any theory of Nordic superiority," it has been "a rational and logical method . . . to best preserve the sociological and cultural balance in the population of the United States." Patrick A. McCarran of Nevada, chairman of the Senate committee in charge, was militant in defense of the current system, warning of the need to ensure that there be no augmentation of those "hard-core, indigestible blocs which have not become integrated into the American way of life." The formal Senate Report routinely made use of popular racial categories (white, yellow, black, red, brown—this last referring to Malayan; and to Teutonic, Latin, and Slavic as "principal divisions of the white race"), and, as Robert A. Divine concluded, "though most congressmen refused to disclose their views . . . , there can be little doubt that their support of the national origins plan rested on a continuing belief in the ethnic theory so popular in the 1920s."

A new Immigration and Naturalization Act (commonly known as the McCarran Act) was passed by large majorities and, after overriding President Truman's veto, went into effect on December 24, 1952. In general, it codified into a single law the practices and policies of the recent past. One important change was the removal of all barriers of race or sex to the right of naturalization; thus there were no more "barred zones," and a quota of at least 100 was assigned to each independent country. However, the total annual allocation was increased only slightly, and this continued support for proportional selection and severe limitation was strongly reinforced by renewed concern over foreign enemies and subversion. The debate took place during the Korean War, a superheated introductory phase of the Cold War. As the staff director of the McCarran Committee proudly reported to the Daughters of the American Revolution, "the 1952 act, for the first time in our history, supplies the Immigration Service with adequate weapons to deal with the Communist penetration and plan of 'conquest by immigration.'"

Upon his reversal by Congress, Truman immediately created a President's Commission on Immigration and Naturalization, which hastily held hearings in several cities and submitted a proposal to abolish the national origins formula, considerably enlarge the intake, and provide for temporary asylum for up to 100,000 annually. Taking office soon thereafter, Eisenhower called for a greater openness to refugees as part of America's responsibility in world leadership, and the topic of how the United States should use immigration policy in the shaping of its growth and character continued to be a lively controversy.

In the longer view of American history the surprising thing is not this era of restrictions but the fact that for more than 120 years there were no restrictions whatever on the overall number of immigrants. Through much of the nineteenth century Americans saw themselves as a new people building a new form of society in a New World of unlimited opportunity, and they welcomed—needed—others to join in the great task. As President John Tyler stated in a message to Congress in 1841, "We hold out to the people of other countries an invitation to come and settle among us as members of our rapidly growing family," and for several decades thereafter political leaders periodically reaffirmed such welcomes to "emigrants and exiles from the Old World," recognizing the obvious truth that such infusions had "added so much to the wealth, development of resources, and increase of power to the nation." Oscar Handlin has well emphasized the common assumption essential to that stance: that simply "being in America would make Americans of them"— "that any man who subjected himself to the American environment was being Americanized." (There were always some who doubted the power of this benign process, especially with reference to Roman Catholics, whom they accused of remaining subjects of a foreign ruler.)

The great shift in attitude toward immigration in the early twentieth century was a response to great increases in volume and variety, in ethnic clustering and perceived problems of assimilation, and adoption of restriction and selection was a direct product of an intensified and narrowed nationalism generated by war. Reluctantly, belatedly, caught up in a great conflict that it was deeply ambivalent about, disappointed and confused about what had been accomplished and what its role in the world ought to be, experiencing in the aftermath a strong outburst of political unrest at home that was widely blamed on "alien agitators," the United States determined to withdraw behind the Atlantic moat and turn away from the "poisons of disorder, revolt, and chaos" in Europe.

America's emotional act of severance was itself but one part of a more "general recrudescence of chauvinistic nationalism" that was especially virulent in Europe, and immigration restriction may be seen as an American assertion of its own national "self determination"—"a second Declaration of Independence," as the chief legislative architect of the 1924 act put it. That the United States had a sovereign *right* to select its immigrants was now often emphasized as if a newly found principle. In this broader view many features of the immigration debates appear more than a little akin to those often deplored—and ominous—postwar European obsessions with problems of peoples and territories. American expressions of such anxieties may be summarized within a few common categories of those geopolitical concerns.

1. *National Unity.* "America is a nationality," not just a geographical expression or an aggregation of people, nor is it "a matter of birth or ancestry," said the sociologist Henry Pratt Fairchild in one of his major books on the immigration problem; "it is a question of spiritual affiliation, loyalty, and allegiance. Any one who responds implicitly, spontaneously, and unreservedly to the appeal of American values is an American." That could be a generous interpretation, but, of course, it depended on how loyalty and values were defined. During the war a fervent patriotism—"Americanism"—promulgated by the government as if national unity required unanimity, had worked to suppress any criticism of the national effort. Fairchild deplored such panicky reactions but joined in the widespread conclusion that the clamoring of "hyphenated Americans" (such as André Siegfried had observed) showed, as Isaiah Bowman, the nation's leading political geographer of the time, put it, "the old bonds between the immigrant and the home country to be so strong that we could

not count upon a united country when wide-ranging destructive forces were loosed, as in 1914–1918." That was enough to dispel "the delusion that there was some magical potency about American soil or American life which would produce without conscious effort" the "wholesome transformation" of immigrants into Americans.

2. *A National People.* Thus many Americans, leaders and public alike, concluded that the "melting pot" ("so badly cracked by the concussions of the great conflict") was a great mistake, for "what was being melted . . . was the American nationality itself." Therefore "the idea of assimilation has become paramount," requiring a shift in policy from the "amalgamation" of diverse groups (which only leads to "the further dilution of our national stock") to the selection of those who will "fuse easily" without trace into American society (all "traits" of the immigrant's "original nationality . . . must be *abandoned*"). The guiding principle, as one congressman put it, was that "the stability of a country depends upon the homogeneity of population"; the goal, said another, was "one race, one country, one destiny."

3. *Selection of Peoples.* "The year 1924 is thus one of the decisive dates of American history, marking . . . the beginning of a new epoch of national reconstruction and racial stabilization that should normally culminate in a *re-forged America.*" "America must be kept American," said Calvin Coolidge, and ardent restrictionists readily adopted the president's characteristically terse statement as a slogan. Such a stance implied a society already formed in content and character that immigration must be made to reinforce. "Racial stabilization" meant preserving "the blood of the United States in its present proportions" (all such discussion generally referring to the Euro-American population), and that became the rationale of the national origins formula favoring "the 80 percent of us who were born in this country" so that "each year's immigration is to be an exact miniature of what we are as a stock."

Supporters of this adopted formula for selection often insisted that it was not "an imputation of inferiority against" any particular people, but the entire debate was permeated by just such characterizations, which were explicitly endorsed by current "racial" and "eugenics" theories propounded in books well known on both sides of the Atlantic, *The Passing of the Great Race,* by Madison Grant (lawyer, chairman of the New York Zoological Society, trustee of the Museum of Natural History, and councilor of the American Geographical Society) being America's most notorious contribution: "These [recent] immigrants adopt the language of the native American, they wear his clothes, they steal his name and they are beginning to take his women, but they seldom adopt his religion or understand his ideals and while he is being elbowed out of his own home the American looks calmly abroad and urges on others the suicidal ethics which are exterminating his own [Nordic] race." "Anglo-Saxon" and "Nordic" were the most common terms used in describing the superior American stock ("Aryan" made an occasional appearance), the peoples of Southern and Eastern Europe (with often specific mention of Jews) as those who "dilute and weaken our national character." Thus our immigrant stream needed to be purified of "its worst elements," for "trouble grows out of a country composed of intermingled and mongrelized people." As Divine notes, this kind of "racial nationalism" (as it was called at the time) "reduced all peoples of a country [or religion] to a generalized stereotype."

4. *Minorities*. In the United States as in many states in Europe, the hypernationalism of the 1920s directed special attention to peoples who seemed to be resisting full integration into the national society. "The American people was at last quite fully awake to the failure of assimilation" and to the fact that "our foreign population had to a large extent formed itself into segregated distinct colonies"; with each "colony" having its own churches, schools, social clubs, shops, newspapers, and local leaders, these people were not "actually living in America." Since "assimilation" is largely advanced by "contact between the newcomer and the native-born population," it becomes "primarily a matter of distribution," but there was no suggestion that the national government should undertake a program of redistribution of those present or direct the geographical placement of those arriving (any such proposal would have encountered powerful public resistance). The only feasible solution was to "cut down the stream of raw material drastically at the source" and give added support to various local efforts to accelerate assimilation. As in Europe, language was fundamental, but insufficient by itself: "the English language is unquestionably the first gateway which leads to Americanization. But it is not Americanization."

5. *Boundaries*. With the collapse of empires, creation of new states, and the gains and losses of victors and vanquished, nearly a third of Europe's 10,000 miles of international boundaries were new, imposed by various treaties associated with the World War. The boundaries of the United States were unchanged, but there were new border issues, and America imposed its own kinds of boundaries on the rest of the world as a means of coping with its internal problems. The creation of the Border Patrol and concern over the increasing immigration from Mexico were new internal matters. Externally, U.S. immigration laws divided the world into excluded, restricted, and unrestricted territories (fig. 36), and further subdivided Europe between areas of relatively generous annual quotas and areas of severe restriction. Like European colonial powers, the United States also had to make decisions about migration into the nation from its own overseas imperial territories.

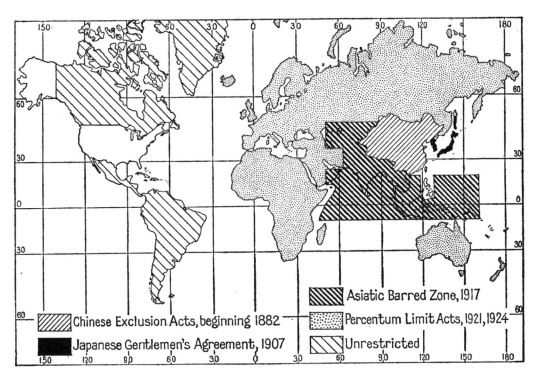

36. World Areas Defined by U.S. Immigration Laws.
(Reproduced from Bowman, *New World* [1928])

As Handlin concluded, the postwar United States was "a society that had moved to a restricted view of itself, of a culture that was beginning to think of itself as fixed rather than fluid, of a society tempted to prefer conformity over diversity." The great focus of national attention and urgency of the matter of restriction "gave official sanction . . . that immigrants were separate from and inferior to the native-born" and thereby "intensified the group consciousness of immigrant peoples," who created instruments of care and defense against the hostility their presence seemed to engender. It also seems reasonable to add that even without the fervid intensifications associated with the war, some considerable reduction in the annual intake of immigrants would have been imposed before the century was much older, for the influx was very large and increasing and the problems of integration into American society were real. Reduction in the number admitted required some formula for selection, and there was no obvious best means. Whether grounded in literacy, age, sex, skills, ethnicity, religion, or some combination of these or other features, any such formula would appear to be discriminating against some of the very kinds of people who had already become valued citizens. The national origins formula, con-trived and flawed as it was, was an attractive concept for a country increasingly self-conscious of its maturity as a nation and concerned with continuing stability and coherence in what seemed an increasingly unstable and dangerous world—and it was supported much more broadly than might be inferred from its most prejudiced proponents.

World War II was a vastly different domestic experience. Foreign-born and native-born joined together in work and war, and celebrated together the victory and sudden emergence of their country as the superpower of the Western World. But Europe was once again in ruins, its boundaries redrawn, with millions of dis-placed persons, and American immigration policy again a major topic. Although political asylum became the most pressing issue, the McCarran hearings and act of 1952 revived the rhetoric of 1924 and reaffirmed much of its framework, even though the national origins formula had clearly failed to ensure that "each year's immigration . . . [was] an exact miniature of what we are as a stock." They also re-flected even greater concern in a newly Global America over aliens as potential en-emies and ensured that immigration would remain of special national concern.

Midcentury demographers, however, assessing their many enumerations, drew quite a different picture and focused on a rather different prospect. Over this forty-year span, net immigration totaled 5,536,000, about 60 percent of it from Europe. Such figures represented a great decline from the period just before World War I (when the "million-a-year" incomers became a large fixed target of restrictionists). As a result, in the 1950 census only 7.5 percent of the White population was for-eign-born, half of what it had been in 1915, and the American-born of foreign-born parents totaled 11 percent. With the total population now increasing rapidly, the foreign element seemed destined to fade with the years into insignificance. As one demographer put it: "today, the average foreign-born American is on the verge of retirement and his average son is approaching middle age."

2. Regionalism, 1920s–1950

The ever-pertinent but often underappreciated truth that the United States was, from its beginnings, a set of regions, as well as a federation, a nation, and an empire, received unusual academic, public, and political attention during the years be-tween the great wars. The regional movements of the time were a diffuse upwelling of varied actors and conditions, differing in methods and objectives, uneven in ar-eas and impact. We shall focus attention on only a few kinds of these distinctly ge-ographic expressions of concern and how they reflected some of the larger changes in the nation as a whole.

AS RESISTANCE

Some of the most passionate forms of regionalism arose as a reaction to an emergent Neotechnic America, a confrontation with some powerful trends of the times: Rural *versus* Urban, Agrarian *versus* Industrial, Indigenous *versus* Metropolitan— the first term in such formulations standing for resistance against secularism and consumerism, centralization and standardization, mobilization and acceleration of tempo—all those "acids of modernity" that seemed to be dissolving local, regional, traditional ways of life. Yet such movements were caught in a paradox, for Americans everywhere were eagerly adopting automobiles, electricity, radios, and the cinema even as they deplored some of the broader social changes driven by such powerful instruments. Furthermore, few Americans anywhere were ready to challenge basic—deeply traditional—attitudes and institutions that were shaping this modern America. Thus, as Catherine McNicol Stock found in her fine study of rural Dakota during these times: "to be a Dakotan, then, meant balancing fundamentally contradictory, but equally heartfelt impulses: loyalty to individuality and community, to profit and cooperation, to progress and tradition."

Leaders of such movements sought ways to stem the tide of change and reinvigorate threatened ways of life. Common themes were the need to halt the decline in the number of farms (the "demographic death" of rural America), preserve the family farm against a pervading commercialization ("agrarianism is not the theory that everybody should be farmers; it is rather the theory that farmers should farm for a living rather than for a profit in the price system"), and restore some greater balance of power among the various sections of the country ("regionalism means social and economic equilibrium"). This conflation of rural and sectional themes expressed the current economic crisis in the great farm belts, suffering from low prices and higher costs, overproduction and little help from national policies, but broader and deeper virtues of regionalism were also widely invoked.

In 1930 twelve Southern humanists issued a set of essays entitled *I'll Take My Stand* in which they declared their fervent support of "a Southern way of life against what may be called the American or prevailing way." Subtitled *The South and the Agrarian Tradition*, it was a composite polemic against the materialistic, mechanistic values and trends of modern life, a harsh critique of the American celebration of "progress." It was a deeply emotional production by men who loved their native ground and clothed it with a mythology of origin, experience, and character that offered a highly selective version of what the South had been, was, and might yet be. All emphasized some sort of rescue and reinvigoration of a conservative rural society; there was a common fear of the "instability" of "a 'floating' populace concentrated in large urban industrial centers, unattached to that tremendous social anchor, land." The more moderate recognized that although the South could not escape industrialization, its leaders must seek to limit its disruptive impact ("to see how the South may handle this fire without being burnt badly"). The whole promulgation exhibited that "the words *region* and *regionalism* lose all exactness when they enter the literary vocabulary," as the poet and critic Donald Davidson, one of its best-known contributors, put it (in a subsequent supportive work), but appearing during the first year of the Great Depression, it became one of the tracts of times pointing toward more specific critiques and prescriptions.

Such militant traditionalists were not alone in their "dissatisfaction with the culture, or pseudo-culture that has accompanied the diffusion of industrialism." Lewis Mumford, apostle of the new technology, was a far more penetrating critic of that "pseudo-culture"—but of such traditionalist pronouncements as well: "The besetting weakness of regionalism lies in the fact that it is in part a blind reaction against outward circumstances and disruptions, an attempt to find refuge within an old shell against the turbulent invasions of the outside world, armed with its new inventions: in short, an aversion from what is, rather than an impulse toward what may be." Mumford insisted that "recognition of the region as a basic configuration in human life" was essential to the taming and shaping of that relentless turbulent world: "the re-examination and re-building of regions, as deliberate works of collective art [like their corresponding artifacts, the cities] . . . is the grand task of politics for the opening generation."

Mumford was not the first to propose such a task. Some years before the war Josiah Royce, California-born Harvard philosopher, had spoken extensively on the need for development of a "Higher Provincialism" as a makeweight against "vast" and "paramount" forces of "national unity" and "social consolidation." But such a re-examination and re-building of regions did not get under way until the 1920s. It was a form of resistance, a "revolt of the provinces"—as Robert L. Dorman entitled his extensive examination of the topic—an attempt to break the megalopolitan "stranglehold on the life of the hinterland." Perhaps the most famous seats of such opposition were the art colonies at Taos and Santa Fe, which "exerted a powerful shearing pull against the New York–Hollywood cultural axis," but there were many less prominent centers, varied in character, each some sort of cluster of artists, writers, folklorists, publishers, or other specialists (and sometimes a single person rather than a group, such as H. G. Merriam, founder and editor of *The Frontier* at Missoula). Several university presses, notably Oklahoma and North Carolina, initiated strong regional programs. Thus, in addition to the places mentioned (and the major efforts of Mumford and associates "headquartered, as it were, in and around the camp of the enemy—New York City"), Dorman's "cultural-intellectual map of the regionalist movement in America, circa 1930," included Albuquerque, Dallas, Austin, Lincoln, Iowa City, Nashville, Charlottesville, and (somewhat later) Baton Rouge. New interpretations of American literature, such as that of Vernon Louis Parrington, and the series of volumes by Van Wyck Brooks, gave emphasis to regional historical context, and in his last years Frederick Jackson Turner was extolling a positive form of sectionalism as "inevitable and desirable"; such regional cultures, he said, "serve as restraints upon a deadly uniformity. They are breakwaters against overwhelming surges of national emotion. They are fields for experiment in the growth of different types of society, political institutions, and ideals," and he called for a new kind of interdisciplinary study to enlarge understanding of these regional-national realities.

Walter Prescott Webb's *The Great Plains* and Rupert B. Vance's *Human Geography of the South* were fresh, unorthodox regional interpretations of the early 1930s, and soon the New Deal offered a whole new level of sponsorship and funding, initiated to put artists, actors, writers, photographers, and related professionals back to work. The politics of funding, with allocations to each state, ensured wide distribution and important impact on many regional programs. One of the most notable and extensive was the Federal Writers' Project (FWP), which produced a detailed guidebook on each state, D.C., Alaska, and Puerto Rico, as well as many on individual cities, various special areas (such as Death Valley and Cape Cod) and travel routes (such as the Ocean Highway along the Atlantic Coast). The character and quality of these books was unprecedented; devoid of the usual boosterism and business advertisements, they answered the need for a new form of guidebook for the inquiring, perceptive automobile tourist, and they were a great enrichment of regional literature. Other federal agencies undertook many detailed community or regional studies (such as the Rural Life Studies of the Bureau of Agricultural Economics and *Rural Regions of the United States*), usually focusing on current problems. The stark photographic coverage of rural Southerners (the South "found itself photographed, stereotyped, and scrutinized" more than any other region), Dust Bowl farmers, and poverty-stricken California-bound migrant families by the Farm Security Administration offered powerful documentation of regional crises—although public awareness of such problems owed much more to newsreels and the large weekly format of the new *Life* magazine. All such programs ended with the onset of war, however, and reappearance of federal support for anything like the FWP had to await President Lyndon Johnson's Great Society (his own variation of the New Deal) and the creation of the National Endowment for the Arts and the National Endowment for the Humanities.

AS RATIONAL MANAGEMENT

All this while another set of regionalists was getting under way with the grand task of the "re-building of regions" in plan, if not in performance. Benton MacKaye set forth his "philosophy of regional planning" in 1928, phrasing it as a choice and contest between the "Indigenous World" and the "Metropolitan World." The former, referring to the domesticated countryside, was "under invasion by the iron glacier . . . spreading, as a 'metropolitan flow,' out along the highways from each metropolis, large and small—out of New York and out of 'Zenith'" (the latter referring to the fictional Midwestern city of Sinclair Lewis's *Babbitt*). Only comprehensive planning could halt these radiating slums of commerce, which were welding together villages and towns in "a common suburban mass without form or articulation," and reinvigorate "through modern instrumentalities" ("the electric wire and motor vehicle") local economies and communities. Like Mumford, his idealized Neotechnic America was a form of resistance to what he saw as the uncontrolled formless reality of America, but he gave closer attention to where geographic "controls" should be applied to effect the protections and nurturings envisioned. His book is full of detailed maps and diagrams; he had helped initiate a statewide regional plan for New York and was working on a similar program for Massachusetts. When the president of the United States, faced with a gigantic national crisis, voiced strong support for such geographic planning, regionalism—and the young profession of planners—suddenly took on a new potency.

"Many hard lessons have taught us the human waste that results from the lack of planning," said the former governor of New York in 1933. "Here and there a few wise cities and counties have looked ahead and planned. But our Nation has 'just grown.' It is time to extend planning to a wider field." His New Deal famously extended some degree of planning to a very wide field indeed. We have already touched on this with reference to highways, rural electrification, and population redistribution. All of these and many other programs had important regional dimensions, and a formal assessment of "Regional Factors in National Planning and Development" was soon undertaken.

The committee assigned to the task (including George T. Renner as staff geographer) made an extensive effort to define and clarify the regional concept. Its members recognized that although regional consciousness has been ever present, "the fluidity of American society on the march has retarded precise regional delineation." Any delineation depended upon purpose; there were as many possible regions as there were things to be enregioned. After a review of major types, they surveyed the variety of existing governmental programs operating through territorial units intermediate in scale between State and Nation. These included metropolitan planning agencies overlapping state boundaries (such as at Kansas City, St. Louis, Chicago, Philadelphia, New York City, and Washington), the seven-state Colorado River Compact, the Port of New York Authority, and two new regional planning commissions (New England and the Pacific Northwest). Turning to the operations of federal departments, they found 108 separate regional schemes employed by the various agencies in carrying out their specialized tasks. While recognizing the highly varied purposes underlying these many territorial divisions, they did suggest the desirability of some greater concordance, and especially of the grouping of administrative headquarters into a few regional centers. Finally, the report offered a set of maps of "possible planning regions" for the nation, each map depicting a different basis for regionalization, such as river basins, metropolitan influence, and what were, in effect, broad human geographic regions (with common "composite planning problems") (fig. 37).

Meanwhile, private foundations had funded a new focus on regionalism at the University of North Carolina under the direction of the sociologist Howard W. Odum. Its first product, *Southern Regions of the United States*, published in 1936, was a vast compendium of facts and figures (270 charts and tables, 329 maps) that did much to focus attention on the South, heightening both regional and national awareness of the ordinary people of the area and of an "extraordinary chasm" between resource potentialities and current conditions. "Envisaged in terms of testing grounds of American regionalism," *Southern Regions* was soon followed by *American Regionalism*, co-authored by Odum and Harry Estill Moore, in which they defined a set of "composite group-of-state major societal regions" as "a comprehensive frame of reference for research and planning" (fig. 38):

> a sixfold regional America to comprehend the *Northeast* and the *Southeast*, the *Northwest* and the *Southwest*, the *Middle States* and the *Far West*. These are realistic extensions of the earlier historical "sections." They represent two "Souths," two "Norths," and two "Wests." Still more historically literal, they represent one "East," one "South," and four "Wests." These are *major* regions approximating a greater degree of homogeneity measured by a larger number of indices for a larger number of purposes and classifications than any other regional framework.

Subtitled *A Cultural-Historical Approach to National Integration*, the book proclaimed regionalism as a "tool and technique for various objectives of planning and of attaining equilibrium and balance, decentralization and distribution, in particular as these relate to population, to wealth, and to sovereignty"—in effect, a benign instrument for radical national reconstruction.

Regional planning most commonly focused on problems of resource development and conservation, on "the continued adjustment and readaptation of the nation to its geography, of the people to its land," as Odum and Moore put it. Much the greatest planning project of the New Deal was the Tennessee Valley Authority, initiated in the first months of the new administration. As noted earlier, selection of the Tennessee for this unprecedented program stemmed directly from the controversial government involvement at Muscle Shoals. In addition, in 1930 the Army Corps of Engineers had submitted plans for a series of dams on that river as part of its studies to lessen the dangers of Mississippi floodings (especially severe in

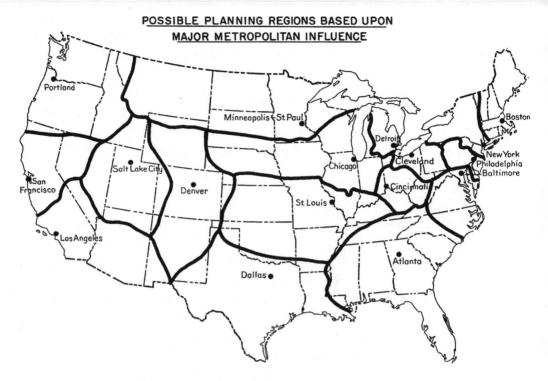

POSSIBLE PLANNING REGIONS BASED UPON
MAJOR METROPOLITAN INFLUENCE

POSSIBLE PLANNING REGIONS BASED UPON
COMPOSITE PLANNING PROBLEMS

37. Possible Planning Regions.
These seventeen metropolitan regions show considerable variation from the oft-cited importance and success of the twelve Federal Reserve districts. The 12 Composite Planning Problems
map obviously reflects the large framework of human-use regions. (Source: *Regional Factors in
National Planning and Development*)

Odum and Moore

MAJOR GROUP-OF-STATE SOCIETAL REGIONS

38. Socioeconomic Regions.
Odum and Moore's regions are here labeled with the titles of the chapters devoted to the description of each in *American Regionalism*.

1926 and 1927). Furthermore, the Tennessee made a long looping traverse of more than 800 miles across one of the most poverty-stricken areas of the nation; potentially rich in resources but with 2 million people living, on average, far below general American standards, the Tennessee Valley was an inviting target for a massive relief program (and all except its upper basin was solid Democratic territory).

Formed out of a half dozen streams rising in the Ridge and Valley and the Great Smoky Mountains, fed by some of the highest rainfall in eastern North America, the Tennessee becomes a mighty river in the southern reaches of the Great Valley, breaking out across the full width of northern Alabama before making a sharp turn north across western Tennessee and Kentucky, and draining a basin of 40,600 square miles into the Ohio River at Paducah (fig. 39). The creators of the TVA specified its main purposes to be flood control, navigation (a nine-foot channel between Paducah and Knoxville), generation of electricity, manufacture of fertilizer, proper use of marginal lands, reforestation, and "the economic and social well-being of the people living in said river basin," and they gave it extraordinary powers to accomplish these. It was designed to be "a corporation clothed with the pow-

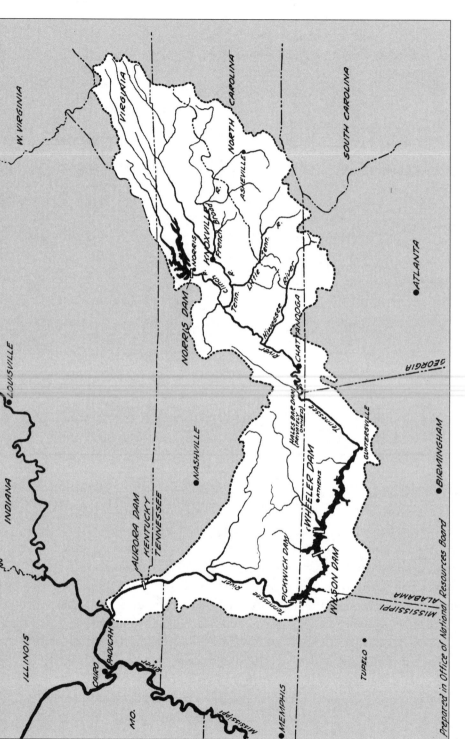

Prepared in Office of National Resources Board

39. Tennessee Valley Authority Area.

This early depiction shows the first four dams and their reservoirs then under construction, with the Wilson and Wheeler dams covering Muscle Shoals. The proposed Aurora Dam on the lower river was shifted downstream and renamed Kentucky Dam. The TVA was not rigidly limited to the drainage basin but was also authorized to serve "such adjoining territory as may be related to or materially affected by the development consequent to this Act." The first electric power was sold to Tupelo, Mississippi, beyond the bounds of the basin. (Adapted from *Regional Factors in National Planning and Development*)

ers of government but possessed of the flexibility and initiative of a private enterprise," including the right to buy and sell real estate, construct new towns, and exercise the power of eminent domain.

Setting up headquarters in Knoxville, the three-man directorate recruited a cadre of managers, scientists, and technicians, began extensive mapping and land-use surveys, and initiated a flurry of projects (which, by decree, used local labor). By 1940 six major dams had been completed, electricity was becoming widely distributed, several hundred demonstration farms were active (private farmers formally cooperating with agricultural specialists), marginal lands were being reforested, and improvement of the regional economy was getting under way. War brought sudden demands for enormous increases in power production (and installation of the first coal-fired plant) to serve chemical and aluminum factories and the secret atomic installation at Oak Ridge, a few miles west of Knoxville.

By 1953, twenty years after inception, the TVA had essentially accomplished its basic objectives. It had been the most consummate neotechnic project in America: a "natural region" transformed under comprehensive planning, featuring hydroelectric power, chemical fertilizers, the application of science to agriculture and forestry, disease control (virtual elimination of malaria), special attention to public recreation (especially in the extensive reservoirs created behind its twenty-three dams), civic and domestic improvements under the tutelage of specialists. Even if these uplands had not all become the "salubrious seats of living" that Mumford had envisioned, most of the now nearly 3 million people of the Tennessee Valley surely enjoyed an improved "economic and social well-being." (Of course, so did nearly all Americans—just how much of this improvement was the result of TVA rather than the wartime economy would remain uncertain and controversial; per capita income in the region had risen from 40 percent of the national average to 60 percent.)

Moreover, this bold experiment was world famous, a magnet drawing politicians and planners, engineers and scientists from around the world, and many TVA personnel had been hired to help with river-basin developments abroad (in India, Palestine, Mexico, Peru, Brazil, and Australia). Admiration and imitation abroad, but no duplication at home. In his originating message to Congress, Franklin D. Roosevelt had said that "if we are successful here [in the Tennessee Valley] we can march on, step by step, in a like development of other great natural territorial units within our borders," but in spite of many proposals and bills in Congress no other such multipurpose regional "authority" has ever been approved, for the TVA fostered a formidable array of opponents as well as admirers.

The loudest voices in opposition were probably the least important. The private power industry was relentless in its denunciations and warnings, and the whole project was derided as a gigantic misuse of taxpayers' money ("a river basin draining seven states, an authority draining forty-eight states"). Within the region thousands of people (125,000 by 1953) had been uprooted, mostly from the relatively rich bottomlands, to clear the way for dams and reservoirs. More broadly there was some expectable resentment that the concept, design, and most of the leadership were by "outlanders," and there was resistance to the massive promotion of the project by the Roosevelt administration and its allies. State officials were understandably fearful of encroachments upon their own realms of responsibility, as were, more importantly, various federal departments that saw this new "integrated" authority assigned a role in soil conservation, agriculture, forestry, water resources, flood control, transportation, and social welfare, each of which was already an established responsibility of one or more agencies. Such governmental jealousies bring us closer to the fundamental issue: the fear of radical geopolitical change of the federal structure, a topic of some serious discussion during this time.

AS A RADICAL GEOPOLITICAL FORMATION

As the Hoover-appointed assessment of *Recent Social Trends* reported in 1933, the "maladjustment and readjustment of governmental areas are . . . one of the significant marks" of the twentieth century. The automobile has "operated with devastating effect upon local boundary lines," a large proportion of the 3,000 some counties in the United States "are too small both in area and population, for efficient public administration under present day conditions," and "broadly speaking, industrial and social relations overflowed the banks of the states and swept out over the nation in a flood too great to be controlled by any one state, as in the case of corporations transacting business in many different commonwealths. Industry, education, the United States government, began to recognize various 'regions' as important units in their activity" (as in the twelve districts of the Federal Reserve Bank).

Critique of the states as inefficient and unresponsive political systems was already well established and had given rise to the new field of public administration (as represented by the public policy focus of the Brookings Institution established in 1920 and the founding of the Maxwell School of Citizenship at Syracuse University in 1924). They seemed unable to cope with twentieth-century problems, such as urbanization ("the states will neither govern the cities nor permit them to govern themselves"), and few "possessed enough vitality to resist the inevitable march toward federal centralization." Thus, as Odum and Moore noted, it was "only natural that the proposal should be heard that the feeble state be replaced by a region large enough and representative enough of a characteristic area of the nation to make its voice heard and its influence felt."

The topic was given voice in books, professional journals, government reports, newspapers, and public forums (in 1930 the Chicago *Tribune* ran a contest for the best proposals for a new set of states). It was the central theme of the 1935 book *The Need for Constitutional Reform*, by William Yandell Elliott, professor of government at Harvard, who argued that "redrawing the political map into areas more suited to the cultural and economic needs of modern America" was basic to the reinvigoration of democratic government. The states should be supplanted by about a dozen "regional commonwealths," but he did not fix these on the map, at one point saying that the present Federal Reserve districts (with perhaps one more in the West) would serve and later suggesting a grouping of the states into eleven new units. Like many others, Elliott was appalled by the "extraordinary overrepresentation of small [in population] states in our powerful Senate," and his reforms aimed at making these new regions "roughly equal in population and economic importance" and at giving them greater power in a revised federation—thereby also reducing "the terrific waste of multiplied capitals, legislatures, and bureaucracies." (He would retain the states as a residual framework—like "English counties"—for minor administration and historical and cultural associations.)

The very idea of abolishing the states may seem preposterous, an academic—and popular—discussion with no possibility of enactment, as most regionalists of the time acknowledged. Referring to this current discussion of "substituting regions for states," Derwent Whittlesey, in his monumental *The Earth and the State*, concluded: "Quite clearly it will take a revolution in the political affairs of the country to alter the present pattern of States." Odum and Moore agree: "The irreducible criterion of reality is the historical, constitutional, and organizational status of the 48 states, which are the very warp and woof of the national fabric" (and therefore they fitted their planning regions upon groups of states). Yet the topic was a telling commentary on the times. Elliott's book was subtitled *A Program for National Security*, and it was driven by his reading of world trends, of "a continuing condition of industrialized nationalism," totalitarianism and economic autarchy (he had written on fascism and syndicalism), and therefore the need to overhaul the "machinery of government" if democracy was to survive, for "we are living in an atmosphere of temporary truce with war just over an uncertain horizon." Few regionalists had such an international view, but in the 1930s all were working on assumptions of future population stability and chronic economic distress in a context of unprecedented federal experimentation.

If the states could not be abolished, they could be usurped, and that brings us back to what had happened in the Tennessee Valley. The TVA was an anomalous geopolitical entity, discordant with the federal structure, imposed upon the states by the central government, with no attempt at local public endorsement ("it is certain that this does not express any well-developed popular movement built up across the years," said the National Planning Board in 1934). It was a territorial unit the size of a major state (about equal in area to the whole State of Tennessee, or Kentucky, or Ohio) and it had some of the powers of a state, but it was nothing like a state in its essential character. It had no citizenry or elected officials; its directors were appointed by the president and confirmed by Congress and were accountable only to the same.

The TVA directorate recognized its contested intermediate position, worked hard to establish cooperation with local agents of federal and state departments, eventually won the support of many in the region, leaders and public alike, and proclaimed their work as an effective decentralization in the actual application of federal authority. Although Roosevelt tried to emphasize that perspective ("national planning should start at the bottom . . . [with] the problems of townships, counties, and states") in his 1937 proposal for seven large regional authorities spread across the nation for a similar development of resources, the firm resistance of Congress to the creation of any more TVAs marked the effective end of that design for the shaping of America. By then the very idea of *national* planning implied an alarming degree of centralization, and the very idea of *planning* was increasingly viewed as foreign to "the American way of life."

AS SECTIONALISM

In the preface to a widely distributed 1938 report Franklin Roosevelt declared: "The South presents right now the Nation's No. 1 economic problem—the Nation's problem, not merely the South's. For we have an economic imbalance in the Nation as a whole, due to the very condition of the South." Although based on the work of Odum and his institute, focused on an area eager for more federal largesse, and intended to strengthen Southern support for New Deal policies, "it was almost as if the President had rung a bell that activated the conditioned reflex of the sensitive South." Some thought the characterization suggested a retarded, inferior South, a mark of shame, whereas the real cause of the imbalance, so they insisted (and the report implicitly suggested), was a relentless "colonial degradation" under an imperial North. The more fundamental response, however, was "the reassertion of a more traditional kind of sectionalism based on an antipathy toward the New Deal" (now magnified by Roosevelt's concurrent attempt to purge his party of conservative opponents) "and a determination to protect the South's special interests, above all the institution of white supremacy" (although, so far, the administration had yielded on that issue: "agencies like TVA were allowed to discriminate in everything from housing to employment").

It was not surprising that such a reassertion should arise in this always most self-consciously defensive of regions, but it sounded an alarm to regional planners for they regarded sectionalism as a divisive, selfish, confrontational geopolitical stance, whereas their "new science of the region" was integrative and national. But national planning with an avowed aim of redressing "an economic imbalance in the nation as a whole" was, necessarily, a revolutionary program. Not only would it require fundamental changes in the regions to be aided, it posed a threat to those regions and interests that enjoyed a preponderance of power and prosperity. In fact, no national plan actually addressed the fearsome problem of how to effect such a radical transformation of the deep-rooted "imbalances" in the regional structure of America. Any initiative in that direction generated strong opposition. A presidency empowered to set priorities on public works and to administer resource development under TVA-type authorities would be a direct threat to congressional power and existing regional and local systems of allocation. As Barry D. Karl emphasizes, "from the earliest days of our national history, the distribution of national resources had been governed by local and regional politics"—it was "the lifeblood of a congressman's career." And so it remained, and many geopolitical realities of regionalism were on display in voting patterns in every session of Congress and in periodic statewide and national elections.

For all its evocations of the rich possibilities of regional florescence and a better-balanced America, regionalism was never an effective geopolitical movement. Largely a product of academics, planners, and social visionaries, it assumed that clear, careful exposure of regional problems would lead to a consensus for ameliorative action in the "national interest," whereas, as Dorman concluded, all their "powerful and evocative . . . critiques and visions . . . were impotent without concrete expression in the requirements of modern politics—platforms, programs, candidates, organization, funding, lobbying, bureaucratic and other means of control. That regionalism was an ideology intended to do away with most of these necessities [especially true of planning] meant, in the finally analysis, that it was to be no ideology at all." The Congress was dominated by Southern Democrats and small-town Midwestern Republicans "whose faith in localism and individualism" coalesced into "a militant antifederalism that associated programs formulated in Washington with radicalism"—in other words, associated them with the subversive intentions of a managerial elite.

On the threshold of war, national planning shifted in focus and purpose, and over the next decade World War II and its aftermath transformed America in such ways as to alter the context of and perspectives on regional-sectional problems. Much the greatest single postwar act of national development was the Interstate Highway System, which, as we have seen, was shaped not by a national planning authority but by the forty-eight states and a set of powerful interests in a classic, prolonged political battle. Important individual studies continued to appear from unorthodox creative regionalists, such as Wilbur Cash, Carey McWilliams, and James C. Malin, but regionalist movements were fading from view. A symposium held at the University of Wisconsin in 1949 and the papers therefrom published as

Regionalism in America has been called "the high point of 'regionalism' as a scholarly concern"; it may also be taken as the end of an era, of a diverse and diffuse intellectual fascination with the possible regional reconstruction of American society, economy, and polity.

3. A Reconnaissance of Regions

"It must be clear," said Max Lerner in his monumental midcentury interpretation *America as a Civilization*, "that regionalism is not so much a 'movement' as a fact—one of the massive facts about America." He was referring to "regional culture—the fusion of place, people, and tradition"—"as a primary datum of American life." In that sense it had always been a massive fact and, as our long historical perspective on the shaping of America has displayed, an ever-changing fact.

Ever-changing, indeed, but not on the same scale, nor at the same rate or in the same ways. The nineteenth century featured huge annexations, conquests, and colonizations, as well as transforming transportation and economic developments, whereas (as noted in *Transcontinental America*), the United States entered the twentieth century with a new sense of maturity, consolidation, and completion: the colonization frontier closing, national boundaries firmly set, the federation soon to be filled out with forty-eight contiguous states, a great dominating urban-industrial belt formed, and a nationwide railroad network completed. Even the emergence of those magical instruments of the new technological age seemed to herald no great disturbance of the broad regional patterns of national life: "improvements in communications, such as the automobile, the telephone, radio, and moving pictures, have diminished localism rather than sectionalism," noted Frederick Jackson Turner in 1922, and the regionalist movements that followed seemed to confirm this. Nevertheless, underneath that relatively stable framework of regions some important structural changes were taking place during the interwar years, as already implied in our brief review of migrations. The great upsurge of industrial and military activities during World War II had important regional impacts, and such a sharp comprehensive contrast with the Great Depression years was generally regarded as a decisive transition into a new era. Thus a regional reconnaissance noting some recent changes and a general overview around midcentury will provide both a look at some reconfigurations that were just appearing and a basis for assessing major geographic reshapings of America that would follow.

The four cardinal points—north, south, east, and west—had long provided the broadest sense of regional divisions in America, though often understood more as pairs of contrast and contention, sectionalism in its most general form—North *versus* South, East *versus* West, or South and West *versus* a domineering North/East—than as four grand quarters of the nation. Underneath these broad sections were various other well-known and loosely defined subdivisions, such as those Odum and Moore recognized in their meticulous "scientific" attempt at a useful grouping of states. Meanwhile, geographers and rural sociologists, sensitive to basic physical conditions of terrain, soils, water, vegetation, and climate, and ignoring political boundaries (as well as political cultures and most political issues), were defining "human use regions," areas of some dominant or special combination of economic activities. First set forth prominently by J. Russell Smith in his lively, opinionated *North America* in 1925, these works featured generalized crop regions and major physical areas and subdivisions thereof (a sharpening of focus carried to the extreme of identifying 264 rural subregions in Mangus' 1940 study); in some accounts industrial areas were also given separate regional status. All such systems are perceptions dependent upon particular perspectives and purposes. The massive regional fact was the obvious existence of large and important differences from area to area in this transcontinental expanse, not some formal master set of clearly bounded regions.

MEGALOPOLIS

We begin our reconnaissance by making use of a new name that suddenly appeared in the vocabulary of American regions. *Megalopolis* was conferred by the French geographer Jean Gottmann as the appropriate title for his American-sponsored study of "an almost continuous system of deeply interwoven urban and suburban areas" along a 600-mile national "Main Street" linking the Washington and Boston metropolitan areas, a concentration of more than 20 percent of the nation's population on less than 2 percent of its area. As Gottmann made clear, the name might be new, but the region had long been forming and it merited special definition and study not only because it was the main seat of the colossal new superpower—"the most active crossroads on earth, for people, ideas, and goods, extending its influence beyond the national borders"—but because it had become the "most impressive and largest urban system" in the world. His major study was undertaken to illuminate this massive American metropolitanization, with the further possibility that it might also serve as "a laboratory of urban growth" in the modern world. (Its centerpiece, New York City, had already served as a laboratory of urban *overgrowth* for Lewis Mumford, who regarded it as an example of gigantism, of incessant mechanistic, capitalistic agglomeration—"megalopolis" indeed, not as a regional name, but as a stage in a long cycle of urban change, displaying to Mumford all the symptoms of incipient decline.)

Our concern is not with these larger implications but with continuity and change in the American regional pattern. This particular multi-urban axis has been the principal seat of power and anchor of the national system since the foundation of the Republic, and its relative density and complexity had long been evident. Gottmann's description of "this interstratified and complex structure" in the 1950s seems an echo of an historian's summation of the 1850s: "Like some complex sea organism, the society of the Northeast had grown older and even more structured, piling up layer upon layer of occupations and social groups, adding function to function through complex interdependent internal markets and contractual arrangements." Viewed as a whole, the most obvious geographic change was the spread of dense settlement far and wide around every city, an expansion initiated by railroads and streetcars, but greatly accelerated in the automobile age, creating along its outer margins "an irregularly colloidal mixture of rural and suburban landscapes." In addition to the great daily tides of movement within these urban systems were weekly and seasonal tides reaching out to uplands and seashores—Poconos, Catskills, Berkshires, and the White Mountains, Chesapeake, Jersey Shore, the Hamptons, Nantucket, Cape Cod, and the Maine Coast—broadening the direct economic and social impact of this metropolitan world. There were almost continuous built-up strips along the main trafficways from one end of the region to the other, and new highway bridges and tunnels across or under the Delaware and the Hudson (and to Staten Island and Long Island) bound it all more tightly together, but it was not one vast urban coalescence; the several great metropolitan clusters remained apart and apparent on the population map (fig. 40).

This set of five great cities had undergone relatively little basic change in their long developing, differentiated roles and character. However, within the last fifteen years Washington had grown by more than half a million in population and become a much more powerful national and international political center. The great extension in the role of the central government made Washington a major financial power, providing massive relief programs during the Great Depression to corporations, states, municipalities, and persons, even more massive outlays for wartime needs, and thereafter the main source of funds for relief and rehabilitation of a war-torn world. Thus at midcentury Washington was sharing more equally with New York the full role of national capital—it was even becoming a cosmopolitan place, shedding its long reputation as a sleepy Southern town seasonally enlivened by congressional sessions.

As we have seen, the major population change affecting Baltimore, Philadelphia, and New York was the influx of Blacks from World War I onward. They had been, of course, a notable presence in these cities since early colonial times and had grown sufficiently in numbers and generations to form recognizable clusters, internally stratified by class and sustaining local businesses and professions, as well as various lesser enclaves. The Great Migration massively enlarged these numbers, with powerful impact upon general metropolitan as well as ghetto patterns and tensions. By 1940 the New York area contained more than half a million Blacks,

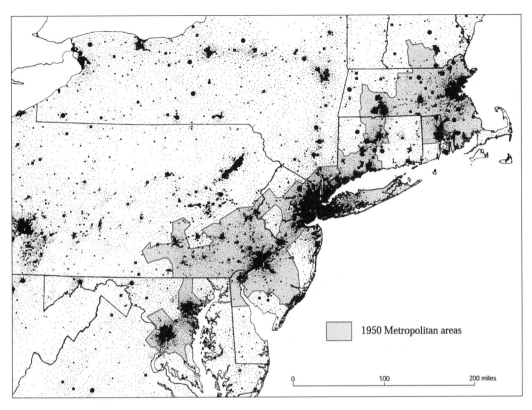

40. Megalopolis.

Gottmann's "almost continuous system of deeply interwoven urban and suburban areas" between Washington and Boston shows up clearly on this Bureau of the Census population distribution map of 1950. The shaded metropolitan areas are also the bureau's delineations.

Philadelphia a quarter million, and both nearly doubled in size during the next ten years. Much the most famous development was the creation of Black Harlem (fig. 41). Initiated by early footholds in an overbuilt housing speculation, by 1910 an "On to Harlem" movement was under way, and by the 1920s Blacks were creating "a city of their own, a cosmopolitan . . . spiritual capital of Black America" in this attractive northeastern corner of Manhattan. Although a majority of the newcomers were from the rural South, an important minority came from the West Indies (a movement propelled in part by "Panama money" earned by the tens of thousands whose work on the Canal was completed in 1914). These immigrants from Barbados, Jamaica, and other British and French islands were distinct as a group and by specific source in language, religion, manners, and experience; they arrived with generally more education and skills and this "first significant urban contact between multiple cultures of the African diaspora . . . produced an interchange of

41. Black Harlem.
"For Respectable Colored Families Only." Street scene, c. 1918–20. (Brown Brothers)

ideas, people, and institutions" that helped spark the cultural and political florescence of (what would later be called) the Harlem Renaissance and "made Harlem,
black metropolis, the center of the African world." Spanish Harlem, just to the
south, also included many Blacks from different countries, and the heavy post–
World War II influx of Puerto Ricans enlarged the Hispanic presence here and elsewhere in the city, but such a change did not as yet appear to be a major modification
of the always highly variegated population of this famous entryway.

On closer view, each of these great cities and the overall mass of Megalopolis
would become intricately complicated mosaics of peoples, communities, and social
groups, broadly sorted by common American conceptions of cultural identities
based on race, religion, and national origin, further subdivided by combinations of
these categories into interacting communities, and these, in turn, finely graded by
social status as defined by family, education, and employment, and displayed in
houses and cars, churches and clubs, dialect, dress, and decorum. There was a
strong territorial dimension to all these levels of assumed or ascribed identities. As

Gottmann repeatedly noted, amid the intensive complexities of modern metropolitan life, Americans seek to conduct their more personal social life "in a small homogeneous world of their own," resulting in a partitioning of every city and suburb into quite distinct local areas, "each of which seems tolerant of the neighboring ones on the condition of being able to keep them out of its own enclosure." (Such areas were of course rarely real "enclosures," and Gottmann commented that they were less rigidly provincial than their counterparts in Europe; under relentless American pressures of growth, migration, and social mobility they were also far less stable.) Protection of such social space engendered fervent support of local political autonomy. Partitioned among ten states, more than fifty counties, and hundreds of incorporated places, the whole region displayed the most complicated of common American patterns of political territoriality. Such fragmentation within a generally weak hierarchy of territorial governments made intergovernmental relations and any kind of geographical planning complex and difficult in American metropolitan regions.

MANUFACTURING BELT

This metropolitan seaboard remained the highly diversified Atlantic anchor of the American Manufacturing Belt. The principal change was the long decline in cotton textile production, the number of spindles in the South surpassing that in New England in 1924. In spite of continued prominence in many specialties (such as brass, hardware, cutlery, guns, jewelry, and woolens), New England was a weakened corner. The plight of mill towns "carrying a staggering burden of old buildings" obsolete in machinery, design, and location, as well as the long, slow depopulation of the rougher, colder uplands, leaving behind abandoned farms, cutover woodlands, and dwindling villages, had become the subject of numerous regional and national studies.

Looking westward, there had been no significant change in the general extent of the Manufacturing Belt, but Detroit was a greatly magnified center and the automobile and its many adjuncts had stimulated production in industrial cities large and small all across the western half of the region. The enormous industrial power of the United States, displayed in such wartime totals as 2.6 million army trucks, 86,000 tanks, 300,000 airplanes, and a long list of other prodigious sums, remained primarily seated within this long-established belt (78 percent of the facilities receiving government aid were within its bounds). Although Southern California and Seattle became famous for massive aircraft production, Long Island, Buffalo, St. Louis, and a huge new bomber factory near Detroit (and another in outlying Wichita) were also major contributors. Steel capacity was now 60 percent greater than in 1920, but 90 percent of it remained anchored in the same localities in this region. The mining of bituminous coal (now producing most of the electricity) had expanded southward deep into West Virginia and eastern Kentucky but had not drawn manufacturing with it; production of anthracite, once a preferred domestic fuel, was less than half that of 1920, leaving an array of depressed towns in the valleys of northeastern Pennsylvania.

As in Megalopolis, the most important population change was the influx of Blacks from the rural South, and here, too, there was a strong focus on a few cities. The Black population of Chicago doubled during the 1920s and was well over half a million by 1950; that of Detroit tripled during the great blossoming of the automobile industry and surged again during World War II to surpass 300,000 at mid-century. Similar growth rates but far smaller numbers had an important impact on several other cities involved in the same industry. Although not matching the fame of Harlem, jazz came up the river from creole New Orleans before diffusing eastward to New York, and Chicago's "Black Metropolis," "a narrow tongue of land, seven miles in length and one and one-half miles in width," was a more common illustration of the problems and prospects of such swollen urban districts ("understand Chicago's Black Belt and you will understand the Black Belts of a dozen large American cities"). These heavy in-migrations created severe racial tensions. The worst riot of the strife-ridden summer of 1919 took place in Chicago, and much the worst during World War II erupted in Detroit (causing the federal government to send in 6,000 troops).

Chicago continued as the unrivaled Second City of America by any measure of size, growth, or power; it was the centropolis of every continental system, the heart of the Heartland (of "Chicagoland," as Colonel McCormick of the strident *Chicago Tribune* would put it). It also became—well before *Megalopolis*—a laboratory, in this case for a widely influential "Chicago School" of sociologists who undertook intensive systematic study of neighborhoods and groups in the search for theory and understanding of the social ecology of urban life. Toward midcentury geographers added their focus on the patterns and dynamics of urban structure and extended the succession of spatial models of urban growth: concentric zones (Burgess), sectoral (Hoyt), multiple-nuclei (Harris and Ullman). From Robert E. Park's first proposal in 1915 to use Chicago as "a laboratory or a clinic," through a long series of studies by various specialists, it was clear that this massive, teeming metropolis, expanding inland rapidly and radially from its lakeside core, was regarded as the most instructive exhibit of the "modern city"; here more fully, powerfully, blatantly than anywhere else was "urbanization—American-style" (fig. 42).

MIDDLE WEST

Chicago was the pinnacle of an extensive hierarchy of tributary cities spaced across this vast central region, and these lesser centers were also attractive to sociologists

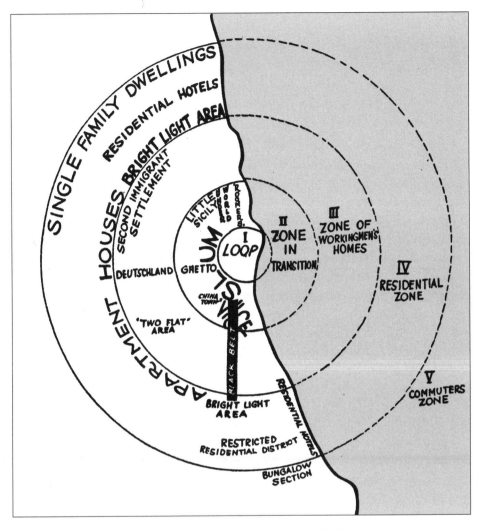

42. Urbanization—American Style, 1925.
We have shaded the Lake Michigan half of Ernest W. Burgess's concentric model to show the half-centric inland expansion of Chicago. Numerous bases for subsequent sectorial and multiple nuclei urban models are apparent. (Adapted from Park, Burgess, and McKenzie, *The City*)

in search of places "as representative as possible of contemporary American life." *Middletown: A Study in American Culture*, by Robert S. and Helen Merrell Lynd, became a great landmark in community studies from its first appearance in 1929. Seeking a relatively small compact city within "that common-denominator of America, the Middle West," the Lynds selected Muncie, Indiana (population 38,000 in 1924). They did caution readers that it must not be taken as a "typical" city of its size because concerns about the sheer complexity of their unprecedented task led them to choose a place with a largely "homogeneous native-born population, even though such a population is unusual in an American industrial city." While one may still sympathize with such pressures of research design, the exclusion or marginalization of Muncie's immigrant (15 percent) and Black (6 percent) populations from such an influential study stands as an implicit endorsement of common attitudes of the time about what best constituted "American" society and culture.

Chicago's agricultural hinterland also provided a compelling exhibit of what many commentators (and residents) regarded as the best of American farming and rural life: the vast level or gently rolling landscape of highly productive, family-operated, commercial grain-livestock farms of the Corn Belt, ordered within the checkerboard of well-fenced quarter-sections (160 acres), with tractors and machinery, trucks and automobiles clustered around houses, barns, and corncribs, all knit together by county and state roads lined with electric and telephone wires, and served by repetitive patterns of villages, towns, and cities (fig. 43). If this scene could not be taken as typical—for there were, of course, many kinds of farming in the United States—it could be proudly declared to be the best representation of what fully *modern agriculture* and farm life could be. Furthermore, this area, too, became a laboratory for social scientists. This common pattern of Middle Western settlement provided the nearest thing to that combination of featureless plain developed rapidly under uniform conditions by a homogeneous population sought by theorists in search of regularities over space and time in the formation and function of a hierarchy of retail trade centers. Initiated by rural sociologists in the 1920s, such studies were expanded and essentially completed in the elaboration of central-place theory by geographers in the 1960s (fig. 44).

However fine an exhibit of modern production and efficiency the Corn Belt or the Wheat Belts might be, world agricultural prices collapsed after World War I, farmers were marginal partakers of the boom of the 1920s, and the crisis of the Great Depression, severely exacerbated by drought, generated a rash of federal programs struggling to shore up this beleaguered sector. World War II brought an upsurge in prosperity, but longer-term prospects were uncertain. Increases in production, especially from hybrid seeds, further mechanization, and general substitution of soybeans for oats (with the replacement of horses by tractors) raised fears of a renewal of depressed prices. Even though the Middle West remained a stronghold of rural life, the farm population was declining, and evocations of pastoralism as a regional signature, as in the bounteous depictions by Grant Wood, John Steuart Curry, Thomas Hart Benton, and other artists of the 1930s, now seemed a shallow nostalgia.

Furthermore, life in the towns and small cities of this "representative" American region had been harshly critiqued. The boosterism, business values, and "progressive optimism" of Middletown and "hundreds of other scaled-down, would-be

43. Corn Belt Landscape, 1950.

The famous rectangularity of the rural Middle West is classically displayed by these half dozen farmsteads, each on its own quarter-section within a frame of county roads on a nearly level stretch of the southernmost margins of glaciation about twenty-five miles northwest of Des Moines. (Courtesy University of Iowa Libraries Map Collection)

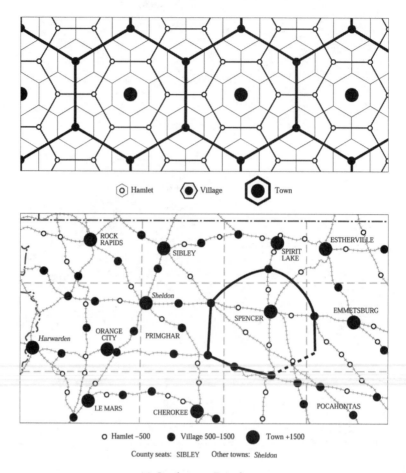

44. Settlement Regularity.
In classic central-place theory the spacing of the hierarchy of market centers is hexagonal. The
1930 pattern in a dozen counties in the northwest corner of Iowa displays a semblance of such
patterns, modified by railroad lines; the example of Spencer, seat of Clay County, is closest to the
model.

Chicagos" had been exposed by Sinclair Lewis in his widely popular novels *Main
Street* and *Babbitt* even before being quelled by the Great Depression. Even though
Graham Hutton, an astute foreign interpreter intimately familiar with the Middle
West during the 1940s, might still find the "extraordinary profusion of quiet and
well-ordered, modern small towns in the region: towns with between 10,000 and
50,000 inhabitants, dependent on one or more big factories or industries" still very
attractive (he named Quincy, Winona, Mason City, and a dozen other examples),
he recognized that the great faith in material progress "came to an end in 1929.
That year marked the high noon of the Midwest."

Beyond the Mississippi the more purely agricultural domain of the Middle West extended across the rich prairie soils to the arc of Gateway cities (Minneapolis–St. Paul, Sioux City, Omaha–Council Bluffs, St. Joseph, and Kansas City), each a collection, processing, and service center for a large subregion. Beyond these the great Wheat Belts stretched across hundreds of miles of higher, drier plains where the farms were much larger, settlement was thinner, and prospects were always less certain. "The last great plow-up," turning grassland into farms, took place on the eve of World War I in eastern Montana, the influx of settlers accompanied by the usual booming of towns and formation of new counties, but in 1918 drought wiped out the crops and ushered in a twenty-year period of poverty and decline. Montana was the only state to experience a net loss of population during the 1920s, and some geographers began to focus on such marginal lands (here and elsewhere in the world) as "zones of experiment," a laboratory for development of a "science of settlement" using the new tools of tractor, truck, and automobile, radio, weather forecasting, and tillage techniques to make settlement more secure, ease the isolation and deprivation, and make farm life more tolerable for the family. The severe drought and walls of dust that darkened skies eastward across the continent and famously compounded the Great Depression broadened such concerns to the whole of the High Plains. A chorus of critics now blamed earlier governments, bankers, railroads, boosters, and speculators for luring settlers to lands that should never have been plowed. Within a few years, however, the return of rains and wartime prices resulted in successful harvests from most of these lands. On the western margins any science of settlement was giving way to speculative capitalistic farming based on the purchase or lease of thousands of acres in various localities with men and equipment appearing only seasonally for seeding and harvesting. Such "suitcase farmers" were becoming much more common amid the remnant of resident farm families (as might be expected, the various Germanic and Slavic settlements were the most strongly anchored to the land).

THE COTTON SOUTH AND OTHER SOUTHS

While some sociologists were reconnoitering the Middle West for cities and towns representative of contemporary American life, others were confirming that Southern spokesmen routinely asserted their own homeland as "the most American part of the nation," meaning, contrarily, that it was the most distinctive and separate part of the country, containing the fewest foreigners and the most thoroughly White Anglo-Saxon Protestant population, retaining thereby "more of the early 'Americanisms' than any other region." That such a characterization ignored half of the population—Black, Afro-American Protestant—was left unsaid.

The period between the two world wars was the peak of this Southern distinctiveness and the nadir of its economic fortunes. The broad extent of regional poverty and lag in adoption of neotechnic facilities was in the making well before documented by sociologists and various New Deal agencies. The boll weevil, first detected as an invader in southern Texas in 1892, completed its devastating spread across the Cotton Belt in thirty years, and the combined collapse of cotton production and world prices plunged this famous farming system into prolonged crisis. Combating the weevil required investment and close management, involving new methods of field preparation, seeds, fertilizers, and pesticides. Response was least effective in some of the oldest and once richest districts, such as the Georgia Piedmont, Alabama Black Belt, and Natchez hinterland, where depleted soils, entrenched credit and sharecropping systems, and passive landlords resulted in widespread failure. In other areas, such as the Yazoo Delta, Central and West Texas, and adjacent Oklahoma, more favorable environmental conditions and more aggressive management sustained the continuation of cotton as a plantation staple.

The curse of the old cotton system was its dependence upon masses of cheap labor, but a mechanized alternative was long delayed by its diverse and exacting seasonal tasks. Tractors might replace one-mule plows but were uneconomic if used only for that purpose when weeding and picking remained dependent upon resident laborers. The simple hoe for "chopping cotton" was not effectively replaced until the development of special herbicides. Cotton-picking machines were being tested in the 1930s, but they produced a trashy cotton, lower in price and harder to gin, and there was no rush to adopt until further adaptations were made. As Charles S. Aiken summarized, "a complete set of machines and chemicals that effectively reduced labor in all three phases of cotton production was not available to cotton planters until 1955." Thus the full onset of an agricultural revolution would coincide—and be intimately connected—with a profound social revolution initiated after a unanimous decision of the Supreme Court in 1954 that the concept and practice of racially segregated public schools was unconstitutional.

Meanwhile, "the cultural landscape long confirmed the decline" that afflicted the region before these great transformations: empty houses and shacks amid former fields taken over by broom sedge and pine, the decay of big houses, merchant stores, and ginneries—and the absence of half or more of the former Black population from the countryside. As earlier noted, the Great Migration to the North was initiated by wartime jobs and a chance to escape the repressive regional caste system, and was continued by the deepening depression of the agricultural system. "Accustomed to an abundant supply of cheap labor, whites panicked when blacks began to leave in droves. But no serious effort was made to hold blacks by increases in wages, improvements to housing and schools, or amelioration of segregation." As local economies collapsed, that great northward, urbanward migration of Blacks became noteworthy not only for its volume and unprecedented direction of interregional movement but because it was impelled in many districts by the prospect of utter destitution—even starvation—if Blacks remained in place. (As Aiken notes, almost all of the famous New Deal–era publicity about poverty-stricken sharecroppers focused on Whites. When James Agee and Walker Evans were assigned to make a study of Southern sharecroppers, which resulted in their eventually acclaimed *Let Us Now Praise Famous Men*, their editors at *Fortune* "made clear that they didn't want to include blacks; blacks had always been poor and were expected always to be poor, so their plight was not considered to be newsworthy.")

The Virginia–North Carolina sector of this Old South was much less severely afflicted. Agriculture was always more diversified, and although cotton declined in Carolina, tobacco, the cash staple across much of this area, expanded with the great popularity of cigarette smoking, and tobacco acreages and income were stabilized by New Deal policies. Furthermore, several large synthetic fiber factories (first rayon, later nylon) were added to the Piedmont textile complex. Even though this industry relied on White labor, the exodus of Blacks from the larger region was comparatively minor.

The plight of the Appalachian South received much publicity and became a focus of federal attention in the TVA. The popular view that it was an isolated region of colorful but primitive mountain folk—"hillbillies"—bypassed by modern progress glossed over the fact that it was an area deeply penetrated and altered by industrial capitalism. The penetrating instrument was the railroad, the lure was vast tracts of timber and huge deposits of coal, and the most obvious human geographic change was the shift of large numbers of local people from their subsistence farms into company towns and camps. Exploitation got under way in the 1880s, and "by the end of the 1920s few residents of the region were left untouched by the industrial age." Unfortunately, this kind of industrial touch brought few if any of the benefits but some of the most severe woes of that age. Before this onslaught agents had roamed the region buying up huge acreages of timberlands and mineral rights from families for whom a few extra dollars seemed an unexpected wealth and the physical and social consequences were an unforeseen change. By the 1920s much of the mountain forest had been felled and coal mining had ravaged hills and valleys and streams. Most of the nearly 500 company towns imposed upon the region provided little more than bare shelter and a company store. This kind of crude resource exploitation under absentee ownership in such a confining physical environment offered little impetus for more ordinary town development featuring local retail enterprise, civic services, social institutions, and improved roads. Any sense of community remained anchored on kinship as families did their best to hold onto homesteads in the valleys and coves with part-time farming an important basis of subsistence and a preferred way of life. Migration to Northern industrial cities in World War I and after relieved some of the pressures of large families on limited resources, but it was commonly "considered a temporary expedient." Such Appalachian migrants found "adjustment to urban life difficult" and unattractive, and (like many Southern and Eastern European migrants in those same receiving cities) they formed close ethnic clusters fostering familiar patterns of living and worked to earn only enough money to return to their original locality and live in greater security and comfort. Such behavior was a strong expression of Appalachia as one form of the more generalized rural folk culture still so dominant over the whole South—and a marked distinction from the adjacent North.

Such generalized distinctions continued westward across a wide variety of Upland South areas, on beyond the fertile "islands" of the Bluegrass and Nashville basins to the Knobs and Western Coalfield of Kentucky and across the Mississippi to the broad Ozarks and Ouachita Mountains, much of which was, in effect, a cultural extension of Appalachia, a sequence of highlands of mostly subsistence farming amid cutover forest land, punctuated here and there by coal or lead mining (with reluctant migrants clustered on the margins of industrial St. Louis).

Texas, harboring a small Appalachia in its own Hill Country, was, as always, a more complicated set of subregions, with East Texas an obvious physical and cultural extension of the rural Deep South and the plains of West Texas becoming a major seat of a modernizing revivified cotton plantation system. Central Texas persisted as an area of ethnic diversity unusual across the South even though no longer augmented by European immigration. Texas had long served as a great frontier for Southern expansion, but it was also famous for an Anglo-Texan chauvinism that insisted on its own distinct identity grounded in its earliest formation and historical experiences. In location and character it was a Southwest, the meeting ground of the cotton plantation and the Western ranch, and it contained within its bounds three of the strongest polarities in American society: White and Black, Anglo and Hispanic, Protestant and Roman Catholic. All along the borderland the dual society of separation and subordination persisted. "In the farm areas of South and West Texas, the Caucasian schools were nearly always divided into 'Anglo schools' and 'Mexican schools,' the towns into 'white towns' and 'Little Mexicos,' and even the churches and cemeteries followed this . . . division of people"—"a separation as complete . . . as any in the Jim Crow South."

The most dramatic change during the period before midcentury was the impact of oil, initiated by an enormous gusher near Beaumont in 1901 and followed by a continuing series of discoveries, large and small, spotted through almost every region in Texas (and spreading into Louisiana and Arkansas). Thus the touch of industrial capitalism came to many a rural county in the form of an oil boomtown. Such places, full of feverish competition and social disorder, were shallow-rooted fragile communities, but the broader impact was very different from that of coal in the Southern Appalachians. Oil not only brought wealth to some local landowners and speculators, it fostered large supply, equipment, transport, and refining businesses, and an increasingly diverse chemical industry. Many small cities were sustained in whole or in part by oil, and Houston, which with the completion of its Ship Canal in 1915 had released itself from dependency upon Galveston as its ocean port, became a major national center of the petroleum industry and tripled in population during the interwar years.

The spread of the oil industry eastward along the Gulf Coast became another capitalist invasion of a strongly localized rural society. Cajuns responded to new opportunities for work and became important in the operation of supply boats along the coast and bayous, but giant corporations with their English-speaking personnel were now laced throughout their homeland. A larger encompassing French Louisiana persisted under even more varied pressures as a distinct and complex ethnocultural enclave. Meanwhile cosmopolitan New Orleans was undergoing unprecedented physical expansion made possible by "one of those potent inventions that people in later years would take for granted" (like the high-speed elevators that "changed the geography of New York City"). In this case it was a heavy-duty pump that could lift rapidly huge volumes of water a short distance, which made settlement of the broad back-swamp possible, releasing the city from its precarious perch upon the natural levees along the Mississippi. Although the pump was invented near the end of the century, reclamation remained a slow and costly process, and only in the economic boom of the 1920s was the creep northward toward Lake Pontchartrain accelerated, creating a large new residential area (mostly White) with California house types now added to the city's long distinctive local architecture. In the 1930s federal funds aided a major lakefront development, including an airport; in 1935 the new Huey Long Bridge upriver offered the first vehicular connection across the Mississippi.

World War II brought "a new kind of prosperity to the South." The Maritime Commission had resisted expansion there because of racial problems and the lack of skilled labor and all kinds of "white collar brains," but "the whole process of selecting and rejecting was done under heavy political pressure," and over the course of the war a dozen new shipyards were spaced along the Gulf and South Atlantic coasts. A new steel works was built near Houston, and the majority of the more than forty government-sponsored synthetic rubber factories were located in existing petrochemical complexes along the Texas-Louisiana coast (only two were built in Akron). When natural rubber from Southeast Asia was again available after the war, the government mandated minimum proportions of synthetic rubber in tires and other products, and these new plants supplied about half of the national consumption. Aluminum—first commercially produced in 1888 and expensive and minor for years thereafter—came of age with electricity and airplanes, but in 1940 the United States had only four aluminum reduction plants (American money, however, had built the world's largest facility on the Saguenay River in Quebec). Reduction of alumina powder to metal requires large amounts of electricity (it was one of the first industries attracted to the Niagara Falls project), and wartime factories were built in the Tennessee Valley, in Texas (powered by natural gas), and in Arkansas near local supplies of bauxite. Fort Worth became the only large aircraft manufacturing center in the region; Oak Ridge, a new city of 30,000, suddenly emerged west of Knoxville as an atomic city.

This wartime industrial impact was limited in kind and place, it was accompanied by local rural-to-urban migrations but no large influx from other regions, and it did not greatly alter the South's chronic subservience within the national economy. In another way, however, the war had greater relative impact on this part of the country than elsewhere, and a hint of this regional selection had appeared in 1917. In World Wars I and II the United States faced the sudden need for an enormous expansion of its normally meager military forces—and therefore of places and facilities to house and train them. In April 1917, the Army had just over 200,000 men on active duty, more than half of whom were in recently activated National Guard units and stationed along the turbulent Mexican border. With the initiation of national conscription a month later, preparations for the quick intake of a million men got under way and the quartermaster general began construction of sixteen national army cantonments. Each of these "great military cities" was designed to house 45,000 men and to serve as the main induction center for a specified source region. Thus the pattern of the sixteen was a general reflection of the national population distribution, although each cantonment was not necessarily central to its own designated territory (Camp Lewis, near Tacoma, served eight western states, including California) (fig. 45). In addition to these standardized wooden-barracks complexes ("pine cities"), the Army also created sixteen "tent cities" for National Guard units called up from the states. As these were temporary housing for troops being readied for overseas service, all but two were located in the southern and southwestern states, where costs of construction and heating were at a minimum. All of these camps as well as the enlargement of regular army posts brought a sudden flurry of work and income to adjacent localities, but it all faded quickly after the twenty-month war. Within a few months after the Armistice, the nearly 4 million men (and a few thousand female nurses and clerks) in service had been reduced to little more than the prewar level—and soon well below that.

However, armies may suddenly swell and as suddenly fade from the scene, but their impress lingered even though their direct impact was brief. The U.S. government retained control of most of these campsites, and when the next emergency arose they again became major centers and were soon amid a much denser pattern of bases for far larger forces and more varied military needs. In 1939 fewer than 200,000 men were on active Army duty, and the total armed forces (not including

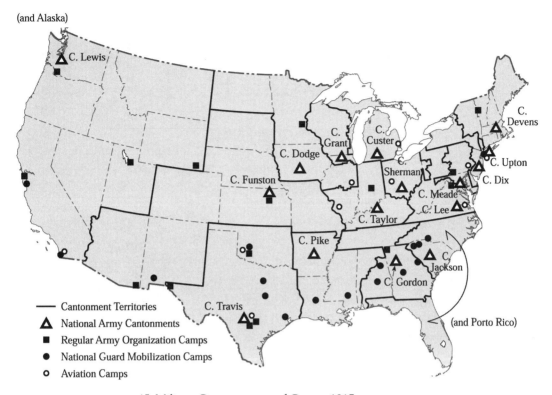

45. Military Cantonments and Camps, 1917.
(Adapted from map in Showalter, "America's New Soldier Cities")

the Coast Guard, which in peacetime was attached to the Treasury rather than the War Department) numbered about 330,000. As war spread in Europe and Asia, plans called for an increase to a million, and America's entry into the war brought a sudden enormous expansion, so that by August 1945, the Army numbered 8,266,000 and the armed forces totaled 12,294,000 (including 274,000 women). Housing and training such a multitude impressed an extensive new military geography upon the American landscape.

The Air Force remained technically part of the army until July 1947, but it had famously taken on a life and geographic presence of its own. Whereas World War I had prompted the creation of ten small "aviation camps" (and none in the South beyond Hampton, Virginia), some 500 airfields and related installations within the continental United States supported the massive air power of World War II (72,000 planes were in service at the end of the war). The heavy concentration of these in the South was a military preference (fig. 46). As a general responded to a Northern senator, "with the exception of some areas on the Pacific Coast, in general, it can be stated that the difficulty of continuous flying training is in direct pro-

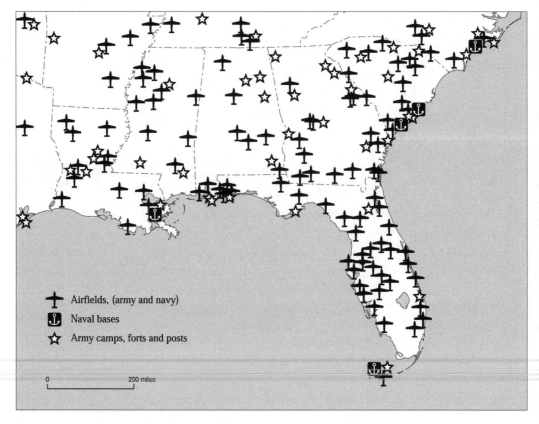

46. Military Bases in the Southeast.
(Adapted from *Rand McNally Map of the United States Military Posts, 1944*)

portion to the distance north of approximately the 37th parallel"—that is, north of southern Virginia and Cairo, Illinois, or, as another officer put it: "wherever you can grow cotton you can grow aviators." The "wide open spaces" and much good flying weather of western Texas and Oklahoma and Kansas extended this southerly pattern.

The attractions of warm climate, cheap land and labor, and the sustained power of Southern senators and representatives on pertinent committees, as well as any preferences of military leaders (the "American officer corps continued to draw disproportionately from people of southern birth and education") resulted in a heavy concentration of all kinds of military bases in the South and Southwest (but not in the rugged Appalachians or Ozarks). The apparent anomaly of proportionately few military bases across the heavily populated northeastern quadrant (except for the immediate Atlantic coastal strip) may be explained by the much higher costs of land and labor, the existing heavy ground and air traffic, the avoidance of diverting labor and supporting services from the critical needs of the industrial belt—and perhaps less intensive concern by regional congressmen of the need to shore up local economies by this kind of military presence (how else to explain Georgia's twenty-two bases compared with Wisconsin's four?).

However varied in size and character, these new or enlarged military installations had an impact upon hundreds of cities, towns, and villages, some of them doubling or more in size almost overnight (such as Fayetteville and Jacksonville in North Carolina, or Killeen in Texas); all were swollen with traffic, the roads between town and camp lined with new opportunistic businesses. Moreover, it was not merely a frantic wartime episode. Although a good many smaller airfields and bases were deactivated, most remained in some degree of service for some years to come (in this, too, congressmen had a strong role in resisting reductions in their district); thus many places, and especially in the South, received stimulating injections of income and population, and achieved a new level of commercial and civic activity.

Southerners, Blacks and Whites, had participated heavily in this vast national effort, and wartime experiences must have broadened perceptions of many in this largely rural population, but the fundamentals of Southern society had not been changed. In 1950 the "Solid South" appeared to be what its chauvinistic spokesmen had long insisted it was: "a nation within a nation," its White leaders determined to preserve a distinctive Southern "way of life."

THE FAR WEST AND THE CALIFORNIAS

The general framework of regions and subregions within the Far West had become essentially set before World War I. By that time all the apparent resources had been tapped, colonization completed, trade areas delimited, and the spacing and hierarchy of towns and cities fixed in place. For twenty years after the war chronic low prices of minerals, lumber, beef, wool, grain, fruit, and sugar (beets) resulted in little growth over most of this huge area—a sharp and widely dispiriting change from the great era of regional formation so recently past.

It was an especially difficult era for the famous subnation in the midst of this West. With no further lands open to their preferred group colonization, the Mormon domain was geographically delimited, the "Gathering" (the bringing in of new converts to their Zion-in-the-Mountains) had lost its momentum, and accommodation of their strongly sanctioned growth of large families posed a serious problem for this self-conscious, cohesive society. The export of surplus youth to cities outside the region was a reluctant response to the prospect of progressive rural impoverishment.

There was nothing akin to that scale of internal pressure in the Inland Empire, but Spokane's utter stagnation after its meteoric rise from a village to a regional capital of 100,000 during the railroad-building era was a deflating experience for civic leaders who only in the mid-1930s could begin to pin their hopes on the Grand Coulee Dam and huge Columbia Basin irrigation project. Meanwhile, here, as with the Mormons, there was a continuing drift of population to the Pacific Coast, in this case mainly to Portland and Seattle, which grew moderately (industrial Tacoma was stagnant). Denver, suffering from a similarly depressed hinterland, worked hard to make itself the "Little Capital of the United States" by luring regional headquarters of the expanding number of federal agencies. With no rival big city anywhere near, by 1940 it had more such offices than any other place in the country, thereby enlarging its depression-proof employment base and extending its regional reach. Also, even in those hard times, the automobile brought a welcome expansion of tourism along the Rocky Mountain Front, the most accessible West to the millions of the midcontinent. In the Southwest the much smaller cities of Albuquerque, Tucson, and Phoenix, benefiting from California-bound traffic, tourism, winter sojourners, or agricultural expansion in the Salt River oasis, nearly, or in some cases more than, doubled their population in the interwar years. In Nevada, emptiest of states and long dependent on a now nearly moribund mining industry, reduction of the residence requirement for divorce (to three months in 1927, further reduced to six weeks in 1931) and legalized gambling (1931) had not yet generated much urban growth (Reno 21,000, Las Vegas 8,000 in 1940).

California was, as always, the great exception. Even though much of the state's agriculture and industry suffered from common problems of the time and the big postwar real estate boom faded, people kept coming in: more than a million and a half during the 1920s, nearly a million more during the Great Depression, and the total population of the state doubled in twenty years. The sheer magnitude of this "apparently uninterruptible tendency of the population of the United States to gravitate westward" (as Bay Area chambers of commerce hopefully put it in 1931) generated growth in many sectors, for whether these people came with money or in poverty they were consumers and potential producers; whether they became taxpayers or public charges they required expansions of services; in 1950 as in 1850, massive immigration was a mighty engine of California development.

Although there was little expansion in agricultural acreage during this interwar period, there were further increases in the remarkable variety and specialization of products (including a major expansion of cotton) and in concentration of ownership. The "family farm" so long characteristic in most parts of America—and idealized nationally—had never been the dominant form in California. Here the most common mode was "factories in the fields" and the fields as but an initial stage in the processing and marketing of (often perishable) products, all by a single or interlocking set of corporations. Two-thirds of all the farmland was held in units of more than a thousand acres, and most small commercial growers depended on long-term contracts with such companies. Such a system was built upon a plentiful—or, better, an overplentiful—supply of cheap, docile labor for brief, critical periods. Such migratory workers had been supplied in large part by a succession of immigrations—Chinese, South Asians (commonly referred to as "Hindus" but including Sikhs as well), Mexicans, Filipinos—and in the 1930s a new source appeared from within America itself. As Don Mitchell has detailed, "the influx of angry, desperate migrants from the Dust Bowl was both a blessing and a curse to California agribusiness." A new supply—surplus—of labor was welcomed, but, as the entire nation would become aware through book and film of John Steinbeck's *Grapes of Wrath*, White American citizens were not so easily subdued and exploited under such appalling conditions and coercions. Earnest attempts by federal agents to establish camp facilities and to support basic civil rights were vigorously opposed by the corporations and local officials and had limited impact on living conditions and festering tensions. As the "Okies" and others began to move into wartime industries, agribusiness leaders instigated the bracero program for regulated seasonal admission of workers from Mexico. As Carey McWilliams (who was for a time in charge of some of these federal efforts) concluded in 1949: "the farm labor problem in California" remained "encysted, i.e., embedded, in the very structure of the state's agricultural economy."

As California farming was different so local towns were different. Industrialized agriculture begets industrialized communities, with sharp class differentiations between a small number of farm operators, managers, and business proprietors and a large body of laborers, themselves often divided into separate racial or ethnic groups. Such towns offer little evidence of common American civic life; places of several thousand people may remain unincorporated, unstable agglomerations. Such generalizations gloss over numerous variations and exceptions. Sprinkled unevenly through the Great Valley were older, more substantial towns in the midst of specialized districts of small family farms, as, especially, in the productive Fresno area. Nevertheless, the sudden large influx of poor White Americans from the western South and recurrent additions to the migrant and resident Mexican population were much the most important social change in rural California.

There are, of course, two American Californias and two very distinct metropolises. San Francisco remained the "Wall Street of the West," serving not only much of the Far West (most of which was in its Federal Reserve district) but important parts of the Pacific World (East Asia and Europe were well represented by branch banks), and it continued to be the equipoise of New York in so many other ways as well: a cosmopolitan social and cultural capital full of old families and old and new immigrants, a world city in many respects. In 1939 the China Clipper beginning weekly seaplane mail and passenger service across the Pacific was the exact counterpart of the Yankee Clipper hopping across the Atlantic, and in that same year each city opened an international exposition to boost its economy and lift the spirits of a public enduring ten years of depression. Even the impact of the automobile was similarly dramatic in these insular and peninsular settings, with the Golden Gate and San Francisco–Oakland bridges even more spectacular than those across the Hudson and East rivers (more mundane was the ensuing congestion in these high-rise downtowns and the heavy increases in truck traffic, the latter greatly promoted in the Bay Area by a 1927 bridge across Carquinez Strait providing a direct link with the Sacramento Valley).

That compelling image of Southern California, rows of bungalows amid the orange groves, was under relentless modification on the ground even as it persisted in external perceptions (fig. 47). Although throughout this interwar period Los Angeles County remained first in the nation in the value of its agricultural production, housing and highways, shopping centers and industries ate away at the land under cultivation as the population of the Los Angeles Basin nearly tripled in twenty years to surpass 3 million by 1940. The region thrived on a set of new or expanded industries: a series of big new oil fields; automobile assembly plants and tire facto-

47. Southern California Suburbia.
Bungalows and young palms in Anaheim, early 1920s. (Courtesy Department of Special Collections, Charles E. Young Research Library, UCLA)

ries; airplane manufacture; a creative fashion center and leading manufacturer of sportswear; tourism in summer and winter (nearly 2 million visitors a year); and, most important, the cinema and world-famous "glamour" of Hollywood (and the closely associated production of radio programs).

As McWilliams noted, the movies, the largest industry in Los Angeles between 1920 and 1940 (producing 90 percent of all films made in the United States), "fit the economic requirements and physical limitations of the region like a glove": requiring few raw materials, creating a product, a roll of film, which "could be shipped anywhere in the world for almost nothing; but which at the same time, poured forth an enormous sum in payrolls and expenditures." "What could be more desirable than a monopolistic non-seasonal industry with 50,000,000 customers, an industry without soot or grime, . . . an industry whose production shows peaks but few valleys?" Moreover, as Reyner Banham later emphasized, "the cultural consequences" were even more important than the economic, for "Hollywood brought to Los Angeles an unprecedented and unrepeatable population of genius, neurosis, skill, charlatanry, beauty, vice, talent, and plain old eccentricity, and it brought that population in little over two decades, not the long centuries that most metropolitan cities have required to accumulate a cultured and leisure class." The formation of that class was fortuitously accelerated and intensified by the influx of thousands of refugees from Adolf Hitler's Europe—famous and aspiring authors, artists, musicians, academics, architects, scientists, physicians, psychiatrists, and others, mostly Jewish (but not all, among the most renowned exiles was the austere German Protestant Nobel Prize novelist, Thomas Mann). These émigrés were added to the influx of American and British writers, artists, and other professionals (but not many academics; Cal Tech, emerging from an earlier polytechnic school in 1920, soon became nationally famous in science, but UCLA, long a subordinate southern branch, was just settling into its new Beverly Hills campus, and most of the many others were still small denominational colleges; the Huntington Library was being converted into a historians' haven). Banham's added remark that Hollywood was thus "the end of innocence and provincialism—the movies found Los Angeles a diffuse fruit-growing super-village of some eight hundred thousand souls and handed it over to the infant television industry in 1950 a world metropolis of over four million" may be taken as a rhetorical summation of a Southern California dominated since the 1880s by the great Protestant, middle-class Middle Western influx being transformed into a far more variegated, looser, unstable amalgam, infamous for its faddish social and political movements and new religious sects but creative in important ways. As Kevin Starr concluded: "in the 1930s a golden age of California as a regional American civilization would soon be asserting itself in architecture, landscaping, interior design, film, fiction, painting, photography, public works, the research and writing of history, sport, competitive athletics, and the good life—all of it coexisting with and running parallel to scenes of unprecedented wretchedness in the fields where the grapes of wrath would soon be harvested."

That new society, featuring leisure and casual living as a positive good, was surely a sharp break from long-asserted Middle American mores. It was obviously a lifestyle that made the most of a distinctive geographic setting; patio, swimming pool, tennis court, and backyard barbecue were perfectly suited to these sunny sub-tropics, but other regions could partake of them in varying degree. Just as Southern California developers and designers showed the nation how to shape a landscape to serve the automobile, so a rapid succession of California house types—bungalow, pseudo-Spanish mission, modern minimalist, and, most popular of all, suburban ranch house with broad built-in garage—penetrated every part of the country, ac-companied by California designs of furnishings and fashions for daily living. In its area of origin this citrus-grove suburbia was not sub-urban in the traditional literal sense, for it was not closely tied to a major downtown center; ever more dispersed and flexible in its residential-commercial relationships, it was a new form of an old antiurban American predilection. As David Brodsly put it: "Los Angeles emerged as America's first essentially middle-class metropolis. . . . Los Angeles' appeal lay in its being the first major city that was not quite a city, that is, not a crowded indus-trial metropolis. It was a garden city of backyards and quiet streets, a sprawling small town magnified a thousandfold and set among palms and orange trees under a sunny sky."

The impact of World War II was extraordinarily dramatic and extensive in the Far West. Unlike the East, where an important share of the industrial effort was a matter of putting long idle plants and workers back into production, the sudden vast demands for ships and airplanes, together with the gigantic military campaigns in the Pacific, required new basic industrial plants and the attraction of hundreds of thousands of new people to various centers, which in turn generated massive pres-sures on housing, highways, shops, schools, and every kind of service. For five in-tense years an array of government agencies and private interests variously com-peted or combined to respond to such problems.

The Pacific Coast shipyards were almost entirely new (eventually 110 berths compared with a mere seven in 1940, and building more than half of all wartime ships). The concentration in the San Francisco Bay area was the largest in the na-tion; those in Portland and nearby Vancouver ranked second on the coast. South-ern California was far in the lead in aircraft production, with seven large factories, and Boeing in Seattle quickly became a world-famous center. Both of these indus-tries required new basic facilities: the production of steelplate at entirely new big works at Geneva, near Provo, Utah, pivotal for rail shipment to all Pacific ports, and at Fontana, near San Bernardino in the Los Angeles Basin; and new aluminum reduction plants at several points along the lower Columbia River and at Spokane.

The established naval bases at San Diego, San Pedro, San Francisco Bay, and Bremerton on Puget Sound and other older military facilities obviously underwent major expansion, but many remote inland areas also became sudden new participants. As Richard White noted, "for military planners all the old liabilities of the West suddenly became virtues": isolation, emptiness, and arid climates became attractions for new airfields, bombing ranges, storage and testing of weapons, and research and production of secret materials. Thus large tracts in New Mexico, Utah, Nevada, Idaho, central Washington, and empty portions of California were put to new military use. Much the largest of these facilities was the Hanford Works along an arid stretch of the Columbia built to produce plutonium for atomic bombs; much the most famous—once it was no longer secret—was Los Alamos, the New Mexican scientific headquarters of that project. Wartime research on electronics, radar and sonar, jet propulsion and missiles, radiation and chemical warfare, and much else created numerous clusters of scientists and engineers in the West, and especially in California.

At the end of this great war, Westerners who had for years complained in the Congress and other forums about the concentration of economic power in the East and the "desirability of decentralizing industry" might take some real satisfaction from what had taken place in four years' time. Even though in national terms the regional shift was small in percentage and had been more the result of expediency than of national planning to redress chronic economic imbalance, the legacy of wartime development was major in substance and potential. At that moment, however, there was also a good deal of anxiety over just how permanent it all would be. With the grim memory of ten years of the Great Depression still strong, "the haunting fear of 'reconversion recession,'" present in some degree nationwide, was especially prominent in the West, which had gained so much in so short a time. The future seemed to hang upon two great questions: How many of the people who came to the West in wartime would choose to stay? How many facilities and how much research and development would the federal government continue to support?

Answers were quickly apparent. A large proportion of those who had come for work or had done a tour of military duty in the West elected to settle there. Thus the demand for housing and associated services was much greater in many parts of the West than that which was common in the nation following the fifteen-year interlude of depression and war. Emergency barracks-type quarters, such as at Vanport, housing 40,000 shipyard workers on a Columbia River floodplain, were not meant to be permanent (and Vanport was wiped out by floods in 1948), but the prefabricated, mass-production techniques used could now be applied to the rapid creation of single-family housing. In Southern California housing factories were set up at the edges of large tracts laid out to receive thousands of new dwellings. Similar expansions on a lesser scale responded to the tens of thousands of newcomers in other regional centers, such as Phoenix, Albuquerque, Denver, Seattle, and the Wasatch Oasis.

The answer to the second big question became clear in 1950, when the Communist conquest of Mainland China and the onset of the Korean War ensured that the vast United States military position in the Pacific was more than a temporary imperial expansion (awaiting the reformation of an occupied Japan for peaceful readmission to international relations). The American armed forces, which had been reduced to a million and a half, were soon doubled in size, and research and development of new weaponry and defense systems, much of it based in the Far West, was greatly accelerated. Within a few years "there were more aircraft employees in Washington and California . . . than there had been in 1944."

Thus at midcentury the American West had "a vastly expanded regional market, a new industrial infrastructure, and a new base of workers and wealth." "The East's influence over the region had faded," and "the main agent of the liberation from dependence on eastern capital was the federal government" (including massive hydroelectric and other projects during the 1930s). For much of this West "the four short years of the war had brought a maturation . . . that in peacetime might have taken generations to accomplish," and "scores of writers and public figures were actively involved in [an] effort to create a new self-image" of unlimited opportunity to replace that of an internal "colonial" economy and society. In all of this, California was, as usual, exceptional, for its writers, public figures, and most of its ordinary citizens had never doubted its importance or its future. The war had simply been another in a succession of "gold rushes" that had magnified its national and world importance.

4. Midcentury Morphology

NATIONAL CORE AND MODIFICATIONS

Amid the flurry of fresh attention to "nation building" and related geopolitical topics upwelling in the aftermath of World War II, the "remarkable dominance" and "self perpetuating momentum" of the American Core area offered an important example of "uneven development" and structural rigidity. The general economic dimensions of this pattern were readily measurable; as a major study of "regions, resources and economic growth" concluded: "after more than a half century of 'filling in' and probing of new wealth and new opportunities across the vast continent. . . . clearly *this area is still the very heart of the national economy and the very center of the national market for goods and services*." A series of maps in a succinct article by the geographer Edward Ullman offered both a careful delineation of that dominant area

and additional measures of concentration, such as the locations of corporate headquarters, members of national scientific societies, patents issued, books published,
prestigious universities, largest libraries. In 1950 this Core contained 43 percent of
the nation's population on 7.7 percent of its area, 68 percent of its manufacturing
employment, and 70 to more than 90 percent of its most notable cultural institutions.

Although the general framework of this great dominating structure had remained stabilized astride its New York–Chicago axis for half a century, the internal
tensions between its two great parts that had been so prominent before World War
I—between, in current terms, Megalopolis and the Middle West—had undergone
important modification. As James R. Shortridge summarized, "over the course of
the 1920s the East stopped viewing the Middle West as a competitor for the leadership of the nation" and "the reign of the Middle West as the self-confident symbol
of the United States was remarkably short-lived." Like most of America, the Middle West at midcentury was growing in its cities, not in its rural countrysides. At its
center was the most widely studied model of American metropolitan development,
and it also contained the new symbol and seat of American industrialism: not paleotechnic Pittsburgh with its massive mills amid the fire and smoke in the Appalachian valleys, but neotechnic Detroit, the birthplace of "Fordism," turning out
millions of shiny automobiles year after year for an eager public—that was universally understood to be America's greatest and original contribution to the modern
industrial world (fig. 48). In volume of sales, Detroit was now second only to New
York City as an industrial headquarters. History and geography had made the Atlantic World and the American Heartland indelibly different regional realms, and
that difference would continue to be reflected in life and landscape, in all sorts of
social and political matters large and small; yet contrary to the shrill, at times para-
noid, voice of the *Chicago Tribune*, the contentious regionalisms within the thousand-mile breadth of the American Core that had emerged so strongly early in the
century had been eased by the common experiences of wars and depression and the
shared promises and problems of an urbanizing, industrializing neotechnic age.
Megalopolis, Chicago, and Detroit increasingly provided bases for a common rather
than competing versions of America.

However, Neotechnic America was also being shaped where a rapidly evolving
California Suburbia was emerging as a powerful symbolic landscape, the setting for
a compelling new version of an American way of life, a marked departure from an
increasingly discredited Main Street of Middle America. This now world-famous
southwestern corner of the nation thereby became the first region to challenge the
power of the Northeastern Core. New York–Chicago–Los Angeles was a much-
augmented transcontinental axis; San Francisco, primary gateway to an oceanic
sphere hugely magnified in significance, had also gained symbolic stature: "The

48. A Modernist River Rouge, 1931.

Under Charles Sheeler's "precisionist" brush even the coal dock at River Rouge is given the clean, bright, geometric image of modernism. A professional photographer as well as a painter, Sheeler was commissioned in 1928 to produce a set of views to be used in a massive advertising campaign to introduce the Model A, successor to the Model T. He spent six weeks in the plant and was awed by the sheer scale and power of the place. After completing his assignment he soon produced a set of paintings that established him as "a leading iconographer of the machine age." However, appearing in the early 1930s amid massive unemployment and Ford's brutal response to labor unrest, his immaculate, almost humanless depictions were controversial from the start and have often been taken as marking an artistic end to the neotechnic "cult of the machine." Sheeler himself did not indulge in social comment and continued to produce impressive work. (Photograph copyright © 2000 Whitney Museum of Modern Art)

stream of troops and munitions was still pouring westward from the Golden Gate when in February 1945, San Franciscans were electrified by the announcement from the leaders of the 'Big Three,' meeting in far-off Yalta in the Crimea: 'we have agreed that a conference of the United Nations should be called to meet at San Francisco, in the United States, on April 25, 1945.'" The U.N. Headquarters would arise on Manhattan Island, the now-unchallenged fulcrum of the Atlantic World, but the U.N. Charter was shaped by delegates meeting for two months in that famous equipoise on the Pacific.

At midcentury California's challenge to long-established patterns was most obvious in these special cultural and strategic terms, but other destabilizing trends were also discernible. Its combination of a much-enlarged population and distance from the Manufacturing Belt favored extensive local industrial development and marketing services to most of the Far West. Less apparent but potentially more significant were the formal geopolitical implications of its phenomenal population growth during these interwar and wartime years, for any major reshaping of the population surface must result in a reshaping of political power.

By law, the House of Representatives must be reapportioned among the states following each decennial census. However, the 1920 census, the first to document that the United States had become more urban than rural, "grabbed the attention of the American public," and for the first (and only) time in American history, no such reapportionment was made during that decade. That report got such attention not because the public were close readers of the census but because of the alarm sounded by those who were deeply concerned about the implications of that urban growth. Heretofore the expansions of metropolitan and industrial centers had been more or less balanced by continued westward colonization and agricultural expansion (in the 1910 reapportionment the Northeastern Core states had gained twenty-one seats, the Plains and Western states twenty-two—the South only six), but while industrial expansions continued, indeed spurted during the war, agriculture had not, and the rural states of the Midwest and South were faced with a considerable reduction in representation. Furthermore, such a shift in the balance of power might now be compounded by an actual loss of seats in Congress, sharply increasing the political pain of such decennial change. Up until this time no states had had to give up seats, for the House had simply been enlarged each decade to take care of the number added. But with the admission of the last of the contiguous territories (Arizona and New Mexico in 1912) and completion of the transcontinental federation of forty-eight states, and with a House of Representatives of 435 seats, there was strong pressure (in part for practical, operational reasons) to hold to this size, meaning that any gain in seats must be offset by an actual loss of representation from low-growth or stagnant states. (Every state, no matter how small its population, is allotted at least one seat in the House.)

Thus this contentious matter in the internal geopolitical structure of the Congress was added to all the other pressures and problems faced by that Congress in post–World War I America. "The debate began in 1921 and lasted virtually the entire decade," and the rural opposition to reapportionment became stridently anti-urban and specifically anti-immigrant. They raised the fear that allotting more power to the great industrial centers might lead to repeal of the stringent immigration controls just begun by Congress (hardly a realistic prospect at the time, given the huge margin in favor of the 1924 act, but an accurate focus on the areas of support, for "nearly one-half of the 'No' votes came from five cities, New York, Chicago, Boston, Cleveland, and Detroit," and nearly all the rest were from similar districts—the South and Far West were unanimous in favor of the bill). Reapportionment was not primarily a party matter; the opposition included many urban Republicans from the Northeast as well as Democrats from the rural South. Finally, in 1929, with President Hoover's support, a bill approving decennial reapportionment "with automatic calculations based on a House fixed at 435 seats" was passed.

Thus the 1930 reapportionment reflected twenty rather than ten years of population change and resulted in a shift of twenty-seven seats, a third of the gains going to California, with New England, Pennsylvania, the agricultural Heartland, and the South all suffering the first actual loss of seats in Congress (fig. 49). Over the full span of this period (in this matter measuring from 1910 through 1950) there was a net shift of forty-four seats (just over 10 percent of the House membership), with exactly half of the gains accruing to the Pacific Coast states and California far in the lead with nineteen additional seats; only ten other states shared the rest. With Pennsylvania's big loss of six seats (coal and heavy industry) offset by Michigan and Ohio gains (automobile industry) the net decline in the states of the Core was only three.

In politics as in most everything else, California was exceptional. As Carey McWilliams remarked: "sociologically detached from the rest of the country, and notably from the rest of the West, California functions in its own right, has its own patterns of political behavior and exists as a kind of sovereign empire by the western shore." Nevertheless, it was also evolving into a position of power in the encompassing empire. A gain of nineteen seats at the expense of other parts of the nation was a major enhancement on the national scene, not least in the Electoral College (where each state is allocated votes in presidential elections equivalent to its total representation in the Congress). California's electoral power rose from thirteen in the 1920s to thirty-two in the election of 1952—and Richard M. Nixon, California native and representative, became vice-president.

That California's politics were unusually independent and inward-looking underscored that, unlike the sustained sectionalism of the South or regionalist movements of the interwar years, California's challenge to established national patterns was not a protest, not a program to redress chronic regional imbalances, but the cumulative result of its own self-confident growth arising from massive spontaneous migrations. Its different version of an American way of life was presented and generally received not as a conflict with the existing order but as a benign, inviting alternative on display in the region and presented incidentally and implicitly by a new powerful entertainment industry. Developers, corporations, and govern-

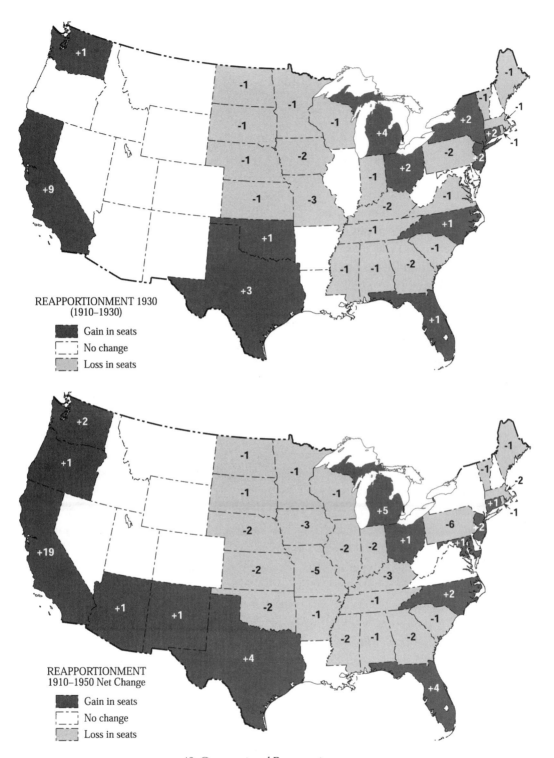

REAPPORTIONMENT 1930
(1910–1930)

◼ Gain in seats
☐ No change
▨ Loss in seats

REAPPORTIONMENT
1910–1950 Net Change

◼ Gain in seats
☐ No change
▨ Loss in seats

49. Congressional Reapportionments.
(Adapted from Martis and Elmes, *Historical Atlas of State Power*)

ments—local, state, and national—were of course intricately involved in this magnification of California's influence, but individual and family decisions of millions of Americans were basic to this reshaping of national patterns.

REDISTRIBUTION OF THE BLACK POPULATION

The migration of Southern Blacks to the Urban North was also a major reshaping of human geography and a challenge to long-established patterns, a regional change of national importance. Throughout these years Blacks continued to constitute about 10 percent of the total population of the continental United States, but whereas in 1910, 89 percent lived in the South, in 1950 only 63 percent of the now 15 million Blacks remained in that old homeland and fully a third of the total resided in the North. Such an extensive redistribution altered common perceptions of what was routinely called "the Negro Problem." No longer could that old embarrassing topic be regarded as a regional aberration best left to the South to resolve in its own manner and time. For reasons well beyond—but bound up with—this geographic change, "race relations" were now clearly a national problem, a challenge directly shared by North and South.

The challenge might be shared, but the geographic context of Black settlement was markedly different in these two broad sections. The Great Migration was a transfer of rural Blacks into large cities. In American racial terms they were not a new presence, for Blacks had always been in those cities, but to many of those long resident there the sudden arrival of large numbers of "uncouth," often illiterate Southern country folk was regarded as an invasion (not unlike the reaction of comfortably successful German Jews in America to the subsequent influx from the ghettos of Eastern Europe). In cities such as Philadelphia, the long-established middle-class Black community, used to relatively stable if limited relations with Whites, found itself lumped together with these newcomers as an unwelcome swollen mass that Whites now sought to contain within firm residential boundaries. Thus former looser clusterings of Blacks were transformed into rigid ghettos, maximizing segregation, severely restricting Black relations with Whites, introducing new diversities that altered stratifications within the Black community, and exaggerated cultural differences between Blacks and Whites. The receiving group feared that "it had been permanently drowned by a torrent of migration," and a later study confirmed that since "1915, the status of Northern Negroes has fallen perceptively"; however, the rapid increase in population also enlarged internal potentials for businesses and professions, and some political leaders would begin to see advantage in such large, racially homogeneous blocs.

Given the great volume of migration, Whites could not completely prevent spatial expansion of these racial enclaves, but they were generally successful in limiting and shaping them. Overt racial zoning ordinances setting aside specific areas for Blacks and Whites were outlawed by the Supreme Court in 1917, but nine years later the Court upheld the use of restrictive covenants between property owners not to sell or rent to unwanted categories of people. It was estimated that 80 percent of Chicago housing became so covered, and the real estate board in that city (from which Black realtors were excluded), insisting that scattered sales to Blacks would result in "an unwarranted and unjustifiable destruction of real estate values," urged support of a policy that "each block shall be filled [with Negroes] and that further expansion shall be confined to contiguous blocks." Intense pressures for housing gave rise to "blockbusting," whereby some realtors specialized in gaining control of bordering properties, selling to a few Blacks, and fostering tension and conflicts to induce Whites to flee; thus ghetto expansion did tend to be contiguous, advancing along some narrow corridor bounded by railroads or other sorts of barriers. As a result, said Harold M. Rose in his defense of the controversial label "Black Ghetto," most Black Americans found themselves confined "to residential areas from which there is little chance to escape, . . . an enclave in which ultimately the only competitors for housing were members of a single race"—a reality powerfully reinforced by the credit policies of banks and the Federal Housing Administration.

In the dominant patterns of American life Blacks were "excluded from assimilation" and "imprisoned as a subordinate caste." Such imposed residential and social segregation was the reverse of the pressures and expectations placed on European immigrants, who were expected to give up group loyalties and assimilate as individuals into American society. In this special case group identity and exclusions required general recognition of distinct peoples in daily practice, categorizations in the census, and formal definitions in laws dealing with official discriminations. This deep-rooted American obsession with race was most commonly expressed in simple terms of "white" and "colored" or "Negro" as if such a distinction was readily recognizable; assignment to the subordinate caste was often spelled out in some form, such as "persons in whom there is a visible and distinct admixture of African blood" (as in an Arkansas statute). The long American history of "admixture" and White determination to penalize the persons resulting from it led to various quantitative generational measures defining "any person of African descent" as one having one-quarter, one-eighth, one-sixteenth, or (in a general Virginia law) "all persons in whom there is ascertainable any quantum whatever of Negro blood." Fearful, ruthless, capricious applications of such preposterous simplifications to the unsearchable complexities of human populations exacerbated all aspects of "the Negro Problem."

Southern White leaders were correct that race prejudice would "rise with the proportion of Negroes present in Northern communities," but their hope that this great interregional migration would thereby "lay the basis for a more unified national opinion on how to treat Negroes" was not fulfilled. In contrast to their comprehensive presence across much of the South, these new millions in the North were heavily concentrated in a few large cities, were only a very small presence in most others, and virtually absent from small towns and countrysides. Northerners readily discriminated against them whenever they thought they might "cause problems," but there were no formal Jim Crow laws, no elaborate patterns of deferential etiquette, no legal restrictions on voting (big city political machines often encouraged and used Black votes), no dual systems of public education. As the author of the most extensive study of this American situation concluded in 1942, "one of the most inclusive definitions of the South . . . is that based on legal segregation in schools"; whereas in sixteen Southern states and the District of Columbia all schools were required to be segregated, a racial basis for separation was specifically prohibited in thirteen Northern states (and three Western ones). Various options were permitted in several Border states, and even in the North, school boards under local pressure might adjust district boundaries or use other tactics to avoid or minimize integration, but the basic regional contrast in laws was stark (fig. 50). Thus "the color line in the North is not a part of the law or of the structure of buildings and so does not have the concreteness that it has in the South"—or, as a 1940 *Fortune* magazine report on regions put it: "the South begins in the Washington airport terminal where the signs on the two doors read 'MEN (White only)' and 'WOMEN (White only).'"

The growing numbers of Blacks in the North stimulated important changes in responses to White domination. A flurry of popular interest in Marcus Garvey's anti-assimilationist Black Nationalism quickly deflated as his extravagant Back-to-Africa program foundered, but it displayed the potentials of mass response to charismatic leadership. More enduring was the New Negro Movement of the 1920s emphasizing the existence of a distinct, vital, creative culture. White fascination with its most famous expressions in the Harlem Renaissance faded after 1929, but it left a permanent mark on American music, dance, and literature. Meanwhile churches, social organizations, and newspapers proliferated in the ghettos, and the first Black congressman since Reconstruction days was elected in Chicago. While the National Association for the Advancement of Colored People (NAACP,

---

50. Black Population and the Color Line.
The Greater South as defined by legal school segregation. Segregation of high schools was also allowed in Arizona if at least twenty-five Blacks were present and local voters approved; New Mexico, Indiana, and Maryland allowed separate schools if local boards of education so approved; Kansas authorized several urban boards to establish separate schooling (in some cases Whites in the morning and Blacks in the afternoon in the same facilities); in Wyoming the option to segregate if fifteen or more "colored children" were present was never exercised. Other formal or tacit segregation of children by "race" or some "otherness" (American Indian, Asian, Mexican) was allowed in various states.

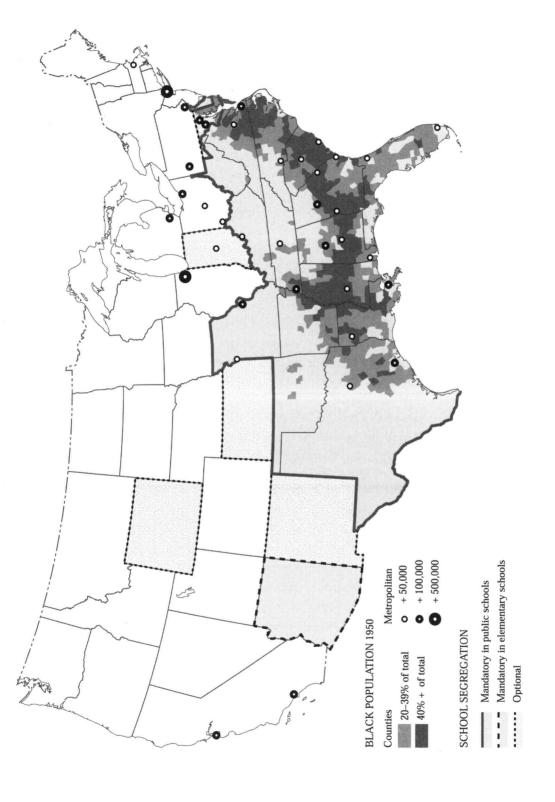

BLACK POPULATION 1950

Counties   Metropolitan

20–39% of total   ○   + 50,000

40% + of total   ◉   + 100,000

                  ◉   + 500,000

SCHOOL SEGREGATION

———   Mandatory in public schools

- - -   Mandatory in elementary schools

·····   Optional

founded in Springfield, Illinois, on the hundredth anniversary of Lincoln's birth, 1909), under joint Black and White leadership, expanded its legal challenges to discrimination, more militant protest organizations were also being formed.

Fundamental to this growing self-confidence was the scholarly assault upon the widespread White view of Blacks as "a caste of people . . . lacking a cultural past and assumed to be incapable of a cultural future." An "upsurge of nativist and racial ideologies and practices" in the 1920s helped provoke intensive critiques by anthropologists and sociologists of contemporary theories of racial inferiorities and distinctions; historians and social scientists undertook studies of Black societies in the Americas and Africa "to discover a cultural tradition for American Negroes" (*The Journal of Negro History* began in 1916; the Schomburg Center for Research in Black Culture was established in 1925 and became part of the New York City Public Library). This learned movement reached a culmination in *An American Dilemma*, a massive landmark study involving many Black and White scholars under the direction of and in the words of the Swedish social scientist Gunnar Myrdal (carefully selected by the funding Carnegie Corporation as a highly respected scholar from a country "with no background or tradition of imperialism which might lessen the confidence of the Negroes in the United States as to the complete impartiality of the study and the validity of its findings"). Completed in 1942, concluding that "the treatment of the Negro is America's greatest and most conspicuous scandal," and published "in the year of D-Day, the *Dilemma* helped secure a strategic beachhead in the battle for racial equality. Its influence would spread quickly and widely during the formative years of the Truman era."

Myrdal's major theme that White Supremacy contradicts the American Creed and thus, in the long run, that "the Negroes in their fight for equality have their allies in the white man's conscience," was given a great boost by World War II. However, it took a good deal of Black pressure to stir the White conscience. Serious threat of a massive "March on Washington" in 1941 resulted in a federal order against racial discrimination in employment of workers in defense industries and in the federal government, but the ruling had meager powers of enforcement. At the outset, the armed forces were completely segregated; Blacks were allowed only as servants in the Navy; none were admitted to the Marines, and none had as yet been accepted in the Army Air Force. Under mounting complaints and pressures all military services (including new women's corps) were opened to Blacks, but segregation and limitations continued; the general policy was that Blacks should constitute about "the same proportion . . . as in the general population of the country" (10 percent). The war provided new experiences for millions of Blacks as well as Whites, whether in military service or not, broadening outlooks, loosening old patterns, and, especially, blatantly displaying the great contradictions between Black status and American democratic ideals. As Wendell Wilkie, recent Republican presidential candidate, said to the NAACP, "our very proclamations of what we are fighting for have rendered our own inequities self-evident." In 1947 the United Nations Charter comprehensively affirmed basic human rights.

In postwar America Black impatience and expectations had been greatly heightened. Having long suffered under rulings from courthouses and state capitals, Blacks were "unanimous . . . for centralization": they looked to Washington for justice. In 1948 President Truman outlawed racial segregation in the American armed forces, and the Supreme Court ruled that anti-Black housing covenants were "unenforceable as law and contrary to public policy"—by midcentury important moves had been made, but there was a long way to go.

RELIGION AND ETHNICITY

A large literature of the time attests that the early 1950s—like the 1850s—was a period of "a great upsurge in church life," an unprecedented "pervasiveness of religious identification," a time when religion was "accepted as a normal part of the American Way of Life." The change was on display in the landscape: "We did not need the evidence of polls or church attendance to confirm what we could so easily observe—the walls of new churches rising in every town and countryside wherever we went," reported Barbara Ward, one of the many keen European commentators on the postwar American scene. Churches, and especially the remarkable variety of them, had long been of particular interest to foreign visitors. This "unprecedented rate" of construction could even be regarded as a special expression of "the country's architectural renaissance" as well as its ecclesiastical revitalization—most any traverse of the Upper Midwest would reveal the impress of "Swedish modern" in new Lutheran churches.

The "religious revival" observed by Ward and others was more than an obvious response to renewed prosperity and opportunity following fifteen years of depression and war; it was an important new era in institutional religious character. The tremendous "Americanizing" experience of World War II, a nation united in support of and widely participating in a righteous cause (one generally defined in broader humanitarian terms than the extreme chauvinism of World War I), resulted in a marked lessening of ethnic and religious animosities. The usual generational fading of immigrant ethnicity was accelerated (the national presence of such "foreign stock" had already been diminished by the severe restrictions on entry); the Roman Catholic Church ceased to be regarded as a "foreign" presence and was increasingly itself an ethnic "melting pot." The unspeakable horrors that destroyed the European roots of American Jewry made anti-Semitism no longer tolerable in public and much reduced in private life; the creation of the State of Israel gave Jews an unprecedented international presence; the role of refugees in the intensifications of American intellectual and artistic life was ever-more apparent (as in the New School for Social Research and Brandeis University)—these and many related matters accentuated an identity and pride in "Jewishness" and respect and acceptance by the general society. The American concept of assimilation never required a change of faith; indeed, it was now emphasized that it fully endorsed "the diversity or separateness of religious community" (even though it had long remained suspicious of other-than-Protestant faiths). Therefore, as a detailed study of Detroit concluded: "the successor to the ethnic subcommunity is the religious subcommunity, a group united by ties of race and religion."

For all kinds of Americans the upheavals of war, migrations, new jobs, new homes, suburbanization, and family formation led to a search for community, a need for "belonging" that led to "religious self-identification among the tripartite scheme of Protestant, Catholic, Jew" as the most common resolution. The emergence of this "triple melting pot" marked an important change in the structure of American society, another phase in its complex, unstable pluralism (as always, Blacks were essentially excluded from such common processes of integration). Will Herberg (whose book employing those three terms in the title was an influential analysis of this new era) also concluded that a considerable amount of this movement seems to have been driven by "sociability" and represented a thin "religiousness without religion." Wilbur Zelinsky, concurring that "this is a nation in which religious feeling tends to run shallow," emphasized that, nonetheless, "the sense of religious difference—as distinct from religious feeling *per se*—is a powerful and often highly emotional element in the minds of Americans that works to bind together or separate people." It was also apparent that major differences in religious beliefs and practices often correlated closely with important differences in social and political attitudes and behavior. Thus the varied regional patterns of those three broad categories of religion and of specific denominations (and groupings of types) became an important focus of geographic inquiry into this "structural pluralism"—with Zelinsky leading the way and soon followed by Edwin Scott Gaustad's *Historical Atlas of Religion in America*.

A 1952 inventory, *Churches and Church Membership in the United States*, published by the National Council of Churches, supplied the data for such mapping (the Bureau of the Census having suspended its controversial gathering of detailed statistics on the topic some years earlier). In spite of serious problems inherent in such surveys (such as different definitions of membership, uneven reliabilities of the numbers reported, and the failure of some denominations to respond; the most serious omission was the Black churches, which apparently did not compile comparable data), the denominational patterns summarized important national variations and regional distinctions built up over the course of American history (figs. 51, 52).

The one obvious religious region was that created by design under centralized religious authority in the Intermountain West. Mormondom was a genuine subna-

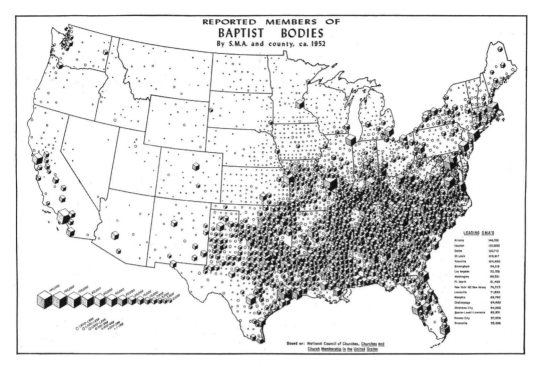

51. Baptist Members.
Baptist churches, the largest Protestant body, were nationwide, but much the heaviest concentration was almost coincident with usual definitions of the Greater South. Two special features deserve mention: Baptists come in many kinds and from different origins, and the Northern Baptists of New England and westward Yankeelands look back to Roger Williams and dissident Rhode Island and became quite distinct in organization and attitudes from their far more numerous Southern brethren; the density of Baptists in the South and in large Northern cities would be much greater if Black churches had been included in this enumeration. (Source: Zelinsky, "Approach to Religious Geography"; reproduced with permission of the Association of American Geographers)

tion, a dual society wherein all non-Mormons were designated by a special name—"Gentile"—though in no way segregated or subordinated. Even after a century of "outsider" penetration there were many towns and even entire counties with only the Mormon Church present. Only by shifting focus onto much smaller areas could a comparable homogeneity be brought into view elsewhere.

The most commonly recognized religious region, the "Bible Belt," was a very different kind: a conglomerate of many denominations that were assumed to share a general type of belief and expression. The pervasive presence of Baptist churches therein often sufficed to vindicate use of the term, but they were themselves a loose association of various kinds, White and Black, and the characteristic religiosity of

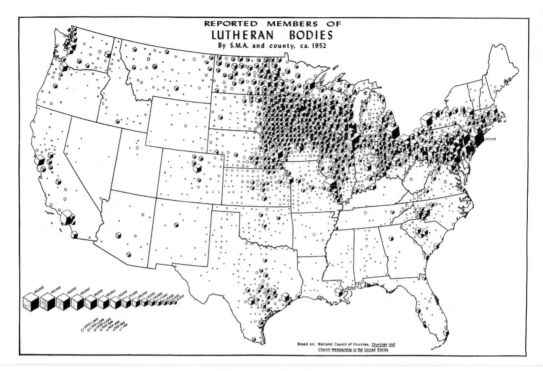

52. Lutheran Members.

This distinctly Northern church dates from German colonization in colonial Pennsylvania, later German immigrations spreading across the industrial belt and into Western farmlands, followed by German and Scandinavian domination of the Upper Midwest. Churches in the Far Western states stem mainly from Midwestern migrants; those in Texas from early immigrations; and the Carolina cluster from pioneers moving via the Great Valley from the Pennsylvania hearth. (Source: Zelinsky, "Approach to Religious Geography"; reproduced with the permission of the Association of American Geographers)

the region was shaped as well by various Fundamentalist, Adventist, and Pentecostal churches and sects (and, as R. Laurence Moore has cautioned, no matter how one defines such groups, "one risks joining together in Christian fellowship a lot of people who would prefer to remain apart").

In the realm of religion as in so much else, the Northeast, and especially the Core area, held the greatest concentration of the great variety of American churches; Roman Catholics and all of the main Protestant denominations were an important presence over all this region, as were Jews in every city (figs. 53, 54), Black churches in many of the larger ones, and various other faiths, lesser in size but distinctive in kind, such as Friends (Quakers), Unitarian, Mennonite, Nazarene, Polish National Catholic, and various ethnic Orthodox churches, were strong in selected districts. Here religion, ethnicity, class, and family were interlocked most

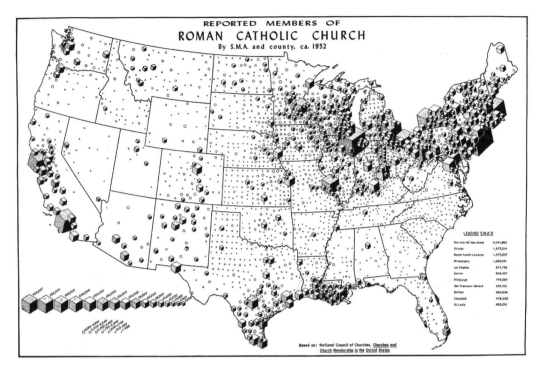

53. Roman Catholic Members.
Roman Catholics accounted for 40 percent of the total church population recorded in the 1952 survey (the scale showing membership is therefore markedly different from the other three maps shown here). Although a nationwide presence, the church clearly shows its immigrant and imperial origins, with the heaviest concentrations in the Manufacturing Belt and in French Louisiana and former Mexican lands (although large numbers in the Hispanic borderlands stemmed from recent immigrations). The thinness across the South of this largest of religious bodies is especially apparent. (Source: Zelinsky, "Approach to Religious Geography"; reproduced with permission of the Association of American Geographers)

complexly and visibly in America, and here, therefore, was where the emergence of the "triple melting pot" was identified and—insofar as it was an accurate assessment—had the most significance in reshaping American life.

Aside from the conspicuous exception of Mormonland, the Far West was an area of both considerable religious diversity and the least in church membership. Both features reflected the continuing influx of migrants from all parts of the country: on one hand, newcomers reestablishing links with the familiar church of their native ground; on the other, drifting free of old ties. The latter group became targets of new movements and sects that had become a famous feature of Southern California. Such innovations were, of course, far from new in the United States; the amazing plethora of religions (the 1953 *Yearbook of American Churches* listed 251 de-

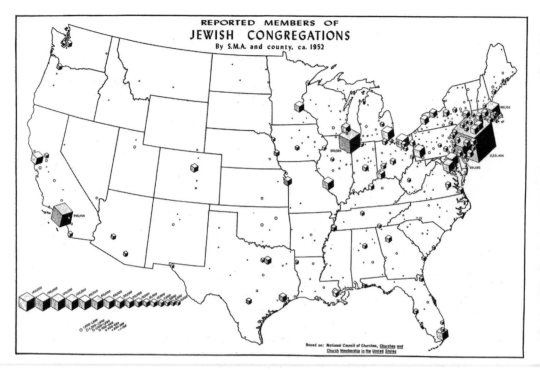

54. Jewish Congregations.

The heavy concentration of Jews in Megalopolis is strikingly apparent. They accounted for a third of the total religious membership reported for the New York–Northern New Jersey Metropolitan Area (and almost as high a proportion in their Florida outlier in Miami). Their extension westward to other cities in the Core was initiated as part of early German migration routes. The recent influx into Los Angeles overshadows the early prominence of San Francisco on the Pacific Coast. (Source: Zelinsky, "Approach to Religious Geography"; reproduced with permission of the Association of American Geographers)

nominations) was the product of what had long been "a free market religious environment that exposed religious organizations to relentless competition," as well as of several centuries of highly varied immigrations.

Our reconnaissance has reflected concern with the ongoing shaping of America rather than an attempt to define a formal comprehensive set of regions. Our focus has been on selected areas of special power, influence, contrast, contention, or change with reference to an overall national structure and system. Thus we began with the *Core*, by definition the dominant region, the most heavily populated and complexly developed, the focus and seat of authority over national systems and most important source of influence upon American culture. All the rest of the contiguous United States was the American *Domain*; that is, an area firmly integrated into national systems and fully American in general character, but subordinate in power, lesser in development, and differentiated into an array of variously distinct regions.

A simple outline of these many areas on the map displays a pattern that was essentially formed by 1915 (fig. 55). More difficult to depict are the different degrees of regional distinctiveness, the sharpness of some boundaries, and the vagueness of others—the great unevenness in the sociopolitical surface of the nation. A comparison of the western and southern boundaries of the American Core offers an illustrative contrast. A modest kind of distinction between regions was the lessening of density and complexity of settlement and economy westward from the rather arbitrary margins of the Core into the increasingly rural and agricultural Middle West, where countrysides and the thinner pattern of cities contained many of the same peoples and extended the same patterns of political culture as those in the more urban-industrialized Middle West. In sharp contrast, the southern boundary of the Core touched upon the most important cultural borderland within the nation; the state boundaries traced through that zone marked a formal separation in social laws and practice between the dominant North and a resisting South, a self-proclaimed subnation resolute in sustaining its own deep-rooted version of an American way of life. This vast folk province contained important socioeconomic subdivisions as well as a culturally distinct French Louisiana and the increasingly Northern exclave of Peninsular Florida. The strident Texan sense of identity based upon unique geopolitical origins and its self-directed expansive development and dominion over a large area support recognition of the state itself amid other regional patterns. The Far West remained a regional set of Wests greatly varied in distinctiveness and significance in the American mosaic, with Mormondom the most sharply defined.

California was much the most famous and vivid West, but here state and region were not at all concordant. For Americans the name had always referred to the Eden beyond the mountains, and in the twentieth century the image and attraction were mainly confined to Coastal California, where two quite unlike metropolitan areas now competed in national importance.

While those regional distinctions were clearly "one of the massive facts about America," Max Lerner also cautioned that "it is possible, of course, to overestimate the importance and endurance of regional differences. American change moves at two levels, and by two clocks, the one being changes common to the nation, the other those peculiar to the region and locality." Although our geographic perspective has focused on endurances and changes at the regional level, it is nonetheless certain that in the aftermath of World War II a surging nationalism had further submerged regionalism and ethnic and religious particularities. "The United States is a nation and the most nationally conscious of all nations," exclaimed André

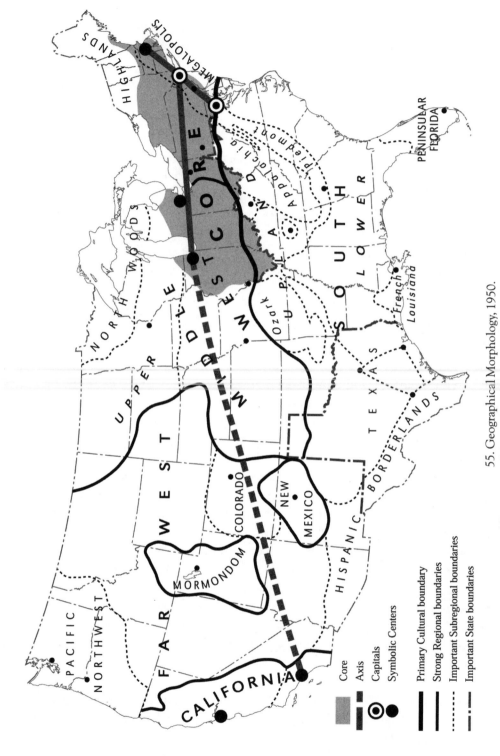

55. Geographical Morphology, 1950.
(Core area as delimited by Ullman, "Regional Development")

Core
Axis
Capitals
Symbolic Centers

Primary Cultural boundary
Strong Regional boundaries
Important Subregional boundaries
Important State boundaries

PENINSULAR FLORIDA

HIGHLANDS

MEGALOPOLIS

CANADA

Piedmont

Appalachia

SOUTH

LOWER

French
Louisiana

NORTH WOODS

UPPER

Ozark

MIDDLE WEST

TEXAS

HISPANIC BORDERLANDS

COLORADO

NEW MEXICO

MORMONDOM

FAR WEST

PACIFIC NORTHWEST

CALIFORNIA

Siegfried in the conclusion of his latest assessment of the country, *America at Mid-Century*. He was referring primarily not to the hyperconsciousness of a people who had participated together so successfully in a great war but to "the material uniformity" and "the high degree of standardization" of the much-vaunted "American Way of Life," and to the fact that "this monotony is not only accepted but even highly esteemed." Such widespread evidence and common attitudes reflected the remarkable assimilation of a great variety of peoples on a continental scale and confirmed that "the American nation can thus be considered a single entity."

If all this seemed remarkable even to a European long familiar with the United States, it was likely simply taken for granted by most Americans. It was a uniformity made possible by ever-greater efficiencies of an ever-expanding infrastructure of this neotechnic age and made especially effectual by the movements and migrations of millions of ordinary Americans. Such features were a huge compelling exhibit of the crucial importance of the mobilization of populations into core areas, growth of cities, the "lift-pump" effect of investment in and integration of a succession of areas and peoples, and related processes in knitting a whole populace "together in an ever greater network of communications and complementarity" being emphasized at this time by new theoreticians of nation building.

Frank Thistlethwaite, a well-informed Englishman immersed in interpreting American development and character to British students, concluded that "the American variant of western society is a new thing, which I have attempted to define as 'the mobile society.'" Writing at midcentury, he added that despite an apparent end to some important features that had shaped America (such as colonization and immigration), "the United States has continued to develop with astonishing velocity"—and, indeed, as we have already shown with respect to some selected features, it was at that very time showing signs of acceleration.

5. Altering the Federation and Internal Empire

In 1912 the basic shape of the Federal Republic seemed at last to be complete. With the admission of New Mexico and Arizona in that year, thirty-five new states had been added to the original thirteen, and the solid block of forty-eight member units filled out the transcontinental areal framework that had become established fifty-nine years earlier with the Gadsden Purchase; a world-famous geographical form had become indelibly impressed upon perceptions of the United States. It would be nearly half a century before two noncontiguous units would be added to the federation—and probably much longer than that before common perceptions of the new shape of the nation would take hold.

As has been recurrently apparent in this continuous shaping of America, the addition of a new state, altering the distribution of representative power in the na-

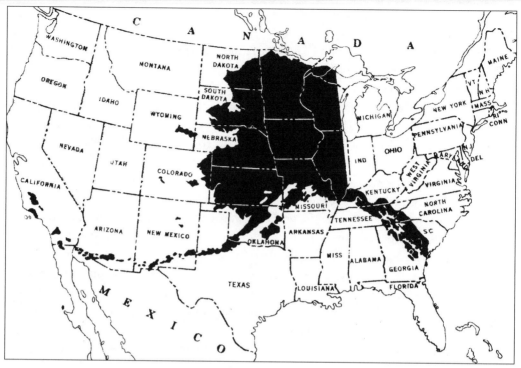

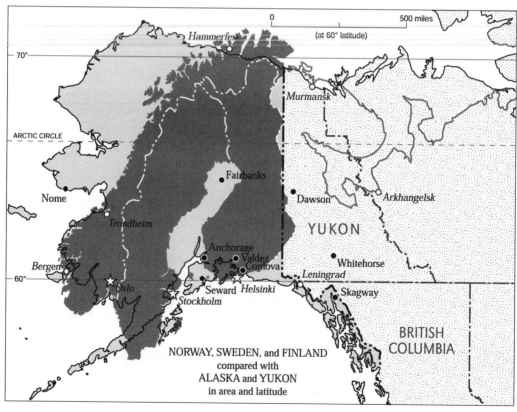

NORWAY, SWEDEN, and FINLAND
compared with
ALASKA and YUKON
in area and latitude

tional congress, is always an important and controversial topic, usually generating divisive factions within the aspiring territory as well as within the national body, and often becomes a process of many years before completion. The cases of Alaska and Hawaii were not uncommon in this general sense: serious local agitations for statehood began in the 1920s, received little congressional or national interest until after World War II, and were not effectuated until 1959. Aside from this timing and being the first noncontiguous applicants, these incipient states were strikingly different from each other in character and the specific issues involved. A review of both states and a brief look at another potential candidate will be followed by a shift in focus to a different scale to consider important changes in the formal geopolitical relations of a great array of peoples and territories long embedded within the structure of the federation and empire.

ALASKA

Long after the United States purchased this vast distant northwest corner of the continent, Alaska remained an imperial holding meager in population and development and of little sustained popular or governmental interest. It did not become a formally incorporated Territory until 1912, at a time when the population was declining after the sudden brief influx from the "Alaska Gold Rush" (the Klondike was in Canadian territory, but there were smaller rushes to Nome and elsewhere). The 1920 census recorded a total of 55,000, half of whom were Native Americans thinly spread over much of the area; almost all of the 27,000 remainder were clustered in a few small footholds. Proponents inevitably touted Alaska as the Last Frontier needing only the right kind of people—"those possessing the vision, spirit and virility of our pioneer forefathers" to develop its vast resources—to make it America's Scandinavia (fig. 56). "If the Finns owned Alaska," said Warren G. Harding, "they would in three generations make it one of the foremost states of the Union." But the Finns had worked for many generations with the only land they had, and the Baltic gave them ready access to the biggest European markets, whereas Americans were still busy exploiting and developing their immense transcontinental expanse, and Alaska was as yet far too remote, difficult, and ex-

56. Alaska and Two Common Comparisons.
The simple Scandinavian overlay does not show the critical contrast in ocean currents: in the North Atlantic warmth from the Gulf Stream bathes the entire Norwegian coast, providing year-round open water as far as Hammerfest and Murmansk; whereas in the North Pacific the Kuroshio (Japanese) Current provides only an eddy of warm water along southern Alaska, leaving the western and northern coasts subject to Arctic cold and ice. The overlay showing the size and extent of Alaska compared with the forty-eight states is from Van Zandt, *Boundaries of the United States*

pensive. General federal policy was to establish large reserves of forest and mineral lands to await future initiatives. The one great resource readily exploitable was the fishery, chiefly salmon, but it was a seasonal activity conducted very largely by fleets based in Seattle and with only modest impact on the mainland.

President Harding had gone to Alaska to drive the golden spike of the 470-mile Alaska Railroad that the federal government had completed between Seward and Fairbanks. He was the first president to visit the Territory, and upon his return to Seattle he spoke of its great potentials and remarked that "in a very few years we can set off the Panhandle and a large block of the connecting southeastern part as a State." Harding died a week later, but local support for a partition and a request to Congress to create a Territory of South Alaska were soon under way. This narrow strip along the rugged glaciated edge of the continent contained the deep-channeled, island-studded waterway to Juneau, the territorial capital, and on up a long fjord to Skagway, which had railroad connection to the upper Yukon. A northern sector of the Northwest Rainforest, this mildest and most accessible region, contained more than 40 percent of the White population of Alaska. The House Committee on Territories held hearings and soon ruled against partition or any prospect of statehood at this time; President Coolidge declared that the cost of administering the Territory was "so far out of proportion to the number of inhabitants" as to require reductions and simplifications in federal oversight.

Noncontiguity—the more than 500 miles from the State of Washington to the nearest corner of Alaska, the three days to travel the thousand miles by steamship between Seattle and Juneau—was an unavoidable issue for statehood proponents and a chronic problem for residents and businesses. Alaskans regarded themselves, with good reason, as victims of the Jones Act of 1920. This legislation required all sea traffic between domestic ports to be carried in U.S. vessels; service to U.S. Territories was exempt—*except* for Alaska. In the States competition by sea and by rail kept rates low; in Alaska, with limited and highly seasonal traffic, no land connection and often in most places with a single company offering service, shipping costs were unusually high. The telegraph and telephone system and radio network were operated by the Army Signal Corps from a Seattle base; all mail moved through that same port. Alaska was, in effect, an "overseas territory," and its dependence upon Seattle for all shipping, supplies, and services, together with its "vassalage" under federal control of its lands and its very limited government kept the statehood issue alive even if not always vigorous. For a brief time the Matanuska Colony excited considerable interest nationwide but became controversial in Alaska as an imposition in concept and colonists from "Outside." It was also an expensive project, and a congressional report in 1937 concluded that "an appraisal of the national interests indicates that there is no clear need to speed the development of Alaska."

Meanwhile other means of improving and diversifying its links with the States were being pursued. Alaska got a quick start into the Air Age with intrepid bush pilots providing contact with a wide scattering of settlements. By the mid-1930s regular mail and some passenger service were established internally, but an external link was not in place until Pan American began its Seattle-Ketchikan-Juneau flights in June 1940, thereby reducing the time between the territorial capital and the outside world from three days to seven hours.

The idea of a highway to Alaska gathered increasing attention during the 1930s, first as a relief project, later from growing concerns about Japanese aggression. Any such American proposal, however, ran into deep Canadian fears of "penetration" and "domination." In 1937 President Roosevelt discussed the idea with Prime Minister Mackenzie King, and each country created a special highway commission to negotiate a plan (fig. 57). In a letter to his secretary of State, Roosevelt noted he did not approve of a suggestion "that Skagway be ceded to Canada" as an inducement of their participation, "but I believe that the ends which the Canadians seek, namely an outlet to the sea in northwestern Canada, might be secured by making Skagway a free port." (Canada had tried but failed to achieve its own port in the boundary arbitration of 1903.) These two national commissions identified possible routes but could not agree on which was best; moreover, the Canadians saw little need for such an expensive undertaking and continued to be wary of American involvement, while American proponents were dismayed by their own War Department's repeated declarations that "the military value of the proposed Alaska Highway is so slight as to be negligible."

In 1940, however, with Canada already in the war, the United States decided to join with Canada's Northwest Staging Route program to create a chain of airfields from north of Edmonton to the Yukon and Alaska. After Pearl Harbor, U.S. Army Engineers undertook to complete "a minimum road at the earliest practicable date" from the Canadian railhead at Dawson Creek along a route linking these new air bases and connecting with an existing road in Alaska leading to Fairbanks. Opened in November 1942, this crude Alaska Highway did not follow exactly any of the routes that had been proposed by various interests. The military choice was well inland in a corridor of better flying weather than the others and connected through Edmonton with railroad links to Middle Western industrial and supply centers. Most of the wartime cargo was in support of the chain of airfields, which supported the military in Alaska and the shuttling of nearly 8,000 warplanes to the Soviet Union. After 1943, with the Japanese threat fading, this gravel road received minimal maintenance, and in 1946 the Canadian sector was, as planned, turned over to the Canadian army. Little improvement of the road or service facilities was made until the 1960s.

The war had an immense and quite unanticipated impact on Alaska. Although in 1934 the famous air power advocate, Brigadier General William Mitchell, had

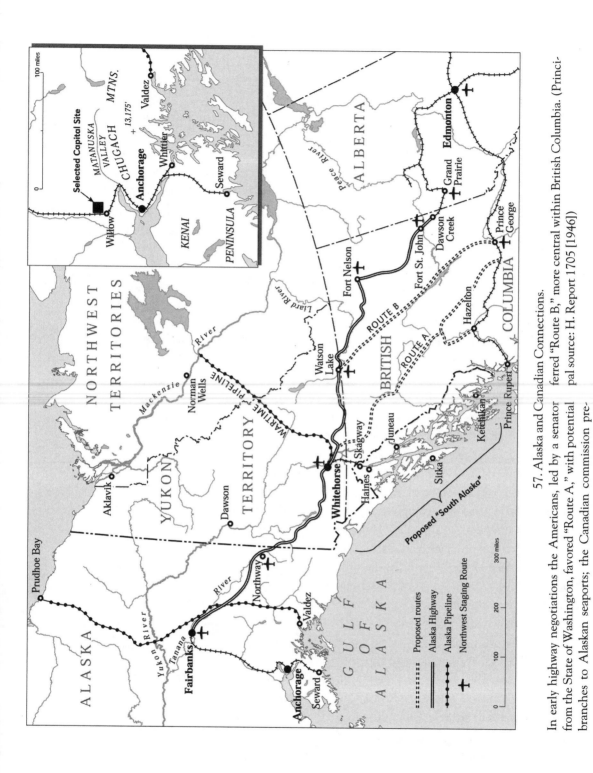

57. Alaska and Canadian Connections.

In early highway negotiations the Americans, led by a senator from the State of Washington, favored "Route A," with potential branches to Alaskan seaports; the Canadian commission pre-ferred "Route B," more central within British Columbia. (Princi-pal source: H. Report 1705 [1946]) argued that Alaska had become "the most important strategic place in the world," his superiors did not agree, and Congress provided few funds for military bases of any kind. In 1940 the armed forces in Alaska totaled fewer than 1,000; in 1942, subsequent to a Japanese air raid and invasion of the Aleutians, they had swollen to 150,000. Rapid reductions toward the end of the war were soon reversed because of the emergence of the Cold War and the Korean conflict. Similarly, the large wartime legacy of new docks, airfields, roads, housing, and other facilities was soon augmented by a new wave of military investment in what was now called America's "first line of defense." Major airlines offered service not only from Seattle to several Alaskan cities but from Chicago to Anchorage and on to Japan (a Great Circle route first explored by Charles Lindbergh in 1931). Between 1940 and 1960 the total population more than tripled to 226,000; in addition to the 150,000 non-Native Alaskans there were 32,000 military in residence. The geography of population had been drastically reshaped: a third of the civilians were now concentrated in and around Anchorage, and well over half lived in Anchorage or Fairbanks; the 35,000 in the Panhandle—"South Alaska"—represented only 15 percent of the total.

These changes in populations and perceptions of Alaska's strategic position invigorated the statehood movement. Not all Alaskans supported a change in status. Many warned that state operations would require much heavier taxes; some feared that expanding development would destroy the very attractions that had lured them to Alaska. But most business and political leaders were avid supporters. Calling for an end to the "second-class citizenship" of this "stepchild of the American family," Governor Ernest Gruening insisted that Alaska constituted not only a new West and "the last frontier," its "unique geographical position—the only part of the country which extends westward into the Eastern Hemisphere and northward far beyond the Arctic Circle" made it of crucial importance to America's new relationships with Asia, the Pacific, and "the great airways of the future." He called for an end to "American colonialism," taking his definition of it from a college textbook: "a geographic area held for political, strategic, and economic advantage" of the colonial power "—precisely what the Territory of Alaska is."

Federal and congressional responses were mixed. Noncontiguity, the small population so unevenly spaced over so large an area, and the whole territory so heavily dependent on federal expenditures were serious concerns. Control of public lands became a major controversy. The federal government regarded itself as the proper custodian of these vast tracts until they were needed for appropriate development; statehood proponents insisted that distant and disinterested bureaucratic control had long been a major impediment to development and that Alaska had never received proper allocation of lands in support of roads, schools, and other public services. The idea of partition kept cropping up in various Washington responses:

carve a state out of the more populous southeast and central regions and set aside most of the west and north as a territory. The Eisenhower administration indicated its support of some such separation, especially because "Alaska's strategic importance required full freedom of federal action" in those northern regions. Throughout these postwar discussions, salmon, mining, and transport companies, and the Seattle Chamber of Commerce lobbied intensely against statehood.

President Truman favored the admission of Alaska and Hawaii whenever their citizens decided they were ready. In 1950 the House passed an Alaska statehood bill, but the Senate took no action. As had often been the case with other applicants, the prospect of two additional senators impinged upon the relative power of national parties, an issue further complicated in the 1950s by civil rights pressures on Southern senators (most of whom consistently voted against Alaska). A 1955 bill for joint admission of Alaska and Hawaii (the first expected to be Democratic, the second Republican) was not successful. After the 1956 elections new proposals, further compromises on public lands and defense concerns, and, for the first time, the endorsement of President Eisenhower, brought approval in both houses in 1958, and after a strong favorable vote in a required local referendum, Alaska became the forty-ninth state in January 1959.

This new formal part of the "continental United States" (as the statehood bill defined it) was much the largest in size (586,000 square miles compared to Texas' 267,000) but the smallest in population (226,000 compared with Nevada's 285,000 in 1960), and its "lack of self-sustaining basic economic activity" was the "dominant characteristic" facing its leaders; in 1959, 27 percent of the workforce were federal employees. The capital remained at Juneau, but Anchorage interests mounted a strong campaign to move it. That effort was interrupted in 1964 by an earthquake (the strongest ever recorded in North America) that devastated the Anchorage area, but ten years later voters approved a referendum to move it to a more central location—but not within thirty miles of Anchorage or Fairbanks. The Selection Committee nominated three sites along the narrow Rail Belt connecting those two cities, and in 1976 voters chose a block of land near Willow, seventy miles north of Anchorage (fig. 57, inset). However, voters have subsequently rejected financing the huge costs of the project, and the capital remains where it has been since 1906.

Evidence of oil in Alaska was widespread and long known. A few small fields along the Gulf of Alaska coast were tapped early, and in 1923 a large Naval Petroleum Reserve was set aside where seepages were apparent along the Arctic. A promising discovery on the Kenai Peninsula in 1957 brought a small boom at statehood time, but the limited Alaskan market and severe competition elsewhere were serious handicaps. The transforming event was the discovery at Prudhoe Bay of the

largest oil deposit ever found in North America. However, the costs, and the problems and controversies about its development were formidable: the dangers of a
pipeline across ecologically fragile tundra and unstable mountains (Valdez, the
eventual terminal, was a new town on a new site following destruction by the 1964
earthquake); the hazards of huge oil spills, especially along a rugged coast rich in sea
life; competing routes (across Canada to the main U.S. markets?); unresolved
Native land claims. Years of delay came to a sudden end in late 1973 amid the
worldwide oil crisis resulting from the huge increase in prices imposed by the Organization of Petroleum Exporting Countries (OPEC). An 800-mile pipeline from
Prudhoe Bay to Valdez was completed in 1977 and the Great Euphoria began.

Suddenly awash in funds, the Alaskan government abolished or reduced taxes,
began an annual payment to each resident, and offered various subsidies for housing, businesses, local governments, schools, and construction projects. Oil revenues made up more than 80 percent of state government funds, and state spending
accounted for about a third of all jobs. The Great Boom collapsed in the mid-1980s
amid a national oil glut and low prices (by federal law Alaska oil could be marketed
only in the United States). Economic recession and exodus followed. It had taken
22,000 workers to build the pipeline, but more permanent additions to industrial
employment were limited. During the 1980s, 448,000 migrants came to Alaska, but
420,000 residents departed during those same years. The 1990 census reported
550,000, a doubling in thirty years of statehood and surpassing that of Wyoming,
now the least populous state. There had been no great change in pattern; 40 percent lived in Anchorage.

Alaska remains a highly distinctive place and part of the Union. In its still strong
sense of colonial status it resembles some of the earlier states of the Far West: an assertively individualistic, independent stance harshly critical of federal control over
much of its land and resources yet heavily dependent upon federal installations and
expenditures; a "tenuous and volatile economy subject to uncontrollable and dimly
understood external forces" and, as in all those states today, a citizenry deeply torn
between those wanting more development and those hoping to fend it off for fear of
losing something magnificent and irreplaceable. But Alaska is something other
than just the newest Western state. It remains distant and detached and above all
Northern—"no other state extracts such a high price in isolation and discomfort
from its residents," and in no other is there such a strong sense of permanent residents and "outsiders." With such a heavily transient population (much of it built
into the normal economy—seasonal workers, the military, federal employees), attempts to discriminate in state benefits by years of residence have been passed but
overturned by courts. Finally, in no other state does the Native American population represent such a large proportion of the total (16 percent—it, too, doubling,

to 86,000, in thirty years), occupy such a large proportion of territory, and play such an important role in the life of the state.

Hawaii presents a special paradox in some fundamentals impinging upon movements toward statehood: a century-long prelude of relentless "Americanization," yet over much of that time a population increasingly "alien," indeed, widely considered to be inherently or defiantly "unAmerican." The very existence of such a paradox obviously depended upon perceptions among those most involved, locally and nationally, in decisions relating to admission; the tensions arising from this contradictory combination would be powerfully affected by larger events during the sixty years of actual U.S. possession of these islands before statehood.

The abrupt annexation of the Hawaiian Islands during the Spanish-American War consummated what the *haole* (this term for foreigner had become commonly narrowed to refer to Euro-Americans) oligarchy had sought following its recent seizure of control of the government from the Hawaiian queen. A significant number of American leaders had been highly critical of that local takeover and of American imperial expansion in the Pacific. When the islands were formally defined in 1900 as an "incorporated territory," attempts to specify that no promise of eventual statehood was implied in such a designation were defeated, and within a few years a series of court cases ruled that such a territory was an "integral part of the United States" and therefore, technically, might become a state after a period of pupilage. However, the more obvious fact, then and for long thereafter, was that Hawaii was an imperial holding, a tropical plantation colony based on sugar and pineapples and imported labor. The haoles completely dominated the economic and political life of the territory but in 1930 were no more than about 7 percent of the resident population (excluding military personnel on temporary assignment). The Native Hawaiians (full or part) who had lost their kingdom and most of their land were about 14 percent, and the succession of imported plantation laborers and their descendants—Chinese, Japanese, Portuguese, Spanish, Puerto Rican, Korean, Filipino—constituted the rest. By the 1920s the Japanese, numbering well over 100,000, were much the largest group. Hawaii, therefore, seemed more akin to a tropical colony like, say, Trinidad or Fiji than an "inchoate state" (as the courts had sometimes called it).

For thirty-five years its initial elementary status was undisturbed. The ruling oligarchy (commonly called the Big Five, referring to the companies controlling plantations, shipping, banking, and other modern services) was content with an appointed governor, minimal interference, and occasional crucial support (such as special immigration legislation allowing importation of Filipino laborers). The national government focused on Hawaii as a strategic outpost, triangulated with the Panama Canal and California coast, and (after completing dredging and docks at Pearl Harbor) the oceanic anchor of the long, thin American line across the Pacific. The one great feature shared by the oligarchy and Washington was concern over the diversity and numbers of the various peoples on these islands. Anti-annexationists had warned that "no candid American would ever think of making a State of this Union out of such a group of islands with such a population as it has or is likely to have," and political leaders on the mainland as well as on the islands long agreed. The xenophobia of World War I and Japanese expansionism in East Asia and the western Pacific accentuated the antipathy toward "Orientals" and suspicion of the loyalty of Japanese on the islands.

The first statehood movement emerged in the aftermath of the Sugar Act of 1934. That legislation, in the midst of the world depression, reduced the Hawaiian quota of the U.S. market by 10 percent and increased that of rival mainland producers. The failure of the nonvoting territorial delegation and its allies to counter the power of Louisiana, Florida, and the sugar beet states convinced some of the Hawaiian leadership that statehood would provide better protection for their highly vulnerable economy. In congressional hearings that followed, proponents pointed to a territorial period of thirty-five years, a population greater than that of four existing states (Nevada, Delaware, Wyoming, Vermont), and an economy that contributed more in federal taxes than paid by fifteen states. Beyond the obvious concern over noncontiguity, opponents had only to point to population categories—64 percent "Oriental" in the 1930 census—and warn of the dangers of ethnic bloc-voting and the potential electoral power of the Japanese plurality. Both sides might agree that the most critical issue was "Americanization," but they disagreed on just what it meant and what had been achieved. In 1935 the House committee concluded that "it would be wiser to wait until another generation of American citizens of Oriental ancestry . . . had an opportunity to absorb American ideals and training."

Americanization had been going on for a long time. Churches, schools, language, laws of property, and constitutional government had dramatically reshaped Native Hawaiian society. Hawaiians had protested annexation without their consent, but by then they were only a quarter of the population. Some continued to adapt to American ways (they were much intermixed with Whites and were a majority in the early Territorial legislature); others did their best to continue "the old fish and poi economy" in a scattering of rural havens of "refuge." In general, the haoles and Hawaiians agreed in their distrust of the Asian population. The Chinese, first in the sequence of laborers, had soon left the plantations and now dominated small businesses across the islands. The Japanese seemed to pose the greatest problem. They were widely assumed to be unassimilable, a self-enclosed society reinforced by local Japanese newspapers and radio, and especially by after-hours Japanese-language schools, staffed mostly by teachers from Japan. However, the proportion of *nisei* (American-born and therefore citizens) was rapidly rising, and many were leaving the plantations for Honolulu and urban life. The public school system was a major instrument of Americanization (the haole elite had long been served by good private schools), and by 1930 the Japanese were a majority in Honolulu schools (highly regarded and influential McKinley High School became known—with pride or alarm—as "Tokyo High"). A set of English Standard grammar schools, open only to those passing an examination in the use of English, was begun in 1924. Initiated more as a covert means of racial and class segregation by excluding those who knew only "pidgin English" (a Hawaiian creole widely used by Asians), by 1940, 20 percent of the students were Asian.

From 1936 on Japan's aggression against China cast a darkening shadow over prospects for Hawaii statehood; the attack upon Pearl Harbor seemed to black them out completely. The senior general proclaimed martial law. Hysterical cries to expel or confine all Japanese (as was done on the western mainland) quickly collapsed under the impracticalities of removing more than a third of the population and critical labor force. However, civil rights were suspended for all residents, newspapers censored or suppressed, workers restricted from leaving plantations without a permit or from changing jobs without a release from their employer; the search for subversives was intense. Japanese members of the local National Guard were sent to Wisconsin as the cadre for a provisional nisei battalion. In 1943 a new all-Japanese unit was authorized, quickly oversubscribed by volunteers, and became the 442d Regiment famous for its heroics and medals in the Italian campaign. Military government of Hawaii was ended in October 1944. The national administration defended its use in such an emergency in a vulnerable territory; the Supreme Court later declared it to have been unconstitutional.

The war changed the whole context of Hawaii and its relations with the nation. The response of the Japanese as soldiers and citizens left no doubt about allegiances. "No member of Hawaii's Japanese community was ever found guilty of collaborating with the enemy during the Pacific war," and the great majority "strove self-consciously to demonstrate their Americanization and commitment." Japan's surrender and peaceful acceptance of American occupation completely altered the larger international context. The experiences of military government by residents and of military service by soldiers convinced Japanese, Chinese, and others that equality as a state was the only hope of achieving genuine democracy and equality of opportunity, and their leaders were now determined to assert their power in postwar politics. Many haoles agreed with the general objective, statehood was also endorsed by the Truman administration and such famous military leaders as Admiral

Chester Nimitz and General Douglas MacArthur, and Hawaii was now far more visible to and appreciated by the American public. Thus "Hawaii emerged from World War II more confident of its Americanization, more prominent in American politics, more convinced of the need for immediate statehood, and more united in the conviction that admission was not only appropriate but imminent." Island and mainland polls supported that hope.

Proponents could cite these many changes and endorsements as well as the national embarrassment of having the United Nations classify Hawaii as a "non-self-governing territory," yet it took twelve more years to win Senate approval. The principal obstacle to statehood was not simply the addition of two senators from an outlying area, but the persistent resistance of a solid bloc of Southern senators to representation from a largely non-White society. This issue was compounded by renewed fears of subversion, especially after a long, bitter maritime strike by "communist-led" unions (largely Japanese in membership on the islands) that had disrupted the postwar economy, and accompanying lurid publicity that fueled further congressional and newspaper opposition to admitting these "polyglot people," this "Oriental" place. Meanwhile, the rapid rise in political participation by Asians in Hawaii strengthened local hesitations about statehood, especially among new residents from the mainland as well as the old elite. President Eisenhower had initially endorsed statehood for Hawaii (employing a common political euphemism: here "East meets West" and the results "display a unique example of a community that is a successful laboratory in human brotherhood"), but the margins of party control in both houses of Congress were so thin as to inhibit change. Not until the late 1950s, when it became clear that the Southern bloc could no longer suppress even a weak civil rights bill and after the Democrats had won a huge majority, did congressional opposition to new states fade. On April 21, 1959, Hawaii became the fiftieth state and sent to Washington its two senators (one White and one Chinese) and single representative (Japanese).

The delay in admission brought a considerably more "Americanized" and connected Hawaii into the Federation. At the time, James Michener stated, "Hawaii is by far the most advanced state culturally that has ever been admitted to the Union." He was referring to the schools, university, churches, libraries, museums, symphony, and the like (admitting that much of it had been created by old haole wealth). His statement might have been broadened to include American consumer culture, for there had been a postwar flurry of mainland investment in hotels and other businesses. The single air connection provided by Pan American had been augmented by two more major airlines providing links with Los Angeles, San Francisco, Portland, and Seattle, and far more traffic in both directions (before the war few Hawaiians had traveled to the States). The agricultural export economy was still important but was now surpassed by the defense industry, which employed 25 percent of the workforce; tourism had grown but was well below these leading activities.

The population of 633,000 (larger than seven other states) reflected a strong upsurge during the 1950s. The number of Whites was now equal to that of the Japanese, each about a third of the total; altogether the Asian population was just over 50 percent, but the usual categories were ever-more blurred, with an estimated third of marriages crossing commonly assumed racial lines. If it was a society widely acculturated to mainland ways, it also remained strongly pluralistic in structure, with family life still segmented along ethnic lines. It was also ever-more concentrated on one island: Oahu, with only 9 percent of the land, contained nearly 80 percent of the population. The outer islands had been losing population for thirty years, a movement accelerated by increasing mechanization on plantations and expanding employment opportunities on Oahu. Honolulu, with over 300,000 in 1960, was the single big city; and it was not technically a separate entity within the island, for Hawaii was divided into four counties and has "no incorporated villages, towns, or cities." As Zachary Smith and Richard Pratt emphasize, Hawaii "has the most centralized system of governance of any American state" (including a single, centralized system of 225 schools). "It is the only state in which the institutions of governance" have "evolved downward from a centralized authority rather than—with classic American reluctance—upward from local jurisdictions." That concentration originated in the long dominant role of a small oligarchy, together with the limited need for local government in a plantation society where basic services were supplied by the company on each estate. In this case, centralization is reinforced by the more limited and marginal locations of cultivable land on the other volcanic islands and by the efficiency of a single focus on the best port for trunkline traffic.

Within a few years this new state would be transformed more quickly and fully than any other by technology and policies originating entirely beyond its borders. In 1959 the first jet passenger plane landed, cutting the ten- to eleven-hour travel time from San Francisco in half. In 1960 about 250,000 tourists visited, nearly five times the total in 1952. In 1964 Japan lifted restrictions on overseas pleasure travel, Hawaii quickly became a favorite destination, and Hawaii's annual tourist population soon exceeded the resident population. In 1970 jumbo jets appeared and the really mass tourism era began; eight years later domestic airline fares were deregulated, and soon nonstop service from several big airports across the continental United States was available. In 1980 nearly 4 million passengers arrived; by 1990 almost 7 million, two-thirds of them from mainland United States, about 20 percent from Japan.

Such an acceleration of growth made tourism much the greatest base of the economy and generated a massive construction boom fueled in part by large investments from Japan (whose firms own about a third of the hotel space and were much involved in the building of shopping centers and golf courses). The impact on landscape and life has been heavy. Whereas before the war and even for a time after Honolulu was a rather quiet tropical city with a small downtown and mostly modest embowered residential districts, "the 'awakening' of Honolulu during the 1960s and many of the outer-island towns during the 1970s has not been gentle." What Lewis Mumford, in an invited 1938 critique of Honolulu, had characterized as "a great park, partly disfigured by a careless weedy undergrowth of buildings" had become a towering, rampant overgrowth, turning Waikiki into a dense maze of hotels and shops, and, studded with high-rise buildings, pressing thickly up nearby steep slopes, eastward to the base of Diamond Head and on farther to Hawaii-Kai; to the west, beyond the military reserves around Pearl Harbor, industrial and urban development spread inland to new towns on former rich plantation lands. Traffic, always constricted by the narrow strand and its backdrop of ravines and ridges, now flows through tunnels on the Pali Highway to expanding bedroom communities on the wet windward side. As might be expected, planners lament that "the trend was toward mainland big city modernism" and that "Honolulu, which could have had its own colorful tropic character, matured as carelessly and as drearily as any other American metropolis." But high-rise residences are a response to intense pressures for housing in such an exceptional site, and any more idealized pattern would have required far more stringent and powerful controls than are to be found anywhere in urban America. Even with this heavy impress of common commercial design it remains a remarkable setting and townscape, dotted at a lower level with Shinto shrines, Buddhist temples, as well as churches and other buildings displaying versions of "Oriental" architecture, and at its statehood focus, across the park from the handsome Iolani Palace (the royal house of the last Hawaiian king and queen), stands the new (1969) capitol building full of symbolic natural and cultural touches that, as Richard Saul Wurman put it, achieve "a camaraderie with the elements, reflecting the islands without resorting to thatched-roof theatrics" (fig. 58).

There has been strong growth in most of the outer islands as well, and by 1990 the total resident population had surpassed a million, with, as usual, nearly 80 percent on Oahu. With statehood common American racial classifications in the census (white, Negro, and "other races") were applied, with results far cruder than common Hawaiian usage. However, later census refinements offer reasonable comparisons with earlier ethnic figures: in 1990 Whites made up a third of the population, Asians just under a half, with persons of Japanese descent about 22 percent. Small, but recently more prominent, were the numbers from other Southeast Asian countries and Pacific islands. And more than ever, all such classifications obscure the amount of ethnic mixing and personal choices in such categorizations. Beyond

58. Hawaiian Capitols.

In the foreground stands Iolani Palace, completed in 1882 for King Kalakaua as "the perfect backdrop for his elaborate court life." After the coup that ousted Queen Liliuokalani and the monarchy in 1893 it continued as the seat of the Hawaiian government and remained so under American rule from 1898 until the completion of the new state capitol on these old royal grounds in 1969. Tastefully incorporating many indigenous features in materials and design, the new statehouse is a bold contrast to the high-rise steel, glass, and concrete towers of modern Honolulu just beyond the right of this photo. (Courtesy Hawaii State Archives)

these standardized identities, "everyday discourse is replete with distinctions and identifiers that differentiate between insider and outsider, local and transient, old-timer and newcomer, real Hawaiian and poseur."

Hawaii continues as a major strategic center. It is the headquarters of the American Pacific Fleet and of the Pacific Air Forces; a relatively large proportion of its small area is owned or leased by the military, and its personnel and dependents make up nearly 10 percent of the total population. In other ways "the dream of Hawaii as an international financial and communications center for the Pacific basin" has not been realized, but the government-supported East-West Center has been in important training and meeting ground for varieties of professionals from the Pacific World.

Small size and noncontiguity exact a high price from residents: almost everything, including all fuel, has to be imported, and there is little outbound cargo. The cost of becoming a world-famous tourist mecca has exacted an even heavier price in many ways, creating a basic economy highly vulnerable to external business and political changes, and transforming life and landscape in drastic and largely irreversible ways: "it is harder and harder to reconcile the images of paradise and its presumably leisurely lifestyle with the actualities of an ongoing struggle between Oahu's accelerating urbanization and rapid statewide economic development, and with the commitment of residents and Native Hawaiians to hold onto what each group sees as irreplaceable physical and cultural qualities." Like Southern California, America's earlier Eden, Hawaii is foundering from its own compelling attractions.

Near the end of the twentieth century as the anniversaries of one hundred years as an American Territory and forty years of statehood neared, official celebrations were faced with rude reminders of what those years of "Americanization" meant to deeply committed Native Hawaiians:

> Hawai'i, of course, is a supreme example of American aggression. Despite promises to support Hawaiian independence in the nineteenth century, the American invasion of Hawai'i in 1893 was a prelude to the extinguishment of Hawaiian sovereignty in 1898 when, against the expressed wishes of the Hawaiian people, Hawai'i became a territorial possession of the United States.

> For us nationalist Hawaiians, the lesson of statehood is a lesson of loss and despair: the loss of land, of self-government, of language; the despair of cultural prostitution, of economic exploitation.

> As Hawaiians enter the new century, they are well grounded in the lessons of the past: We are Hawaiians, not Americans.

Such embittered cries remind us that America is, as always, an empire, as well as a nation, a federation, and a set of regional societies.

PUERTO RICO

Statehood advocates in Puerto Rico were jubilant over the admission of Hawaii in 1959. It demonstrated that there were no fundamental congressional barriers to the addition of a distant insular territory with a largely non-Anglo-Saxon population; a new association, "Citizens for State Fifty-One," was soon formed to further their campaign. As the British historian Raymond Carr later noted in his commissioned study of the island, Puerto Rican opponents of statehood were "quick to point out that this jubilation was based on a misreading" of the Hawaiian case. Although acquired in the same year (1898), "Hawaii had been an incorporated territory since

1900, and as early as 1940, seventy percent of Hawaiians had voted for statehood in a yes/no referendum; by 1958 opposition to statehood was virtually non-existent." Such a corrective was well based, and the differences in the two cases were extensive and complex.

In contrast with Hawaii, Puerto Rico was made an "unincorporated territory," a new concept contrived to deal with an unanticipated acquisition with which the imperial government did not yet know what its longer-term relationship should be, and its people were declared to be citizens of Puerto Rico—whatever that might mean—rather than of the United States. In Puerto Rico, as in Cuba and the Philippines, the new imperial power disdained to recognize or work closely with existing political elites. It sent a sequence of mostly inept, willfully ignorant, non-Spanish-speaking minor political appointees to govern the million people of this poor mountainous island of marginal interest or concern to American politics or public. Such treatment humiliated and embittered the local leadership, which had initially welcomed the American flag and, having recently won a large measure of self-government and representation in the Cortes in Madrid, had expected at least as much autonomy from Washington. In the face of such retrogression Puerto Rican politics became obsessed with changing its relationship with the United States. In 1917 Congress conferred U.S. citizenship on Puerto Ricans, but such action (taken without consultation) did not make them equal in privileges and programs available to mainland citizens. In 1919 Congress was formally petitioned to hold a plebiscite on Puerto Rican preference of status: statehood, autonomy, or independence.

Meanwhile the United States treated Puerto Rico as a tropical colony under the general assumption that while this densely populated island had no room or attractions for colonists from the mainland, "modernization" would steadily erode Puerto Rican culture and result in an ever-more thorough "Americanization." Big corporations took charge of sugar production, the U.S. government built water and sanitation systems, roads and bridges, and established agricultural experiment stations, public schools, a university, and (in 1926) a school of tropical medicine. English was imposed as the official language, and until 1916 all school classes were in English; thereafter Spanish was allowed in the lower grades, English required in the higher. In 1922 the Supreme Court cautioned that despite the grant of citizenship, Puerto Ricans should not infer "an intention to incorporate in the Union . . . distant ocean communities of a different origin and language from those of our continental people." At the same time, the governor of Puerto Rico (a Kansas City businessman) advised a local political leader to "publicly renounce independence and break loose from your pernicious and anti-American associates."

Three decades of paternalism, subordination, and marginalization fostered a Puerto Rican nationalism that erupted into violence during the extreme impoverishments of the Great Depression (magnified by two devastating hurricanes). Taking his cue from the Irish Republican Army, a charismatic leader (graduate of Harvard and Yale) declared a republic and instigated assassination and terrorism. The revolt was not widespread and was soon repressed, but the official inquiries that followed exposed the economic and political conditions that gave rise to such anti-Americanism. In 1936 Senator Millard Tydings (Maryland), who had recently coauthored the act setting out the ten-year path to independence for the Philippines, filed a bill to grant the same to Puerto Rico over a four-year span. The proposal was a shock to island leaders; putting it so quickly beyond the tariff borders and subsidies of the United States would be an economic disaster, and the proposal was generally regarded as a threat aimed at quelling the independence movement. President Roosevelt had visited the island before these confrontations, and he transferred its imperial supervision from the War Department to the Department of the Interior, and in cooperation with Luis Muñoz Marín, a major political figure (who had spent much of his younger years in the United States), formed a Puerto Rican Reconstruction Administration to initiate an array of relief projects, labor reforms, and economic diversifications, all accompanied by numerous studies of island conditions and prospects. With the approach of world war a retired admiral was appointed governor and the military presence was greatly expanded.

During the war Congress held several hearings, and a variety of bills and resolutions ranging from statehood through various degrees of autonomy to independence were discussed, but a lot of it was more a reflection of American party rivalries than a careful consideration of major alternatives and there was a general reluctance to make any change until the war was over. In 1947 Puerto Rico was granted the right to elect its own governor, and in January 1949, Luis Muñoz took office. A former *independentista*, Muñoz was now head of a new party committed to finding an acceptable alternative, for, as he put it, "if we seek statehood we die waiting for Congress, if we adopt independence we die from starvation—in any case we die." The idea of some sort of "dominion" status, an "Estado Libre Asociado," modeled in general on the self-governing members of the British Commonwealth, had often been proposed. In 1950 Congress authorized Puerto Ricans to draft a constitution for internal self-government (soon followed by riots and an attempt by radical independence supporters to assassinate President Truman); in 1951 more than 76 percent of voters in Puerto Rico approved the document, and in July 1952 the Commonwealth of Puerto Rico was proclaimed.

As head of this new government, Muñoz asserted that this "compact" was "a free and voluntary association" and proclaimed that "the people of Puerto Rico have reached the highest possible level of political equality; and of political dignity." The new relationship, however, was "riddled with legal ambiguities," and Congress and the courts soon made clear that although Puerto Rico had been granted a large measure of autonomy, it remained a dependency, its status ultimately controlled by Congress. Beyond home rule the critical features were exemption from all federal taxes and remaining within the tariff wall of the United States. Congress still determined the application of federal programs to the island. After extensive political negotiations by U.S. and Puerto Rican officials the United Nations recognized that the people of the island "have been invested with the attributes of political sovereignty which clearly identify the status . . . of an autonomous political entity" (not all Latin American states agreed). Participation in the Olympic Games under their own flag since 1948 has become of great symbolic importance to Puerto Rican politics. In 1967 commonwealth status was endorsed by 60 percent of voters in a plebiscite (which a much-weakened independence party boycotted).

Statehood was supported by nearly 40 percent in that poll, and the statehood party has been a major force in island politics. As Carr noted, "the emotional core of the statehood case" was always "the dignity of first-class citizenship and the justice of being treated on an equal footing with fellow American citizens" (Puerto Ricans, for example, cannot vote in presidential elections and, of course, have no voting representatives in Congress—they are a constituency of no one in power). In recent decades "statehooders maintain that American federalism is sufficiently flexible not only to allow, but to welcome, the admission of a culturally distinctive Puerto Rico as a State." However, in serious debates in San Juan and in Washington "culturally distinctive" becomes quickly narrowed to a focus on *language*. In a major report on the status of Puerto Rico in the 1960s a powerful U.S. senator declared: "We welcome diversity; therefore the distinctive culture of Puerto Rico presents no bar as such to Statehood. The unity of our Federal-State structure, however, requires a common tongue. . . . A condition precedent to Statehood must be the recognition and acceptance of English as the official language." Although those insisting on such a uniform policy express no wish to suppress the common use of Spanish, the ideal of a bilingual island population has so far proven to be far from attainable despite long and varied efforts ("practically every type of language policy for the teaching of English in the public schools of Puerto Rico has been tried with the exception of having English and Spanish as the language of instruction on alternate days"). A 1980 census reported that fewer than one in five Puerto Ricans could speak English with relative ease, well over half none at all.

In 1991 the Puerto Rican legislature designated "Spanish as the official language of Puerto Rico, while retaining English as a mandatory subject in schools"; two years later the statehood party, newly in power, rescinded that legislation—not, however, because of any less determination to sustain Spanish but to suppress such an obvious irritation to and symbolic separation from the United States. All parties agree on the need to preserve the island's cultural identity—considered to have been in the making for 500 years—and most express concern over the threat of "engulfment" by the relentless spread of American materialistic values (anti-state-hood leaders have long tarred their opponents as advocating "political and cultural assimilation with the United States"). Yet there appears to be little general rejection of the material elements of the "American Way of Life," and the U.S. passport not only allows free entry into a vast labor market but also a guaranteed possibility of testing, appraising, and even selecting to join in mainland American life (though, in effect, as an Hispanic "immigrant," at whatever level one can afford). Intensive surveys on the island confirm that few Puerto Ricans consider themselves "Americans" in any way beyond that narrow legal sense; nevertheless, "the greatest catalyst for changing the Puerto Rican 'identity'" is that more than 40 percent of all Puerto Ricans now live within the United States, with much continuing family traffic between mainland and island. There is a strong sense on the island of "Nuy-oricans" as a new subculture, and concern over that change. Furthermore, Puerto Ricans in the United States are dispersing from their heavy concentration in the New York City metropolitan area. For example, in recent years newspapers in San Juan became "full of advertisements for houses in Central Florida," where migrants from New York seeking family security and the chance to own a house and garden had begun to cluster. As the ties between the continent and the island multiply the processes of cultural change are surely being affected.

In 1979 the U.S. Congress offered to grant Puerto Rico statehood should a "substantial majority" of island voters support such a change. In the following year the statehood party was defeated in elections and obviously no such majority existed as yet. Moreover, various members of Congress warned that the resolution stating the offer was no guarantee of admission on Puerto Rican terms. It has never been clear that Congress would welcome Puerto Rico as the fifty-first state. In addition to issues of language and culture, this small island (larger only than Rhode Island and Delaware), would be greater in population (3,528,000 in 1990) than twenty-five states and would thereby not only add two senators but would qualify for eight representatives (which seats would have to be taken from existing states). It would also be much the poorest state, with a per capita income no more than half that of the poorest in the present Union. In a 1993 plebiscite 48 percent voted for commonwealth, 46 percent for statehood; in 1998 the U.S. House of Representatives approved a bill to offer Puerto Rico its usual three options (with a ten-year transition to statehood or independence), but the Senate took no action, and the formal relationship remained unchanged.

All Puerto Rican parties chafe under their perceived status as a marginalized entity—"the oldest colony in the world." The present commonwealth has not generally been regarded as a permanent design and has been aptly described as "a haven for the undecided" and "a buffer zone between the extremes of complete integration and total separation." Thus "the conflict between cultural identity and the search for economic survival [that] has been the crux of Puerto Rico's political status dilemma," and "has perplexed the island for the past century" seems assured of continuing to do so well into the current one.

INTERNAL EMPIRE

Three kinds of geopolitical sovereignty are recognized within the United States: federal, state, and tribal. The basic relationship between the first two were defined in the Constitution; those between the federal and the tribal were formalized in individual treaties between the central government and specific Indian groups. Those documents were "filled with the language of mutual concession and mutual recognition," but, as we noted with reference to the main era of these treaties, such ostensible mutuality was in reality "the language of empire, drawing upon the standard vocabulary of diplomacy, the formal etiquette of adversaries, the rhetorical disguise of actual power relations and feelings between the two parties." During that same era, "Indian Tribes" (who appear by name in the Constitution only with reference to the power of Congress to regulate commerce, and exclusion from the count for apportioning taxes and representation) became formally defined by the Supreme Court as "domestic dependent nations." Their dependency within the body of the empire was obvious and repressive, but the sovereignty recognized in their group identity and territorial status, even though subject to emending and impairing redefinition, has been residual and crucial to their enduring special presence. Ever since those first treaties Americans and Indians have been locked together in a struggle "to answer the riddle of tribalism in a modern nation-state."

In simplest terms that struggle can be seen as having two broad phases: the first, stemming from the completion of conquests in the latter nineteenth century on through (with one significant interruption) the 1950s, was a period of imperial management and policies aimed at deep cultural change in all these captive peoples; the second, dating from the 1960s, has been marked by the rise of "Red Power" and incremental shifts in imperial policies toward recognition of tribal integrity and authority and official acceptance of the special status of several hundred Indian groups as a continuing presence within the American nation. Here our concern is with some geopolitical aspects of this "Indian Problem" rather than with any fuller consideration of the complexities of this long, festering, vexing relationship between indigenous peoples and the ruling power (some essential foundations of which have been treated in the preceding volumes of this historical geographical perspective).

"It is my fixed purpose to bring about the speedy individualization of the Indian," said Cato Wells, commissioner of Indian Affairs during the Woodrow Wilson administration. Wells was simply adhering to the established goal of "de-tribaliza-

tion" and eventual assimilation of Indians as individual citizens and full participants in the "American Way of Life." Principal instruments of this imperial policy
were the suppression of all tribal political authority within the reservations; "allotment," by which each Indian household was to be assigned a parcel of private property and the "excess" reservation lands released to Whites; and federally operated
boarding schools "conceived in terms of driving a wedge between children and parents and thus hastening the process of cultural assimilation" through prohibition of
all Indian language, dress, and customs (initially these schools, some on and others
at great distances from the reservation, were allocated to various religious denominations, but the federal government soon began to take more direct charge of education programs).

Thus Indians were in effect (and formally declared to be) *wards* of the federal
government under the guardianship of the Bureau of Indian Affairs (BIA), whose
resident agents exercised complete power, consulting Indians only if they wished to
do so. And thus treaties turn out to mean whatever the dominant power wants
them to mean. By the twentieth century the government did not regard this relationship as an imperial program to control potential enemies but as a national program to convert helpless peoples into ordinary citizens—to Americanize them in
order to save them from the deep poverty and despair of captive societies that could
no longer sustain themselves by traditional ways of life. As an Indian commissioner
had bluntly put it in 1889: "this civilization may not be the best possible, but it is
the best Indians can get. They cannot escape it, and must either conform to it or be
crushed by it."

The 1920s would prove to be the nadir of American Indian societies. Contrary
to a popular assumption, they were not really "a vanishing race" (the nearly
250,000 enumerated in the decennial, and not very careful, census was about the
same as had been recorded over the past thirty years), but they were certainly a beleaguered one. They had lost well over half of their treaty lands from a chaotic and
corrupt allotment program; the reservations of the famous Five Civilized Tribes in
Oklahoma had been completely dissolved, but the tribes remained there on loose
clusters of individual lands and under some degree of control. On any close examination the Bureau of Indian Affairs was a bloated bureaucracy engaged in perpetuating itself and, in effect, the perpetual dependence of Indian tribes. The school
program was largely ineffective and the whole Americanization process stultified.
The Indians had neither conformed nor been crushed, but their physical well-
being was precarious. Concerns about such matters led to various investigations,
official and private, culminating in the Meriam Report of 1928. Initiated by the
secretary of the Interior, following tumultuous congressional hearings, and conducted by the Brookings Institution, the report confirmed these many failures and
revealed appalling levels of poverty, disease, and mortality. Although recommend-

ing extensive reform of the system, the report endorsed the intent of federal policies—yet hinted at a possible shift in focus: the Indian Service, it said, should be
"devoting its main energies to the social and economic advancement of the Indians, so that they may be absorbed into the prevailing civilization or be fitted to live
in the presence of that civilization at least in accordance with a minimum standard
of health and decency." Further, the report emphasized that "scrupulous care must
be exercised to respect the rights of Indians. . . . [to] recognize the good in the economic and social life of the Indians in their religion and ethics, and . . . seek to develop it and build on it rather than to crush out all that is Indian."

A strong move to shift the focus of federal policy and recognize Indian group integrity began with the appointment of John Collier as Franklin Roosevelt's commissioner of Indian Affairs. Long a strong advocate of cultural pluralism and an ad-
mirer of the virtues of community life, Collier had become a crusader for Indian
rights after a visit to Taos Pueblo in 1920. In 1934 Congress passed the Indian Re-
organization Act (IRA), ending land allotments, closing many boarding schools,
encouraging tribal self-government (but requiring an American-style constitution
and system of courts), and opening the way for tribal business corporations. Collier
was an assertive leader, and his program was controversial among Indians as well as
Whites. The IRA was officially endorsed by 70 percent of the 258 voting tribes, but
half of those approving did not accept his design for tribal government. Congressional opponents accused Collier of "re-Indianizing the Indians," whereas he was
resolute in the need to "strip the word tribe of its primitive and atavistic connotations" and "divest ourselves of the lingering fear that tribalism is a regression."

This remarkable change in policy proved to be a twelve-year interlude followed
by a period of "barren years" under strongly anti–New Deal postwar Congresses.
The establishment of the Indian Claims Commission in 1946 was a transitional
move. It marked formal recognition of Indian grievances over lands taken from
them illegally; however, the form of restitution was not land but, in effect, conscience money given by the government in the hope that "it could free itself once
and for all of the moral burden of the wrongs" it had perpetrated and take further
steps toward dissolution of these sovereign relationships. Payments were made on
the estimated value of the lands when lost (with no interest) and acceptance pre-
cluded any future claims. Several hundred cases were adjudicated, but many tribes
refused to enter into this form of settlement.

The Eisenhower administration moved firmly toward "termination" of the reservation system. Without consulting tribes, the BIA drew up a list of those it considered ready to manage their own affairs and be released from federal supervision.
Such Indians were to become ordinary citizens of the state in which they resided
(U.S. citizenship had been conferred—without consultation—upon all Indians in
1924, but states did not usually accept them as local citizens and sought to avoid as-

suming responsibilities for them). Under this new policy Indians could remain as tribal members and tribes could be eligible for federal social and economic aid just as local governments were. Indians who had served in the armed forces and wartime jobs had induced the first sizable influx of Indians into urban areas, and the BIA sought to enlarge this movement by offering subsidies to help them move off the reservation and establish "new homes in ordinary American communities" (this "Operation Relocation" was under the direction of the man who had been in charge of the removal and internment of Japanese Americans from West Coast cities). "Between 1954 and 1966 Congress terminated over one hundred tribes, most of them in Oregon and California"; most of these were very small and only about 3 percent of the total Indian population was directly affected. Nevertheless, most of these tribes were strongly opposed to or at least deeply split about such a drastic change. Legally, termination was firm proof that "Congress has virtually unlimited authority to regulate Indian affairs," that it can "either assist a tribal government or destroy it." Empires rest ultimately upon force, and it is not surprising that the prevailing Indian view was—and is—that "in practice termination is used as a weapon against Indian people in a modern war of conquest."

The objective of termination was assimilation; the result of these midcentury initiatives was quite the opposite. For example, "relocation backfired. Instead of promoting widespread assimilation of Indians into the general society as intended, relocation simply produced Indian people with urban savvy to argue and demonstrate for Indian rights before the general public"—and thus American nationalism begot Indian nationalism. Such a response was in keeping with the general geopolitical principle that revolt within an imperial system is most likely to be led by those "trained in the tools of empire," "those who know the language and understand the social and political institutions, those who have had their horizons broadened by participation in the larger imperial society." Once under way their own "provincial culture is the model and imperial influences a taint"; if the imperial state is one of great cultural prestige and power, "the rebellious leadership at least seeks control over the processes and degree of cultural change."

The inherent difficulty in this particular case was the extreme fragmentation— more than 250 federally recognized tribes—of the resisting peoples. The upwelling of "Pan-Indianism" in the 1960s was a strategic response to that problem. "A genuine phobia about the intentions of the federal government" was prompting a growing number of intertribal "all-Indian" gatherings and organizations to bring the general cause and crisis of Indian America to national attention (tribal traditionalists continued to resist the term "Indian" as an imposed concept, but both popular and legal use were firmly entrenched). Taking a cue from the success of Blacks, the more militant factions (very largely urban Indians and students) proclaimed "Red Power," staged sit-ins at various federal facilities (seizure and lengthy occupation of vacant Alcatraz Island garnered much publicity), led a "March on Washington," occupied the BIA headquarters, and, in what began as an intratribal dispute, ended with a prolonged confrontation and clash with federal officials on the powerfully symbolic site of Wounded Knee, South Dakota. All of these and related activities were aimed at achieving a radical redefinition of federal-Indian relationships; the larger context of the times—the civil rights movement, War on Poverty, Vietnam and anti-colonialism, newfound pride in race and ethnicity—helped immeasurably to make that possible.

Termination was halted in 1966, and President Nixon officially proclaimed a new era in 1970 when he forthrightly declared that the policy had been "wrong" and that the new goal of the federal service should be "to strengthen the Indian's sense of autonomy without threatening his sense of community." The BIA has been increasingly led and staffed by Indians, and a long series of federal actions have resulted in unprecedented recognition and assistance—but not always on Indian terms. As in preceding eras, this new Indian policy at times invoked fundamental American concepts that were not in accord with those of Indian societies. For example, the Indian Civil Rights Act applied to individuals and required conflicts to be adjudicated in tribal courts, all in profound contrast with the traditional sense of community and consensus handling of disputes. Or, at the opposite scale, to qualify in general for special development funds Indians had, in effect, "to pose as another American domestic minority"—as a single category of people warranting various kinds of "affirmative action." The American ideal of "self-determination" was now applied in measured degree to Indian tribes, but such federal policies inevitably raised the questions who is an Indian? What is a tribe?

The BIA had long recognized many tribes, but as federal assistance became much more available in various forms, additional Indians groups began to petition for such services, and in 1978 the government decreed that to receive official recognition these petitioners must provide evidence that "a single Indian group has existed since its first sustained contact with European cultures on a continuous basis to the present; that its members live in a distinct, autonomous community perceived by others as Indian; that it has maintained some sort of authority with a governmental system by which its members abide; that all its members can be traced genealogically to an historic tribe." By 1997, 185 petitions had been received but only 37 resolved by this long and demanding process; the total number of federally recognized tribes exceeded 300, many of them very small in membership.

"The determination of who is 'Indian' has a long history of ambiguity" and remains highly controversial, subject to widely divergent interpretations. Tribes maintain their own membership rolls, and these are generally recognized by the federal government. On the other hand, since 1960 the Bureau of the Census had invited individuals to declare an ethnic identity, and the returns for that year recorded 524,000 Indians (compared with the 345,000 reported by the BIA); by 1980 this number approached a million and a half, and in 1990 nearly 2 million. Such "'unnatural leaps" in the Indian population beyond the plausible demographics of natural increase surely reflect this new "ethnic self-determination," but just how much and why are not readily determined (those most concerned about this recent inflation tend to speak of "invented Indians," "ethnic fraud," and other derogatory labels). There has obviously been an unprecedented upsurge of pride in being "Indian," even if very partially so in ancestry; there has also been an incentive to claim tribal affiliation in order to benefit from Indian programs. In recent years "tribal enrollment review committees have been swamped with applications and inquiries," a pressure arising primarily from the astounding economic success of Indian gaming, especially casinos, many of which are owned by very small and recently certified tribes (the Foxwoods Casino about halfway between New York City and Boston on the Connecticut reservation of the Mashantucket Pequots, a tribe of about 300 members, "is the largest casino in the western hemisphere").

Near the end of the century "142 Indian tribes or communities operated 281 casinos and bingo halls in twenty-four states," with more in preparation, and this sudden proliferation made the presence of an Indian reservation or tribal-owned lands a cause for alarm in the states. Only two (Nevada since 1933, and New Jersey since 1978) had allowed full-scale casinos; however, all but three (Hawaii, Tennessee, Utah) had authorized various forms of gambling, and thirty-seven had turned to state lotteries as a means of raising revenues. With billions of dollars and ramifying effects on cities and localities at stake, the states have sought strong powers from Congress and the courts to regulate Indian gaming. Various negotiations between individual tribes and states have taken place, but the matter remains an unresolved clash of sovereignties, with neither the states nor the Indians united in their respective positions.

For those Indians engaged in creating these alluring facilities, the sudden increase in wealth has been by far the "greatest boon to reservation economies and tribal government resources" ever experienced. The profits have been applied to housing, health, education, and other social needs and to fostering other reservation industries; cash payments have been distributed to tribal members, and in 1998 the Oneidas, operators of a casino in Upstate New York, became the first to return the BIA's annual subsidy for social programs back to the federal treasury (they also shared their profits with twenty other small Indian groups in the East and South). It is generally assumed that these profits are potentially vulnerable to new patterns of competition and regulation, but they have already had a powerful impact on a large number of tribes (although some major ones have not joined in this particular pursuit of wealth). Frank Pommersheim, commenting on the alarm that this Indian success has produced in the states, noted the irony that "the colonized are almost always overtly encouraged to succeed and pull their own weight, but there is often a covert subtext not to do too well for fear they will undermine the privileged economic status of the colonizer." In this American case it is the privileged *geopolitical* status of these colonized peoples that allows them to entice and exploit their colonizers.

Indians residing on reservations constitute about a quarter of the nearly 2 million who identify themselves as Indians in the U.S. census (fig. 59). Those living off the reservations are often categorized as "urban Indians" and are most heavily concentrated in a relatively few metropolitan areas: Los Angeles (whose nearly 100,000 include some migrants from Latin America), San Francisco, San Diego, and Seattle; Phoenix and Tucson; Tulsa and Oklahoma City with half of that state's 200,000; Denver, Minneapolis, and Chicago; and New York City, whose 50,000 is much the largest in the East. Each of these populations represents a great variety drawn from near and far, but most Indians retain their tribal affiliation and some contact with their reservation. Thus although bound together by intricate networks of kith and kin, most tribes contain these two physically separate groups and experience some degree of internal tension between them. In general, those on the reservation tend to be more traditional, concerned with preserving language, oral history, and tribal customs, deeply suspicious of federal agents and programs, intent on ensuring a degree of insulation from the encompassing culture. In contrast, urban Indians living daily in the midst of that culture cannot avoid making adaptations, and some, especially those with regular jobs and homes, become extensively involved with American ways, attending public schools, knowing English far better than their tribal tongue, and many intermarrying with Whites. More often scattered rather than tightly clustered within the metropole and perhaps associating as much with members of other tribes as with their own, they find "Indian" their most strategic public identity. Such characterizations scarcely touch the diversities and complexities of Indian and tribal life, but they suggest the likelihood of disagreement on various issues: on tribal membership, for example, with traditionalists holding to much stricter rules than urban Indians of more diluted ancestry. Whereas some Indians approve of modern exploitation of valuable mineral and timber resources on tribal lands (such as the massive coal mines and power plants on the Navajo Reservation), others regard it as a despoliation and a surrender to an alien impersonal capitalist system; although games and gambling are an ancient part of Indian life, tribes can be deeply split over the operation of casinos as modern money machines.

In recent years relations with the federal government have undergone dramatic change. A series of congressional and executive acts have formally endorsed the survival and revitalization of Native American languages, religions, and cultural traditions, and encouraged the repatriation of sacred and ceremonial objects and

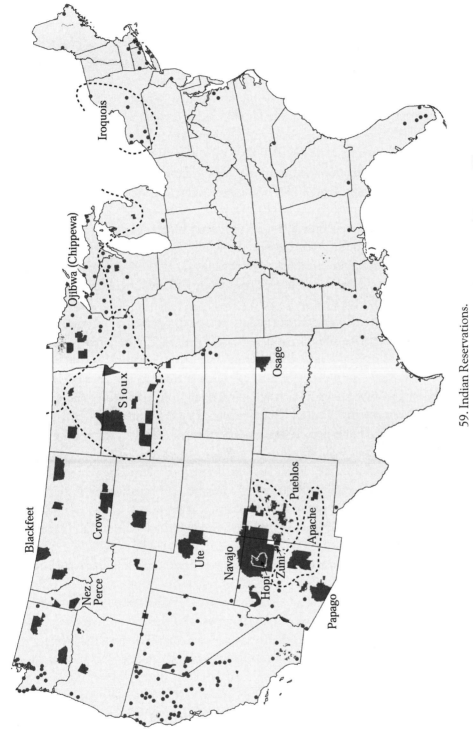

59. Indian Reservations.

Only a few large tribal reserves and groupings are identified; the Hopi and Zuni are Western Pueblo peoples; other large reserves are not named because they contain two or more separate or "federated" nations. The Iroquois and Ojibwa also have reservations in Canada.

skeletal remains; in September 2000, the Bureau of Indian Affairs marked its 175th anniversary with an expression by the commissioner (a Pawnee) "of profound sorrow for what the agency has done in the past" and acceptance of "the moral responsibility of putting things right." Tribal governments now have much greater control over their affairs. Within the bounds of the reservation they exercise civil jurisdiction, with power to maintain law and order, and broad authority to regulate private property and economic activity and to exclude non-Indians from tribal ground (at the height of the Red Power movement, Vine Deloria, Jr., a major leader, called for a rejection of outsiders—chiefly anthropologists—using reservations as "living laboratories"; today it is usually difficult and often impossible to obtain tribal permission for field work). They have charge of education and most other social services, aided by a variety of federal programs. There are now about thirty Indian community colleges in the United States and several four-year schools. The first of these, established by the Navajo in 1969, is now Diné College, with a four-year program including "knowledge of Navajo culture, history, language, values and principles."

"Indians have preserved the idea of nationhood or peoplehood throughout their period of contact with the non-Indian world." In the 1970s a coalition of tribal leaders, emphasizing "the importance of acting as a nation" and "taking their case to other nations," sent a delegation to the United Nations to participate in hearings on "Discrimination against Indigenous Populations." Such an exposure of the internal empire of the United States may have accelerated changes in policy already under way. By the end of the twentieth century Indian tribes were participants in a much more substantial government-to-government relationship; although clearly subordinate, these "nations within" now held a degree of sovereignty that placed them "in a status parallel to, but not identical with, that of the states" within the federal system. However, such a status was not yet legally stabilized (as Barsh and Henderson note, a really firm tribal federalism would require an amendment to the Constitution), and answers to "the riddle of tribalism in a modern nation-state" will require continuing adjustments on both sides over a long period of time.

Geopolitically, the archipelagoes of Indian reservations have been expanded by the addition of many tiny islets sprinkled across California, Nevada, the Northeast, and elsewhere (and several terminated reserves have been restored). In several cases reservations overlap state boundaries, a reminder not only that these sovereign territories are distinct from the states but that in the West most were imprinted on the map by the United States government before most of those states were admitted to the Union. The Navajo Reservation is much the largest in area (about the size of West Virginia) and population (more than 150,000 tribal members within its bounds) and in its very active government and range of facilities seems to resemble a state in important ways. In contrast, the Sioux are fragmented among more than a dozen reserves in the Upper Middle West. However, while the loss of huge tracts of hunting grounds was crippling to traditional economies, a large, single contiguous reserve was not fundamental for traditional tribal government because the Sioux, like many others, were a loosely associated set of generally related peoples, with four large branches subdivided into many local bands of a few dozen or more families, a size appropriate to a communal, consensual polity. The centuries-old sociopolitical distinction of each Pueblo Indian reserve in New Mexico is perhaps the most compelling illustration of this common scale of Indian life.

Whatever their size and population, Indian reservations are *homelands*, residual ground of a drastically reduced Native America, anchors for the tenacious hold of tribal peoples on their own identities, redoubts for survival and dignity amid the powerful pressures of the encompassing society, cultural islands seeking stronger demarcation on the legal map of America.

The particular histories of the newest, noncontiguous states underlie an important addendum to this review of tribal sovereignty. Most congressional legislation on Indians over the past half century has initially or eventually "explicitly included Alaska Native villages as 'tribes'—for the purposes" of those acts. However, the geopolitical status of Alaska Natives was and is critically different from that of American Indians in the contiguous United States. Alaska Natives consist of three general groups: Eskimos in the North and West, Aleuts on the island chain, and Indians, these last making up about a third of the total and subdivided into those of the Northwest Coast Culture (chiefly Tlinglit and Haida) and those of the central Interior (Athapascans). Except for the relatively focused disruptions of the several gold rushes and the very few cities and towns, Alaska Natives had not, until recently, been pressured to surrender their lands; indeed, most are still living in ancestral villages and districts. Thus, aside from one unique case (that of the Metlakatla at the southern tip of Alaska, a community under the leadership of a White minister relocating from nearby British Columbia in 1887 and welcomed by U.S. officials) there have never been Native reservations in Alaska like those elsewhere in the United States—and therefore tribal sovereignty and government-to-government political status were never documented and institutionalized as elsewhere.

This difference became crucially apparent in bitterly contested claims to land following statehood in 1959. The new Alaskan government was given the right to select 103 million acres from the federal public domain. Selection was a slow process, but it quickly alarmed Native leaders, who formed a general association and submitted their own claims to ancestral lands. Thus state and federal authority were brought into confrontation. As guardians of Native rights and welfare, federal officials had designated many areas as fishing and hunting reserves and offered other support and protections; although the statehood act and Alaska constitution referred to Native land rights, statehood advocates had vigorously resisted any concept of formal territorial reservations or any special status for Native Alaskans (who had also been made American citizens in 1924). In 1966 the secretary of the Interior declared a "land freeze," and with the discovery of oil at Prudhoe Bay two years later the pressures for resolution of the matter became intense, leading to the Alaska Native Claims Settlement Act (ANCSA) of 1971.

ANCSA represents a complex compromise of state, federal, and Native interests. Native Alaskans were granted 44 million acres and nearly $1 billion. Title to these lands, however, was given not to tribal governments but to state-chartered, Native-administered business corporations. The entire state was subdivided into twelve regions, each approximating the area of a broadly distinct Native group (such as Aleut, Arctic Slope Eskimo, and Northwest Coast Indians), within which a regional corporation might operate; nearly 200 village corporations were also formed. The act "extinguished aboriginal hunting and fishing rights as well as aboriginal land title." Finding that Native subsistence was thereby at great risk, Congress subsequently intervened to clarify subsistence rights—but, to appease the state, made these available to all eligible rural residents, not just Natives. So far most Native-owned corporations have not enjoyed much business success, and other Alaskans have recurrently challenged Native privileges in courts.

As McBeath and Morehouse conclude in their review of the topic, this 1971 act "is an equivocal product of overlapping termination and self-determination eras of federal Indian policy. It speaks the language of self-determination, but it does so with a distinct accent of termination and assimilation." "Politically, ANCSA emphasized Natives' formal equality with all citizens, not their special status." Thus "the challenge confronting Alaska Natives . . . requires, somewhat paradoxically, that Natives participate effectively in mainstream politics as equal citizens in order to enhance their status as aboriginal Americans." Native Alaskans have homelands and may be secure in their own identities, but they do not have sovereign status within firmly bounded legal territories—a critical geopolitical difference.

Meanwhile, in still another reverberation of empire-building, a vociferous Native Hawaiian movement emulating Red Power has followed a formal apology and admission by the U.S. Congress in 1993 that "the indigenous Hawaiian people never directly relinquished their claims to their inherent sovereignty as a people or over their national lands to the United States" with an insistence on an end to "State Wardship" and "federal recognition of Hawaiians as a Native nation with all the rights of nationhood extended to Indian nations"—including "a land base as the anchor of Native sovereignty."

6. Populations and Policies, 1950s–1990s

By the close of the twentieth century the population of the United States had doubled in the fifty-four years since the end of World War II, rising from 140 million to 281 million. The sudden spurt of growth during the postwar years was followed by a slowing rate but steady strong decennial increments (24, 23, 22 million) between 1960 and 1990, and then (in one of those recurrent surprises to demographers— but largely because of increased immigration) a sharp upturn, adding 31 million, during the final decade.

During that same period the urban population had risen from 60 percent of the total to more than 75 percent, and by 1990 the rural farm population had slipped below 2 percent. Both of these trends had been going on for more than a century. The Census Bureau continued to create new categories to measure this relentless urbanization. In 1960 it delimited 212 Standard Metropolitan Statistical Areas (SMSAs), each a county or set of counties related to one "central city" of at least 50,000 inhabitants. In 1975 it began to distinguish "consolidated" areas consisting of two or more SMSAs, including at least one with a population of a million or more; toward the end of the century five levels of metropolitan population clusters were being marked upon the national map (fig. 60). As always, there were major migrations and shifts in the regional balance of populations. Measured by five-year intervals about 10 percent of Americans moved from one state to another during such time. For example, in 1980 in six states (in addition to characteristically transient Alaskans)—Florida, Arizona, Nevada, Colorado, Wyoming, Oregon—a majority of the population was born elsewhere. Most important was an unprecedented shift in the direction of interregional migration so great as to result in a profound reshaping of the nation, giving rise to a new set of regional terms—a new popular image of the geography of America.

INTERNAL MIGRATIONS

Migration patterns of earlier decades continued well into the 1960s: the broad general movement to the Far West, and especially to California; the continued contraction of rural populations in the Middle West, especially from the High Plains; the selective Northerner colonization of Peninsular Florida; and the net migration of people, Whites as well as Blacks, from the South.

The Great Migration of Blacks continued strongly for twenty years after World War II. Their proportion in the total American population rose only slightly (to 11–12 percent), but by 1970 the number residing in the North was essentially equal to that in the South (10,216,000 compared to 10,673,000, calculated using the more pertinent regional division along the Potomac rather than the standard census use of the Mason-Dixon Line). The concurrent transformation of the Cot-

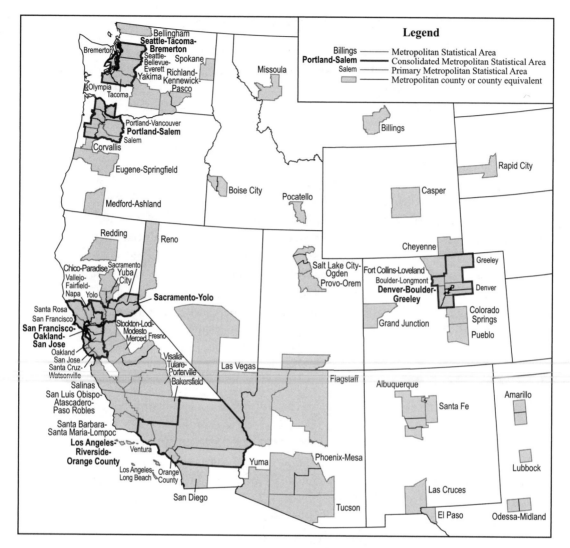

60. U.S. Census Metropolitan Areas, 1999.
An illustrative portion of a map of the United States and Puerto Rico.
These MSAs were further categorized by population size.

ton Belt was rapid: in 1958, 25 percent of the richest lands were harvested by machine, in 1966, 95 percent, and thus the 1933 prediction of O. E. Baker, government agricultural geographer, that "should the use of the cotton picker become common" it "may compel a migration of a magnitude unparalleled in our history from the hill lands as well as from the level lands of the cotton belt to the cities," came to pass. The largest single interstate migration was from Mississippi to Illinois, and by 1970 only 18 percent of the Black population remained in the rural

South. During this same time the interracial revolution was also fully under way. The federally mandated integration of schools was contentious all across the South, boycotts and civil rights initiatives were soon intensified by more confrontational sit-ins and marches; race relations became far more turbulent and dangerous—and a further reason to leave.

A generation of unbroken contacts between sources and destinations continued to channel migration into a selected set of Northern industrial cities. The bigger the Black ghetto the stronger the lure, for such clusters offered the greatest security and services. By 1970 the proportions of Blacks within these cities, situated well beyond the old border footholds of Baltimore, Cincinnati, and St. Louis, rivaled those in Southern cities:

Newark	54.2%	Atlanta	51.3%
Gary	52.8	New Orleans	45
Detroit	43.7	Savannah	44.9
Cleveland	38.3	Birmingham	42
Philadelphia	33.6	Richmond	42
Chicago	32.7	Jackson	39.7
Dayton	30.5	Memphis	38.9
Flint	28.1	Macon	37.3
Hartford	27.9	Chattanooga	35.8

A critical feature of this comparison is the fundamental geopolitical fact that these proportions refer to residents within city limits, not to total metropolitan populations. In the largest Northern cities the great growth in these Black populations was countered by an even greater loss of Whites to suburbs beyond the boundaries of the corporate city.

The late stages of this migration coincided with "urban renewal" and superhighway constructions that resulted in massive disruptions and displacements of populations—and massive unrest, exploding into riots in many Northern (and Western) cities. Furthermore, in the 1960s industrial America began to undergo basic structural changes leading to major reductions in older heavy industries, relocations of many others to suburbs, other regions, or overseas, all resulting in a drastic shrinkage of jobs accessible to these expanding inner-city populations. Thus, in broad terms, a Black population expelled from a modernizing rural South found itself stranded in a declining industrial North.

In 1969, in what would prove to be an astute and influential geopolitical analysis, Kevin B. Phillips emphasized that "from the Charleston-Savannah-Jacksonville coastal strip to California's urban south the conservative 'Sun Belt' of the United States is undergoing a massive infusion of people and prosperity. . . . Spurred by high pensions, early retirement, increased leisure time and technological innovation, the affluent American middle class is . . . [seeking] the comforts of the end-less summer, which they can escape at will in swimming pools and total refrigera-tion." As obvious in the title of his book, *The Emerging Republican Majority*, Phillips was focused on party and electoral issues, but his assessment was based on funda-mental geographical changes, and he introduced a new regional term to the popu-lar American vocabulary and was perhaps the first to give appropriate general rec-ognition to a transforming neotechnic innovation.

Climate has always been a defining characteristic of the American South. As North America's great sector of the world pattern of humid subtropics, with hu-midity magnified by the great body of warm water in the Gulf of Mexico, for three hundred years much of the pace and patterns, activities and architecture, of a dis-tinctive Southern Way of Life were adaptations to long, relentless steamy summers. As Raymond Arsenault relates, the "'air conditioning revolution' . . . was actually an evolution—a long, slow, uneven process stretching over seven decades." In the South it was first applied in textile mills and tobacco warehouses; in the 1920s it began to appear in the main theaters, hotel lobbies, and banks; during the 1930s major government buildings were becoming air-conditioned (until World War II Congress routinely adjourned and fled the Potomac Valley in summer), and not un-til 1939 was a successful office tower system installed (in Macon, Georgia). Appli-cation to homes was mainly limited to a wealthy few until 1951, when an "inex-pensive, efficient window unit finally hit the market, and sales skyrocketed, especially in the South"; within a few years central air-conditioning systems further propelled that market. By 1970, 50 percent of all Southern households were par-takers of this wonderfully welcome amelioration, and the *New York Times* com-mented that "the humble air-conditioner has been a powerful influence in circulat-ing people as well as air in this country."

That comment was based on the current census, whose own demographers noted "the sudden and unexpectedly large volume of migration to the Sunbelt." Some Northerners had been moving south for many years, but the first net inflow, into selected areas of the traditional South—the Carolinas, Georgia, and Texas—was recorded in 1965–70; during the next decade this pattern was apparent across almost the entire South, and in the 1980s it became a flood. Although comprehen-sive air-conditioning was an essential (use in cars followed about the same timing and trajectory as in homes), this migration was the product of many other factors as well. At this point we need only note the unusually heavy aerospace and defense contracts, rapid emergence of new and expanded light industries, new ease of mar-keting to much of the nation over the interstate highway system and improved air services, and marked easing of racial tensions in the South; once such a movement was well under way, the sheer growth in population sustained increases in con-struction and in wholesale and retail marketing.

In journalistic commentaries on this remarkable shift, the alluring Sun Belt quickly gave rise to a losing "Snow Belt" or "Frost Belt"; as serious economic problems arising from the world oil crisis, heavy inroads of foreign manufactures, inflation, and other woes began to erode the great American Manufacturing Belt in the 1970s, much of this North became known as the "Rust Belt." Such gross generalizations gloss over complex geographic patterns of change, but they point to broad regional demographic shifts: between 1970 and 1990 a major net outflow of people from the American Core states (New England through Wisconsin, north of the Potomac and Ohio) and an unprecedented and large net inflow to the Southern states. During those twenty years the Northeast had a net addition of 4,300,000 to its total (New York State, long the most populous state until this period, actually lost a quarter of a million), but the South added 21,800,000. Florida nearly doubled its population during those years and Florida and Texas together accounted for more than half of that regional growth, but all Southern states gained and the region as a whole was approaching a third of the nation's total population, equaling a position it had not held since 1880.

An important detail within these interregional changes was the participation of Blacks. Throughout their great exodus from the South "people were forever coming and going" between their new Northern place and the old home-place; family visits, seasonal and longer sojourns were shared by all ages. In the early 1970s the balance of this two-way traffic shifted in favor of a greater net flow southward, a countermovement that increased during the 1980s, drawing most heavily from Megalopolis. Although the numbers and local proportions of Blacks in Northern cities generally continued to increase, by 1990 a million more were now recorded residing in the South than in the North, a small but significant part of the larger national redistribution.

The widespread popular acceptance of these new regional terms eventually prompted a sharp critique from geographers as "a case of sloppy regionalizing." Contrary to our focus up to this point on the traditional South and Florida, the Sun Belt as defined by Phillips was a transcontinental expanse from the Carolinas to Southern California—a "Southern Rim," to use Kirkpatrick Sale's favorite term in his even more emphatic emphasis on the unprecedented "power shift" that was gaining such serious attention in the 1970s. To the geographer, the Sun Belt is a generalization superimposed upon deeply different natural and historical regions. Recent migrations have not significantly subdued those differences and should not be assumed to reflect responses to factors common across the full reach of that southerly belt. To put it simply, to lump the Carolinas and the Californias together in the same "region" obscures more than it illuminates about the late twentieth-century reshaping of America.

Obviously there was nothing new about the simple fact of American migration to California as thousands had been going there year after year for a century. Coastal California was air-conditioned by its natural summer-dry, mild winter,

Mediterranean-like climate—"America's Italy." Mechanical air-conditioning was no doubt welcomed by residents of the Central Valley to mitigate the oven-like heat of late summer, but it was not fundamental to the area's strong growth. Only in the new urbanlands of the Southwest deserts, such as Las Vegas, Lake Havasu City, and the metropolitan sprawl of Central Arizona, has air-conditioning been essential to the attraction of large numbers of new residents (in 1950 Las Vegas was barely a city of 25,000, and the Phoenix area was more noted for "snowbirds": winter sojourners from the northerly Western states who returned home before the onset of blistering summer heat).

Huge government research and development investments and the revolution in transport and communications were stimulants to migration to California and the Southwest as they were to Texas and the Southeast, but the larger regional contexts remained sharply different. Whereas the South expanded by drawing heavily upon a declining or impaired industrial North, the western sector of the Sun Belt was part of a larger expanding Far West. California was not only a great focus of migration from the eastern half of the nation, it became an important source of migrants into Far Western states. During the national economic troubles of the 1970s California sent almost as many people out, mostly to Oregon and Washington, as came in from other states, and during a similar subsequent pulsation (1985–91) California contributed a third of the two and a half million in-migrants to other states west of the Rockies. In such swirls of movement the regional frame of a Sun Belt is constrictive and misleading as to the processes and patterns of change (vigorously growing Seattle has the least annual hours of sunshine of any American metropolitan area). Furthermore, whereas the easing of racial tensions was important to the recent attractiveness of the South (and must have helped induce some return migration of Blacks from California to the South), a rising concern over crime and immigration is clearly implied by many Whites queried about their reasons for leaving California. More generally new residents of Eugene, Bend, Coeur d'Alene, Boise, St. George, and dozens of other small Western cities who say they were seeking a better "quality of life" were fleeing a California now foundering on its own famous attractiveness, on its vast, intense, and diverse metropolitan growths.

With nearly 20 million recorded in the 1970 census, California passed New York to become the most populous state in the Union, and by the end of the century its nearly 34 million constituted 12 percent of the national total and accounted for more than half of that of the vigorously growing West as a whole. Such total populations, of course, reflect natural increase and immigration as well as net change from internal migrations, and California had experienced strong growth in all three in recent decades. A simple comparison of regional populations and proportions between those of 1950 and 2000 displays the general shift in balances over this half century of strong growth and change (figs. 61, 62). The reversal of South-

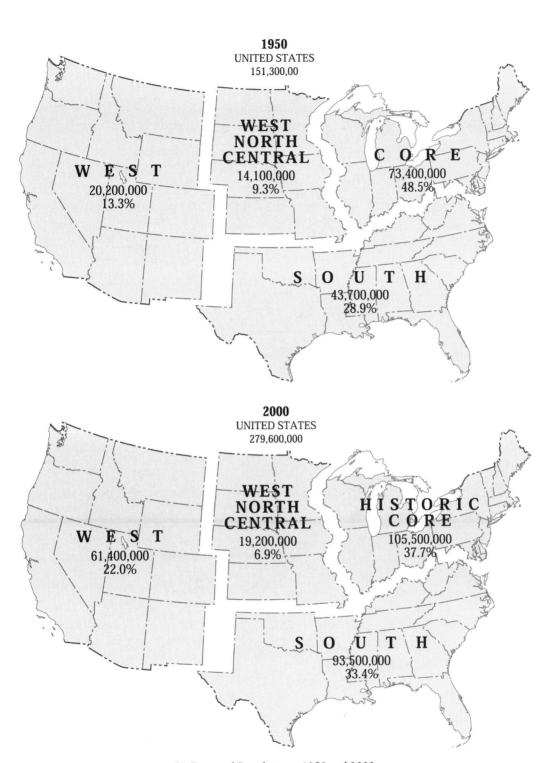

1950
UNITED STATES
151,300,00

WEST
NORTH
CENTRAL
14,100,000
9.3%

C O R E
73,400,000
48.5%

W E S T
20,200,000
13.3%

S O U T H
43,700,000
28.9%

2000
UNITED STATES
279,600,000

WEST
NORTH
CENTRAL
19,200,000
6.9%

H I S T O R I C
C O R E
105,500,000
37.7%

W E S T
61,400,000
22.0%

S O U T H
93,500,000
33.4%

61. Regional Populations, 1950 and 2000.
The boundary between the Core and the South has been shifted to the Potomac River rather than follow the Bureau of the Census use of the Pennsylvania-Maryland boundary. Inclusion of Alaska and Hawaii would add 1,800,000 to the total population in 2000.

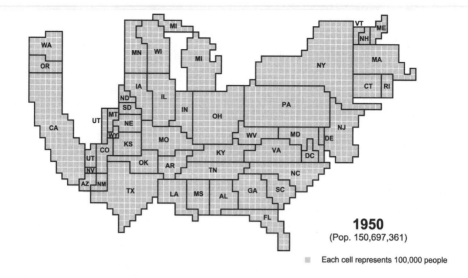

1950
(Pop. 150,697,361)

▨ Each cell represents 100,000 people

2000
(Pop. 281,421,906)

▨ Each cell represents 100,000 people

▨ Increase of more than 20% from 1990 to 2000

62. State Populations, 1950 and 2000.
Cartograms showing state areal size proportioned by population offer a far more striking view of these shifts. (Designed by Joseph W. Stoll)

ern decline and its overall growth was the most unexpected—and now famous—change (although Texas and Florida together account for almost 40 percent of the current population of the region). Given the widespread publicity of the Sun Belt phenomenon it is important to note that the historic Core, though markedly depleted in proportion, remains the most populous section of the nation. As a census demographer cautioned: "During the 1970s extensive media attention was directed at the redistribution of population from a number of Frostbelt states (especially the Rustbelt segment) to many Sunbelt states. Underlying the net movements, however, are far more extensive gross flows, and net migration is typically only a small percentage of the total in and out movements. The net outmigration states of the Northeast and Midwest are not distinguished by high rates of departure among their residents."

Less publicized but of great local and regional importance was the emptying of rural counties in the Farm Belt, a process under way in the 1960s, accelerated by the economic depression of the early 1980s, and slowing somewhat in the 1990s (yet forty-seven of North Dakota's fifty-three counties experienced losses between 1990 and 2000); especially severe in the High Plains, declines were notable all across the Middle West (the entire State of Iowa lost population during the 1990s).

The arrival of millions of newcomers along old and new streams of international migration would of course further affect these internal patterns of population change.

IMMIGRATION IN GENERAL

The McCarran Act of 1952 can now be seen as an extension of what became a forty-year phase within the history of American immigration. Retaining the central concept of severe restrictions on numbers and sources it succeeded in bringing about a steady reduction in the "foreign element" in an expanding national population. In the 1960s the foreign-born slipped below 5 percent of the total, well under half the proportions of the 1920s.

Such a policy was sustained in part by rapid intensification of the Cold War and fears of world communism. Yet all the while the numbers of immigrants were rising, and convulsions within that superpower confrontation sent sudden large clumps of refugees to American shores, most notably following the abortive Hungarian uprising against communist rule in 1955 and the exodus of hundreds of thousands of Cubans to Miami following Fidel Castro's seizure of power at the end of that decade. Such events combined with long-standing dissatisfactions over the complexities and biased selectivities of the 1924/1952 acts led to a complete overhaul of policy during the liberal Johnson administration. The 1965 Immigration and Naturalization Act replaced the national-origins quota system with hemispheric allocations: 170,000 annually for the Eastern Hemisphere (with no more than 20,000 from any one country), and 120,000 for the Western Hemisphere (the first quota ever applied to that half of the world). Furthermore, immigrant visas were to be allocated according to a new system of preferences: family unification (with immediate relatives of legal U.S. residents not charged against numerical quotas), a list of designated skills and employer needs, and refugees. Although various details have since been altered or added (such as a 20,000-per-country limit for the Western Hemisphere, broadening family preference quotas, changes in preferred skills, removal of refugees from regular quotas) this general policy remains the framework for American immigration.

From the time this new act became fully operative in 1968 the number, sources, types, and destinations of immigrants have all markedly changed. In view of the sharp increase in number (almost year by year and certainly decade by decade) to a cumulative total of more than 20 million by the end of the century, the whole era has been referred to as the Second Great Migration. The foreign-born are again almost 10 percent of the American population, and immigration was actually playing a greater role in the nation's overall population growth than it had during the last years of the great inflow before World War I (in part because of a marked decline in the birth rate of the native-born population).

General numbers relating to this topic always need further interpretation. People leave the United States as well as move to it, but "demographic information on emigration" continued to be "particularly scarce and elusive." Special studies have concluded that while annual immigration during the 1990s was averaging about 800,000, an estimated 300,000 residents left the United States, reducing the net yearly increase to half a million (Europeans had the highest rate of departure). Yet these numbers refer to legal immigration, whereas illegal entrants have been much the greatest cause of public and political concern. Here, too, no reliable numbers exist, but recent studies suggest that about 200,000–300,000 enter each year (thus nearly offsetting the number of emigrants), and while it is commonly assumed that most of these sneak across the Mexican border, often as many as 50 percent or more are persons who actually entered legally at some point as nonimmigrants (tourists, students, temporary employees, and so on) and have overstayed their allotted time. The cumulative number of illegal immigrants became so large and intractable that Congress passed an amnesty program in 1986 to legalize those already here who sought to become regular residents. Thus during the 1989–92 about 2,700,000 persons took advantage of that opportunity (thereby inflating the immigration numbers recorded for those particular years).

Refugees from a wide scattering of war-torn lands and oppressive regimes have continued to add unevenly to immigrant totals. Much the largest number arrived in the wake of the U.S. defeat and withdrawal from Vietnam. Many continued to come from Cuba. Before—and just after—the collapse of the Soviet Union a considerable number arrived each year from that country and its East European satellites. Iran, Afghanistan, Ethiopia, Yugoslavia, El Salvador, and various other places have sent brief surges of refugees and asylum seekers. The intent and prospects of such immigrants are likely to remain uncertain for some years after their arrival. Some may seek to stay, others may wish to return to their homeland as soon as practicable. The unpredictable fate of such uprooted populations is well displayed in Miami, where a Cuban business and professional class had expected to return home soon, once Castro had been overthrown.

As Alejandro Portes and Rubén G. Rimbaut note in their introduction to a study of this new era of immigration:

> The human drama remains as riveting, but the cast of characters and their circumstances have changed in complex ways. . . . The heterogeneous composition of the earlier European waves pales in comparison to the current diversity. Today's immigrants came in luxurious jetliners and in the trunks of cars, by boat and on foot. Manual laborers and polished professionals, entrepreneurs and refugees, preliterate peasants and some of the most talented cosmopolitans on the planet—all are helping to reshape the fabric of American society.

THE ASIAN INFLUX

Throughout nearly a century of mass immigration Europe was the great source region, New York City the great gateway, and the Statue of Liberty and nearby Ellis Island became the world-famous symbols of the Open Door—the Front Door welcoming newcomers to America. A major intent of the 1965 act was to provide entry for the backlog of family members from Italy, Greece, and other hitherto low-quota countries seeking to join their relatives in the United States; this liberalization produced an immediate response and continuation of earlier patterns, funneling these Europeans to New York and spreading them on across the American Core.

Much the most important change, however, was a shift from that historic pattern by an influx from East and South Asia unprecedented in volume and variety. By 1970 the number of Filipinos admitted surpassed that from any European country, and China, Korea, and India emerged as important sources. The large protracted surge of refugees from Vietnam, Cambodia, Laos, and Thailand soon followed (including many Chinese residents of those states), as well as further increases from other countries. During the 1980s four times as many of these Asians arrived as Europeans, and by 1990 they outnumbered Europeans among the foreign-born in the United States.

Thus San Francisco once again became a portal for Asian immigration, though it could not become the singular great focus it had been in Gold Rush days nor imitate the role of New York as the great Front Door for this new migration. The air age provided many doors to America, and the much greater variety in status, intentions, and prospects of these new arrivals allowed many of them to disperse quickly from any entry point. Many did enter at San Francisco and settle in the Bay area, augmenting its long-established Chinese, Japanese, and Filipino populations (giving it the highest proportion of Asian population—nearly 15 percent in 1990 —of any mainland metropolitan area; Honolulu, also receiving many immigrants, remained far in the lead in that category). A considerably larger number came by way of Los Angeles and settled in Southern California. Overall, California was certainly a preferred destination, as was displayed in the aftermath of the government's Vietnam resettlement program: to cope with the sudden influx of so many and to avoid overloading social services in Southern California, these refugees were flown in to four army bases located in different sections of the country (including one in Southern California) and, with the help of church and refugee organizations, dispersed to more than 800 towns and cities across all fifty states; with no further restriction on movement, five years later the 20 percent originally assigned to California had been nearly doubled by those who had moved there (Texas had also gained from the large number dispersed across the South).

However, many Asians were well suited for more ready dispersal on their own than had been usual among immigrants. Thousands went directly to New York City, Boston, Washington, Chicago, Houston, and lesser cities in every section of the country. Many came with resources and skills, as entrepreneurs and engineers (Indians became especially prominent in Silicon Valley), physicians and professors, nurses and teachers; armed with college degrees and some command of English (most Filipinos and Asian Indians had learned it at home as well as in school) they were readily employed by American firms and institutions. Others created their own niche through family-run shops and small businesses, or ethnic networks focused on some specialty; thus Chinese, Thai, Korean, Indian restaurants and Oriental groceries now appear in the common American commercial scene alongside those of Italians, Greeks, and others from earlier generations of immigrants; and thus Koreans dominate the greengrocer business in New York City and Indians own more than a quarter of America's motels. Although in the largest reception areas a Koreatown and Little India might emerge as had Chinatowns and Little Tokyos in earlier days, the varied status of recent Asian immigrants and general lack of severe discriminations against them has meant far less segregation within American urban areas than was the case with earlier ethnic groups.

In the 1990 census Asians constituted 25 percent of the foreign-born, and more than 7 million Americans identified themselves as Asian in ancestry, a doubling in number in ten years (this general census category includes Pakistan, Afghanistan,

Iran, and smaller Middle Eastern countries, but their numbers are not large enough to invalidate these generalized proportions and totals here attributed to South and East Asia). The Chinese, earliest of Asian Americans, remained the largest group at 1.6 million, followed closely by Filipinos, from America's one-time colony, at 1.4 million; Japanese, Indians, and Koreans ranked next in order; the 615,000 Vietnamese were by then being augmented by regular immigrants rather than by refugees.

HISPANIC IMMIGRANTS

Although Asian immigration was the great new feature of the late twentieth century, the large influx from Mexico (itself a twentieth-century phenomenon) was much the most controversial and complex in this always complicated topic. Mexico has been the largest single source of immigrants since the mid-1950s, totaling just under half a million during the decade of the 1960s and rising to more than a million and a half during the 1980s. By the mid-1990s Mexico had contributed more than 3 million legal immigrants during the past thirty-five years. Such figures need refining for they say nothing about the number moving back to Mexico (which may run high in some years and is not regularly recorded) or about illegal entrants, the number of whom resident in the United States in recent years is estimated to be greater than that cumulative total of legal arrivals (Mexicans accounted for 70 percent of the more than 2 million applying for amnesty during the brief period of that provision). A useful corollary to these general measures is the 1990 census report that natives of Mexico, numbering 4,300,000, accounted for 21.8 percent of the foreign-born in the United States, 23 percent of whom were naturalized citizens and 30 percent had arrived since 1985 (and these figures can mislead about the growing Mexican-American presence since they do not include the American-born children of these immigrants).

The 1,950-mile boundary between the United States and Mexico bisects one of the world's great cultural borderlands (fig. 63). Even though our concern at this point is with immigration, that topic is deeply embedded in the human geography of this binational zone, and cross-border flows have been a powerful force in shaping some of its most important features. Perhaps the most compelling illustration of that impact is the immense recent growth of Tijuana. That this city in this farthest northwest corner of Mexico, an area of few local resources lying hundreds of miles across the Sonoran Desert from any other populous district in Mexico, is now approaching a million people attests to the enormous pull of California on Mexican workers and to the creation of special new industrial attractions on the Mexican side of the border in an effort to reduce the volume of emigration to the United States.

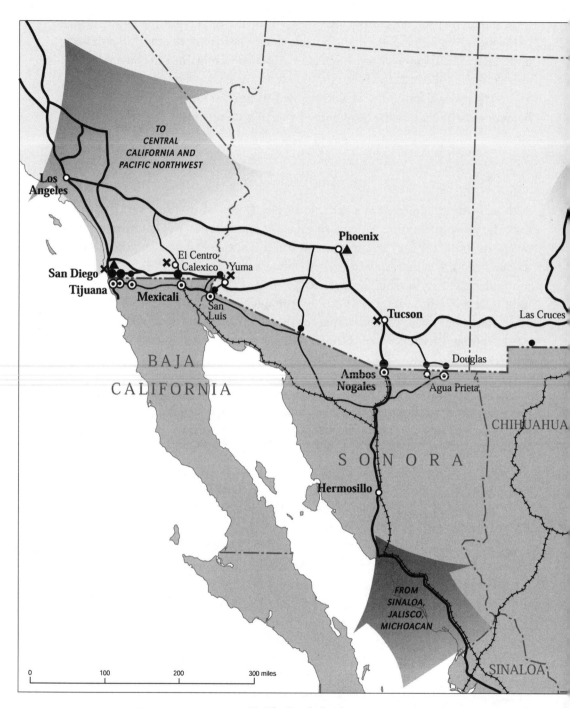

TO
CENTRAL
CALIFORNIA AND
PACIFIC NORTHWEST

Los
Angeles

Phoenix

El Centro
Calexico   Yuma

San Diego
Tijuana

Mexicali

San
Luis

Tucson

Las Cruces

BAJA
CALIFORNIA

Ambos
Nogales

Douglas

Agua Prieta

CHIHUAHUA

S O N O R A

Hermosillo

FROM
SINALOA,
JALISCO,
MICHOACAN

SINALOA

0   100   200   300 miles

63. The Borderland.
Nearly all Mexican states contribute some migrants; those listed for the several channels within
Mexico are the leading sources.

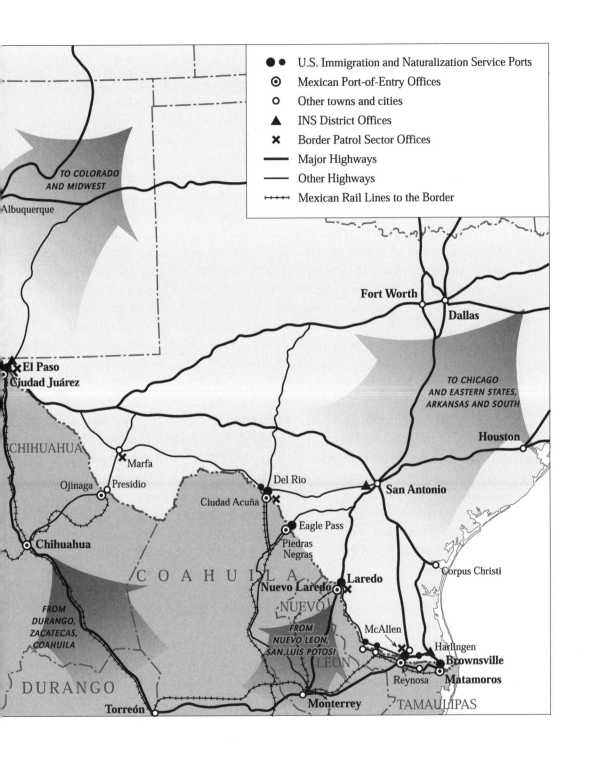

U.S. Immigration and Naturalization Service Ports
Mexican Port-of-Entry Offices
Other towns and cities
INS District Offices
Border Patrol Sector Offices
Major Highways
Other Highways
Mexican Rail Lines to the Border

TO COLORADO AND MIDWEST

Albuquerque

Fort Worth

Dallas

TO CHICAGO AND EASTERN STATES, ARKANSAS AND SOUTH

Houston

El Paso
Ciudad Juárez

CHIHUAHUA

Marfa

Del Rio

San Antonio

Ojinaga   Presidio

Ciudad Acuña

Chihuahua

Eagle Pass

Piedras Negras

Corpus Christi

C O A H U I L A

Nuevo Laredo   Laredo

NUEVO

McAllen

Harlingen

FROM DURANGO, ZACATECAS, COAHUILA

FROM NUEVO LEON, SAN LUIS POTOSI

LEON

Brownsville

DURANGO

Reynosa   Matamoros

Torreón

Monterrey   TAMAULIPAS

On the eve of World War II Tijuana had just over 20,000 residents. A booming business from American tourists and wartime jobs in nearby San Diego brought a spurt of growth to 65,000 by 1950s, but not until that early postwar period did Baja California become bound into the national transport system by a long railroad line from Sonora across the empty desert to Mexicali, and shortly thereafter a paved road and interstate bus service, opening the way for Mexicali and especially Tijuana to become major portals to California. Much later the Border Industrialization Program, allowing tax-free import of raw materials and export of finished products, spurred the creation of large numbers of foreign-owned factories (*maquiladoras*), greatly expanding the local economic base. The heavy influx of migrants through this busiest of borderland corridors has spread thickly over many parts of California urban and rural, rapidly expanding the long-established Hispanic presence to a quarter or a third or more of the total population across much of Southern California and many areas of the Central Valley. The old Mexican barrio in East Los Angeles has been greatly enlarged, and many other current clusters are anchored on farmworker *colonias* or railroad yards and industrial neighborhoods of an earlier era, but there has been a much wider dispersal as well, reinforcing both the perception and the reality of the powerful impact of recent immigration upon the famous Golden State.

Nogales, on the old main route serving the Pacific states of Mexico, still provides entry for many California-bound migrants as well as lesser numbers of those finding jobs in Arizona's rapidly growing cities (expanding very largely from non-Hispanic-American migrants—the Phoenix metropolitan area is only 16 percent Hispanic). Earlier cross-border links in railways, mining, smelting, agriculture, and ranching are now much less significant, but there are maquiladoras at the border and large American industrial plants in Hermosillo, the Sonoran capital, and this route is an important commercial trafficway connecting Sinaloa's California-style agribusiness with American markets.

Ciudad Juárez–El Paso, with a combined population of 1,300,000, is much the largest single, interdependent, borderland metropolis. The American city was in origin and development almost wholly a product of this strategic borderland position, and 70 percent of its half million people are Hispanic. Juárez has much the largest number of maquiladoras, and local cross-border traffic is heavy. The north-south route crossing here has long been an important commercial and migrant passageway connecting central Mexico with the central United States. Recent migrants are drawn to long-established Mexican districts in Kansas City, Chicago, St. Paul, Detroit, and other industrial centers and to Denver and newer feedlot and meat-packing centers on the High Plains, such as Garden City, Kansas (where they compete with new Southeast Asian immigrants for jobs in the world's biggest beef-packing plant).

The heaviest commercial traffic between the two countries flows through Laredo, a trunk line connecting the eastern half of the United States with northern Mexico's largest industrial center at Monterrey and through there to the core of the country. This route leads immigrants straight across 150 miles of open country to San Antonio, with easy dispersal from there to Houston, Dallas–Fort Worth, and beyond. The several crossings in the Lower Rio Grande Valley lead directly into an old Hispanic homeland later invaded by American settlers. Here a million people live on each side of the border; more than 85 percent of those on the American side are Hispanic, and six separate crossing places are mainly for local traffic. Brownsville, near the mouth of the Rio Grande, serves as a port more for Mexico than for its small American hinterland.

The cities and towns at the many crossing points vary greatly in size, volume of traffic, and character. Several major ones, Ambos Nogales, Ciudad Juárez–El Paso, Los Dos Laredos, Matamoros-Brownsville, are interdependent dual cities, separated only by a fence or bridges, their economies and societies a creation of their transnational relationships. In marked contrast San Diego developed as a thoroughly American city for which Tijuana, fifteen miles to the south, was no more than a day-trip tourist attraction. American migrants and new industries powered its rapid growth after World War II during which one corridor of expansion spread southward. Whereas Tijuana continued to be almost completely dependent on its relationship with the United States, only recently has San Diego annexed San Ysidro, the community directly on and of the border, and undertaken the development of a special industrial park adjoining Tijuana (uncoordinated with analogous developments on the Mexican side); Mexican immigrants are a rising proportion of the population in this southern extension (and some Anglo-American citizens have moved to the Mexican side in search of cheaper housing).

Beyond these portals, two borderland metropolitan areas are especially important in Mexican migration flows. Los Angeles has the largest Mexican and Hispanic population in the United States, the latter amounting to more than a third of the total. Yet this sprawling metropolis contains such a variety of immigrant groups (including many Hispanics from other sources) dispersed among so many locales and the whole human complex is so full of movement and change that the Mexican impress is not as striking as its numbers might suggest; here, especially, "powerful social, cultural and economic forces . . . are drawing Mexicans into the mainstream of American life." In contrast, San Antonio, where the Mexicans have been a continuing presence since its Spanish foundation, is, as Daniel Arreola has well maintained, the real "Mexican-American cultural capital." Mexican Americans make up half of the metropolitan population, and immigrants arriving on the West Side encounter and reinforce a deep-rooted society sustaining much of the familiar forms of language, religion, endogamy, and other social customs; it is also an unusually well-organized political society, arising from a strong consciousness of "Mexican" in opposition to long-dominant Anglo-Texans (and thereby has contributed Mexican-American leaders to state and national politics). However, San Antonio is not a major growth area and therefore serves more as a staging place for further immigrant dispersal than as a main destination (less than 15 percent of its Hispanic residents are foreign-born).

Mexicans have spread into all American regions and nearly all of the fifty states (Mexico recently opened consulates in Anchorage and Honolulu), but mounting concerns about this particular immigration have naturally stressed changes in California and the Southwest and especially the volume of illegal entry into the United States. From the latter 1970s onward there have been strident calls to "regain control of our borders," recurrent augmentations of the Border Patrol, expansion of fences, walls, and various instruments of surveillance at major crossings, and larger numbers of "undocumented" (a more neutral term in common official use) aliens apprehended and expelled ("voluntary departure," as the immigration authorities call it). Yet a 1997 official report stated "that it was as yet impossible to determine whether the billions of dollars spent in this effort in recent years had actually reduced the flow of undocumented Mexicans into the United States."

"The movement of people across the border has been and remains breathtaking. In 1996 280 million legal land crossings were made from Mexico into the United States." Most of this, of course, was "cross-border commuting in binational twin cities—to work, to shop, use services, or socialize," local travel "facilitated by the possession of a U.S.-issued border-crossing card by more than 5 million Mexican residents." Immigration is a generally different category of movement but one deeply affected by the scale and routine of these borderline complexes, which also serve as major "springboards" and "recepticales" for more distant movements into and out of the United States. These portals can serve as a reminder that some of these localities were a homeland of Hispanic settlers long before American conquest and colonization ("some of us have been here for three hundred years, some for three days") and that long after the boundary was drawn crossings were routine and generally unregulated. Mass immigration is a phenomenon of the past half century, following the bracero program and concurrent with the enormous growth of the U.S. economy, and that relationship can serve as a reminder that "Mexican immigration . . . originated in deliberate recruitment by North American interests and was not a spontaneous movement"; subsequent inflows have strongly reflected formal or tacit mutual interests of American employers and Mexican workers.

Once under way such movements tend to acquire their "own momentum and become progressively more widespread" within both originating and receiving countries. Familial and locality networks become increasingly efficient channels between Mexican regions and "daughter" communities in the United States, the ease and volume of travel between them aided by improvements in highways and transport services in both countries. (Houston's old barrio "has become the Mexican gateway . . . for all the Eastern and Central United States. Hispanic bus and van lines feed passengers from as far away as Chicago, Miami, and New York to destinations as distant as Mexico City and Oaxaca, but to Monterrey most of all.") Thus most Mexican immigrants stay in touch with their home communities, strategies of recurrent migration—repeated movements back and forth and stays of varied length at either end—are common, "sentimental attachment to their native culture" remains strong, and the issues of settlement and integration into American society "remain problematic and ambiguous" for many migrants. Such maintenance of transnational ties and Mexican identities and resistance to full assimilation on the usual American terms underlie much of the concern expressed about this immigration.

Mexicans are of course but one nationality among the varied body of Hispanic immigrants (the latter a term now in common use by government agencies for what was earlier classified as "Spanish-origin population"). These same overland routes and portals have also been used by Central Americans, especially Salvadorans and Guatemalans (many of them refugees from civil wars in which the United States had intervened), who now number about half a million in Los Angeles. Others from that region might enter at New Orleans or Miami. Much the most famous and unusual Hispanic influx was the sudden invasion of Miami by Cuban exiles in the early 1960s. Although there had long been close personal and commercial connections between the two countries (and occasional small groups of political exiles), in 1959 there were only about 50,000 Cubans in the United States, and relatively few in Miami. During the 1960s, 350,000 arrived, and although the U.S. government attempted some dispersal, most either stayed in Miami or soon returned there (Union City, New Jersey, with an early small Cuban community became another smaller exile enclave—"Havana on the Hudson"—a "sister city" of Miami with much contact between the two). As the initial influx was mainly of middle- and upper-class families with skills, connections, and entrepreneurial experience they soon created a thriving Cuban community, a Little Havana, that was able to absorb the shock of the sudden exodus of another 125,000 in the early 1980s; these later newcomers were a much broader representation of Cuban society and completed the transformation of Miami into "the mythical capital of the so-called Cuban Exile Country," a sustained cultural-national enclave unprecedented in size and character within the body of the United States. By 1990, 800,000 Cubans had come to the United States, and a majority lived in Florida.

The Dominican Republic became the source of another rapid upwelling of immigration in the 1980s, with so many fleeing that poor, crowded country across the narrow seas to Puerto Rico that Congress authorized a Border Patrol unit for the latter island. San Juan thereby became an important portal, but it has been only a stopover en route to New York, where Dominicans now number at least 400,000, second in size to Puerto Ricans among the city's varied Hispanic residents. (The growing tensions between these two may not ease soon: a recent Santo Domingo newspaper poll reported that "half of all Dominicans now have relatives in the United States and more than two-thirds would move there if they could.")

All Hispanic-American countries contribute immigrants to the United States, nearly a million in total in 1990, with yearly numbers from particular countries often reflecting episodic political pressures as well as chronic economic stress; they also represent most all levels of society, with many professionals dispersing to metropolitan centers across the United States. (It is worth noting that non-Hispanic Brazil, with much the largest population in Latin America, sends very few: only 4,200 in 1990.)

OTHER NORTH AMERICANS

The non-Hispanic West Indies continued their lesser but influential streams: 20,000 or so each year from Jamaica and from Haiti, with smaller numbers from the many other islands. New York was their principal destination but Miami a growing one, especially for Haitians (and West Indian Blacks long resident in the New York area were becoming increasingly responsive to the tropical lures of Florida). Often generalized as part of the larger Caribbean diaspora, these movements continued to sustain and invigorate a Greater Afro–North American World.

Movements across America's northern border continued to be mostly routine and of little political concern in the United States. The two countries have long exchanged residents and citizens, the balance commonly southward and reflecting relative economic opportunities. In the late 1960s and early 1970s the number of Americans moving to Canada was at times double the number of Canadians moving south, a reflection in part of those crossing the border to avoid the draft during the Vietnam War. Canada has since instituted strict controls on immigration. The number of Canadian immigrants to the United States has averaged about 12,000– 15,000 annually in recent years (half of what it was in the 1960s); Canadians ranked third in the number of foreign-born in the United States (755,000 in 1990), following Mexico and the Philippines, and just ahead of Cuba.

CONCERNS AND COMPLEXITIES, OLD AND NEW

During the latter years of the twentieth century immigration once again became "one of the most contentious topics of debate in the United States." Amid congressional campaigns for much more stringent controls and a polemical literature featuring such titles as *The Immigration Invasion* and *Alien Nation*, the debate seemed in many ways a recapitulation of those early in that century. Once again, there was concern over the sheer scale of "mass immigration," over distinctively new sources of peoples, over America's ability to integrate and absorb such diversity, over the impact on the nation's traditional values and character.

Although "Americans have always been ambivalent toward immigration," they have only rarely taken major comprehensive action on the topic. As Nathan Glazer observed during the latest upwelling of concern: "When one considers present immigration policies, it seems we have insensibly reverted to mass immigration, without ever having made a decision to do so." He was referring especially to the act of 1965 that had ended sixty years of narrow Old World selectivity. Enacted while Congress and the public were much more concerned about civil rights, that legislation had set a relatively modest annual quota, together with provisions for some special cases. The unanticipated results flowing from that act and other world developments over the next twenty years fueled the movement for another comprehensive assessment of policies and portends. Citing the drastic reduction following the act of 1924 as a valuable "breathing space" that allowed integration and assimilation of the great pre–World War I influx, some restrictionists advocated "a five-year moratorium on immigration" to assess recent results and determine what new policies might best serve the nation. In the 1990s major bills in Congress, bipartisan federal commissions, and numerous opinion polls of a variety of American groups (including the foreign-born) all supported marked reductions and firmer controls of immigration—with little effect.

All of these attempts at major immigration reform foundered on the deep conflicts of interest and complexities of attitude long inherent in the topic. Broadly, the principal grounds for dispute were economic and sociocultural. As for the former, general arguments that immigrants were taking away jobs from American citizens, lowering wages, undermining labor unions and standards, as well as becoming a burden on taxpayers for local services were countered by those who insisted that immigrant labor and skills were essential in a wide range of industries and that they contributed far more to the national economy than they cost. The topic was so complex and measurement of effects so difficult that one might well conclude with Glazer "that economics in general can give no large answer as to what the immigration policy of a nation should be." American business leaders, however, had a large and ready answer: their opposition to any reductions in foreign worker intake "was overwhelming" (the *Wall Street Journal* has long called for "open borders").

The debate over the impact on the fundamentals of the American national character was even more intense and insoluble, mired in deeply different views of what kind of society the United States was, is, might, or ought to become. Expressions of alarm over changes attributed to or expected from the new sources and characteristics of recent immigrants were countered by expressions of confidence in the long-demonstrated ability of American society to integrate and assimilate diversity, and admiration of the enrichment derived therefrom ("the doctrine of the melting pot may not be good history but it is powerful ideology"). Clichés of America as "a nation of immigrants" and a haven for the oppressed continued to have a powerful appeal, in Congress and out. In the end, "when pressure built to 'do something' about immigration, illegal aliens were a natural target. And that is precisely what Congress did" (in 1996)—without, as yet, major effect.

Although much of this debate was a rehearsal of old arguments, there *were* important differences in this recent upsurge. "What is new is global migration from the farthest reaches, across the greatest distances, involving all the world's populated regions and migrants as diverse as the peoples of the world, and accomplished by foot, car, ship, and jet." The propensity to migrate on such a scale "is a direct consequence of the dominant influence attained by the culture of the advanced West in every corner of the globe," creating "a sinewy web of relationships" with the United States "at the core." Drawing the greatest number from the greatest variety of places—"more immigrants than all other countries combined," from nearly 200 different political states or colonies—such magnetic power was surely one of the defining features of a Global America.

A second major difference is more geographically specific: the volume and character of movement across the U.S.-Mexican boundary. Given the great asymmetry between the two countries in national economies and distributions of wealth among their citizens, together with high population growth in Mexico (doubling to 100 million over the past twenty-five years), and assuming a continuing availability of jobs and much higher wages in the United States, a high volume of movement will presumably continue to take place even though public policies in either country may attempt to reduce it. Furthermore, the character of much of this immigration differs in its implications: a vast folk movement maintaining footholds and families in both countries, ambivalent about where "home" should be. Although the same may have been true for some immigrants from Europe, the scale and propinquity of this relationship makes it of unprecedented social and geopolitical significance. Having long ago created a shared borderland, in recent decades Mexicans and Americans have been in effect creating a shared continent. Indeed, together with the historic ease over crossings of the U.S. northern boundary, Canadians, Americans, and Mexicans (and Puerto Ricans, Cubans, and Dominicans) seem to be creating a "'peoples' North America," featuring volumes and complexities of movements from one country to another with or without official permissions. Although many citizens and leaders of the "naturally" dominant nation of North America may be disturbed by this concept and prospect, it is already a powerful force in the continuous reshaping of the internal character of the United States.

7. Some Reconfigurations

Accelerating changes during the last half of the twentieth century were little short of revolutionary in many respects. Because in longer perspective these represent a re-acceleration following the relatively stable urban and regional formations of the first half of that century, changes during this latest period in the shaping of America can be generally measured from our earlier regional reconnaissance and mid-century morphology.

METROPOLITANIZATION

In the summer of 1947 Levitt & Sons, Inc., broke ground in a former potato field on Long Island for "the largest private housing project in American history." The Levittown created on this 4,000-acre tract in the Town of Hempstead, twenty-five miles east of Manhattan, eventually contained 17,500 houses and 82,000 residents—and even more quickly became the foremost exhibit of a new American "suburbia." Suburbs were of course not new in general and Levittown was not wholly new in type, yet its scale, efficiency, uniformity, and affordability became a model for others soon emerging on the outskirts of every American city during the late 1940s and 1950s. Financed by generous new federal mortgage and loan policies ("if it weren't for the Government the boom would end overnight"), these large new additions became the symbol and substance of "a new way of life," of progress and prosperity for a much-broadened class of homeowners. As Kenneth T. Jackson put it, "the early Levitt house was as basic to post–World War II suburban development as the Model T had been to the automobile. In each case, the actual design features were less important than the fact that they were mass-produced and thus priced within reach of the middle class" (fig. 64). It became quickly understood that a young family could buy a brand new *modern* house in the suburbs more cheaply than it could buy or even rent an older one in the city; once that differential had been legislated into the American housing market, expansion outward—"suburban sprawl"—was guaranteed, and some inward contraction and depression of older parts of the city were almost certain to follow.

Nevertheless, this first great surge of postwar expansion was literally *sub-urban*: residential tracts anchored on a central city. Schools, churches, recreation grounds, and small shopping centers for daily necessities were included within, or sprang up near, these large developments, but the jobs remained in the city; 80 percent of the men in Levittown commuted to Manhattan, 80 percent or more of the women remained at home, raising children ("in Levittown, all activity stops from 12 to 2 in the afternoon; that is nap time"). All across the country Central Business Districts (CBDs) remained the great focus of shops, offices, government, big churches, entertainment, and all bus routes. These downtowns, too, were modernizing, cover-

64. Levittown.
The basic character of this mammoth project is starkly displayed in this 1948 view. Each of these Cape Cod boxes was filled with modern appliances; no garage or carport was included. (Courtesy Levittown Public Library)

ing turn-of-the-century façades with sleek claddings and stylish trim, yet there was relatively little real expansion, whereas the suburbs, having met the most pressing postwar demands for housing, continued to expand and diversify to cater to higher levels of income and taste; soon they were luring major businesses as well as people. By the late 1950s concerns over "the exploding metropolis" and the contrasting vitality of center and suburbs had become matters of nationwide attention.

During the next phase of this "suburban revolution" the rise of large shopping centers and clusters of major motels and other services at outlying freeway interchanges rapidly drained prosperity from most downtowns. In response, civic leaders, with unprecedented help from the federal government (which had long "fastidiously avoided involvement in municipal affairs"), initiated massive programs of "urban renewal." Under the direction of special planning agencies large portions of the historic centers were demolished and "a new geography" was imposed "on the face of the town" featuring office towers, parking garages, and new civic buildings usually standing alone amid open spaces on newly formed superblocks; in the larger cities massive, dense public housing projects on former "blighted areas" were an important part of the program. Such "renewal" involved the "traumatic uprooting of many thousands of individuals and families" and displacement or destruction of many small shops and services with little recognition of existing neighborhood ties or the complexities of social problems. While some high-quality buildings and attractive spaces were added to townscapes, the commercial vitality of most centers continued to fade, and this kind of radical program, having generated considerable local resistance, was soon abandoned. The whole approach expressed a narrow view of cities as economic utilities. As Carole Rifkind concluded in her 1977 photograph history of "the face of urban America": "Ironically, American optimism, faith in progress, energy, technical innovation—the qualities that built a great urban nation . . . —these very same qualities were now galvanized in a vast unbuilding. . . . Time-honored landmarks, at the heart of the town, were sacrificed as obsolete. . . . Homogeneity replaced diversity. Order obliterated vitality. Space succeeded place."

The emergence of Edge Cities, with gigantic shopping malls, office complexes, and new light industries, marked the most critical new phase of metropolitanization (fig. 65). Concurrent with completion of interstate highways and outer beltways, these new centers were largely detached from daily dependence on the central city. Traffic was increasingly circumferential, connecting the ring of warehousing and other outlying service centers, serving the flow of employees from all directions and at greater distances. ("Corporate executives living on their nearby estates often move their head offices to the edge city. A short journey to work is still important to them, as it was for owners of old perched in their grand houses on the hill overlooking their mills and worker's villages.") Housing tracts were no longer sub-urban in the older sense; they were also largely empty during the day as women joined the nondomestic workforce in far greater numbers and variety of employment (and as two incomes were judged to be necessary to keep a household abreast of ever-rising levels of American middle-class "standards of living").

Central cities tended to remain strongholds of government, finance, information networks, large medical complexes, major arts facilities, and convention centers. In the more prosperous places new office towers went up—and the sidewalks emptied. To attract more downtown life, the emphasis shifted from demolition to preservation and restoration. The 1950s cladding was removed from business blocks and the elaborate detail of old façades highlighted by fresh paint; nearby well-built but run-down housing was "gentrified" by young professionals with good jobs in the center's healthy institutions; fountains and "festival centers" were created (Baltimore's Harbor Place among the most elaborate and famous). Yet such

65. Edge City.

The loose cluster of offices and shops in Addison and Prestonwood fifteen miles north of downtown Dallas. The LBJ Freeway (I-635) in the middle distance is the inner metropolitan beltway.
(Courtesy C. Troy Mathis)

costly contrivances could not halt more fundamental trends, and "none of these
central city rebounds should be misinterpreted as city renewal."

Urban historians have appropriately emphasized that "the trend toward the
super-city had long been present in American life." Until the 1950s that trend was
generally understood as an ever-greater urban massing around a primary center;
thereafter this concentric model was becoming loosened and altered so rapidly as to
raise fears that most Americans would soon "be living in fifteen great, sprawling,
nameless communities—which are rapidly changing the human geography of the
entire country." By the end of the century most of them were indeed living within
or in easy reach of such giant clusters, although most of these continued to be identified with a major city. "Megalopolis" had come into considerable use for the oldest and greatest of these conglomerates, but the individuality of its deeply rooted
great cities was never lost in the mass (nor, fortunately, subsumed by such geography jargon as "Boswash" or "Bosnywash"). The need to slow, shape, and limit such
powerful spatial expansion—this uncontrolled formless reality of America that
Benton MacKaye was decrying eighty years earlier—has become ever more widely
expressed, but with as yet little general effect. Attempts by incorporated places to

impose more restrictive zoning, higher development fees, annual limits on the number of new houses, or even growth moratoriums, run into powerful opposition from the building industry. More fundamentally, a population increasing by 2 to 3 million a year needs more housing and services, more space, and most Americans do not want governments—local, state, or national—to specify where that space must be found. American courts have always been wary of limitations on American mobility and on individual and corporate property rights.

Recent American metropolitanization is something more than just a vast sprawl; it is not really formless, but a common generic term for its patterning has not readily emerged. It is "a patchwork" that includes an old central city with its own characteristic areas, "inner suburbs, large suburban centers, office parks, retail centers, a few manufacturing communities . . . , and even low density rural territory—in addition to the stereotypical bedroom communities" (and these last highly varied by class and taste); it is a set of complexly related parts, not all focused toward the city: "more like a constellation than a solar system." The geographer Peirce Lewis drew a similar analogy and offered a term for it: "on the map, this new urban morphology looked like a galaxy of stars and planets held together by mutual gravitational attraction, but with large empty spaces between them" (fig. 66). He further noted that the process of creating these great clusters "was endemic, but it was not new. The skeletal structure of the *galactic city* was already in place in Los Angeles by the end of the 1920s" (emphasis added).

A more fundamental pattern was the geopolitical fragmentation of most American metropolitan areas. Such patchworks of legal territorial entities varying greatly in size, population, and character, in politics, problems, and power, had enormous implications for the vitality of urban systems. The emergence of this feature became prominent after World War I. In earlier times American cities tended to expand their political boundaries more or less in keeping with their spreading physical extent. Not only had a growing city been generally regarded as a source of regional pride, a symbol of progress and sophistication, but cities could offer important services to bordering areas: good streets, water and sewage systems, police and fire protection, better schools. By the 1920s, however, the sheer scale of big industrial cities, their ever-greater ethnic and racial variety and problems of governance, had generated more attention to the pathologies of urban life than to its attractions; the automobile provided new means of escape and the suburbs incorporated to resist annexation. During that decade major campaigns by St. Louis and Pittsburgh failed, and in the American Core, at least, urban annexation was essentially over.

However, cities are legal creatures of the state with specified powers and duties, and the states differ in their internal geopolitical structure and the power granted to various levels of local authority. Municipal annexation is not even authorized by law in some states and is allowed only under stringent procedures in many others;

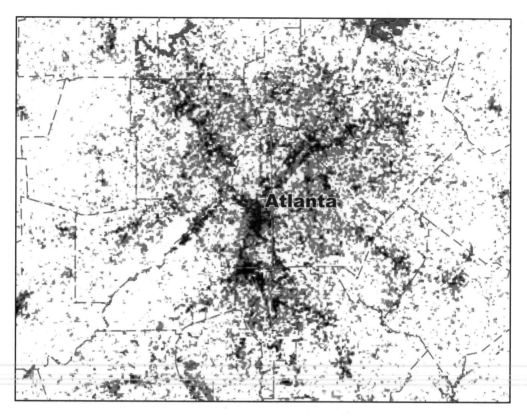

66. Galactic City.
Urbanization ("dense" and "sparse" by shadings) spread across a dozen counties within a forty-mile radius of central Atlanta. (Adapted from land use images by NASA/Goddard Space Flight Center Scientific Visualization Studio)

yet a few have given cities strong annexation powers. Similarly, the ease of local incorporation of suburbs or other settlements within rural countrysides varies widely from state to state. David Rusk, an urban specialist (and former mayor of Albuquerque) has popularized his concept of "elastic" and "inelastic" cities with regard to the relative ease or difficulty of central city expansion by annexation or by other comprehensive means (such as city-county consolidation). A map based on his detailed assessment of American metropolitan areas reveals strong regional contrasts in this feature (fig. 67). As he notes, "in effect, the geopolitical map of New England, New Jersey, New York, and Pennsylvania is set in concrete," and the western half of the historic American Core is not greatly different (Indianapolis consolidated with its county only by a special act of the state legislature). Whereas most of the older large cities in the South have been no more than moderately elastic, some states, notably North Carolina, Florida, and Texas, have been strongly supportive

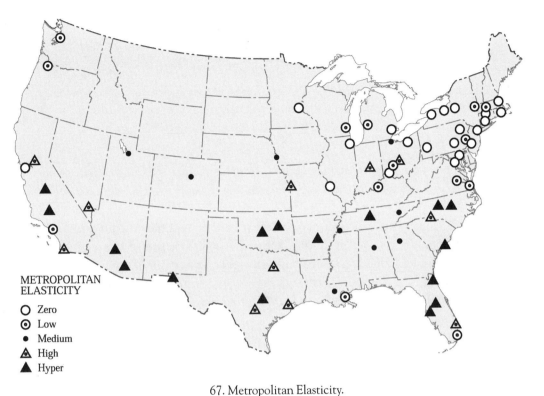

67. Metropolitan Elasticity.
Based on the categories calculated by David Rusk in *Cities without Suburbs* for metropolitan areas of at least 500,000.

of urban annexation. Jacksonville became the largest city in area in the United States; Houston was allowed to annex unincorporated rural areas by simple city council decision. Similarly, most of the recent-growth cities in the West have expanded by annexation, a process made easier in some cases by the dependence of new development on the extension of city water systems.

The current importance of this geopolitical topic arises not simply from the unprecedented scale of American metropolitan growth but from its direct bearing upon "the toughest issue in American society." Whereas urban annexation was earlier presented as a matter of efficiency—the need for better management of routine services for a growing population—recent concerns also stress urban elasticity as a matter of equity. As Rusk summarizes:

An inelastic area has a central city frozen within its city limits and surrounded by growing suburbs. It may have a strong downtown business district as a regional employment center, but its city neighborhoods are increasingly catch basins for poor Blacks and Hispanics. With the flight of middle-class families, the city's population has dropped steadily (typically by 20 percent or more). The income gap between city residents and suburbanites steadily widens. City government is squeezed between rising service needs and eroding incomes. Unable to tap the areas of greater economic growth . . . , the city becomes increasingly reliant on federal and state aid. The suburbs are typically fragmented into multiple towns and small cities and mini school systems. This very fragmentation of local government reinforces racial and economic segregation. Rivalry among jurisdictions often inhibits the whole area's ability to respond to economic challenges.

Proponents do not suggest that elasticity is by itself a cure for difficult urban problems, and certainly not for "the toughest issue," but it can provide a basis for a much more comprehensive approach and an easing of disparities in burdens and resources. While "cities without suburbs" may not be feasible literally, political strategists look for ways of "stretching" cities through some sort of limited metropolitan government based on shared authority and coordination in a common purpose. (The Portland Metropolitan Services District, created by the Oregon legislature and involving three counties and twenty-four municipalities, is often cited as an example.)

However, as Jackson has noted, whereas "efficiency and the regional character of many contemporary problems point to the necessity of government that is metropolitan in authority and planning," that stance is only one side of "a dilemma that has confronted American cities for two hundred years," for "democracy seems to call for government to remain small and close to the people." Americans have been famously inclined in general to value the latter, but that preference has had special imperatives and connotations in this context. As Jon C. Teaford concludes in his assessment of the matter, urban reform has "repeatedly collided with the implacable realities of social and ethnic separation: most Americans desired not a unified metropolis but a fragmented one, where like-minded people lived together untroubled by those of differing opinions, races, or life-styles. . . . Thus, Americans opted for the dissolution of the city and with the aid of the automobile, created the dispersed and fragmented metropolitan world of the late twentieth century."

Cities have, of course, always been a mosaic of social neighborhoods ranging from an upper class displaying "a clear material statement of status, power, and privilege . . . in the most picturesque real estate," on down through gradations of status to the meanest streets, and from those same dominantly White Anglo-Saxon Protestant preserves on across a variety of ethnoreligious and racial neighborhoods. The fragmentation of new postwar areas was in general a continuation of such sociogeographical patterning ("not a single one of Levittown's 82,000 residents was black"), with controls and exclusions only somewhat lessened by a sequence of federal actions. In large part this may be seen as a search for protection, for "resistance to annexation is symptomatic of the view that metropolitan problems are unsolvable and that the only sensible solution is isolation." That, too, is a continuation: moving away from local problems is as old as American frontiering. It may also represent a search for identity amid the mass of the modern metropolitan world, a concern for place rather than mere space, a recognizable, named locality rather than just a street, house number, and ZIP code. It would be less easy to make the case that resistance to annexation to a larger political body represents strong support for vitalized local government, simply because Americans have not generally been that concerned about civic management and have so widely allowed themselves to be placed "in the thrall of corporations." American cities have, of course, always been bold projections of the primacy of privatism and capitalism, developed and redeveloped under conditions of intense competition by thousands of entrepreneurs. The great postwar difference was not just in the scale of development but more especially in the concentration of corporate power: huge enclosed malls replacing Main Street, and office parks, edge cities, and whole new towns controlled by a single or, at most, a few developers, in contrast with the much more incremental growth by small-scale investors and households typical of earlier eras.

As emphasized in *Atlantic America,* from the earliest days of the Republic "the basic dynamics of American expansionism were unprecedented," and they continue to be, now prominently expressed in metropolitan form. Late in the twentieth century calls for a "new urbanism"—featuring greater housing densities, neighborhood shopping, green space, and other amenities—and attempts to exert greater local and regional political authority to limit and shape spatial expansion were some of the louder reverberations from this continuing metropolitan "explosion." But the United States was not running out of space, nor were Americans reducing their dependence on automobiles, and this form and mode of expansionism would not likely be altered to any significant degree unless the immense infrastructure basic to it all could no longer be expanded to serve it well and the traffic congestion, costs in time and energy, and other discomforts gave rise to popular resistance from its daily participants and thereby set in motion search for alternative American ways of life.

DECENTRALIZATION

If we shift our focus from a metropolitan to a national scale some broadly analogous patterns of change over the past half century come into view: strong growth beyond the long-established center (the historic American Core), resulting in some contraction and depression of that dominant area and diminution of its power and prestige; this continuing expansion outward (in the American Domain) transformed rural into urban, bound old small centers into mushrooming complexes, and resulted in the emergence of major metropolises of more than regional signifi-

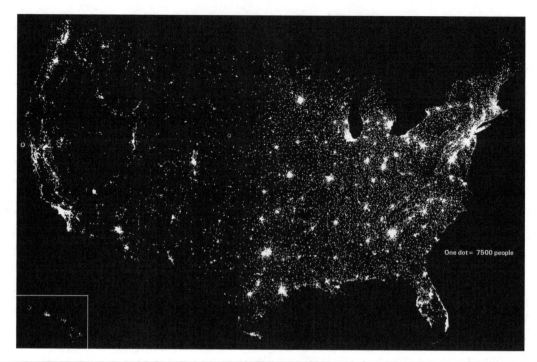

68. National Galaxy.

Population distribution in the United States, 2000. Hawaii in lower left box; a large box show-ing Alaska in the original has been excluded to keep the map at this scale. (Prepared by Geogra-phy Division, U.S. Department of Commerce, Economics Statistics Administration, U.S. Cen-sus Bureau)

cance (Atlanta, Houston, Dallas, and Denver are old cities, but the large extent of their physical newness and influence makes them not unlike edge cities on the pe-riphery of the old center). On the map this new national morphology also "looked like a galaxy of stars and planets . . . with large empty spaces between them" (fig. 68), and it, too, remained geopolitically fragmented (among the states) and could be managed as a whole only through limited specialized agencies and continual ne-gotiations among its many (federal) parts.

Furthermore, expansive developments beyond the Historic Core were also pow-erfully aided by policies of the national government. The federal tax code (as with Federal Housing Administration mortgage and loan policies) was not specifically discriminatory by area, but "the investment tax credit and the allowances for accu-mulated depreciation, have consistently favored new plants over older ones, and new investment over maintenance as a survival strategy." So, too, the Interstate Highway System (like beltways around the metropolis) created a new level of na-tionwide connectivity, deeply undermining old patterns of locational advantage. Much the most direct impact on regional development came from the unprecedented and prolonged "militarization of the economy," growing out of World War II and sustained by the Cold War. The high-tech revolution in electronics was an outgrowth of wartime innovations, and federal dollars supported at least 60 percent of the research and development that has since had a major impact upon virtually every industry. As Ann Markusen summarized: "The sheer size of these government-engendered sectors and the unique geopolitical and strategic forces which shaped their regional distribution explain in large part why the United States has had such massive postwar internal redistribution of productive capacity, unlike any other major industrial nation."

Shifts in regional shares of the value of prime military contracts offer a simple measure of this influence on general patterns of change. During World War II the long-established Manufacturing Belt received about three-quarters of such contracts; by the early 1960s this had been reduced to just over half of the total, and California and the West accounted for nearly one-third; by 1990 the South had overtaken the West by a small margin, each having just under 30 percent, leaving the Frost Belt with 43 percent. In 1990 half of the states each received over a billion dollars of this federal expenditure, but half a dozen received half of the 124 billion total (fig. 69). In these postwar years Department of Defense programs had shifted rapidly into electronics and communications, missiles, and space systems, as well as continued developments in aircraft. Major new government facilities, such as the NASA space centers in Houston and Florida and Redstone Arsenal in Huntsville, Alabama, were added to new high-tech private firms clustered mainly in New England and California (in 1990 California alone received nearly 20 percent of Defense Department contracts). The main loser in these regional shifts was the Middle Western half of the old Manufacturing Belt, so heavily based on steel, automobiles, and other heavy capital and consumer goods. Michigan, a great focus of that sector, ranked twenty-fourth in the state list of military contracts.

The automobile industry, long the greatest emblem of the industrial Middle West, illustrates important regional change in the private sector. During the last quarter of the twentieth century American automakers came under unprecedented pressure from foreign imports. Japanese companies rapidly gained a significant share of the huge California market and steadily penetrated the nation; as sales grew (and to counter political pressures for restrictive quotas) they set up assembly plants, and eventually whole factories. Subsequently, German companies (Mercedes and BMW) also established factories in the United States. Such competition has forced a massive overhaul of the American auto industry, including adaptation of manufacturing and management methods characteristic of these foreign firms. Although the American-owned industry remains strongly based in the Middle West and Japanese companies have also been drawn there (both siting new plants in small towns away from older automotive locales), there has been rapid recent expansion in the South. Initiated in 1990 by a new General Motors factory near

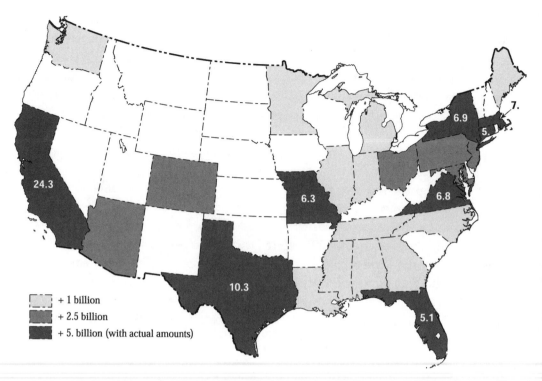

69. Military Prime Contracts, 1990.
All states received some contracts. That prime contractors might subcontract some of the work to a firm in another state would not significantly modify this general pattern. (Source: *Statistical Abstract of the United States*)

Nashville (for Saturn), Japanese and German companies have since established factories in Alabama and South Carolina, as well as assembly plants in Kentucky and Mississippi. As James M. Rubenstein has noted and mapped, whereas the automotive industry (vehicles and thousands of parts) was long concentrated in Michigan and nearby areas of adjacent states, today it stretches in a dense but relatively narrow swath from central Michigan on south across Kentucky and Tennessee into Alabama and Georgia, an industrial corridor anchored on I-75 and I-65, with these superhighways providing the essential means for "just-in-time" assembly of finished vehicles.

THE SOUTH

These new automotive factories are bold exhibits of the lure of the much-publicized "business climate" of the South, featuring ample supplies of labor, lower wages, absence of or weak unions, and, as the late John Paterson (an English geographer long devoted to the study of America) added, a labor force "that is also more prepared to regard working in industry as a means of gaining status rather than losing it" (as were immigrants during an earlier era of industrialization in the North). Coupled with these proclaimed advantages in labor was a second major feature: a politically friendly environment at all levels, as evident in massive tax concessions, infrastructure subsidies, and looser regulations by state and local governments. Such attractions were especially strong to Northern companies faced with the need to modernize and expand old facilities. (The South also had its "rust spots," if not a "belt," such as the steel and rubber industries in Birmingham and Gadsden—a contraction making the new Honda factory at Lincoln, Alabama, especially welcome.)

To these oft-cited advantages were important changes already noted, such as air-conditioning, the influx of people from the North, the easing of racial relations. As Southern cities prospered and diversified in population, schools improved, research centers emerged, and new suburbs at all levels expanded across the green countryside; Northern corporate response might follow in stages: first a small branch plant, next relocation of an entire low-wage service sector, then a new primary facility, and finally a shift of company headquarters, bringing a clientele for the most exclusive country clubs, golf courses, and private retreats.

This postwar transformation of the South has been called "the Second Reconstruction," and it bore more than a little resemblance and even some continuity with Reconstruction following the Civil War, when most of the region was a formal imperial province of the victorious North (*Transcontinental America*, 187–226). The most fundamental feature of this recent change was initiated by federal courts and Congress—even with the use of federal troops (in Little Rock to counter the governor's attempt to use the Arkansas National Guard to block school integration). The subsequent civil rights revolution was largely carried out by Southern Blacks themselves, but the much-publicized participation by Northern activists ("outside agitators"—imperial agents) and essential constitutional support for crucial changes in society and polity may be seen as a long-delayed consummation of the "regeneration" of the South advocated by Radical Republicans a century earlier. Progress in this difficult social transformation was followed by efforts of governments, corporations, and institutions that in effect reasserted the aims of a quite different set of original Reconstructionists: "to bind the South more effectively into the nation and help it partake of all the commercial, industrial, and modernizing trends of the times." Once again opportunists "flocked to the best areas," this time to attractive cities and towns rather than to the richest cotton lands. The great divergence between these successive great transformations comes with the large migrations of Northerners to the South—a "colonization" advocated a century earlier as a means of changing Southern mores, now carried out by millions migrating to improve their own well-being but an influx often regarded by Southerners as "an alien invasion."

Northern leadership and capital were essential and avidly recruited to advance the new economy of the South, but the result was not simply a new phase of the colonial economy of the past but a vigorous regional sector of a far more balanced nationwide system. Indeed, the sudden burst of high-rise office towers in downtown Charlotte in the late 1980s marked its sudden emergence as a national banking center; a decade later one of its megabanks took over Bank of America and moved the headquarters of that famous giant from San Francisco to North Carolina. Such remarkable developments were made possible by changes in interstate banking laws initiated by various states at the urging of the industry (economists viewed prohibitions against interstate banking as a crude form of protectionism). Southern states began their campaigns to lure Northern industry in the early 1960s; by the late 1970s the images and self-confidence of the two regions had undergone a historic reversal. Whereas the South was for the first time undergoing expansion and diversification and enjoying an upsurge of civic and regional confidence, the North was in the midst of painful industrial changes, losses of business and skilled workers, declines in tax revenues, deterioration of schools and civic services, and seemingly intractable racial problems in the large numbers of segregated inner-city poor.

However, these changes in the South were geographically uneven within the region, concentrated on metropolitan areas large and small. Northern investment and corporate leadership had long been prominent in the biggest centers (Atlanta, Dallas, Houston) and continued to be; much of the recent growth has been in physically attractive areas with universities, research centers, and recreation amenities, such as the North Carolina Piedmont, Nashville Basin, Knoxville and the Southern Appalachians, Lexington and the Bluegrass. Such places are fringed with Yankee suburbs and new country clubs whose residents and members may have little social connection with deep-rooted Southern families at any level. New industries often seek open country at urban edges; there is plenty of space to spread into, and as the range of commuting by car or pickup is very wide, this new metropolitan impact can reach far into the Southern countryside.

Yet there remain extensive areas beyond that reach, in the Piney Woods, Delta, Ozarks, and Appalachia, and others obviously avoided: "although manufacturing companies and state officials do not publicly confirm it, for certain industries a black population of 30 to 35 percent within a county is the threshold for exclusion from consideration for factory location." As Charles Aiken's detailed studies make clear, such avoidance is based on general assumptions about Blacks: poorly educated, poor health, poor attitudes toward work—legacies of centuries of suppression that are still apparent in many areas. Small Black-governed communities have been heavily dependent on federally funded aid (housing, clinics, water and sewage systems, and so on) and many "are among the places . . . where what is termed 'environmental racism' exists," when, desperate for funds and jobs, these communities accept hazardous waste landfills, incinerators, federal prisons, and other usually unwelcome facilities. Such areas represent the sharpest contrast with the prospering South.

Settlement patterns continue to evolve across the Southern countryside: rural hamlets, all Black or all White, Black "ghetto towns" (incorporated places Whites have fled), and the more common largely White towns with all-Black clusters on the outskirts. At the opposite scale, Blacks are a majority within the city limits of some large places (Atlanta, Birmingham, Memphis, Richmond), and in various lesser cities Black mayors work with Black and White civic leaders, each representing a substantial business and professional class; modern Black suburbs are a common part of the larger metropolitan scene (fig. 70). Although a high degree of segregation remains (as elsewhere in the nation), race relations have generally evolved toward mutual toleration during recent years of urban growth and relative prosperity. As presidential aspirant Jimmy Carter proclaimed in 1976, "The Voting Rights Act [of 1965] did not just guarantee the vote for black people. It liberated the South, both black and white. It made it possible for the South to come out of the past and into the mainstream of American politics." And, indeed, the South's coming out of the past radically transformed both regional and national politics. The Solid South ("Civil War Democrats") was shattered, conservative Republicans rapidly gained strength, and at the end of the century, in the closest election in American history, the Republican candidate won every Southern state.

Destruction of the formal racial caste system opened the way for the South to move into the mainstream of American life, but the ensuing changes did not dissolve all regional distinctions. The majority of households across the South were native to the region, and even if an unprecedented proportion were now typically middle class in employment and education as well as income, old characterizing features were still much in evidence even if subdued in effect. Wide kinship networks within the "great family" of the traditional South remain, and visiting, periodic gatherings, and trips to the old home-place and country cemeteries are still common features of Southern family life. The role of the church remained unusually strong and distinctive; "rural-to-urban migrants in the South take their church with them," and unlike elsewhere "educated business and professional people make up one of the most churchgoing groups in the region." Gospel preaching and gospel music are a pervasive presence in local broadcasting, and the Bible Belt an appropriate term for the dominant style of religious expression. Even though far more Southerners now live in urban areas, access to the countryside, to woods and streams, backcountry coves and mountains, low-country marshes and estuaries is generally easy and attractive; hunting and fishing, boating and stock-car racing,

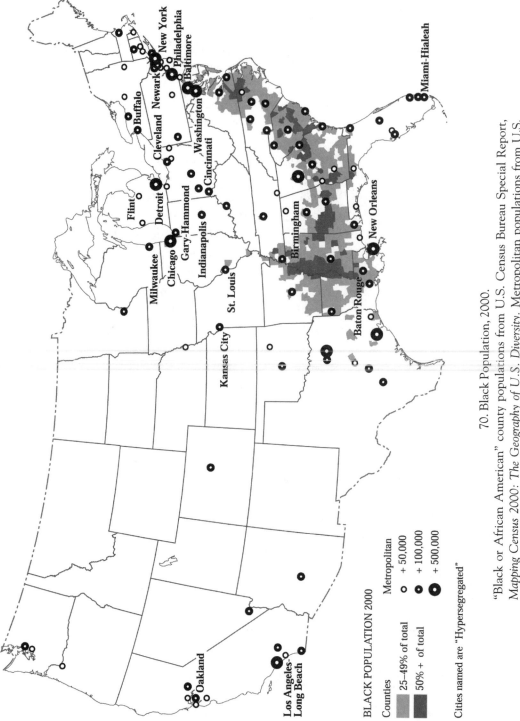

70. Black Population, 2000.

"Black or African American" county populations from U.S. Census Bureau Special Report, *Mapping Census 2000: The Geography of U.S. Diversity*. Metropolitan populations from U.S. Census supplied by Lewis Mumford Center for Comparative Urban and Regional Research, SUNY-Albany. "Hypersegregated" based on Nancy Denton's study of 1990 census as reported in Kaplan and Holloway, *Segregation in Cities*.

BLACK POPULATION 2000

Counties

25–49% of total

50% + of total

Metropolitan

○ + 50,000

◉ + 100,000

⦿ + 500,000

Cities named are "Hypersegregated"

New York
Philadelphia
Baltimore
Newark
Cleveland
Buffalo
Washington
Cincinnati
Miami-Hialeah
Flint
Detroit
Gary-Hammond
Indianapolis
Milwaukee
Chicago
St. Louis
Kansas City
Birmingham
New Orleans
Baton Rouge
Oakland
Los Angeles-Long Beach

and relaxed country ways with dogs, horses, and cattle are common diversions. And although air-conditioning has worked its welcome revolution and urban dwellers might "travel in an arctic circle from home to car to office and back without ever braving the sweltering heat," climate remains a powerful presence. This Sun Belt of short, open winters and generally little snow invites outdoor activities, but it also features some of the most violent weather in the nation: heavy downpours, floods, tornados and hurricanes, hail and ice storms, as well as that long season of sweltering heat; such things still impinge upon Southern living and Southern regional consciousness. Long-famous distinctions in diet, dialect, and deportment remain apparent even though, as always, varied among places and classes, and now modified by modernizations and integrations.

It is important to emphasize that all of these regional distinctions apply to both Blacks and Whites long joined in the creation of this regional culture. Even though diminished in numbers by exodus, the continuing presence of rural and small town Blacks remains a distinguishing feature of Southern society. Furthermore, the presence of all those newcomers—"Yankees," Northerners, "outsiders"—all those non-Southern Americans coming in upon this deep-rooted regional society, is a new distinctive feature of the South. The sociocultural effects of this invasion and interaction upon natives and newcomers and their life together will need another generation or two to assess. If it was obvious that the South was no longer the militant "nation within a nation" whose social system was not to be tampered with, there remained leaders with keen sensitivities about relationships between region and nation; as Georgia Senator Zell Miller warned in the second year of the twenty-first century, any suggestion of "submission to outside forces of 'political correctness,'" or, worse still, any indication that "they were being looked down upon," would encounter widespread resentment and quiet resistance among native Southerners.

HEARTLAND

One of the most important reconfigurations has received little notice beyond the region directly affected: the quiet, relentless attrition of vast numbers of traditional family farms, losses of rural population, and decline of towns all across the agricultural heartland. As James R. Shortridge has noted, "the prosperity of the 1950s," a decade of world food shortages following upon years of wartime high prices, probably "represented the closest that many Plains communities have ever come to fulfilling the dreams of their founders"—that is, of independent farmers and townsfolk prospering and secure in the Garden of the World. Thereafter, with only brief exceptions, vast surpluses and the collapse of world prices, new modes of agriculture and processing, and high costs of equipment and land put farmers under heavy pressure, especially severe in the 1980s when a wave of bankruptcies and foreclosures stirred much anger and even attempts at militant local resistance.

If in popular terms the change marked a shift from the family farm to agribusiness, a closer view was more complicated, but a shift in scale was readily apparent. In the Corn Belt the continuing family farms were now more likely to be a full section (640 acres) or more, rather than the traditional quarter-section (160 acres), and the family business was likely a formal corporation to handle the investments, regulations, and operations essential to successful farming; in the wheat belts the increases were similar in pattern, on a larger scale. The emergence of a few giant corporations that "control not only the buying and selling of grain but the shipment of it, the storage of it and everything else" was not wholly new in kind, but the widespread, accelerating "landshed"—the transfer of large acreages from retiring or departing farmers into the control of farm management corporations—was new in scale and consequence because few young persons could afford the huge costs, nor be lured by the very uncertain prospects, of individual farming in modern America.

In this region, as in parts of the South and Colorado Piedmont, the most blatant displays of the role of agribusiness are the giant meat factories for hogs, beef, poultry. Whereas the fattening of small lots of hogs and cattle was an integral and most profitable part of traditional Corn Belt farming, this practice has increasingly given way to huge corporate operations feeding and processing tens of thousands of animals a year (and creating enormous local environmental problems).

Much larger farms needing even less labor than before, the demise of most local processing of farm products, and the ease of travel over long distances have led to reductions in rural and small town populations across much of the prairie and plains country. The business blocks of once-stable trade centers of a few hundred or even a few thousand people may stand half empty, their houses mostly occupied by older people, and services—educational, religious, medical, recreational—severely limited, if available at all. However, within forty or fifty miles another town has turned into a small city, serving as the main trade center for an area of several counties. Located on an Interstate or other main highway, often with a small airport, perhaps a state college, a cluster of various government offices, and subdivisions of new houses, such places are a thriving contrast with those in their hinterlands. These places, in turn, are linked to larger, long-established regional trade centers. Thus the settlement hierarchy has been reordered: the base level thinned in population and services, the next levels fewer in number and serving larger areas. With commuting ranges much extended, small towns and old farmsteads around these main service centers are now mostly filled with a nonfarm population. By 1990 the farm population of the nation fell below 2 percent of the total resident population, and it was a continually declining proportion all across this agricultural heartland.

CALIFORNIA

"California. The Nation Within a Nation" boldly proclaimed the cover of a 1967 issue of *Saturday Review* largely devoted to the topic. The use of this characterizing concept by this long-popular magazine of issues and ideas did not suggest any analogy with or succession to the role of the South. There was nothing deep-rooted or militant about California. The metaphor applied to the sheer scale, distinction, and influence of this one massively growing state on the shaping of America, a role that California had been playing for more than forty years. That it was about to become the most populous state, had an economy that would rank it sixth among the world powers, and was the source of a highly attractive American lifestyle was worth examining, but hardly news. (Although some of the reports coming out of such places as Berkeley, Haight-Ashbury, and Big Sur were of avid national interest and what would soon become known as the "counterculture" would further compound California's reputation and influence.)

For thirty years after World War II California received most of the attention devoted to the ever-stronger "westward tilt" of the nation (to use Neil Morgan's title of his detailed report on the topic). During those years a flight across the Southwest might reveal the faint framework of roads and lot lines of large tracts roughed out on the desert floor, and the nationwide marketing of opportunities—for home, recreation, retirement, investment—in raw Western lands was an imitation of earlier mass promotions in California and Florida (one on a high mesa northwest of Albuquerque offered 172,000 lots). But they were not very successful. Even though many areas had felt the impact of the war economy and all the main cities were centers of growth, much of the West remained the land of wide open spaces, "the Empty Quarter," regions of spectacular scenery and traditional economies (ranching, mining, lumbering, irrigation agriculture). Only as California began to supply large numbers of people to other western states did the Far West as a whole begin to take on much of the image and pattern—and problems—of its most famous part (fig. 71).

The early 1970s was a time of troubles in America that produced "a new and urgent concern over national unity, political stability, and law and order." Riots and disorders had caused widespread anxiety over "crime in the streets," and polls reported that six out of ten adults living in metropolitan areas would leave for smaller places if it were feasible. Such fears gave rise to a new genre of guidebooks, one of the first popular ones being *Safe Places* by a New York City couple, David and Holly Franke, based on detailed research on 600 possibilities and a long transcontinental reconnaissance. Their volume on the West (like another on the East) offered a choice of two dozen places of various sizes and kinds, but aside from three quiet suburbs (including Bellevue, Washington, not yet famous as the home of Microsoft's Bill Gates), most were small towns remote from cities, such as Moscow and

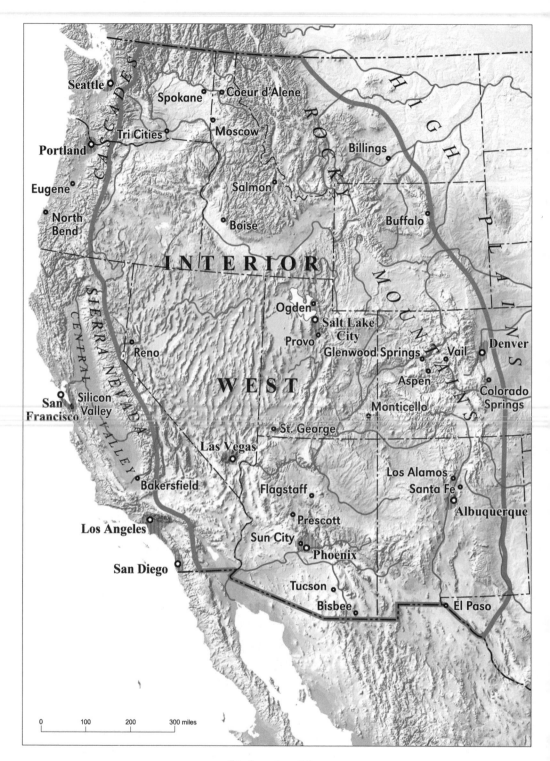

71. American West.

The map is simply a general reference for places mentioned in the text. The boundaries of the Interior West are those used in *Atlas of the New West*. (Base: *National Atlas of the United States*)

Salmon, Idaho; North Bend, Oregon; Monticello, Utah; Buffalo, Wyoming; Glenwood Springs, Colorado. Such books were no doubt far more productive of dreams than of actual migrants, but even in 1971 the Frankes found that natives of neighboring states were concerned about the new influx of persons from California "aghast at what overpopulation has done" to their former home. As general American affluence broadened and as freedom of choice in residence expanded (and national political crises subsided), newcomers began to arrive in growing numbers in cities and towns, large and small, and also spread into often remote countrysides all across the Interior West (and the variety of national guidebooks for potential migrants rapidly expanded in number and specialty; Rand McNally's first *Places Rated Almanac: Your Guide to Finding the Best Places to Live in America* appeared in 1981). Unlike the South, the business climate had relatively little to do with Western growth. The West was a "chosen land," populated by newcomers lured by a new kind of landscape and lifestyle and "by native-born residents who explicitly resisted moving away."

This rapid recent growth has given Western cities an increasingly distinct form and image. Older regional capitals, such as San Francisco, Seattle, Salt Lake City, and Denver, were focused, hierarchical urban centers distinguished only by particular—spectacular—sites and settings from cities of the East. But Los Angeles and Southern California provided the prototype for postwar development. Linear and horizontal, uncentered and unbounded, its attractions were more than merely utilitarian for the Automobile Age. Vast tracts of similar architecture and obvious sprawl might be regarded as positive signs of newness and spaciousness, of a democratic openness and social equality more apparent in the West than elsewhere. As the problems of and outflow from California have grown, this urban image has been imprinted ever-more strongly on cities all across the rest of the West. As Carl Abbott concluded, "in the second half of the twentieth century, Western cities have become leaders as much as followers, setting their own styles and creating their own problems. Changes in the sources of population, capital, and commerce have lessened their real and perceived dependence on the country's old industrial capitals." Furthermore,

> Western cities also represent the national future as environments for a new multiethnic culture. . . . Eastern cities from the 1840s to the 1940s struggled with adapting the narrow culture of North Sea Protestantism to the full range of European languages, religions, and national loyalties. . . . Newer cities in the Southwest and West now have to incorporate a much wider range of racial and cultural types—European-American, African-American, Mexican-American, Asian-American, and Native American.

Although the West is surely a distinct section of the nation, with closer relationships among its many parts and greater coherence as a whole than in the past, such generalizations require further regional refinement. There are still several Wests within the West, even if the borders and distinctions of these have become blurred.

The two Californias, each famous in its own way, have undergone further distinguishing developments. In the 1960s the San Francisco Bay area was the vortex of a swirl of social and political upwellings that, reverberating across the country as the counterculture, had at first a shocking and then a surprisingly rapid and extensive impact upon American society and behavior. In the 1970s the environmentalist movement, long prominent in Northern California (the Sierra Club was founded there in 1892), began a far more aggressive challenge to routine American acceptance of unlimited growth, consumption, corporate power, and technological proliferation. In detail, these complex movements were diverse in origin, character, and support, but San Francisco and the Bay Area played an unusually strong role. The later sudden emergence of the hypercapitalistic Silicon Valley phenomenon may seem a very different, even contradictory, development, but it is a further expression of a characteristic creativity and openness and has added to the fame and attractions of the area.

Having been a powerfully creative influence upon the shaping of America for more than sixty years, Southern California seemed to be in grave danger of foundering on its own attractiveness. James Q. Wilson (a native son who was then at Harvard) could emphasize in 1967 that "the important thing to know about Southern California is that people who live there, who grew up there, love it. Not just the way one has an attachment to a hometown, any hometown, but the way people love the realization that they have found the right mode of life." But in the 1970s a "tarnished golden state" became the main source of migrants to other parts of the Far West (carrying that mode of life with them, of course, insofar as possible); by the 1990s it had become the primary national focus of concerns about how to manage growth, how to cope with great volumes and varieties of immigrants, how to restructure a heavily militarized economy, and "whether any common identity and purpose can be forged in an urban future in which workers commute hours from distant suburbs and where the poor, the middle class, and the rich live in isolation from one another." Rather than America's Eden and the primary receiving ground from the westward tilt of the United States, the region might now be more appropriately characterized as the greatest focus of the Borderland and as the Ellis Island of the Pacific Coast, and thereby as the primary environment for the emergence of the "new multiethnic culture of the national future."

The Central Valley was an increasingly different California, an agribusiness cornucopia rather than a sprawling metropolis or exurban arcadia. Its southern half, the San Joaquin and Bakersfield areas, was the stronghold of a subculture evolved from Dust Bowl migrations. From a cohesion born of early exploitations and discriminations, these Okies gained in number, security, and self-esteem to become a people noted for their highly emotional religious sects (a "radical fringe of evangelical Protestantism" far more prominent here than in the South), their country music, and what has been termed their "plain-folk Americanism," all of which have become more generally influential. In recent years their proportion of the population has been reduced by the influx of Hispanics.

OTHER WESTS

Oregon began to feel the impact of California migrants in the 1970s. Eugene was an attractive university town to those seeking an alternative to Berkeley and other huge, conflicted multiversities; Portland, a rather quiet metropolis in a handsome setting. The influx of Californians (and others) was so strong as to seem threatening to common amenities of this well-rooted regional society. Tim McCall must surely have been the first American governor publicly to plead with outsiders to enjoy a visit but please don't stay; in 1973 he endorsed a statewide planning program "to halt the ravenous rampage of suburbia in the Willamette Valley." Over the next twenty years 400,000 people were added to the Portland metropolitan area, but the new controls, metropolitan-wide government, and a traditionally cautious conservative leadership have made the city on the Willamette, backed by forested hills on one side, with the towering cone of Mt. Hood on the other, one of the most attractive, humane urban environments in America.

While Portland remained a major regional commercial center, the leaders of its rival, Seattle, sought a larger role for their city. "Entrepreneurial and expansive," they staged "a successful world's fair, developed convention and sports facilities, provided essential infrastructure . . . and revitalized the port"; meanwhile the state university and research centers expanded in size and quality, and together with Boeing aerospace and newer companies many highly skilled people were attracted— all this before the sudden enormous impact of Microsoft. Thus Seattle became an important hub in national and international "networks of finance, investment, tourism, and trade that link the North American and East Asian core regions of the world economy"—and the addition of a million people to this naturally constricted site has inflicted many of the usual congestions and problems of mass growth.

Probably no region in the United States surpasses the Pacific Northwest in general public consciousness of its magnificent natural endowments and of concern over the human impact upon its environmental systems. Fishing, forestry, recreation, trafficways, urbanization are all enmeshed in controversies over the appropriate management of lands and waters. Under pressures from environmentalists federal officials are even considering breaching a series of large dams on the lower Snake River (built to serve local barge traffic) in the hope of restoring salmon runs.

Although superhighways bind it more closely to Portland and Seattle, the dry Columbia Interior remains a different world from the Raincoast, its traditional economies subdued, its population growing much more slowly, but Spokane and smaller scenic centers, such as Coeur d'Alene (its once famous mining hinterland now closed down and heavily polluted), are attracting an increasing number of Californians and others. At the center of the Columbia Basin lies the worst of American environmental cases: the nuclear graveyard of the Hanford Works, full of radioactive waste in leaky storage, contaminating ground and water, including the mighty Columbia.

The most powerful—and in some ways paradoxical—impact of the California exodus has been felt in the famously contrasting society of Utah. The Mormons had always fostered growth of their own kind, by large families or by welcoming Saints from afar to their Zion-in-the-Mountains, but through most of the twentieth century local resources were inadequate to sustain large increases and the region was long an exporter of people, especially to always-expanding California. Such experience made the church look with favor on most any kind of local economic development. Government projects in World War II gave an industrial boost, but only later in the high-tech boom did a large number of companies respond to Utah's alluring business climate—low taxes, minimal regulations, good schools, young, dependable workers, scenic settings—with church and government joining in the welcome. As a recent report noted, the governor was making this "pitch to Silicon Valley decision makers: Salt Lake City is cheaper than Seattle, closer than Austin, not as hot as Phoenix or Albuquerque, and the ski slopes are much closer to downtown than in Denver." A newcomer executive remarked that Provo and Utah Valley (the most thoroughly Mormon part of the Wasatch metropolis) seemed "identical to my eyes to Silicon Valley 30 years ago, the mix of residential, industrial and rural"—and at the present rate of development, in thirty years or less the rural will have disappeared.

Mormons returning to or finally attaining a foothold in Zion were part of this large influx of recent years, but church policy had long since shifted from the Gathering to taking temples to the people. The first of these was dedicated in Los Angeles in 1956, and concurrent with a much-expanded missionary program many more, on every continent and in the South Pacific, were constructed to serve a membership that grew from just over 1 million in 1950 to 10 million claimed in the 1990s. As a result, its leaders were eager to stress that Mormonism could "no longer . . . be thought of as the 'Utah church,' or as an 'American church,'" but as "a universal religion." Nevertheless, not only the headquarters of this hierarchical system but the central base of this self-conscious society remained firmly anchored in its mountain homeland, with half of the U.S. membership still within a long-established Mormon Culture Region, and more than half of these within the Wasatch core (fig. 72). The Mormons of course have always had to accept other people

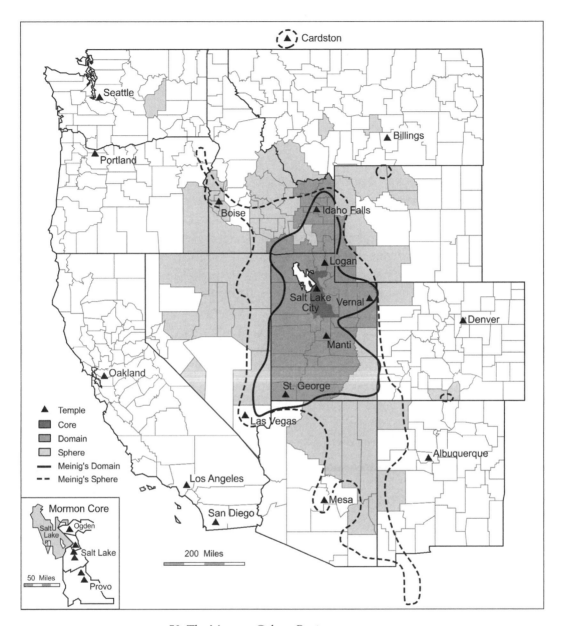

Temple
Core
Domain
Sphere
Meinig's Domain
Meinig's Sphere

72. The Mormon Culture Region.

Lowell C. Bennion has updated my 1960s attempt to define the geographical morphology of this subnation. His 1990 Domain includes counties where Mormons are a majority of residents specifying some kind of religious affiliation; his Sphere comprises those counties where they number at least 10 percent. The addition of ten temples since the first outreach to Los Angeles reflects recent policy changes. (Richard L. Nostrand and Lawrence E. Estaville, *Homelands: A Geography of Culture and Place across America*, 202. © 2002. Reprinted by permission of the Johns Hopkins University Press) within their remarkable religious region, but the Mormon majority has never achieved comfortable accommodation with its Gentile minority, and the strength and character of this recent insurge has heightened social tensions. If, as Paul Starrs and John Wright have put it, "growth is the universal solvent of historic cultural landscapes," its power in this case has been exaggerated by "a California-bred unconcern for 150 years of cultural traditions and sensibilities." Such changes are heavily concentrated in the Wasatch metropolis (Gentiles are a majority within the narrow political limits of Salt Lake City) and were compounded by preparations for the eagerly sought 2002 Winter Olympics. Living within Mormondom has not always been comfortable for Gentiles either, and especially not for some of these newcomers. However, a really head-on "collision of Mormon and West Coast values" is even more apparent in St. George, the nearest corner of the Mormon domain directly across 400 miles of desert from Los Angeles. The population of this gateway to Zion, nestled 3,000 feet below the High Plateaus, has increased fourfold in twenty-five years, with Californians accounting for "about half of what locals call move-ins, a term that is not one of endearment." Marketed by developers as "The Other Palm Springs," this famous Mormon town (Brigham Young's winter capital in "Utah's Dixie") now features golf courses, exclusive walled residential tracts, and shuttle buses to Las Vegas, as well as industries and franchises of nationwide companies. Even though encouraged by church and state, such growth must surely make a people who have long been "wary of 'Babylon' and its worldly influences" uneasy.

Within the Southwest, Central Arizona, nearest in location and character to Southern California, has undergone much the greatest growth. The Phoenix metropolitan area, with just under a million people in 1970, doubled in twenty years and added another million during the 1990s. Like the Los Angeles Basin, expansion has been horizontal, at the edges of several early small centers, much of it a conversion of agricultural land and water to urban use, resulting in one vast sprawling, low-density, contiguous complex. Californians have contributed to this growth, but Arizona has long drawn much more broadly, with special attractions for retirees from northern climates. Small tracts catering to such people had been common (as in California and Florida), but in 1960, in the midst of irrigated cotton fields twelve miles northwest of Phoenix, Sun City offered a new concept of such a place: a separate community, in appearance more like a vacation resort than a normal town, and open only to buyers at least fifty years old. Designed by the developer to convey what a good retirement life should be, it was a great success, houses and facilities were recurrently expanded and upgraded to respond to wishes of more affluent buyers, and by 1980 it had 48,000 inhabitants. Sun City was the most famous age-segregated community in America; "developers throughout the country, and especially in the Sunbelt, took it as a model, and observers of the elderly viewed its 'solutions' to the problems of aging as ones that could be emulated." Many other newcomers have avoided this metropolitan mass and brought marked growth to a wide scattering of smaller cities and towns in the higher country (such as the Prescott and Flagstaff areas) or desert margins (Tucson and Bisbee).

New Mexico, with mostly higher lands and no tropical oasis equal to Central Arizona and more dependent on federal research money, has grown much more slowly, most of it concentrated at Albuquerque. Located where the westward-moving Anglos cut through the old Hispanic riverine axis, this pivotal place has long been a bicultural city, but, as in the state as a whole, the role of the deep-rooted Hispanic population has been continually eroded by the ever-heavier Anglo influx. Santa Fe, the oldest Euro-American settlement, has long drawn a special class of residents attracted by life and landscape at the very center of the Pueblo-Hispano-Anglo Southwest, but although it remains a small city, newer immigrants and influences (such as the Los Alamos scientific community) have broadened its cultural and artistic attractions beyond the regional to the international (such as the Santa Fe Opera) and have intensified local problems.

Even though military, energy, tourism, and other developments have had a heavy impact upon many towns and districts, the special ethnocultural complexity of the region persists and evolves. Tribal territories are bold on the map, and even if they are mostly small in population, the geopolitical autonomy of each Indian society has been strengthened, and resistance to assimilation continues—that of the Pueblos persevering since the arrival of the Spanish 400 years ago. The native Hispanic population (product of that Spanish conquest) is much larger in size but less secure in its hold upon its homeland: its rural areas impoverished and penetrated by Anglo residents and activities, its town and city presence a declining proportion of the whole; yet Hispanics are still important participants in local and state politics (and in the late 1960s a radical, confrontational movement to recover lost lands briefly flared under charismatic leadership). As in earlier stages, the New Mexico so defined is a culture region discordant with state boundaries and rather separate from the Mexican-American Borderland, and it remains the most extensive and complex display of the American imperial legacy within the United States.

Colorado is famous as a place, a name invoking a strong image in the public mind, but rather less cohesive and clear as a region than it was during the formative railroad age. Traditional economies of mining, ranching, and agriculture are much subdued, but tourism is far stronger than ever, and recreational facilities and activities have undergone enormous growth; mountainous Colorado has become one of the main choices of affluent Americans who can afford to live—year around or seasonally—wherever they wish. Whole towns and nearly empty districts have been transformed. Aspen, a remote, moribund mining town, was an early influential case. Selected in 1949 by a Chicago philanthropist for a new Institute for Humanities Studies, it quickly became a world-class center for arts festivals, intellectual gatherings, and skiing. Vail, begun in 1962, was an early example of an entirely new place, inspired by the success of Squaw Valley (created in California for the Winter Olympics) and by the prospect of superhighway tunnels through the Rockies directly west of Denver. As Charles Wilkinson notes, Vail "has grown into one of the immensely rich enclaves of the New West"; he lists a dozen others in half a dozen states that "all have one thing in common: they are inlaid in natural splendor." More generally, small towns and cities in scenic settings in every Western state have lured people of more modest means to growing local economies now sustained by tourism and recreation.

Denver, too, has been transformed: from its secure position as capital of its limited Colorado hinterland (Piedmont, High Rockies, Western Slope), ruled by a complacent conservative establishment, into an aggressive growth center and national metropolis. Texas investors were major initiators of change, breaking open the real estate market and transforming Denver's skyline with new office towers (Texans had long been rather resented and feared, especially those who bought Colorado ranches more for fishing and hunting than for running cattle). During the energy development boom of the 1970s Denver became a major base of corporate operations and has since expanded into a metropolitan area of more than 2 million spread along the base of the mountains, with a huge new airport on the High Plains proclaiming its national aspirations. The largest metropolis between Chicago and San Francisco (having surpassed Kansas City in the 1970s), Denver had finally attained the position envisioned by its first territorial governor, William Gilpin, in his "1,000 mile" theory of four great metropolises spaced across the continent from New York to California. It was also a major node on a more specialized, longitudinal line: the petroleum–energy industry axis anchored on Houston and reaching northward to Billings, Calgary, Edmonton (and episodically to the Yukon and Alaska).

The most phenomenal growth of all has taken place in what a few decades ago would have been thought one of the least likely areas for such a change: from a small railroad and highway oasis of 8,000 in 1940 to a metropolis of more than a million sixty years later (fig. 73). The extraordinary image and power of Las Vegas are world famous, and it is appropriate for Carl Abbott to remind us that it has been a "special creation of the federal government," as well as of Nevada's unique laws, casino entrepreneurs, and cheap airfares. Its first growth came with the construction of Boulder Dam, World War II brought an air base, and in 1951 the Nevada Test Site, sixty-five miles northwest, brought in thousands of government jobs and made Las Vegas a proud "nuclear city" (the chamber of commerce provided schedules and road maps to the best vantage points); in 1963 testing went underground, but even after that ended, atomic and military activities continued to expand. At

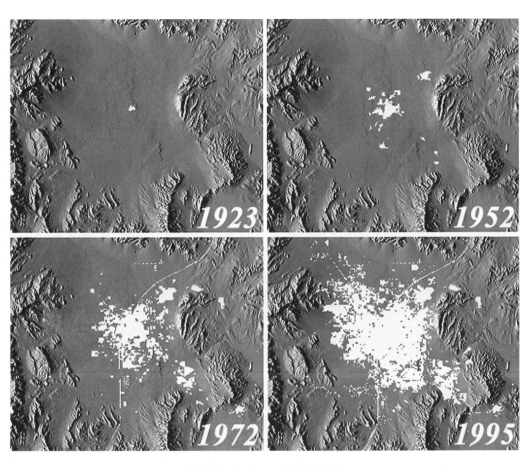

73. Urban Explosion in the Desert.
In 1923 Las Vegas was a railroad servicing stop and a county seat of 2,500. The 1952 image shows suburban expansions, a cluster around the Air Force base (to the northeast), and small settlements southeast along the road to Boulder (Hoover) Dam. In 1972 the urbanized area shown had about 250,000 residents, and by 1995 over 800,000. (Courtesy Leonard J. Gaydos, from U.S. Geological Survey)

the outset "the entertainment theme was the Wild West" (hotels and casinos with names like Last Frontier, Pioneer, El Rancho) with the weekend crowd from Southern California the main clientele; "by the 1960s Las Vegas was trying to define itself as a universal and generic resort rather than simply a western gambling den." The city constructed a convention center and a large airport, and the jet age opened up the flood of visitors and dollars for the continuing transformation. Rather unexpected has been the rapid increase of residents: many retirees, but also many young families (fifty-two new public schools were opened during one four-year period in the 1990s), including many Asian and Hispanic immigrants who find jobs awaiting in the massive service industry. In its famous role Las Vegas is an extravagant theme park, a worldly rather than a particularly Western place; but Las Vegas is also the greatest exhibit of the power of Americans to suburbanize the desert, and like all such horizontal growth, even though the ability to spread out is a great attraction, the common problems of concentration—traffic congestion, smog, and in this case pressure on water supplies—are generated by the addition of so many so rapidly with, as yet, little sign of amelioration.

Las Vegas is the most startlingly new presence in the galaxy of the West, but many older, lesser ones also glow with greater intensity: Tucson, Colorado Springs, Reno, Boise, Billings, Tri-Cities. Each of these clusters stands out amid the relatively empty spaces of the Interior West, and their common experience has helped give rise to labeling this entire area as the *New West:* new in its rapid recent growth and prosperity, in the massive influx of new people and activities affecting every corner of this huge expanse, and new in the problems and tensions generated by such changes. Much of this newness is Californian in origin or character, but the regional experience has been different. Whereas California (and especially Southern California) was built upon a continuous influx of newcomers, who for the most part sought and readily adapted to the way of life they found there, recent migrants to the Interior West are more like an invasion, bringing a new set of interests and values threatening to traditional economies and the casual ease of small city and town life in an uncrowded land. Local "westerners' innate suspicion of the East," of big business and big government, was compounded by the unexpected menace of Californians. Conservationists and environmentalists have generated widespread tensions between old residents and new, upwelling in the "Sagebrush Revolution" wherein politicians of these states have sought to block federal changes in traditional uses of public lands and waters (an attempt to assert "states' rights" over economic issues, rather than social issues as in the South). An age-old fear of planning (such as federal programs for river basins) has caused fierce contests over restrictions on property rights in attempts to limit and manage growth. A 1962 ruling by the Supreme Court has shifted legislative power from rural counties to urban voters in many of these states, further strengthening the newer forces against the old.

Although western Oregon and western Washington have experienced some of the same changes characteristic of the New West, the results have been less severe in these metropolitan-dominated subregions. Thus it is not inappropriate to recognize the broader pattern of Coast and Interior, separated by the mountain barrier of the Cascades–Sierra Nevada–Southern California ranges, as two Wests distinguished not only by their obvious physical contrasts but by their different timings and impacts of transforming developments in their human geography.

The West as a whole, of course, remains a famous and vivid half (more exactly, third) of the continental United States, undiminished in its mythical and symbolic power, an alluring and different kind of country whose people enjoy a sense of separation and superiority over what they view as an old, depleted East. Early in the twentieth century James Bryce, referring to the lure and the kind of society emergent there, suggested that "the West might be called the most distinctly American part of America because the points in which it differs from the East are the points in which America as a whole differs from Europe." By the end of the century the migrations spreading over the whole of the West indicated that a large proportion of Americans seemed to think that they would have a better chance of Life, Liberty, and the pursuit of Happiness there than elsewhere.

8. Reshaping the Nation

REGIONAL STRUCTURE

"Regional domination has virtually disappeared in the United States," wrote James E. Vance, Jr., in 1987; there was "no longer any disadvantaged periphery." Even though such an observation was becoming more obvious by that date, it nonetheless pointed to a truly fundamental geographical change. That the massive Core of the United States that had been firmly in place for a century could have become so eroded and countered in its power in so short a time (seemingly in little more than a couple of decades—although many factors had been much longer at work) represented a drastic restructuring of the nation.

As Vance's comment makes clear, it was a change in kind rather than a shift in place, a dispersal of populations and economies so depleting the once-dominant section and augmenting others as to undermine the existence of a traditional core area (or analogous center-periphery, heartland-hinterland relationships). Yet that historic core remained the most populous section of the nation, and several of its great cities were still seats of power over national systems. What had taken place was a complicated restructuring that featured marked changes in the relative position of particular cities and subregions—and in several cases particular states—rather than broad regions or sections.

To the changes already noted in the South and West, those in the Historic Core should be added. The most obvious has been the idling or complete demolition of huge iron and steel plants in Bethlehem, Buffalo, Pittsburgh, Youngstown, and the Chicago District. Not only have imports increased and production capacity decreased (by a third), but the industry has shifted to smaller plants using newer processes and more scrap, and it is more widely dispersed. Over the past thirty years the competition of foreign imports and the shift of manufacturing to other countries by American firms has affected every industry and has heavily reduced or even eliminated domestic production of a wide array of consumer goods; even world-famous producers of specialized products (such as Kodak) have been affected. Nevertheless, this region remains the principal manufacturing belt, with about 45 percent of the nation's industrial employment (compared with 68 percent in 1950). It still produces most of the country's machine tools, motor vehicles, heavy equipment, farm machinery, and much else; it has high-tech clusters and many centers of research and development. Thus a reconnaissance of the region would reveal a complex, differentiated economic landscape with many pockets of industrial poverty and most of its cities in various stages of rather severe economic readjustment, with central cities, especially, under financial and social distress (the map of Metropolitan Elasticity—see fig. 67—displays the ghost of the American Core). Yet some cities have done much better, and there are prosperous local seats of affluence. Such a complex mixture of the demolished, decaying, adaptive, rehabilitated, and new make this once dominant region the principal exhibit of "a chronology of ascension, dominance, degeneration, and redemption"—"the basic plot of U.S. urban histories."

The concept of a core region is simply a geographical generalization useful in the assessment of some major features common to many countries during particular eras. The Historic American Core took on its full shape during the railroad era, when whole sectors of the national economy (iron and steel, machinery, textiles, and so on) became regionally concentrated to take maximum advantage of raw materials, power, labor, markets, and transport costs. The current pattern of business operations has taken advantage of new revolutionary changes in transportation and communications to do the opposite: to disperse the internal operations of individual firms among various locations, often far apart in different regions, countries, continents, to take advantage of the economies of specialization and least cost for research, design, manufacture, assembly, marketing, and management—but all under the control of a central headquarters. The number of such control centers has been reduced and their power increased by a great surge of mergers among similar companies and the rise of conglomerate corporations exercising control over a variety of specialized companies, each producing a different kind of product. Such concentration has left most American cities with few, if any large, independent, locally based companies. Thus these radical changes in the mode of operations have altered the pattern of dominance over national systems from a regional one to that of a few metropolitan places.

Some years earlier than his remark about the disappearance of regional domination, Vance had called attention to a particular shift of balance within the nation: "in a fascinating cultural-geographic isostasy, the Bay Area, California, and the West Coast have risen in their impact on American settlement structure as New York and Megalopolis have sunk." Written in 1971 when New York City was threatened with bankruptcy and the Bay Area had become famous as the primary source of the counterculture, such a statement may have exaggerated episodic change, but it was a useful reminder of more than simple economic measures of regional change. The rise of California continued to be marked by various indicators of its widening influence upon American ways. In the late 1970s major publishing houses were moving whole divisions or setting up new ones in San Francisco or Los Angeles to tap into new trends and talents as well as a growing market (only a few years earlier, Harper & Row had decided to warehouse its trade books near Scranton, Pennsylvania, following an old formula that this location, near a new Interstate crossroads, would be in easy reach of 80 percent of the market). Like publishers, national broadcasters shifted important operations from New York City to Los Angeles to be in close touch with the movie industry, program production, and recording studios. In the 1990s automobile manufacturers also responded directly to Californian creativity. Japanese firms set up "a base to study Americans' style of living and the kinds of features they desire in an automobile"; Ford moved the headquarters of several divisions, including all of its European lines (Jaguar, Aston Martin, Volvo), to Southern California because "we want to get connected to the California attitude" and be "at the forefront of automotive trends." During that decade the Silicon Valley phenomenon was so powerful as to induce Harvard Business School and the Wharton School of the University of Pennsylvania to set up offices or programs in the Bay Area.

By the end of the century "bicoastal" was becoming a popular reference to the special significance of California and Megalopolis in American affairs (fig. 74). Meanwhile, an important uplift was taking place all across the country, bringing a greater degree of equality in many aspects of national life. For example, national media and pertinent agencies were confirming that no region now lacked a growing variety of high-level cultural institutions, such as symphonies, opera companies, museums, and galleries ("American Art Scene Spreads from New York"). Probably much the most important development (as Vance noted) was the great increase in the quality and availability of higher education. The long-prestigious private colleges and universities of the East as well as the best of those in the Midwest continued to rank high on any assessment, but such lists now include many other state institutions (and several private ones in the South, among them Duke, Vanderbilt, Emory, Tulane, and Rice). Here again, California magnified its long-established reputation by creating a huge statewide system of universities, state colleges, and junior colleges to serve every potential student, a postwar program widely influential upon, if never equaled by, other states (including New York, which had heretofore left the task largely to its many private schools).

The nationwide expansion of major league sports is an obvious and important display of an unprecedented equality of regional participation. Driven by the attraction of broadcasting markets as well as by attendance, every large metropolitan

B. Smaller

"I was raised in New York and Nancy is from L.A.,
but we're bringing up the children bicoastal."

74. Regional Consciousness.
The late James E. Vance, Jr., who hated planes and loved to cross the continent by train, commented, characteristically, that with the advent of nonstop jet travel "it is not surprising that . . . coastal parochials began . . . to divide American space between the home of the cognoscenti which they placed on either coast, and Middle America, . . . where it was assumed, much was benighted and all was provincial." Vance, a Massachusetts man who spent most of his life in Berkeley, was richly aware of the differences the cartoonist is suggesting by the term "bicoastal." (*The New Yorker* Collection © 1998 Barbara Smaller from cartoonbank.com. All Rights Reserved)

area now has one or more professional teams. Baseball best illustrates the historical geography of this expansion. Playing daily games over a long season, any league was limited in extent by travel time. Thus from the formation of the two-league system in 1902 baseball was confined during the railroad age to the largest cities within the American Core (fig. 75). Once transcontinental air service was well established, baseball expanded in the late 1950s to Los Angeles and San Francisco, the two largest unserved markets. Subsequently, during the jet age and rapid growth of other metropolitan areas, baseball has increased its number of teams and established them in other regions.

Similar changes were so common and the results are now so obvious as to need no further illustration that decentralization and leveling had led to a "national set-

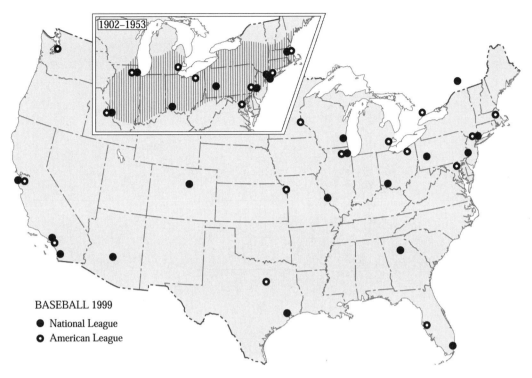

75. Major League Baseball.
The inset shows the pattern within the Core. The first changes, in 1954, were also within that frame: Boston to Milwaukee (N) and St. Louis to Baltimore (A). The great shift came in 1958: Brooklyn to Los Angeles (N) and New York to San Francisco (N). In 1961 the Washington team was moved to Minneapolis, and the nation's capital has never regained a club. Toronto and Montreal were long members of the International League before gaining major league status.

tlement system . . . composed of broadly similar metropolitan regions sprawling across the national landscape, mutually interdependent parts of a completely urbanized society." "Completely urbanized" referred to such a heavy blurring of "rural" and "urban" that all now lived within relatively easy reach of and under the prevailing influence of a metropolitan world; "broadly similar" pointed to generalized structure and services and nationwide imprints of standardized designs upon all newer sectors, despite the particularities of settings and histories. "Interdependent parts," of course, did not mean equality of parts, for the national system was, as always, hierarchical and differentiated in function.

Although size is important, it is not a reliable guide to how this system of cities actually works, and students have used a variety of measures to illuminate rank and relationships, such as banking services, corporate headquarters, corporate services (legal, media, advertising, consulting, lobbying, and so on), volumes of air traffic

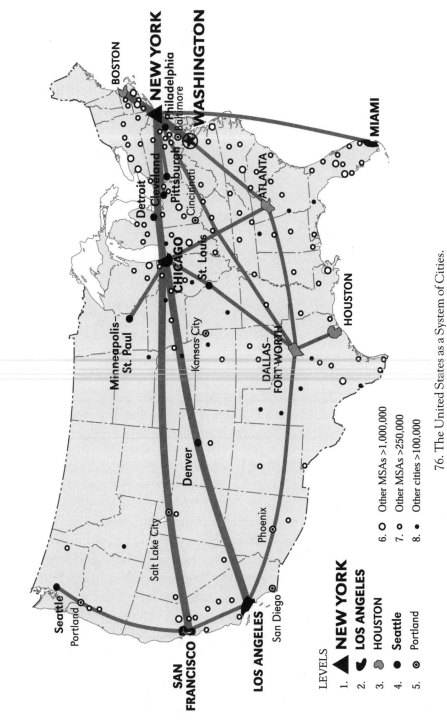

LEVELS
1. ▲ **NEW YORK**
2. ◣ **LOS ANGELES**
3. ⬤ **HOUSTON**
4. ● **Seattle**
5. ◎ **Portland**

6. ○ Other MSAs >1,000,000
7. ○ Other MSAs >250,000
8. • Other cities >100,000

76. The United States as a System of Cities.

Only the higher levels of the network of metropolitan connections are suggested; any recent volume of the annual *Rand McNally Commercial Atlas and Marketing Guide* will delimit the trade areas of these 150 centers.

(parcel more than passenger because the latter includes leisure travel as well as business), and, recently, capacity of Internet connections. From these and other data some sense of a national network can be inferred and some of its special features identified (fig. 76).

New York City, the "command-and-control center" of corporate America, stands unchallenged at the top of the national system and is now the undisputed world "capital of capitalism" (surpassing its old rival, London, during the oil crisis of the 1970s). The two positions have become interlocked, for to be the focus of the world's greatest domestic market is fundamental to its power in the global marketplace. New York is obviously a "world city" by any of the various definitions recently offered for that geographic category. San Francisco was long cited as a counterpart—an equipoise—arising on the opposite side of the country. It continues to be an impressive cosmopolitan financial center of national and international importance, but Los Angeles, its archrival (and in some ways functional complement) is now more obviously America's second great "world city." Even though it remains relatively weak as a corporate "command center," it is a highly varied and expansive industrial area, and it handles the majority of trans-Pacific trade. More important, its fame as a sociocultural trend- and pacesetter has made it, in Edward W. Soja's characterization, "the epitomizing world-city" of "postmodern" form and function, and is thereby fostering a "Los Angeles School" of urban studies of such "polycentric, polycultural, balkanized, polarized" metropolitan areas being shaped by "global restructuring." Chicago, long the Second City of the American system (and earlier prototype), continues to be a powerful national center, and sustained by Chicago's productive hinterland, its commodity markets set world prices. It is second to New York as a base of major corporations, a position publicized and enhanced by Boeing's recent shift of its headquarters from Seattle to Chicago (rather than to Dallas or Denver, the other finalists in a short, intense competition). And yet, its industrial hinterland has suffered declines, this midcontinent area is one of low population growth, and Chicago will likely undergo some erosion of its relative position.

Somewhere below New York and these three other great metropolises, but anomalous in its history and role, is Miami. It has been called a "global city" where we can "see, almost in laboratory-like fashion, how a new international corporate sector can be implanted in a site." But all this took place under unusual, dramatic geopolitical circumstances, and it required not only the skills and initiatives of the Cuban business class but massive governmental assistance and investment (including the largest Central Intelligence Agency station in the world) over several decades to change Miami from an American resort into a financial, commercial, and traffic center for the West Indies and Caribbean. Miami has many foreign banks and the largest free trade zone in the United States; it is a haven for refugees, an immigration portal, and a major tourist, shopping, and seasonal residence center for affluent Latin Americans (who seek above all "privacy, exclusivity, and security").

At the next level, the position of Boston, long a major financial and intellectual hub, has been reinforced by its role in the new technology, while the other cities are new to such importance within the national system. Houston, which long prided itself as the "money center" of the South and Southwest, underwent an enormous, uncontrolled expansion during the oil boom of the 1970s and drew much attention from students of urban form and affairs (Ada Louise Huxtable called it "an exciting and disturbing place"). The deflation of that boom depressed its vaunted vitality, but it remains the premier seat of the world's oil business and of NASA, as well as a major focus of the Gulf Coast. Meanwhile, Dallas–Fort Worth equaled Houston's growth (about doubling in twenty-five years) and became an important financial, corporate, and national transportation center (gaining the headquarters of American Airlines and Union Pacific). Atlanta, similar in its great expansion (now having the longest average commuting distance of any metropolitan area) and anchoring the national network in the Southeast, completes this level.

The next tier is a mixed group, some of rapid recent growth (Denver and Seattle), one long-established major regional capital (Minneapolis–St. Paul), and several big industrial cities in various stages of restructuring. Detroit remains the headquarters of American automobile companies (Chrysler is now owned by a German firm), but its one cluster of great office towers overlooks one of America's most devastated and segregated central cities; in St. Louis, the graceful Gateway Arch frames another display of extensive decline in what was long the southwest anchor of the American Core. The various shifts in balance and performance within this national network would become clearer on detailed examination of these and other levels, but the general change from the regional morphology of midcentury is apparent.

The sheer volume and velocity of this continuing reshaping of America is unparalleled elsewhere in the world. Such dynamics are often assumed to be evidence of the freedom and flexibility inherent in American values and basic to its preeminent productive system. Any general geographic view of this "flexibility" draws attention to changes among places—cities, metropolitan areas, states, regions—and the most obvious result of such changes is the emergence of "winners" and "losers." Thus the often exalted dynamism of the American system generates fears as well as opportunities. This intense competition between places is endemic in the United States—and it is not new:

> A curious outgrowth of the rivalries of American cities, is the practice that obtains so generally of offering bonuses and pecuniary inducements to manufacturers to move their plants. . . . Any factory or established business employing labor can have its

choice, nowadays, from a long list of cities, new and old, any one of which will give it a site for a factory, pay the expenses of moving, and perhaps contribute substantially toward the construction of a new building. . . . The result is that the migratory disposition already so pronounced in these days is intensified, and it has become a familiar thing not merely for individuals to move, but for great aggregations of working men to shift the scene of their activities from one city to another, sometimes thousands of miles away.

So commented an editor of *Scribner's Magazine* in September 1890. He thought this was "a passing phase" and that the country's industrial pattern would become stabilized even as "travel will go on increasing"—and his prediction was generally correct for more than half a century, as the existence of an American Manufacturing Belt attests. Yet the competition among places never ceased. Lewis Atherton has described the rather frantic struggles of small Midwestern towns during the decades before World War II to lure a factory that would elevate them above their farm center status and the "footloose" companies that preyed on them (never delivering all they promised and leaving for another eager town within a few years).

Such competition, waxing and waning over the years, reached unprecedented levels from the 1970s onward concurrent with and critically connected to the reshaping of the nation's economic geography. Much of this was generated at local levels by "coalitions of banks, developers, local newspapers and local governments," but these groups almost always sought crucial assistance at the state level. Incentives to move—or to stay—involve general statewide conditions, such as the status of taxes, social welfare costs, and labor laws, as well as special aids for particular cases, such as tax credits, easing of regulations, free sites, access roads and other infrastructure, low-interest loans, and wage subsidies (relating to the number of jobs created). While local governments can offer some of these, the states become the principal combatants in these intensifying contests, and the press frequently offers current "business-friendly" rankings of the states.

The enticement of Northern companies by Sun Belt states has been much publicized, often successful, and costly for Northern states to resist. The avid participation of Southern states in the competition may appear to be a reassertion of sectionalism, but these states have also vied intensely with one another to be chosen for relocations as well as for entirely new facilities (Alabama, desperate to jump start a new industrial economy in a state long perceived as poor and unattractive to investors, provided $253 million in incentives for Mercedes-Benz to build an assembly plant and employ 1,500 workers—"Subsidy: $169,000 for Each Job"). However, some of the most intensive competitions have been between adjacent states elsewhere, especially where a metropolitan area overlaps a state boundary, as in the case of Kentucky versus Ohio in the Cincinnati area, and in the three-state New York Metropolitan Area. New Jersey, which has successfully lured many companies from New York City ("Chase Manhattan collected $235 million to stay in New York" rather than move across the Hudson), recently found itself threatened by a Pennsylvania working to develop the once heavily industrial Lehigh Valley, which, with Interstate highways, can aspire to be an attractive outlier of Greater New York.

The usual economic rationale for such public grants to private corporations assumes that such costs are necessary to provide growth (or sustain a local economy by stopping a move) and will be eventually recovered in greater income from taxes and further growth. However, this entire system of "economic incentives" ("they never call it 'corporate welfare'") has been harshly criticized: it "wastes public dollars, subsidizes shareholders . . . , fosters unfair competition and diverts policymakers from making long-term improvements in their communities' business climates" (such as better schools, medical care, cultural institutions, and general infrastructure). Whatever merit these arguments may have (and states differ greatly in their modes and degree of participation), the obvious general cause of such behavior is the fact that under the American federal system the states are engaged in economic warfare with one another and believe that one state cannot "unilaterally disarm" unless there is "an armed truce among all the states." As *Time* magazine headlined, in a series of articles on the topic, "There Are Solutions to the Corporate Welfare Mess—But Who Goes First?" In such a polity, it appears that the federal government would have to go first (agreements against poaching on one another have been tried between some states, but never sustained). Two proposals have received considerable attention. One would have Congress "define state location incentives as taxable income for companies receiving them, and to tax that income at a 100 percent rate." A second proposal seeks to outlaw state incentive payments as illegal obstacles to interstate commerce: "Congress has the authority . . . under the commerce clause of the Constitution to end this war between the states."

Proponents of national action point out that incentives to shift jobs from one place to another do not create more jobs for the nation as a whole; further, that in many cases (but difficult to know how many) such subsidies are "giveaways, . . . providing a bonus for someone who would have taken the same course of action anyway" (would Boeing not have gone to Chicago had there been no subsidies?); and that corporate welfare "tilts the playing field in favor of the largest or most politically influential or most aggressive businesses." More serious is the impact on the places involved: "we are funneling tens of billions of dollars into shifting jobs from one state to another . . . that should be going to schools and roads and other public outlays," said an Ohio congressman (whose state has been a major target of Southern states), with the further result that state and federal governments are under pressure to provide the funds needed for those local public outlays. One of the worst—and least discussed—impacts of these hyperdynamics is the destabilization and depression of communities; those that lose major companies not only lose jobs and taxable resources, they often lose important community leadership and civic vitality. As always, much more than economics are affected by shifts in economic geography, and these state interventions magnify the instabilities inherent in unregulated free-market capitalism.

Despite growing concern over the problem toward the end of the twentieth century, there appeared to be little likelihood of any formal resolution early in the next. This system of economic subsidies has been operating for a long time, and "a corporate welfare bureaucracy of an estimated 11,000 organizations and agencies has grown up with access to city halls, statehouses, the Capitol and the White House." Most politicians at all levels are willing participants. The American system is anchored more in local districts than in political parties and "congressional life consists largely of a 'relentless search' for ways of claiming credit for making good things happen back home," and as long as American election campaigns require the raising of enormous amounts of money, there is little prospect of angering business patrons by imposing controls over the movement of capital or the amount of money that can be extracted out of eager or defensive communities.

FEDERAL STRUCTURE

Although many specialists in government and the economy have concluded that it would be better if state investment incentives were abolished, a majority of congressional and state lenders do not agree. Not only have there been winners as well as losers (although it is impossible to determine the exact role of incentives in the results), the proposed solutions would impinge upon the power of each state to set the rules and shape the character of its business climate for particular cases. Interstate competition may lessen following this recent unusually intense period of change, but it is not likely to cease, for it is deeply built into the American geopolitical system. A federal structure of fifty extensively autonomous civil republics spread across a continental expanse and beyond, varied in physical character, historical experience, and economic development, yet bound together by nationwide commercial systems and wide open to population movement, provides the possibility for peculiarly intense and continuous competition among places. There is nothing remotely equal to this "strong territorialization of American political power, embodied in the federal Constitution" and its influence upon the dynamics of economic location.

The exercise of a state's power within the national government is of course closely related to the number of its members in the Congress (modified by party affiliations, chairmanships, and personal influence). When we shift our focus from the system of cities to the system of states the changes in state representation be-

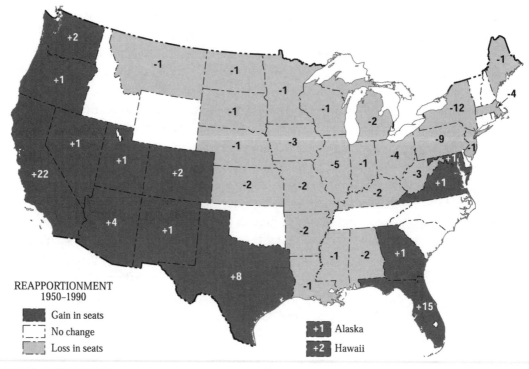

REAPPORTIONMENT
1950–1990

■ Gain in seats

▢ No change

▨ Loss in seats

+1 Alaska

+2 Hawaii

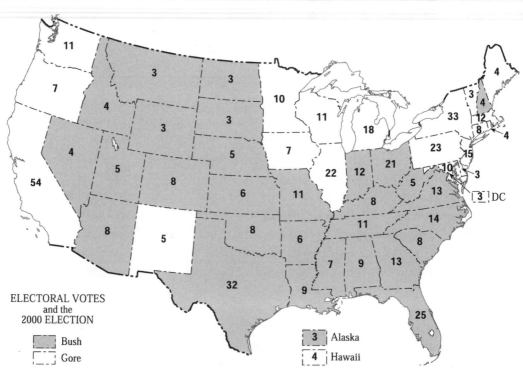

ELECTORAL VOTES
and the
2000 ELECTION

▨ Bush

▢ Gore

3 Alaska

4 Hawaii

tween 1950 and 2000 display how heavy and selective the shifts in balance were toward the West and the South (fig. 77). Aside from Texas, most of the traditional
South experienced loss or no gain (Virginia's additional seat, like that of Maryland,
may be attributed to suburban growth around the District of Columbia). The bitter,
protracted, unprecedented contest over Florida's twenty-five votes in the 2000
election was a reflection of how complex that nontraditional, rapidly growing
Southern state had become. The states of the Historic Core lost fifty-three seats
over this forty-year span.

The capital of this geopolitical hierarchy has in form and character become a
more representative "American" place than in earlier eras: Washington, D.C., politically separate, declining in total population (by 25 percent in thirty years),
which is becoming increasingly Black (two-thirds in 1990), with affluent Whites
confined to a few districts (early gentrified Georgetown the most famous)—all this
amid a metropolitan area that has rapidly expanded not so much from direct increase in the federal bureaucracy as from the vast array of ancillary agents and activities lured by a compelling interest in the making and the workings of laws and
regulations. The grand design of the capital and its monumental symbols of power
and heritage make the city a major national and international tourist center. Its
universities have also attracted students from across the nation and from abroad.
As Carl Abbott summarizes: "Washington at the end of the twentieth century has
experienced substantial and almost certainly permanent accommodation to the
public values of the North and has been integrated into the communications network of the northeastern core. At the same time improvements in transportation
and communication have enhanced its role as a metropolitan focus for Southern
culture." Suburban character reflects this variety, with northern ones akin to those
of Philadelphia and New York, those in Virginia to those of Atlanta or Dallas, and
the southeast developing areas of middle-class Blacks as well as areas of Whites;
closer connections with Baltimore, the Chesapeake, and along Interstate 95 all the
way to Carolina now form a much-extended metropolitan hinterland.

These changes and links in Washington invite attention to changes in the political cultures of the states and districts sending representatives to this highest
level of political authority. The imprint of the major regional societies shaping the
early nation—those four versions of America (*Continental America*, 264–96)—are
still discernible but considerably modified in strength, extent, and clarity. Much

---

77. Reapportionment and Electoral Power.
The number of electoral votes in the 2000 election was based on the reapportionment following
the 1990 census. The state totals reflect the number of seats in the House of Representatives plus
two senators. In 1964 the District of Columbia (which has no seat in the Congress) was granted
three electoral votes, bringing the total number to 538, and thus 270 needed to win.

the greatest change has been the drastic reduction of the crassly authoritative *hegemonic* society to scattered remnants across the former Cotton Belt in locales only marginally altered by the civil rights movement. The broader and more moderate *traditionalistic* politics of Southern society ("Virginia Extended") has been modified by the civil rights "emancipation" of the South and by the influx of large numbers of Northerners, most of whom came from areas of strongly *individualistic* political societies. The fourth variety, a *moralistic* concern for the commonwealth, is still apparent in much of its early imprint in New England and on across the Upper Middle West (as well as in its special version in Mormondom). These northern sectors are areas of low growth and therefore of declining influence, but this kind of citizen concern for broader community interests has become reinforced by environmental and related movements in the Raincoast and several other districts of the Far West. Any assessment within such broad ("Elazaran") categories must emphasize the widespread increase in the *individualistic* practical "politics of the marketplace," wherein elected officials are primarily brokers mediating conflicts among competing interests. Emerging out of the great diversities of peoples and enterprises in the New York–Philadelphia nucleus, this form spread throughout the Core and far afield to industrial areas across the West. It has been strengthened by interregional and rural-to-urban migrations—relocations from the familiar patterns of home ground—and especially by the rise of giant metropolitan clusters and the rising American malaise about politicians and the political process.

SOCIETAL STRUCTURE

Some other broad and basic patterns have undergone rather similar change. The regional distributions of religious denominations at midcentury are still readily discernible in Edwin Scott Gaustad and Philip L. Barlow's *New Historical Atlas of Religion* of 2001, but with some marked changes in growth, extent, and substance. The general postwar upsurge in church life faded in the 1970s, and by the 1990s most of the major denominations reported declines in total membership. As always, such figures are highly uneven in definition and quality among the many religious bodies; more telling of institutional vitality are declines in seminary enrollments, religious orders, schools, and other church societies. The Roman Catholic Church registered large gains in membership (much of it from immigration) but has experienced declines in the number of priests and nuns, and about 4,000 of the 13,000 schools operating in 1965 have been closed (but it still operates more than 200 colleges and universities). There have been obvious regional differences in these changes: closures or mergers of many local churches in the North, and new or expanding churches in Southern cities and suburbs (and to a lesser extent in the West).

There are also important exceptions to these generalizations. Southern Baptists have doubled in membership and are much the largest Protestant church, now present over much of the country, heavily dominant across almost the entire South, and strong in areas of Southern migration. Furthermore, other fundamentalist denominations (such as Churches of Christ and Assemblies of God) and the diverse category of Adventist, Pentecostal, and Holiness churches have also experienced strong growth; they reinforce the Baptists in any definition of the Bible Belt and are expansive in small towns and "rural suburbia" in much of the country and especially in the West. All of these groups are American in origin, emerging as loosely organized, unstable associations following a particular leader or style of worship, reacting against the formal, doctrinal, institutionalized religion of the churches of older ancestry. The recent strong growth of these long categorized, marginalized, and even stigmatized religious bodies in the open spiritual marketplace of America marks a discernible shift within the religious life of the nation—a change often translated in political terms as the "rise of the Religious Right."

Thus while the pattern of specific religious denominations remains a deep impress on the geographic shape of America, important in itself and in relation to other basic matters, it has lessened in prominence and power. The renewal of mass immigration has enlarged the presence of Muslims, Hindus, and Buddhists, and many others, widening the range of sects and folk cults from many parts of the world, furthering the astounding diversity of religion in the United States.

The "triple melting pot" of Protestant-Catholic-Jew defined a "structural pluralism" of subsocieties, each with its own set of primary social relations and institutions, attitudes and behavior (especially endogamy), while also responding and readily adhering to more general American principles and ideals. This early postwar interpretation of the shaping of American society, however, was soon undermined (quite apart from the long secular pressures of modernity) by strong sociocultural movements. The counterculture of the 1960s challenged all formal institutions of the ruling society. It promoted a search for individual identity and transforming experience through esoteric, quasi-religious practices (as well as other means), and although that movement faded, a general trend toward "religious individualism" has strengthened. As Gaustad and Barlow conclude: "Religion in the United States continues its perpetual reconfiguration, manifest at the beginning of the 21st century less by an upsurge of scepticism than by a privatization of belief and weakening of institutional loyalty."

Challenges to the melting pot (of whatever number) and to pressures toward an American conformity also arose from a very different source. Michael Novak, speaking especially for Eastern and Southern Europeans in America, attacked the "wealthy, suave, and powerful" Protestant establishment that "sets the tone" and governs "the instruments of education and public life" for its condescension toward what it regarded as a residual ethnicity, impeding the emergence of "rational" universal values. His call for a richer, multicultural, yet truly national society was backed by Roman Catholic bishops in 1981, who issued a statement on "cultural pluralism" in which they protested a lingering anti-Catholic nativism and rejected pressures for assimilation to any single version of "American."

By that time the simple pluralistic concept of three broad religious categories had markedly weakened and blurred (exogamy was becoming common), and any model for a homogeneous nation seemed a fantasy. The tumultuous events of the previous fifteen years—war, economic crisis, political scandal, civic unrest, racial protests—had discredited leadership and disturbed common assumptions about American character and values, and about its history and prospects. Thus, further compounded by mass immigration of new peoples, much attention was devoted to an unprecedented search for identity at both individual and group levels; "multiculturalism" came into vogue, "ethnicity" became an accepted badge, "diversity" a valued national and institutional characteristic. In 1980, following new guidelines for federal agencies, the Census Bureau opened the door to self-definition of race and ancestry. The primary categories are White; Black or African American; Hispanic or Latino ("may be of any race"); Asian; Hawaiian and Pacific Islander; and American Indian and Alaskan Native. A proposal to include "mixed race" was rejected, but individuals could write it in or specify more than one race. Beyond these, a person could declare a single or multiple ancestry from a long list of suggested categories, mostly national (such as Belgian, German, Iranian, or Burmese), some broader (such as Arab, Chinese, or West Indian), and some narrower (Acadian, French Canadian, Scotch-Irish, Hmong), with the further option of writing in whatever they wished to claim (which federal officials would then assign to some recognized category).

The morass yielded by such recording may be regarded as marking a culmination of two centuries of official categorization of the American population in some such terms, beginning with White, Colored, Indian, enlarging with successive new sources of immigration and being reinforced by an array of federal laws regarding quotas and equality of treatment for designated "minorities." As might be expected the whole topic generates intense political pressures and strong public reactions. Some groups favor further expansion of categories (a proposed Middle Eastern classification foundered on whether it would include both Arab Americans and Jewish immigrants from Israel); others, such as older civil rights organizations, fear diminution of their clientele (if those of "mixed race" should be treated separately). More generally, the arbitrary character of these "pseudoprimal categories" came under heavy scholarly criticism: as David Hollinger noted, "this ethnical-racial pentagon . . . supposed to contain us all" is "a remarkable historical artifact, distinctive to the contemporary United States." Furthermore, the invitation to iden-tify one's ancestry served only "to emphasize our differences and make people more conscious of them" rather than bring them together, said Arthur Schlesinger, Jr.; "the attack on the common identity is the culmination of the cult of ethnicity" and it could threaten "the brittle bonds of national identity that holds this diverse and fractious society together."

Alarms about a "disuniting of America," however, are countered by assessments that suggest that "something resembling an American 'core' ideology has reemerged —but an ideology subject to change and contestation"; and that for those of Euro-pean ancestry at most what remains is better described as a "symbolic ethnicity"— not central to daily life, even if emotionally satisfying in certain ways. Indeed, for this majority of Americans assimilation has gone so far as to create *Euro-Americans*— who rarely think of themselves as members of such an ethnic group. The percep-tion of such a category has been sharpened by the rapid growth and prominence of other ostensible "panethnicities," especially Hispanic Americans and Asian Amer-icans, both of which encompass many distinct—ethnic—peoples among whom any such broad sense of group consciousness is highly uneven and unstable, open to sociopolitical manipulation.

The case of Black Americans is deeply different. Their long, large presence (1 million enumerated in the 1800 census) and centuries-old enforced subordination had been the compelling reasons for official classification of the population by "race" at the formation of the nation. That imposed group identity has been broad-ened and reinforced through every phase of national development, culminating in the most explosive expression and effective assertion of Black consciousness in the civil rights movement of the 1960s. That epic struggle—which galvanized and pointed the way for Hispanics, American Indians, and other groups—won formal legal equality, laws against discrimination on the basis of race, and various forms of special assistance decreed by the federal government toward greater equality of op-portunity in education, housing, and jobs. Yet it was a volatile, factionalized strug-gle, marked by sharp differences in strategies and goals. In simplest terms, there were those (such as Martin Luther King, Jr., and his followers) who sought true in-tegration, with full access to assimilation—"Americanization"—to whatever de-gree any individual might wish to have; in contrast and contention were those (such as Malcolm X and the Nation of Islam) who sought to cultivate Black Pride and to assert a cultural separateness and the virtues of African origins. The first of these programs sought a marked easing and eventual erasure of racial identities and a comfortable sharing of vaunted American ideals of freedom and equality. The second, despairing of any such deep transformation of White attitudes and regard-ing total assimilation to an essentially Euro-American society and culture "as a confession of cultural inferiority," fostered the creation of a coherent African-American cultural ethnicity, cultivating distinct hair styles, clothing, and deportment, music, dance, and theater, language, festivals, and personal names. Alex Haley's highly publicized *Roots*, relating his search back through many generations to family origins in Gambia, served to equate Black Americans with immigrants having a homeland in the Old World (as one Black leader noted, if Haley had traced his paternal line his search would have led him to Ireland), and in a rapidly expanding polemical literature the former "Dark Continent" was transformed into a seat of civilization.

The emergence of "African American" as a preferred term of identity might be read as a beneficent shift from racial to ethnic categorization (Afro-American had long been in use, but was never the most common). However, African American may be panethnic in application but not necessarily in self-reference, for various West Indians, Dominicans, Black creoles of Louisiana, and certainly Cabo Verdeans, resist being grouped with the larger body of Black Americans. Yet this new label cannot hide—and might better be understood as confirming—that segregation is a far greater reality than integration for the vast majority of Black Americans. Ironically, while achieving legal equality through the responses of the federal government, the tensions generated and the failure to break open paths to greater social and economic equality for Blacks as a whole resulted in a far more reactive and prominent polarization. Thus the presidentially initiated Kerner Report of 1968 opened with a severe warning: "Our nation is moving toward two societies, one black, one white—separate and unequal." A generation later, the very title of Andrew Hacker's widely publicized personal report confirmed that assessment: *Two Nations: Black and White, Separate, Hostile, Unequal*. The Kerner Report, noting the dichotomy of rapid growth of the Black population in central cities and of whites in the suburbs, had stated that "white society is deeply implicated in the ghetto. White institutions created it, white institutions maintain it, and white society condones it"; twenty-four years later, Hacker put it this way: "not only is the taxpaying electorate overwhelmingly white, but it is also middle class, middle-aged and—increasingly—ensconced in insulated suburbs. In short, our time is not one receptive to racial remedies."

The upwelling of multiculturalism toward the end of the twentieth century is yet another phase in a recurrent attempt to reformulate what "American" means with reference to the nature and goal of the general society, culture, nation. If it now seems clear that the concept represents a new openness and possibilities for a more inclusive acceptance of diversity and equality, it is also obvious that in daily life and prospects not all groups are included within that wider compass. As with the special case of American Indians, various Hispanic clusters, and small self-insulated groups such as the Amish, the United States has long been a segmented society, and a stratified, biracial one as well. As Hacker emphasizes, given the continued polarization and subordination of so large a body of African Americans, rather than simply recognizing multiculturalism as an appropriate new general formulation "it would be more accurate to say that the United States will continue to have a dominant culture."

PART THREE
MISSION: ASSERTIONS
AND IMPOSITIONS

I believe that for the rest of the world, contemporary America is an almost symbolic concentration of all the best and the worst of our civilization.

*Václav Havel, president of the Czech Republic,
in Washington, 1997*

Prologue

We now broaden our focus to fit our title and bring into view panoramas in time and space of where and in what form this great national growth and power and momentum, this unparalleled dynamism, has been applied to or impinged upon other parts of the world.

America's obvious early lead in neotechnic modernization as well as its more recent role in the technologies and systems of "globalization" was each widely recognized in its time. Much more abrupt, overt, and contentious were its assertions of itself as not only the leader but the model for a new World Order. Initially defined in the aftermath of its brief participation in the Great European War, but then failing to win the support of the nation, this ambition was strongly reasserted a generation later following victory in a massive World War—whereupon the United States then found itself firmly opposed and directly endangered by another mission-driven superpower.

As always, our concern is narrowly selective. What follows is a spare geopolitical sketch of American policies and positions through several distinct phases of a dauntingly complex reshaping of the world.

1. Assertions: America and Europe

PRELUDE

"In Chicago, Americans flaunted the cheap mass products, the dazzling technology, and the alluring mass culture that, in the coming century, they would spread throughout the world," said Emily S. Rosenberg, featuring the great Columbian Exposition of 1893 as an important impetus for *Spreading the American Dream*. At that same international fair Frederick Jackson Turner had set forth his famous thesis on the closing of the settlement frontier and thereby the close of "the first period of American history." However, he also declared that "he would be a rash prophet who should assert that the expansive character of American life has now entirely ceased. Movement has been its dominant fact, and unless this training has no effect upon a people, the American energy will continually demand a wider field for its exercise." Propelled by the imperial triumphs of 1898, the United States did move quickly into the next and wider field of its history.

At the beginning of the twentieth century London was the nearest thing to a world capital that history had ever known. Britain's empire (formal and de facto) was huge on every continent, its navy ruled the seas, its merchant fleet carried most of the world's cargo, its sterling dominated world finance, its telegraph network bound the globe together. Yet, at that same time, the power and potential of the United States was on display and had become a topic of considerable interest and concern in Europe, and especially in Britain. The eventual rise of America had been foretold many years before as an inevitable next stage in the westward "geographical march of history," and thus William Gladstone, musing between premierships in 1879, could accept that "at a coming time" the United States "can and probably will wrest from us our commercial supremacy. . . . If she acquires it, she will make the requisition by the right of the strongest and the best. We have no more title against her than Venice or Genoa or Holland has against us." But the sheer scale and rapidity of American growth became ever more awesome. It was "without a precedent in history . . . [and] is perhaps the greatest political and economic fact of the age," declared economist Sir Robert Giffen in 1904—a view H. G. Wells echoed more vividly two years later: "Now my picture of America is . . . one of a gigantic process of growth, of economic coming and going, spaced out over vast distances and involving millions of hastening men; I see America as towns and urgency and greatness beyond, I suppose, any precedent that has ever been in the world." Journalists were quick to respond to this new presence, and in *The Americanisation of the World* (1902), William Thomas Stead urged the creation of a great "United States of the English-speaking World" as Britain's only hope for continuance as a world power in the new century; as Giffen admitted, a "sense of being dwarfed will probably increase in time."

Other than its magnetic lure of European migrants, however, American influence on European ways of life was as yet narrow in kind and limited in scope. The single immediate focus of European concern was "alarm at the American penetration of customary European markets." By 1914 U.S. industrial exports had surpassed its large agricultural surpluses. In the broader view, this commercial competition was simply a new phase in those "intensely dynamic reciprocities of America and Europe" that had been apparent for half a century. Industrialization had proceeded rapidly on both sides of the Atlantic World, with America importing engineers and other skilled workers, tools, and science (such as metallurgists and the Bessemer furnace), while Europe borrowed techniques and systems of machine mass production (as in firearms, locks, and sewing machines). Europeans had invested heavily in American railroads and industries; American firms, such as Colt, Singer, McCormick, Otis, and Kodak, had built factories in Europe. As the new century unfolded the United States became much less dependent on foreign funds, and propelled by that wider field of marketing which, as President Taft declared, "will soon be indispensable to our prosperity," its leaders began aggressively promoting a commercial creed of "free enterprise, free trade, free men" toward the creation of an economic world patterned on its own success.

Such pretensions were but one part of a broader belief and proclamation of the United States as the symbol of progress, the obvious model for a twentieth-century society. However, beyond the industrial-commercial sector, American example had made little penetration of the European world. A half dozen or so of its writers were well known and respected (Mark Twain received an honorary degree from Oxford in 1910), as were half as many of its innovative architects (especially Louis Sullivan and Frank Lloyd Wright), but American society was widely perceived by European writers and travelers to be a shallow, restless, materialistic mass offering little to emulate and much to fear. If during this era "a combination of provincialism and arrogance" made American propagandists claim superiority over an aging Europe, Americans of means (and some with little) continued to go abroad to tour those famous old societies and savor culture.

BREAKTHROUGH

World War I resulted in a tectonic shift in the balance between America and Europe. Whereas the United States emerged "rich and buoyant," the world's leading nation by many measures, Europeans were left economically and psychologically exhausted, depleted of millions of young men, deeply in debt, disillusioned with their own leaders, societies, and prospects.

The radical reshaping of the world economic system was the most obvious and measurable change. By 1915 Britain and France were drawing heavily upon American material and financial resources; American entry into the conflict quickly displayed the enormous capacity of its systems of production and transoceanic application. The stalemate on the Western Front had destroyed the principal industrial region of France and Belgium; Germany, the leading economic power of Europe, was defeated, diminished in area and resources, and saddled with heavy reparations. For the first time in its history the United States emerged as a creditor nation—the sole great creditor power. After a brief postwar interlude, a flood of

American consumer goods "began to pour into Europe out of the apparently limit-less, mechanized cornucopia of the United States." Moreover, an increasing pro-portion of those goods were coming from branch plants and shops of American firms directly operating in Europe (such as Woolworth's, Safeway, Montgomery Ward, and Ford) whose success exerted a strong influence on the whole mode of European retailing—on the types of shops, goods, and fashions, management tech-niques, advertising styles, electric signs, and much else (and European business leaders, social theorists, and journalists came across the Atlantic for the grand tour of the American commercial scene: Manhattan, great department stores, mer-chandise marts, Sears, Roebuck, and various associated services).

The "American invasion" (as it was widely viewed by Europeans) involved more than consumer goods. In much greater numbers and variety, Americans flocked to Europe as tourists, students, sojourners, expatriates (there were 40,000 residing in Paris in 1929). They brought their own tastes and talents and ideas and partook lib-erally of what they found, and thereby a major increase and rebalancing of cultural exchanges took place, as in the famous case of jazz going eastward and modern art westward across the ocean. Students of this traffic generally agree that much the most powerful instrument of American influence was the cinema. As Thomas J. Saunders put it: "Parallel with America's rise to global importance, it emerged as the dominant form of people's entertainment and enlightenment." Moreover, "cin-ema was, as it remains, the first and most consequential medium to transcend geo-graphic, linguistic and cultural barriers" (and during the "era of screen silence [in-cluding most of the 1920s] the cinema offered the closest approximation to a universal language—Esperanto based on images"). Thus "as a vehicle for exporting the American way of life and stimulating demand for American products it proved unrivaled. Hollywood became the promotional guardian of the American dream and the primary instrument for domesticating American culture in Europe." By the mid-1920s European states were establishing import quotas on American films in the hope of sustaining their own cinema industries and stemming the tide of Amer-ican influence.

During the war Congress created a Committee on Public Information to spread, what its director called, "the Gospel of Americanism" abroad; after the war a gen-erally similar message was carried through the activities of Rotary International, the YMCA, and other nongovernmental agencies. Such propaganda met strong re-sistance from a wide spectrum of European commentators. When Sinclair Lewis was awarded the Nobel Prize in 1930 his compatriots generally took it to mark America's coming of age in the world of literature, whereas European critics noted that he had earned it by his accurate, devastating portraits of typical American scenes and society in *Main Street* and *Babbitt*.

It is ironic that Henry Ford, who during these years became a viciously bigoted, hate-filled, antiforeign propagandist, was, in a broad sense, the most influential American abroad. The term "'Fordism' . . . was ubiquitous in 1920s Europe"; its reception was ambivalent. When referring to efficient, modern ways of organizing work that emphasized machines and mass assembly production that undergirded the rising American standard of living it could be regarded as "a progressive idea: future-oriented, flexible, and melioristic." Yet this emphasis upon machine and mass was also what many Europeans denounced and feared most about "Americanisation." With its enormous power and lead in neotechnic transformations America inevitably became "metaphor and symbol for modernization" in the 1920s, but it did not directly shape a modern Europe in its own image. After all, Western Europeans had shared and sometimes led in the development of the new technology—in electricity, telephones, radio, in automobiles and aviation. Each society there was under way in its own distinctive way, influenced but far from simply imitative, with this great change (as was especially apparent during the brief years of Weimar Germany).

In the immediate aftermath of the Great War, President Woodrow Wilson had been a powerful voice proclaiming American political ideals of popular sovereignty and of freedom of trade and peaceful economic expansion as the foundation for a new world order. His Republican successors endorsed the same theme but to little effect at home or abroad. The huge imbalance in transatlantic financial conditions and conflicting attitudes toward its cause and cure defied solution. The primacy of business in American foreign policy locked its leaders into insistence on repayment of massive European war debts. As Frank Thistlethwaite put it, "the persistence of a debtor mentality in a creditor state, of small-town banking ethics in the most powerful nation in the world, was one inevitable result of the strains imposed on a people so suddenly arrived at world power." The resultant strains on the European states proved unbearable, and they ultimately defaulted as the world economic system collapsed into the Great Depression.

The shared trauma of that experience undercut American prestige and influence. The country turned inward to focus upon its own problems. In doing so it continued to contradict in practice its own evangelical commercial creed about free enterprise and free trade by its tacit support for international cartels and by raising tariffs to new highs. European powers likewise sought their own solutions, with Germany quickly demonstrating (as the Soviet Union struggled to do) that modernization featuring masses and machines need not follow the "liberal" American path. Cultural influences continued to make Atlantic crossings in both directions. America's emergency concerns for social welfare programs, public housing, and city planning drew upon well-advanced European experience, while the TVA experiment fascinated Europeans as well as other foreigners. By any measure, much the most important crossing was from east to west: the great diaspora from Hitler's

Germany to the United States: "the greatest collection of transplanted intellect, talent, and scholarship the world has ever seen." It was not part of a mass migration but, rather, an often accidentally or arbitrarily selective influx, severely restricted by immigration laws. Unforeseen, not particularly welcomed, and resisted by many American officials and public alike, but aided by a few organizations and determined individuals, the impact of this intelligentsia on virtually every professional field in science, social science, and the humanities would soon prove what a great gift it was to the cultural and scientific richness and power of America. As these refugees and their offspring took root, joined earlier arrivals, and emerged as civic leaders in the postwar generation it began to appear ever more clearly that any American city that lacked a good quota of Jews was culturally deprived.

The United States has always represented both a continuation and an invention: a westward extension of Europe and a new version of Western Society. These interwar years marked an important new phase in this relationship. For the first time Europeans widely acknowledged that the full-grown child was directly, importantly, even fearfully affecting the shaping of parental societies. Of course this assertive nation had long sought to extend its influence beyond its own borders, and with considerable success in North America, as our periodic cartographic depictions of its spheres of influence have shown. The 1920s did not add any European territory to the American sphere, but there had been important kinds of penetration and a general shift in the balance of influences, as a shift in focus now to more directly geopolitical relations will further affirm.

2. Impositions: War and Interwar, Europe and Asia

PRELUDE

In the early twentieth century "the United States had definitely become a Great Power. But it was not part of the Great Power System." That it was a military as well as an economic Great Power was manifested in the famous "globe-encircling parade" of President Theodore Roosevelt's Great White Fleet of battleships in 1907–8, but it had long adhered to a national policy of no "entangling alliances" with other Powers. Nevertheless, its famous declaration of 1823 that "the American continents . . . are henceforth not to be considered as subjects for future colonization by any European power" was and long remained implicitly dependent upon the unchallenged supremacy of the British fleet (the British had proposed a joint declaration, but President Monroe agreed with his secretary of State, John Quincy Adams, that it would be more "dignified" to go it alone "than come in as a cockboat in the wake of a British man-of-war").

The United States also achieved recognition as one of the Great Imperial Powers. A treaty with Great Britain in 1902 recognized U.S. supremacy in Tropical America and opened the way for building and controlling an isthmian canal on its own and intervening as it pleased in this American Mediterranean, where it had taken over the last of the Spanish colonies. Aside from a long-developing involvement in the Hawaiian Islands, America's sudden extension across the Pacific and into the China seas was entirely new and unplanned. The annexation of the Philippines was highly controversial at home and provocative abroad within a realm of intense Great Power competitions. America's Open Door commercial policy did not disturb the other five Great Powers in their imperial spheres of influence over large portions of the feeble Chinese Empire. In 1902 Britain formally recognized Japan's supremacy over its own strategic waters, three years later Japan had defeated Russia in the Far East, and the American position was looking increasingly vulnerable. After ten years of a Republican "Americanization" program, the Democratic platform of 1912 condemned this "experiment in imperialism as an inexcusable blunder" and called for "independence of the Philippine Islands as soon as a stable government can be established."

Through all these years the American public displayed a "pervading sense of security" and "a placid indifference to world affairs." As war was breaking out between the Great Powers in Europe, President Woodrow Wilson told reporters that the situation there "is perhaps the gravest in its possibilities that has arisen in modern times, but it need not affect the United States unfavorably in the long run" (the focus of the discussion was upon economic rather than military dangers). Reacting to the flurry of emotional nationalistic responses by various Euro-Americans in New York City and other immigrant centers the president made a formal "appeal to the American People" against "passionately taking sides," urging them to exhibit the dignity of self-control and to be "neutral in fact as well as in name, . . . impartial in thought as well as action." Certainly the hope for at least military neutrality remained strong and widespread among American leaders and public even as the pretense of such Wilsonian repose and purity evaporated as this war, originating in a conflict between Austria-Hungary and Serbia, quickly evolved into the Great War—war of a kind and on a scale quite unforeseen.

Whereas the United States was generally regarded by Europeans as foremost in the development of machines and mass techniques, when viewed in the later and larger perspective of world historian William H. McNeill, "the really impressive achievements of human engineering" of these times were "concentrated in the military sphere." "As a result, the first weeks of World War I presented the amazing spectacle of vast human machines, complete with replaceable parts, operating in a truly inhuman fashion and moving at least approximately according to predetermined and irreversible plans." As millions marched and a million died in the early stages of this conflict without achieving any of the combatants' objectives, it was soon apparent that the Great Powers of Europe had become mired in a prolonged horror. Warfare had taken on new forms primarily because of technology. In simplest terms, for example, machine guns and barbed wire had made defense superior to offense on land, resulting in the stalemated Western Front and the massive killings of trench warfare. On the seas submarines provided a new offensive weapon superior to early defensive responses, resulting in a heavy toll in shipping. Very early the British deployed their superior surface fleet to form a blockade on ships with cargo bound for Germany; in response, the Germans declared a submarine war zone surrounding the British Isles. The risks of travel amid this new mode of warfare were soon apparent, the legal rights of neutral passengers and shipping uncertain, but President Wilson took a strong stand in support of American travelers and against unrestricted submarine attacks.

Our concern here is not with details of the U.S. entrance and performance in the war in Europe but with America's influence in shaping the peace in the wake of a shattered Great Power System. Suffice to note that an "intellectual fog . . . rolled in across the Atlantic after the outbreak of war in Europe and eventually surged westward, blanketing the country with rumors, half-truths, and even falsehoods," which, together with a mounting sequence of notorious German actions—overrunning neutral Belgium, sinking of passenger vessels, conniving with Mexico, and exhibiting crude "Prussian militarism"—stimulated military preparedness in the United States and strengthened public favor toward Britain and France. More substantial was the American economic boom and deepening financial stake in supplying those Allies with their massive wartime needs. Important regional variations in such reactions were recurrently expressed in congressional debates. "Midwestern agrarians interpreted the world war as the outgrowth of a rivalry among European powers for colonial possessions" and wanted no part in it. Southerners viewed a large standing army and any strengthening of central government "with deep distrust," and, not untypically, a Texas congressman accused the East of promoting war "hysteria" to sustain military "preparedness" because "the money is poured out along the Atlantic seaboard. It goes straight into the pockets of Bostonians, New Yorkers, and Philadelphians."

Woodrow Wilson was certainly no isolationist; indeed he was a strong internationalist—"we are participants, whether we would or not, in the life of the world"—but he clung to neutrality, as Walter A. McDougall notes, not "because the American people were almost unanimously in favor of staying out of the war," but "because he believed that remaining above the battle was the only way that he, Wilson, could exert the moral authority needed to end the war on terms that would make for a lasting peace." The Wilson administration made recurrent attempts to initiate peace talks among the belligerents, but to no avail. Addressing the Senate in January 1917, Wilson reported on the latest failure and then spoke at some length about the principles that must serve as "the foundations of peace among the nations," including, first of all, that "it must be a peace without victory." Unfortunately for his cause it was by then known that the warring sets of powers had already made secret deals about the division of spoils and new geopolitical designs to ensure their predominance in a postwar world, and thus it became increasingly clear that a neutral United States would likely have little influence over any eventual settlement. The president was thereby faced with the awful paradox that "to practice peace, he had to wage war." Within a few weeks a renewal of submarine sinkings ("a warfare against mankind"), revelation of German overtures to Mexico, and rising fear of a German victory in Europe provided Wilson with the rationale that war "has been thrust upon us" and America responds in order "to vindicate the principles of peace and justice in the life of the world." Thus in April 1917 the United States joined the battle as an "associated" not "allied" power, a distinction meant to keep it untainted by existing wartime agreements among Britain, France, Italy, Russia, and Japan (and war was declared initially only against Germany, later against Austria-Hungary, and never against Bulgaria or Turkey). By December 200,000 American troops were in Europe; thrust into battle against a major German offensive in the spring of 1918 such fresh forces tipped the balance amid war-depleted combatants and intensified pressures toward the Armistice of November 11, 1918. In total 2 million American soldiers were sent to Europe, 600,000 were engaged in battle, at a cost of 53,400 killed. This last figure was minute when viewed against the estimated 13 million lost by all the other powers but quite enough to sear on the national memory this brief but vigorous participation in a Great World conflict, and enough to ensure an American voice at the peace table.

ATTEMPT AT A WILSONIAN PEACE

Woodrow Wilson's message had already been widely proclaimed. He had often addressed his remarks to the people of the world, and his propaganda machine had scattered 60 million pamphlets and leaflets preaching Wilsonian principles of a new world order; in 1919 he was welcomed to Europe by throngs of ordinary people. He arrived in Paris determined to seek a "scientific peace" based upon rational, equitable long-term considerations, and he brought with him a team of specialists and a large volume of studies that had been prepared by a Commission of Inquiry working out of the American Geographical Society (AGS) in New York and in conjunction with its staff. Our concern here must be limited to a few general geopolitical issues in the dauntingly difficult problems facing the negotiators.

The president had declared his most important geopolitical principle in an address to Congress on February 11, 1918: "There shall be no annexations. . . . Peoples are not to be handled about from one sovereignty to another by an international conference or an understanding between rivals and antagonists. National aspirations must be respected; peoples may now be dominated and governed only by their own consent. 'Self determination' is now an imperative principle of action which statesmen will henceforth ignore at their peril." "Self determination" would prove to be a powerful slogan—and a principle whose perils statesmen could never escape. The Great War of 1914–18 and its aftermath was one of the great turning points in geopolitical history. Four great interlocking empires—German, Austro-Hungarian, Russian, Ottoman—were shattered by military defeat and internal explosions. Seven newly independent states emerged (not counting ephemeral ones from the collapse of the Russian Empire), the boundaries of thirteen others were altered, and several subordinate units were transferred to new imperial control.

Wilson's favorite term was an endorsement of nationalism, a revolutionary instrument reasonably well tamed and strongly lodged in parts of Western Europe, but in much of Eastern Europe many peoples "were still locked into the complex multiple loyalties of kinship, territory and religion" and populations exhibited "a chaotic ethnographic map of many dialects and ambiguous historical or linguogenetic allegiances." Wilson was made aware of the problem by his panel of specialists (Leon Dominian's *Frontiers of Language and Nationality in Europe* had been published by the AGS in 1917), but references to boundary issues in his famous Fourteen Points glossed over such explosive problems ("readjustment . . . along clearly recognizable lines of nationality" [Italy]; "along historically established lines of allegiance and nationality" [Balkans]). In his later attempts to convince the American public of the virtues of the treaty his narrow faith in rational processes and good will was on prominent display: "There are regions where you can not draw a national line and say these are Slavs on this side and Italians on that [he is holding up a map]. You have to approximate the line. You have to come as near to it as you can, and then trust to the processes of history to redistribute, it may be, the people that are on the wrong side of that line." Or, "we will let the people that live there decide. We will have a referendum. Within a certain length of time after the war, under the supervision of an international commission."

Such faith in and fostering of such deceptively simple geopolitical concepts was the despair of Robert Lansing, his secretary of State (who was granted little influence upon such matters): "When the President talks of self-determination, what unit does he have in mind? Does he mean a race, a territorial area, or a community? Without a definite unit which is practical, application of this principle is dangerous to peace and stability. . . . The phrase is simply loaded with dynamite. It will raise hopes which can never be realized. It will, I fear, cost thousands of lives. . . . What a calamity that the phrase was ever uttered! What misery it will cause!" The phrase may not have caused the misery, but it surely intensified and extended it. The growing pressures of nationalism now erupted to feverish levels across Central and Eastern Europe faced with the imposition of new national boundaries across multi-national areas. What constituted a "national state" was fearfully uncertain. Until Austria-Hungary's collapse, Wilson had shared some hope that that historic frame-work might be generally preserved as a federation of national republics, and the large composite units of Czechoslovakia and Yugoslavia were preferred over new Montenegros. But whatever the resultant pattern, the general consequences would have been similar. As Wilson's chief geographic adviser, Isaiah Bowman, observed in 1921, "the danger spots of the world have been greatly increased in number, the *zones of friction* lengthened, . . . the sources of possible trouble between unlike and, in the main, unfriendly peoples" has increased. No phrase or formula would resolve such geopolitical disputes peacefully (fig. 78).

The Wilsonian principle of "absolute freedom of navigation upon the seas, out-side territorial waters, alike in peace and in war," was firmly rejected by Britain; his corollary that landlocked nations must be allowed direct access "to the great high-ways of the sea" was of course keenly supported by such states and became the source of bitter disputes over the Polish Corridor and Danzig, Fiume, Thrace, Con-stantinople and the Zone of the Straits, some of which were resolved by local forces rather than by Paris negotiators.

Germany's overseas colonies in Africa and the Pacific had been occupied by and divided among the Allied Powers early in the war. Self-determination was gener-ally not considered to be appropriate as yet for these non-European peoples. How-ever, Wilson's resistance to simple seizure and transfer of peoples from one sover-eignty to another led to the technical allocation of these territories as "mandates" to victorious powers that were "to act as trustees and not as their masters," all to be monitored by a permanent commission of the League of Nations. Although this was in effect a division of the spoils of war and such international oversight carried limited powers of intervention, the concept of trusteeship had been established. Arab areas released from Turkish rule were also placed under this system in a sepa-rate class anticipating independence within a shorter period. The Allied Powers urged the United States to be mandatory of Armenia (a newly defined territory) and Constantinople; Wilson accepted the first as a "Christian duty" to a (Chris-tian) people who had suffered genocidal attacks from the Turks, and the second as a disinterested power taking on a job "like the Panama Canal job—one of keeping the Black Sea passage open." The U.S. Senate rejected any such involvement, and the Turkish nationalist uprising soon put an end to all Great Power designs for post-war Asia Minor.

Wilson always regarded the war above all as "a struggle for a just and secure peace" that could be obtained by not "a balance of power, but a community of power." His was the great voice for such a community, he was chairman of the com-mission that drafted the Covenant of the League of Nations, his insistence made it

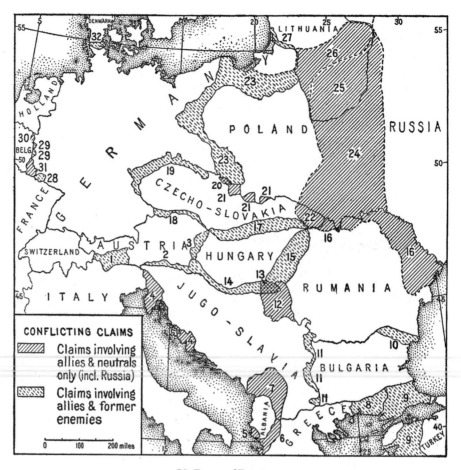

78. Zones of Friction.
Overlapping territorial claims in Central Europe as depicted in Isaiah Bowman's *New World* (1921). The thirty-two areas are listed by name in his caption.

an integral part of the peace treaty, and he was—and is—universally regarded as its great founder (the general idea was not new). The long, bitter political battle and eventual failure of the U.S. Senate to ratify the Versailles Treaty is a famous episode in domestic and international politics and need not be related here. Suffice to note that although Wilson had already compromised on nearly every other point, he refused to budge on Article 10 requiring every member to join in preserving "the territorial integrity and existing independence of every other member," whereas the Senate feared that "acceptance would permanently embroil the United States in European conflicts, and would deprive Congress of its constitutional right to declare war."

Woodrow Wilson was a great American missionary. A skilled sermonizer, his message was always grounded upon what he regarded as fundamental truths. The United States "had entered the war to promote no private nor peculiar interest of our own. . . . We had formulated the principles upon which the settlement was to be made," and these (as he had earlier emphasized in presenting his Fourteen Points) were "American principles, American policies," those "of forward looking men and women everywhere, of every nation, of every enlightened community. They are the principles of mankind and must prevail." Thus American troops had arrived in Europe as "a great moral force" and became "recognized as crusaders." Once the war was over "there can be no question of our ceasing to be a world power. The only question is whether we can refuse the moral leadership that is offered us. . . . The stage is set, the destiny disclosed. It has come about by no plan of our conceiving, but by the hand of God who led us into this way."

Wilson was thus the leader of the Chosen People, an authoritarian reformer determined to make the world "safe for democracy" through universalization of the American civil creed, believing "that he had the power to impose the new order upon Europe." He took pride in his Southern, Scotch-Irish background, but his message was a deep departure from Presbyterian Calvinism. His was a faith grounded in Enlightenment and Progress, in science, rationality, and the basic goodness of humankind, confident that a free people knowing the facts of any particular case will seek an equitable settlement and live in peace—a utopian vision of a sinless world.

Historians have often noted that Wilson was not the only figure at that moment in world affairs who was "possessed of an idea," preaching a social gospel based upon the "goodness of the people," the voice of a chosen nation steeped in millennial "utopian thought." For while Wilson was providing an ideology for the Allied cause, Lenin was proclaiming that "the transition to classless communism was immanent" and that "Russia was destined to provide ideological regeneration for the decaying West." In November 1917, Lenin had proposed an immediate armistice leading to a "democratic peace without annexations and indemnities, and on the basis of self-determination of nations." Wilson's Fourteen Points speech was a response to Lenin and to the chaotic uncertainties of the revolution and included an article calling for "the evacuation of all Russian territory" (by foreign troops) and "obtaining for her an unhampered and unembarrassed opportunity for the independent determination of her own political development and national policy." Lenin defied all attempts to keep Russia in the war, signed a separate peace treaty with Germany, and eventually defeated Western-supported anti-Bolshevik forces. For years thereafter, "'the Russian experiment' seemed the most important political thing in the world. . . . bringing hope to some fear to others," reviving the pertinence of Alexis de Tocqueville's famous observation of the United States and Russia in the 1830s as "two great nations" starting from different points but tending toward the same end; each "marked out by the will of Heaven to sway the destinies of half the globe." However, as Hans Kohn noted, "the situation in which Washington and Moscow faced each other in 1918 . . . lasted only a short time. The United States voluntarily withdrew into isolation; Russia was forced by weakness to abandon attempts to decide the course of history" until it could get its own system in working order.

AFTERMATH

"Isolationism" is a common but overly simple term for American foreign policy following World War I. It might better be said that the United States was "a nation struggling to avoid the inevitable consequences of having become a World Power" in political as well as economic terms, and it chose to follow an "independent internationalism." It continued to be involved in Europe, Asia, and the Americas; in two of these realms more or less on its own terms, in the other increasingly, uncomfortably pressed by a rival.

The United States signed a separate peace treaty with Germany differing little from the Versailles design. Any idea of a "peace without victory" had evaporated in the fervors of warfare (highly enflamed within the United States as elsewhere). Yet after an unavoidable phase of punishment, Wilson hoped for full participation of a democratic Germany as an inherently important power within the League of Nations. To a security-obsessed France he even offered to join with Britain in a formal alliance to defend France against German attack (also rejected by the U.S. Senate). The United States had entered the war to tip the balance against a superior Continental European Power; lacking formal commitments for the future it thereafter relied on an old implicit relationship of new significance: an independent Great Britain, guarded by its navy behind its narrow moat, with options of intervening on the Continent as needed. As Nicholas J. Spykman, writing twenty years later, put it: "The position of the United States in regard to Europe as a whole is, therefore, identical to the position of Great Britain in regard to the European Continent: the scale is different, the units are larger, and the distances greater, but the pattern is the same." German science, technology, and economy as well as military strength had been impressive; Britain was both a buffer and potential offshore base against the reappearance of such a threatening Continental Power. Such a geopolitical reading was not commonly discerned by the public or politicians on either side of the Atlantic. With the great imbalance in power and potential now obvious, relations between Britain and the United States were neither close nor cordial. America's European involvement reverted to economic policies, and animosities were deepened by its focus on war debts (as a British leader complained, whereas previously "the Bank of England rate controlled the interest rate everywhere," today "London is harnessed to Wall Street").

American and Western European leaders did share a common fear: Bolshevism. It took several tumultuous years to find out just what the extent of its hold would be. It welled up briefly in Central Europe, and the United States joined in faltering attempts to prop up more conservative forces in Russia. In the meantime, the creation of a tier of independent states separating Revolutionary Russia from a revengeful Germany was considered strategically imperative by the remaining Great Powers in Paris. Halford J. Mackinder, British geographer and member of Parliament, earnestly advocated the same in a short book completed just as the peace negotiations got under way. Starting with the simple principle that "there is in nature no such thing as equality of opportunity for nations," and elaborating upon a brief sketch of his ideas presented in 1904, he set forth his reasoning "that the grouping of lands and seas, and of fertility and natural pathways, is such as to lend itself to the growth of empires, and in the end of a single world-empire." Coining a set of key geographic terms, he phrased his warning against such a fearful eventuality in a stunningly simple formula:

> *Who rules East Europe commands the Heartland:*
> *Who rules the Heartland commands the World-Island:*
> *Who rules the World-Island commands the World.*

Mackinder's warning had no direct bearing on national policies at the time; with the collapse of continental empires the tier of independent states was created, and the need to curb German power was foremost in the minds of the Allies. Mackinder's formulation would become famous only after the collapse of that geopolitical solution a generation later. As for command of the world, perhaps most Western Europeans who thought about the matter might have found Bertrand Russell's early 1920s view plausible: "It is, of course, obvious that the next Power to make a bid for world empire will be America. America may not, as yet, consciously desire such a position, but no nation with sufficient resources can long resist the attempt. And the resources of America are more adequate than those of any previous aspirant to universal hegemony." Such talk of "empire," whether by Mackinder, Russell, or others, commonly referred to national states with commanding political jurisdiction and military power over vast territories and other peoples (as in examples then extant or of recent memory). The United States had always been an empire of that kind, and it was, in fact, already a conscious "aspirant to universal hegemony" on its own terms—a world-empire of another type. From the outset of the twentieth century the United States was seeking economic empire, a world of the "open door" ("the removal, as far as possible, of all economic barriers," as the Third of Wilson's Fourteen Points put it), a world open to American investment, access to markets, and control of materials.

At the end of the war "the continental United States . . . enjoyed a measure of security unapproached by any other great nation in modern times." It had no further territorial ambitions, it shunned Great Power alliances, and it refused to join the League of Nations that its president had so extensively shaped. Its formal interest in Europe was essentially economic; its hatred of Bolshevism was so great that it did not respond to Lenin's brief opening for Western investment and did not recognize the Soviet Union as an acceptable member of the world of nations until 1933, but it had no military fear of that struggling state. Yet the United States continued its massive naval expansion with a declared aim of having the most powerful fleet in the world.

EAST ASIA AND THE PACIFIC

On a gray winter day in late December 1918, ten battleships, "looming one after another through the mist" of swirling rain and snow, steamed slowly past the cheering crowds lining the waterfront of lower Manhattan welcoming their return from wartime operations in the Atlantic; as Harold and Margaret Sprout state about this vignette, "it was fitting that the rise of American naval power, begun in hostility to Great Britain, should thus approach its climax" in this return "from intimate association in a common cause with the world's first naval power." A little more than two years later these great dreadnoughts and many other vessels—the bulk of the American fleet—would be in the Pacific on maneuvers, as naval strategists rehearsed contingent plans for war against a rival force.

The United States and Japan had become generally recognized Great Powers during the same moment in history, and relations between them became strained soon thereafter. This developing enmity was twofold in character: geopolitical and psychological. The former might be obvious to anyone who examined a map showing their new Pacific empires; the latter was stridently expressed in perceptions and prejudices of each society for the other, in fears and fervors generated by contact of the two peoples with one another.

Having undertaken its radical transformation toward a Western-styled modernization so late, Japan soon saw itself as having to catch up in imperial expansion as well. Three years before the United States had precipitously thrust itself across the Pacific into East Asian affairs, Japan had defeated China (to the world's surprise) and taken a large step southward with the annexation of Formosa (Taiwan), the first large island north of the Philippines. Ten years later its defeat of Russia (another surprise) opened the way for a vigorous move onto the continent, taking over Korea, South Manchuria, and poised for moving in upon North China. There followed a succession of attempts by the United States to gain from Japan formal declarations of respect for its own exposed position in the Far East, including its Open Door policy regarding foreign concessions in China. It was understood that the United States would have to offer something in return. As his ambassador in Tokyo informed President Wilson (by way of Colonel Edward M. House): "We cannot meet Japan in her desires as to land and immigration, and unless we make some concessions in regard to her sphere of influence in the East, trouble is sure, sooner or later to come." Thus the Lansing-Ishii Agreement of 1917 acknowledged that "territorial propinquity creates special relations between countries, and consequently, the Government of the United States recognizes that Japan has special interests in China, particularly in the part to which her possessions are contiguous" (language "which was to haunt future American-Japanese diplomacy").

The ambassador's reference to being unable to meet Japan's "desires as to land and immigration" pointed directly at the intersection of the geopolitical and the psychological in the relations between these two powers. In the early twentieth century Japanese became successors to Chinese in the "Yellow Peril," in American fears of "invasion" and even a "complete Orientalization of the Pacific Coast." Local discriminations were severe; in 1913 California barred Japanese from owning land (and later attempted to prohibit even leasing it); negotiations at the highest diplomatic levels attempted to limit emigration; courts ruled Japanese immigrants ineligible for citizenship; and an "Asiatic Barred Zone" was initiated in 1917. The Wilson administration sought to quell such moves as needlessly provocative; Japan regarded each one as "a national insult."

Out of its long, rigid, self-imposed isolation and its unusual homogeneity of race and culture, the Japanese brought into the world an extreme national self-consciousness with a keen sensitivity to respect and rank among nations. Its rapid Westernization was admired and it soon won status as a Great Power, but it was obviously regarded as something apart, an anomaly within a Western-dominated world permeated with a strong sense of racial and cultural differences. In 1919 Japan initiated an amendment to the League of Nations Covenant declaring "the equality of nations [as] a basic principle" and specifying that "all alien nationals" within member states be accorded "just treatment in every respect, making no distinction, either in law or in fact, on account of their race or nationality." They were bitterly disappointed at its failure (the United States was content to let Britain and Australia be its firmest opponents).

Geopolitically, however, these times were a great success for Japan. It took from Germany (as a Mandated power) its Pacific Islands north of the Equator (Britain, Australia, and New Zealand were allotted those south of that line), and also its port and special privileges in Shantung province; with the collapse of the Russian Empire it had no effective rival for Manchuria (fig. 79). The United States was ambivalent about this overall pattern of expansion: discerning a real threat in the Pacific, wanting to be protective of China, but regarding Japanese movement into "contiguous" Manchuria as "unavoidable," and perhaps advantageous: "the diversion of the tide of Japanese migration toward Manchuria may somewhat relieve the situation on our own Pacific Coast." In his 1921 survey of world political geography Bowman wrote that because of the pressure of population Japan was "a country that must overflow its boundaries" and "looks westward across the sea, where she beholds fair lands thinly populated." Manchuria was such a rare attraction in that part of the world because the Manchus, long rulers of China, had kept settlers out of their pastoral homeland. Only as the Western powers began to parcel large portions of the moribund empire among themselves were concessions granted to Russia. Although Japan had taken these over and established a program for farmer emigrants, few of its own were attracted to such a land; as Bowman noted ten years later in his study of the remaining "pioneer fringes" of the world, Manchuria was rapidly filling up with Chinese in "the greatest folk movement in the world today," while the Japanese there were town dwellers at work on its large industrial resources.

In an attempt to apply Wilsonian principles aggressively to world problems, the United States convened the Washington Naval Conference in late 1921, boldly proposed dramatic reductions in existing and planned fleets, and sought agreement on solutions for various Pacific and Far Eastern problems. The most famous outcome was the 5–5–3 ratio established for the United States, Great Britain, and Japan, respectively (but applied only to battleships, not to entire fleets as first proposed). In addition the Anglo-Japanese Alliance of 1902 was replaced by a Four-Power Treaty that included the United States and France as other Pacific powers, and treaties offering general endorsements of the Open Door and respect for the territorial integrity of China were signed. But Japan was "an unwilling participant" in these proceedings. It accepted this naval ratio only after the United States and Britain agreed to refrain from building further fortifications beyond Pearl Harbor and Singapore. And it held its own interpretations of its geopolitical position. As its foreign minister later declared to the American secretary of State, Japan's "special interests" in China were inextinguishable—"realities deriving from nature and geography . . . and not benefits conferred on Japan by the United States." To Japan the insistent pressures of these and other negotiations before and after "seemed to be clear evidence of an Anglo-American lineup against Japan. For many Japanese it seemed that race and culture were the ultimate determinants."

Thus the geopolitical positions of these rival powers were starkly different, and increasingly divergent. The United States had a big navy backed by huge domestic resources, but it had given notice of its limited commitments in the Far East. The Philippines was not to be a major forward base for possible Asian warfare, nor had it become the great commercial base at the threshold of China that fervent annexationists had predicted (American companies accounted for only 6 percent of foreign investment in China, and U.S. trade with Japan was much more important). The eventual withdrawal from the Philippines declared in 1916 had become specified as 1946. The U.S. insistence on respect for the territorial integrity of China

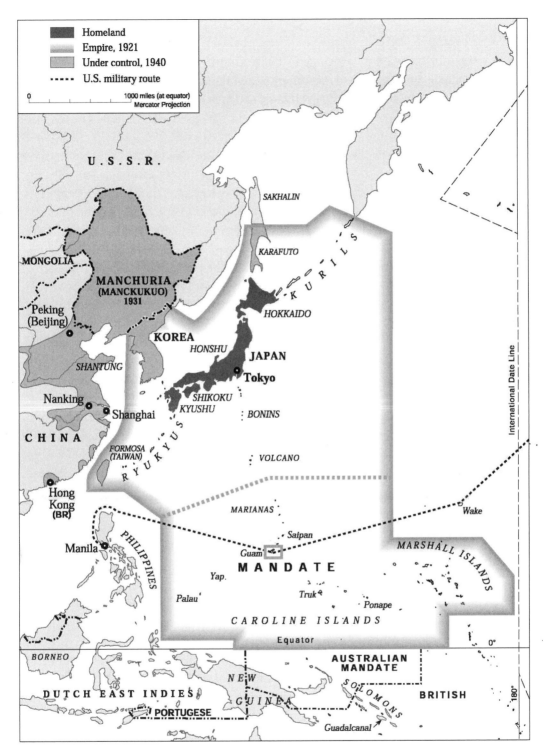

79. Japanese Position, 1940.

arose from its late entry into imperial competition, rested on general principles, was nurtured by well-publicized missionary and philanthropic work in that famous civilization undergoing wrenching change, and was intensified by obvious Japanese imperial intentions. Its policy focused on formal agreements among contending powers because China "was not and never had been a truly vital American national interest" and such treaties or understandings lay "beyond our will or power to support by force."

Japan had been allocated the dominant navy in East Asia and the Western Pacific. It had won a huge set of positions on the adjacent mainland ("Peking lives under the Japanese shadow. All the northern gateways are sentineled by the Japanese fleet"), and it held a dense array of Micronesian archipelagoes (Palau, Caroline, Marshall) stretching nearly 3,000 miles across the equatorial seas, and these tethered to the homeland along a narrow north-south line of islands (Bonins, Volcanos, Marianas) cutting across the widely spaced east-west American links at Guam, 3,300 miles west of Pearl Harbor (see fig. 79).

The shock of the Great Depression, bringing higher tariffs and crippling markets around the world, "seemed to threaten the very existence" of a Japan of 65 million people crowded on a mountainous homeland smaller than California and an expanding industrial economy heavily dependent on imports and exports. A militant Japanese leadership accelerated imperial expansion as the obvious response. In 1931 the army "rode the crest of a tidal wave of patriotism" in a complete conquest of Manchuria; in 1932 Japan attacked Shanghai but withdrew under pressure from the League of Nations (primarily from Britain) and unexpectedly strong Chinese resistance. In 1933 Japan resigned from the League and in the following year served notice that it would resign from the Washington Naval Treaty in 1936. In 1937 it began a major invasion of China. The United States sent a protest, and a portion of its Asiatic fleet to evacuate American citizens from China.

In negotiations with the Americans, Japanese diplomats often likened its aspired position in East Asia to that of the United States in the Western Hemisphere. The usual American response insisted that the Monroe Doctrine was not a claim of "paramount interest" in Latin America but only a guardianship to ensure the self-development of those countries, free from European interference. Given its keen sensitivity to rank and respect and the opposition and critique that its actions encountered, it is not surprising that "Asia for the Asians" emerged as a Japanese slogan in the 1930s and that prominent military and public leaders came to insist upon the geopolitical "reality" that only those nations ruling great continental or sea empires could hope to survive independently in a Great Power World.

3. Impositions: Western Hemisphere

MIDDLE AMERICA

Early in his presidency, Woodrow Wilson, vexed by problems arising from the Mexican Revolution, instructed the State Department to draft a statement to be sent to all the European Powers to remind them in "strong and direct language" that "the United States was the nation of paramount influence in the Western Hemisphere" and to warn them not to "antagonize and thwart" it from carrying out its sole responsibility to intervene when necessary in the political affairs of any state therein. Although his State Department counselor talked him out of sending such a crude, provocative note, it was commonly understood in Europe and the Americas that such was indeed the basic stance of the United States.

Such hegemony had been formally declared ten years earlier in Theodore Roosevelt's Corollary to the eighty-year-old Monroe Doctrine, wherein he stated that "flagrant cases of wrongdoing" or "impotence" on the part of a lesser state may force the United States, as the major "civilized nation," to intervene and exercise "an international police power" to resolve the problem. The case of the Dominican Republic that had prompted his proclamation became the first example and well represented the general geopolitical focus of such actions thereafter. As an American secretary of State put it in the year before Wilson's election: "The logic of political geography and strategy, and now our tremendous national interest created by the Panama Canal, make . . . Central America and the zone of the Caribbean of paramount interest to the Government of the United States."

During the twenty years following that first action American troops and officials were sent again to the Dominican Republic, to Nicaragua (several times), Haiti, and Panama to quell civil disorders threatening American lives and property and to impose controls over national financial institutions to protect American and other foreign investors. Such occupations (and almost annual "naval visits") made these countries de facto protectorates, akin to (but less comprehensive than) that imposed on Cuba in 1902. Some generated strong resistance; the third intervention in Nicaragua in 1927 was countered by a guerrilla leader, Augusto Sandino, who enjoyed strong local support, and the ensuing protracted struggle involving 5,600 American troops came under heavy criticism in the United States. Meanwhile, as Walter La Feber notes, "United Fruit controlled not only the banana market, but the rail systems, shipping, banking, and governments in Costa Rica and Honduras," making official intervention unnecessary. Purchase of the Danish Virgin Islands in 1917 (completing an earlier rebuffed attempt) further augmented the American position in the region (fig. 80).

Mexico was a very different case. The chaos of the early stages of the revolution threatened American lives and property, but this was surely not to be resolved by

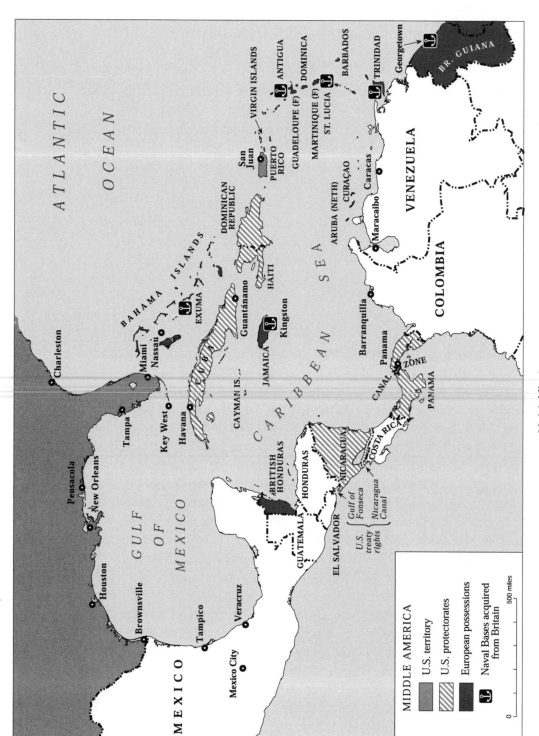

80. Middle America.

the intervention of a contingent of U.S. Marines and Treasury officials. Unlike the small states of Hispaniola and Central America, Mexico was a large country undergoing a major social revolution, a contention among "classes, regions, ideologies" as well as "feuding elites." The likelihood of reverberations within the broad shared borderland of the two countries was soon apparent, magnified by the importance of northern Mexico in the conflict. The revolt was ignited through the plotting of a defeated presidential candidate from his San Antonio refuge; many of the principal leaders were *norteños* and much of the fighting took place in their region. Various districts were affected by raids and pursuits across the border, refugees and opportunists flowed back and forth through the main crossings, and since the United States was a critical source of supplies, especially of arms and munitions, the approaches and access to Nogales, El Paso, Eagle Pass, Laredo, Brownsville, and the Rio Grande Valley became major strategic objectives.

While the long, open Porfirian era was an important prelude to this widespread complex uprising, most of its contending leaders were not militantly against foreign investment, even though they aspired to greater control over the direction of Mexican development. There were of course outbursts of xenophobia, and some American mines and other properties were ravaged (the big copper camps were not seriously disrupted), but much the most prominent and profitable American presence endured because "oil money was a significant factor in financing the Mexican Revolution, in the form of taxes, forced loans, and outright theft." Production had begun in 1901, soon after the famous Spindletop gusher had revealed the immense deposits in the salt domes of southeastern Texas, and the same feverish speculation that opened fields in many parts of Texas and Oklahoma spread to the Tampico Embayment and soon made Mexico a major world producer. These oil districts were essentially foreign enclaves ("Tampico is the most American city in Mexico and the Mexicans themselves call it 'Gringolandia'"), and the U.S. Navy routinely patrolled Gulf waters and kept a warship at Tampico. In 1914 a petty incident involving some sailors ashore, followed by an admiral's arrogant insistence on a national apology from Mexico, led to the first American intervention.

Woodrow Wilson struggled to apply his "moral imperialism" to the larger case. He was generally interested more in good leaders and better governments than in protecting American investments, but he blundered badly in this situation by seizing control of Veracruz, Mexico's leading port, with loss of life on both sides, and becoming mired for months in an embarrassing stalemate. He regarded an early de facto Mexican president as unsuitable, and his later endorsement of Venustiano Carranza caused another rival, Pancho Villa, to pillage the border town of Columbus, New Mexico, killing Americans. (The United States had previously allowed Carrancista troops to move by rail through American territory from El Paso to Douglas, Arizona, to try to halt Villa's raids in this northern sector.) Given the instant uproar for retaliation, Wilson had little choice but to send General John Pershing with 6,000 troops in pursuit of Villa, but leaders of both countries worked to restrain their citizens and parried with one another to avoid any enlargement of conflict. "In this case the humiliation of having a foreign army ranging deep into Mexican territory was matched by the embarrassment of Pershing's failure to catch any of the attackers, and an eventual diplomatic conciliation was achieved." Wilson was always far more concerned about the war in Europe than about annoying episodes in Mexico; the deployment of 120,000 American troops, including federalized National Guard units, to the Borderland proved to be important preparation for the far greater task (the last of the punitive forces were quietly withdrawn from Mexico just two months before the United States declared war on Germany).

A coup in 1920 that deposed Carranza and placed Alvaro Obregón in power marked the end of the main military phase of the revolution but did not end serious tensions between the two countries. Disputes over the status of foreign oil companies festered for years, with Mexico insisting on national control over subsoil rights and the companies insisting on the legality of their original concessions. Initial strong U.S. government and popular support for the companies began to fade following the domestic Teapot Dome scandal, and oil production (which had expanded greatly during the revolution) was declining and the companies were finding better prospects in Venezuela; in 1928 a new, unusually capable, American ambassador brokered a compromise representing "the triumph of . . . moderate, pragmatic interests over the imperialist ideologues and the petroleum militants" by which Mexican national rights were recognized, but the original American developers were granted some of their special privileges. Historians have regarded this settlement as "an important step in the 'retreat from imperialism'" and a "turning point" whereby for American administrations "the word 'Mexico' came to represent a neighbor nation and not a recurring problem"—though in fact this very problem did recur ten years later when, confronted by company defiance of labor regulations, a Mexican president suddenly, reluctantly, nationalized the oil industry.

This unanticipated act in 1938 was enormously popular, hailed as the winning of economic independence—"Mexico for the Mexicans." By that date it had become clear that the United States had a new kind of neighbor on its southern border. A bloody war among regional *caciques* had evolved into broader contentions among expanding popular reformist movements, and these became selectively incorporated into an increasingly consolidated and centralized state under the leadership of a single national party enjoying, and manipulating, mass support. It was an indigenous transformation independent of other revolutions in the world, strongly nationalistic but not anticapitalistic. Mexico had become a developing country with a drive for material improvements and social reforms under middle-class business leaders and bureaucrats. Nor was it widely anti-American. Mexican leaders could never be seen as yielding to American pressure, but the American example had long been important to those seeking to create a more liberal and prosperous republic. Despite recurrent episodes during the civil war, Alan Knight pointed to a more important endemic "Hispanophobia" directed against Spanish "landlords, estate managers, foremen, shopkeepers, pawnbrokers, and wholesalers," as well as to the hierarchy of the Catholic Church. During the 1930s numerous problems arose, but none caused serious disruption of relations. The expulsion of many Mexicans from the United States during the Great Depression was resented, but the two countries worked together to resolve the oil seizure crisis; the U.S. government never challenged the Mexican right to nationalize and insisted only on fair recompense for the companies. Very soon the United States was confronted with much larger questions of hemispheric cooperation, and Mexico was an essential partner.

PAN AMERICANISM

Following President Monroe's famous Doctrine of 1823 orators in various American countries, North and South, might wax grandiloquently upon the larger meanings of this wonderful geopolitical separation of the free peoples of the New World from the control and contaminations of the Old—this near political concordance with Nature's grand design—but it was many years before any move to bind all these states together was made.

In 1889 Secretary of State James G. Blaine convened a First International American Conference, with delegates from seventeen states, but the concept, purpose, and auspices of such a gathering encountered considerable resistance and skepticism. A Union of American Republics agency was established, but to little effect. Blaine's radical proposals for a customs union, common coinage, and other ties were firmly rejected because of correct perceptions of their purpose: an attempt to redirect Latin American commerce with Europe to the United States.

Once the United States intervened in the Cuban Revolution, took over the island remnants of Spain's American empire, and assumed firm control over the American Mediterranean, inter-American relations perforce became a major geopolitical issue for all hemispheric states. Failure of this "Colossus of the North" to join the League of Nations "was regarded as proof that American imperialism was resolved to accept no external control, and that southward economic penetration . . . was to continue in new strength" (U.S. firms had expanded vigorously in South America as European countries sold off assets to finance their war). Eighteen Latin American countries joined the League hoping "that the spirit of the covenant would tend to provide protection against the overweening influence of the United States."

The very term "Pan American" (the new common name for periodic conferences and the secretariat of the Union) was generally regarded by the other states as a concept imposed by the United States and could not easily be separated from long-standing presumptions of Anglo-Saxon superiority and its "civilizing" mission. Deep differences in cultural heritage provided little basis for a common ideology, and the gross imbalances in economic power provided ample basis for a common fear. Thus a 1922 speech by an Argentine intellectual to a distinguished Mexican audience carried a not uncommon theme and tone:

> We are not, we no longer wish to be, we no longer can be pan-Americanists. The famous Monroe Doctrine, which for a century seemed to be the guarantee of our political independence against the threat of European conquests, has gradually proved to be a declaration of the American right to protect us and to intervene in our affairs. Our powerful neighbor and meddlesome friend, having developed to its highest level the capitalist mode of production, during the past war has attained world financial hegemony. This development has been accompanied by the growth in voracity of the American privileged caste, which has increasingly pressed for an imperialist policy and converted the government into an instrument of its corporations. . . . Among the ruling classes of this great state, the urge to expand and conquer has grown to the point where the classic "America for the Americans" actually means "America—our Latin America—for the North Americans."

The scene and the speaker were a compelling combination for such remarks because U.S. relations with Mexico, its nearest neighbor, were closely watched by all the other states as a critical test of American policies and practices, while Argentina, the most remote of these "neighbors," was a persistent leader in the opposition to U.S. hemispheric pretensions. This most European of Latin American states not only resented U.S. assumptions of protection and dominance, its cultural, demographic, and commercial ties with Europe were in fact far more vital to its well-being.

At the 1923 Pan American conference the U.S. delegation blocked a Uruguayan proposal "for an American League of Nations based on the absolute equality of nations"; at the next, in 1928, it led the defeat of a resolution supporting the principle of nonintervention. There was nothing surprising in these oppositions (in the latter one it was supported by three states under U.S. occupation and only one other). However, American involvements were coming under heavy criticism at home as well as abroad and were not as successful as expected (especially in Nicaragua). In 1928 President-elect Herbert Hoover made a goodwill tour of eleven Latin American countries and soon initiated a shift in policy, beginning with a formal repudiation of the Roosevelt Corollary. Interrupted by the economic crisis, further steps were taken under Franklin D. Roosevelt, who in his inaugural address dedicated "this nation to the policy of a good neighbor." Later that year the United States agreed to an Argentine-sponsored proposition that "no state has the right to intervene in the internal or external affairs of another." In 1934 the formal protectorate over Cuba (the Platt Amendment of 1902) was abrogated and removal of U.S. Marines from Haiti begun (and Congress ratified independence for the Philippines to take effect ten years hence). In 1936 Roosevelt attended the Pan American conference in Buenos Aires—to great acclaim—and the principle of consultation among all these states for collective security was affirmed. Meanwhile the American practice of recognizing stable dictatorships became quietly more apparent.

Although fear and distrust of the United States was somewhat softened by such changes, there was no doubt that "collective security" meant U.S. security. Insistence on ever-closer relations was powered by the fact that "the Pan American system served primarily as a means by which the US could maintain its hegemony in the western hemisphere." That geopolitical concept represented the strategic policy of a Great Power that was still reluctant to become part of a Great Power System, for that system was seated in the Northern Hemisphere operating (in these simple terms) in a world halved latitudinally at the Equator rather than longitudinally through the oceans, as a renewal of the Great War would soon make clear.

Pan American conferences and agencies produced many agreements on routine practicalities of doing business with one another. A more prominent geographical scheme was topical but neither routine nor practical. The 1924 proposal for a Pan American Highway, endorsed by the Union in 1928, was a successor to the grandiose idea in Blaine's time of a railway from Canada to Tierra del Fuego. Sponsored by the United States, it was a magnification of the Good Roads Movement. As Robert N. Seidel put it: "the final list of backers of the . . . Commission read like an honor roll of American engineering, finance, government [e.g., Thomas MacDonald], and automotive related industry." But whereas the idea of a transcontinental Lincoln Highway within the United States made obvious good sense, the idea of a linear road paralleling the open ocean for most of its 7,000 miles or so made almost no sense at all as a long-distance transportation link (fig. 81). In the 1930s the United States financed initial surveys of the 3,265-mile Laredo–Panama Canal section, and that portion of this symbolic scheme took on new strategic significance after Pearl Harbor but was not completed until well after the war. (Mexico declined American construction aid and completed its part in 1954.)

Before anything whatever had been accomplished by the Pan American Highway Commission, Pan American Airways had a far more extensive system in service. It was essentially the creation of an American entrepreneur, Juan Trippe, working closely with the U.S. Post Office. Beginning in October 1927, with a mail contract to fly between Key West and Havana, Trippe obtained exclusive foreign landing rights from Cuba and thereby was in a position to take immediate advantage of subsidies provided by the Foreign Mail Act passed by Congress in early

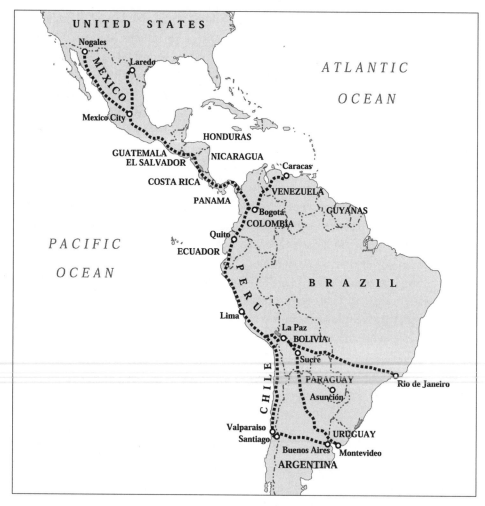

81. Proposed Pan American Highway.
(Adapted from Wilgus, *Latin America in Maps*)

1928. Mail contracts were awarded by the postmaster general, and thus the same man who was shaping the domestic trunk-line system, Walter Folger Brown, made Pan American the nation's chosen instrument for all of Latin America and the West Indies. In less than five years from its first flight, Pan American, by its own rapid extensions and absorption of lesser local companies, had a hemispheric network, anchored on Miami, encircling both the Caribbean and the main body of South America, plus a Mexican section connecting with the U.S. system at Brownsville (fig. 82). As so many of these links were across water or along coastlines, the company became a leader in the development of seaplanes, which by

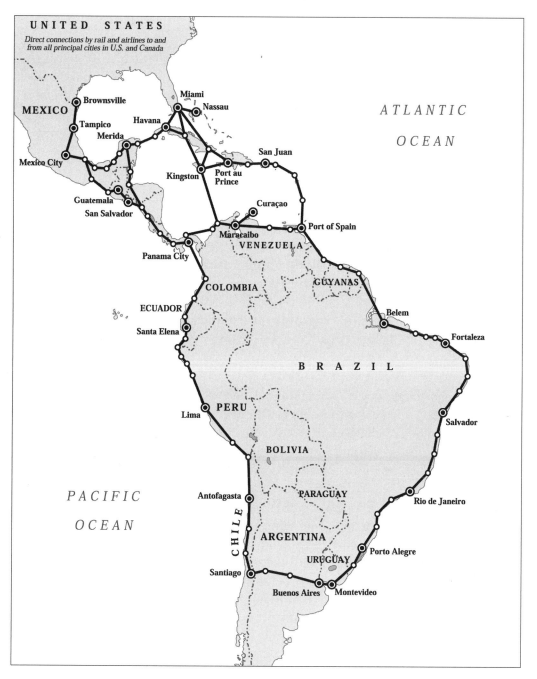

82. Pan American Airways, 1932.

(Adapted from company map reproduced in Hugill, *World Trade*, and from Davies, *Airlines of the United States*)

1934 featured four-engine Sikorsky flying boats capable of carrying thirty-four passengers, mail, and cargo over a distance of 750 miles.

Thus within an amazingly short time communications within a large sector of the world that had few rail or road connections between, or even within, most countries were transformed: an almost instant neotechnic, geographic revolution. If "at first regarded with suspicion, if not open hostility, by governments justifiably apprehensive of a new kind of United States colonialism, Pan American gradually came to be recognized as a symbol, not of aggrandizement, but of progress."

NORTH AMERICA

When the Union of American Republics was reorganized as the Pan American Union in 1910 and built a handsome headquarters on the edge of the Mall in Washington, "the Canadian coat of arms was placed with those of the twenty-one American republics on the cornices of the inner court of the House of the Americas, and a chair, inscribed 'Canada,' was made for future use at the Council Table." Canada was indifferent to the whole project and remained so for thirty years. It was obviously not a republic and it was heavily engaged in furnishing and filling its own spacious room within the northern wing of the "House of the Americas"; yet, as always, it was deeply concerned about relations with its powerful neighbor in the adjacent room, the two separated by thin walls and many doors.

The outbreak of war in Europe in 1914 triggered an immediate response from the British Dominions. Canada sent a large force to the Western Front and suffered heavy losses. The 48,000 killed were only slightly fewer than the total suffered later by the United States with a population more than ten times greater; as a Canadian historian commented to an American audience: "It was good to know that the Yanks had come after so long, but it was hard to be told that they had won the war." Such a response and sacrifice were a great impetus for revising imperial relationships toward recognition of the Dominions as essentially independent allied states. Canada signed the Versailles Treaty and became a member of the League of Nations. A series of Imperial Conferences led to the declaration in 1926 that the Dominions (Canada, Newfoundland, Australia, New Zealand, South Africa, and Irish Free State) are "autonomous Communities within the British Empire, equal in status, in no way subordinate one to another in any aspect of their domestic or foreign affairs, though united by a common allegiance to the Crown, and freely associated as members of the British Commonwealth of Nations." In 1927 the first Canadian minister was assigned to Washington, and an American counterpart was sent to Ottawa.

In the 1920s it became increasingly obvious "that Canada was moving out of the orbit of the British Empire and into that of the United States. Canada, however, wished no more to be a satellite of America than a dependency of Britain"—but that would prove to be an ever more challenging problem. The United States became Canada's largest market and Canada the greatest focus of American investment, and as (Canadian-born) Isaiah Bowman noted in 1928, "the great population and industrial power of the United States had laid serious economic servitudes upon Canada." The seeds of servitude had been planted earlier in the century, nurtured, ironically, by Canada's National Policy of high protective tariffs to foster industrial development. Faced with such barriers American companies built branch plants. Although some Canadians expressed fears about this response, it had been strongly supported by many interests and—in true American fashion—"every Canadian province, every Canadian city, every Canadian hamlet pursued its own 'national policy' of offering all possible incentives to capitalists and developers to come into its territory and establish manufacturing enterprises." However, any reassuring assumption that such firms would become "Canadianized" amid an expanding national economy dissipated with the ever-greater disparity in scale and power between the two countries. Big American companies competed with or bought out smaller, often family, firms and soon dominated important sectors of the Canadian economy.

Many Canadian nationalists regarded the "cultural invasion" as at least as alarming and more insidious. American magazines outnumbered the home-produced by eight to one, and radio threatened to compound the problem. Canada negotiated with the U.S. Federal Radio Commission (FRC) for recognition of its main broadcasting channels and for limitation on the power of American stations near its cities. But the Canadian public avidly and routinely consumed the much greater variety and power of American productions in all these forms. Self-conscious nationalist attempts to create a literature and arts "commensurate with Canada's new status as an independent nation" led to stiff duties imposed on some categories of American publications and, in 1932, to the creation of the government-owned CBC to assure, as the prime minister put it, "complete Canadian control of Broadcasting from Canadian sources, free from foreign interference or influence." Such moves were recurrent tactics within a national strategy in an endless struggle.

Despite such anxieties, some Canadian historians, now shifting focus from long-standing imperial perspectives, undertook to reexamine "continentalism" in less ominous terms than in the past. For some "even the word 'Americanization' came to connote not deliberate imitations or influence, but similar responses to the American continent and modern industrial life generally"—adjacent nations undergoing common processes of "modernization." Such a "North American" interpretation was the general theme of a twenty-five-volume series that explored the highly diverse interconnections between the two countries; the impetus and much of the substance of this product came from Canadian-born scholars resident at U.S. institutions (their very presence south of the border an increasingly common feature and problem for Canadian nationalism). Sponsored by the Carnegie Endowment for International Peace, the overall project was conceived as a rational, non-ideological examination of a relationship that might become "a model of how nations might learn to live together peacefully." As a Canadian scholar remarked in 1937, this postwar generation was the first "for whom the spectre of annexation to the United States has never risen above the political horizon."

The Great Depression "which stopped the world's strongest economy in its tracks staggered vulnerable Canada." The plight of both countries was deeply affected by their structural interdependence. Canada was heavily dependent on exports from farms, mines, forests, and fisheries and on imports of industrial goods and American capital, while the United States needed Canada as its largest outlet for goods and investment. Canada had sought a lowering of American tariffs for some years; having failed in this (and having held back Canadian approval of a St. Lawrence Seaway partly as a retaliation), it was now offered an alternative in this world crisis when Britain abandoned free trade and initiated an Imperial Preference program to make the Empire a more self-sustaining commercial system. In itself this proved of limited help to Canada, but the threat of such an alignment led to a Reciprocity Trade Agreement with the United States in 1935, a long-resisted change adopted by the Americans as a means of further "disengaging Canada from the British Empire."

Sharing this broad continent lying between two great oceans and having shared in the bloody mess in Europe induced an isolationism in Canada "almost as profound as that of the United States" (although Canada had its own internal reasons as well, especially the strains on English-French relations produced by war and military conscription). However, isolation "was a new and not a characteristic attitude" in the Canadian experience, and the sentimental ties of Empire and Commonwealth retained considerable strength. As Canada emerged toward independence in a dangerous world the fundamentals of its geopolitical situation became clear. In 1922 it had been the most insistent on replacing the Anglo-Japanese Alliance of 1902 in order to remove any possibility that Canada might be drawn into conflict with American interests anywhere in the Pacific. As the clouds of war once again expanded and darkened Canadians welcomed Franklin D. Roosevelt's declaration in August 1938 in Kingston (where he had received an honorary degree from Queens University after opening the Thousand Islands bridge): "We in the Americas are no longer a far-away continent, to which the eddies of controversies beyond the seas could bring no interest or no harm. . . . The Dominion of Canada is part of the sisterhood of the British Empire. I give you an assurance that the people of the United States will not stand idly by if domination of Canadian soil is threatened by any other Empire."

World War I demonstrated that America's Atlantic moat had become significantly narrowed. As Bowman noted in 1921, "the use made of the submarine by Germany during the late war and the powerful strides in aerial navigation and radio communication have greatly increased the width of those border protective zones that all commercial nations seek to control." Further technical advances in such instruments continued to alter perceptions and realities of distance and time for geopolitical strategists.

The two greatest naval powers had important interrelated but not directly coordinated interests. Great Britain's primary concerns were the Atlantic approaches to the homeland and the Mediterranean-Suez route to the main sectors of Empire; those of the United States were the American Mediterranean and Panama Canal, and its Hawaiian outpost guarding the Pacific approaches to the mainland. With Japan as its only rival, most of the American fleet was stationed in the Pacific. Nevertheless, its primary concern was the Panama Canal and the Caribbean, and even though in 1902 Britain had formally yielded naval supremacy in those waters, U.S. sensitivity in that area—together with the latent antipathy to a European geopolitical presence in the Americas—remained acute and might be expressed in surprising form. During a 1929 meeting on naval affairs in Washington between President Hoover and Prime Minister Ramsay MacDonald (focused mainly on ratios and reductions in preparation for a broader international conference), Hoover proposed that "the British abandon their naval bases in the Western Hemisphere in return for the Americans building none in the Eastern Hemisphere." Rebuffed on that, Hoover recorded in his memoirs that he also verbally "suggested that the British consider selling us Bermuda, British Honduras, and the island of Trinidad. . . . I wanted Bermuda and Trinidad for defense purposes, and I wanted to have British Honduras as an item to use in trading with Mexico" to resolve certain problems. His offer to pay for these small parcels of empire by absolving Britain of most of its war debt received no response (leaving Hoover to surmise that MacDonald did not take repayment of such debts seriously).

The significance of these proposals, small ploys amid broader negotiations, lies not so much in naval strategy as in American attitudes toward territorial transfers. Purchase, of course, had been a preferred means of expansion during the great century of nation building, with offers made for a variety of territories beyond those actually obtained (and other than the "purchase," under duress, of Indian lands).

Having bought the Virgin Islands from Denmark only twelve years earlier, Hoover's attempt to pick up more such islands may seem nothing out of the ordinary. Yet the very idea that Britain would *sell* Bermuda—its oldest holding in the Americas, permanently settled for more than 300 years, a lively and attractive royal colony since 1684, and an important station in imperial networks (as well as a resort for wealthy Americans)—must have appeared as yet another display of American insensitivity and arrogance in such matters. Furthermore, the bargaining of the people and territory of British Honduras for geopolitical ends would be an application of widely denounced practices of European sovereigns and a direct contradiction of Wilsonian principles. In the broader view, perhaps the only surprising feature of these proposals was that they came from a president of widely respected humane qualities and unusually broad experience in world affairs.

The years of the Great Depression sharply strengthened U.S. isolationism, not only because of crucial struggles with its own economic and social problems but because "having waged a war to make the world safe for democracy, the country watched in bitter disillusionment the rise of dictatorships and the ensuing recrudescence of aggression and conflict. On all sides it was felt again that the European system was basically rotten, that war was endemic on that continent, and that somehow the Europeans had only themselves to blame for their plight." (As another historian remarked with reference to any such characterization, the "American people never realized . . . how deep was the feeling of betrayal among the European peoples at the withdrawal of the United States from its position of ideological leadership" of the League of Nations and its failure to bring its great power to bear upon such ominous developments.) But if "the very idea of aligning the United States with any power was anathema to the isolationist," the logic of defending the New World from aggressions by the Old was unassailable (whatever the quarrels over military budgets and specific policies). In 1938, following the Munich crisis in Europe and with Japan engaged in war with China, Franklin Roosevelt made his pledge to defend Canada and, in a momentous conference with his military leaders, declared that "the United States must be prepared to resist attack on the western hemisphere from the North Pole to the South Pole, including all of North America and South America." Development of a shared Pan American foreign policy conforming to this U.S. stance got under way.

However, those in charge of strategic planning were not ready to affirm U.S. capabilities of such a complete hemispheric defense, at least not without a much greater buildup of forces and additional bases. Plans approved in August 1939 (as war was breaking out in Europe) defined the essential defensive area as extending from Wake Island in the Pacific to 30° W in the Atlantic (the western edge of the Azores) but to only 10° S. This southern limit was designed to include the Pacific approaches to the Panama Canal and, on the east, the northeastern promontory of

Brazil. The former included the Galápagos Islands (Ecuador) and the tiny Cocos Islands (Costa Rica) that were under consideration as possible bases; the latter was the American key to command of the narrow waist of the Atlantic, which even though distant from Panama or the United States, was considered to be a major danger zone (fig. 83). In the mid-1930s, before Pan American Airways had established its transatlantic service, German and French airlines had flights along the Saharan coast to Dakar or the Cape Verde Islands, thence across the ocean to Natal, and on to Rio de Janeiro and Buenos Aires. German propaganda cultivated the large German and Italian immigrant populations of Brazil and Argentina, fostered Nazi-like organizations, fomented hatred of the United States, and, it was feared, plotted revolutions. In the face of such threats Roosevelt insisted that the United States must always speak publicly of full hemispheric defense because exclusion of southern South America would (in the words of one of his generals) "be catastrophic in its effect. It would void the Monroe Doctrine, [and] tend to throw all the most powerful countries of South America into the axis camp." Thus the U.S. Navy and the Air Force urged "the absolute necessity for a base of operations in or near the eastern extremity of South America."

In September 1939, a Pan American conference established a Neutrality Zone several hundred miles wide around the Americas south of Canada "from which all belligerent warships were to be excluded." The futility of such an encompassing design was soon apparent when the German commerce raider *Admiral Graf Spee* was intercepted by British cruisers off the Brazilian coast, heavily damaged in battle, driven toward the La Plata estuary, and scuttled off Montevideo. As there were no American warships within thousands of miles, the formality of such an oceanic zone was abandoned (it had never been accepted by other powers), and patrols remained concentrated in critical areas much closer to home; formation of a permanent Atlantic fleet did not take place until early 1941.

The German defeat of the British and French forces on the continent in June 1940 resounded portentously across the Atlantic. The fate of European colonies in the Western Hemisphere was suddenly acute. French warships under a Vichy-collaborationist admiral in Martinique were neutralized only through U.S. threats and negotiation. To avert Latin American opposition to Yankee expansionism or opportunistic occupation by Latin American neighbors (Brazil would welcome a trusteeship over the Guianas; Venezuela eyed the Netherlands West Indies just offshore), a Pan American conference adopted a "no-transfer doctrine" within the hemisphere but left open the possibility of emergency military action. The most immediate concern was to ensure no interruption of strategic supplies, such as bauxite from Surinam and oil from Aruba and Venezuela.

In September 1940, American military positions were greatly augmented by the famous "destroyers-for-bases" deal in which fifty U.S. warships (overage but adapt-

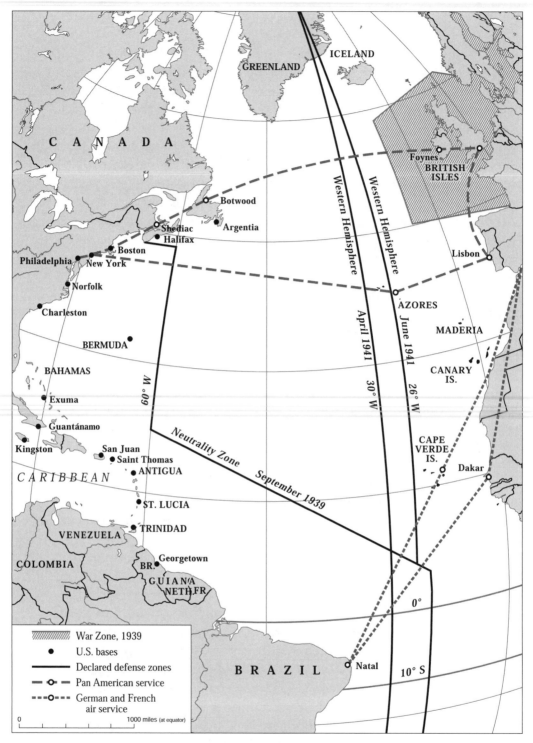

83. Hemispheric Defense: The Atlantic.
Halifax was a vital part of the system but not a U.S. base.

able to convoy duty) were transferred to Great Britain in return for control of naval stations and airfields in eight British territories that, added to Canada's Halifax and to U.S. bases, provided a complete shield of outposts from Newfoundland to British Guiana. The impetus for this exchange came much more from a beleaguered Britain than from an unscathed United States but represented the Roosevelt administration's conviction that the British fleet was vital to American security in the Atlantic. At this same time a Joint Board on Defense was formed with Canada. A few months earlier, after the Germans conquered the Low Countries, Denmark, and Norway, Canada had proposed a guardian force for Greenland, but the United Stated opposed this on the ground that the Japanese might invoke a similar excuse to occupy the Netherlands East Indies. A year later, when the German menace seemed far greater, U.S. forces did occupy Greenland, replaced British troops that had set up guard over Iceland (which had declared itself a republic), and began naval protection of convoys that far across the Atlantic; an undeclared war soon followed from German submarine attacks on U.S. warships.

In early 1941 German plans seemed to pose a serious threat to the one strategic hemisphere sector still unguarded. By this "Gibraltar-Africa scheme" Germany, with the cooperation of Vichy France and Franco Spain, would seize Gibraltar, occupy Morocco and the Azores, and extend its control clear to French West Africa. The United States rather frantically drew up contingency plans to take over the Azores and perhaps even to send an expeditionary force to Dakar. Roosevelt warned Congress that war was "approaching the brink of the Western Hemisphere itself." Despite protracted efforts, the United States had not as yet gained permission from Brazil for a base in Natal. (Latin American countries resented any appearance of American troops on their soil; Mexico insisted that American military use of designated airfields on a route to Panama be operated only by U.S. civilians ostensibly employed by Pan American Airways.) This alarming threat soon faded (Spain had refused to cooperate); in June 1941 Hitler invaded Russia.

In a letter to the president his secretary of War called this German eastward turn "an almost providential occurrence," giving the United States time to reinforce the Western Hemisphere and Britain relief from immediate threat of invasion. Through all these years a large majority of the American people were opposed to any direct participation in the war, and Roosevelt faced, in Congress and out, shrill critics of his increasingly open alignments with Britain. In the 1940 presidential campaign both he and his opponent, Wendell Wilkie, "felt compelled to say that they had no intention of getting the United States into the war or of ever permitting American boys to be sent overseas to fight." However, as Stetson Conn and Byron Fairchild further note, Secretary of State Cordell Hull spoke forthrightly at the time about the perils even a well-defended hemisphere might face:

There can be nothing more dangerous for our nation than for us to assume that the avalanche of conquest could under no circumstances reach any vital portion of this hemisphere. Oceans give the nations of this hemisphere no guarantee against the possibility of economic, political, or military attack from abroad. Oceans are barriers but they are also highways. Barriers of distance are merely barriers of time. Should the would-be conquerors gain control of other continents, they would next concentrate on perfecting their control of the seas, of the air over the seas, and of the world's economy; they might then be able with ships and with planes to strike at the communication lines, the commerce, and the life of this hemisphere; and ultimately we might find ourselves compelled to fight on our own soil, under our own skies, in defense of our independence and our very lives.

Here was a Mackinder-like warning about control of the "World-Island" shortly before Halford Mackinder became known in the United States and his geopolitical thesis became fashionable.

4. Redividing the World

GRAND DESIGNS, AGGRESSIONS, FAILURES

In the preamble of a pact signed on September 27, 1940, the governments of Japan, Germany, and Italy declared that they considered "the prerequisite of a lasting peace that every nation in the world shall receive the space to which it is entitled. They have, therefore, decided to stand by and co-operate with one another in their efforts in Greater East Asia and the regions of Europe. . . . In doing this it is the prime purpose to establish and maintain a new order of things." They also referred to "other spheres of the world," and the Japanese premier notified the American government that if it would assent to the objectives of this pact, the Three Powers would "recognize the guiding position of the United States on the American continent." For the time being, the Soviet Union was another "sphere" (nonaggression pacts had been or would be signed with it), but its future was obviously compromised in various other assertions about this "new order of things."

These New Order geopolitical programs were broadly similar in concept and exposition. In each case the Greater Sphere consisted of a densely populated homeland and industrial core, a nearby critical defensive area, a vast colonization and resource hinterland, and the whole organized under firm central control of the single dominant power. Expansion would be by stages, by whatever means proved necessary, with ultimate limits left unfixed, depending upon opportunities.

Japan's homeland on the four main islands was complete and solid, with no important minority problems. Island chains to the northeast and southwest, together with its hold on Korea and Shantung, provided an inner defensive perimeter;

Manchuria and, eventually, the Russian Far East (which Japanese troops had occupied during the chaotic collapse of that empire), a major resource and colonization area. Japan's long insistence on its "special interests" in China, on the creation of an imposed but functioning Sino-Japanese relationship, was essential to its Pan-Asian aspirations. Southeast Asia, mainland and East Indies, was a critical resource hinterland (especially for oil and rubber); with much of Micronesia already under imperial control, further insular expansion southward was primarily for naval defense (tropical Australia was tempting, but Australia and New Zealand together appear in only the more extreme versions of this New Order).

Germany's program was more complex, deeply rooted, and philosophically formulated. In contrast to Japan a German homeland was imprecise in concept and insecure in location. German identity was shaped by nineteenth-century pseudo-racial and linguistic concepts and nationalist movements. German speakers were widely distributed through central and eastern Europe, and the vision of a German-dominated "Mitteleuropa" was recurrently asserted in various forms. An unstable "Deutschland" economic association had appeared in the nineteenth century, succeeded by a Prussian-imposed German Empire, which was defeated and diminished in 1918. In 1926 Austrian-born Adolf Hitler asserted in *Mein Kampf* that "the supreme point of view of every foreign policy" is "*to bring the land into consonance with the population,*" and thus the frontiers of prewar (1914) Germany were "anything but logical" because "*the German Reich, as a State, should include all Germans.*" Policy therefore must be exclusively directed toward increasing "the area of the motherland itself." "*Germany will be either a world power or it will be not at all.* To be a world power, however, it requires that size which nowadays gives its necessary importance to that power, and which gives life to its citizens." "Never regard the Reich as secure while it is unable to give every national offshoot for centuries his own bit of soil and territory." Sloganized as *Blut und Boden* and the pressing need for *Lebensraum,* vitalized by the idea that a healthy state is an expanding state, spatial designs of this continental imperium were set before the public by various writers, and most famously by the German "school" of *Geopolitik* under the influence of the academic-propagandist Karl Haushofer.

Sketches of this Greater Germany commonly included a homeland of the Germany of 1914 plus Austria, German Switzerland, Sudetenland, and other margins of predominantly German-speaking populations (fig. 84). Defense in the West assumed at least the defeat of France and subordination of the Low Countries and Denmark, and in the East defeat and repulsion of the Soviet Union so as to open a vast expanse from the Gulf of Finland to the lower Danube to German colonization and economic exploitation (an area commonly characterized in this literature as already permeated by the influence of German speech and culture). That such a gross geopolitical program was serious (and antedated the Nazis) was apparent in

84. Greater Germany.
As commonly defined by geopolitical propagandists (superimposed on 1990 boundaries; Austro-Hungarian Empire as of 1914).

the plans readied for that great hinterland following the collapse of the Russian Empire and the Treaty of Brest Litovsk with the newly emergent Soviet Union. During the brief interval before the defeat of Germany, the Ukraine, considered to be the greatest prize, was a German puppet state. From that time on the famous Berlin-to-Baghdad *Drang nach Osten* might be said to have become redirected to Kiev, although in its largest visions this Pan-Germanic Europe included domination of the Near East and all of Africa following the defeat of the Western colonial powers.

Simply noting the existence of a set of Great Powers and a sketch of some geopolitical aspirations does not of course explain why particular collisions between them actually occurred. Jack Snyder, examining "the central myth of empire," concludes that "the idea that the state's security can be safeguarded only through expansion" originates "as a justification for the policies of domestic political coalitions formed among groups having parochial interests in imperial expansion, military preparedness, or economic autarky." Once initiated such programs may take on momentum and amplitude that actually exceed the aims of any one of those groups; early successes may gain public support, empower the slogans of expansion, and make it impossible for more moderate interests and leaders to control. Germany and Japan represent extreme cases of "domestic pathologies" that unleashed "extraordinarily aggressive states." Both were late industrializing nations seeking greater control over large resource areas. In Germany widespread public support for drastic revision of a humiliating peace treaty became militantly focused by a fanatical dictator who rapidly built upon one expansive success after another before challenged in war. In Japan the modern political system allowed great power to the military, which experienced early successes against China and Russia, but was increasingly resisted and at times thwarted by Western powers in its primary objective of dominating mainland East Asia (and thereby preventing the emergence of a potentially much greater power in China).

By the time of that late 1940 Three Power Pact, Japan and Germany (and Italy as a distinctly lesser associate) were well under way with their intended redivision of the world. It is pertinent to note just how far each of these ruthlessly aggressive powers was able to extend its reach before yielding to counterforces. The Japanese had almost achieved the outer limits of their proclaimed Greater East Asia Sphere; the one—highly significant—missing piece was interior central and southern China (fig. 85). Germany's effort was no less impressive. On the west it controlled the coast of Europe from Narvik in northern Norway to the Bay of Biscay; in the east its armies laid siege to Leningrad, came within a few miles of Moscow, reached Stalingrad in the Lower Volga, and thrust deeply along the north Caucasus almost to the Caspian Sea; to the south, together with the Italians, it dominated the Balkans, Greece, and Crete, and with the Vichy French held all of northern Africa to within a few miles of Alexandria and the Suez Canal (fig. 86). In each case, given the size of the homeland base, the scale of these conquests represented a prodigious military effort—and a staggering challenge to the Great Powers under attack.

The assault on Pearl Harbor was a surprise to American military and political leaders, and it was understood to be a high risk by many military and political leaders in Japan. As we have noted, an enmity between the two countries had been growing for many years, and the possibility of an overt clash was a common feature of war plans in both countries. The probability of hostilities increased from the date of the Three Power Pact when Japan, emboldened by Germany's victory in the West, began to occupy northern French Indochina (Vietnam); the United States

85. Japanese Conquests.

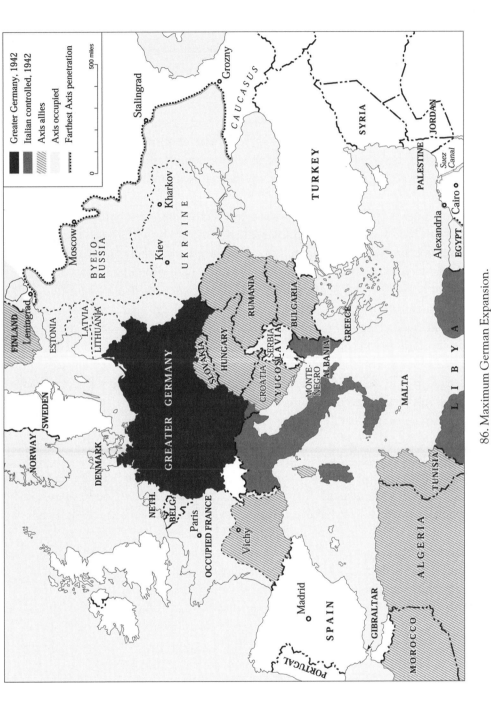

Legend:
- Greater Germany, 1942
- Italian controlled, 1942
- Axis allies
- Axis occupied
- Farthest Axis penetration

500 miles

86. Maximum German Expansion.

It is important to note that Finland's role as an ally was as an opportunistic retaliation for losses recently suffered. In 1939 the
USSR pressured Finland for major territorial concessions. Re-
fusing to capitulate, Finland staged a vigorous, skillful defense
during the famous Winter War of 1939–40, winning the admiration of, but no effective aid from, the West, and it was ultimately forced to yield. The United States never declared war
against Finland during World War II.

sharply protested and embargoed shipments of aviation fuel and scrap metal to Japan. In negotiations during many months thereafter the United States kept insisting on Japan's withdrawal from China, the Japanese insisting on recognition of their paramount interest there. When in July 1941 (following Hitler's invasion of the Soviet Union, thereby deflating perceived dangers from the USSR in East Asia) Japan moved in upon southern Indochina, the United States embargoed all strategic materials, impounded Japanese funds, and closed the Panama Canal to Japanese shipping. American priorities were focused on sustaining and strengthening Britain, and "since Japan was pictured as inferior militarily and economically to the United States, it was not expected to risk American retaliation by precipitous action."

Japan's military government was faced with a crisis: either retreat in some fashion from its hard-won positions in the country most fundamental to its Pan-Asian aspirations or embark upon a desperate war against a potentially far greater power. The Japanese resolution of this psychological and geopolitical dilemma was at once "a symbol of Asia's revolt against the West" and a gross miscalculation of the resoluteness latent in the American portion of that West. In their view the United States had made clear that the Western Pacific and East Asia were not vital to its national interests; it was preparing to free the Philippines; it had declared the International Date Line to be the Pacific limit of its Western Hemisphere security zone; its Congress and public seemed steadfast against joining the war in Europe. Japanese leaders, moreover, assumed that their hard-disciplined military forces would be more than a match for soft Americans, especially in severe tropical fighting. Thus, if it could cripple the U.S. Navy and have two years to fortify its Pacific perimeter and consolidate its control over East Asia, Japan could make it so costly in American lives that it would bring the United States to the negotiating table and work out a new understanding of Great Power world regions. The Japanese did indeed make it very costly, but the only new understanding reached was "unconditional surrender" and extreme geopolitical reduction to their four main-islands homeland—a "Least" rather than a Greater East Asia.

With the U.S. declaration of war against Japan "a great irony became apparent"; as Walter La Feber goes on to state: "For nearly two years, FDR had prepared to fight Germany, but now he had to ask for war only against Japan. Roosevelt was not certain that a declaration of war against Germany was possible. On December 11, however, Hitler solved the dilemma by declaring war on the United States. He evidently did so because of his treaty ties to Japan; but more important were his beliefs that the Japanese had perhaps mortally wounded the Americans and that FDR's growing aid to the British and Soviets had to be stopped by force."

The Germans rapidly applied their own force against these American supply lines, and over the next year their submarines took a massive toll of Atlantic shipping, sinking hundreds of vessels off the East and Gulf coasts of the United States and throughout Caribbean and West Indies waters. The failure of Germany to defeat or induce any compromise with Britain was critical to any counteroffensive by the West. (Hitler was apparently genuinely puzzled by the lack of British response to some sort of understanding between what he considered to be peoples with a shared Anglo-Saxon-Germanic past.) Great Britain became (in the words of the aged Mackinder's wartime updating of his thesis) the key "moated forward stronghold" and "aerodrome . . . essential to amphibious power." At least as important was Hitler's underestimate of the strength of Soviet resistance and counteroffensive (aided in some degree by supplies and airplanes from the United States by way of Murmansk, Iran, and Alaska).

AMERICAN DESIGNS

The United States rolled back those avalanches of conquest by means of "the American way of war": a reliance on "firepower and the massive use of force." And whereas its Great Power partners were in a fight for their very survival, the United States, unharmed in its homeland and confident of victory, had from the beginning clothed its larger purpose in its own distinct ideology. "We are now in the midst of war, not for conquest, not for vengeance, but for a world in which this nation, and all that this nation represents, will be safe for our children," Franklin Roosevelt proclaimed to Congress and the nation on December 8, 1941, "we are going to win the war and we are going to win the peace that follows." Support for this resounding Wilsonian echo had already been obtained from Great Britain four months earlier when the president, in a meeting aboard a U.S. warship off Newfoundland, had pressed upon a Winston Churchill desperate for greater American participation in the war co-sponsorship of what became known as the Atlantic Charter, containing a set of familiar principles: no territorial aggrandizement; no territorial changes contrary to the wishes of the people concerned; the right of peoples to choose their own form of government; access by all nations to the trade and raw materials needed for their prosperity; freedom of the high seas; the need to lighten the crushing burden of armaments pending establishment of a wider and permanent system of general security. Shortly after Pearl Harbor the twenty-six states by then formally allied in the war against the Axis Powers issued a "Declaration of the United Nations" that contained an endorsement of the Atlantic Charter.

"The war aims expressed by the Churchill-Roosevelt declaration are almost precisely of the same import as those of President Wilson's 'Fourteen Points,'" noted Herbert Hoover at the time, and he drew upon his close experience with that "First Crusade" to offer words of caution on the Second. Revelations of the full horrors of the Nazi regime readily sustained such feelings as expressed by General Dwight D.

Eisenhower that "this war was a holy war . . . more than any other in history this has been an array of the forces of evil against those of righteousness." But, like the First, this Second Crusade envisioned much more than military victory. Once again the United States assumed the role of missionary to the world, evangelist for a faith grounded in a set of principles for all sorts and conditions of nations and peoples: the American Way to peace and prosperity.

Yet, as before, even the preaching of principles—to say nothing of attempts at their direct application—may exacerbate geopolitical problems. In effect the Atlantic Charter endorsed self-determination and nationalism, was hostile to colonial empires, favored the strongest economic power, and implicitly assumed a common preference for the American concept of democracy. And, once again, well before the war was won disputes and deals between co-belligerents compromised general objectives for the peace: Roosevelt was strongly against partitioning the world into Great Power spheres of influence, seeking instead "a broader system of general security in which all countries great and small will have their part." Yet Europe was clearly going to be divided at least temporarily under occupying armies, and decisions of the most profound importance would have to be made about a more enduring geopolitical design of a New Europe.

CREATING TWO EUROPES

Important features of that new design had been formed at the outbreak of the war and later confirmed by the imminent Soviet victory. In 1939, after Hitler invaded Poland, the Soviet Union had annexed the three Baltic states and the largely Belorussian and Ukrainian portions of eastern Poland (thereby approximating what had been proposed as the eastern boundary of the newly formed state at the 1919 Peace Conference, and reclaiming area lost by the USSR in a brief war with Poland in 1920). It became understood that Poland would be compensated by annexing some portions of eastern Germany. Given the Soviet Union's enormous losses and massive role in the defeat of Germany it was obvious that the USSR would insist upon the creation of a broad security zone west of its own borders. Churchill, concerned about Soviet intentions and methods, had made an agreement with Stalin in late 1944 to recognize Soviet domination of Romania and Bulgaria in return for British influence in Greece (thereby holding the USSR away from the Mediterranean). Many of the issues about postwar Europe were under negotiation at the Yalta Conference in February 1945. That Germany would be parceled into occupation zones and subjected to major territorial reductions was reconfirmed in general. Roosevelt pressured for implementation of the Atlantic Charter, and Churchill joined in seeking at least some gesture toward democratic governments in newly liberated states, but Stalin held firmly to his own geopolitical imperatives. As the war entered its final phase in Europe, Churchill (in the absence of a fatally ill Roosevelt), hoping for some Western leverage, sent an emergency message to General Eisenhower stating: "I deem it highly important that we should shake hands with the Russians as far east as possible" and urged that American armies push directly to Berlin and Prague. But American generals regarded this as a typical British geopolitical complication that would divert them from tracking down the remnants of Hitler's armies as quickly as possible. When they completed that task a month later and moved toward Prague, Stalin sent a vehement protest and the U.S. army withdrew, allowing the Russians to occupy the Czech capital a day after the war had ended. The Americans also had to pull back to allow Soviet forces to establish full control over their allocated zone in Germany. Berlin, lying within that zone, was itself divided into occupation areas (as was Austria, but Vienna was placed under joint control).

In the wake of this broad Russian advance across the Elbe into central Germany, a Soviet-sponsored Polish government laid claim to all of Germany east of the Oder-Neisse line (East Prussia having already been divided between the USSR and Poland). Just where the western boundary of Poland's compensatory territory should be had been discussed but never resolved at various summit conferences. Technically this westward reach remained an "occupation" pending formal treaties; actually, it became a rapid and permanent transformation as most of the German population fled and were replaced by Poles.

Shortly after the victory in Europe, Churchill sent a telegram to Harry Truman warning him about Soviet intransigence. The new president was determined not to be seen as a weak or uninformed successor to Roosevelt, and at the next meeting of leaders, at Potsdam, just outside Berlin, in the summer of 1945, Truman refused to recognize Soviet-installed governments and briefly mentioned the successful test of an atomic bomb. Such a hardened American stance could only intensify Soviet obsessions with security. (Stalin knew about the development of the bomb from informants within the Manhattan Project.)

In early 1946, responding to an invitation from Truman to speak at Westminster College in his home state of Missouri, Churchill (out of office, having lost the postwar election to Clement Attlee) provided the Western World with a memorable metaphor for the radical Great Power redivision of the European World: "From Stettin in the Baltic to Trieste on the Adriatic, an iron curtain has descended across the continent." Stettin was becoming Polish Szczecin and what in critical sectors would become literally an Iron Curtain had been so labeled and more accurately defined in Churchill's early telegram to Truman as a "Lübeck-Trieste-Corfu" (Kérkira) line, thereby including Soviet East Germany and extending along the

Adriatic to the Albanian-Greek border. Thus the rebuilding of a war-ravaged, decimated, and impoverished Europe would take place in two distinct and separated parts under very different and competing programs.

EAST ASIA

Three months after the end of the war in Europe the Soviet Union, as agreed at Yalta, joined the war against Japan. That its move coincided with the dropping of atomic bombs and assured demolition of Japanese resistance made its action less desirable to the United States than anticipated (at the time of Yalta the United States was engaged in a fierce battle for Iwo Jima, and Allied armies had not yet reached the Rhine), however, with one important exception, this late entry had little bearing on territorial changes. The complete dismemberment of the Japanese empire had been agreed upon by the United States, Britain, and Nationalist China in 1943, and the various parts allocated in later conferences. Thus the Soviet Union regained southern Sakhalin (Karafuto), Port Arthur, and specified privileges in Manchuria, and took over the Kurile island chain. The United States had complete command of the Japanese homeland, took over the former mandated territories in Micronesia, and occupied the Ryukyus and lesser island groups. The one jointly occupied territory was Korea, where the 38th parallel was accepted as a convenient line to separate the victorious armies in disarming the Japanese pending the establishment of a unified independent state.

Taiwan was returned to China, but who would be in charge of that long-besieged country was uncertain. As the defeat of Japan became ever more assured, the American-backed Nationalist government became increasingly concerned with the threat from the Chinese Communists, whom they had earlier driven out of central China to a refuge in the northwest. As this civil war flared anew and popular support for the Nationalists was fading the United States sought to bring the two camps together (the USSR agreed in principle to help). In the distant non-Chinese parts of the historic empire, Soviet predominance in Outer Mongolia had been granted in wartime conferences, but the former European spheres of influence along the coast had been formally renounced as a gesture of support for China early in the war. The British, of course, returned to their century-old possession of Hong Kong.

The anticolonial implications of the Atlantic Charter and Roosevelt's recurrent critiques of such systems rankled Churchill, who famously declared that he had not become His Majesty's Prime Minister to preside over the dissolution of the British Empire. The French and Dutch governments were no less resolved to hold on to their large Southeast Asian possessions. The United States warned about the explosive potentials in India when the Japanese army was lodged in Burma with its propagandists preaching "Asia for the Asians"—as if the British needed any re-minder. And even though Asian rule of Asians under the Japanese proved to be brutally exploitative, nationalist movements in Indochina and Indonesia regarded it as an opportunistic interlude leading to a shedding of any imperial control. The United States of course pointed to its programmed independence for the Philip-pines as an appropriate example of an "orderly retreat from empire."

INTERNATIONAL SYSTEMS

Europeans had reason to suspect that U.S. anticolonialism was designed to open the world to freer trade—and its own economic dominance. "The capitalistic sys-tem is essentially an international system. If it cannot function internationally, it will break down completely," said a Roosevelt economic adviser, as the prewar ex-perience of the Great Depression and economic autarky seemed to prove. Thus in mid-1944 the United States called a conference of non-Axis nations at Bretton Woods, New Hampshire, "to ensure an open, capitalist postwar world" and insisted on the creation of two new institutions, the World Bank and the International Monetary Fund, that rested on gold and the dollar (and thus soon overpowered the sterling bloc and the British Imperial Preference system). The Soviet Union re-jected participation in any such economic program, and in early 1946 Stalin an-nounced a new series of Five-Year Plans for the development of his own bloc.

Meanwhile, at Dumbarton Oaks in Washington, the Allied Powers established the design of the United Nations, with a general assembly open to all and a security council made up of two classes of nations: five permanent members (holding veto power), and seven additional seats to be rotated periodically among other states. The permanent members represented very unequal "Great Powers":

China, racked by invasion and civil war, without effective leadership and uncertain national unity, was simply accorded a position as the obvious potential Great Power of East Asia following the diminution and suppression of Japan.

France, politically shattered and humiliated, was accorded membership as a diplo-matic move in support of the Free French movement and the need to keep North Africa and Dakar open to Allied use (at Charles de Gaulle's insistence, France was belatedly given occupation sectors in Germany and Austria).

Great Britain, valiant victor in Europe, with its vast Empire intact or restored, was still commonly recognized as a Great Power, but with a widely damaged homeland, its world commercial system impaired, and ominous political rumblings in Asian sectors of empire.

The *USSR* would emerge victorious with a huge military establishment, but all at an enormous cost; heavily depleted and devastated, it was therefore militantly defensive within its own enlarged sphere.

The *United States*, in stark contrast with all others, emerged from the war wholly triumphant, unharmed in its homeland, possessing massive, unprecedented economic and military power, with armed forces and other official personnel spread across dozens of countries, girdling the globe.

The opening session of the United Nations was held in San Francisco on April 25, 1945; two months later, following the Allied victory in Europe, the U.N. Charter was signed by fifty nations.

"In 1945 the United States held a uniquely preeminent position." As Melvyn P. Leffler further observes about this predominance of power,

> For many officials, businessmen, publicists, victory confirmed the superiority of American values: individual liberty, representative government, free enterprise, private property, and a marketplace economy. Given their country's overwhelming power, they now expected to refashion the world in America's image and create the American century. They intended to promote world peace and foster international stability at the same time that they safeguarded national security, perpetuated American power, and further augmented American prosperity. It was a wonderful image.

Yet, as Leffler goes on to note, this vision of a grandly empowered evangelical assertion of the American creed was ominously beclouded: "even before the guns fell silent, the exhilaration of victory was marred by omnipresent fears that America's relative power would soon erode, its security would be endangered, and its prosperity would prove fleeting."

5. Impositions and Oppositions

AFTERMATH

International war, said the world historian William H. McNeill, is "perhaps the most potent single factor in promoting and accelerating social change—one which . . . has played a distinguished role in human history since at least 2000 B.C." World War II was a grand crescendo in this long, violent, vibrant history. Not only did it result in a drastic change in the scale and pattern of the Great Power system and in the extent of physical devastation, social disruption, and depletion, but it accelerated developments in weaponry to the point of fearfully altering the lethal potential of modern warfare. In so doing, it altered the basic context of state-based international rivalries.

For the United States isolationism was dead, but what kind of program it should undertake to advance and protect its vital interests was far from certain. It emerged preeminent in power, and it presumed to play a major role in the shaping of a new world order. Looking toward some real degree of cooperation among the victorious powers it was commonly assumed that America's vast overseas wartime operations and organizations were a "transitory thing, like the emergency controls imposed upon the domestic economy"; domestic political pressures sought a speedy postwar demobilization. Yet the United States was not secure. The new air age and atomic weapons, products of its own prodigious efforts, left it—like every other country—potentially vulnerable. As its top military leaders soon warned: "In the future neither geography nor allies will render a nation immune from sudden and paralyzing attack should an aggressor arise to plague the peace of the world."

The United States was not at the time fearful of direct attack, but what seemed like aggressive diplomatic encounters with the Soviet Union plagued American designs for the postwar world and warned of eventual unprecedented dangers. Disputes and suspicions had surfaced at Potsdam and rapidly multiplied by the actions and interpretations of both superpowers. For example, the United States was surprised at the implacable resistance to strong American pressures regarding political systems in Eastern Europe and Germany and was forced to reckon with the continuing presence of huge Soviet ground forces, while at the same time Stalin interpreted Churchill's "Iron Curtain" speech as an official warlike declaration from Britain and the United States "that the English-speaking nations, as the only superior countries, should rule over the rest of the nations of the world." Victory had created vast geopolitical vacuums and left only two Great Powers to fill them, and thus "in spite of much reluctance and in face of all traditional obstacles at home and abroad to such radical innovation, the United States . . . recreated the main outlines of the globe-encircling organization of power with which the Anglo-Americans fought the second World War."

That wartime system had not only broadly spanned the Pacific and Atlantic, it included long extensions across North Africa to Egypt, Arabia, the Persian Gulf, and on to India and Burma, a link critical for key resources and getting supplies to beleaguered Russia and China. Even before the war was over the Joint Chiefs of Staff (JCS) began to assess how much of this system should be kept and also gave new emphasis to Arctic air approaches to North America—and stressed the vital need to maintain technical superiority.

EMERGENCE OF THE COLD WAR

Basic American assumptions about its rival superpower were strongly influenced by the assessments of George F. Kennan, one of the most experienced U.S. specialists on the Soviet Union. In a report from Moscow to his secretary of State in February 1946, Kennan emphasized (in telegraphese) how "at bottom of Kremlin's neurotic view of world affairs is traditional and instinctive Russian sense of insecurity." Never enjoying legitimacy from a stable, well-structured polity, Russian rulers have "always feared foreign penetration" and currently see themselves facing "capitalist encirclement." Although Kennan did not regard Soviet behavior as a direct military threat to the United States, he considered its rulers, armed with a ruthless ideology, to be dangerous and insidious competitors in the reshaping of the postwar world. Later that year, Kennan expanded his view of the "Sources of Soviet Conduct" for the new secretary of Defense and stated "that the main element of any United States policy toward the Soviet Union must be that of a long-term, patient but firm and vigilant containment of Russian expansive tendencies." His general proposition had an immediate effect upon government leaders, and when his essay was published (anonymously) in *Foreign Affairs* some months later, *containment* became the common characterization of American foreign policy in response to "an expanding totalitarian state which continues to act on the belief that the world is divided into two irreconcilably hostile camps."

That last was the wording of a State Department reply to the JCS, who were charged with defining the "forces and installations disposed in an outer perimeter" of bases "essential to the security of the United States, its possessions, the Western Hemisphere, and the Philippines." A large number of these were already under firm U.S. control, such as those leased from Britain (in the destroyer deal) and from a newly independent Philippines, and Japan's former Pacific island empire seized and held under U.S. trusteeship. Existing treaties with Canada and Latin American states gave means of negotiation for further needs. However, other desired facilities would require new treaties to secure American use. In June 1946 the JCS asked the State Department to obtain rights for a set of "essential" and (if reasonably obtainable) "required" bases, as well as certain transit rights for American military aircraft (fig. 87).

While the formation of a new American global network was under consideration, new danger zones appeared. In early 1947 Great Britain gave notice that it could no longer sustain economic and military support of the governments of Greece and Turkey. Believing (as Dean Acheson emphasized to wary congressmen) that "Soviet pressure on the Straits, on Iran and on northern Greece had brought the Balkans to the point where a highly possible Soviet breakthrough might open three continents to Soviet penetration," the United States quickly assumed the burden. In doing so the president was determined to clothe this action as the symbol of America's leadership of the free world against oppressive totalitarian regimes. Hailed at home as a "historic landmark in American foreign policy," this Truman Doctrine was the first bold step in the containment policy.

Far more comprehensive moves soon followed. After the end of the war Europe

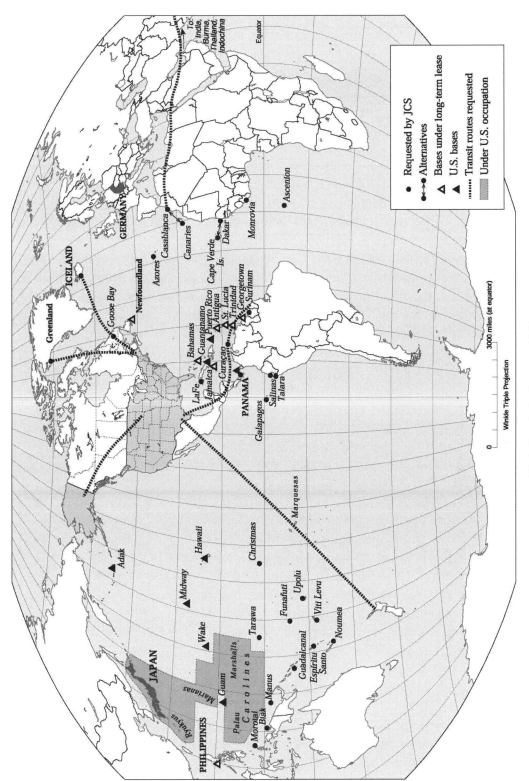

87. A Search for Security, 1946.

experienced two of the coldest winters in memory, leaving these shattered economies in desperate condition: "millions of people in the cities are slowly starving." In response to political fears as well as humanitarian needs, Secretary of State George C. Marshall outlined a massive program for immediate aid and redevelopment, one "directed not against any country or doctrine but against hunger, poverty, desperation and chaos." The Soviet Union considered but ultimately rejected participation because of American insistence on the strengthening of free institutions and open trade under a degree of U.S. supervision; Moscow pressured all Eastern European countries to do the same.

All during this intensifying confrontation in Europe other problem areas had emerged: Turkey, Iran, Palestine, Southeast Asia, China. In September 1949 the Chinese Communists completed their conquest of the mainland, driving their Nationalist opponents into refuge on Taiwan; in that same month President Truman announced that the Soviet Union had exploded an atomic device. In light of these last two events, the National Security Council was directed to "make a reexamination of our objectives in peace and war." It concluded that "Soviet efforts are now directed toward domination of the Eurasian land mass." While as yet the Soviet Union had not technically, militarily breached the peace with the West, it "is animated by a new fanatic faith, antithetical to our own, and seeks to impose its absolute authority over the rest of the world. Conflict has, therefore, become endemic and is waged . . . by violent or non-violent methods in accordance with the dictates of expediency." The report called for a massive increase in American defense expenditures. Presented to Truman in April 1950, it was approved by him shortly after the outbreak of the Korean War.

Thus (although opposed at the time by Kennan as too rigid and militaristic), containment now became a Mackinder-like strategy. Given the massive position of the Soviet Union and its allies, American policy now focused on applying its leadership and power to the Marginal Crescent, or "Rimland" (an alternative geopolitical term that had become well publicized with the posthumous appearance in 1944 of Spykman's *Geography of the Peace*). And thus Samuel Flagg Bemis, America's senior diplomatic historian, concluded a condensed and updated version of his famous work with a "revolutionary USSR" standing "firmly based in the Heartland of Eurasia, one mighty foot by 1950 planted in the Asiatic Rimland of the World-Island, the other poised to tread Atlantic shore." Here he repeated Mackinder's famous formula and simply added that "the best that men could hope for seemed a long armed peace." (In a secret report to the British Cabinet in early 1948 Foreign Secretary Ernest Bevan had also spoken in Mackinderese: "Physical control of the Eurasian land mass and eventual control of the whole World Island is what Politburo is aiming at—no less a thing than that.")

That a long armed peace between what had been the most powerful of wartime allies was the *best* the postwar world could hope for arose from their responses to the vast alterations of the Great Power System. It was as if the great geopolitical "plates" of Eurasia–North Africa had undergone profound tectonic shifts, movements ramifying across half the globe, changing the elevations, shapes, and exposures of large areas, leaving an altered terrain riven with new fractures, tensions, and potential eruptions. Containment was the American attempt to stabilize what was perceived to be a great fault line, a perilous nonconformity of political culture between the vast hard bloc of the Heartland and a long highly varied, uneven, unstable Rimland.

As a result of rather frantic efforts to stabilize that Eurasian girdle around the Communist Bloc as well as ensure the conformity of its Western Hemisphere security zone, by the late 1950s the United States had collective defense treaties with forty-three countries, bilateral mutual defense treaties with four others, agreements with forty-seven countries concerning jurisdiction over U.S. military personnel that might become stationed within their bounds; its armed forces (totaling more that a million, including dependents) were actually on duty in thirty-five foreign lands. Furthermore, its civilian air services girdled the globe, although it had to share many international routes. Near the end of the war American preference for an "open skies" policy generated "a fear on the part of every nation that the United States would exert its powerful air transport strength to acquire world dominance." However, Britain, controlling critical stepping stones across the Atlantic, countered with a "national sovereignty" doctrine, and a bilateral compromise led the way to the formation of an International Air Transport Association (headquartered in Montreal) to negotiate routes, frequencies, and rates. In response to many complaints, President Truman ended Pan American's role as the U.S. "chosen instrument," and international routes were awarded to several other companies (but Pan American was in the lead, opening service from New York via Europe, India, and East Asia to San Francisco in June 1946). Meanwhile state-supported airlines of other Western countries, nearly all of them flying American-built planes and using English as their international operational language, joined in enlarging this global network, just as Russian-built aircraft and the Russian language were binding together Communist-dominated space. International connections between the two were few.

The Cold War has inevitably generated an enormous, controversial historical literature. What follows is merely a brief commentary on the major regions of contention related to the shaping of this American global system, with no more than passing reference to major episodes and phases of that long, dangerous era.

EUROPE

One of the greatest ironies of the postwar world was the extraordinary effort of the United States to rebuild and secure the two enemy nations it had so determinedly defeated. That remarkable reversal arose in part out of the very thoroughness of those defeats. Unlike anything experienced in modern world history, these Great Powers were literally left devastated, harshly diminished in territory, and slated to be firmly locked into an innocuous international status. But problems quickly defeated plans and the ruling policy soon turned to the need for strong economic and political rehabilitation to provide American security in this new bipolar world.

The case of Germany was much the most complex and compelling. It was reduced to three-quarters of its 1937 territory, divided into four zones of occupation, with a similarly divided Berlin standing as a political island within the Soviet sector. The occupying powers were determined never to allow the reestablishment of German dominance within Europe. All entertained the possibility of internationalizing the Ruhr, the greatest seat of German industry; the French, "terrified at the thought of a united Germany," favored further dismemberment (such as detaching the Rhineland); the Soviet Union had even greater reason to insist on firm controls and heavy reparations; the United States initially planned to support the German population at no more than a basic subsistence level.

It was soon apparent, however, that this Germany was the central and critical part of a much more broadly devastated Europe facing the immediate "specter of economic and social chaos." Focusing first on the need to get Ruhr coal to freezing Europe, the United States soon followed with the Marshall Plan. This massive aid to rebuilding is widely regarded as "the most central and creative policy initiative of the postwar period," but an essential geopolitical corollary was the movement, led by Jean Monnet and Robert Schuman of France, declaring that the only way to accept a revived Germany was to bind it firmly within a larger European system. The first stage of such integration was the European Coal and Steel Community formed by France, Italy, Benelux, and West Germany in 1952, followed by the European Economic Community of the same six in 1959, and further degrees of integration and expansions in membership stage by stage over the next forty years—with the German economic contribution ever the most important (fig. 88).

However, the initiation of this great transformation was dependent on still another basic requirement. The Federal Republic of Germany, formed from the combination of the three Western occupation zones, came into being in 1949. Before such a creation could be accepted other European states, led by Great Britain, had insisted that "the vital North American arsenal" and military forces be firmly committed to the defense of Western Europe. Hence the formation of the North Atlantic Treaty Organization (NATO) binding the United States and Canada, along with Iceland, Norway, Denmark, Portugal, and Italy with the earlier Brussels Pact nucleus of Britain, France, and Benelux. Only after this assurance of American support for defense and "U.S. military personnel flooded into Europe" would the shaping of this New Europe get under way.

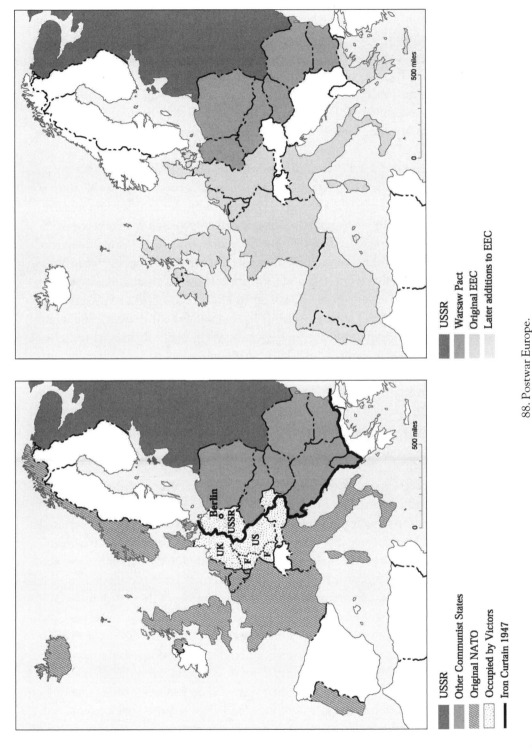

USSR
Warsaw Pact
Original EEC
Later additions to EEC

USSR
Other Communist States
Original NATO
Occupied by Victors
Iron Curtain 1947

88. Postwar Europe.

The four military occupation zones in Germany are shown, but in Austria only that of the Soviet Union, behind the Iron Curtain. Additions to the EEC include those before 1990. The later dis-integration of Yugoslavia is not shown.

Russian fear of Germany was so deep that it would consider unification only if the result was a completely neutralized and demilitarized state. Failing in that, the Soviet Union inadvertently aided German revival and Western European integration by not allowing its occupation zone to participate, for, shorn of old strongholds of Protestantism and Prussianism in East Germany (and the territories lost to Poland), the predominantly Roman Catholic and industrial remnant of West Germany could draw upon political philosophies closely akin to those of France, Belgium, and Italy.

The Kremlin attempted to counter every major Western development: viewing the Marshall Plan as primarily an attempt to rebuild Germany, it quit the postwar Allied Council, blockaded land access to West Berlin (generating the famous airlift as a successful response), and tightened its grip firmly on Czechoslovakia (but Marshal Tito's Yugoslavia defected); following the formation of the Federal Republic of Germany the Soviet zone became the German Democratic Republic; when West Germany became a sovereign state and a member of NATO, this East Germany became sovereign and a member of a new Warsaw Pact of the USSR and its satellites; when a prospering West Germany became the leader of the Common Market and thousands of East Germans began to flock into West Berlin, Nikita Khrushchev erected the formidable Berlin Wall. One positive achievement between these contending powers was an end of occupation and the formal neutralization of a sovereign Austria in 1955.

Although NATO was a mutual defense alliance it is clear that Western Europe was in effect an American protectorate. In an older era of empire that term was more commonly applied to marginal areas of lesser importance in the fringes of more directly ruled territories but the definition of such a relationship—"the promise of protection from external dangers in return for acknowledgement of the exclusive political supremacy of the imperial state," while leaving the subordinated people and territory largely undisturbed—remained apt for this case with pertinent modifications. Here Europe was certainly of primary rather than marginal concern, its recognition of the political supremacy of the United States was more implicit than formal, and the protecting power was heavily involved in economic as well as military affairs. It was commonly understood on both sides of this relationship that this new American role and position was not a case of old-style imperial expansion. Indeed, the Norwegian scholar Geir Lundestad has termed this desire for a strong American military presence as a case of "empire by invitation." It was clearly to Western Europe's advantage to be able to focus on economic rehabilitation and political cooperation without the burdens or fears of heavy military development by each nation, and the invitation could be extended with a reasonable confidence that the United States had no territorial ambitions, that its strategy was not aimed at dominating Europe, that the very idea of such a military alliance was controversial within the United States, and that it was entered into only as the need for a balance of power with its great adversary persisted and not as a long-term commitment. The great successful emergence of an independent West European complex of economic power and political cooperation was the best kind of result envisioned by Kennan in his original concept of "long-term, patient but firm and vigilant containment."

The Soviet Union also sought a balance of power and essentially achieved that goal for several decades, using an opposite political means. As Charles Bohlen, Kennan's diplomatic colleague, observed during the birth pangs of the Cold War: "the Soviet mind is incapable of making a distinction between influence and domination, or between a friendly government and a puppet government." The American policy, reflecting much of the best in its basic principles, was obviously superior in this contest. However, it is well to keep in mind that its generally benign imperial presence hinged on many factors working within Europe, the United States, and the Soviet Bloc. Had European states not agreed about the degree of danger and need for intercontinental defense the United States might have imposed its forces on areas deemed essential to its strategic needs (such as Iceland, where the continued presence of troops on the soil of this proudly national people may yet today be casually referred to as "the American occupation"). Great Powers tend to use force, if needed, to ensure their safety.

MIDDLE EAST

The "Middle East," a general Euro-diplomatic reference to a large area, was not of the slightest official interest to the United States before World War II. Defeating Germany brought the area into intense strategic focus and military action (primarily in North Africa), but with no long-term positions anticipated. Yet after the war this large, complex region became considered so important that the president and Congress soon declared it to be of "vital national interest," and a line of American military facilities was put in place from Morocco to Pakistan. Several major developments prompted this radical geopolitical revision.

The most fundamental was the sudden emergence of a relatively small part of this huge area as the most productive and profitable oil-exporting region in the world. Production itself was not new in the basins fringing the Persian Gulf, having been started by the Anglo-Persian Oil Company in 1908 and augmented later by British developments in Iraq, with growth in importance as a supplier to Europe marked by the completion of pipelines across the desert to Lebanon and Palestine ports shortly before World War II. American explorations brought in the first well in Saudi Arabia in 1938. In 1944 a consortium of major firms formed the Arabian American Oil Company (Aramco), and by 1950 it was the largest and richest in the world (and had made the Saudi ruling family, sharing 50 percent of the profits, among the richest in the world). The Middle East had replaced the Caribbean as the greatest exporting region and become Europe's principal source of this vital product. An even more significant feature of this immense change was that by the early 1950s the Middle East contained well over half of the world's estimated crude oil reserves (and would continue to expand that preponderance, accounting for two-thirds by the century's end).

A second major change, also localized but with wider ramifications, was the creation of the State of Israel in 1948. When, following the collapse of the Ottoman Empire, Britain took over Palestine as a mandate under the League of Nations, it had already officially expressed sympathy with "Jewish Zionist aspirations" and support for the idea of "a national home for the Jewish people" in Palestine—"it being clearly understood that nothing shall be done which may prejudice the civil and religious rights of existing non-Jewish communities." The contradictions of such a policy were soon apparent. Amid local Arab resistance to rising Jewish immigration, the British struggled to find acceptable proposals for shared government or partition, including convening a London conference in 1939 with representatives from major Arab states. Defeated by the heavy influx of desperate Jews following the horrors of World War II, the British turned the territory over to the United Nations, which drew up a plan of partition. Unwilling to accept such a fate, local and bordering Arabs attacked but were defeated by the Israelis, who thereby enlarged their hold in several areas, including a corridor to a divided Jerusalem.

President Truman immediately recognized the new State of Israel (against the advice of his foreign policy team, which favored some sort of U.N. trusteeship for this intractable problem). Truman had his eye on the upcoming election, but beyond his obvious concern for Jewish votes there was a more general American sympathy for a devastated people and support for the establishment of an industrious, modern democratic society in that part of the world. Truman was soon annoyed at Israeli failure to respond with concessions to Palestinian refugees (many of whom had fled the war zone confident of returning after a quick Arab victory); cultivation of Arab governments became newly important, and American entanglement in the bitter, enduring Arab-Israeli conflict was under way.

British withdrawal from Palestine was but one small part of the collapse of the European hold on much of the Middle East, including almost the entire Arab world. Following World War I only Yemen and (what would become) Saudi Arabia, along with Turkey and Iran, had escaped some degree of incorporation within the British, French, or Italian empires; by the mid-1950s only Algeria (its bloody battle for independence achieved only in 1962) and a set of small sheikhdom protectorates along the Arabian Peninsula from Kuwait through Oman and Aden remained. Such a geopolitical transformation in such an era was inevitably accompanied by competition between the superpowers for influence within the independent states, old and new, and such a powerful rivalry and attempted interventions intensified the volatility of this deeply nationalistic, factionalized region.

As earlier noted, the first application of America's containment policy focused on Soviet borderlands in this region. With Turkey apparently secured, attention soon turned to Iran (where a Soviet attempt to create a puppet state in the wake of its wartime presence in the northwest had been withdrawn after Western protest). When a popularly elected leader of Iran nationalized its oil industry (after failing to secure the same sharing of profits with the British company as the Saudis had secured from the Americans) the alarmed British sought U.S. help and the new Eisenhower administration, working through the CIA, toppled him and replaced his government with the shah, who became increasingly an American puppet. Having thus hardened these northern bounds of the Rimland against direct Soviet expansion, attention could be focused on Arabs and oil.

Saudi Arabia was obviously the key state for the Americans. The mutually enriching economic partnership between its rulers and Aramco was soon reinforced by the creation of a major U.S. military base at Dhahran, in return for modern weapons for the regime. The new American line of air bases spanning the 3,000 miles from the Persian Gulf to Morocco augmented the older protection of shipments offered by British naval bases at Aden, Suez, Malta, and Gibraltar. For the British, Egypt was obviously the main key on this route, but their position was weakening here as it had in Iran and American help less likely. American leaders blamed Britain for its unwillingness to accept the end of old-style colonialism and negotiate new permissions for military relationships. British leaders resented such attitudes, regarding their interests and experience in the area as much the greater and, as Anthony Eden said to his cabinet, "should not therefore allow ourselves to be restricted overmuch by reluctance to act without full American concurrence and support." He soon learned the cost of such assumptions. A military coup had brought Colonel Gamal Nasser into fervent leadership of Egypt; provoked by Western pressures he seized control of the Suez Canal and was aiding Algerian rebels. Britain and France, therefore, invited the help of Israel and, without consulting any others, launched air and ground attacks. The Israelis quickly defeated Nasser's armies in the Sinai, but before European troops arrived blunt condemnations of such actions from the Americans (and from the Soviets, who had aided Nasser) brought an ignominious end to this campaign.

This humiliation of Britain and France confirmed American domination but undermined the Western coalition. More than that, the Suez debacle hastened the end of European colonial empires everywhere (independence in Tropical Africa began the next year when Britain's Gold Coast became Ghana), and it exposed the power and leverage new states might exercise amid Great Power rivalries. Containment would face alarming difficulties in this fractured, volatile sector, and in 1957 Eisenhower requested and received congressional authority to use force to help any state in the region to resist "armed attack from any country controlled by international communism." As Warren I. Cohen later noted, "for most denizens of the Middle East . . . the Soviet threat was imperceptible" and "there was little popular support for containment," but "there was a vast quantity of combustible material waiting to be ignited by a leader who would strike out against Israel and reverse the decades of humiliation by the West."

Middle Eastern leaders had other reasons for favoring the Soviet Union. If, as Joel Carmichael has asserted, "Islam since its inception has been grounded on the triple foundation of theocracy . . . , the army . . . , and the intelligentsia," the success of a small group of ideologues in seizing control of a undeveloped state and transforming it into a great industrial and military power made the Soviet Union a more apt model than one espousing Wilsonian ideals. Superpower rivalries fueled local arms races and sustained dictatorial regimes. America's key ally, Saudi Arabia, was the least democratic state in the region. During the Cold War the United States made three direct military interventions (two in Lebanon and the humiliating attempt to rescue hostages held by the new theocratic regime in Iran), all costly failures. When containment was no longer the problem, the United States went to war over oil against Iraq's invasion of Kuwait. By the end of the twentieth century its overall position in the Middle East remained insecure, its sustained popular support of Israel a deep complication in its relationships with Arab and Islamic peoples, whose popular leaders expressed resentment of America's cultural character and imperial presence.

EAST ASIA

The devastating defeat of a Great Power and its occupation and encompassing domination by a sole victorious superpower was an extraordinary situation in modern world history. Having quickly carried out Allied agreements on the dismemberment of the Japanese empire, the United States imposed upon the residual four-island homeland a drastic program of demilitarization, democratization, and economic restriction—a bold attempt at remolding a whole political society.

As for the first of these objectives, the military forces were dissolved, arsenals, armaments factories, naval bases, and shipyards destroyed, and the new U.S.-imposed constitution declared that "the Japanese people forever renounce war as a sovereign right of the nation" and therefore "land, sea, and air forces, as well as other war potential, will never be maintained." That constitution, which came into effect in May 1947, spelled out the framework of a parliamentary democracy based on the sovereignty of the people (with the emperor reduced to being "the symbol of the

State and the unity of the people"). Meanwhile purges of military, political, and industrial leaders deemed responsible for Japan's recent career of conquest, and reforms relating to education, labor, and land tenure were under way. Economic policy called for dismantling the corporate oligarchy (*zaibatsu*), restrictions on the scale of heavy industries, such as steel, machine tools, and chemicals, elimination of some others, such as aircraft and synthetic rubber, and in general confining the restored economy to the levels of 1930–34.

These economic goals were by necessity soon replaced. Given the vast devastation throughout Japan, plus the repatriation of almost 6 million from the empire (the rest of the Far East "was for the most part swept bare of Japanese"), and the release of more than 3 million from the armed services, there was an urgent need for rehabilitation and expansion to provide 80 million people with a minimum subsistence rather than a focus on limiting their war-making capabilities. Thus "American policy shifted from punishment toward reconstruction" and massive American aid.

Moreover, as the containment of international communism emerged as America's foreign policy obsession, its postwar fixation on the repression of Japanese militarism rapidly evolved into a need to ensure Japan as America's key ally in an unstable region. With the success of the Chinese Communists and revolutionary movements under way in Southeast Asia, the United States was looking toward ending the occupation, encouraging Japan to develop a homeland defense force, and assessing the need for American bases. In January 1950 Secretary of State Dean Acheson, recognizing that "a new day . . . has dawned in Asia" and the future would be shaped by the decisions of those countries and peoples, declared that the United States would safeguard the security of Japan, Okinawa, and the Philippines as part of its defense perimeter but would not intervene elsewhere. Six months later the war in Korea would bring surprises and alter perceptions: the invasion of the South by the North surprised the United States; U.S. military intervention surprised the Kremlin; Chinese intervention to halt the sweeping American counteroffensive surprised the United States. Although the final armistice line approximated the original division, larger geopolitical relations were deeply affected.

China was much the greatest presence in that larger picture and Americans were still in the midst of adjusting their view of it. It was now apparent that Sino-American friendship had been a brief asymmetrical relationship. As John King Fairbank put it: Americans "discovered China in an era of dynastic decline and social demoralization, not realizing that it was an interregnum between periods of unity and central power." Confronted with this "strong, chauvinist, and anti-Western China," the new messianic anticommunist Secretary of State, John Foster Dulles, sought to contain this international menace by strong American bases in South Korea, Japan, Okinawa, and the Philippines, and naval protection of the remnant

Republic of China on Taiwan. The end of the occupation in Japan in 1952 was accompanied by a joint security pact with the United States. The Korean War had provided a massive infusion for the Japanese economy, and the United States now regarded a prospering Japan as an essential bulwark against communism and Southeast Asia as Japan's critical economic hinterland. Following the defeat of the French in Indochina in 1954 the United States began its long, incremental, accelerating, compulsive disaster in Vietnam.

"Postwar Asia, like the Balkans before 1914, was an area where the clash of imperial and nationalistic forces created an extremely volatile situation," said Akira Iriye. "The collapse of the Japanese empire and the weakening of the European empires brought about a situation in which it was virtually impossible to produce any clearly recognized sense of regional stability." At the outset the United States sought to control and remake Japan and stay off the continent. The Americans and the Chinese Communists each regarded the other as an ideological enemy but not as a threat to its own security. Driven by its global view of dangers (and by domestic politics), the United States failed to distinguish between nationalism and communism and to recognize that much of the turmoil was rooted in civil strife antedating World War II. By the 1960s it was clear that China was not a Soviet satellite, but unclear to Americans whether revolutionary Vietnam was a Chinese surrogate; it was also obvious that by protecting Taiwan the United States was helping perpetuate China's civil war, but quite uncertain whether it could help a remnant South Vietnam survive.

In Japan, rather than a still virulent nationalism or nascent civil war, the United States experienced peaceful acceptance of the tutelage and protection of an all-powerful victor following traumatic defeat. Here the "revolution" was accomplished by encouragement of changes in political and social structure during the occupation (drawing in part upon indigenous but subdued prewar movements) such that once restored to sovereignty Japan's leaders, taking advantage of fortuitous American and international economic conditions, set their nation upon an "era of high-speed growth" under their own form of bureaucratic capitalism. Thereby the Japanese, who have tended to see "their world as a hierarchy, and . . . to rank the countries of it in order of esteem and importance," would, in a remarkably short time, gain an unprecedented position as a Great Economic Power—and with the continuing advantage of military protection, begin to have a strong impact upon the economy of their conqueror.

LATIN AMERICA

During and after World War II the United States continued its geopolitical policies of alignment and subordination within its Latin American sphere (and a recalcitrant Argentina persevered in its stance, not formally breaking with Germany until late in the war—and then mainly to ensure its membership in the United Nations—and soon willingly harboring Nazis fleeing the prospect of Allied punishment). In 1947 a new Pan American military pact was signed, and in the next year the general hemispheric system was reconstituted as the Organization of American States (OAS).

Expectedly the most difficult topic for this new charter was nonintervention, finally included as an article over the objections of the United States. And, as usual, the United States soon defied that rule and asserted its power when its interests seemed to be threatened. In 1954 a popularly elected leader in Guatemala undertook a land reform program that included expropriation, with payment, of a large body of land held in reserve by a powerful American company. The company resisted, and the U.S. government, fearing the spread of such nationalistic policies and the probabilities of Soviet opportunism, asked the OAS to take action. Upon its refusal (there being no evidence of Kremlin aid), the CIA helped Guatemalan exiles overthrow the government, install a new dictator, and thereby, as Secretary Dulles put it, saved the country from "Communist imperialism." By so defining the threat, the United States was justifying its intervention as consistent with the Monroe Doctrine: keeping external imperial powers from asserting any claim upon independent American states. It would soon help create an obvious case of external intervention, with dangerous, prolonged, and embarrassing results for all concerned.

Since the time of Thomas Jefferson, Cuba has been deemed to be crucial to American security: Havana, the Gibraltar of the New World, must never be allowed to fall into the hands of an unfriendly power. Since the time of James Polk relationships between Cubans and Americans have been close, and at times contentious; under the presidency of Theodore Roosevelt the island became a formal U.S. protectorate; in Franklin Roosevelt's time the formality was ended but Cuba's status as a Great Power satellite continued; as Louis A. Pérez, Jr., summarized: "North Americans controlled every major sector of the national economy. . . . They owned a vast proportion of the national territory. They operated the better schools and presided over the most prestigious social clubs. . . . They were the money-lenders, the landowners, and power brokers. They bought and sold Cuban politicians and policemen the way they bought farms and factories." The United States was concerned with the protection of those interests, with political stability and subordination; beyond that Cuba was no more than a convenient exotic tropical playground.

Cubans had long been deeply ambivalent about the United States. It was the source of modern progress and they "partook freely of American culture," but its "presence in Cuba was so visible, and so privileged" that "it also aroused hostility and resentment" and "Cubans of all classes, in varying degrees, had grievances against the status quo." Thus Fidel Castro's 1959 triumph brought "a joyful nationalist celebration," but as the extent of his revolutionary intent became clear, deep divergences within Cuba and with the United States soon appeared.

Castro understood that serious reform had to be structural, sharply reducing American economic control and influence. When he turned to the Soviet Union (whether motivated by ideology or opportunism remains controversial) to trade sugar for oil, the United States began to prepare for his ouster; the embarrassing failure of an initial attempt was soon followed by the infamous Cuban Missile Crisis, the most dangerous of Cold War escalations. Khrushchev was delighted to support a leader who had seized control of what had long been America's quasi-colony ninety miles offshore. In documents released much later he is recorded as telling his advisers that "since the Americans have already surrounded the Soviet Union with a ring of military bases and various types of missile launchers, we must pay them back with their own coin . . . so they will know what it feels like to live in the sight of nuclear weapons." The Soviet Union retreated from this confrontation (and Khrushchev was soon removed from office), but there was ample humiliation for all concerned. Castro, eager manipulator, was left isolated from much of the world, his country a remote ally and economic dependent of a superpower struggling to provide a decent living for its own people. The United States, frustrated by its failure to interrupt the revolution, was left with what it regarded as a festering sore within its own sphere, on its own boundary, with all Cuban-American relations, domestic and foreign, profoundly altered.

As part of its resolution with the Soviet Union, the United States agreed not to invade Cuba, but the Kremlin's intervention had confirmed American obsessions about the worldwide threat of "international communism." A few years later, President Lyndon Johnson, in a "feverish determination to prevent 'another Cuba,'" sent a large force of marines into the Dominican Republic, and subsequent presidents intervened directly or covertly, heavily or tentatively, in numerous other countries in the West Indies, Central America, and even (and decisively) in distant Chile. Massive aid was supplied to client regimes, military schools were set up in the United States to train Latin American forces, American "advisers" directed "counterinsurgency" tactics to suppress "subversive" change. But Latin America was a seething cauldron of problems crying out for change, for which the United States had no solution. Americans might generally support the ideals of "democracy" and "progress," but feared upwellings of popular movements and the radical changes that any serious attempt at reform would necessarily involve. The failed American intervention in Cuba made Castro a hero; its support of military coups and oligarchies reinforced fears and resentments of its policies among many Latin

Americans and magnified the human costs of attempts at social change (especially in Guatemala, El Salvador, and Nicaragua).

Once Soviet missiles were withdrawn from Cuba no return of such a threat was plausible had not the United States been so fearful of "international communism." The massive forces of the United States, operating from dozens of bases in or near critical sectors (including Guantánamo Bay in Cuba itself) ensured the country's security from any serious threat within its "own hemisphere"—as the grotesque asymmetry of the U.S. attack upon Grenada displayed. Communism was certainly present in name and slogan, for some Latin American intellectuals and politicians found Marxism (in whatever form) an attractive alternative to local exhibits of American capitalism. But popular movements were powered by people and leaders seeking direct, tangible improvements in daily life and prospects, whatever the ideology. Had the United States not been so embarrassed by Cuban defiance at its very borders, it might have relied more effectively on its experience a generation earlier with its far larger bordering nation to the west. Woodrow Wilson's brief armed interventions were utterly fruitless, and Mexico was left to endure its civil wars, which, as we have earlier noted, evolved into an indigenous revolution, resulting in a consolidated, centralized state, strongly nationalistic but not anticapitalistic, that undertook a program of modest, incremental reform and development without serious harm to any basic American interest. During World War II and after Mexico was a strong, stable partner in support of larger U.S. concerns. It is perhaps ironic that whereas Latin American leaders had long regarded U.S.-Mexican relations as a basic test of American foreign policy, America's postwar leaders apparently ignored the lessons of that example.

POLAR CONFRONTATION

In June 1937 even the few Westerners who had paid any attention to prior talk of such a thing "were confounded when a Russian plane nonchalantly flew non-stop from Moscow to the United States via the North Pole," landing across the river from Portland at Vancouver, Washington; two weeks later a second plane extended the route to within eighty miles of the Mexican border in Southern California, setting a new world long-distance record (6,262 miles). Although "the world applauded" their feat, nothing came of their ostensible intention of demonstrating the feasibility of a Moscow–San Francisco air service. Nevertheless, Vilhjamur Stefansson, well-known Arctic explorer, suggested at the time that if a monument were built to commemorate the achievement of these Russian pilots it might well be engraved: "They found the world of transportation a cylinder; they left it a sphere."

Cylinder-type maps, wrapping the globe at the equator, cannot show the poles at all and grossly distort the higher latitudes. A cartographic shift from such Merca-tor-like maps to polar and other air-age projections, offering a more sphere-like view of the Northern Hemisphere, began to appear during World War II to give Americans a more appropriate "geographical sense of our time," a "strategic" rather than a conventional view of the world. Thus the Fortune-sponsored *Look at the World*, featuring the richly vivid designs of Richard Edes Harrison, opened with a north polar projection, followed with a set of highly unconventional (no north-at-the-top) perspectives on major geopolitical relationships, and concluded with a de-piction of great circle airways. Such maps were critical to any understanding of the revolutionary change in America's strategic position. A few years after those widely applauded Russian flights of 1937, advances in aircraft and weaponry had trans-formed what had been an impenetrable barrier into a potential thoroughfare of mu-tual destruction.

The United States and Canada agreed on the general need for Arctic defenses, but Canadian leaders, ever conscious of "the fearful asymmetry" of relationships in North America, were cautious about such undertakings. Canada had welcomed the extension of its defense ties into a broader NATO as providing "the prospect of a multilateral counterpoise to U.S. influence"—an enlargement and a reinforce-ment of the older North Atlantic Triangle concept of the United States, Canada, and Britain. Yet, as their prime minister well knew, "if the Americans felt security required it [they] would take peaceful possession of part of Canada" (as they had with the Alaska Highway), and by 1950 the two countries, "at American insis-tence," began construction of what would become a vast set of three continent-wide radar defense systems (fig. 89). In 1957 a joint North American Air Defense (NORAD) agreement placed the air forces of both countries under command of an American general at Colorado Springs (with a nominal Canadian deputy at a base near Montreal).

Canadian leaders understood and accepted the obvious situation of Canada as an essential American security zone in a bipolar world of growing danger. Never-theless, every move in the formation of this collaboration had been intensely de-bated in parliament and the press. A good many Canadians came to see Washing-ton as the seat of "a powerful bureaucracy with a vested interest in demonizing the Soviet Union" and fostering an unbalanced fear and fervor over a direct Soviet threat to North America. Even those who sided more closely with the American point of view could not have been comfortable with the news that during the Cuban Missile Crisis NORAD forces had been put on high alert without notifying Ottawa. With the development of intercontinental missiles strategies shifted more to retaliation than interception and the emplacement of nuclear weapons became a divisive issue in Canada. Through all these developments the junior partner was

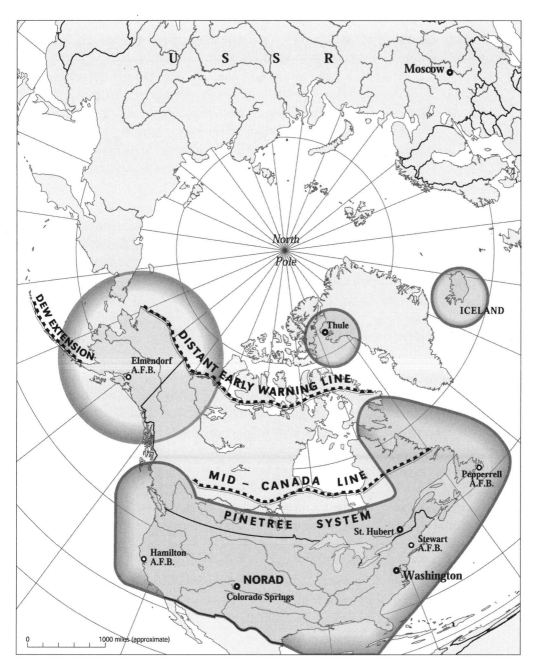

89. Detection and Deterrent Systems.

These radar networks to detect Soviet long-range bombers were augmented by continual air and sea patrols in the North Pacific and North Atlantic. Strategic Air Command (SAC) forces of bombers under the control of NORAD were stationed at many bases. In the late 1950s these systems became inadequate against intercontinental missiles.

hyperconscious about infringements on Canadian sovereignty, while the Americans were relentlessly focused on their control over the design, timing, and operation of the system.

In the face of heavy American pressure, and at times obvious annoyance, Canada asserted some freedom of action in its own foreign policy (especially in its direct relationships with Castro's Cuba and Communist China). In North American military matters, however, Canada was an American satellite. In 1940, on the second anniversary of Franklin Roosevelt's Kingston speech assuring Canada of American protection, the two countries' leaders met at Ogdensburg, New York, and formed a Permanent Joint Board on Defense. With Canadian forces already committed to the war in Europe, Mackenzie King explained that the main point of such an agreement was to further Canada's support of the British Commonwealth. Roosevelt, however, was armed with a revised interpretation that the main object of the Monroe Doctrine "is actually to keep war off the American hemisphere," and his signature was, in effect, a formal step "in the completion of American hegemony in the western hemisphere."

FROM CONTAINMENT TO COLLAPSE

Containment began as a simple term for a complex policy focused on the only other Great Power. It quickly evolved into a confrontation of great enemies that shaped U.S. policy for forty years. The shock and challenge of the change of the Soviet Union from wartime ally to postwar adversary triggered a strong characteristic response from the United States. Containment quickly evolved into another American crusade to save the world. As President Eisenhower phrased it: "Forces of good and evil are massed and armed and opposed as rarely before in history. Freedom is pitted against slavery, lightness against dark."

It was easy to demonize the Soviet Union, even before the full force and extent of Stalinist policies was generally understood in the West; it was obviously a massive totalitarian regime, and its rigid stance against American plans for postwar Europe was a warning of trouble ahead. But more important, "the Soviet Union had an ideology which gave the capitalist West ample cause to be nervous." Marxism's call for revolution was notorious, and, as Reinhold Niebuhr observed, it was "obviously not simply an economic and social theory but a scheme of redemption" for all humankind, "a new political utopian religion"; as George Steiner later confirmed: "we recognize in the history of Marxism each of the attributes . . . characteristic of a mythology in the full theological mould. . . . Above all, it offers a contract of messianic promise concerning the future." Already seductive to intellectual critics of the capitalist West, to many more in the radically altered and troubled postwar world "the communist system seemed a viable form of political modernity." Such a heresy so firmly rooted in a strong rival power generated a full evangelical counter-attack from the assertive leader of the "free world" and "democracy." "The strength of their own fervent religious convictions made many Americans particularly sensitive to the crusading tone of Moscow's communism," and Wilsonian ideals became clothed in anticommunism as an ideology grounded in America's own quasi-Christian missionary creed. And so, "caught in a maelstrom of mutual distrust," the contending powers "spun dizzily downward until the Cold War was universalized, ideologized, institutionalized, and then militarized."

Senator William Fulbright, commenting in 1966 on "the tendency of great nations to equate power with virtue and major responsibilities with a universal mission," noted also the possibility that "the missionary instinct in foreign affairs . . . may reflect a deficiency rather than an excess of national self-confidence." Such conditions tend to reinforce stereotypes of societies, suppress dissent, and becloud assessments of alternative policies. As history well records, crusades tend to go awry, leading to the sack of Constantinople rather than recovery of the Holy Land. As recent history records, such observations seem like axioms well fitted to both sides in this global contest.

Containment was complicated by fear that international communism's appeal to discontented (often majority) populations would cause the toppling, in geographic succession, of one state after another (the oft-cited "domino effect") by insurgent forces working out of an expanding Communist Bloc. Ideological estimates of this subversive power soon transformed containment into a more general confrontation policy far beyond the Rimland, inducing interventions as far afield as Angola and Chile, "as events in every corner of the world became defined in terms of American security concerns."

Insecurity—fear—was a major feature on both sides in rallying domestic support for foreign policies and international interventions. In this effort the United States was peculiarly vulnerable to what might be called the paradox of democracy, wherein mobilization of strong popular support of a relentlessly sloganized cause injects a rigidity into national policy facing re-endorsement every two years: "the surest way to lose an election was to be accused of being 'soft on communism.'" Such fears drive internal exposés of doubters or critics and impositions of loyalty oaths. Much the most ominous product of insecurity on both sides was the massive militarization of society. The United States was especially infected with "Cold War threat inflation," marked by recurrent alarms (Soviet atomic success, "missile gaps," Sputnik, first man in space) followed by feverish expansions in numbers and quality of armaments and "space spectaculars." After the Bay of Pigs disaster, Kennedy, needing "a dramatic gesture designed to recover pride at a moment of national embarrassment," authorized the man-on-the-moon project, "the most costly enterprise in history . . . undertaken by a nation that was only vaguely aware of what 'practical' purpose, if any, it might serve." Such escalating responses became built into the system: "big budgets for the military, big contracts for military suppliers, big contributions for campaign funds, and a never-ending Mississippi of consultant money for experts in think tanks"; to which should be added huge budgets for the CIA, and extremely restricted political oversight of it and other intelligence agencies. The National Security Council, created in 1947, was soon more powerful than the State Department in foreign policy.

The first major steps to ease this arms race were taken in the mid-1980s. In December 1987 President Ronald Reagan and Chairman Mikhail Gorbachev agreed to dismantle a complete class of threatening weaponry. From this point on Gorbachev began his attempt to reform the entire Soviet system and ease controls over its East European satellites. In 1989, after he refused to send troops to prop up those failing regimes, most of them were overturned; that November the Berlin Wall was demolished. Although the Soviet Union (and France and Britain) opposed any immediate unification of the two Germanys, the leader of West Germany, with U.S. backing, soon brought it about. In 1991 Moscow announced the dissolution of the Warsaw Pact that had bound all those subordinated states to the Kremlin. An even more stunning revolution—haplessly resisted by Gorbachev—quickly followed. As controls from Moscow eased or faltered, first the Baltic republics and soon after the other members of the USSR began to assert their independence. On December 25, 1991, Boris Yeltsin, the new president of the Russian Republic, announced that the Union of Soviet Socialist Republics ceased to exist.

The quickness and completeness of this collapse astounded the world, yet there had been signs that this system had been under increasing strain for a generation. Thus the end of the Cold War revealed "a barely functioning Soviet economy, a cynical and despairing populace with a falling lifespan, technology primitive in all but a few areas of military hardware, a worthless currency, a degraded environment, allies eager to break free." Critical to all of this deterioration was the loss of faith in the ruling ideology by the leaders, a sclerotic bureaucracy, and the general public— though probably most did not foresee nor welcome the foundering of the routine socioeconomic system. Thus the Soviet Union became a striking example of the disintegration of empire by "collapse from within because the center has become so enfeebled as to be unable to serve or deploy force upon outlying provinces . . . [;] because empires are a patchwork they tend to come apart at the seams," and the former subordinate territorial units "provide the framework for successor states." That none of the member republics chose to remain under the rule of Moscow attested to the reality of the USSR as an empire and to the complete failure of its relentless suppression of "national deviations" from its totalitarian program for the creation of a new uniform "Soviet" citizenry.

Thus the "evil empire" disappeared from view and the United States was suddenly left as the sole Great Power. However great the relief, it was not a comfortable moment for its leaders. As President George Bush said in 1991, the Soviet Union is no longer the enemy (he had flown to Kiev to urge Ukraine to stay under Moscow): "No, the enemy is unpredictability. The enemy is instability." The United States had immense military power but no program ready, no clear vision of what its mission should be in the wake of such drastic change. The view from Washington looked out upon a world with an enormous variety and complexity of peoples, nations, problems; the United States had never shown itself very adept at dealing with such things beyond its own borders.

6. America and the World

SOME POSTWAR WORLDS

The cover of *Time* magazine for March 17, 1947, featured a portrait of an English historian against a dramatic background of figures struggling, clinging, dangling on a sheer cliffside. Inside, the text tied this depiction to a recent geopolitical event:

> That implacable educator, History, at last assigned a lesson that even the duller members of the class could grasp. Britain, its Government had announced, no longer possessed the resources to continue its comparatively puny military aid to Greece. India had all but left the Empire. Burma and Malaya were going. South Africa was tugging at the tether. In the citadel itself were hunger, cold and socialism.
>
> History was moving with 20th Century acceleration. Americans . . . heard the news almost with awe. For they grasped the fact that this was no merely political or military crisis; it was a crisis in Western civilization itself.

Americans had been told of their political and military response that very week when their president had set forth his Truman Doctrine before Congress. As for "what a civilization is" and what to do about such a crisis, the man on the cover, Professor Arnold Toynbee, was "the one man in the world probably best equipped to tell them"—and he was lecturing in the United States that week. Henry Luce's introduction of this scholar to American readers (a long essay in *Life* followed some months later) was complemented by the appearance of a one-volume condensation by an American scholar of the first six volumes of Toynbee's *A Study in History*. Thus the concept of *civilizations*, rather than nations or empires, as the essential "intelligible field" of historical study was given unprecedented attention (fig. 90).

A generation earlier Oswald Spengler's *Decline of the West* had caused a flurry of serious interest in a comparative "morphology of world history," but his powerful, ponderous presentations of the life cycle of a set of vast, distinct, and separate cultures was harshly criticized for its organic determinism and mystical presumptions. Toynbee's work was more directly comparative, explicit about analogous develop-

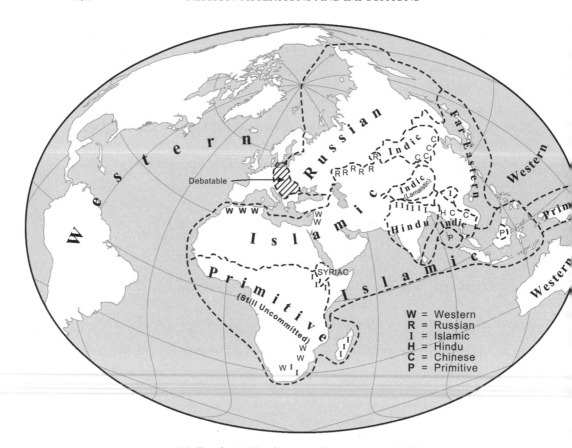

90. Toynbee's "Civilizations Current in A.D. 1952."
Adapted and simplified from Toynbee and Myers, *Historical Atlas and Gazetteer*, vol. 11, *A Study of History* (1959).

ments, and featured a less deterministic "challenge-and-response" theory (those figures on the cliffside representing the responses of different peoples to the challenge of cultural progress). Both authors stressed the fundamental importance of great religions and philosophical systems.

As might be expected from their times of composition (1910s and 1930s) and from their emphasis upon origins and decisive periods of early creativity and growth, the United States was no more than a shallow outlier in these panoramic metahistories. At midcentury, however, the sheer power and momentum of this Global America contrasted with a Europe in ruins must surely invite a revisioning of its significance in any contemporary interpretation. Luce, having predicted in 1941 an emergence of "the American Century," was confident that its moral and political leadership and example would be the essential response to any challenges facing the Western World. The massive crisis of World War II had itself brought a fresh emphasis upon Western Civilization among scholars and teachers, and the dramatic change in America's relative position in the world soon generated an enormous literature assessing its character and prospects. American Studies emerged as a formal topic in college curricula.

Perhaps the most pertinent single exhibit in this literature is *America as a Civilization*, a 950-page assessment by Max Lerner (with informal assistance acknowledged from a long list of prominent scholars), published in 1957. Lerner set out "to draw a portrait—the portrait of the American as the 'Archetypal Man of the West' who has focused on the characteristic energies of the modern world." Although such a theme acknowledged "the idea of American integration into the broader Western pattern," his entire text was devoted to America as a great creative culture, a civilization with "a way of life and a world view" that was leaving "a deep imprint" on human experience. While our concern is with this book as a prominent mark of its time, we could (without adopting his titular characterization) readily relate some of his central themes to our narrower geographical perspective, especially his recurrent stress on the revolutionary dynamic and expansionism of American development, with technological change empowering mobilization and acceleration on a continental scale.

Although Lerner capitalized on the sudden popularity of the civilizations concept and made occasional references to Spengler and Toynbee, he adopted nothing of their categories or methods; yet such was the currency of ostensible long historical cycles of these vast complexes that he concluded his own capacious work with a speculative commentary on "the destiny of a civilization." Writing in the mid-1950s he was confronted with "the polarizing pressures of the two superpowers," and he readily translated this into a rivalry between "two civilizations." Given the time of writing, his assessments of possible longer-term relationships and outcomes were well drawn; Lerner was confident that "the American experience embodied a more authentic revolution" in human affairs than Marxist-Leninism, and "in the generations to come, the image of an open society" should be America's most effective single weapon. He was less confident that Americans would make the best use of it.

Today we might well take Lerner's title and concluding topic as marking the end of a decade of prominent attention to civilizations as the ultimate framework for history. Popular interest had responded to speculations about current conditions as a repetition of stages in the life cycle of earlier civilizations. ("Is the whole Western world destined to become part of an American empire similar to the Roman empire?") But the topic was so vast, complex, and imprecise that it was treated seriously by relatively few historians and almost totally shunned by social scientists (Carroll Quigley and Philip Bagby representing important exceptions).

More important, Cold War immediacies demanded short-term, simpler geopolitical views of the world. The very idea of a solid Communist Bloc made up of the Soviet Union, Eastern Europe, and China might seem to confirm the modern irrelevancy of older historical delineations, while U.S. proclamation of the Free World, though grounded in some fundamental ideals of Western Civilization, was obviously an opportunistic slogan for all states allied with its anticommunist cause, whatever their cultural affiliations. However, any such bipolar geopolitical simplification was soon complicated by the emergence of the "Third World." Formally proclaimed at a gathering of Asian and African leaders at the Bandung Conference in Indonesia in 1955, the term was coined to distinguish their countries from the West (First World) and the Soviet Union (leader of the Second World), not necessarily in political alignments but to insist that the agenda of world politics must include major attention to the needs of other countries and peoples across much of the globe. Soon joined by many more newly independent states, this Third World became a "vast geographical zone not yet committed to a particular path to modernity," a complicated unstable arena for Cold War programs and interventions.

Serious attention to the concerns of this new disturbing voice together with the obvious and growing disparities between the rich nations and the poor gave rise to a great volume and variety of international aid projects, some under the sponsorship of new postwar institutions, such as the World Bank, most of it backed by American capital. All of this was directed at countries in what now became commonly known as the "Underdeveloped World." Less offensive than "backward," the term implied both the need and possibility of lifting whole populations to some acceptable world standard of living. The nations of the industrialized West, and especially the United States, were the obvious models for new theories of development that sought to identify the critical features of their success. These tended to focus on economic change, on "stages of economic growth," diffusion from economic centers to peripheral regions, and related themes. Yet the whole topic was dauntingly complex. The variations in internal character and current levels of development from country to country and the multitude of factors involved were quite beyond the compass of any general theory. Clearly "development" could not simply be diffused or transplanted, and changes resulting from wider adoptions of modern science and technology and operational systems could be deeply disturbing in general and narrowly selective in the sectors of social benefit. Increasingly critics, in the West as well as elsewhere, charged that attempts to impose Western-style "progress" tended to perpetuate the very inequalities and injustices it was ostensibly designed to mitigate and extend the domination of those already holding power.

During the brief euphoria following the collapse of the rival Soviet path to modernization in 1991, "globalization" suddenly emerged as a topic of intense interest (as Anthony Giddens remarked, the term "has come from nowhere and is almost everywhere"). Its appearance was related to an intensified American emphasis on the triumph of deregulated, privatized, market-based economies being reinforced by the unprecedented power of new communications and information processing networks in an expansive capitalist world system.

Various commentators soon pointed out that globalization of this general sort was not an entirely new feature in world history. As already noted, in 1900 London was the center of a worldwide system. British political power and economic tentacles encircled the globe and together with other European and American empires and spheres of influence had left an indelible imprint upon the rest of the world. At this stage Westernization and modernization were indivisible. The Western powers had imposed their locational systems and time zones upon the globe and had completed and formalized the world's politico-territorial framework. All the transforming technologies, operational systems, and associated cultural practices were of Western origin; a multitude of informal marks of modernization followed (with the adoption of Western dress, initially by business and political elites, among the more telling).

Adoption of these new ways, whether imposed or welcomed, varied greatly across the breadth of the non-Western World. Japan's decisive, decreed mimetic response was the most unusual case (but not its first, having reacted rather similarly upon its "discovery" of China in the seventh and eighth centuries). Its official systematized adoption of modern tools and a selection of modern ways (even the young Meiji emperor, "restored" as a link with the ancient past, appeared at times in Western dress), while sustaining a distinctive and defensive national culture, laid the groundwork for a divergence between modernization and Westernization.

While Britain and other Western European powers were completing this first great phase of modern globalization the United States was absorbed in its own great task of nation building on a continental scale and was relatively indifferent to other world affairs. To some degree this sense of separation worked both ways. Thomas P. Hughes, in his book on the creation of "the modern technological nation," refers to "The Second Discovery of America" by Europeans: "the first discovery had been that of the virgin land, nature's nation; the second was of technology's land, America as artifact. Some foreigners continued to associate the United States with the frontier, but others realized that for more than a century the nation had been the world's most active construction site." The early phase of that massive development was the railroad age—coal-iron-steam—Europe's paleotechnic on a larger scale. But as the twentieth century unfolded "Europeans perceived the transformation to be more than a technological and industrial revolution, that it bore the seeds of a cultural mutation as well." The United States "was leading the world into a uniquely modern era." At first, Americans themselves perceived this leadership largely in technological terms: the neotechnic of the automobile, electricity, household appliances; mass production and mass consumption; a revolutionary change in general material standards of living. But after intellectual leaders in Europe (especially from Germany) had been subdued or driven out (mostly to the United States) and their countries lay in ruins, America's cultural transformation as well as its economic power became apparent to all and modernization became synonymous with "Americanization."

This phase of modernization was therefore concomitant with the Cold War, and our treatment of that topic has suggested some special contexts associated with that global confrontation: an extensive system of military bases on foreign soil, military alliances and shared weaponry and facilities, military occupancy and imposed programs of national reconstruction, massive economic aid projects. To these should be added heavy investments in foreign resources, vigorous marketing of American goods and services, and American corporate control of previously local foreign firms. But as this transformation succeeded, the global spread of the imprint of modernization became less and less distinctively American and more and more generic in form: the worldwide standardizations of automobile landscapes and international airports, of skyscrapers and convention centers, of hotels and banks and the bold names and symbols of major corporations—with no obvious clues as to where actual control resides; meanwhile the real basics, such as electricity, water systems, sanitation, modern medical care, and schools were commonly operated by local governments. Furthermore, in the 1970s American power and prestige were waning (Vietnam and the petroleum exporter states had taken a heavy toll), while in international economic affairs those of Japan and some European countries were rising.

In the 1990s the upsurge of American confidence in its world leadership associated with the end of the Cold War and the vigor of its high-tech revolution was countered by much more overt opposition to any such superpower domination or universalization of the American "mission." And thus, ironically, the sudden emergence of globalization (based so heavily on those two events) was faced with the reemergence of a very different view of the fundamentals of global change. In 1997, fifty years after *Time*'s touting of Toynbee, forty years after Lerner's claim for the United States itself, Samuel P. Huntington asserted that "a civilization-based world order is emerging." A civilization, he claimed, is "the highest cultural grouping of people," and these broad levels of identity "are shaping the patterns of cohesion, disintegration, and conflict in the post–Cold War world." His book, *The Clash of Civilizations and the Remaking of World Order,* was a direct challenge to glib assumptions about globalization based largely upon the impact of the communications revolution and to more substantial emphases on the power of economic systems; his argument has altered the agenda of debates about trends in world affairs. Our concern is much narrower than Huntington's topic, but our commentary will connect with his work at numerous points, not only because of America's position in the world order, but because his definitive concepts and culture areas are so closely (but only implicitly) related to those of historical cultural geography (even with specific themes that have occasionally appeared in the latter field: Meinig, "Culture Blocs and Political Blocs: Emergent Patterns in World Affairs" [1956]).

Our long geographical perspective on the shaping of America has emphasized the need always to see the United States—incipient or in being—as a complex structure and in larger context. From the first minimal consolidation of the nation in 1800 we have presented maps and commentaries at selected periods of development setting forth general areal patterns of the principal seats and regions of power, the fully Americanized area, outlying spheres of influence, and the nation's position in relation to bordering lands and peoples. We therefore conclude with such a geographical morphology at the close of the twentieth century (fig. 91).

THE WESTERN HEMISPHERE

The pattern of the central unit of this areal structure has been presented in "Reconfiguration" and "Reshaping the Nation," wherein we noted how decentralization has dissolved the power of the *Historic Core*, metropolitanization has resulted in an ever-tighter hierarchical network anchored on the twin *capitals* of New York City and Washington, and culturally creative California has been a national force. The entire transcontinental expanse is now a closely integrated *domain* in which regional distinctions continue to be apparent but everywhere modified from older patterns and generally facing strong pressures toward uniformity in the most intensely connected and expansive sectors of the settlement system.

Embedded within this national pattern is the highly uneven scattering of Indian reservations, an imperial residue of "nations within" grounded upon the crucial importance of tribal sovereignty. Such areas are too fragmented and permeable to warrant recognition as separate spheres at this scale of generalization. In contrast, although Native Alaskans do not enjoy such sovereign territorial status, they are the majority population across a broad, thinly settled expanse in the west and north much more removed from daily pressures of the ruling society and thus constitute a marginal fringe, a classic type of protectorate and *sphere* within the sovereign bounds of the federal republic. The remainder of the state, colonized Alaska, is an outlier of the American domain, and the Alaska Highway continues as a slender thread of American influence across the northwestern interior of Canada.

As already noted, proximate Canada has long been inescapably within the *sphere* of the United States and the extent and prospects of that influence a chronic matter of concern within that country. The post–World War II era brought some important changes in the context and character of these relationships. In 1949

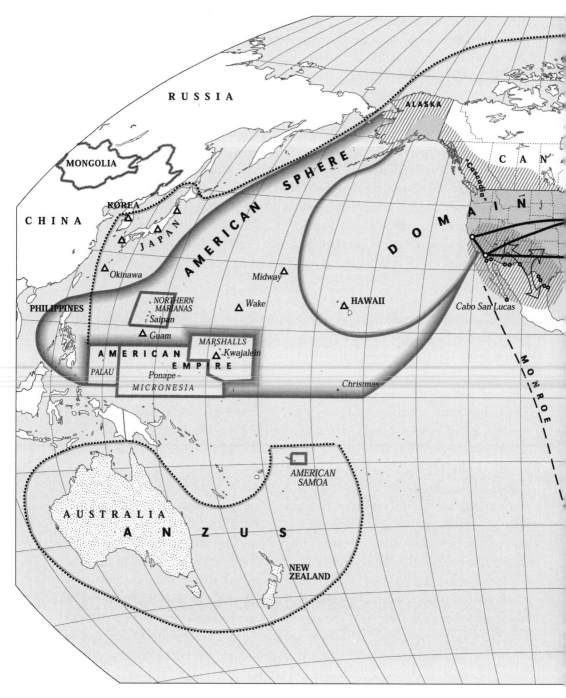

91. The United States in the World.

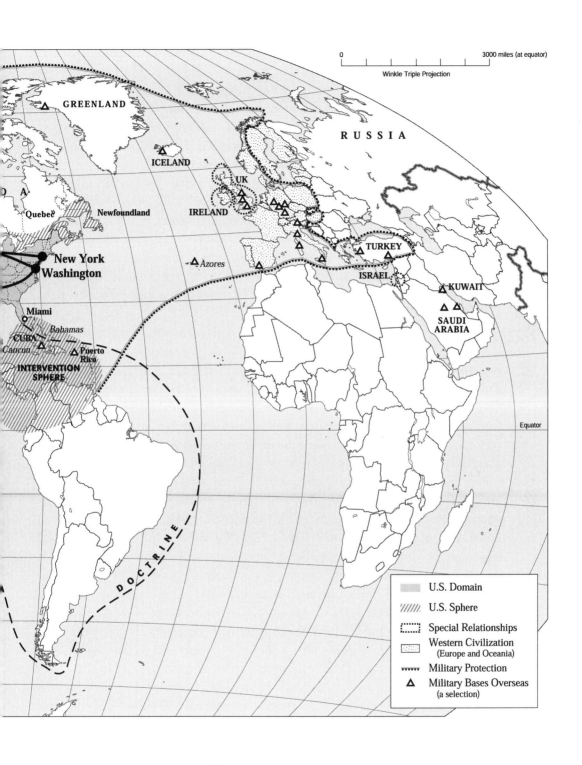

GREENLAND

ICELAND

UK

IRELAND

RUSSIA

Quebec   Newfoundland

New York
Washington

Azores

TURKEY

ISRAEL

KUWAIT

SAUDI
ARABIA

Miami

Bahamas

CUBA
Cancun

Puerto
Rico

INTERVENTION
SPHERE

Equator

D O C T R I N E

0   3000 miles (at equator)

Winkle Triple Projection

U.S. Domain

U.S. Sphere

Special Relationships

Western Civilization
(Europe and Oceania)

Military Protection

△   Military Bases Overseas
(a selection)

Newfoundland, "Britain's Oldest Colony," became "Canada's Youngest Province." It was a change intensely debated and only narrowly endorsed (52.3 percent) by island voters, the opposition favoring a return to virtual self-government or a further period as a colony managed from London. (In 1864 Newfoundland representatives had attended an early conference on forming a Canadian federation but soon decided not to join.) As for Canada, this addition would clearly be a costly burden in at least the near term, but there was fear that Newfoundland might "drift" into some kind of relationship, "even political union," with the United States; as Canada's Minister of External Affairs noted, his country's "place in world affairs would be better preserved by a territory which extended right out to the broad ocean and if access thereto was not closed to Canada by another sovereignty over the territories of Newfoundland and Labrador." Canada, however, had only a short while to enjoy the satisfaction of this geopolitical expansion before it was confronted with an upwelling new in strength and portent of its oldest and most serious internal problem.

A century after the Confederation was created as a political framework to accommodate the two Canadas, French and English, as deeply distinct but essentially—equivocally—equal partners, what would become known as the "Quiet Revolution" emerged in an energetically modernizing and increasingly secularizing Quebec. At a time when elsewhere in the world empires were dissolving and new states were emerging, its leaders now spoke more of a national future than of an historic past and sought formal recognition of *l'Etat Québécois* (they avoided the word *province*) as requiring some sort of special relationship with Canada. In 1980 a cautiously drafted referendum in Quebec seeking a "mandate to negotiate" a new "sovereignty-association" with Canada was rejected by a 60–40 margin (but francophone voters were about evenly split). Meanwhile a languages act of 1969 had established French and English as having "equality of status and equality of rights" in all the institutions of the federal government, but in 1977 Quebec made French *the* official language, with preferred status over English. As a result of this continuing agitation several major Canadian companies and many thousands of Anglophone residents (who had constituted an affluent quarter of the population and the dominating leadership) began to leave Montreal. Attempts by government to amend the constitution to recognize Quebec as a "distinct society" with special status have failed to be ratified by all provinces. In 1995 a second, rather more directly separatist, referendum was very narrowly rejected (50.6 percent) by Quebec voters. Although these insistent but highly controversial political aspirations have not succeeded, under vigorous Québécois leadership a long beleaguered province and people have been transformed into a modern, productive, assertively distinct society, a formal, quasi-autonomous French North American nation (but one that has not paid much attention to nor necessarily pleased francophone populations elsewhere in Canada).

Major changes in western provinces have produced further, if less ominous, geopolitical reverberations. Postwar developments of major oil, gas fields, and coal mines in Alberta brought a surge of growth and welcome diversification, booming Calgary into a major corporate center. British Columbia has experienced even stronger growth, accompanied by heavy shipments of timber, coal, and grain to Asian (especially Japanese) markets, and an unprecedented influx of Asian (chiefly Chinese) immigrants, including many with skills and wealth (particularly those from Hong Kong), transforming Vancouver into a thriving, highly attractive, cosmopolitan, Pacific Rim metropolis. The West has long been the generator of political dissent with the Laurentian core, and these recent developments have further altered the balances and representations of political power within the Confederation.

Such internal changes found further expression in external relations. All through this half century it was generally accepted that Canada needed ready access to American markets and capital, innovations and expertise, but there was always concern over how this close but asymmetrical relationship could be managed so as "to strengthen Canada rather than smother it." Thus beyond the common tool of tariffs, government intervention in various forms—limitations on foreign control, Canadian content quotas, subsidies for arts and institutions—was extensive. However, the 1988 Free Trade Act with the United States, followed five years later by the North American Free Trade Agreement (NAFTA), which brought in Mexico, marked an important shift in practice and perspectives. The acts themselves were obviously an endorsement of an important degree of "continentalism," and they gave new life to an old debate. Historically the term has referred to an inexorable eventual triumph of "natural geographic" north-south regional alignments over the "artificial" east-west line of political separation.

Recent talk of "Cascadia" provides the most prominent display of developments in that direction. Promoted by various business and nongovernmental groups in British Columbia, Washington, and Oregon, it combines "various visions and agendas at diminishing the barrier effect of the Canadian–United States border," especially along the "Cascade Corridor" between Vancouver and Eugene. A variety of (not always compatible) organizations, alliances, and conferences focus on improving infrastructure, the high-tech economy, commercial and cultural links with Asia, tourism, environmental, and a host of other issues, resulting in a heightened regional consciousness. A Western sense of alienation from Ottawa and Toronto has also promoted a "Greater Cascadia" to include Alberta, along with Alaska, Idaho, and Montana. In either case, these developments point more toward ad hoc transnational planning regions than to any serious attempt to shift the international boundary.

On the other side of the continent, whereas Quebec leaders in the past had feared social contamination from the materialistic republic and proclaimed their country as a "refuge . . . amid the immense sea of saxonizing Americanism," recent ones have been strong proponents of these free trade agreements, confident of advantageous participation, secure in their francophone stronghold, and eager for tourists and cultural exchanges. Meanwhile Ontario, long the main seat of a "branch plant economy," has prospered on earlier automobile industry agreements and remains closely locked into larger continental relationships, with Toronto a major center in a North American metropolitan hierarchy.

The United States had no expansionist program to subordinate Canada. (American leaders were careful to assure Ottawa that Quebec separatism was entirely an internal matter and fended off Québécois attempts to prefigure any American response.) To Americans continentalism was simply an incremental expansion of mutual benefits: free trade would enrich the larger whole, culture was a set of marketable commodities serving common demands, and greater cooperation was a logical response to shared problems. On the other side, George Grant, one of the strongest voices of Canadian nationalism, directed his famous *Lament for a Nation* of 1965 at his own compatriots for allowing Canada to become "a branch-plant society of American capitalism." "The power of the American government to control Canada," he said, "does not lie primarily in its ability to exert direct pressure; the power lies in the fact that the dominant classes in Canada see themselves at one with the continent on all essential matters"—noting, as well, that "branch-plant economies have branch-plant cultures." In such polemics the power of continentalism may be exaggerated. Canadian supporters of an open "North American regional marketplace" insisted "that 'system' need not be synonymous with 'hegemony.'" As Randy Widdis has emphasized, "Canada still exists as a country with many layers of identity"; "over time, Canada developed national economies and political-cultural institutions which transcended internal regional boundaries and provided a counterbalance to the North-South integrative forces existing within transborder regions." As Cole Harris, another strong Canadian voice, has observed about "lived-in Canada" (those five major compartments lying along the boundary), it has been bound together by "a web of experiences" giving an "emotional structure" to its internal regionalism and, considering its larger geopolitical context, a remarkable stability. Canadians have long shared a continental house with a giant and have adapted to that situation in many ways; it remains a duplex, each furnished and run differently despite much borrowing by the smaller household from the larger. Canada cannot escape from the U.S. sphere of influence, but it has not become simply a northern "America."

Relations with the southern neighbors of the United States are far more complex. In Mexico a few recently developed resort centers, such as Cabo San Lucas and Cancún, are in effect rather isolated exclaves of pervasive Americanization. The Mexican halves of the interdependent binational cities spaced along the border are clearly within the American *sphere,* and the well-recognized norteño regionalism marks a further gradation of influence. Beyond these, however, the pattern and concept becomes much more blurred. As Octavio Paz put it, for Mexicans the United States is "an *other* that is inseparable from us and that at the same time is radically and essentially alien." It is "another civilization . . . another language; . . . another time (the United States is running after the future while we are still tied to our past). . . . Yet . . . it is right next to us. The United States is always present among us, even when it ignores us or turns its back on us: its shadow covers the entire continent. It is the shadow of a giant." Thus even as NAFTA and welcomed modernizations multiply reciprocal economic ties and as millions of Mexicans have direct experience or active connections with communities in the United States, such people "have shown a remarkable capacity for *not* adapting to American society. . . . In Mexico it has not been the professionals of anti-imperialism who have put up the strongest resistance, but the humble folk who make pilgrimages to the Sanctuary of the Virgin of Guadalupe. Our country survives thanks to its traditionalism." Those professionals, however, are ever alert to the threat of U.S. hegemony in any form and in a sense retaliated in 1998 by formally approving dual citizenship for Mexicans born or naturalized in a foreign land. Thus, given the strong increases and impact of the Mexican presence within the United States and these continuing relationships with their ancestral homeland, it is perhaps appropriate to recognize a special category of overlapping national-cultural spheres of influence.

As earlier noted, Puerto Rico exhibits some of these same features in special form: a century of influence wherein modernization was obviously Americanization and, with cheap air travel, a half century of close interactions between homeland and mainland and 40 percent of Puerto Ricans now resident on the continent; yet in terms of history, culture, and homogeneity the island "possesses all the attributes of a nation," Spanish remains the dominant tongue despite efforts to impose English, and few consider themselves American beyond a narrow legal sense. Puerto Rico's special commonwealth status remains an uneasy compromise between nationalist and statehood movements, both of which are keenly sensitive to matters of equality and dignity in relations with the United States.

Cuba represents a truly paradoxical case within this American *sphere:* embargoed and ostracized by the United States, but deeply fettered and affected by the presence of the large expatriate community in the United States. As Louis A. Pérez, Jr., has emphasized, the evolution of a Cuban nation "involved Cubans in the appropriation of American forms, adapting them to their own needs, reshaping them to their own image," and all this "took hold not through compulsion or coercion but by way of assent and acquiescence." Cubans admired American achievements and even as the United States intervened politically and economically did not generally regard themselves as subjugated. Only in the new conditions of the postwar world did it become obvious that "Cubans had fashioned a version of the North in the tropics, one that created high expectations but had no capacity to deliver." The revolution of 1959, intent on "Cubanizing Cuba," was such an abrupt shift in national direction that it soon impelled a mass exodus of much of the business and professional classes to Miami. The United States, obsessively involved in the Cold War, sought to overthrow Castro; when that failed and the Cuban Missile Crisis was resolved, the United States imposed a punitive policy of isolation and deprivation designed to demonstrate the high cost of such defiance of American interests and "serve as an object lesson to other Western Hemisphere countries."

"The Cuban revolution not only transformed Cuba but dictated the course of America's Caribbean policy. . . . Preventing another Castro became the overriding American goal," and this American Mediterranean has continued to be a vast interventionist sphere with American military operations and political pressures asserted in more than a dozen states spanning this highly fragmented geopolitical arena from Belize to Grenada and Trinidad, including the "war against drugs" in Colombia and other Andean states, and strategic concerns over Venezuelan oil.

In view of this pervasive concern the American withdrawal from Panama at the end of the century stands as an important and unusual geopolitical change. Panamanian nationalists had long sought enhancements of Panamanian presence and diminution of the American, symbolic and functional, in their country. Periodic riots pressured toward revisions in relationships, and a sequence of new treaties was negotiated. In 1964 President Lyndon Johnson announced an American intention to build a new sea-level canal (not necessarily in Panama) and recognize Panamanian sovereignty over the existing one, with the United States continuing to operate and defend it; the ensuing treaties created a storm of dissent in Congress and were rejected by both countries. Renewal of agitations in the 1970s raised the same problems, but in the aftermath of Vietnam and Watergate, weary of such protests, and reassured by the Joint Chiefs of Staff that the military bases were no longer essential and that a friendly Panama would be better than a chronically antagonistic partner, the American administration signed new treaties in 1977 that abolished the Canal Zone and replaced it with a joint commission (five Americans, four Panamanians) to run the canal until December 31, 1999, with American bases to continue only by Panamanian permission after that date. The usual vociferous protests about "giving away our canal" were countered by support from shipping lobbies, banking interests, and others, and by larger diplomatic concerns, especially widespread criticisms from the Organization of American States. A serious clash between U.S. and Panamanian forces in 1989 hastened preparations, and by the end of 1999 the canal was turned over to Panama; all American bases had been closed and forces relocated to Puerto Rico, which became the military headquarters for this entire sector.

The Bahamas and about half of the Lesser Antilles have become independent states, the rest continuing under some degree of British, French, Dutch, or American rule; all are linked with migrant communities in and by general ties of language, customs, and economies with their respective imperial homelands. A strong localism persists in all this insular Afro-Caribbean World, yet even though its Virgin Islands are the only U.S. holding (an unincorporated territory of 115,000 residents), the rapid rise and pervasive impacts of air travel, cruise ships, recreation, and tourism have brought this region under ever-stronger influences of American mass culture. Propinquity and the sheer variety and density of these asymmetrical relationships in addition to century-old security priorities have made the entire circum-Caribbean an American sphere.

Beyond this active interventionist sphere the remainder of Latin America remains a set of countries involved with the United States in important ways but continuing to resent and resist the pressures of a now even greater Colossus of the North with its own formulations of Pan Americanism. In Ibero-America, initiated from a distinctly different European culture hearth and, as Octavio Paz put it, having "had neither the intellectual revolution" of the Reformation and Renaissance, "nor a democratic revolution of the bourgeoisie," modernization has been delayed, impeded, and warped by powerful traditional sociopolitical structures; the North American example has often inspired Latin American liberals, but over most of the twentieth century, the United States has been more generally regarded as "the protector of tyrants and the ally of the enemies of democracy."

AMERICA IN THE PACIFIC

In the Pacific the American position still stands astride the thin imperial line suddenly formed a century ago (Hawaii–Midway–Wake–Guam–the Philippines) but with further additions and modifications to form what is now a broadened sphere of quite disparate parts.

The granting of statehood to Hawaii in effect certified it as an acceptably "Americanized" area, a *domain* fully equal in status with its federal associates on the mainland (with Native Hawaiians, like Indians, a remnant typical of imperial expansion). At the other end of the line, the Philippines evolved in an opposite direction to full independence, yet the impress of America holds it more or less willingly within the American *sphere*. As H. W. Brands noted, "When Philippine independence arrived, it resulted less from a Filipino desire to have done with

America than from an American desire to have done with the Philippines"; thus "in the ninety year process by which power shifted from Americans to Filipinos, . . . the transfer of sovereignty in 1946 signaled no abrupt change. The devolution of power traced a reasonably smooth course, with formal imperialism shading into informal imperialism." This latter term referred especially to the continuance of military bases and alignment with American policies on China and Southeast Asia in return for continuing economic aid. As in Panama, the bases became a chronic source of political agitations, and a special "parity" agreement, by which American citizens and corporations retained the same rights of Filipinos to own property, resources, industries, and public utilities became a rasping exhibit of "continuing colonialism." In 1974 parity was unilaterally terminated by the Philippine president, and five years later he successfully pressured for formal recognition of Philippine sovereignty over U.S. bases and five-year review periods of this relationship. By this time the United States was assessing whether such bases were worth the trouble and cost (in economic aid and accusations of imperialism). When even more severe pressures were renewed in 1991, the United States decided to pull out (its big air base had been ruined that year by a volcanic eruption).

These political agitations were powered by a striving for national dignity rather than any strong anti-Americanism. Filipinos have long been open to many American influences; school texts detail how their American heritage has contributed to their distinctive cultural identity, English is a co-official "national" language (along with Tagalog); it is widely spoken and regarded by many of the middle class and elites as their "native" tongue. A general emphasis on strong extended family networks and the persistence of a small dominating elite exhibit basic resistance to some important American values, but a half century of American tutelage followed by even more pervasive American contacts—including close ties with the million and a half Filipinos resident in the United States (and long-standing recruitment of Filipinos for the U.S. Navy)—have kept this independent nation closely associated with its former imperial ruler.

The abandonment of bases in the Philippines left the American strategic front in the Pacific defined by military installations in Okinawa, Japan, and South Korea. The United States recognizes Japan's residual sovereignty over the first of these (and has returned the rest of the Ryukyu chain to Japan), but its huge set of bases dominates the island. Japan and South Korea are, of course, deeply distinct societies, and no matter how influential fifty years of American policies have been in various matters at various times these countries are military protectorates, and their national aspirations surely do not include any subordination to the United States.

Having conquered the Japanese empire in the Western Pacific, the United

States was determined to hold onto this vast scattering of archipelagoes across an ocean expanse equal in breadth to that of the continental United States. In 1947 it arranged to govern these islands as a Strategic Trusteeship under the jurisdiction of the United Nations Security Council (on which of course it had veto power). All Japanese residents (about 85,000 in 1940 but many lost in war) were repatriated, leaving small indigenous populations (totaling about 50,000) on the best of the thousands of these atolls or volcanic isles. American policy for this sudden expansion of empire has gone through three phases. The first was entirely focused on military use, most notoriously for the testing of atomic bombs on Bikini and Enewetok atolls, whose residents had been persuaded to evacuate "for the good of mankind and to end all wars" (winds blew the radioactive fallout across their new island homes); in another corner of this expanse Tinian became a military base, and the CIA took over Saipan for the training of Chinese guerrillas. Public access was severely restricted, and local populations were encouraged to follow traditional ways. In the 1960s a program of American modernization was undertaken, featuring schools and other social services, airports and roads, and various forms of economic aid.

In the 1970s more locally responsive longer-term relationships with the different sectors of this island empire were begun. The Chamorro people of the Northern Marianas had earlier sought to reintegrate with adjacent Guam (separated from the rest by American acquisition in 1898); but Guam, much the largest, most populous, and developed of the chain, rejected any such amalgamation. Therefore in 1975 the Marianas voted strongly in favor of a commonwealth status, whereby they would become American citizens and enjoy local self-government under the constitution and protection of the United States. On January 1, 1978, these islands, with their 20,000 people, became a formal territorial addition to the United States.

The Polynesian people of Micronesia elected to go in a different direction, resulting in the formation of the Freely Associated States of Micronesia (with a capital at Kolonia, on Ponape), subdivided into the Republic of the Marshall Islands, Republic of Palau, and the Federated States of Micronesia (the Carolines). The United States treats these areas "in large measure as independent countries" having received authority from their own people in an act of self-determination and entered into a contractual relationship with the United States. Their 135,000 people are not American citizens and the U.S. Constitution does not apply. In 1986 the U.N. Trusteeship was terminated. The United States remains in charge of foreign affairs, defense, and the right to deny other countries any military presence. The most important American presence is the Kwajalein Army Missile Base. Local economies are heavily dependent on fishing and tourism.

Two thousand miles south of Hawaii is American Samoa, the nation's only out-

post in the South Pacific. It remains an unincorporated territory under the Department of the Interior; the 35,000 Samoans are not U.S. citizens and govern themselves under a Samoa Code of customary law incorporated into their 1960 constitution. Their nearest neighbors, Western Samoa, Tonga, and Fiji, are independent
states; farther to the west New Caledonia, and to the east French Polynesia, remain
under French authority, which has generated strong local protests, especially when
the French resumed nuclear testing in Polynesia in the 1990s. Samoa has not been
militarized, the United States looking to New Zealand and Australia as formal and
reliable allies in this distant sector. However, its own nuclear-powered naval vessels
have not been welcomed in New Zealand, and its foreign policies have been frequently criticized in both countries.

The United States has been the sole Great Power of the Pacific for more than
fifty years, but perspectives and positions have changed. Its strategic front, formed
in the 1950s as a Rimland bulwark against the Communist Bloc, has been reduced
in scale and become less certain in purpose with the strong emergence of China as
the Great Power of East Asia. Its bases, especially in South Korea and Okinawa,
have generated popular local protests even though still providing a military shield
not unwelcome to political leaders of those countries who must adjust to living
with their rapidly developing neighbor. West of Hawaii the enlarged American island empire is of little economic or cultural interest and, aside from Kwajalein, is
primarily a preventive occupation to deny use to any other power.

AMERICA AND EUROPE

The shape of America's position across the Atlantic displays some similar features
but is far more deeply rooted and complex than that in the Pacific.

An outer line of formal military protection extends from the Arctic base of
Thule in Danish Greenland to Keflavík in Iceland, includes several large bases
shared with the Royal Air Force in Britain, a large number of ground and air bases
in Germany, others in western Turkey, Italy (including Sicily and Sardinia), Atlantic Spain, and the Azores (Portuguese). The central purpose of this NATO system, created by the Cold War, became suddenly less clear in the 1990s. The United
States began to encourage an increasing role for European forces to deal with European problems, as in the difficult case of Bosnia, and in 1999 the alliance was extended eastward to include the former Soviet satellites of the Czech Republic,
Hungary, and Poland—to the unease of an uncertain Russia.

This military network generally encompassed the emerging European Community, but although the United States had an important role in assisting the initial
formation of that remarkable geopolitical experiment (especially in Germany, and

overall with critical economic aid), and although relationships of many kinds at all levels between America and Western Europe thrive as never before, these nations (Austria, Sweden, and Finland were added in 1995) are resistant to any expression of subordination to American pressures and, notably in the case of France, overtly critical of American pretensions.

There are, of course, gradations to all such generalizations, and any geocultural overview must recognize the "special relationship" between Britain and the United States. This hackneyed expression is reflective of obvious American foundations, and even as the new nation focused on its westward expansion and for a time regarded Britain as a rival those "dynamic reciprocities" across the Atlantic were strengthening. In economic and larger geopolitical terms the United States was the more dependent during the nineteenth century, followed by an inexorable reversal of roles in the twentieth. The significance and basis of this broad shift in power was aptly put by Otto von Bismarck in his 1898 response to a query as to what he considered to be the decisive factor in modern history: "The fact that the North Americans speak English." Americans who might currently assume that the role of English as a global language was largely of their own making need to understand that much the greatest foundation for that dominance was laid by the British Empire—formal (political) and informal (financial and commercial). Aside from the growth of the United States itself, the American role has largely been an accompaniment of their own much shorter superpower status and leadership in the recent computer and communications revolution. Sharing a language has of course been a major factor in the volume and intensity of transatlantic interactions, such as the attraction of American academic posts to British-trained faculty and their considerable influence on many fields (including geography). Despite various geopolitical strains (such as during the dissolution of Britain's empire), this relationship has never been fundamentally endangered.

Ireland represents its own variation of a special relationship. The presence within the United States of a large, self-conscious Irish ethnic population together with the high intensity of modern Irish nationalism has bound together the peoples (but not governments) on either side of the Atlantic. The traffic between the two has long been high and become somewhat more balanced in recent years during unprecedented Irish prosperity. Individual American politicians and other leaders as well as large amounts of American money have played a role in Irish affairs for years.

The case of Israel is far more complex. Israel is not in Europe, but it was essentially European in both the positive and negative aspects of its immediate origins as a national state. American Jews have helped populate Israel and sustain and shape U.S. policy toward the state, and cultural, scientific, and various professional as well as familial relations between the two countries have been close. The U.S. government has given economic and especially military aid and has become the de facto guarantor of Israel's security in a volatile region. Yet this fifty-year relationship has been fraught with tensions and frustrations on both sides because while the nations share certain values and interests, their overall concerns and strategies diverge on critical matters. Whereas the United States seeks stability and continued access to oil in the Middle East, Israel seeks to consolidate its hold and expand its settlements in contested Palestinian lands. While Israel has been to some degree a client state it is certainly no satellite; in some sense its insistent independent policies hold the United States hostage by its aggressive actions against local Arabs; attempts by several American administrations to broker a peace between Israelis and Palestinians have failed.

Underlying these particular relationships is the general sharing of Western Culture. The great modern geographical feature of that dominant civilization is the existence of distinct creative core areas on either side of the Atlantic; a persistent historical feature has been ideological tensions between these two centers despite their intricate ties. Beyond all practical concerns over shifts in the balances of economic and political power have been contrasts in cultural characteristics and assumed or relegated roles. Long expressed in clichés about Old and New, Past and Future, Static and Dynamic, such stereotypes are grounded on substantial differences. There is much in the American model and example that goes against the grain of European values and experience and generates fears about distinct American versions of freedom, democracy, individualism, progress, and related ideals. These concerns are further aggravated by their Wilsonian propagation. As the *New York Times* editorial noted on the final day of the twentieth century: "The idealistic desire to make the world over is the deepest mystery of the American character and our signature national trait." The sheer scale and momentum of this single, self-confident American republic contrasted with a recurrently war-torn, multinational Europe further accentuates these intramural tensions. Complaints, of course, flow both ways across the Atlantic. American criticisms of Europe can be quite as severe, even if rather less common and intense—more indifferent and dismissive than consistently and deeply concerned. Our emphasis here is simply to suggest the complications as well as the fundamentals of America's situation within this larger civilizational complex.

A WIDER PERSPECTIVE

Beyond this historic familial Western frame the structure of America's position is limited and fragile. The United States offers military aid and has "security assis-

92. Paradox of Power.

The United Nations Headquarters represents the dream and the role of the United States in its creation. The United Nations itself was very much a product of Franklin D. Roosevelt's insistent Wilsonian vision of a New World Order, its location in the United States and on Manhattan an obvious result of America's unrivaled global and New York City's national power. The specific site, a 17.5-acre parcel being assembled for speculative commercial development, was a gift of the Rockefellers. The architecture represents a consensus of an international team (under the direction of an American architect closely associated with the Rockefellers) that this sleek, slender, modernist slab, a "functional" design transcending national and cultural associations, would best convey the vision of a rational, peaceful, progressive world. (As Jane C. Loeffler notes, the curious little dark dome over the long Assembly building was hastily added as "a nod to tradition" in hopes of appeasing the U.S. Congress and obtaining a loan for construction costs.)

The paradox arises from the presence of this international organization seated in its own exclusive district (a formal legal exclave) within the body of the United States. Many Americans were and are suspicious of the United Nations as a rival, even subversive agency loaded with petty states and a bloated bureaucracy, threatening to interfere with American interests and actions in the world; the United States was often at odds with its programs and in arrears in its dues. Yet the United States also turned to it to legitimate some of its own actions and has welcomed U.N. assumption of various welfare and peacekeeping tasks. After half a century in its East River home the United Nations remains the one great truly global forum and an active instrument for worthy causes; even its modernist architecture, harshly criticized at the outset—then duplicated in every modern city—stands here as a monument to the vision of a creative historical moment. (© Royalty-Free/CORBIS)

93. Capital of Capitalism.

Conceived in the 1950s, under construction in the 1960s, dedicated in 1973, but not completed until 1977, the World Trade Center spanned eras so different as to raise serious doubts about its purpose or prospects. Very much the product of David Rockefeller's vision to do for the financial district of Lower Manhattan what Rockefeller Center had done for Midtown in the 1930s and 1940s, and of the concern of the powerful bistate (New York, New Jersey) Port Authority to revitalize New York's role as a premier world port, this massive development arrived in full form amid a city in financial crisis, a collapsed real estate market, a shift of seaborne traffic to new docks in New Jersey, and heavy criticism of any such gigantic, intrusive "urban renewal" project (and these were the world's tallest buildings for only a month after their dedication—yielding to the Sears Tower in Chicago).

David Rockefeller insisted on something exceptional, exciting, a creation of "catalytic bigness" to dramatize his grand project. Seattle-born Minoru Yamasaki responded with these towers as an expression of his own sense that "beauty through structure and technology" would be specifically reflective of American culture. His design engendered a torrent of derision from other architects and urban specialists ("stolid, banal monoliths"; "an arrogant intrusion into the jagged splendor of the beloved skyline"—to quote two architectural guidebooks), but this simple, slender, soaring pair of towers captured the imagination of the public as an irresistible icon, a new, unchallenged focal point, and an instant world symbol of America. It took years and lures to banks, insurance companies, brokerage firms, and others beyond the realm of international trade to fill all that space, but it became the workplace of 40,000. Shocking confirmation of its symbolic importance came on February 26, 1993, when foreign terrorists drove a truck loaded with explosives into a basement garage hoping to blast out a corner and topple a tower; the tower

withstood the blast, but six died, 1,000 were injured, and major changes were made in the plaza and lower levels.

At the far right in this photograph stands a more venerated and powerful symbol relating to another aspect of America and the world. (© Joseph Sohm; ChromoSohm Inc./CORBIS)

tance personnel" working with local military forces in many countries, and in times of special need, such as the Gulf War in 1991, friendly states may make facilities available to U.S. forces (as by Egypt, Oman, and Saudi Arabia in that case), but any American base in Saudi Arabia is intrinsically as vulnerable to political upheaval as was a large air base in Libya in the 1960s or the intensive political partnership with Iran before 1978. The United States has shown great flexibility in its military adjustment to changing geopolitical conditions, but our concern is with physical presence and cultural influence rather than the striking range of air forces and fleets, and those revolutionary responses of Islamic nationalism are, in that sense, merely one of the more extreme reactions to foreign presence and pressures.

However much the non-Western world has been disturbed, destabilized, or forced to undergo what Theodore Von Laue has called "an internal revolution of reculturation," it remains anchored in specific societies, great and small. Whether these are denoted as "civilizations," "culture worlds," or a complex array of "culture areas" is a problem of classification that need not divert us from our limited theme;

suffice to recall William McNeill's 1950s conclusion that "of all the problems which today confront mankind, the antipathy between races and cultures seem likely to endure the longest and prove the most difficult to handle because it is the most permanently and deeply rooted in human instinct and impulse."

American popular culture in its many forms readily spreads onto the surface of these other societies, or at least sectors thereof, and it may become a symbol or tool of those seeking internal change of traditional ways, but its consumption does not represent an enduring American imprint. The United States is the greatest seat of economic power, but, as Agnew and Corbridge suggest, the recent "globalization of modern life" is best viewed as a complex form of "transnational liberalism," an emerging hegemony of "a new ideology *of the market* . . . embedded in and reproduced by a powerful constituency of liberal states, international institutions, and what might be called the 'circuits of capital' themselves." Capitalism is obviously adaptable to a wide range of different societies, and not only is the American version not replicable elsewhere, some of its more extreme forms of freedom, individualism, and privatism, its seemingly blind worship of perpetual economic growth and mass consumption regardless of social and environmental impacts, are not widely admired. That technical innovations may foster social changes in such directions is a product of modernization that is far from exclusively American.

Furthermore, global economic and informational systems have not noticeably weakened deeply emotional *nationalisms*—least of all that of the United States. As geographer Marwyn Samuels noted, "One of the central lessons to be learned from the much blood-soaked history of the twentieth century is that place prevails as an object of intense loyalty," and "the much heralded 'death of place' is counterfactual or at least as absurd as the more recently proclaimed 'death of history.' . . . This is not to deny large-scale, global processes, but to deny that these processes work everywhere, or mean the same thing everywhere in the same way, and without resistance."

The end of the Cold War brought an upsurge of triumphalism that seemed to display to the rest of the world the most feared features of modern American nationalism: its universalism and its militarism—the American Mission and the American Empire—Superculture as well as Superpower (figs. 92–94). The strength of opposition to such pretensions and assertions was likely more extensive and effective than generally appreciated by Americans, and therefore our map of the positions of the United States in the world may be more confined than common impressions about its influence and impact might suggest. American society is so fundamentally, peculiarly, geared to movement and change that its people are likely to misread the potential for similar alterations elsewhere in the face of the conservatism at the core of most societies.

94. Massive Seat of Militarism.

Washington is a highly symbolic capital, its landscape larded with powerful icons of American political concepts, its leaders, and its historic experience. But across the Potomac in Virginia in a massive, dull, functional building surrounded by immense trafficways and parking lots lies the most basic symbol of national power. Laid out during World War II, it has emerged as a new *citadel*, housing the "modernized megamachine commanding 'absolute' powers of destruction." As the Cold War was well under way and Eisenhower was giving his farewell warning about the "military-industrial complex," Lewis Mumford, writing his final summation of the city in history, issued his own, more penetrating, commentary: "in less than a decade, have come one-way communication, the priestly monopoly of secret knowledge, the multiplication of secret agencies, the suppression of open discussion, and even the insulation of error against public criticism and exposure through a 'bi-partisan' military and foreign policy, which in practice nullifies public reaction and makes rational dissent the equivalent of patriotic disaffection, if not treason. The dismantling of this repressive citadel will prove a far harder task than the demolition of the baroque fortifications" (an example of the latter shares the photographic page with the Pentagon in *The City in History*). Unlike some of Mumford's perspectives and polemics, this symbolism of the Pentagon remained pertinent, year by year, through the remainder of the century. (Aerial view of the Pentagon, 1962; AP/WIDE WORLD PHOTOS)

This last feature, however, also points toward a sharp counter to all these foreign resistances and fears. As we earlier noted, one of the defining features of Global America has been an immigration as diverse as the peoples of the world, drawn to the United States from nearly two hundred foreign lands. In such movements individuals, families, and groups are necessarily involved in social change and an orientation to the future. Moreover, immigrants are only one category of the multitudes who have been attracted to America. A continuing, widening stream of people—students and teachers, nurses and doctors, scientists and researchers of all kinds, writers, artists, and entertainers, casual visitors and keen opportunists, people at all levels of society—have chosen to spend many months or years in this country. However varied their exposure and experience or their likes and dislikes in what they have encountered, sojourners and settlers alike perpetuate the fame of the United States as an Open Society, a welcoming "dynamic society, endlessly moving on, rebuilding itself, with little reverence for the past and few fixed boundaries."

The willingness to accept and ability to integrate a widening range of immigrants has been one of the defining (and at times intensely debated) features of American society for two centuries. The attraction of a large number of energetic, creative, seriously interested sojourners is more recent, reflecting not only the high quality of many American institutions but also a widely assumed need of direct experience with the ways and means of this sole superpower for eventual use at home. Power projected outward is thereby converted to power drawing inward. As a result of these movements there are people in virtually every country of the world with kinship, neighborly ties, or personal experience with some part or parts of the United States and with the American people. Whatever the feelings might be at other levels about international policies of the American government, these human bonds continue. Thus *America as Magnet*, creating those close personal links on a scale utterly unequaled elsewhere, must be recognized and emphasized, even if impossible to measure or map for our depiction of America and the World.

Just as the creation of an Atlantic World was the essential broad view for the beginning of our study, we have concluded our 500-year perspective on the shaping of America with a view spanning three-quarters of the globe. In between, in this geographic examination of history as place and space, we have focused on a wide range of scales—localities, towns, and cities, colonies, districts, and regions, territories and states, sections and the nation, as well as continent, hemisphere, and other large sectors of the world—whatever seemed appropriate to the continuous processes of areal formation and function. In the terms of Henry Glassie's epigram for the entire work, we have chosen prospects at various heights, mapped selectively what we have seen, and provided an extensive set of maps of the past to be useful to the modern traveler.

Sources of Quotations

PART ONE

p. 4 "roads in the United States are said to be the worst": Joy, "Transcontinental Trails," 160

p. 4 *The Horseless Age* declaration: Flink, *America Adopts the Automobile*, 22

p. 4 "a horseless city" . . . a "flyless city": Karolevitz, *This Was Trucking*, 26

p. 4 "The motor vehicle . . . accepted as an integral part of American life": Flink, *America Adopts the Automobile*, 51

p. 4 "the problem of good roads is not surpassed in importance": H. Doc. 1510, 63d Cong., 3d sess., January 21, 1915, 14

p. 5 "for practical purposes, the railway station is the terminus of roads": Rep. Dorsey W. Shockleford, quoted in U.S. Dept. of Transportation, FHA, *America's Highways*, 86

p. 5 "This 'corvée,' or forced-labor system": Shaler, *American Highways*, 24, 23

p. 5 "Today, in the rich state of Iowa not a wheel turns": Henry Joy, quoted in Hokanson, *Lincoln Highway*, 97

p. 7 on Progressive reforms: Seely, *Building American Highway System*, 25, 33

p. 7 sequence of quotations from 1916 act: S. Report 250, 64th Cong., 1st sess., March 10, 1916, 1, 15, 4, 8

p. 7 Wilson's interest in "the nationalization of America": *Papers*, vol. 38, 415

p. 8 Wilson, "transportation problem is exceedingly serious": *Address of the President*, H. Doc. 1, 64th Cong., 1st sess., December 7, 1915, 13

p. 10 "four years of conflict have put us in a new era": *Engineering News-Record* 81, November 28, 1918, 967

p. 10 "sudden" and "complete" failure of roads: BPR report, 1918, quoted in *America's Highways*, 117

p. 10 "present day traffic descended . . . like an avalanche": Seely, *Building American Highway System*, 72

p. 10 "a national system of highways . . . by the Federal Government": *Engineering News-Record* 81, December 19, 1918, 1108, 1145ff.

p. 10 "crystallizing element": Mehren, "Suggested National Highway Policy," 1114

p. 10 "Coast-to-Coast Rock Highway": Hokanson, *Lincoln Highway*, 6

p. 10 "the most enduring memorial": Joy, "Transcontinental Trails," 165

p. 10 "establishment of a continuous improved highway": Hokanson, *Lincoln Highway*, 11

p. 11 "blossomed into a dense and unruly matting of named roads": Hokanson, *Lincoln Highway*, 105

p. 11 "the dignity of a separate major arm of government": Mehren, "Suggested National Highway Policy," 116

p. 13 "expedite the completion of an adequate and interconnected system": Holt, *Bureau of Public Roads*, 87

p. 13 Pennsylvania system of "the main travelled roads" and California statute for roads "so laid out and constructed": H. Doc. 1510, 63d Cong., 3d sess., 165, 123

p. 13 BPR index revealing major centers "through which diagrammatic routes could be laid out": Edwin W. James, in charge of project, quoted in *America's Highways*, 108

p. 13 "100 mi. seemed to have marked the limit of such hauls": MacDonald, "Classification and Uses of Highways," 985

p. 15 numbering system and shield "to give them a conspicuous place": James, "Making and Unmaking a National System," 16

p. 17 "cross-country highways . . . unnecessary": *America's Highways*, 39

p. 17 "It has been well said that the railroads decided": Smith and Phillips, *North America*, 140

p. 17 "the whole population of the United States . . . could have been put into automobiles": Keir, *March of Commerce*, 312

p. 18 "Our main roads are merely connected neighborhood roads": *Engineering News-Record* 117, August 27, 1936, 317

p. 18 "Germany has the roads while we have the traffic": quoted in Seely, *Building American Highway System*, 148

p. 18 "We are proceeding on the principle that the utilization of the highways": quoted in Seely, *Building American Highway System*, 161

p. 18 "not the reasoned thought of engineers": editorial, *Engineering News-Record* 120, February 17, 1938, 256

p. 19 Geddes, *Magic Motorways*, 4, 3, 11, 280–81

p. 20 "in a startling way how dependent the United States had become": *America's Highways*, 148

p. 20 "so located as to connect by routes . . . the principal metropolitan areas": *Highway Needs*, H. Doc. 249, 81st Cong., 1st sess., 71

p. 20 "there was no thought of requiring that every mile of the system": *America's Highways*, 158

p. 23 "what they managed to secure . . . was federal funding": Rose, *Interstate*, 98, 96

p. 23 "few industries have arisen so rapidly": Hilton and Due, *Electric Interurban*, 3

p. 23 "a transitional step from . . . steam railroad to automobile": Hilton and Due, *Electric Interurban*, vii

p. 25 trucking "grew like a field of weeds": Goddard, *Getting There*, 86

p. 25 "coordination of all existing transportation agencies": Little and Cunningham, *Historical Development*, 88

p. 25 "I believe that there is a place . . . for both the railroad and the truck": Joseph H. Hays, *Proceedings of Nat. Assoc. of RR and UC*, 152

p. 26 "the tide of heavy trucks rolling northward": *Delaware*, American Guide Series, 319

p. 27 "It is probable that no invention . . . was ever diffused with such rapidity": *Recent Social Trends*, 172

p. 27 The automobile has touched our "national soul": cited in Flink, *Car Culture*, 161

p. 28 loss of "community" from the changing "*structure* of rural social life": Berger, *Devil Wagon*, 212

p. 29 "stupendous difficulties and expense": U.S. Congress, *Toll Roads and Free Roads*, 94

p. 29 "ran counter to the most deeply ingrained tradition": *American Highways*, 159–60

p. 30 "Detroit automobile makers set off the most effective Yankee invasion": Thomas D. Clark, quoted in Flink, *Car Culture*, 152

p. 30 Stewart on "motoring": *U.S. 40*, 27

p. 30 "Travel for necessity and travel for the sake of travel": *Recent Social Trends*, 186

p. 31 "young bloods . . . talking golf, polo, and motor cars": Pomeroy, *In Search of the Golden West*, 126

p. 31 "the first real monument to the Motor Age" and "first linear downtown": Banham, *Los Angeles*, 84

p. 31 "the Fifth Avenue of the West": Krim, "Imagery in Search of a City," 252

p. 32 Los Angeles had a "chance . . . of showing the right way of doing things": quoted in Foster, "Model-T," 481

p. 33 "essential expression of the automotive culture of Los Angeles": Krim, "Imagery in Search of a City," 59

p. 33 "as it flickered before Middle America in darkened movie halls": Kevin Starr, quoted in Foster, "Role of the Automobile," 189

p. 33 Stewart on his generation having "grown up . . . with the automobile": *U.S. 40*, 29

p. 33 Mumford on "the new machines followed not their own pattern" and "this private locomotive": *Technics and Civilization*, 236

p. 34 "safety, comfort, speed, and economy": Geddes, *Magic Motorways*, 16

p. 34 great achievement "was to free the common man from the limitations of his geography": J. R. T. Hughes, quoted in Rae, *Road and Car*, 51–52

p. 35   on men whose approach "was from the engine to the vehicle": Rae, *American Automobile Man-ufacturers*, 24

p. 36   "motor car for the great multitude": Wik, *Henry Ford and Grass-roots America*, 233

p. 37   "the world's most widely used single piece of large mechanical equipment": Donovan, *Wheels for a Nation*, 100

p. 40   River Rouge complex "which almost literally converted coal, iron ore, and other materials into a finished automobile": Faulkner, *American Economic History*, 516

p. 41   it would "be difficult to find a city more highly specialized": McCarty, *Geographic Basis*, 552

p. 44   "the brilliant execution of the great Niagara project": Hunter and Bryant, *History of Industrial Power*, 254

p. 44   "electrification was fragmented and individualized": Nye, *Electrifying America*, 139

p. 45   Hoover, "The time is ripe for a great national program": Baum, *Atlas of U.S.A. Electric Power Industry*, 1

p. 45   "somewhat comparable to the relation of the Federal Reserve District banks": Baum, *Atlas of U.S.A. Electric Power Industry*, 3

p. 45   a "natural monopoly" and "cannot be regulated by competition": Pinchot in "Giant Power," ix

p. 45   Cotton South would need to adopt "a more balanced program of agriculture": Brown, *Electricity for Rural America*, 9

p. 45   "unsocial practices must give way": Garwood and Tuthill, *Rural Electrification Administration*, 39

p. 46   Franklin D. Roosevelt on "four great government power developments": quoted in Abrams, *Power in Transition*, 22

p. 46   REA definition of "rural": Garwood and Tuthill, *Rural Electrification Administration*, 7

p. 46   TVA given "full responsibility for meeting all power supply requirements": *National Power Survey*, 1964, 23

p. 46   "for all practical purposes American agriculture was electrified": Brown, *Electricity for Rural America*, 113

p. 47   Electricity was "a commodity in the marketplace": Nye, *Electrifying America*, 387

p. 47   rather like "the successful railways that have emerged out of the maze": Baum, *Atlas of U.S.A. Electric Power Industry*, 3

p. 50   California with "the largest interconnected system in the world": Baum, *Atlas of U.S.A. Electric Power Industry*, preface, n.p.

p. 50   "where mankind wishes to go, copper wires can go too": "Giant Power," 96

p. 50   Henry Ford on "what can be done with water power": quoted in Hubbard, *Origins of the TVA*, 71

p. 50   Ford on "enough water power on this continent to run railroads, factories, homes": quoted in Nye, *Electrifying America*, 298

p. 50   Muscle Shoals "only the first of a whole series of such projects": Hubbard, *Origins of the TVA*, 39

p. 51   Ford on his proposal as "an industrial philanthropy": quoted in Hubbard, *Origins of the TVA*, 42

p. 51   Ford on running "power lines 200 miles in every direction": quoted in "Ford Politics in Muscle Shoals," 15

p. 51   "The instruments of a neotechnic civilization are now at hand" and "By means of the motor car the upland areas . . . can be thrown open to commerce": Mumford, *Technics and Civiliza-tion*, 214–15, 238–39

p. 51   Ford on "why should the factory stay in the city?": quoted in "Giant Power," 91

p. 51   "The dramatic evolution of the radio": *Recent Social Trends*, 211

p. 52   "to give Uncle Sam the same relation to wireless messages": Hugill, *Global Communications*, 121

p. 52 "the feeling that broadcasting was a key to influence and power": Barnouw, *Tower in Babel*, 4

p. 52 "could serve the whole country adequately": Barnouw, *Tower in Babel*, 95

p. 53 Radio Act of 1927: Socolow, *Law of Radio Broadcasting*, vol. 1, 388

p. 53 "it is inconceivable that we should allow so great a possibility for service": quoted in Barnouw, *Tower in Babel*, 96

p. 53 "deluged with requests for admission to their 'chains'": Schubert, *Electric World*, 291

p. 53 networks designed on the basis of "population and purchasing power": Robinson, *Radio Networks*, 39

p. 53 "the natural tendency was to admit the stations with the greatest audiences": Schubert, *Electric World*, 291

p. 55 "equality of radio broadcasting service": Socolow, *Law of Radio Broadcasting*, vol. 1, 408

p. 55 "social effects" of radio: *Recent Social Trends*, 153–56

p. 56 "by keeping the Wabash Railroad in sight": Leary, *Pilots' Directions*, 56, 51, 61

p. 56 saving "a complete working day between the two biggest business centres": Davies, *Airlines of the U.S.*, 25

p. 56 secretary of Commerce "to designate and establish airways": Davies, *Airlines of the United States*, 35

p. 58 Boeing B247 as "first modern airliner": Davies, *Airlines of the United States*, 180

p. 58 Walter Folger Brown as "architect of the major U.S. airline route networks": Davies, *Airlines of the United States*, 117

p. 58 "from the outset, the C.A.B. controlled roughly half of the world's airline activity": Davies, *Airlines of the United States*, 675

p. 60 TWA "took air transport another step forward": Davies, *Airlines of the United States*, 206

p. 60 "an air transport explosion" and "Feeder Airline" classification: Davies, *Airlines of the United States*, 389

p. 61 "a great tidal wave of federal money": Lewis, *Divided Highways*, 87

p. 61 "automobile was the passport to the postwar American dream": Lewis, *Divided Highways*, 80

p. 64 chambers of commerce "as their chief clientele": Barrow, "Politics of Interstate Route Selection," 196

p. 64 "the node joining national, regional, and local worlds": Schein, "Interstate 70 Landscape," 347

p. 64 "divided the land into four quadrants": Lewis, *Divided Highways*, 212

p. 64 "the triple pillars of American roadside commerce," "new players in the exit game," "at least five thousand new but nameless 'places'": Norris, "Interstate Highway Exit Morphology," 29, 31, 24

p. 64 "a rim connecting the spokes of the radial expressways": Browning, "Rise of Beltways," 18

p. 67 on railroads—"no civic authority in America could or wanted to resist the intrusion": Meinig, *Continental America*, 371

p. 67 "as two-dimensional abstractions the lines looked harmless": Lewis, *Divided Highways*, 123

p. 68 on neighborhoods "particularly vulnerable to freeway disruption": Federal Highway Administration policy statement quoted in Moon, *Interstate Highway System*, 56

p. 68 "Over the full span of American history": Lewis, "Landscapes of Mobility," 36

p. 68 "in 1986, an informal group . . . began to discuss the future": Sussman, "ITS," 115

p. 68 "a fundamentally new kind of urban structure," railroads "lost substantial market," "rush-hour conditions . . . often extended through the day": Sussman, "ITS," 122, 115

p. 69 "would have to be addressed by means other than . . . conventional highways"; "to create something wholly new in the world of transportation": Sussman, "ITS," 116, 118

p. 69 "multimodal service corridors" and "Coast-to-Coast in One Day": Grava, "Thoughts toward the Next Transportation System," 516, 507

p. 69 Kay on "our vaunted mobility is obstructed by a car culture": *Asphalt Nation*, 8

p. 69 "the fast, individually controlled vehicle . . . is as close to the ancient flying carpet": Grava, "Thoughts toward the Next Transportation System," 505

p. 69 Goddard on the "epic struggle": *Getting There*, 5

p. 70 "prompt merger without friction of all carriers' lines": Little and Cunningham, *Historical Development*, 69

p. 70 ICC directed to "prepare and adopt a plan for the consolidation": Daggett, *Principles* (1934), 585

p. 70 "became the first major industry in which large combinations were looked upon with favor": Leonard, *Railroad Consolidation*, 63

p. 70 "competition shall be preserved as fully as possible": Daggett, *Principles* (1934), 585

p. 70 Senator Cummins: "from the unguided, uncontrolled right of owners to build railroads": Little and Cunningham, *Historical Development*, 74

p. 71 "present or future public convenience and necessity": Daggett, *Principles* (1934), 584

p. 71 "collectively the greatest and most important industry," etc.: U.S. Congress, *National Transportation Policy* (Doyle Report), 264

p. 73 "General consolidation of railroads in the near future": U.S. Congress, *National Transportation Policy* (Doyle Report), 15

p. 73 intercity passenger service "meets no important needs," "in the foreseeable future, there is no means of transportation that offers the combination of economy and dependable service," consolidation should begin in "the northeast area": U.S. Congress, *National Transportation Policy* (Doyle Report), 322, 267, 16

p. 74 "it was a thunderclap that shook all railroading": Saunders, *Railroad Mergers*, 89

p. 75 "merger, rather than a panacea, was the catalyst for collapse": Saunders, *Railroad Mergers*, 4

p. 75 "the *Titanic* of the railroad merger era": Martin, *Railroads Triumphant*, 382

p. 75 "the most miserable fiasco in American business"; "The East was a railroad graveyard," but "the ICC insisted it was not possible to dismantle vast sections": Saunders, *Railroad Mergers*, 294, 295, 307

p. 75 "in the late Seventies it seemed inevitable in Washington": Blaszak, "Megamergers," 41

p. 77 "The Great Railway Bazaar": Frailey, "Colossus of Roads," 51

p. 78 "served every major region . . . [and] preservation of the passenger train had wide geographic" and political support: Hilton, *Amtrak*, 13

p. 78 "that Amtrak trains be given priority over freight trains": Hilton, *Amtrak*, 24

p. 80 Klein: "Every road was a sovereign state": see Meinig, *Transcontinental America*, 245

p. 80 "railroaders inhabited a closed world": Klein, *Unfinished Business*, 150

p. 80 "railroads are in a transitional phase": Wilner, "Truth about Mergers," 45

p. 81 "no common carriage of consequence on the Mississippi": Daggett, *Principles* (1955), 37

p. 81 "wherever a navigable river runs beside railroads" and "It is common knowledge that the railroads are no longer able to move crops and manufactures rapidly enough": Theodore Roosevelt, quoted in Willoughby, *St. Lawrence Waterway*, 73

p. 81 Hoover: "we have wasted vast sums of money": *Memoirs*, vol. 2, 121

p. 82 Hoover on "three great trunk lines of water transportation": *New Day*, 184

p. 82 Hoover: "I know of nothing that should so appeal to the imagination": epigram, Mabee, *Seaway Story*

p. 84 Roosevelt: "United States needs the St. Lawrence Seaway for defense": Mabee, *Seaway Story*, 131

p. 85 "the economic consequences to the Midwest could be tragic": General Lewis Pick, Army Corps of Engineers, quoted in Mabee, *Seaway Story*, 150

p. 85 waterways as "free highways": U.S. Congress, *National Transportation Policy* (Doyle Report), 197

p. 85 "the key to the completion of the Seaway": Mabee, *Seaway Story*, 155

p. 85 Truman on the Seaway: Hills, *St. Lawrence Seaway*, 83

p. 88 trunk lines as "a national asset": Davies, *Airlines of the United States*, 495–96

p. 88 jet engine, "the greatest single advance in technology" and "the term jet conveyed an image": Davies, *Airlines of the United States*, 507, 513

p. 89 "matching equipment now became mandatory": U.S. Congress, *National Transportation Policy*, 704, 705

p. 90 "the worst in aviation history": quoted in Fleming, "Competition," 201

p. 90 "what remains is a rather small number of very large airlines": Fleming, "Competition," 207

p. 92 "the flow of passengers through these complex networks": Fleming, "Competition," 194

p. 93 "the tendency of the largest city . . . to act as the receiving point": Taaffe, "Air Transportation," 222–23

p. 94 "the U.S. air express industry went from infancy to adulthood": Ligon, "Development of U.S. Air Express Industry," 293

p. 95 Tysons Corner, "halfway between Dulles Airport and the Pentagon": Garreau, *Edge City*, 76

p. 95 "civic pride . . . will prompt cities to demand service": U.S. Congress, *National Transportation Policy*, 705

p. 95 "there are not a few pockets of pain" and "Sky-High Fares Hurting Local Business": *Syracuse Herald-Journal*, February 16, 1999, quoting attorney general of Iowa and front-page headline

p. 96 "it is possible to reach almost anywhere within continental North America": Hugill, *World Trade*, 295

p. 96 "some passengers get bargains while other passengers subsidize those bargains": Fleming, "Competition," 205

p. 96 "to build up market share" and "there is very little in American law": Fleming, "Competition," 204, 210

p. 97 "this industry should not choose the winners and losers": attorney general of Iowa, quoted in *Syracuse Herald Journal*, February 16, 1999

p. 97 government taking possession of "each and every telegraph and telephone system": President Wilson's proclamation, quoted in Brooks, *Telephone*, 151

p. 97 AT&T as "network manager" and commitment "to continue expansion": Stone, *How America Got On-Line*, 31, 32

p. 98 "much of our telephone transmission network is a splicing of different types of technologies": Hyman, Toole, and Avellis, *New Telecommunications*, 43

p. 98 FCC's "first priority was to provide at least one television service to all parts of the United States": Inglis, *Behind the Tube*, 198

p. 99 barred use of "terrain features . . . as a basis for reduced spacing": Inglis, *Behind the Tube*, 201

p. 99 "a fundamental change in the technological basis of society": Preer, *Emergence of Technopolis*, 57

p. 99 "information must not be confused with meaning": Winston, *Media Technology and Society*, 153

p. 100 "the computer survived the Second World War *in utero*": Winston, *Media Technology and Society*, 181

p. 100 Santa Clara Valley as "an almost endless orchard": *San Francisco: The Bay and Its Cities*, 460

p. 102 "gained fame as Silicon Valley": Saxenian, "Genesis of Silicon Valley," 20

p. 102 "in the mid-1960s the complexity of a chip was comparable to the network of streets": Rogers and Larsen, *Silicon Valley Fever*, 98

p. 102 definition of "technopolis": Preer, *Emergence of Technopolis*, 55

p. 102 Frederick Terman on "Stanford's secret weapon": Rogers and Larsen, *Silicon Valley Fever*, 35

p. 103 "inventive and entrepreneurial talent thrived in a milieu": Saxenian, "Genesis of Silicon Valley," 29

p. 103 "the formula for creating a technopolis": Preer, *Emergence of Technopolis*, 29

p. 104 Albert Gore and highway analogy: quoted in Adams, "Cyberspace and Virtual Places," 158

p. 106 e-mail "makes at least a quick stop . . . in Schaumburg": Specter, "Your Mail Has Vanished," 98

p. 106 Internet "ranks among the most complex and organized entities": Starrs and Anderson, "Words of Cyberspace," 151

p. 106 "like the network of back roads" and "message from one computer to another": Johnson, "From Two Small Nodes"

p. 106 "message from one computer to another chopped up into many little packets": Johnson, "From Two Small Nodes"

p. 106 "The growing use of fibre optic systems": Sassen, "On Concentration and Centrality," 73

p. 106 "I cannot think of a comparable change so rapidly adopted": Starrs, "Sacred, Regional, Digital," 212

p. 107 Pickles on the "information highway": *Ground Truth*, ix

p. 107 "a system for producing something valuable from virtually nothing": Rogers and Larsen, *Silicon Valley Fever*, 276

p. 109 Silicon Valley phenomenon as "a special kind of supercapitalism": Rogers and Larsen, *Silicon Valley Fever*, 273

p. 109 "each new communication agency bids for public favor": *Recent Social Trends*, 167

p. 109 "to be without a telephone": *Recent Social Trends*, 199

p. 109 "an untroubled zeal for technology": Lohr, "Reluctant Conscripts"

p. 109 on "one is faced here with a magnified form of a danger": Mumford, *Technics and Civilization*, 240–41

PART TWO

p. 114 dwarfing "any previous growth the nation has known": Bogue, *Population of United States*, 760

p. 114 "the annual volume of movement and migration": Bogue, *Population of United States*, 377

p. 116 "primarily a phenomenon of late adolescence and early maturity": Bogue, *Population of United States*, 381

p. 117 "In recent years the most spectacular movement of the population": *Recent Social Trends*, 566

p. 121 "Americans were finding the problem of where to go more perplexing": Goodrich et al., *Migration and Economic Opportunity*, 660, v

p. 121 Matanuska Valley as the "most conspicuous current case": Goodrich et al., *Migration and Economic Opportunity*, 7

p. 121 "never before in the history of our country has there been so great a shuffling and redistribution": census report quoted in Labatut and Lane, *Highways in Our National Life*, 137

p. 122 sequence of quotations by Siegfried: *America Comes of Age*, 3, 9, 119, 11

p. 122 "Germany seems to have lost all her foreign possessions": quoted in Jones, *American Immigration*, 270

p. 122 Milwaukeeans and German war relief: Ostergren and Vale, *Wisconsin Land and Life*, 392

p. 122 "millions of war-torn Europeans were about to descend": Divine, *American Immigration Policy*, 6

p. 123 Republican party platform statement: Hutchinson, *Legislative History*, 633

p. 123 quotas "were to be computed on the basis of the national composition": Divine, *American Immigration Policy*, 17

p. 123 "percentage of the white blood in the population": Petersen, *Population*, 103

p. 123 "Since the passage of the Immigration Act of 1924": Davie, *World Immigration*, 372, 383

p. 124 "10,000,000 . . . American refugees who have been walking the streets": Rep. Will Taylor (Tennessee), quoted in Divine, *American Immigration Policy*, 98

p. 124 "full and complete investigation of our entire immigration system": Bennett, *American Immigration Policies*, 109

p. 126 "we have locked the front door but left the side door open": Davie, *World Immigration*, 382, 213

p. 126 "to complete the established policy of immigrant restriction": H. Report 898, 71st Cong., 2d sess., March 13, 1930, 12, and Part 2, 1

p. 127 "lower classes of the Mexican population": H. Report 898, 71st Cong., 2d sess., March 13, 1930, 3, 4

p. 127 "turned into a bitter contest": Divine, *American Immigration Policy*, 61

p. 127 "infiltration and differential fecundity . . . will in a comparatively short time change the complexion": H. Report 898, 71st Cong., 2d sess., March 13, 1930, 12, 4, 28

p. 127 on census classification of Mexicans: Petersen, *Population*, 125

p. 128 national origins has "provided a fixed and easily determined method": S. Report 1515, 81st Cong., 2d sess., April 20, 1950, 448–49, 455

p. 128 "hard-core, indigestible blocs": Patrick McCarran, quoted in Bennett, *American Immigration Policies*, 173

p. 129 "principal divisions of the white race": S. Report 1515, 81st Cong., 2d sess., April 20, 1950, 7

p. 129 "though most congressmen refused to disclose their views": Divine, *American Immigration Policy*, 181

p. 129 "the 1952 act, for the first time in our history": Bennett, *American Immigration Policies*, 179

p. 129 President Tyler's invitation: quoted in S. Report 1515, 81st Cong., 2d sess., April 20, 1950, 47

p. 129 political leaders reaffirmed welcomes: quoted from political platforms of 1852 and 1864, in Hutchinson, *Legislative History*, 622, 623

p. 130 Handlin on "being in America would make Americans of them": *Uprooted*, 265, 270

p. 130 "poisons of disorder, revolt, and chaos" in Europe: Kennedy, *Over Here*, 87, quoting from Screiber, *Wilson Administration*, slightly condensed

p. 130 "general recrudescence of chauvinistic nationalism": Fairchild, *Immigration*, 426

p. 130 "a second Declaration of Independence": Stoddard, *Re-Forging America*, 191

p. 130 "America is a nationality": Fairchild, *Immigration*, 417

p. 130 Bowman on "the old bonds between immigrant and the home country": *New World*, 695

p. 131 "the delusion that there was some magical potency": Fairchild, *Immigration*, 414

p. 131 melting pot "so badly cracked": Fairchild, *Immigration*, 396

p. 131 "what was being melted . . . was the American nationality": Fairchild, *The Melting Pot Mistake*, quoted in Kohn, *American Nationalism*, 170

p. 131 "the idea of assimilation has become paramount," "further dilution of our national stock," all traits "must be abandoned": Fairchild, *Immigration*, 396, 460, 431

p. 131 congressmen on "stability of the country" and "one race, one country, one destiny": Divine, *American Immigration Policy*, 14, 15

p. 131 "The year 1924 is thus one of the decisive dates": Stoddard, *Re-Forging America*, 192

p. 131 Coolidge, "America must be kept American": Stoddard, *Re-Forging America*, 191

p. 131 preserving "the blood of the United States in its present proportions": Rep. William Vaile (Colorado), quoted in Stoddard, *Re-Forging America*, 205

p. 131 "the 80 percent of us who were born in this country": Sen. David Reed (Pennsylvania), quoted in Bennett, *American Immigration Policies*, 47

p. 131 "each year's immigration is to be an exact miniature": Stoddard, *Re-Forging America*, 203

p. 131 not "an imputation of inferiority": Fairchild, *Immigration*, 460

p. 131 quotation from Grant, *Passing of the Great Race*, 91

p. 132 "dilute and weaken our national character": Bowman, *New World*, 695

p. 132 purified of "its worst elements": Stoddard, *Re-Forging America*, 208

p. 132 "trouble grows out of a country composed of intermingled and mongrelized people": *Cong. Record*, April 5, 1924, quoted in Divine, *American Immigration Policy*, 14

p. 132 Divine on "racial nationalism": *American Immigration Policy*, 18

p. 132 sequence of quotations under "Minorities": Fairchild, *Immigration*, 396, 414, 418, 432 (slightly rearranged), 420

p. 133 Handlin on "a society that had moved to a restricted view of itself": *Uprooted*, 299, 294, 295

p. 134 Petersen, *Population*, 117

p. 135 "to be a Dakotan": Stock, *Main Street in Crisis*, 10

p. 135 "demographic death": Dorman, *Revolt of the Provinces*, 219

p. 135 "agrarianism is not the theory that everybody should be farmers": Vance, *Regionalism and the South*, 63

p. 135 "regionalism means social and economic equilibrium": Davidson, *Attack on Leviathan*, 51

p. 135 "a Southern way of life against what may be called the American . . . way": *I'll Take My Stand*, xix

p. 135 "a 'floating' populace . . . unattached to that tremendous social anchor, land": Lyle H. Lanier, *I'll Take My Stand*, 150

p. 136 "to see how the South may handle this fire": John Crowe Ransom, *I'll Take My Stand*, 22

p. 136 "the words *region* and *regionalism* lose all exactness": Davidson, *Attack on Leviathan*, 228

p. 136 "dissatisfaction with the culture, or pseudo-culture": Davidson, *Attack on Leviathan*, 10

p. 136 "The besetting weakness of regionalism": Mumford, *Technics and Civilization*, 292

p. 136 "recognition of the region as a basic configuration in human life" and "the re-examination and re-building of regions": Mumford, *Culture of Cities*, 306, 349

p. 136 "Higher Provincialism," etc.: Royce, *Basic Writings*, vol. 2, 1070, 1083

p. 136 megalopolitan "stranglehold on the life of the hinterland": B. A. Botkin, quoted in Dorman, *Revolt of the Provinces*, 149

p. 136 "exerted a powerful shearing pull": Dorman, *Revolt of the Provinces*, 35

p. 136 "headquartered, as it were, in and around the camp of the enemy" and "cultural-intellectual map": Dorman, *Revolt of the Provinces*, 46, 45

p. 137 sectionalism "inevitable and desirable": Turner, "The Significance of the Section," in *Frontier and Section*, 131

p. 137 "serve as restraints upon a deadly uniformity": Turner, "Sections and Nation," in *Frontier and Section*, 152

p. 137 "found itself photographed, stereotyped, and scrutinized": Burl L. Noggle, quoted in Grantham, *South in Modern America*, 148

p. 138 "under invasion by the iron glacier" and "a common suburban mass without form or articulation," etc.: MacKaye, *New Exploration*, 224, 161, 163, 164

p. 138 "Many hard lessons have taught us the human waste": FDR, April 10, 1933, quoted in Abrams, *Power in Transition*, 199

p. 138 "the fluidity of American society on the march": *Regional Factors in National Planning*, 139

p. 139 Odum on an "extraordinary chasm" in the South and his study "envisaged in terms of testing grounds": *Southern Regions*, ix

p. 139 Odum and Moore on a "composite group-of-state major societal regions": *American Regionalism*, 32, 34, 640

p. 139 "the continued adjustment and readaptation of the nation to its geography": Odum and Moore, *American Regionalism*, 639

p. 141 "the economic and social well-being of the people living in said river basin": Hodge, *Tennessee Valley Authority*, 48

p. 141 "a corporation clothed with the powers of government": *Regional Factors in National Planning*, 83

p. 143 "if we are successful here we can march on, step by step, in a like development": quoted in Owen, *Tennessee Valley Authority*, 14

p. 143 "a river basin draining seven states, an authority draining forty-eight states": quoted in Odum, *Southern Regions*, 107

p. 144 "maladjustment and readjustment of governmental areas," automobile has "operated with devastating effect," counties "are too small both in area and population," "broadly speaking, industrial and social relations overflowed the banks": *Recent Social Trends*, 1491, 1495

p. 144 "the states will neither govern the cities nor permit them to govern themselves": C. E. Merriam, quoted in Graves, "Future of American States," 25

p. 144 few states "possessed enough vitality to resist the inevitable march toward federal centralization": Elliott, *Need for Constitutional Reform*, 191

p. 145 Elliott on "redrawing the political map," "extraordinary overrepresentation," reducing "the terrific waste of multiplied capitals": *Need for Constitutional Reform*, 207, 186, 36, 192

p. 145 "Quite clearly it will take a revolution: Whittlesey, *Earth and State*, 577

p. 145 "The irreducible criterion of reality": Odum and Moore, *American Regionalism*, 33

p. 145 "we are living in an atmosphere of temporary truce": Elliott, *Need for Constitutional Reform*, 243

p. 145 "it is certain that this does not express any well-developed popular movement": National Planning Board, *Final Report*, 93

p. 146 "national planning should start at the bottom": quoted in Karl, *Uneasy State*, 165

p. 146 "The South presents the Nation's No. 1 economic problem": quoted in Grantham, *South in Modern America*, 166

p. 146 "it was almost as if the President had rung a bell": Tindell, *Emergence of the New South*, 599

p. 146 "colonial degradation": Davidson, *Attack on Leviathan*, 298

p. 146 "reassertion of a more traditional kind of sectionalism": Grantham, *South in Modern America*, 139

p. 146 "agencies like TVA were allowed to discriminate": Karl, *Uneasy State*, 217

p. 146 "new science of the region": Odum and Moore, *American Regionalism*, 3

p. 147 "from the earliest days of our national history, the distribution of national resources": Karl, *Uneasy State*, 165, 161

p. 147 "powerful and evocative . . . critiques and visions . . . were impotent": Dorman, *Revolt of the Provinces*, 251

p. 147 "whose faith in localism and individualism": Karl, *Uneasy State*, 217

p. 148 "the high point of 'regionalism' as a scholarly concern": John Shelton Reed in Vance, *Regionalism and the South*, 155

p. 148 "It must be clear that regionalism is not so much a 'movement'": Lerner, *America as a Civilization*, 203, 204

p. 148 "improvements in communications, such as the automobile": Turner, "Sections and Nation" in *Frontier and Section*, 152

p. 149 "an almost continuous system of deeply interwoven urban and suburban areas": Gottmann, *Megalopolis*, 7, 9, 776

p. 149 Mumford on Megalopolis: *Culture of Cities*, 275–77

p. 150 "interstratified and complex structure": Gottmann, *Megalopolis*, 725

p. 150 "Like some complex sea organism": William N. Parker, quoted in Meinig, *Continental America*, 418

p. 150 "an irregularly colloidal mixture": Gottmann, *Megalopolis*, 5

p. 151 "a city of their own, a cosmopolitan . . . spiritual capital": *New York City Guide*, 257–58, inverted sequence

p. 151 "first significant urban contact": Watkins-Owens, *Blood Relations*, 175

p. 153 conduct personal life "in a small homogeneous world of their own": Gottmann, *Megalopolis*, 723

p. 153 "carrying a staggering burden of old buildings": Wright, *New England's Prospect*, 338

p. 154 on Chicago's "Black Belt": Glaab and Brown, *History of Urban America*, 287

p. 154 Chicago as "a laboratory or a clinic": Park, Burgess, and McKenzie, *The City*, 46

p. 155 on Middletown: Lynd and Lynd, *Middletown*, 7, 9, 8

p. 156 "progressive optimism": Stein, *Eclipse of Community*, 63

p. 156 "hundreds of other scaled-down, would-be Chicagos": Hudson, *Crossing the Heartland*, 22

p. 158 "extraordinary profusion of small towns" and progress "came to an end in 1929": Hutton, *Midwest at Noon*, 160, 322

p. 159 "The last great plow-up": Malone and Roeder, *Montana*, 194

p. 159 "zones of experiment" for a "science of settlement": Bowman, *Pioneer Fringe*, v, vi, vii, 93

p. 159 "the most American part of the nation": Odum and Moore, *American Regionalism*, 520

p. 160 "a complete set of machines and chemicals": Aiken, *Cotton Plantation South*, 109

p. 160 "cultural landscape long confirmed the decline" and "accustomed to an abundant supply of labor, whites panicked": Aiken, *Cotton Plantation South*, 88, 82

p. 161 "made clear that they didn't want to include blacks": Maharidge and Williamson, *Their Children after Them*, 70

p. 161 "by the end of the 1920s few residents of the region were left untouched": Eller, *Miners, Millhands, and Mountaineers*, xix

p. 162 migration "considered a temporary expedient" and "adjustment to urban life difficult": Luebke and Hart, "Migration," 52

p. 162 "In the farm areas of South and West Texas": Montejano, *Anglos and Mexicans*, 252

p. 163 "one of those potent inventions": Lewis, *New Orleans*, 61

p. 163 "a new kind of prosperity to the South," Mississippi congressman quoted in White, *Billions for Defense*, 42

p. 163 "white collar brains" and "the whole process of selecting and rejecting": Lane, *Ships for Victory*, 49, 151

p. 165 on military preference for airfields south of the 37th parallel: quoted in Abbott, *Metropolitan Frontier*, 9

p. 166 "American officer corps continued to draw disproportionately": Abbott, "Dimensions of Regional Change," 1387

p. 168 "apparently uninterruptible tendency of the population . . . to gravitate westward": Scott, *San Francisco Bay Area*, 224

p. 169 "the influx of angry, desperate migrants from the Dust Bowl": Mitchell, *Lie of the Land*, 180–81

p. 169 "the farm labor problem in California": McWilliams, *California: The Great Exception*, 155

p. 171 movies "fit the economic requirements and physical limitations of the region," etc.: McWilliams, *Southern California Country*, 339, 341, 340

p. 171 "Hollywood brought to Los Angeles an unprecedented and unrepeatable population": Banham, *Los Angeles*, 35

p. 171 "in the 1930s a golden age of California as a regional American civilization": Starr, *Material Dreams*, 393–94

p. 172 "Los Angeles emerged . . . and Los Angeles' appeal": Brodsley, *L.A. Freeway*, 137, 4

p. 173 "for military planners all the old liabilities of the West became virtues": White, *It's Your Misfortune*, 497

p. 173 "desirability of decentralizing industry": S. Doc. 35, 77th Cong., 1st sess., March 31, 1941, 23

p. 173 "the haunting fear of 'reconversion recession'": Abbott, *Metropolitan Frontier*, 36

p. 174 "there were more aircraft employees in Washington and California": White, *"It's Your Misfortune,"* 513

p. 174 "a vastly expanded regional market, a new industrial infrastructure": Abbott, *Metropolitan Frontier*, 4

p. 174 "The East's influence over the region had faded": White, *"It's Your Misfortune,"* 462, 461

p. 174 "the four short years of the war had brought a maturation" and "scores of writers and public figures were actively involved": Nash, *American West Transformed*, viii, 207

p. 174 on "nation-building": Perloff et al., *Regions, Resources and Economic Growth*, 49–50, and Ull-man, "Regional Development," 184

p. 175 Shortridge quotation: *The Middle West*, 54, 39

p. 175 "The stream of troops and munitions": *San Francisco, the Bay and Its Cities*, 11

p. 177 1920 census "grabbed the attention of the American public": Martis and Elmes, *Historical Atlas of State Power*, 166

p. 177 "The debate began in 1921": Martis and Elmes, *Historical Atlas of State Power*, 164

p. 178 "nearly one-half of the 'No' votes came from five cities": Bennett, *American Immigration Policies*, 54

p. 178 McWilliams on California politics: *Southern California Country*, 313

p. 180 "it had been permanently drowned by a torrent of migration": Gregg, *Sparks from the Anvil*, 25

p. 180 since "1915, the status of Northern Negroes has fallen": Myrdal, *American Dilemma*, 601

p. 181 "an unwarranted and unjustifiable destruction of real estate values": Brown, "Access to Housing," 68

p. 181 Rose on Black ghettos: *Black Ghetto*, 5

p. 181 Blacks "excluded from assimilation": Myrdal, *American Dilemma*, 54

p. 181 "persons in whom there is a visible and distinct admixture" and "all persons in whom there is ascertainable any quantum": Mangum, *Legal Status of the Negro*, 9, 6

p. 181 prejudice would "rise with the proportion of Negroes present": Myrdal, *American Dilemma*, 200–1

p. 182 "the color line in the North is not a part of the law": Myrdal, *American Dilemma*, 677

p. 182 "the South begins in the Washington airport": "The Regions," *Fortune*, 48

p. 182 "a caste of people . . . lacking a cultural past": Myrdal, *American Dilemma*, 54

p. 182 "upsurge of nativist and racial ideologies": Williams, *From Caste to Minority*, 116

p. 184 "to discover a cultural tradition for American Negroes": Myrdal, *American Dilemma*, 750

p. 184 scholar from a country "with no background or tradition of imperialism": K. P. Keppel, president, Carnegie Foundation, in foreword to Myrdal, *American Dilemma*, vi

p. 184 "the treatment of the Negro is America's greatest scandal": Myrdal, *American Dilemma*, 1020

p. 184 "in the year of D-Day, the *Dilemma* helped secure a strategic beachhead": Southern, *Gunnar Myrdal*, 99

p. 184 "the Negroes in their fight for equality": Myrdal, *American Dilemma*, 1009

p. 184 Blacks should constitute about "the same proportion . . . as in the general population": Myrdal, *American Dilemma*, 420

p. 184 Wendell Wilkie's statement to NAACP: Myrdal, *American Dilemma*, 1009

p. 185 covenants were "unenforceable as law and contrary to public policy": Jackson, *Crabgrass Frontier*, 208

p. 185 "a great upsurge in church life," etc.: Herberg, *Protestant-Catholic-Jew*, 51, 47, 257

p. 185 "We did not need the evidence of polls or church attendance," quoted in Herberg, *Protestant-Catholic-Jew*, 1

p. 185 "unprecedented rate" of construction: Ahlstrom, *Religious History*, 961

p. 185 "the diversity or separateness of religious community": Herberg, *Protestant-Catholic-Jew*, 38

p. 186 "religious self-identification among the tripartite scheme": Herberg, *Protestant-Catholic-Jew*, 256

p. 186 "religiousness without religion": Herberg, *Protrestant-Catholic-Jew*, 260

p. 186 Zelinsky on "religious feeling": "Approach to Religious Geography," 166

p. 188 "one risks joining together in Christian fellowship": Moore, *Religious Outsiders*, 151

p. 190 "a free market religious environment": Finke and Stark, *Churching of America*, 2

p. 191 "it is possible . . . to overestimate the importance of regional differences": Lerner, *America as a Civilization*, 204

p. 193 Siegfried on American nationalism: *America at Mid-Century*, 248, 113

p. 193 knitting a whole populace "together in an ever greater network": Deutsch, "Growth of Nation," 184

p. 193 Thistlethwaite on America: *Great Experiment*, xii, xiii

p. 195 "those possessing the vision, spirit and virility": *Alaska Railroad*, 21

p. 195 "If the Finns owned Alaska": quoted in Naske and Slotnick, *Alaska*, 100

p. 196 "in a very few years we can set off the Panhandle": quoted in Naske and Slotnick, *Alaska*, 142

p. 196 Coolidge on cost "so far out of proportion": Colby, *Guide to Alaska*, 39

p. 196 "an appraisal of the national interests indicates that there is no clear need": Naske and Slotnick, *Alaska*, 117

p. 197 Roosevelt on Skagway: quoted in Remley, *Crooked Road*, 235

p. 197 "the military value of the proposed Alaska Highway . . . is negligible": H. Report 1705, 79th Cong., 2d sess., March 13, 1946, 6

p. 197 "a minimum road at the earliest practicable date": Remley, *Crooked Road*, 15

p. 199 "the most important strategic place in the world": quoted in Naske and Slotnick, *Alaska*, 122

p. 199 America's "first line of defense": Naske and Slotnick, *Alaska*, 138

p. 199 Gruening on Alaskan statehood: *Battle*, 49, 4, 40, 78

p. 200 "Alaska's strategic importance required full freedom of federal action": Naske, *Interpretative History*, 133

p. 200 "lack of self-sustaining basic economic activity": Naske and Slotnick, *Alaska*, 160

p. 201 "tenuous and volatile economy" and "no other state extracts such a high price": McBeath and Morehouse, *Alaska Politics*, 56–57, 21

p. 203 "no candid American would ever think of making a State of this Union": Carl Schurz; see Meinig, *Transcontinental America*, 367

p. 203 House committee conclusion, "it would be wiser to wait until another generation": Bell, *Last among Equals*, 64

p. 203 "the old fish and poi economy": Lind, *Hawaii's People*, 46

p. 204 "Tokyo High" and "pidgin English": Fuchs, *Hawaii Pono*, 290, 276

p. 204 "No member of Hawaii's Japanese community was ever found guilty": Bell, *Last among Equals*, 80

p. 205 "Hawaii emerged from World War II": Bell, *Last among Equals*, 91

p. 205 "polyglot people" and "Oriental": Bell, *Last among Equals*, 241, 253

p. 205 Eisenhower on "East meets West" and Michener on "Hawaii is by far the most advanced state culturally": Lineberry, *New States*, 113, 67

p. 206 "has the most centralized system of government" and "the only state in which the institutions of governance" have "evolved downward": Smith and Pratt, *Politics and Public Policy*, 215, 2

p. 207 "the 'awakening' of Honolulu": Chow, "Urbanization," 178

p. 207 Mumford on Honolulu: "Report on Honolulu," 77

p. 207 "the trend was toward mainland big city modernism": Creighton, *Lands of Hawaii*, 79–80; also quoted in Chow, "Urbanization," 178

p. 207 Wurman on "a camaraderie": *Hawaii Access*, 95

p. 208 "everyday discourse is replete with distinctions": Smith and Pratt, *Politics and Public Policy*, 148

p. 208 "the dream of Hawaii as an international . . . center": Fuchs, *Hawaii Pono*, xi

p. 209 "it is harder and harder to reconcile the images of paradise": Smith and Pratt, *Politics and Public Policy*, 1

p. 209 three statements of Native Hawaiians: Trask, *From a Native Daughter*, 49, 89, 79

p. 209 Carr on jubilation over Hawaii statehood: *Puerto Rico*, 147

p. 210 should not infer "an intention to incorporate in the Union": Leibowitz, *Defining Status*, 147

p. 210 "publicly renounce independence": Wagenheim, *Puerto Rico*, 70

p. 211 "if we seek statehood we die waiting for Congress": Carr, *Puerto Rico*, 76

p. 211 "compact . . . a free and voluntary association": Bhana, *United States and Puerto Rican Status*, 171

p. 211 "the people of Puerto Rico have reached the highest possible level": Leibowitz, *Defining Status*, 170

p. 211 "riddled with legal ambiguities": Carr, *Puerto Rico*, 4

p. 212 "have been invested with the attributes of political sovereignty": Bhana, *United States and Puerto Rican Status*, 175

p. 212 "the emotional core of the statehood case": Carr, *Puerto Rico*, 152

p. 212 U.S. senator declared: "We welcome diversity": Sen. Henry Jackson (Washington), quoted in Leibowitz, *Defining Status*, 160

p. 212 "practically every type of language policy for the teaching of English": quoted in Wagenheim, *Puerto Rico*, 172

p. 212 "Spanish as official language": Morris, *Puerto Rico*, 58

p. 213 "political and cultural assimilation with the United States": Morris, *Puerto Rico*, 59

p. 213 "the greatest catalyst for changing Puerto Rican 'identity'": Wagenheim, *Puerto Rico*, 160

p. 213 "full of advertisements for houses in Central Florida": Rohter, "Puerto Rican Boom," A10

p. 213 statehood should be a "substantial majority": Carr, *Puerto Rico*, 154

p. 213 "the oldest colony in the world": Trías Monge, *Puerto Rico*, subtitle

p. 213 "a haven for the undecided": Wagenheim, *Puerto Rico*, 266

p. 213 "a buffer zone between the extremes": Trías Monge, *Puerto Rico*, 191

p. 213 "the conflict between cultural identity and the search for economic survival": Wagenheim, *Puerto Rico*, 9

p. 214 treaties "filled with the language of mutual concession": Barsh and Henderson, *The Road*, 279

p. 214 "the language of empire, drawing upon the standard vocabulary of diplomacy": Meinig, *Continental America*, 188

p. 214 "to answer the riddle of tribalism": Barsh and Henderson, *The Road*, 286

p. 214 "It is my fixed purpose to bring about the speedy individualization": Kvasnicka and Viola, *Commissioners*, 244

p. 215 boarding schools "conceived in terms of driving a wedge": Spicer, *Short History*, 116

p. 215 "this civilization may not be the best possible": Kvasnicka and Viola, *Commissioners*, 194

p. 215 quotations from Meriam Report: document excerpt in Spicer, *Short History*, 243–44; also in Deloria and Lytle, *Nations Within*, 44

p. 216 "re-Indianizing the Indians," and Collier on the need to "strip the word tribe of its primitive and atavistic connotations": Spicer, *Short History*, 125, and document excerpt, 247–48

p. 216 "it could free itself once and for all of the moral burden": Frantz, *Indian Reservations*, 33

p. 217 "new homes in ordinary American communities": Kvasnicka and Viola, *Commissioners*, 295

p. 217 "Between 1954 and 1966 Congress terminated over one hundred tribes": Pevar, *Rights of Indians*, 57

p. 217 "Congress has virtually unlimited authority to regulate" . . . "in practice termination is used as a weapon": Pevar, *Rights of Indians*, 52, 58

p. 217 "relocation backfired": Nancy Oestreich Lurie in Sutton, *Irredeemable America*, 366

p. 217 on general geopolitical principle of revolt within an empire: Meinig, *Atlantic America*, 374–75

p. 217 "A genuine phobia about the intentions of the federal government": Kvasnicka and Viola, *Commissioners*, 311

p. 218 termination "wrong" and new goal "to strengthen the Indian's sense of autonomy": Nagel, *American Indian Ethnic Renewal*, 217

p. 218 "to pose as another American domestic minority": Deloria and Lytle, *Nations Within*, 216

p. 218 standard for official recognition as a tribe: Josephy, Nagel, and Johnson, *Red Power*, 269; also Nagel, *American Indian Ethnic Renewal*, 242

p. 218 "The determination of who is an 'Indian' has a long history of ambiguity" and "unnatural leaps" in population: Shoemaker, *American Indian Population Recovery*, 5

p. 219 "tribal enrollment review committees have been swamped": Shoemaker, *American Indian Population Recovery*, 103

p. 219 quotations on Indian casinos: Winchell, Lounsbury, and Sommers, "Indian Gaming," 5, 1, 10

p. 219 Pommersheim on irony of Indian economic success: *Braid of Feathers*, 182

p. 222 Bureau of Indian Affairs apology: *New York Times*, September 9, 2000

p. 222 rejection of reservations as "living laboratories": Frantz, *Indian Reservations*, 6

p. 222 "knowledge of Navajo culture, history, language, values and principles: Josephy, Nagel, and Johnson, *Red Power*, 184

p. 222 "Indians have preserved the idea of nationhood" and "taking their case to other nations": Deloria and Lytle, *Nations Within*, 263, 241

p. 222 "in a status parallel to, but not identical with, that of the states": Barsh and Henderson, *The Road*, 270

p. 223 legislation "explicitly included Alaska Native villages as 'tribes'": McBeath and Morehouse, *Alaska Politics*, 102

p. 224 "extinguished aboriginal hunting and fishing rights": McBeath and Morehouse, *Alaska Politics*, 112

p. 224 McBeath and Morehouse on 1971 act: *Alaska Politics*, 112, 115

p. 224 quotations on Native Hawaiian movement: Trask, *From a Native Daughter*, 221, 69; and Trask in Smith and Pratt, *Politics and Public Policy*, 252

p. 226 "should the use of the cotton picker become common": Baker, in *Recent Social Trends*, 110

p. 227 Phillips on the "Sun Belt": *Emerging Republican Majority*, 436, 437

p. 228 Arsenault on air-conditioning: "End of the Long Hot Summer," 613

p. 228 *New York Times* on "the humble air-conditioner": quoted in Arsenault, "End of the Long Hot Summer," 618

p. 228 "the sudden and unexpectedly large volume of migration to the Sunbelt": Long, *Migration and Residential Mobility*, 3

p. 229 "people were forever coming and going": Cromartie and Stack, "Reinterpretation," 300

p. 229 "a case of sloppy regionalizing": Browning and Gesler, "Sun Belt-Snow Belt," subtitle

p. 230 Californians seeking a better "quality of life": Egan, "Eastward, Ho!"

p. 233 "During the 1970s extensive media attention was directed": Long, *Migration and Residential Mobility*, 98

p. 234 "demographic information on emigration": Smith and Edmonston, *New Americans*, 39

p. 235 "The human drama remains as riveting": Portes and Rumbaut, *Immigrant America*, xviii, xvii

p. 241 "powerful social, cultural and economic forces . . . are drawing Mexicans": Skerry, *Mexican Americans*, 375

p. 241 "Mexican-American cultural capital": Arreola, title

p. 242 "that it was as yet impossible to determine whether the billions of dollars spent": Spener and Staudt, *U.S.-Mexico Border*, 245

p. 242 "The movement of people across the border has been and remains breathtaking": Spener and Staudt, *U.S.-Mexico Border*, 237

p. 242 "springboards" and "recepticales": Herzog, *Where North Meets South*, 61

p. 242 "some of us have been here for three hundred years, some for three days": Skerry, *Mexican Americans*, 25

p. 242 "Mexican immigration . . . originated in deliberate recruitment": Portes and Rumbaut, *Immigrant America*, 225

p. 242 movements acquire their "own momentum and become progressively more widespread": Massey et al., *Return to Aztlan*, 109

p. 243 Houston's old barrio "has become the Mexican gateway": Myerson, "On the Road"

p. 243 "sentimental attachment to their native culture" remains strong, and issues "remain problematic and ambiguous": Massey et al., *Return to Aztlan*, 6

p. 243 "the mythical capital of the so-called Cuban Exile Country": Gonzalez-Pando, *Cuban Americans*, xiii

p. 244 "half of all Dominicans now have relatives in the United States": Rohter, "Flood of Dominicans"

p. 244 "one of the most contentious topics of debate": Isbister, *Immigration Debate*, 5

p. 245 "Americans have always been ambivalent toward immigration": Smith and Edmonston, *New Americans*, 13

p. 245 "When one considers present immigration policies, it seems we have insensibly reverted": Glazer, "Closing Door," 46

p. 245 "a five-year moratorium on immigration": Reimers, *Unwelcome Strangers*, 116

p. 245 "that economics in general can give no large answer": Glazer, "Closing Door," 42

p. 245 opposition "was overwhelming": Reimers, *Unwelcome Strangers*, 138, 66

p. 246 "the doctrine of the melting pot may not be good history": Isbister, *Immigration Debate*, 191

p. 246 "when pressure built to 'do something' about immigration": Reimers, *Unwelcome Strangers*, 147

p. 246 "What is new is global migration": Barkan, *Asian and Pacific Islander Migration*, 9

p. 246 "is a direct consequence of the dominant influence": Portes and Rumbaut, *Immigrant America*, 13

p. 246 "a sinewy web of relationships" with the United States "at the core": Barkan, *Asian and Pacific Islander Migration*, 39, 49

p. 246 "more immigrants than all other countries combined": Isbister, *Immigration Debate*, 5

p. 247 "the largest private housing project": Jackson, *Crabgrass Frontier*, 234

p. 247 "If it weren't for the Government": "Housing" in *Time*, 68

p. 247 "the early Levit house was as basic": Jackson, *Crabgrass Frontier*, 236

p. 247 "in Levittown, all activity stops": "Housing" in *Time*, 69

p. 248 "fastidiously avoided involvement in municipal affairs," "a new geography" was imposed, "Ironically, American optimism, faith in progress": Rifkind, *Main Street*, 237, 230, 239

p. 249 "traumatic uprooting of many thousands": Mayer, "Four Decades of Change," 386

p. 249 "Corporate executives living on their nearby estates": Lemon, *Liberal Dreams*, 4

p. 250 "none of these central city rebounds should be misinterpreted": Frey, "New Geography of Population Shifts," 314

p. 250 "the trend toward the super-city": Glaab and Brown, *History of Urban America*, 305

p. 250 "fifteen great, sprawling, nameless communities": Christopher Tunnard, quoted in Strauss, *Images*, 254

p. 251 "a patchwork" that includes "inner suburbs, large suburban centers": Frey, "New Geography of Population Shifts," 311

p. 251 "more like a constellation than a solar system": Calthorpe and Fulton, *Regional City*, 6

p. 251 "looked like a galaxy of stars and planets": Lewis, "America between the Wars," 432

p. 252 "in effect, the geopolitical map of New England": Rusk, *Cities without Suburbs*, 103

p. 253 "the toughest issue in American society" and Rusk's summary of "an inelastic area": Rusk, *Cities without Suburbs*, xv, 47

p. 254 "efficiency and the regional character of many contemporary problems": Jackson, *Crabgrass Frontier*, 154–55

p. 254 "repeatedly collided with the implacable realities of social and ethnic separation": Teaford, *Twentieth-Century American City*, 169

p. 254 "a clear material statement of status, power, and privilege": Higley, *Privilege, Power, and Place*, 127

p. 254 "not a single one of Levittown's 82,000 residents was black": Jackson, *Crabgrass Frontier*, 241

p. 254 "resistance to annexation is symptomatic": Jackson, *Crabgrass Frontier*, 155

p. 255 "in the thrall of corporations": Lemon, *Liberal Dreams and Nature's Limits*, 45

p. 255 "the basic dynamics of American expansionism were unprecedented": Meinig, *Atlantic America*, 417

p. 256 "investment tax credit" and "militarization of the economy" and "The sheer size of these . . . sectors": Markusen, *Regions*, 100, 106, 112–13

p. 257 On Southern labor force: Paterson, *North America*, 329

p. 259 "the Second Reconstruction": Smith, *Myth, Media*, 67

p. 259 "to bind the South more effectively into the nation": Meinig, *Transcontinental America*, 188

p. 261 on excluding Black counties from factory location and on "environmental racism": Aiken, *Cotton Plantation South*, 356, 360

p. 261 Jimmy Carter on "The Voting Rights Act": quoted in Smith, *Myth, Media*, 56

p. 261 "rural-to-urban migrants in the South take their church with them": Reed, *One South*, 135

p. 263 urban dwellers might "travel in an arctic circle": Crewdson, "Houston's Lifeline"

p. 263 "submission to outside forces": Miller, "Democratic Party's Southern Problem"

p. 263 On "the prosperity of the 1950s": Shortridge, "Expectations of Others," 125

p. 265 "a new and urgent concern": Franke and Franke, *Safe Places*, 13

p. 267 "aghast at what overpopulation has done": Franke and Franke, *Safe Places*, 22

p. 267 West was a "chosen land": Findlay, *Magic Lands*, 270

p. 267 On Western cities: Abbott, *Metropolitan Frontier*, 195, 194

p. 268 On Southern California: Wilson, "Reagan Country," 37

p. 268 "whether any common identity and purpose can be forged": Reinhold, *New York Times*, August 24, 1993

p. 269 "radical fringe of evangelical Protestantism" and "plain-folk Americanism": Gregory, *American Exodus*, 199, 141

p. 269 "to halt the ravenous rampage of suburbia": Abbott, *Metropolitan Frontier*, 146

p. 269 On Seattle: Abbott, "Regional City and Network City," 306–7, 317

p. 270 "the pitch to Silicon Valley decision makers": Lee, "There's Silicon in Them Thar Hills"

p. 270 "no longer . . . be thought of as the 'Utah church'": Bennion, "Geographic Dynamics," 25

p. 272 On California impact: Starrs and Wright, "Great Basin Growth," 433, 430, 433, 431

p. 272 "wary of Babylon": Bennion, "Mormondom's Deseret Homeland," 209

p. 272 Sun City as a model: Findlay, *Magic Lands*, 212

p. 274 Vail as one of "immensely rich enclaves": Wilkinson, "Paradise Revised," 18

p. 274 On Las Vegas: Abbott, *Metropolitan Frontier*, 71

p. 276 "westerners' innate suspicion of the East": Gressley, "Regionalism and the Twentieth-Century West," 201

p. 277 On the West: Bryce, *American Commonwealth*, vol. 2, 315; also quoted in Morgan, *Westward Tilt*, 25

p. 277 "Regional domination has virtually disappeared": Vance, "Revolution in American Space," 438

p. 278 "a chronology of ascension, dominance, degeneration, and redemption": Beauregard, *Voices of Decline*, 282

p. 278 "in a fascinating cultural-geographic isostasy": Vance, "California and the Ideal," 205

p. 279 Japanese firms set up "a base to study": Levin, "Motor City"

p. 279 Ford "to get connected to the California attitude": Cassidy, "Comeback," 127

p. 279 "at the forefront of automotive trends": Peterson, "3 Luxury-Car Makers"

p. 279 "American Art Scene Spreads": *Wall Street Journal*, June 8, 1979

p. 280 decentralization and leveling had led to "a national settlement system": Berry, "'The Nature of Cities' and Beyond," 438

p. 283 New York City, the "command-and-control center": Wheeler, "Corporate Role," 370
p. 283 "capital of capitalism": Abu-Lughod, *New York, Chicago, Los Angeles*, 320
p. 283 On Los Angeles: Soja, *Postmodern Geographies*, 223, 244
p. 283 "Los Angeles School": terms taken from Dear and Flusty, "Postmodern Urbanism," 52, 59
p. 283 on Miami as a "global city": Sassen, "On Concentration and Centrality," 69
p. 284 seek above all "privacy, exclusivity, and security": Nordheimer, "Nesting"
p. 284 Houston "an exciting and disturbing place": Huxtable, "Deep in the Heart"
p. 284 *Scribner's* on "a curious outgrowth": "Point of View," 396
p. 285 "coalitions of banks, developers, local newspapers": Cox, "American Politics," 5
p. 285 "Subsidy: $169,000 for Each Job": *Time*, November 9, 1998, 40; also Donahue, *Disunited States*, 101
p. 286 "Chase Manhattan collected $235 million": Donahue, *Disunited States*, 93
p. 286 "they never call it 'corporate welfare'": Bagli, "Known as Poacher"
p. 286 "wastes dollars, subsidizes shareholders": Mulder, "States Compete," quoting Corporation for Enterprise Development stance
p. 286 one state cannot "unilaterally disarm": Bagli, "Known as Poacher"
p. 286 proposals for solutions to state location incentives: Donahue, *Disunited States*, 116
p. 286 Uchitelle, "Taxes Help Foot Bill"; *Time*, November 30, 1998; Bagli, "Known as Poacher"; *Time*, November 9, 1998
p. 287 "a corporate welfare bureaucracy has grown up": *Time*, November 9, 1998
p. 287 "congressional life consists largely of a 'relentless search'": Cox, "American Politics," 21
p. 287 "strong territorialization of American political power": Markusen, *Regions*, 3
p. 289 On Washington: Abbott, "Dimensions of Regional Change," 1392
p. 291 "structural pluralism": Gordon, *Assimilation*, 132
p. 291 "Religion in the United States continues its perpetual reconfiguration": Gaustad and Barlow, *New Historical Atlas*, 353
p. 291 "wealthy, sauve, and powerful" Protestant establishment: Novak, *Further Reflections*, 10, 13–14
p. 292 "ethnical-racial pentagon," Hollinger, "Ethno-Racial Pentagon," 199
p. 293 "rather than bringing them together": Schlesinger, "Disuniting of America," 221; and "the brittle bonds of national identity," quoted in Kazal, "Revisiting Assimilation," 464 n
p. 293 a reemerging "core" ideology: Kazal, "Revisiting Assimilation," 438
p. 293 "symbolic ethnicity": a term credited to Herbert Gans, in Hollinger, "Ethno-Racial Pentagon," 205
p. 293 "panethnicities": Zelinsky, *Enigma*, 38
p. 293 "as a confession of cultural inferiority": Frederickson, *Comparative Imagination*, 209
p. 294 Kerner Report quotations: Boger, "Kerner Commission," 9, 11
p. 294 "not only is the taxpaying electorate overwhelmingly white": Hacker, *Two Nations*, xiii
p. 295 "it would be more accurate to say": Hacker, *Two Nations*, 11

PART THREE

p. 299 "In Chicago, Americans flaunted": Rosenberg, *Spreading the American Dream*, 6
p. 300 Turner on "the expansive character of American life": "The Significance of the Frontier," in *Frontier and Section*, 61
p. 300 Gladstone on America: quoted in Denny, *America Conquers Britain*, 403
p. 300 Giffen on American growth "without a precedent" and a "sense of being dwarfed": quoted in Thistlethwaite, *Great Experiment*, 277, 276
p. 300 H. G. Wells on America: *Future in America*, 248
p. 300 "alarm at the American penetration of . . . European markets": Rodgers, *Atlantic Crossings*, 47

p. 301 on foreign markets as "indispensable" and American commercial creed: Rosenberg, *Spreading the American Dream*, 58, 23

p. 301 "a combination of provincialism and arrogance": Henretta et al., *America's History*, 680

p. 301 U.S. emerged "rich and buoyant": Costigliola, *Awkward Dominion*, 19

p. 302 American consumer goods "began to pour into Europe": Rodgers, *Atlantic Crossings*, 370

p. 302 Saunders on influence of American cinema: *Hollywood in Berlin*, 1, 9, 1

p. 302 "the Gospel of Americanism": Rosenberg, *Spreading the American Dream*, 79

p. 303 on "'Fordism'": Rodgers, *Atlantic Crossings*, 371, 373

p. 303 America became "metaphor and symbol for modernization": Costigliola, *Awkward Dominion*, 22

p. 303 Thistlethwaite on war debts: *Great Experiment*, 280

p. 304 "the greatest collection of transplanted intellect, talent, and scholarship": Peter Gay in Fleming and Bailyn, *Intellectual Migration*, 12

p. 304 "United States had definitely become a Great Power": Kennedy, *Rise and Fall*, 248

p. 304 "globe-encircling parade": Sprout and Sprout, *Rise of American Naval Power*, 284

p. 305 Monroe Doctrine: LaFeber, *American Age*, 86, 85

p. 305 Democratic platform on "inexcusable blunder": Meinig, *Transcontinental America*, 373–74

p. 305 "pervading sense of security": Sprout and Sprout, *Rise of American Naval Power*, 303

p. 305 Wilson on situation in Europe and "appeal to the American People": *Papers*, vol. 50, 535; vol. 30, 393–94

p. 305 McNeill on "the really impressive achievements": *Rise of the West*, 742

p. 306 "intellectual fog . . . rolled in": Sprout and Sprout, *Rise of American Naval Power*, 322

p. 306 "Midwestern agrarians interpreted the world war": Bensel, *Sectionalism*, 107, 106

p. 306 "we are participants, whether we would or not": McDougall, *Promised Land*, 122, 132

p. 307 Wilson principles of "foundations of peace": *Papers*, vol. 40, 534, 536

p. 307 "to practice peace, he had to wage war": LaFeber, *American Age*, 296

p. 307 war "has been thrust upon us": *Papers*, vol. 41, 521

p. 307 "scientific peace": Wimer, "Wilson and World Peace," 147

p. 307 Wilson address, February 11, 1918: *Papers*, vol. 46, 321

p. 308 "were still locked into the complex multiple loyalties": Gellner, *Nations and Nationalism*, 100

p. 308 boundary issues in Fourteen Points: *Papers*, vol. 45, 537, 538

p. 308 "There are regions where you can not draw a national line": *Papers*, vol. 63, 13–14

p. 308 "When the President talks of self-determination": quoted in Kohn, *American Nationalism*, 217

p. 309 "the danger spots of the world": Bowman, *New World*, 3

p. 309 "absolute freedom of navigation" and access "to the great highways of the sea": *Papers*, vol. 45, 536; vol. 40, 537

p. 309 on "mandates": *Papers*, vol. 61, 431, 436, 240

p. 309 "a struggle for a just and secure peace": *Papers*, vol. 40, 535

p. 310 Senate feared that "acceptance . . . would embroil": Chambers, Grant, and Bayley, *Age of Conflict*, 437

p. 310 Wilson as American missionary: *Papers*, vol. 61, 435; vol. 40, 539; vol. 61, 428, 436; vol. 41, 525

p. 311 "that he had the power to impose": Hoover, *America's First Crusade*, 3

p. 311 characterizations of Lenin: Billington, *Icon and Axe*, 528, 529

p. 311 Lenin proposal of armistice: Pratt, *Challenge and Rejection*, 162

p. 311 "'Russian experiment' seemed the most important political thing": Chambers, Grant, and Bayley, *Age of Conflict*, 234

p. 311 Tocqueville: *Democracy in America*, vol. 1, 452

p. 312 Kohn on the 1918 situation: *American Nationalism*, 218

p. 312 United States "a nation struggling to avoid": Chambers, Grant, and Bayley, *Age of Conflict*, 453

p. 312 Spykman on United States in Europe: *America's Strategy*, 124

p. 312 "Bank of England rate controlled": Denny, *America Conquers Britain*, 27, 170

p. 313 Mackinder on growth of empires: *Democratic Ideals and Reality*, 2, 150

p. 313 Russell on America and world empire: Denny, *America Conquers Britain*, 16

p. 313 "continental United States enjoyed a measure of security": Sprout and Sprout, *Rise of American Naval Power*, 383

p. 314 on battleships "looming one after another": Sprout and Sprout, *Rise of American Naval Power*, 1

p. 315 "We cannot meet Japan in her desires" and language "which was to haunt": Curry, *Woodrow Wilson*, 185, 118

p. 315 Lansing-Ishii Agreement: Griswold, *Far Eastern Policy*, 216

p. 315 American fears of "invasion" and "complete Orientalization": Iriye, *Across the Pacific*, 105

p. 315 Japan regarded each as "a national insult": Reischauer, *United States and Japan*, 17

p. 315 amendment on "equality of nations": Griswold, *Far Eastern Policy*, 247

p. 315 Japanese into Manchuria as "unavoidable" and "the diversion of the tide may somewhat relieve": Curry, *Woodrow Wilson*, 180, and (quoting State Deparmtnet official), 116

p. 316 Bowman on "a country that must overflow its boundaries": *New World*, 502, 505

p. 316 Bowman on Manchuria: *Pioneer Fringe*, 280

p. 316 Japan "an unwilling participant" and special interests in China inextinguishable: Griswold, *Far Eastern Policy*, 298, 401

p. 316 "seemed . . . clear evidence of an Anglo-American lineup": Jansen, *Japan and Its World*, 81

p. 318 China "was not and never had been a truly vital American interest": Griswold, *Far Eastern Policy*, 466

p. 318 "beyond our will or power to support": Stevens and Westcott, *History of Sea Power*, 423

p. 318 "Peking lives under the Japanese shadow": Bowman, *New World*, 497

p. 318 "seemed to threaten the very existence" of Japan: Reischauer, *United States and Japan*, 24

p. 318 "rode the crest of a tidal wave of patriotism": Griswold, *Far Eastern Policy*, 421

p. 319 Wilson's "strong and direct language" to European Powers: Cline, *United States and Mexico*, 149

p. 319 Roosevelt Corollary: Bailey, *Diplomatic History*, 558

p. 319 "the logic of political geography and strategy": Bailey, *Diplomatic History*, 582

p. 319 "United Fruit controlled not only the banana market": LaFeber, *American Age*, 261

p. 321 Mexican Revolution as a contention among "classes, regions, ideologies": Knight, *U.S.-Mexican Relations*, 106

p. 321 "oil money was a significant factor": Hall and Coerver, *Revolution on the Border*, 94

p. 321 "Tampico is the most American city in Mexico": "Oily Mexico," 40

p. 322 "In this case the humiliation of having a foreign army ranging deep . . . was matched by": Meinig, *Transcontinental America*, 352, with map and further context

p. 322 oil compromise as "the triumph of . . . moderate pragmatic interests": Knight, *U.S.-Mexican Relations*, 44

p. 322 "an important step in the 'retreat from imperialism'": Cline, *United States and Mexico*, 212

p. 322 "the word 'Mexico' came to represent a neighbor nation": Knight, *U.S.-Mexican Relations*, 2

p. 323 Knight on "Hispanophobia": *U.S.-Mexican Relations*, 66

p. 323 U.S. failure to join the League "was regarded as proof": Chambers, Grant, and Bayley, *Age of Conflict*, 450

p. 323 "that the spirit of the covenant would tend to provide protection": Callcott, *Western Hemisphere*, 220

p. 324 speech by Argentine intellectual in Mexico: Holden and Zolov, *Latin America and United States*, 123–24

p. 324 FDR's "policy of a good neighbor" and U.S. agreement that "no state has the right to intervene": Bailey, *Diplomatic History*, 732, 737

p. 325 "Pan American system served primarily" to maintain U.S. "hegemony": Berger, *Under Northern Eyes*, 50

p. 325 Seidel on Pan American Highway Commission: *Progressive Pan Americanism*, 282

p. 328 Pan American Airways "at first regarded with suspicion": Davies, *Airlines of the United States*, 239

p. 328 "the Canadian coat of arms" in the Pan American Union: Nicholson, *Canada*, 115

p. 328 "It was good to know that the Yanks had come": Morton, *Canadian Identity*, 70

p. 328 1926 declaration on Dominions as "autonomous Communities": *Statesman's Year-Book 1931*, 75; also Cornell, et al., *Canada Unity in Diversity*, 418

p. 328 "that Canada was moving out of the orbit": Morton, *Canadian Identity*, 71

p. 329 Bowman on "serious servitudes" laid upon Canada: *New World* (1928), 711

p. 329 "every Canadian province, every Canadian city": Bliss: "Canadianizing American Business," 33

p. 329 "commensurate with Canada's new status" and "complete Canadian control of Broadcasting": Morchain, *Sharing a Continent*, 189, 191

p. 329 "even the word 'Americanization' came to connote": Berger, *Writing of Canadian History*, 148

p. 330 "a model of how nations might learn to live together": Berger, *Writing of Canadian History*, 156

p. 330 "for whom the spectre of annexation to the United States": Chester Martin, quoted in Berger, *Writing of Canadian History*, 137

p. 330 Great Depression "which stopped the world's strongest economy": Morchain, *Sharing a Continent*, 141

p. 330 "disengaging Canada from the British Empire": Stewart, *American Response*, 185

p. 330 isolationism "almost as profound as that of the United States": Morton, *Canadian Identity*, 73, 74

p. 330 FDR's Kingston address: *United States Presidential Addresses*, 11; and Cook, *Canada*, 223–24

p. 331 "the use made of the submarine by Germany": Bowman, *New World* (1921), 570

p. 331 "the British abandon their naval bases in the Western Hemisphere": McKercher, *Transition of Power*, 41

p. 331 Hoover to MacDonald on selling Bermuda, etc.: *Memoirs*, vol. 2, 345–46

p. 332 "having waged a war to make the world safe for democracy": Langer and Gleason, *Challenge of Isolation*, 13

p. 332 the "American people never realized . . . how deep was the feeling of betrayal": Chambers, Grant, and Bayley, *Age of Conflict*, 437

p. 332 "the very idea of aligning the United States with any power as anathema": Langer and Gleason, *Challenge of Isolation*, 142

p. 332 "the United States must be prepared to resist attack . . . from the North Pole to the South Pole": Conn and Fairchild, *Western Hemisphere*, 3

p. 333 exclusion of southern South America would be "catastrophic in its effect": Callcott, *Western Hemisphere*, 396

p. 333 "the absolute necessity for a base of operations in or near the eastern extremity of South America" and Pan American Neutrality Zone: Conn and Fairchild, *Western Hemisphere*, 13, 23

p. 335 "Gibraltar-Africa scheme" and was "approaching the brink of the Western Hemisphere": Conn and Fairchild, *Western Hemisphere*, 77, 114

p. 335 German invasion of Russia "an almost providential occurrence": Conn and Fairchild, *Western Hemisphere*, 127

p. 335 Roosevelt and Wilkie "felt compelled to say that they had no intention of getting the United States into the war": Conn and Fairchild, *Western Hemisphere*, 89

p. 336 Cordell Hull's speech, "There can be nothing more dangerous for our nation": Conn and Fairchild, *Western Hemisphere*, 89–90

p. 336 declaration of Japan, Germany, and Italy: Fifield and Pearcy, *Geopolitics*, 20–21, 97

p. 337 "the supreme point of view of every foreign policy": Hitler, *Mein Kampf*, 944

p. 337 other quotations from *Mein Kampf*: 601, 950, 964

p. 339 "the central myth of empire," "domestic pathologies," "extraordinarily aggressive states": Snyder, *Myths of Empire*, 1–2, 152, 320

p. 342 "since Japan was pictured as inferior" and "a symbol of Asia's revolt": Iriye, *Across the Pacific*, 217

p. 342 LaFeber on "a great irony became apparent": *American Age*, 405

p. 343 Mackinder "moated forward stronghold" and "aerodrome": "The Round World and Winning the Peace" in *Democratic Ideals and Reality*, 274, 277

p. 343 "the American way of war": Strachan, *TLS*, 7

p. 343 FDR, "We are now in the midst of war": quoted in McDougall, *Promised Land*, 147

p. 343 "The war aims expressed by the Churchill-Roosevelt declaration": Hoover, *America's First Crusade*, vii

p. 344 Eisenhower, "this war was a holy war": quoted in Carroll, *Constantine's Sword*, 257

p. 344 "a broader system of general security": Smith, *America's Mission*, 130

p. 345 Churchill, "I deem it highly important that we should shake hands as far east as possible": quoted in Link and Catton, *American Epoch*, 308

p. 345 Churchill, "Iron Curtain" speech: *Churchill Speaks*, 881

p. 347 "orderly retreat from empire": Smith, *America's Mission*, 126

p. 347 "The capitalistic system is essentially an international system" and Bretton Woods conference "to ensure an open, capitalist postwar world": LaFeber, *American Age*, 431

p. 348 "In 1945 the United States held a uniquely preeminent position": Leffler, *Preponderance of Power*, 3

p. 348 McNeill, *Past and Future*, 178

p. 349 overseas system a "transitory thing": McNeill, *Past and Future*, 73

p. 349 "In the future neither geography nor allies": Schnabel, *History of Joint Chiefs of Staff*, 91

p. 349 "that the English-speaking nations, as the only superior countries": *Pravda*, quoted in Walker, *Cold War*, 43

p. 349 "in spite of much reluctance": McNeill, *Past and Future*, 76

p. 350 "at bottom of Kremlin's neurotic view of world affairs": U.S. Department of State, *Foreign Relations, 1946*, vol. 6, 699

p. 350 "the main element of any United States policy": Kennan, *American Diplomacy*, 119 (reprint from *Foreign Affairs* 25 [July 1947]: 566–82)

p. 350 "an expanding totalitarian state": Schnabel, *History of Joint Chiefs of Staff*, 92

p. 350 "forces and installations disposed in an outer perimeter": Schnabel, *History of Joint Chiefs of Staff*, 148, 310, 313–14

p. 350 "Soviet pressure on the Straits": Walker, *Cold War*, 48

p. 350 "historic landmark in American foreign policy": Leffler, *Preponderance of Power*, 145

p. 352 "millions of people in the cities are slowly starving" and Marshall Plan "directed not against any country": Walker, *Cold War*, 50, 51

p. 352 "make a reexamination of our objectives in peace and war": U.S. Department of State, *Foreign Relations, 1950*, vol. 1 (NSC 68), 236, 238, 237

p. 352 Bemis on a "revolutionary USSR . . . firmly based in the Heartland": *United States as a World Power*, 463

p. 352 Bevin on "Physical control of the Eurasian land mass": Gaddis, *Long Peace*, 46

p. 353 on American "open skies" policy: Davies, *Airlines of the United States*, 370

p. 354 "terrified of the thought of a united Germany": Eisenhower, quoted in Leffler, *Preponderance of Power*, 68

p. 354 "specter of economic and social chaos": Leffler, *Preponderance of Power*, 64

p. 354 "the most central and creative policy initiative": Cronin, *World the Cold War Made*, 36

p. 354 "the vital North American arsenal": Gaddis, *Long Peace*, 45

p. 354 "U.S. military personnel flooded into Europe": LaFeber, *American Age*, 492

p. 356 definition of "protectorate": Meinig, *Continental America*, 172

p. 356 "empire by invitation": Lundestad, *American "Empire,"* 55

p. 357 Bohlen on "the Soviet mind": Gaddis, *Long Peace*, 53

p. 357 Middle East of "vital national interest": Cohen, *America in Age of Soviet Power*, 114

p. 358 "a national home for the Jewish people": Balfour Declaration, in Chambers, Grant, and Bayley, *Age of Conflict*, app. E, xxx

p. 359 Eden, "should not therefore allow ourselves to be restricted": Walker, *Cold War*, 98

p. 360 to resist "armed attack from any country controlled by international communism": LaFeber, *American Age*, 567

p. 360 Cohen on Soviet threat and containment: *World the Cold War Made*, 109

p. 360 Carmichael on "Islam": *Arabs Today*, 141

p. 360 on the Japanese constitution: Reischauer, *United States and Japan*, 351, 350

p. 361 Far East "swept bare of Japanese": Reischauer, *United States and Japan*, 241

p. 361 "American policy shifted from punishment": Allinson, *Japan's Postwar History*, 53

p. 361 Acheson on "a new day . . . has dawned in Asia": Iriye, *Across the Pacific*, 284

p. 362 Iriye on "Postwar Asia": "Asian Perspectives," 488

p. 362 "era of high-speed growth": Allinson, *Japan's Postwar History*, 83

p. 362 Japanese have tended to see "their world as a hierarchy": Jansen, *Japan and Its World*, 5

p. 363 Dulles on "Communist imperialism": LaFeber, *American Age*, 547

p. 363 Pérez on Cuba: "'So Near and Yet So Foreign,'" 7, 23

p. 364 "since the Americans have already surrounded the Soviet Union": LaFeber, *American Age*, 598

p. 364 Lyndon Johnson's "feverish determination to prevent 'another Cuba'": Steel, *Pax Americana*, 235

p. 365 on Russian polar flights: *Time*, June 28, 1937, 34

p. 365 "They found the world of transportation a cylinder": George B. Eisler in introduction to Raisz, *Atlas of Global Geography*, 5

p. 366 "geographical sense of our time": Harrison, *Look at the World*, 7

p. 366 "the fearful asymmetry" of relationships and Canadian responses: Thompson and Randall, *Canada and the United States*, 166, 192, 166, 197

p. 366 Washington as seat of "a powerful bureaucracy with a vested interest": Thompson and Randall, *Canada and the United States*, 180

p. 368 object of the Monroe Doctrine "to keep war off the American hemisphere": Stewart, *American Response*, 154, 155

p. 368 Eisenhower on "Forces of good and evil": Kennedy, *Rise and Fall*, 372

p. 368 "the Soviet Union had an ideology which gave the capitalist West ample cause": Walker, *Cold War*, 27

p. 368 Niebuhr on Marxism: *Pious and Secular America*, 9, 21

p. 368 Steiner on Marxism: *Nostalgia*, 9–10

p. 368 "communist system seemed a viable form": Smith, *America's Mission*, 186

p. 369 "The strength of their own fervent religious convictions": Smith, "American Imperialism," 46

p. 369 "caught in a maelstrom of mutual distrust": McDougall, *Promised Land*, 166

p. 369 Fulbright on "the tendency of great nations": *Arrogance of Power*, 9, 21

p. 369 "as events in every corner of the world became defined": Smith, *America's Mission*, 143

p. 369 "the surest way to lose an election": Smith, *America's Mission*, 207

p. 369 "space spectaculars" and moon enterprise as "most costly in history": Boorstin, *Americans*, 595, 597

p. 369 Kennedy, needing "a dramatic gesture": Fulbright, *Arrogance of Power*, 220

p. 370 "Cold War threat inflation," "big budgets," and end of Cold War revealed "a barely function-ing economy": Powers, "Secret Intelligence Wars," 33

p. 370 Soviet Union as example of disintegration of empires: Meinig, *Atlantic America*, 373

p. 371 Bush, "No, the enemy is unpredictability": LaFeber, *American Age*, 755

p. 371 *Time* on Toynbee: "The Challenge," March 17, 1947, 71

p. 373 "to draw a portrait": Lerner, *America as a Civilization*, 54, 65; on "the destiny of a civilization," 937, 938, 905

p. 373 "Is the whole Western world destined to become part of an American empire . . . ?": Bagby, *Culture and History*, 210

p. 374 Third World as a "vast geographical zone": Agnew, *Geopolitics*, 113

p. 374 "has come from nowhere and is almost everywhere": Giddens, *Runaway World*, 25

p. 375 Hughes on "the modern technological nation": *American Genesis*, 295

p. 376 Huntington on "a civilization-based world order": *Clash of Civilizations*, 20, 43

p. 380 on Newfoundland with reference to the U.S. and to Canada: Eggleston, *Newfoundland*, 54, 74

p. 380 Quebec's "mandate to negotiate": Balthazar, *French Canadian Civilization*, 20

p. 381 "to strengthen Canada rather than smother it": Smith, *Doing the Continental*, 8

p. 381 "various visions and agendas": Alper, "Idea of Cascadia," 1

p. 382 a "refuge . . . amid the immense sea": Henri Bourassa, 1918, quoted in Grant, *Lament*, 81

p. 382 Grant on "branch-plant society": *Lament*, 40, 41

p. 382 "North American regional marketplace": Smith, *Doing the Continental*, 23, 17

p. 382 Widdis on "Canada still exists": "Borders," 61, 49

p. 382 Harris on "a web of experiences": "Emotional Structure," 25

p. 383 Paz on Mexico and the U.S.: *One Earth*, 137, 154

p. 383 Puerto Rico "possesses all the attributes of a nation": Leibowitz, *Defining Status*, 140

p. 383 "involved Cubans in the appropriation of American forms" and "Cubanizing Cuba": Pérez, *On Becoming Cuban*, 7, 9, 493, 482

p. 384 "serve as an object lesson": Pérez, *Cuba and the United States*, 258

p. 384 "Cuban revolution not only transformed Cuba": Langley, *U.S. and the Caribbean*, 251

p. 385 Paz on Ibero-America: *One Earth*, 163, 169

p. 385 "When Philippine independence arrived": Brands, *Bound to Empire*, 350, 352

p. 387 evacuations "for the good of mankind": Leibowitz, *Defining Status*, 602

p. 387 Micronesian states treated "in large measure as independent countries": Leibowitz, *Defining Status*, 117

p. 389 "dynamic reciprocities": Meinig, *Continental America*, 398

p. 389 Bismarck on "The fact that the North Americans speak English": Crystal, *English as a Global Language*, 76–77

p. 390 "The idealistic desire to make the world over": *New York Times*, December 31, 1999

p. 393 "internal revolution of reculturation": Van Laue, *World Revolution*, 334

p. 394 "of all the problems which today confront mankind": McNeill, *Past and Future*, 171

p. 394 Agnew and Corbridge on "globalization of modern life": *Mastering Space*, 164

p. 394 Samuels, "One of the central lessons to be learned": "To Rescue Place," 602, 603

p. 396 "dynamic society, endlessly moving on": Dickstein, "The Fifties Were Radical Too," 15

Bibliography

Following the pattern set in Volume III, works used in the preparation of *Global America* are subdivided by chapters wherein they were first or most extensively used. A good many were pertinent to more than a single chapter, but titles have not generally been repeated. In Part Three, especially, there are numerous works applicable to all or much of the period since 1915, and reference to previous chapter listings may be necessary to find the full reference for a particular quotation. As in previous volumes a wide array of generally standard references, such as census reports, statistical abstracts, and maps and atlases, have also been consulted, and for this volume especially, the *New York Times* and the *Times Literary Supplement* (*TLS*) on a daily and weekly basis over many years.

GENERAL

Conzen, Michael P., Thomas A. Rumney, and Graeme Wynn. *A Scholar's Guide to Geographical Writing on the American and Canadian Past.* Chicago: Univ. of Chicago Press, 1993.

Elazar, Daniel J. *The American Mosaic: The Impact of Space, Time, and Culture on American Politics.* Boulder, Colo.: Westview Press, 1994.

Garrett, Wilbur E., ed. *Historical Atlas of the United States.* Washington, D.C.: National Geographic Society, 1988.

Henretta, James A., W. Elliot Brownlee, David Brody, and Susan Ware. *America's History.* Chicago: Dorsey Press, 1987.

Hugill, Peter J. *World Trade since 1431: Geography, Technology, and Capitalism.* Baltimore: Johns Hopkins Univ. Press, 1993.

———. *Global Communications since 1844: Geopolitics and Technology.* Baltimore: Johns Hopkins Univ. Press, 1999.

Paterson, J. H. *North America: A Geography of the United States and Canada.* 9th ed. New York: Oxford Univ. Press, 1994.

Zelinsky, Wilbur. *The Cultural Geography of the United States.* Revised ed. Englewood Cliffs, N.J.: Prentice Hall, 1992.

PART ONE
1. Automotive Revolution

Auto Road Atlas of the United States. Chicago: Rand McNally, 1926.

Banham, Reyner. *Los Angeles: The Architecture of Four Ecologies.* New York: Harper & Row, 1971.

Batchelder, A. G. "The Immediate Necessity for Military Highways." *National Geographic Magazine* 32 (November–December 1917): 477–99.

Berger, Michael L. *The Devil Wagon in God's Country: The Automobile and Social Change in Rural America, 1893–1929.* Hamden, Conn.: Archon Books, 1979.

Brilliant, Ashleigh Ellwood. "Social Effects of the Automobile in Southern California during the Nineteen-Twenties." Ph.D. dissertation, Department of History, Univ. of California, Berkeley, 1964.

Childs, William R. *Trucking and the Public Interest: The Emergence of Federal Regulation, 1914–1940.* Knoxville: Univ. of Tennessee Press, 1985.

Daggett, Stuart. *Principles of Inland Transportation.* New York: Harper & Brothers, 1934.

Donovan, Frank. *Wheels for a Nation.* New York: Thomas Y. Crowell, 1965.

"Express Roads for Express Traffic." *Engineering News-Record* 117 (August 27, 1936): 317.

Fellmann, Jerome Donald. *Truck Transportation Patterns of Chicago.* Research Paper 12. Chicago: Department of Geography, Univ. of Chicago, 1950.

Flink, James J. *America Adopts the Automobile, 1895–1910.* Cambridge: MIT Press, 1970.

———. *The Car Culture.* Cambridge: MIT Press, 1975.

———. *The Automobile Age.* Cambridge: MIT Press, 1988.

Foster, Mark S. "The Model-T, the Hard Sell, and Los Angeles's Urban Growth: The Decentralization of Los Angeles during the 1920s." *Pacific Historical Review* 44 (November 1975): 459–84.

———. *From Streetcar to Superhighway: American City Planners and Urban Transportation, 1900–1940.* Philadelphia: Temple Univ. Press, 1981.

———. "The Role of the Automobile in Shaping a Unique City." In *The Car and the City: The Automobile, the Built Environment, and Daily Urban Life,* ed. Martin Wachs and Margaret Crawford, 186–93. Ann Arbor: Univ. of Michigan Press, 1992.

Geddes, Norman Bel. *Magic Motorways.* New York: Random House, 1940.

Genet, Arthur S. *"Profile of Greyhound!": The Greyhound Corporation.* Princeton, N.J.: Newcomen Society, 1958.

Goddard, Stephen B. *Getting There: The Epic Struggle between Road and Rail in the American Century.* New York: Basic Books, 1994.

"Highway Progress and Problems in the Mid-South." *Engineering News-Record* 91 (July 26, 1936): 128–32.

Hilton, George W., and John F. Due. *The Electric Interurban Railways in America.* Stanford: Stanford Univ. Press, 1960.

Hokanson, Drake. *The Lincoln Highway: Main Street across America.* Iowa City: Univ. of Iowa Press, 1988.

Holt, W. Stull. *The Bureau of Public Roads: Its History, Activities and Organization.* Baltimore: Johns Hopkins Press, 1923.

Hugill, Peter J. "Good Roads and the Automobile in the United States, 1880–1929." *Geographical Review* 72 (July 1982): 327–49.

———. *World Trade since 1431: Geography, Technology, and Capitalism.* Baltimore: Johns Hopkins Univ. Press, 1993.

Hutchinson, Rollin W. "Motorized Highway Commerce." *Scribner's Magazine* 55 (January 1914): 181–92.

Interstate Commerce Commission. "Historical Development of Transport Coordination and Integration in the United States." Bureau of Transport Economics and Statistics Statement, No. 5015. Washington, D.C., April 1950 (mimeo).

Jackson, John Brinkerhoff. *Landscape in Sight: Looking at America.* Ed. Helen Lefkowitz Horowitz. New Haven: Yale Univ. Press, 1997.

Jackson, Kenneth T. *Crabgrass Frontier: The Suburbanization of the United States.* New York: Oxford Univ. Press, 1985.

Jakle, John A. *The Tourist: Travel in Twentieth-Century North America.* Lincoln: Univ. of Nebraska Press, 1985.

Jakle, John A., and Keith A. Sculle. *The Gas Station in America.* Baltimore: Johns Hopkins Univ. Press, 1994.

Jakle, John A., Keith A. Sculle, and Jefferson S. Rogers. *The Motel in America.* Baltimore: Johns Hopkins Univ. Press, 1996.

James, E. W. "Making and Unmaking a National System of Marked Routes." *American Highways* 12 (October 1933): 16–18, 27.

Joy, Henry B. "Transcontinental Trails." *Scribner's Magazine* 55 (January 1914): 160–72.

Karolevitz, Robert F. *This Was Trucking: A Pictorial History of the First Quarter Century of Commercial Motor Vehicles.* Seattle: Superior Publishing, 1966.

Keir, Malcolm. *The March of Commerce.* New Haven: Yale Univ. Press, 1927.

Kelly, Thomas E. "The Concrete Road to MIC; National Defense and Federal Highways." In *War, Business, and American Society: Historical Perspectives on the Military-Industrial Complex,* ed. Benjamin Franklin Cooling, 133–45. Port Washington, N.Y.: Kennikat Press, 1977.

Krim, Arthur James. "Imagery in Search of a City. The Geosophy of Los Angeles, 1921–1971." Ph.D. dissertation, Department of Geography, Clark Univ., 1979.

Labatut, Jean, and Wheaton J. Lane. *Highways in Our National Life: A Symposium.* Princeton: Princeton Univ. Press, 1950.

Lewis, Peirce. "The Landscapes of Mobility." In *The National Road,* ed. Karl Raitz, 3–44. Baltimore: Johns Hopkins Univ. Press, 1996.

Liebs, Chester H. *Main Street to Miracle Mile: American Roadside Architecture.* Boston: Little, Brown, 1985.

Lynd, Robert S., and Helen Merrell Lynd. *Middletown: A Study in American Culture.* New York: Harcourt, Brace, 1929.

MacDonald, Thomas H. "Classification and Uses

of Highways and the Influence of Federal-Aid Acts." *Engineering News-Record* 83 (December 11–18, 1919): 985–88.

———. "Tomorrow's Roads." *Engineering News-Record* 117 (December 17, 1936): 868–70.

Mehren, E. J. "A Suggested National Highway Policy and Plan." *Engineering News-Record* 81 (December 19, 1918): 1112–17.

Meinig, D. W. "Symbolic Landscapes." In *The Interpretation of Ordinary Landscapes: Geographical Essays*, ed. D. W. Meinig, 164–92. New York: Oxford Univ. Press, 1979.

Moline, Norman T. *Mobility and the Small Town, 1900–1930: Transportation Change in Oregon, Illinois*. Research Paper No. 132. Chicago: Department of Geography, Univ. of Chicago, 1971.

Mumford, Lewis. *Technics and Civilization*. New York: Harcourt, Brace, 1934.

"National Highway System Gets Strong Backing." *Engineering News-Record* 81 (December 19, 1918): 1108.

National Highways Map of the United States Showing One Hundred Thousand Miles of National Highways. Washington, D.C.: National Highways Association, November 1915.

Nelson, Howard J. "The Spread of an Artificial Landscape over Southern California." *Annals of the Association of American Geographers* 49, Part 2 (September 1959): 80–100.

"A New Era in Highway Transportation." *Engineering News-Record* 81 (November 28, 1918): 967.

Official Paved Road and Commercial Survey of the United States. Indianapolis: National Map, [1928].

Parmelee, Julius H. *The Modern Railway*. New York: Longmans, Green, 1940.

Pomeroy, Earl. *In Search of the Golden West: The Tourist in Western America*. New York: Alfred A. Knopf, 1957.

Proceedings of Forty-second Annual Convention, National Association of Railroad and Utilities Commissioners. Charleston, S.C. November 12–15, 1930. New York: Nat. Assoc. of RR and UC, 1931.

Rae, John B. *The Road and the Car in American Life*. Cambridge: MIT Press, 1971.

Recent Social Trends in the United States. New York: McGraw-Hill, 1933.

Report of the Postmaster General. November 15, 1915. Washington, D.C.: Government Printing Office, 1916.

Rose, Mark H. *Interstate: Express Highway Politics, 1941–1956*. Lawrence: Regents Press of Kansas, 1979.

Seely, Bruce E. *Building the American Highway System: Engineers as Policy Makers*. Philadelphia: Temple Univ. Press, 1987.

Shaler, N. S. *American Highways: A Popular Account of Their Conditions and of the Means by Which They May Be Bettered*. New York: Century, 1896.

Stewart, George R. *U.S. 40: Cross-Section of the United States of America*. Boston: Houghton Mifflin, 1953.

"Toward New Road Systems." *Engineering News-Record* 118 (April 1, 1937): 493.

Trewartha, Glenn T. "The Unincorporated Hamlet. One Element in the American Settlement Fabric." *Annals of the Association of American Geographers* 33 (March 1943): 32–81.

U.S. Congress. *Address of the President of the United States*. 64th Cong., 1st sess., December 7, 1915. H. Doc. 1.

———. House. *Report of the Joint Committee on Federal Aid in the Construction of Post Roads*. 63d Cong., 3d sess., January 21, 1915. H. Doc. 1915.

———. House. *Toll Roads and Free Roads*. 76th Cong., 1st sess., April 27, 1939. H. Doc. 272.

———. House. *Interregional Highways*. 78th Cong., 2d sess., January 12, 1944. H. Doc. 379.

———. House. *Highway Needs of the National Defense*. 81st Cong., 1st sess., June 30, 1949. H. Doc. 249.

———. Senate. *Federal Aid in the Construction of Rural Post Roads*. 64th Cong., 1st sess., March 10, 1916. S. Report 250.

———. Senate. *Good Roads*. 64th Cong., 1st sess., June 26, 1916. S. Doc. 474.

U.S. Department of Transportation, Federal Highway Administration. *America's Highways, 1776–1976*. Washington, D.C.: Government Printing Office, 1977.

Vance, James E., Jr. *Capturing the Horizon: The Historical Geography of Transportation*. New York: Harper & Row, 1986.

Wachs, Martin, and Margaret Crawford, eds. *The*

Car and the City: The Automobile, the Built Environment, and Daily Urban Life. Ann Arbor: Univ. of Michigan Press, 1992.

Wilson, Woodrow. *Papers of Woodrow Wilson*. Ed. Arthur S. Link. Vol. 38. Princeton: Princeton Univ. Press, 1982.

2. Neotechnic Evolution

Abrams, Ernest R. *Power in Transition*. New York: Charles Scribner's Sons, 1940.

Archer, Gleason L. *History of Radio to 1926*. New York: American Historical, 1938.

———. *Big Business and Radio*. New York: American Historical, 1939.

Barnouw, Erik. *A Tower in Babel: A History of Broadcasting in the United States*. Vol. 1, *—to 1933*. New York: Oxford Univ. Press, 1966.

Baum, Frank G. *Atlas of U.S.A. Electric Power Industry: Outlining Regional Electric Power Districts and Proposed Constant-Potential Transmission Systems for the United States of North America*. New York: McGraw-Hill, 1923.

Bloomfield, Gerald T. "Coils of the Commercial Serpent: A Geography of the Ford Branch Distribution System, 1904–33." In *Roadside America: The Automobile in Design and Culture*, ed. Jan Jennings, 40–51. Ames: Iowa State Univ. Press, 1990.

Boas, Charles W. "Locational Patterns of American Automobile Assembly Plants, 1895–1958." *Economic Geography* 37 (July 1961): 218–30.

Brown, D. Clayton. *Electricity for Rural America: The Fight for the REA*. Westport, Conn.: Greenwood Press, 1980.

Davies, R. E. G. *Airlines of the United States since 1914*. Washington, D.C.: Smithsonian Institution Press, 1988.

The Electric Power Industry: Past, Present and Future. By the Editorial Staff of *Electrical World*. New York: McGraw-Hill, 1949.

Faulkner, Harold Underwood. *American Economic History*. 5th ed. New York: Harper & Brothers, 1943.

"Ford Politics in Muscle Shoals." *Literary Digest* 79 (October 27, 1923): 14–15.

Garwood, John D., and W. C. Tuthill. *The Rural Electrification Administration: An Evaluation*. Washington, D.C.: American Enterprise Institute, 1963.

"Giant Power: Large Scale Electrical Development as a Social Factor." *Annals of the American Academy of Political and Social Science* 118 (March 1925).

"Henry Ford's Bid for Muscle Shoals." *Literary Digest* 72 (January 28, 1922): 10–11.

Hounshell, David A. *From the American System to Mass Production, 1800–1932: The Development of Manufacturing Technology in the United States*. Baltimore: Johns Hopkins Univ. Press, 1984.

Hubbard, Preston J. *Origins of the TVA: The Muscle Shoals Controversy, 1920–1932*. Nashville, Tenn.: Vanderbilt Univ. Press, 1962.

Hugill, Peter J. *Global Communications since 1844: Geopolitics and Technology*. Baltimore: Johns Hopkins Univ. Press, 1999.

Hunter, Louis C., and Lynwood Bryant. *A History of Industrial Power in the United States, 1780–1930*. Vol. 3, *The Transmission of Power*. Cambridge: MIT Press, 1991.

Hurley, Neil P. "The Automotive Industry: A Study in Industrial Location." *Land Economics* 35 (February 1959): 1–14.

Hyman, Leonard S. *America's Electric Utilities: Past, Present and Future*. 5th ed. Arlington, Va.: Public Utilities Reports, 1994.

Leary, William M., ed. *Pilots' Directions: The Transcontinental Airway and Its History*. Iowa City: Univ. of Iowa Press, 1990.

Lewis, Peirce. "America between the Wars: The Engineering of a New Geography." In *North America: The Historical Geography of a Changing Continent*, ed. Robert D. Mitchell and Paul A. Groves, 410–37. Totowa, N.J.: Rowman & Littlefield, 1987.

McCarty, Harold H. *The Geographic Basis of American Economic Life*. New York: Harper & Row, 1940.

Merz, Charles. "Muscle Shoals." *Century Magazine* 108 (September 1924): 615–21.

Mumford, Lewis. *Technics and Civilization*. New York: Harcourt, Brace, 1934.

National Power Survey. A Report by the Federal Power Commission. Washington, D.C.: Government Printing Office, October 1964.

Nye, David E. *Electrifying America: Social Meanings of a New Technology, 1880–1940.* Cambridge: MIT Press, 1990.

Official Guide of the Railways and Steam Navigation Lines of the United States, Porto Rico, Canada, Mexico and Cuba. New York: National Railway Publication, November 1933.

Radio Service Bulletin, February 28, 1929, No. 143. Washington, D.C.: Department of Commerce.

Rae, John B. *American Automobile Manufacturers: The First Forty Years.* Philadelphia: Chilton, 1959.

————. *The American Automobile: A Brief History.* Chicago: Univ. of Chicago Press, 1965.

Robinson, Thomas Porter. *Radio Networks and the Federal Government.* [1943] New York: Arno Press, 1979.

Rubenstein, James M. *The Changing US Auto Industry: A Geographical Analysis.* London: Routledge, 1992.

Schubert, Paul. *The Electric World: The Rise of Radio.* New York: Macmillan, 1928.

Socolow, A. Walker. *The Law of Radio Broadcasting.* 2 vols. New York: Baker, Voorhis, 1939.

Sporn, Philip. *The Integrated Power System as the Basic Mechanism for Power Supply.* New York: McGraw-Hill, 1950.

Taylor, Frank J. *High Horizons: Daredevil Flying Postmen to Modern Magic Carpet—The United Air Lines Story.* New York: McGraw-Hill, 1962.

U.S. Bureau of the Census, Department of Commerce. "Central Electric Light and Power Stations." *Census of Electric Industries, 1917.* Washington, D.C.: Government Printing Office, 1920.

Warren, Kenneth. *The American Steel Industry, 1850–1970: A Geographical Interpretation.* Oxford: Clarendon Press, 1973.

White, Llewellyn. *The American Radio: A Report on the Broadcasting Industry in the United States from the Commission on Freedom of the Press.* Chicago: Univ. of Chicago Press, 1947.

Wik, Reynold M. *Henry Ford and Grass-roots America.* Ann Arbor: Univ. of Michigan Press, 1972.

3. Acceleration: On the Surface

Baerwald, Thomas J. "The Emergence of a New 'Downtown.'" *Geographical Review* 68 (July 1978): 308–18.

Barrow, Robert Van. "The Politics of Interstate Route Selection: A Case Study of Interest Activities in a Decision Situation." Ph.D. dissertation, Department of Political Science, Florida State Univ., 1967.

Bigham, Truman C., and Merrill J. Roberts. *Transportation: Principles and Problems.* New York: McGraw-Hill, 1952.

Blaszak, Michael W. "Megamergers to the Far Horizon." *Trains* 57 (April 1997): 36–46.

Briggs, Ronald. "The Impact of the Interstate Highway System on Nonmetropolitan Developments, 1950–75." In *Beyond the Urban Fringe: Land Use Issues of Nonmetropolitan America,* ed. Rutherford H. Platt and George Macinko, 83–105. Minneapolis: Univ. of Minnesota Press, 1983.

Browning, Clyde E. "The Rise of the Beltways: A Powerful Force for Urban Change." *Focus* (Summer 1990): 18–22.

Clay, Grady. *Close-Up: How to Read the American City.* New York: Praeger Publishers, 1973.

Conzen, Michael P., and Adam R. Daniel, eds. *Lockport Legacy: Themes in the Historical Geography of an Illinois Canal Town.* Chicago: Committee on Geographical Studies, Univ. of Chicago, 1990.

Daggett, Stuart. *Principles of Inland Transportation.* New York: Harper & Brothers, 1934, and 4th ed., 1955.

Doster, James F., and David C. Weaver. *Tenn-Tom Country: The Upper Tombigbee Valley.* Tuscaloosa: Univ. of Alabama Press, 1987.

Drury, George H. *The Historical Guide to North American Railroads.* Milwaukee: Kalmbach, 1985.

Frailey, Fred W. "Powder River Country." *Trains* 49 (November 1989): 40–63.

————. "Colossus of Roads." *Trains* 55 (November 1995): 42–53.

Garreau, Joel. *Edge City: Life on the New Frontier.* New York: Doubleday, 1991.

Goddard, Stephen B. *Getting There: The Epic*

Struggle between Road and Rail in the American Century. New York: Basic Books, 1994.

Grava, Sigurd. "Thoughts toward the Next Continental Transportation System." *Transportation Quarterly* 46 (October 1992): 503–16.

Hatcher, Harlan, and Erich A. Walter. *A Pictorial History of the Great Lakes*. New York: Crown Brothers, 1963.

Hills, T. L. *The St. Lawrence Seaway*. New York: Frederick A. Praeger, 1959.

Hilton, George W. *Amtrak: The National Railroad Passenger Corporation*. Washington, D.C.: American Enterprise Institute for Public Policy Research, 1980.

Hoover, Herbert. *The New Day: Campaign Speeches of Herbert Hoover, 1928*. Stanford: Stanford Univ. Press, 1929.

———. *The Memoirs of Herbert Hoover*. Vol. 2. New York: Macmillan, 1952.

Itzkoff, Donald M. *Off the Track: The Decline of the Intercity Passenger Train in the United States*. Westport, Conn.: Greenwood Press, 1985.

Johnson, Bob. "Showdown for Amtrak." *Trains* 55 (January 1995): 40–49.

Kay, Jane Holtz. *Asphalt Nation: How the Automobile Took over America, and How We Can Take It Back*. Berkeley: Univ. of California Press, 1997.

Klein, Maury. *Unfinished Business: The Railroad in American Life*. Hanover, N.H.: Univ. Press of New England, 1994.

Ladd, Harry. *U.S. Railroad Traffic Atlas*. Orange, Calif.: Ladd Publications, 1995.

Lamb, J. Parker. "Texas' Chemical Coast." *Trains* 59 (October 1999): 36–49.

Larson, Thomas D. "Pennsylvania and the Interstate System." *Transportation Quarterly* 41 (April 1987): 117–32.

Leonard, William Norris. *Railroad Consolidation under the Transportation Act of 1920*. New York: Columbia Univ. Press, 1946.

Lewis, Peirce. "The Landscapes of Mobility." In *The National Road*, ed. Karl Raitz, 3–44. Baltimore: Johns Hopkins Univ. Press, 1996.

Lewis, Robert G. *Handbook of American Railroads*. New York: Simmons-Boardman, 1951.

Lewis, Tom. *Divided Highways: Building the Interstate Highways, Transforming American Life*. New York: Viking Press, 1997.

Little, James A., and Henry M. Cunningham. *Historical Development of Transport Coordination and Integration in the United States*. Washington, D.C.: Interstate Commerce Commission, April 1950.

Mabee, Carleton. *The Seaway Story*. New York: Macmillan, 1961.

Martin, Albro. *Railroads Triumphant: The Growth, Rejection, and Rebirth of a Vital American Force*. New York: Oxford Univ. Press, 1992.

Mason, Joseph B., and Charles T. Moore. "Commercial Site Selection at Interstate Interchanges." *Traffic Quarterly* 27 (January 1973): 19–33.

Mayer, Harold M. "The Changing American Railroad Pattern." In *A Man for All Regions: The Contributions of Edward L. Ullman to Geography*, ed. J. D. Eyre, 108–43. Studies in Geography No. 11. Chapel Hill: Univ. of North Carolina, 1977.

Moon, Henry. *The Interstate Highway System*. Washington, D.C.: Association of American Geographers, 1994.

1995 Status of the Nation's Surface Transportation System: Condition and Performance. Report of the Secretary of Transportation to the United States Congress. 104th Cong., 2d sess. Washington, D.C.: Government Printing Office, 1996.

Norris, Darrell A. "Interstate Highway Exit Morphology: Non-Metropolitan Exit Commerce on I-75." *Professional Geographer* 39 (February 1989): 23–32.

Parmelee, Julius H. *The Modern Railway*. New York: Longmans, Green, 1940.

Richards, Curtis W., and Michael L. Thaller. "United States Railway Traffic: An Update." *Professional Geographer* 30 (August 1978): 250–55.

Saunders, Richard. *The Railroad Mergers and the Coming of Conrail*. Westport, Conn.: Greenwood Press, 1978.

Schein, Richard H. "The Interstate 70 Landscape." In *The National Road*, ed. Karl Raitz, 319–47. Baltimore: Johns Hopkins Univ. Press, 1996.

Solzman, David M. *The Chicago River: An Illustrated History and Guide to the River and Its Waterways*. Chicago: Loyola Press, 1998.

Sussman, Joseph M. "ITS: A Short History and

Perspective on the Future." *Transportation Quarterly* 50 (October 1996): 115–25.

Ullman, Edward L. "The Railroad Pattern of the United States." *Geographical Review* 39 (April 1949): 242–56.

U.S. Congress. *National Transportation Policy*. Preliminary Draft of a Report Prepared for the Committee on Interstate and Foreign Commerce, U.S. Senate, by the Special Study Group on Transportation Policies (the Doyle Report). Washington, D.C.: Government Printing Office, 1961.

———. *Amtrak's Current Situation*. Hearings before the Subcommittee on Railroads of the Committee on Transportation Infrastructure, House of Representatives, 104th Cong., 1st sess., February 7, 10, and 13, 1995. Washington, D.C.: Government Printing Office, 1996.

Wallace, William H. "Freight Traffic Functions of Anglo-American Railroads." *Annals of the Association of American Geographers* 53 (September 1963): 312–31.

Wayman, Norbury L. *Life on the River: A Pictorial History of the Mississippi, the Missouri, and the Western River System*. New York: Crown Publishers, 1971.

Willoughby, William R. *The St. Lawrence Waterway: A Study in Politics and Diplomacy*. Madison: Univ. of Wisconsin Press, 1961.

Wilner, Frank N. "The Truth about Mergers." *Railway Age* 199 (November 1998): 41–45.

4. Acceleration: In the Air

Debbage, Keith G. "U.S. Airport Market Concentration and Deconcentration." *Transportation Quarterly* 47 (January 1993): 115–36.

Fleming, Douglas K. *An Identification and Interpretation of U.S. Air Travel Patterns*. Monograph. Seattle: Department of Geography, Univ. of Washington, September 30, 1976.

———. "Competition in the U.S. Airline Industry." *Transportation Quarterly* 45 (April 1991): 181–210.

Jemiolo, Jerzy, and Clinton V. Oster, Jr. "Regional Changes in Airline Service since Deregulation." *Transportation Quarterly* 41 (October 1987): 569–86.

Ligon, Gray C. "Development of the U.S. Air Express Industry: 1970–1990." *Transportation Quarterly* 46 (April 1992): 279–94.

"Sky High Fares Hurting Local Business." *Syracuse Herald-Journal*, February 16, 1999.

Taaffe, Edward J. "Air Transportation and United States Urban Distribution." *Geographical Review* 46 (April 1956): 219–38.

5. Acceleration: Invisible and Instantaneous

Adams, Paul C. "Cyberspace and Virtual Places." *Geographical Review* 87 (April 1997): 155–71.

Brinkley, Joel. "Information Highway Is Just Outside the Beltway." *New York Times*, October 12, 1999.

Broad, William J. "Doing Science on the Network: A Long Way from Gutenberg." *New York Times*, May 18, 1993.

Brooks, John. *Telephone: The First Hundred Years*. New York: Harper & Row, 1976.

Christensen, Jon. "What Web Retailers Really Need Is a Whole Lot of Shelf Space." *New York Times*, September 22, 1999.

Gladwell, Malcolm. "Clicks and Mortar." *New Yorker*, December 6, 1999, 106–15.

Hall, Peter, and Ann Markusen, eds. *Silicon Landscapes*. Boston: Allen & Unwin, 1985.

Henderson, Jeffrey. *The Globalisation of High Technology: Space and Semiconductors in the Restructuring of the Modern World*. London: Routledge, 1991.

Hepworth, Mark E. *Geography of the Information Economy*. New York: Guilford Press, 1990.

Hybels, Saundra, and Dana Ulloth. *Broadcasting: An Introduction to Radio and Television*. New York: Van Nostrand, 1978.

Hyman, Leonard S., Richard C. Toole, and Rose-mary M. Avellis. *The New Telecommunications Industry: Evolution and Organization.* N.p.: Public Utilities Reports and Merrill Lynch, Pierce, Fenner & Smith, 1987.

Inglis, Andrew F. *Behind the Tube: A History of Broadcasting Technology and Business.* Boston: Focal Press, 1990.

Johnson, George. "From Two Small Nodes, a Mighty Web Has Grown." *New York Times,* October 12, 1999.

Johnson, Kirk. "Where Electronic Money Talks as Fast as It Moves." *New York Times,* February 18, 1997.

Lewis, Peter H. "U.S. Begins Privatizing Internet's Operations." *New York Times,* October 24, 1994.

Lohr, Steve. "Reluctant Conscripts in the March of Technology." *New York Times,* September 17, 1995.

Markoff, John. "A Supercomputer in Every Pot." *New York Times,* December 29, 1988.

———. "Bush Plan Would Aid Computing." *New York Times,* September 8, 1989.

———. "Building the Electronic Superhighway." *New York Times,* January 24, 1993.

———. "The Soul of a New Economy." *New York Times,* December 29, 1997.

Markusen, Ann, Peter Hall, and Amy Glasmeier. *High Tech America: The What, How, Where, and Why of the Sunrise Industries.* Boston: Allen & Unwin, 1986.

Murphy, Todd. "Developers Rush to Meet Demands of E-Commerce." *New York Times,* January 23, 2000.

Pickles, John, ed. *Ground Truth: The Social Implications of Geographic Information Systems.* New York: Guilford Press, 1995.

Preer, Robert W. *The Emergence of Technopolis: Knowledge-Intensive Technologies and Regional Development.* New York: Praeger Publishers, 1992.

Rogers, Everett M., and Judith K. Larsen. *Silicon Valley Fever: Growth of High-Technology Culture.* New York: Basic Books, 1984.

Sassen, Saskia. "On Concentration and Centrality in the Global City." In *World Cities in a World System,* ed. Paul L. Knox and Peter J. Taylor, 63–75. Cambridge: Cambridge Univ. Press, 1995.

Saxenian, Annalee. "The Genesis of Silicon Valley." In *Silicon Valley Landscapes,* ed. Peter Hall and Ann Markusen, 20–34. Boston: Allen & Unwin, 1985.

Specter, Michael. "Your Mail Has Vanished." *New Yorker,* December 6, 1999, 96–104.

Starrs, Paul F. "The Sacred, the Regional, and the Digital." *Geographical Review* 87 (April 1997): 193–218.

Starrs, Paul F., and Julie Anderson. "The Words of Cyberspace." *Geographical Review* 87 (April 1997): 146–54.

Stone, Alan. *How America Got On-Line: Politics, Markets, and the Revolution in Telecommunications.* Armonk, N.Y.: M. E. Sharpe, 1997.

Verhovek, Sam Howe. "Austin Rides a Winner: Technology." *New York Times,* January 31, 1998.

White, C. Langdon. "Sequent Occupance in the Santa Clara Valley, California." *Journal of the Graduate Research Center* (Stanford University) 34 (June 1965): 277–99.

Winston, Brian. *Media Technology and Society, a History: From the Telegraph to the Internet.* London: Routledge, 1998.

PART TWO

1. Populations and Policies, 1915–1950s

Allen, James P. "Changes in the American Propensity to Migrate." *Annals of the Association of American Geographers* 67 (December 1977): 577–87.

Allen, James Paul, and Eugene James Turner. *We the People: An Atlas of America's Ethnic Diversity.* New York: Macmillan, 1988.

Auerbach, Frank L. *Immigration Laws of the United States.* Indianapolis: Bobbs-Merrill, 1955.

Bennett, Marion T. *American Immigration Policies: A History.* Washington, D.C.: Public Affairs Press, 1963.

Bogue, Donald J. *Population Growth in Standard Metropolitan Areas, 1900–1950.* Housing and Home Finance Agency. Division of Housing Research. Washington, D.C.: Government Printing Office, December 1953.

———. *The Population of the United States.* New York: Free Press, 1959.

Bogue, Donald J., Henry S. Shryock, Jr., and Siegfried A. Hoermann. *Subregional Migration in the United States, 1935–40.* Vol. 1, *Streams of Migration between Subregions.* Oxford, Ohio: Scripps Foundation Studies in Population Distribution, No. 5, 1957.

Bowman, Isaiah. *The New World: Problems in Political Geography.* 4th ed. Yonkers-on-Hudson, N.Y.: World Book, 1928.

Davie, Maurice R. *World Immigration: With Special Reference to the United States.* New York: Macmillan, 1949.

Dinnerstein, Leonard, and David M. Reimers. *Ethnic Americans: A History of Immigration and Assimilation.* 2d ed. New York: Harper & Row, 1982.

Divine, Robert A. *American Immigration Policy, 1924–1952.* New Haven: Yale Univ. Press, 1957.

Ehrlich, Paul R., Loy Bilderback, and Anne H. Ehrlich. *The Golden Door: International Migration, Mexico, and the United States.* N.p.: Wideview Books, 1981.

Fairchild, Henry Pratt. *Immigration: A World Movement and Its American Significance.* Revised. New York: Macmillan, 1925.

Fligstein, Neil. *Going North: Migration of Blacks and Whites from the South, 1900–1950.* New York: Academic Press, 1981.

Florette, Henri. *Black Migration: Movement North, 1900–1920.* Garden City, N.Y.: Anchor Press, 1975.

Fuchs, Lawrence H. *Hawaii Pono: A Social History.* New York: Harcourt Brace Jovanovich, 1961.

Goodrich, Carter, et al. *Migration and Economic Opportunity: The Report of the Study of Population Redistribution.* Philadelphia: Univ. of Pennsylvania Press, 1936.

Grant, Madison. *The Passing of the Great Race; or, The Racial Basis of European History.* Revised. New York: Charles Scribner's Sons, 1918.

Hacker, Louis M. *American Problems of Today: A History of the United States since the World War.* New York: F. S. Crofts, 1938.

Handlin, Oscar. *The Uprooted: The Epic Story of the Great Migrations That Made the American People.* New York: Grosset & Dunlap, 1951.
———. *Race and Nationality in American Life.* Garden City, N.Y.: Doubleday Anchor Books, 1957.

Hart, John Fraser. "The Changing Distribution of the American Negro." *Annals of the Association of American Geographers* 50 (September 1960): 242–66.

Hing, Bill Ong. *Making and Remaking Asian America through Immigration Policy, 1850–1990.* Stanford: Stanford Univ. Press, 1993.

Hutchinson, E. P. *Legislative History of American Immigration Policy, 1798–1965.* Philadelphia: Univ. of Pennsylvania Press, 1981.

Jones, Maldwyn Allen. *American Immigration.* Chicago: Univ. of Chicago Press, 1960.

Kennedy, David M. *Over Here: The First World War and American Society.* New York: Oxford Univ. Press, 1980.

Kohn, Hans. *American Nationalism: An Interpretative Essay.* New York: Collier Books, 1961.

LeMay, Michael C. *From Open Door to Dutch Door: An Analysis of U.S. Immigration Policy since 1820.* New York: Praeger, 1987.

Long, Larry. *Migration and Residential Mobility in the United States.* New York: Russell Sage Foundation, 1988.

Moore, Joan W., with Alfredo Cuellar. *Mexican Americans.* Englewood Cliffs, N.J.: Prentice-Hall, 1970.

Ostergren, Robert C., and Thomas R. Vale, eds. *Wisconsin Land and Life.* Madison: Univ. of Wisconsin Press, 1997.

Perloff, Harvey S., Edgar S. Dunn, Jr., Eric E. Lampard, and Richard F. Muth. *Regions, Resources and Economic Growth.* Baltimore: Johns Hopkins Press, 1960.

Petersen, William. *Population.* New York: Macmillan, 1961.

Sernett, Milton C. *Bound for the Promised Land: African American Religion and the Great Migration.* Durham, N.C.: Duke Univ. Press, 1997.

Shryock, Henry S., Jr. *Population Mobility within the United States.* Chicago: Community and Family Study Center, Univ. of Chicago, 1964.

Siegfried, André. *America Comes of Age: A French Analysis.* Trans. H. H. Hemming and Doris Hemming. New York: Harcourt, Brace, 1927.

Stoddard, Lothrop. *Re-Forging America: The Story of Our Nationhood.* New York: Charles Scribner's Sons, 1927.

Stone, Kirk H. *Alaskan Group Settlement: The Matanuska Valley Colony.* Washington, D.C.:

Bureau of Land Management, U.S. Department of the Interior, 1950.

Taeuber, Conrad, and Irene B. Taeuber. *The Changing Population of the United States*. New York: John Wiley & Sons, 1958.

Taylor, Philip. *The Distant Magnet: European Emigration to the U.S.A.* New York: Harper & Row, 1971.

U.S. Congress. House. *Immigration from Countries of the Western Hemisphere*. 71st Cong., 2d sess., March 13, 1930. H .Rept. 898.

————. Senate. *The Immigration and Naturalization Systems of the United States*. 81st Cong., 2d sess., April 20, 1950. S. Report 1515.

Ward, Robert DeC. "Our New Immigration Policy." *Foreign Affairs* 3 (September 15, 1924): 99–111.

Wright, Russell O. *A Twentieth-Century History of United States Population*. Lanham, Md.: Scarecrow Press, 1996.

2. Regionalism, 1920s–1950

Abrams, Ernest R. *Power in Transition*. New York: Charles Scribner's Sons, 1940.

Bogue, Allan G. *Frederick Jackson Turner: Strange Roads Going Down*. Norman: Univ. of Oklahoma Press, 1998.

Cash, W. J. *The Mind of the South*. New York: Alfred A. Knopf, 1941.

Creese, Walter L. *TVA's Public Planning: The Vision, the Reality*. Knoxville: Univ. of Tennessee Press, 1990.

Davidson, Donald. *The Attack on Leviathan: Regionalism and Nationalism in the United States*. Chapel Hill: Univ. of North Carolina Press, 1938.

Dorman, Robert L. *Revolt of the Provinces: The Regionalist Movement in America, 1920–1945*. Chapel Hill: Univ. of North Carolina Press, 1993.

Elliott, William Yandell. *The Need for Constitutional Reform: A Program for National Security*. New York: McGraw-Hill, 1935.

Fesler, James W. "Federal Administrative Regions." *American Political Science Review* 30 (April 1936): 257–68.

Freidel, Frank. *F. D. R. and the South*. Baton Rouge: Louisiana State Univ. Press, 1965.

Grantham, Dewey W. "The Regional Imagination: Social Scientists and the American South." *Journal of Southern History* 34 (February–November 1968): 3–32.

————. *The South in Modern America: A Region at Odds*. New York: HarperCollins, 1994.

Graves, W. Brooke. "The Future of the American States." *American Political Science Review* 30 (February 1936): 24–50.

Hodge, Clarence Lewis. *The Tennessee Valley Authority: A National Experiment in Regionalism*. [1938] New York: Russell & Russell, 1968.

I'll Take My Stand: The South and the Agrarian Tradition. By Twelve Southerners. Intro. Louis D. Rubin, Jr. Biographical Essays by Virginia Rock. [1930] New York: Harper & Row, 1962.

Jensen, Merrill, ed. *Regionalism in America*. Madison: Univ. of Wisconsin Press, 1951.

Karl, Barry D. *The Uneasy State: The United States from 1915 to 1945*. Chicago: Univ. of Chicago Press, 1983.

Kyle, John H. *The Building of TVA: An Illustrated History*. Baton Rouge: Louisiana State Univ. Press, 1958.

Lilienthal, David E. *TVA: Democracy on the March*. New York: Harper & Row, 1953.

MacKaye, Benton. *The New Exploration: A Philosophy of Regional Planning*. New York: Harcourt, Brace, 1928.

Malin, James C. *The Grassland of North America: Prolegomena to Its History*. Lawrence, Kans.: The Author, 1947.

Mangus, A. R. *Rural Regions of the United States*. Works Projects Administration. Washington, D.C.: Government Printing Office, 1940.

Merriam, C. E. "Government and Society." In *Recent Social Trends in the United States: Report of the President's Research Committee on Social Trends*, 1489–1541. New York: McGraw-Hill, 1933.

Mumford, Lewis. *The Culture of Cities*. New York: Harcourt, Brace, 1938.

National Planning Board. *Final Report—1933–34*. Federal Emergency Administration of

Public Works. Washington, D.C.: Government Printing Office, 1934.

O'Brien, Michael. *The Idea of the American South, 1920–1941*. Baltimore: Johns Hopkins Univ. Press, 1979.

Odum, Howard W. *Southern Regions of the United States*. Chapel Hill: Univ. of North Carolina Press, 1936.

Odum, Howard W., and Harry Estill Moore. *American Regionalism: A Cultural-Historical Approach to National Integration*. New York: Henry Holt, 1938.

Owen, Marguerite. *The Tennessee Valley Authority*. New York: Praeger Publishers, 1973.

Raitz, Karl B., and Richard Ulack. *Appalachia: A Regional Geography*. Boulder, Colo.: Westview Press, 1984.

Regional Factors in National Planning and Development. National Resources Committee. Washington, D.C.: Government Printing Office, 1935.

Royce, Josiah. *The Basic Writings of Josiah Royce*. Vol. 2. Chicago: Univ. of Chicago Press, 1969.

Stock, Catherine McNicol. *Main Street in Crisis: The Great Depression and the Old Middle Class on the Northern Plains*. Chapel Hill: Univ. of North Carolina Press, 1992.

Tindell, George Brown. *The Emergence of the New South, 1913–1945*. Baton Rouge: Louisiana State Univ. Press, 1967.

Turner, Frederick Jackson. *Frontier and Section: Selected Essays of Frederick Jackson Turner*. Intro. Ray Allen Billington. Englewood Cliffs, N.J.: Prentice-Hall, 1961.

Vance, Rupert B. *Human Geography of the South: A Study in Regional Resources and Human Adequacy*. [1935] New York: Russell & Russell, 1968.

———. *Regionalism and the South: Selected Papers of Rupert Vance*. Ed. and Intro. John Shelton Reed and Daniel Joseph Singal. Chapel Hill: Univ. of North Carolina Press, 1982.

Webb, Walter Prescott. *The Great Plains: A Study of Institutions and Environment*. Boston: Ginn, 1931.

Whittlesey, Derwent. *The Earth and the State: A Study of Political Geography*. New York: Henry Holt, 1939.

3. A Reconnaissance of Regions

Abbott, Carl. "Dimensions of Regional Change in Washington, D.C." *American Historical Review* 95 (December 1990): 1367–93.

———. *The Metropolitan Frontier: Cities in the Modern American West*. Tucson: Univ. of Arizona Press, 1993.

Aiken, Charles S. *The Cotton Plantation South since the Civil War*. Baltimore: Johns Hopkins Univ. Press, 1998.

Allen, James P., and Eugene Turner. *The Ethnic Quilt: Population Diversity in Southern California*. Northridge: Center for Geographical Studies, California State Univ., Northridge, 1997.

Banham, Reyner. *Los Angeles: The Architecture of Four Ecologies*. New York: Harper & Row, 1971.

Berry, Brian J. L. *Geography of Market Centers and Retail Distribution*. Englewood Cliffs, N.J.: Prentice-Hall, 1967.

Bowman, Isaiah. *The Pioneer Fringe*. New York: American Geographical Society, 1931.

Brodsly, David. *L.A. Freeway: An Appreciative Essay*. Berkeley: Univ. of California Press, 1981.

Clarkson, Grosvenor B. *Industrial America in the World War: The Strategy behind the Line, 1917–1918*. Boston: Houghton Mifflin, 1923.

Cochran, Thomas C. *American Business in the Twentieth Century*. Cambridge: Harvard Univ. Press, 1972.

Coffman, Edward M. *The War to End All Wars: The American Military Experience in World War I*. New York: Oxford Univ. Press, 1968.

Cunningham, John T. *This Is New Jersey*. New Brunswick, N.J.: Rutgers Univ. Press, 1953.

Dickinson, Robert E. "The Metropolitan Regions of the United States." *Geographical Review* 24 (April 1934): 278–91.

Eller, Ronald D. *Miners, Millhands, and Mountaineers: Industrialization of the Appalachian South, 1880–1930*. Knoxville: Univ. of Tennessee Press, 1982.

Garland, John H., ed. *The North American Mid-*

west: A Regional Geography. New York: John Wiley & Sons, 1955.

Glaab, Charles N., and A. Theodore Brown. *A History of Urban America.* New York: Macmillan, 1967.

Gottmann, Jean. *Virginia at Mid-Century.* New York: Henry Holt, 1955.

———. *Megalopolis: The Urbanized Northeastern Seaboard of the United States.* New York: Twentieth Century Fund, 1961.

Green, Constance McLaughlin. *American Cities in the Growth of the Nation.* New York: Harper & Row, 1965.

Groner, Alex. *The American Heritage History of American Business and Industry.* New York: American Heritage Publishing, 1972.

Hart, John Fraser. *The Southeastern United States.* Princeton, N.J.: D. Van Nostrand, 1967.

———. "The Middle West." *Annals of the Association of American Geographers* 62 (June 1972): 258–82.

Hewes, Leslie. *The Suitcase Farming Frontier: A Study in the Historical Geography of the Great Plains.* Lincoln: Univ. of Nebraska Press, 1973.

Hilliard, Sam B. *The South Revisited: Forty Years of Change.* New Brunswick, N.J.: Rutgers Univ. Press, 1992.

Hise, Greg. *Magnetic Los Angeles: Planning the Twentieth-Century Metropolis.* Baltimore: Johns Hopkins Univ. Press, 1997.

Hornbeck, David. *California Patterns: A Geographical and Historical Atlas.* Mountainview, Calif.: Mayfield Publishing, 1983.

Hudson, John C. *Crossing the Heartland: Chicago to Denver.* New Brunswick, N.J.: Rutgers Univ. Press, 1992.

Hutton, Graham. *Midwest at Noon.* Chicago: Univ. of Chicago Press, 1946.

Jackson, Kenneth T. *Crabgrass Frontier: The Suburbanization of the United States.* New York: Oxford Univ. Press, 1985.

Jordan, Terry G. "The Anglo-Texan Homeland." *Journal of Cultural Geography* 13 (Spring–Summer 1993): 75–86.

Junker, Patricia. *John Steuart Curry: Inventing the Middle West.* New York: Hudson Hills Press, 1998.

Lane, Frederic C. *Ships for Victory: A History of Shipbuilding under the U.S. Maritime Commis-*

sion in World War II. Baltimore: Johns Hopkins Univ. Press, 1951.

Lantis, David W., Rodney Steiner, and Arthur E. Karinen. *California: Land of Contrast.* Belmont, Calif.: Wadsworth Publishing, 1963.

Lerner, Max. *America as a Civilization: Life and Thought in the United States Today.* New York: Simon and Schuster, 1957.

Lewis, Peirce F. *New Orleans: The Making of an Urban Landscape.* Cambridge, Mass.: Ballinger Publishing, 1976.

Link, Arthur S., and William B. Catton. *American Epoch: A History of the United States since 1900.* Vol. 2, *1921–1945.* 4th ed. New York: Alfred A. Knopf, 1973.

Lucic, Karen. *Charles Sheeler and the Cult of the Machine.* Cambridge: Harvard Univ. Press, 1991.

Luebke, B. H., and John Fraser Hart. "Migration from a Southern Appalachian Community." *Land Economics* 34 (February 1958): 44–53.

Lynd, Robert S., and Helen Merrell Lynd. *Middletown: A Study in American Culture.* New York: Harcourt, Brace, 1929.

McAlester, Virginia and Lee McAlester. *A Field Guide to American Houses.* New York: Alfred A. Knopf, 1984.

McWilliams, Carey. *Southern California Country: An Island on the Land.* New York: Duell, Sloan & Pearce, 1946.

———. *California: The Great Exception.* New York: A. A. Wyn, 1949.

Maharidge, Dale, and Michael V. Williamson. *And Their Children after Them.* New York: Pantheon Books, 1989.

Malone, Michael P., and Richard B. Roeder. *Montana: A History of Two Centuries.* Seattle: Univ. of Washington Press, 1976.

Map of United States Military Posts. Chicago: Rand McNally, 1944.

Mattson, Richard. "The Bungalow Spirit." *Journal of Cultural Geography* 1 (Spring–Summer 1981): 75–92.

Meinig, D. W. *Imperial Texas: An Interpretive Essay in Cultural Geography.* Austin: Univ. of Texas Press, 1969.

Mitchell, Don. *The Lie of the Land: Migrant Workers and the California Landscape.* Minneapolis: Univ. of Minnesota Press, 1996.

Montejano, David. *Anglos and Mexicans in the Making of Texas, 1836–1986*. Austin: Univ. of Texas Press, 1987.

Mumford, Lewis. *The Culture of Cities*. New York: Harcourt, Brace, 1938.

Nash, Gerald D. *The American West Transformed: The Impact of the Second World War*. Bloomington: Indiana Univ. Press, 1985.

Nelson, Howard J. "The Spread of an Artificial Landscape over Southern California." *Annals of the Association of American Geographers* 49 (September 1959): 80–99.

Newton, Milton B., Jr. *Atlas of Louisiana: A Guide for Students*. Baton Rouge: School of Geoscience, Louisiana State Univ., 1972.

New York City Guide. American Guide Series. New York: Random House, 1939.

Osofsky, Gilbert. "A Decade of Urban Tragedy: How Harlem Became a Slum." *New York History* 46 (October 1965): 330–55.

Park, Robert E., Ernest W. Burgess, and Roderick D. McKenzie. *The City*. Chicago: Univ. of Chicago Press, 1925.

Parkins, A. E. *The South: Its Economic-Geographic Development*. New York: John Wiley & Sons, 1938.

Perloff, Harvey S., Edgar S. Dunn, Jr., Eric E. Lampard, and Richard F. Muth. *Regions, Resources, and Economic Growth*. Baltimore: Johns Hopkins Univ. Press, 1960.

Pomeroy, Earl. *The Pacific Slope: A History of California, Oregon, Washington, Idaho, Utah, and Nevada*. New York: Alfred A. Knopf, 1965.

Preston, Richard E. 'The Changing Form and Structure of the Southern California Metropolis." *California Geographer* 12 (1971): 5–20.

Price, Edward T. "The Future of California's Southland." *Annals of the Association of American Geographers* 49 (September 1959): 101–16.

Robinson, Malcolm. *The American Vision: Landscape Paintings of the United States*. New York: Portland House, 1988.

Rubin, Morton. *Plantation Country*. Chapel Hill: Univ. of North Carolina Press, 1951.

Schroeder, Walter A. *The Eastern Ozarks: A Geographic Interpretation of the Rolla 1:250,000 Topographic Map*. Special Publication No. 13. Normal: National Council for Geographic Education, Illinois State Univ., 1967.

Scott, Mel. *The San Francisco Bay Area: A Metropolis in Perspective*. Berkeley: Univ. of California Press, 1959.

Shortridge, James R. *The Middle West: Its Meaning in American Culture*. Lawrence: Univ. Press of Kansas, 1989.

Showalter, William Joseph. "America's New Soldier Cities: The Geographical and Historical Environment of the National Army Cantonments and National Guard Camps." *National Geographic Magazine* 32 (November–December 1917): 438–76.

Sims, Patterson. *Charles Sheeler*. New York: Whitney Museum of Modern Art, 1980.

Smith, J. Russell, and M. Ogden Phillips. *North America: Its People and the Resources, Development, and Prospects of the Continent as the Home of Man*. [1925] New York: Harcourt, Brace, 1942.

Smith, J. Russell, M. Ogden Phillips, and Thomas R. Smith. *Industrial and Commercial Geography*. 4th ed. New York: Henry Holt, 1955.

Starr, Kevin. *Material Dreams: Southern California through the 1920s*. New York: Oxford Univ. Press, 1990.

Stein, Maurice R. *The Eclipse of Community: An Interpretation of American Studies*. Princeton: Princeton Univ. Press, 1960.

Trice, Andrew Homer. "California Manufacturing Branches of National Firms, 1899–1948: Their Place in the Economic Development of the State." Ph.D. dissertation, Department of Economics, Univ. of California, Berkeley, 1955.

U.S. Congress. Senate. *Investigation of Concentration of Economic Power*. Final Report and Recommendations of the Temporary National Economic Committee. 77th Cong., 1st sess., March 31, 1941. S. Doc. 35.

Vance, James E., Jr. *Geography and Urban Evolution in the San Francisco Bay Area*. Berkeley: Institute of Governmental Studies, Univ. of California, 1964.

———. "California and the Search for the Ideal." *Annals of the Association of American Geographers* 62 (June 1972): 185–210.

Waddell, Eric. "French Louisiana: An Outpost of L'Amerique Française, or Another Country and Another Culture?" Document de Travail/

Working Paper No. 4, Département de géographie, Université Laval, Quebec, January 1979.

Watkins-Owens, Irma. *Blood Relations: Caribbean Immigrants and the Harlem Community, 1900–1930*. Bloomington: Indiana Univ. Press, 1996.

White, Gerald T. *Billions for Defense: Government Financing by the Defense Plant Corporation during World War II*. University: Univ. of Alabama Press, 1980.

White, Richard. *"It's Your Misfortune and None of My Own": A History of the American West*. Norman: Univ. of Oklahoma Press, 1991.

Wright, J. K., ed. *New England's Prospect: 1933*. Special Publication No. 16. New York: American Geographical Society, 1933.

Wyckoff, William. *Creating Colorado: The Making of a Western Landscape, 1860–1940*. New Haven: Yale Univ. Press, 1999.

4. Midcentury Morphology

Ahlstrom, Sydney E. *A Religious History of the American People*. New Haven: Yale Univ. Press, 1972.

Brown, William H., Jr., "Access to Housing: The Role of the Real Estate Industry." *Economic Geography* 48 (January 1972): 66–78.

Calef, Wesley C., and Howard J. Nelson. "Distribution of Negro Population in the United States." *Geographical Review* 46 (January 1956): 82–97.

Davis, George A., and O. Fred Donaldson. *Blacks in the United States: A Geographic Perspective*. Boston: Houghton Mifflin, 1975.

Deutsch, Karl W. "The Growth of Nations: Some Recurrent Patterns of Political and Social Integration." *World Politics* 5 (January 1953): 168–95.

Elazar, Daniel J. *Community and Polity: The Organizational Dynamics of American Jewry*. Revised ed. Philadelphia: Jewish Publication Society of America, 1995.

Finke, Roger, and Rodney Stark. *The Churching of America, 1776–1990: Winners and Losers in Our Religious Economy*. New Brunswick, N.J.: Rutgers Univ. Press, 1992.

Franklin, John Hope. *From Slavery to Freedom: A History of Negro Americans*. 4th ed. New York: Alfred A. Knopf, 1974.

Gaustad, Edwin Scott. *Historical Atlas of Religion in America*. New York: Harper & Row, 1962.

Greeley, Andrew M. *The American Catholic: A Social Portrait*. New York: Basic Books, 1977.

Gregg, Robert. *Sparks from the Anvil of Oppression: Philadelphia's African Methodists and Southern Migrants, 1890–1940*. Philadelphia: Temple Univ. Press, 1993.

Harris, Robert L., Jr. "The Flowering of Afro-American History." *American Historical Review* 92 (December 1987): 1150–61.

Hart, John Fraser. "The Changing Distribution of the American Negro." *Annals of the Association of American Geographers* 50 (September 1960): 242–66.

Herberg, Will. *Protestant-Catholic-Jew: An Essay in American Religious Sociology*. Revised ed. Garden City, N.Y.: Doubleday, 1960.

Krohn, Claus-Dieter. *Intellectuals in Exile: Refugee Scholars and the New School for Social Research*. Trans. Rita and Robert Kimber. Amherst: Univ. of Massachusetts Press, 1993.

Lenski, Gerhard. *The Religious Factor: A Sociologist's Inquiry*. Garden City, N.Y.: Doubleday, 1963.

Lewis, Anthony. *Portrait of a Decade: The Second American Revolution*. New York: Random House, 1964.

Lewis, G. M. "The Distribution of the Negro in the Conterminous United States." *Geography* 54 (November 1969): 410–18.

Mangum, Charles S., Jr. *The Legal Status of the Negro*. Chapel Hill: Univ. of North Carolina Press, 1940.

Martis, Kenneth C., and Gregory A. Elmes. *The Historical Atlas of State Power in Congress, 1790–1990*. Washington, D.C.: Congressional Quarterly, 1993.

Moore, R. Laurence. *Religious Outsiders and the Making of Americans*. New York: Oxford Univ. Press, 1986.

Myrdal, Gunnar. *An American Dilemma: The Negro Problem and Modern Democracy*. 2 vols. New York: Harper & Brothers, 1944.

Perloff, Harvey S., Edgar S. Dunn, Jr., Eric E. Lampard, and Richard F. Muth. *Regions, Resources and Economic Growth*. Baltimore: Johns Hopkins Press, 1960.

"The Regions" in "The U.S.A." *Fortune* 21 (February 1940): 42–49, 146–50.

Rose, Harold M. *The Black Ghetto: A Spatial Behavioral Perspective*. New York: McGraw-Hill, 1971.

Rutkoff, Peter M., and William B. Scott. *New School: A History of the New School for Social Research*. New York: Free Press, 1986.

San Francisco, the Bay and Its Cities. American Guide Series. Works Progress Administration. 2d ed. New York: Hastings House, 1947.

Shortridge, James R. "Patterns of Religion in the United States." *Geographical Review* 66 (October 1976): 420–34.

Siegfried, André. *America at Mid-Century*. New York: Harcourt, Brace, 1955.

Sopher, David E. *Geography of Religions*. Englewood Cliffs, N.J.: Prentice-Hall, 1967.

Southern, David W. *Gunnar Myrdal and Black-White Relations: The Use and Abuse of An American Dilemma, 1944–1969*. Baton Rouge: Louisiana Univ. Press, 1987.

Taeuber, Karl E., and Alma F. Taeuber. *Negroes in Cities: Residential Segregation and Neighborhood Change*. New York: Atheneum, 1965.

Thistlethwaite, Frank. *The Great Experiment: An Introduction to a History of the American People*. Cambridge: Cambridge Univ. Press, 1955.

Ullman, Edward L. "Amenities as a Factor in Regional Growth." *Geographical Review* 44 (January 1954): 119–32.

———. "Regional Development and the Geography of Concentration." *Papers and Proceedings of the Regional Science Association* 4 (1958): 179–99.

Williams, Vernon J., Jr. *From a Caste to a Minority: Changing Attitudes of American Sociologists toward Afro-Americans, 1895–1945*. Westport, Conn.: Greenwood Press, 1989.

Zelinsky, Wilbur. "An Approach to the Religious Geography of the United States: Patterns of Church Membership in 1952." *Annals of the Association of American Geographers* 51 (June 1961): 139–93.

5. Altering the Federation and Internal Empire

Alaska Natives and the Land. Anchorage: Federal Field Committee for Development Planning in Alaska, October 1968.

The Alaska Railroad. Booklet issued by U.S. Department of the Interior. Chicago: Horner Printing, 1937.

"Anchorage and the Cook Inlet Basin." *Alaska Geographic* 10, no. 2 (1983).

Barsh, Russel Lawrence, and James Youngblood Henderson. *The Road: Indian Tribes and Political Liberty*. Berkeley: Univ. of California Press, 1980.

Bell, Roger. *Last among Equals: Hawaiian Statehood and American Politics*. Honolulu: Univ. of Hawaii Press, 1984.

Bhana, Surendra. *The United States and the Development of the Puerto Rican Status Question, 1936–1968*. Lawrence: Univ. Press of Kansas, 1975.

Breidenbach, Michelle. "Oneidas, Mohegans Help Twenty Nations." *Syracuse Herald-Journal*, December 7, 2000.

Carr, Raymond. *Puerto Rico: A Colonial Experiment*. New York: New York Univ. Press, 1984.

Chow, Willard T. "Urbanization: Six Propositions." In *Hawaii: A Geography*, ed. Joseph R. Morgan, 167–85. Boulder, Colo.: Westview Press, 1983.

Colby, Merle. *A Guide to Alaska: Last American Frontier*. American Guide Series. New York: Macmillan, 1939.

Creighton, Thomas H. *The Lands of Hawaii: Their Use and Misuse*. Honolulu: Univ. of Hawaii Press, 1978.

Davis, Mary B., ed. *Native America in the Twentieth Century: An Encyclopedia*. New York: Garland Publishing, 1994.

Deloria, Vine, Jr., and Clifford M. Lytle. *The Nations Within: The Past and Future of American Indian Sovereignty*. New York: Pantheon Books, 1984.

Frantz, Klaus. *Indian Reservations in the United States: Territory, Sovereignty, and Socioeconomic Change*. Chicago: Univ. of Chicago Press, 1999.

Fuchs, Lawrence H. *Hawaii Pono: A Social History*. New York: Harcourt Brace Jovanovich, 1961.

Gruening, Ernest. *The Battle for Alaska Statehood*. College: Univ. of Alaska Press, 1967.

Hanson, Earl Parker. *Puerto Rico: Ally for Progress*. Princeton: D. Van Nostrand, 1962.

Herman, RDK. "The Aloha State: Place Names and the Anti-conquest of Hawai'i." *Annals of the Association of American Geographers* 89 (March 1999): 76–102.

Hunt, William R. *Alaska: A Bicentennial History*. New York: W. W. Norton, 1976.

Johnson, Hugh A., and Harold T. Jorgenson. *The Land Resources of Alaska*. New York: University Publishers, 1963.

Josephy, Alvin M., Jr., Joane Nagel, and Troy Johnson, eds. *Red Power: The American Indians' Fight for Freedom*. Lincoln: Univ. of Nebraska Press, 1999.

Judge, Joseph. "Alaska: Rising Northern Star." *National Geographic* 147 (June 1975): 730–66.

Kvasnicka, Robert M., and Herman J. Viola, eds. *The Commissioners of Indian Affairs, 1824–1977*. Lincoln: Univ. of Nebraska Press, 1979.

Lautaret, Ronald. *Alaskan Historical Documents since 1867*. Jefferson, N.C.: McFarland, 1989.

Leibowitz, Arnold H. *Defining Status: A Comprehensive Analysis of United States Territorial Relations*. Dordrecht: Martinus Nijhoff Publishers, 1989.

Lind, Andrew W. *Hawaii's People*. 3d ed. Honolulu: Univ. of Hawaii Press, 1967.

Lineberry, William P., ed. *The New States: Alaska and Hawaii*. New York: H. W. Wilson, 1963.

McBeath, Gerald A., and Thomas A. Morehouse. *Alaska Politics and Government*. Lincoln: Univ. of Nebraska Press, 1994.

Mid-Century Alaska. Office of Territories. U.S. Department of the Interior. Washington, D.C.: Government Printing Office, 1951.

Morgan, Joseph R. *Hawaii: A Geography*. Boulder, Colo.: Westview Press, 1983.

Morris, Nancy. *Puerto Rico: Culture, Politics, and Identity*. Westport, Conn.: Praeger, 1995.

Mullins, Joseph G. *Hawaiian Journey*. Honolulu: Mutual Publishing, 1978.

Mumford, Lewis. "Report on Honolulu." In *City Development: Studies in Distintegration and Renewal*, 73–128. London: Secker & Warburg, 1947.

Nagel, Joane. *American Indian Ethnic Renewal: Red Power and the Resurgence of Identity and Culture*. New York: Oxford Univ. Press, 1996.

Naske, Claus-M. *An Interpretative History of Alaskan Statehood*. Anchorage: Alaska Northwest Publishing, 1973.

Naske, Claus-M., and Herman E. Slotnick. *Alaska: A History of the Forty-ninth State*. 2d ed. Norman: Univ. of Oklahoma Press, 1987.

Nordyke, Eleanor C. *The Peopling of Hawaii*. Honolulu: East-West Center, 1977.

Pevar, Stephen L. *The Rights of Indians and Tribes: The Basic ACLU Guide to Indian and Tribal Rights*. 2d ed. Carbondale: Southern Illinois Univ. Press, 1992.

Pommersheim, Frank. *Braid of Feathers: American Indian Law and Contemporary Tribal Life*. Berkeley: Univ. of California Press, 1995.

Puerto Rico: A Guide to the Island of Boriquén. Puerto Rican Department of Education. American Guide Series. New York: University Society, 1940.

Remley, David A. *Crooked Road: The Story of the Alaska Highway*. New York: McGraw-Hill, 1976.

Rohter, Larry. "A Puerto Rican Boom for Florida." *New York Times*, January 31, 1994.

Shoemaker, Nancy. *American Indian Population Recovery in the Twentieth Century*. Albuquerque: Univ. of New Mexico Press, 1999.

Smith, Zachary A., and Richard C. Pratt, eds. *Politics and Public Policy in Hawai'i*. Albany: State Univ. of New York Press, 1992.

Spicer, Edward H. *A Short History of the Indians of the United States*. New York: D. Van Nostrand, 1969.

Sutton, Imre, ed. *Irredeemable America: The Indians' Estate and Land Claims*. Albuquerque: Univ. of New Mexico Press, 1985.

Trask, Haunani-Kay. *From a Native Daughter*. Revised ed. Honolulu: Univ. of Hawai'i Press, 1999.

Trías Monge, José. *Puerto Rico: The Trials of the Oldest Colony in the World*. New Haven: Yale Univ. Press, 1997.

U.S. Congress. House. *The Alaska Highway*. 79th Cong., 2d sess., March 13, 1946. H. Rept. 1705.

Van Zandt, Franklin K. *Boundaries of the United*

States and the Several States. Geological Survey Bulletin 1212. Washington, D.C.: Government Printing Office, 1966.

Wagenheim, Karl. *Puerto Rico: A Profile*. 2d ed. New York: Holt, Rinehart and Winston, 1975.

Winchell, Dick G., John F. Lounsbury, and Lawrence M. Sommers. "Indian Gaming in the U.S." *Focus* 44 (Winter 1997): 1–10.

Wurman, Richard Saul. *Hawaii Access*. Los Angeles: Access Press, 1982.

6. Populations and Policies, 1950s–1990s

Allen, James P., and Eugene Turner. *The Ethnic Quilt: Population Diversity in Southern California*. Northridge: Center for Geographical Studies, Department of Geography, California State Univ., 1997.

Arreola, Daniel D. "The Mexican American Cultural Capital." *Geographical Review* 77 (January 1987): 17–34.

Arreola, Daniel D., and James R. Curtis. *The Mexican Border Cities: Landscape Anatomy and Place Personality*. Tucson: Univ. of Arizona Press, 1993.

Arsenault, Raymond. "The End of the Long Hot Summer: The Air Conditioner and Southern Culture." *Journal of Southern History* 50 (November 1984): 597–628.

Baker, O. E. "Agricultural and Forest Lands." In *Recent Social Trends in the United States*, 90–121. New York: McGraw-Hill, 1933.

Baker, Reginald P., and David S. North. *The 1975 Refugees: Their First Five Years in America*. Washington, D.C.: New TransCentury Foundation, 1984.

Barkan, Elliott Robert. *Asian and Pacific Islander Migration to the United States: A Model of New Global Patterns*. Westport, Conn.: Greenwood Press, 1992.

Breckenfeld, Gurney. "Business Loves the Sunbelt (and Vice Versa)." *Fortune* 95 (June 1977): 132–46.

Browning, Clyde E., and Wil Gesler. "The Sun Belt–Snow Belt: A Case of Sloppy Regionalizing." *Professional Geographer* 31 (February 1979): 66–74.

Capaldi, Nicholas, ed. *Immigration: Debating the Issues*. Amherst, N.Y.: Prometheus Books, 1997.

Carlson, Alvar W. "Recent Immigration, 1961–1970: A Factor in the Growth and Distribution of the United States Population." *Journal of Geography* 72 (December 1973): 8–17.

Cromartie, John, and Carol B. Stack. "Reinterpretation of Black Return and Nonreturn Migration in the South, 1975–1980." *Geographical Review* 79 (July 1989): 297–310.

Dunn, Timothy J. *The Militarization of the U.S.-Mexico Border, 1978–1992: Low-Intensity Conflict Doctrine Comes Home*. Austin, Tex.: Center for Mexican American Studies, 1996.

Egan, Timothy. "Eastward, Ho! The Great Move Reverses." *New York Times*, May 30, 1993.

Farley, Reynolds, ed. *State of the Union: America in the 1990s*. Vol. 2, *Social Trends*. New York: Russell Sage Foundation, 1995.

Flanders, Stephen A. *Atlas of American Migration*. New York: Facts on File, 1998.

Frey, William H., and Kao-Lee Liaw. "Immigrant Concentration and Domestic Migrant Dispersal: Is Movement to Nonmetropolitan Areas 'White Flight'?" *Professional Geographer* 50 (May 1998): 215–32.

Ganster, Paul, ed. *The U.S.-Mexican Border Environment*. San Diego: San Diego State Univ. Press, 2000.

Gimpel, James G. *Separate Destinations: Migration, Immigration, and the Politics of Place*. Ann Arbor: Univ. of Michigan Press, 1999.

Glazer, Nathan. "The Closing Door." In *Arguing Immigration: The Debate over the Changing Face of America*, ed. Nicolaus Mills, 37–47. New York: Simon and Schuster, 1994.

Gonzalez-Pando, Miguel. *The Cuban Americans*. Westport, Conn.: Greenwood Press, 1998.

Haverluk, Terrence W. "Hispanic Community Types and Assimilation in Mex-America." *Professional Geographer* 50 (November 1998): 465–80.

Herzog, Lawrence A. *Where North Meets South: Cities, Space, and Politics on the U.S.-Mexico Border*. Austin: Univ. of Texas Press, 1990.

House, John W. *Frontier on the Rio Grande: A Political Geography of Development and Social Deprivation*. Oxford: Oxford Univ. Press, 1982.

Isbister, John. *The Immigration Debate: Remaking*

America. West Hartford, Conn.: Kumarian Press, 1996.

Jamail, Milton H., and Margo Gutiérrez. *The Border Guide: Institutions and Organizations of the United States-Mexico Borderlands*. Austin: Univ. of Texas Press, 1992.

Johnson, Daniel M., and Rex R. Campbell. *Black Migration in America: A Social Demographic History*. Durham: Duke Univ. Press, 1981.

Long, Larry. *Migration and Residential Mobility in the United States*. New York: Russell Sage Foundation, 1988.

McHugh, Kevin E. "Black Migration Reversal in the United States." *Geographical Review* 77 (April 1987): 171–82.

Martínez, Oscar J. *Troublesome Border*. Tucson: Univ. of Arizona Press, 1988.

———. *Border People: Life and Society in the U.S.-Mexico Borderlands*. Tucson: Univ. of Arizona Press, 1994.

Massey, Douglas, Rafael Alarcón, Jorge Durand, and Humberto González. *Return to Aztlan: The Social Process of International Migration from Western Mexico*. Berkeley: Univ. of California Press, 1987.

Moore, Joan W., with Alfredo Cuellar. *Mexican Americans*. Englewood Cliffs, N.J.: Prentice-Hall, 1970.

Mydans, Seth. "Twenty-five Years Later, Vietnamese Still Flock to the U.S." *New York Times*, November 7, 2000.

Myerson, Allen R. "On the Road to Monterrey." *New York Times*, December 18, 1997.

Newbold, K. Bruce. "Race and Primary, Return, and Outward Interstate Migration." *Professional Geographer* 49 (February 1997): 1–14.

Nostrand, Richard L. "The Hispanic-American Borderland: Delimitation of an American Culture Region." *Annals of the Association of American Geographers* 60 (December 1970): 638–61.

Phillips, Kevin B. *The Emerging Republican Majority*. Garden City, N.Y.: Anchor Books, 1969.

Poitras, Guy, ed. *Immigration and the Mexican National: Proceedings*. San Antonio: Border Research Institute, Trinity Univ., 1978.

Portes, Alejandro, and Rubén G. Rumbaut. *Immigrant America: A Portrait*. Berkeley: Univ. of California Press, 1990.

Reimers, David M. *Unwelcome Strangers: American Identity and the Turn against Immigration*. New York: Columbia Univ. Press, 1998.

Reinhold, Robert. "Nation's Land of Promise Enters an Era of Limits." *New York Times*, August 24, 1993.

Rohter, Larry. "Flood of Dominicans Lets Some Enter U.S. by Fraud." *New York Times*, February 19, 1997.

Sale, Kirkpatrick. *Power Shift: The Rise of the Southern Rim and Its Challenge to the Eastern Establishment*. New York: Random House, 1976.

Skerry, Peter. *Mexican Americans: The Ambivalent Minority*. New York: Free Press, 1993.

Smith, James P., and Barry Edmonston, eds. *The New Americans: Economic, Demographic, and Fiscal Effects of Immigration*. Washington, D.C.: National Academy Press, 1997.

Spaeth, Anthony. "The Golden Diaspora." *Time*, June 19, 2000, B26–B28.

Spener, David, and Kathleen Staudt, eds. *The U.S.-Mexico Border: Transcending Divisions, Contesting Identities*. Boulder, Colo.: Lynne Rienner Publishers, 1998.

Takaki, Ronald. *Strangers from a Different Shore: A History of Asian Americans*. Boston: Little, Brown, 1989.

Uchitelle, Louis. "America's Newest Industrial Belt: Northern Mexico." *New York Times*, March 21, 1993.

Weinstein, Bernard L., and Robert E. Firestine. *Regional Growth and Decline in the United States: The Rise of the Sunbelt and the Decline of the Northeast*. New York: Praeger, 1978.

Wood, Joseph. "Vietnamese American Place Making in Northern Virginia." *Geographical Review* 87 (January 1997): 58–72.

7. Some Reconfigurations

Abbott, Carl. "Frontiers and Sections: Cities and Regions in American Growth." In *American Urbanism: A Historiographic Review*, ed. Howard Gillette, Jr., and Zane L. Miller, 271–90. New York: Greenwood Press, 1987.

———. "Southwestern Cityscapes: Approaches

to an Urban Environment." In *Essays on Sunbelt Cities and Recent Urban America*, 59–86. The Walter Prescott Webb Memorial Lectures. College Station: Texas A&M Univ. Press, 1990.

———. "Regional City and Network City: Portland and Seattle in the Twentieth Century." *Western Historical Quarterly* 23 (August 1992): 293–322.

———. *The Metropolitan Frontier: Cities in the Modern American West*. Tucson: Univ. of Arizona Press, 1993.

Bennion, Lowell C. "The Geographic Dynamics of Mormondom, 1965–95." *Sunstone* 18 (December 1995): 21–32.

———. "Mormondom's Deseret Homeland." In *Homelands: A Geography of Culture and Place across America*, ed. Richard L. Nostrand and Lawrence E. Estaville, 184–209. Baltimore: Johns Hopkins Univ. Press, 2001.

Blakely, Edward J., and Mary Gail Snyder. *Fortress America: Gated Communities in the United States*. Washington, D.C.: Brookings Institution, 1999.

Borchert, John R. "Futures of American Cities." In *Our Changing Cities*, ed. John Fraser Hart, 218–50. Baltimore: Johns Hopkins Univ. Press, 1991.

Bryce, James. *The American Commonwealth*. Vol. 2. New York: Macmillan, 1921.

"California: The Nation within a Nation." *Saturday Review*, September 23, 1967.

Calthorpe, Peter, and William Fulton. *The Regional City: Planning for the End of Sprawl*. Washington, D.C.: Island Press, 2001.

Crewdson, John M. "Houston's Lifeline: Tons of Cool Air." *New York Times*, August 6, 1981.

Davidson, Osha Gray. *Broken Heartland: The Rise of America's Rural Ghetto*. Iowa City: Univ. of Iowa Press, 1996.

Egan, Timothy. "Urban Sprawl Strains Western States." *New York Times*, December 29, 1996.

———. "Las Vegas Bet on Growth but Doesn't Love Payoff." *New York Times*, January 26, 2001.

The Exploding Metropolis, by the Editors of *Fortune*. Garden City, N.Y.: Doubleday, 1958.

Findlay, John M. *Magic Lands: Western Cityscapes and American Culture after 1940*. Berkeley: Univ. of California Press, 1992.

Firestone, David. "Search for Efficiency Now Leaves Alabama Town [Gadsden] Behind." *New York Times*, February 21, 1999.

Ford, Larry R. *Cities and Buildings: Skyscrapers, Skid Rows, and Suburbs*. Baltimore: Johns Hopkins Univ. Press, 1994.

Franke, David, and Holly Franke. *Safe Places: West*. New York: Warner Paperback Library, 1973.

Frey, William H. "The New Geography of Population Shifts: Trends toward Balkanization." In *State of the Union*, ed. Reynolds Farley, 2: 271–336. New York: Russell Sage Foundation, 1995.

Garreau, Joel. *The Nine Nations of North America*. New York: Avon Books, 1981.

Glaab, Charles N., and A. Theodore Brown. *A History of Urban America*. New York: Macmillan, 1967.

Goldfield, David R. *Cotton Fields and Skyscrapers: Southern City and Region, 1607–1980*. Baton Rouge: Louisiana State Univ. Press, 1982.

Gregory, James N. *American Exodus: The Dust Bowl Migration and Okie Culture in California*. New York: Oxford Univ. Press, 1989.

Gressley, Gene M. "Regionalism and the Twentieth-Century West." In *The American West: New Perspectives, New Dimensions*, ed. Jerome O. Steffen, 197–234. Norman: Univ. of Oklahoma Press, 1979.

Hart, John Fraser. *The Land That Feeds Us*. New York: W. W. Norton, 1991.

Higley, Stephen Richard. *Privilege, Power, and Place: The Geography of the American Upper Class*. Lanham, Md.: Rowman & Littlefield, 1995.

Hill, Gladwin. "Nation's Cities Fighting to Stem Growth." *New York Times*, July 28, 1974.

"Housing: Up from the Potato Fields." *Time* (July 3, 1950, 67–72.

Jackson, Kenneth T. *Crabgrass Frontier: The Suburbanization of the United States*. New York: Oxford Univ. Press, 1985.

Lee, Jennifer. "There's Silicon in Them Thar Hills, or Will Be Soon." *New York Times*, June 13, 2001.

Lemon, James T. *Liberal Dreams and Nature's Limits: Great Cities of North America since 1600*. Toronto: Oxford Univ. Press, 1996.

Lewis, Peirce F. "The Galactic Metropolis." In

Beyond the Urban Fringe: Land Use Issues of Nonmetropolitan America, ed. Rutherford H. Platt and George Macinko, 23–59. Minneapolis: Univ. of Minnesota Press, 1983.

———. "America between the Wars: The Engineering of a New Geography." In *North America: The Historical Geography of a Changing Continent,* ed. Robert D. Mitchell and Paul A. Groves, 410–37. Totowa, N.J.: Rowman & Littlefield, 1987.

Limerick, Patricia Nelson. "The Significance of Hanford in American History." In *Terra Pacifica: People and Place in the Northwest States and Western Canada,* ed. Paul W. Hirt, 53–70. Pullman: Washington State Univ. Press, 1998.

Lord, J. Dennis. "Banking across State Lines." *Focus* 37 (Spring 1987): 10–15.

Markusen, Ann. *Regions: The Economics and Politics of Territory.* Totowa, N.J.: Rowman & Littlefield, 1987.

Massey, Douglas S., and Nancy A. Denton. *American Apartheid: Segregation and the Making of the Underclass.* Cambridge: Harvard Univ. Press, 1993.

Mayer, Harold M. "Four Decades of Change in Urban North America." In *World Patterns of Modern Urban Change: Essays in Honor of Chauncy D. Harris,* ed. Michael P. Conzen, 353–402. Research Paper No. 217–218. Chicago: Department of Geography, Univ. of Chicago, 1986.

Meinig, D. W. *Southwest: Three Peoples in Geographical Change.* New York: Oxford Univ. Press, 1971.

Miller, Zell. "The Democratic Party's Southern Problem." *New York Times,* June 4, 2001.

Morgan, Neil. *Westward Tilt: The American West Today.* New York: Random House, 1963.

Muschamp, Herbert. "Becoming Unstuck in the Suburbs." *New York Times,* October 19, 1997.

"A New Face for the U.S." Editorial. *Fortune* 56 (September 1957): 117–18.

Reed, John Shelton. *One South: An Ethnic Approach to Regional Culture.* Baton Rouge: Louisiana State Univ. Press, 1982.

Reinhold, Robert. "Nation's Land of Promise Enters an Era of Limits." *New York Times,* August 24, 1993.

Riebsame, William E., gen. ed. *Atlas of the New West: Portrait of a Changing Region.* New York: W. W. Norton, 1997.

Rifkind, Carole. *Main Street: The Face of Urban America.* New York: Harper & Row, 1977.

Rubenstein, James M. "Further Changes in the American Automobile Industry." *Geographical Review* 77 (July 1987): 359–62.

Rusk, David. *Cities without Suburbs.* 2d ed. Washington, D.C.: Woodrow Wilson Center Press, 1995.

Shortridge, James R. "The Expectations of Others: Struggles toward a Sense of Place in the Northern Plains." In *Many Wests: Place, Culture, and Regional Identity,* ed. Michael C. Steiner and David M. Wrobel, 114–35. Lawrence: Univ. Press of Kansas, 1997.

Smith, Stephen A. *Myth, Media, and the Southern Mind.* Fayetteville: Univ. of Arkansas Press, 1985.

Starrs, Paul F., and John B. Wright. "Great Basin Growth and the Withering of California's Pacific Idyll." *Geographical Review* 85 (October 1995): 417–35.

Strauss, Anselon L. *Images of the American City.* New Brunswick, N.J.: Transaction Books, 1976.

Stroud, Hubert B. *The Promise of Paradise: Recreational and Retirement Communities in the United States since 1950.* Baltimore: Johns Hopkins Univ. Press, 1995.

Teaford, Jon C. *City and Suburb: The Political Fragmentation of Metropolitan America, 1850–1970.* Baltimore: Johns Hopkins Univ. Press, 1979.

———. *The Twentieth-Century American City.* Baltimore: Johns Hopkins Univ. Press, 1993.

Tunnard, Christopher, and Henry Hope Reed. *American Skyline: The Growth and Form of Our Cities and Towns.* New York: Mentor Books, 1956.

Vance, James E., Jr. "California and the Search for the Ideal." *Annals of the Association of American Geographers* 62 (June 1972): 185–210.

———. *This Scene of Man: The Role and Structure of the City in the Geography of Western Civilization.* New York: Harper & Row, 1977.

Warner, Sam Bass, Jr. *The Urban Wilderness: A History of the American City.* New York: Harper & Row, 1972.

Wilkinson, Charles. "Paradise Revised." In *Atlas of the New West,* ed. William E. Riebsame, 15–44. New York: W. W. Norton, 1997.

Wilson, James Q. "A Guide to Reagan Country: The Political Culture of Southern California." *Commentary* 43 (May 1967): 37–45.

8. Reshaping the Nation

Abbott, Carl. "Dimensions of Regional Change in Washington, D.C." *American Historical Review* 95 (December 1990): 1367–93.

Abu-Lughod, Janet L. *New York, Chicago, Los Angeles: America's Global Cities.* Minneapolis: Univ. of Minnesota Press, 1999.

Agnew, John A. "Beyond Core and Periphery: The Myth of Regional Political-Economic Restructuring and Sectionalism in Contemporary American Politics." *Political Geography Quarterly* 7 (April 1988): 127–39.

Atherton, Lewis. *Main Street on the Middle Border.* Bloomington: Indiana Univ. Press, 1954.

Atlas, James. "The Million-Dollar Diploma." *New Yorker,* July 19, 1999.

Bagli, Charles V. "Known as Poacher, New Jersey Is Faced by Rival to the West." *New York Times,* March 20, 2000.

Barboza, David. "Chicago, Offering Big Incentives, Will Be Boeing's New Home." *New York Times,* May 11, 2001.

Barlett, Donald L., and James B. Steele. "The Empire of the Pigs." *Time,* November 30, 1998, 52–66.

Beauregard, Robert A. *Atop the Urban Hierarchy.* Totowa, N.J.: Rowman & Littlefield, 1989.

———. *Voices of Decline: The Postwar Fate of U.S. Cities.* Cambridge, Mass.: Blackwell, 1993.

Bender, Thomas. "New York as a Center of 'Difference.'" *Dissent* 34 (Fall 1987): 429–35.

Bennett, Robert A. "New York: The World Financial Market." *New York Times,* March 22, 1983.

Berry, Brian J. L. *The Human Consequences of Urbanization: Divergent Paths in the Urban Experience of the Twentieth Century.* New York: St. Martin's Press, 1973.

———. "'The Nature of Cities' and Beyond." In *World Patterns of Modern Urban Change,* ed. Michael P. Conzen, 437–55. Essays in Honor of Chauncy D. Harris. Research Paper No. 217–218. Chicago: Department of Geography, Univ. of Chicago, 1986.

Boger, John Charles. "The Kerner Commission Report in Retrospect." In *Race and Ethnicity in the United States,* ed. Stephen Steinberg, 8–36. Malden, Mass.: Blackwell Publishers, 2000.

Bradsher, Keith. "Ford Is Moving Lincoln-Mercury Headquarters to California." *New York Times,* January 23, 1998.

Brunn, Stanley D., and James O. Wheeler, eds. *The American Metropolitan System: Present and Future.* New York: John Wiley & Sons, 1980.

Cassidy, John. "The Comeback." *New Yorker* (*California Issue*), February 23–March 2, 1998, 122–27.

"Corporate Welfare." *Time,* November 9, 1998, 38–40.

Cox, Kevin R. "The American Politics of Local Economic Development: From Locality to Center and Back Again." Unpublished paper, Reflections on the "Institutional Turn" in Local Economic Development, Sheffield, England, September 9–10, 1998.

Dear, Michael, and Steven Flusty. "Postmodern Urbanism." *Annals of the Association of American Geographers* 88 (March 1998): 50–72.

Donahue, John D. *Disunited States.* New York: Basic Books, 1997.

Firestone, David. "Suburban Comforts Thwart Atlanta's Plans to Limit Sprawl." *New York Times,* November 21, 1999.

Frederickson, George M. *The Comparative Imagination: On the History of Racism, Nationalism, and Social Movements.* Berkeley: Univ. of California Press, 1997.

Gaustad, Edwin Scott, and Philip L. Barlow. *New Historical Atlas of Religion in America.* New York: Oxford Univ. Press, 2001.

Glater, Jonathan D. "Wharton School to Start Program in San Francisco." *New York Times,* December 13, 2000.

Glazer, Nathan. *We Are All Multiculturalists Now.* Cambridge: Harvard Univ. Press, 1997.

Godfrey, Brian J. "Restructuring and Decentralization in a World City." *Geographical Review* 85 (October 1995): 436–57.

Gordon, Milton M. *Assimilation in American Life: The Role of Race, Religion, and National Origins.* New York: Oxford Univ. Press, 1964.

Graham, Hugh Davis, and Nancy Diamond. *The Rise of American Research Universities: Elites and Challengers in the Postwar Era.* Baltimore: Johns Hopkins Univ. Press, 1997.

Grosfoguel, Ramón. "Global Logics in the Caribbean City System: The Case of Miami." In *World Cities in a World System,* ed. Paul L. Knox and Peter J. Taylor, 156–70. Cambridge: Cambridge Univ. Press, 1995.

Hacker, Andrew. *Two Nations: Black and White, Separate, Hostile, Unequal.* New York: Charles Scribner's Sons, 1992.

Halvorson, Peter L., and William M. Newman. *Atlas of Religious Change in America, 1952–1990.* Atlanta: Glenmary Research Center, 1994.

Hammond, Philip E. *The Protestant Presence in Twentieth-Century America: Religion and Political Culture.* Albany: State Univ. of New York Press, 1992.

Hollie, Pamela G. "California's Banking Shuttle." *New York Times,* March 2, 1979.

Hollinger, David. "The Ethno-Racial Pentagon." In *Race and Ethnicity in the United States,* ed. Stephen Steinberg, 197–210. Malden, Mass.: Blackwell Publishers, 2000.

Huxtable, Ada Louise. "Deep in the Heart of Nowhere." *New York Times,* February 15, 1976.

Kaplan, David H., and Steven R. Holloway. *Segregation in Cities.* Washington, D.C.: Association of American Geographers, 1998.

Kazal, Russell A. "Revisiting Assimilation: The Rise, Fall, and Reappraisal of a Concept in American Ethnic History." *American Historical Review* 100 (April 1995): 437–71.

Knox, Paul L., and Peter J. Taylor, eds. *World Cities in a World System.* Cambridge: Cambridge Univ. Press, 1995.

Kristol, Irving. "Faith à la Carte." *Times Literary Supplement,* May 26, 2000, 14–15.

Leff, Laurel. "More Big Publishers Open Offices on West Coast." *Wall Street Journal,* June 8, 1979.

Levin, Doron P. "Motor City for Japanese in California." *New York Times,* May 7, 1990.

Lubiano, Wahneema. *The House That Race Built: Black Americans, U.S. Terrain.* New York: Pantheon Books, 1997.

Lynch, Jean, and David R. Meyer. "Dynamics of the U.S. System of Cities, 1950–1980: The Impact of the Large Corporate Law Firm." *Urban Affairs Quarterly* 28 (1992): 38–68.

Marvel, Bill. "America's Art Scene Spreads from New York . . . ." *Wall Street Journal,* June 8, 1979.

Massey, Douglas S., and Nancy A. Denton. *American Apartheid: Segregation and the Making of the Underclass.* Cambridge: Harvard Univ. Press, 1993.

Mulder, James T. "States Compete to Lure Business." *Syracuse Herald-Journal,* June 5, 1998.

Newman, Bruce. "From the Land of Private Freeways Comes Car Culture Shock." *New York Times,* October 16, 1997.

Nordheimer, Jon. "Nesting beyond the Snowbirds, Foreigners Flock to Miami's Luxury Condominiums." *New York Times,* February 20, 1996.

Novak, Michael. *The Rise of the Unmeltable Ethnics.* New York: Macmillan, 1973.

———. *Further Reflections on Ethnicity.* Middletown, Pa.: Jednota Press, 1977.

Patterson, Orlando. "What to Do When Busing Becomes Irrelevant." *New York Times,* July 18, 1999.

Peterson, Iver. "Three Luxury-Car Makers to Leave New Jersey." *New York Times,* February 25, 2000.

"The Point of View." *Scribner's Magazine* 8 (September 1890): 396.

Rischin, Moses. *"Our Own Kind": Voting by Race, Creed, or National Origin.* Santa Barbara, Calif.: Center for the Study of Democratic Institutions, 1960.

Schlesinger, Arthur M., Jr. "The Disuniting of America." In *Immigration: Debating the Issues,* ed. Nicholas Capaldi, 221–31. Amherst, N.Y.: Prometheus Books, 1997.

Soja, Edward W. *Postmodern Geographies: The Reassertion of Space in Critical Social Theory.* London: Verso, 1989.

Steinberg, Stephen, ed. *Race and Ethnicity in the United States: Issues and Debates.* Malden, Mass.: Blackwell Publishers, 2000.

Sterngold, James. "In Los Angeles, Tears and a

Feeling of Loss." *New York Times*, March 14, 2000.

Uchitelle, Louis. "Taxes Help Foot the Payrolls as States Vie for Employers." *New York Times*, August 11, 1998.

Vance, James E., Jr. "California and the Search for the Ideal." *Annals of the Association of American Geographers* 62 (June 1972): 185–210.

———. "Revolution in American Space since 1945, and a Canadian Contrast." In *North America: The Historical Geography of a Changing Continent*, ed. Robert D. Mitchell and Paul A. Groves, 438–59. Totowa, N.J.: Rowman & Littlefield, 1987.

Warf, Barney. "Global Dimensions of U.S. Legal Services." *Professional Geographer* 53 (August 2001): 398–406.

Wheeler, David C., and Morton E. O'Kelly. "Network Topology and City Accessibility of the Commercial Internet." *Professional Geographer* 51 (August 1999): 327–39.

Wheeler, James O. "Corporate Spatial Links with Financial Institutions: The Role of the Metropolitan Hierarchy." *Annals of the Association of American Geographers* 76 (June 1986): 262–74.

———. "Corporate Role of New York City in the Metropolitan Hierarchy." *Geographical Review* 80 (October 1990): 370–81.

Wheeler, James O., and Ronald L. Mitchelson. "Information Flows among Major Metropolitan Areas in the United States." *Annals of the Association of American Geographers* 79 (December 1989): 523–43.

Zelinsky, Wilbur. *The Enigma of Ethnicity: Another American Dilemma*. Iowa City: Univ. of Iowa Press, 2001.

PART THREE

1. Assertions: America and Europe

Costigliola, Frank. *Awkward Dominion: American Political, Economic, and Cultural Relations with Europe, 1919–1933*. Ithaca: Cornell Univ. Press, 1984.

Denny, Ludwell. *America Conquers Britain: A Record of Economic War*. New York: Alfred A. Knopf, 1930.

Eaton, Leonard K. *American Architecture Comes of Age: European Reaction to H. H. Richardson and Louis Sullivan*. Cambridge: MIT Press, 1972.

Fleming, Donald, and Bernard Bailyn, eds. *The Intellectual Migration: Europe and America, 1930–1960*. Cambridge: Harvard Univ. Press, 1969.

Rodgers, Daniel T. *Atlantic Crossings: Social Politics in a Progressive Age*. Cambridge: Harvard Univ. Press, 1998.

Rosenberg, Emily S. *Spreading the American Dream: American Economic and Cultural Expansion, 1890–1945*. New York: Hill and Wang, 1982.

Russell, Bertrand, et al. *The Impact of America on European Culture*. Boston: Beacon Press, 1951.

Saunders, Thomas J. *Hollywood in Berlin: American Cinema and Weimar Germany*. Berkeley: Univ. of California Press, 1994.

Strauss, David. *Menace in the West: The Rise of French Anti-Americanism in Modern Times*. Westport, Conn.: Greenwood Press, 1978.

Wells, H. G. *The Future in America: A Search after Realities*. New York: Harper & Brothers, 1906.

2. Impositions: War and Interwar, Europe and Asia

Bailey, Thomas A. *A Diplomatic History of the American People*. New York: F. S. Crofts, 1947.

Bensel, Richard Franklin. *Sectionalism and American Political Development, 1880–1980*. Madison: Univ. of Wisconsin Press, 1984.

Billington, James H. *The Icon and the Axe: An Interpretive History of Russian Culture*. New York: Vintage Books, 1970.

Blouet, Brian W. *Halford Mackinder: A Biography*. College Station: Texas A&M Press, 1987.

Bowman, Isaiah. *The New World: Problems in Political Geography.* Yonkers-on-Hudson, N.Y.: World Book, 1921.

———. *The Pioneer Fringe.* New York: American Geographical Society, 1931.

Chambers, Frank P., Christina Phelps Grant, and Charles C. Bayley. *This Age of Conflict: A Contemporary World History.* New York: Harcourt, Brace, 1946.

Cressey, George Babcock. *China's Geographic Foundations: A Survey of the Land and Its People.* New York: McGraw-Hill, 1934.

Curry, Roy Watson. *Woodrow Wilson and Far Eastern Policy, 1913–1921.* New York: Octagon Books, 1968.

Gelfand, Laurence E. *The Inquiry: American Preparations for Peace.* New Haven: Yale Univ. Press, 1963.

Gellner, Ernest. *Nations and Nationalism.* Oxford: Basil Blackwell, 1983.

Griswold, A. Whitney. *The Far Eastern Policy of the United States.* New York: Harcourt, Brace, 1938.

Hoover, Herbert. *America's First Crusade.* New York: Charles Scribner's Sons, 1942.

Iriye, Akira. *Across the Pacific: An Inner History of American-East Asian Relations.* New York: Harcourt, Brace & World, 1967.

Jansen, Marius B. *Japan and Its World: Two Centuries of Change.* Princeton: Princeton Univ. Press, 1980.

Kennedy, Paul. *The Rise and Fall of the Great Powers: Economic Change and Military Conflict from 1500 to 2000.* New York: Vintage Books, 1989.

Kohn, Hans. *American Nationalism: An Interpretative Essay.* New York: Crowell-Collier, 1961.

LaFeber, Walter. *The American Age: United States Foreign Policy at Home and Abroad.* 2d ed. New York: W. W. Norton, 1994.

McDougall, Walter A. *Promised Land, Crusader State: The American Encounter with the World since 1776.* Boston: Houghton Mifflin, 1997.

Mackinder, Halford J. *Democratic Ideals and Reality* [1919]. Republished with additional papers. New York: W. W. Norton, 1962.

McNeill, William H. *The Rise of the West: A History of the Human Community.* Chicago: Univ. of Chicago Press, 1963.

———. *The Pursuit of Power: Technology, Armed Force and Society since A.D. 1000.* Chicago: Univ. of Chicago Press, 1982.

Pratt, Julius W. *Challenge and Rejection: The United States and World Leadership, 1900–1921.* New York: Macmillan, 1967.

Reischauer, Edwin O. *The United States and Japan.* New York: Viking Press, 1965.

Schwabe, Klaus. *Woodrow Wilson, Revolutionary Germany, and Peacemaking, 1918–1919: Missionary Diplomacy and the Realities of Power.* Trans. Rita Kimber and Robert Kimber. Chapel Hill: Univ. of North Carolina Press, 1985.

Smith, Neil. "Bowman's New World and the Council on Foreign Relations." *Geographical Review* 76 (October 1986): 438–60.

Sprout, Harold, and Margaret Sprout. *The Rise of American Naval Power, 1776–1918.* Princeton: Princeton Univ. Press, 1942.

Spykman, Nicholas John. *America's Strategy in World Politics: The United States and the Balance of Power.* New York: Harcourt, Brace, 1942.

Stevens, William Oliver, and Allan Westcott. *A History of Sea Power.* New York: Doubleday, Doran, 1942.

Tocqueville, Alexis de. *Democracy in America.* Vol. 1. New York: Vintage Books, 1945.

Trewartha, Glenn Thomas. *Japan: A Physical, Cultural and Regional Geography.* Madison: Univ. of Wisconsin Press, 1945.

Williams, William Appleman. *American Russian Relations, 1781–1947.* New York: Rinehart, 1952.

Wilson, Woodrow. *The Papers of Woodrow Wilson.* Ed. Arthur S. Link. 51 vols. Princeton: Princeton Univ. Press, 1966–94.

Wimer, Kurt. "Woodrow Wilson and World Peace." In *Woodrow Wilson and a Revolutionary World, 1913–1921,* ed. Arthur S. Link, 146–73. Chapel Hill: Univ. of North Carolina Press, 1982.

Wright, John Kirtland. *Geography in the Making: The American Geographical Society, 1851–1951.* New York: American Geographical Society, 1952.

3. Impositions: Western Hemisphere

Benjamin, Thomas, and Mark Wasserman, eds. *Provinces of the Revolution: Essays on Regional Mexican History, 1910–1929.* Albuquerque: Univ. of New Mexico Press, 1990.

Berger, Carl. *The Writing of Canadian History: Aspects of English-Canadian Historical Writing: 1900–1970.* Toronto: Oxford Univ. Press, 1976.

Berger, Mark T. *Under Northern Eyes: Latin American Studies and U.S. Hegemony in the Americas, 1898–1990.* Bloomington: Indiana Univ. Press, 1995.

Bliss, Michael. "Canadianizing American Business: The Roots of the Branch Plant." In *Close the Forty-ninth Parallel, etc.: The Americanization of Canada,* ed. Ian Lumsden, 27–42. Toronto: Univ. of Toronto Press, 1970.

Bowman, Isaiah. *The New World: Problems in Political Geography.* 4th ed. Yonkers-on-Hudson, N.Y.: World Book, 1928.

Brebner, John Bartlet. *North Atlantic Triangle: The Interplay of Canada, the United States, and Great Britain.* Toronto: McClelland and Stewart, 1966.

Callcott, Wilfrid Hardy. *The Western Hemisphere: Its Influence on United States Policies to the End of World War II.* Austin: Univ. of Texas Press, 1968.

Cline, Howard F. *The United States and Mexico.* Cambridge: Harvard Univ. Press, 1963.

Conn, Stetson, and Byron Fairchild. *The Western Hemisphere: The Framework of Hemisphere Defense: United States Army in World War II,* Vol. 12, pt. 1. Washington, D.C.: Office of the Chief of Military History, Department of the Army, 1960.

Cook, Ramsay, with John T. Saywell and John C. Ricker. *Canada: A Modern Study.* Toronto: Clarke, Irwin, 1963.

Cornell, Paul G., Jean Hamelin, Fernand Ouellet, and Marcel Trudel. *Canada: Unity in Diversity.* Toronto: Holt, Rinehart and Winston of Canada, 1967.

Davies, R. E. G. *Airlines of the United States since 1914.* Washington, D.C.: Smithsonian Institution Press, 1988.

Gomick, C. W. "Foreign Ownership and Political Decay." In *Close the Forty-ninth Parallel, etc.: The Americanization of Canada,* ed. Ian Lumsden, 43–73. Toronto: Univ. of Toronto Press, 1970.

Hall, Linda B., and Don M. Coerver. *Revolution on the Border: The United States and Mexico, 1910–1920.* Albuquerque: Univ. of New Mexico Press, 1988.

Holden, Robert H., and Eric Zolov. *Latin America and the United States: A Documentary History.* New York: Oxford Univ. Press, 2000.

Hoover, Herbert. *The Memoirs of Herbert Hoover.* 3 vols. New York: Macmillan, 1952.

Knight, Alan. *U.S.-Mexican Relations, 1910–1940: An Interpretation.* San Diego: Center for Mexican Studies, Univ. of California, 1987.

Langer, William L., and S. Everett Gleason. *The Challenge of Isolation: The World Crisis of 1937–1940 and American Foreign Policy.* 2 vols. New York: Harper & Row, 1964.

Langley, Lester D. *The United States and the Caribbean in the Twentieth Century.* 4th ed. Athens: Univ. of Georgia Press, 1989.

McKercher, B. J. C. *Transition of Power: Britain's Loss of Global Pre-eminence to the United States, 1930–1945.* Cambridge: Cambridge Univ. Press, 1999.

Morchain, Janet. *Sharing a Continent: An Introduction to Canadian-American Relations.* Toronto: McGraw-Hill Ryerson, 1973.

Morton, W. L. *The Canadian Identity.* Madison: Univ. of Wisconsin Press, 1961.

Nicholson, Norman L. *Canada in the American Community.* Princeton: D. Van Nostrand, 1963.

"Oily Mexico—Horn of Plenty, or Leaky Sieve?" *Literary Digest* 80 (March 29, 1924): 38–44.

Rippy, J. Fred. *Globe and Hemisphere: Latin America's Place in the Postwar Foreign Relations of the United States.* [1958] Westport, Conn.: Greenwood Press, 1972.

Seidel, Robert N. *Progressive Pan Americanism: Development and United States Policy toward Latin America, 1906–1932.* Dissertation Series No. 45. Ithaca: Latin American Studies Program, Cornell Univ., 1973.

The Statesman's Year-Book: Statistical and Historical Annual of the States of the World for the Year 1931. London: Macmillan, 1931.

Stewart, Gordon T. *The American Response to*

Canada since 1776. East Lansing: Michigan State Univ. Press, 1992.

Thompson, John Herd, and Stephen J. Randall. *Canada and the United States: Ambivalent Allies*. Athens: Univ. of Georgia Press, 1994.

United States Presidential Addresses to the Cana-dian Parliament, 1943–1995. Ottawa: United States Embassy, July 4, 1995.

Wilgus, A. Curtis. *Latin America in Maps: Historic, Geographic, Economic*. New York: Barnes & Noble, 1943.

4. Redividing the World

Bemis, Samuel Flagg. *The United States as a World Power: A Diplomatic History, 1900–1950*. New York: Henry Holt, 1950.

Carroll, James. *Constantine's Sword: The Church and Jews, a History*. Boston: Houghton Mifflin, 2001.

Churchill, Winston. *Churchill Speaks, 1897–1963: Collected Speeches in Peace and War*. Ed. Robert Rhodes James. New York: Barnes & Noble, 1980.

Cornis-Pope, Marcel, and John Neubauer. *Towards a History of the Literary Cultures in East-Central Europe: Theoretical Reflectisons*. ACLS Occasional Paper No. 52. N.p.: American Council of Learned Societies, 2002.

Domarus, Max. *Hitler: Speeches and Proclamations, 1932–1945*. 4 vols. Wauconda, Ill.: Bolchazy-Carducci Publishers, 1990.

Fifield, Russell H., and G. Etzel Pearcy. *Geopolitics in Principle and Practice*. Boston: Ginn, 1944.

Hitler, Adolf. *Mein Kampf*. Complete and unabridged; fully annotated. Editorial sponsors: John Chamberlain, et al. New York: Reynal & Hitchcock, 1939.

Iriye, Akira. "Asian Perspectives on Containment." In *Containment: Concept and Policy*, ed. Terry L. Deibel and John Lewis Gaddis, 2: 481–99. Washington, D.C.: National Defense Policy Press, 1986.

———. *The Globalizing of America, 1913–1945: Cambridge History of American Foreign Rela-tions*. Vol. 3. Cambridge: Cambridge Univ. Press, 1993.

Leffler, Melvin P. *A Preponderance of Power: National Security, the Truman Administration, and the Cold War*. Stanford: Stanford Univ. Press, 1992.

McDougall, Walter A. *Promised Land, Crusader State: The American Encounter with the World since 1776*. Boston: Houghton Mifflin, 1997.

Miller, Theodore R. *Graphic History of the Americas*. New York: John Wiley, 1969.

Polelle, Mark. *Raising Cartographic Consciousness: The Social and Foreign Policy Vision of Geopolitics in the Twentieth Century*. Lanham, Md.: Lexington Books, 1999.

Pounds, Norman J. G. *Divided Germany and Berlin*. Princeton: D. Van Nostrand, 1962.

———. *Poland between East and West*. Princeton: D. Van Nostrand, 1964.

Smith, Tony. *America's Mission: The United States and the Worldwide Struggle for Democracy in the Twentieth Century*. Princeton: Princeton Univ. Press, 1994.

Snyder, Jack. *Myths of Empire: Domestic Politics and International Ambition*. Ithaca: Cornell Univ. Press, 1991.

Strachan, Hew. "The American Way of War." *TLS*, February 16, 2001, 7–8.

Whittlesey, Derwent. *German Strategy of World Conquest*. New York: Farrar & Rhinehart, 1942.

5. Impositions and Oppositions

Allinson, Gary D. *Japan's Postwar History*. Ithaca: Cornell Univ. Press, 1997.

Bailey, Paul J. *Postwar Japan: 1945 to the Present*. Oxford: Blackwell, 1996.

Boorstin, Daniel J. *The Americans: The Demo-cratic Experience*. New York: Vintage Books, 1974.

Carmichael, Joel. *Arabs Today*. New York: Anchor Books, 1977.

Cohen, Warren, I. *America in the Age of Soviet*

Power, 1945–1991. Cambridge: Cambridge Univ. Press, 1993.

Cronin, James E. *The World the Cold War Made: Order, Chaos, and the Return of History*. New York: Routledge, 1996.

East, W. Gordon, and A. E. Moodie, eds. *The Changing World: Studies in Political Geography*. London: George G. Harrap, 1956.

Easton, Stewart C. *The Rise and Fall of Western Colonialism: A Historical Survey from the Early Nineteenth Century to the Present*. New York: Frederick A. Praeger, 1964.

Fairbank, John King. *The United States and China*. Revised ed. New York: Viking Press, 1958.

Fulbright, J. William. *The Arrogance of Power*. New York: Random House, 1966.

Gaddis, John Lewis. *The Long Peace: Inquiries into the History of the Cold War*. New York: Oxford Univ. Press, 1987.

Gibson, James. "Russian Imperial Expansion in Context and by Contrast." *Journal of Historical Geography* 28 (April 2002): 181–202.

Harrison, Richard Edes. *Look at the World: The Fortune Atlas for World Strategy*. New York: Alfred A. Knopf, 1944.

Hoopes, Townsend. "Overseas Bases in American Strategy." *Foreign Affairs* 37 (October 1958): 69–82.

Iriye, Akira. "Asian Perspectives on Containment." In *Containment: Concept and Policy*, ed. Terry L. Deibel and John Lewis Gaddis, 2: 481–99. Washington, D.C.: National Defense Univ. Press, 1986.

Kennan, George F. *American Diplomacy, 1900–1950*. Chicago: Univ. of Chicago Press, 1951.

Kinzer, Stephen. "U.S. and Central America: Too Close for Comfort?" *New York Times*, July 28, 2002.

LaFeber, Walter. *America, Russia, and the Cold War, 1945–1966*. New York: John Wiley, 1967.

Leffler, Melvyn P. *A Preponderance of Power: National Security, the Truman Administration, and the Cold War*. Stanford: Stanford Univ. Press, 1992.

Longrigg, Stephen H. *The Middle East: A Social Geography*. Chicago: Aldine Publishing, 1963.

Lundestad, Geir. *The American "Empire" and Other Studies of U.S. Foreign Policy in a Comparative Perspective*. Oxford: Oxford Univ. Press, 1990.

MacKirdy, K. A., J. S. Moir, Y. F. Zoltvany. *Changing Perspectives in Canadian History: Selected Problems*. Don Mills, Ontario: J. M. Dent & Sons, 1971.

McNeill, William H. *Past and Future*. Chicago: Univ. of Chicago Press, 1954.

Mahant, Edelgard, and Graeme S. Mount. *Invisible and Inaudible in Washington: American Policies toward Canada*. Vancouver: UBC Press, 1999.

Niebuhr, Reinhold. *Pious and Secular America*. New York: Charles Scribner's Sons, 1958.

Pérez, Louis A., Jr. "'So Near and Yet So Foreign': Cuba and the United States, 1860–1960." *Culturefront* 2 (Winter 1993): 4–8, 23, 61.

Powers, Thomas. "The Secret Intelligence Wars." *New York Review of Books*, September 26, 2002, 32–35.

Raisz, Erwin. *Atlas of Global Geography*. New York: Global Press, 1944.

Resnick, Philip. "Canadian Defence Policy and the American Empire." In *Close the Forty-ninth Parallel, etc.: The Americanization of Canada*, ed. Ian Lumsden, 93–115. Toronto: Univ. of Toronto Press, 1970.

Schnabel, James F. *The History of the Joint Chiefs of Staff: The Joint Chiefs of Staff and National Policy*. Vol. 1, *1945–1947*. Wilmington, Del.: Michael Glazier, 1979.

Smith, Tony. "American Imperialism Is Anti-Communism." In *Imperialism and After: Continuities and Discontinuities*, ed. Wolfgang J. Mommsen and Jürgen Osterhammel, 41–48. London: Allen & Unwin, 1986.

Stambuk, George. *American Military Forces Abroad: Their Impact on the Western State System*. Columbus: Ohio State Univ. Press, 1963.

Steel, Ronald. *Pax Americana*. New York: Viking Press, 1967.

Steiner, George. *Nostalgia for the Absolute*. Toronto: Canadian Broadcasting Corp., 1944.

Treadgold, Donald W. *Twentieth Century Russia*. Chicago: Rand McNally, 1959.

U.S. Department of State. *Foreign Relations of the United States, 1946*. Vol. 6, *Eastern Europe;*

the Soviet Union. Washington, D.C.: Government Printing Office, 1969.

———. *Foreign Relations of the United States, 1950*. Vol. 1, *National Security Affairs; Foreign Economic Policy*. Washington, D.C.: Government Printing Office, 1977.

Walker, Martin. *The Cold War: A History*. New York: Henry Holt, 1993.

Wines, Michael. "Bush and Yeltsin Declare Formal End to Cold War; Agree to Exchange Visits." *New York Times*, February 2, 1992.

6. *America and the World*

Agnew, John. *Geopolitics: Re-Visioning World Politics*. London: Routledge, 1998.

Agnew, John, and Stuart Corbridge. *Mastering Space: Hegemony, Territory and International Political Economy*. London: Routledge, 1995.

Alper, Donald K. "The Idea of Cascadia: Emergent Transborder Regionalisms in the Pacific Northwest-Western Canada." *Journal of Borderland Studies* 11 (Fall 1996): 1–22.

Bagby, Philip. *Culture and History: Prolegomena to the Comparative Study of Civilizations*. Berkeley: Univ. of California Press, 1963.

Balthazar, Louis. *French Canadian Civilization*. Washington, D.C.: Association for Canadian Studies, 1989.

Brands, H. W. *Bound to Empire: The United States and the Philippines*. New York: Oxford Univ. Press, 1992.

Buruma, Ian. "The Road to Babel." *New York Review of Books*, May 31, 2001, 23–25.

Bustamante, Jorge A. "The Mexico-U.S. Border: A Line of Paradox." In *Identities in North America: The Search for Community*, ed. Robert L. Earle and John D. Wirth, 180–94. Stanford: Stanford Univ. Press, 1995.

"The Challenge," *Time*, March 17, 1947, 71–81.

Crystal, David. *English as a Global Language*. Cambridge: Cambridge Univ. Press, 1997.

Darton, Eric. *Divided We Stand: A Biography of New York's World Trade Center*. New York: Basic Books, 1999.

"A Defining Century in America." Editorial. *New York Times*, December 31, 1999.

Dickstein, Morris. "The Fifties Were Radical Too." *TLS*, June 8, 2001, 13–15.

Eggleston, Wilfrid. *Newfoundland: The Road to Confederation*. Ottawa: Information Canada, 1974.

Fry, Earl H. "Quebec's Relations with the United States." *American Review of Canadian Studies* 32 (Summer 2002): 323–42.

Giddens, Anthony. *Runaway World: How Globalization Is Reshaping Our Lives*. New York: Routledge, 2000.

Gillespie, Angus Kress. *Twin Towers: The Life of New York City's World Trade Center*. New Brunswick, N.J.: Rutgers Univ. Press, 1999.

Goodno, James B. *The Philippines: Land of Broken Promises*. London: Zed Books, 1991.

Grant, George. *Lament for a Nation: The Defeat of Canadian Nationalism*. Toronto: McClelland and Stuart, 1965; reprinted with an Introduction, Macmillan of Canada, 1978.

Harris, Cole. "The Emotional Structure of Canadian Regionalism." In *The Challenges of Canada's Regional Diversity*. The Walter L. Gordon Lecture Series. Toronto: Canadian Studies Foundation, 1981, 5: 9–30.

Havel, Václav. "The Charms of NATO." *New York Review of Books*, January 15, 1998, 24.

How the World Sees Us. Special Issue. *New York Times Magazine*, June 8, 1997, sec. 6.

Hughes, Thomas P. *American Genesis: A Century of Inventions and Technological Enthusiasm, 1870–1970*. New York: Viking Press, 1980.

Huntington, Samuel P. *The Clash of Civilizations and the Remaking of World Order*. New York: Simon and Schuster, 1996.

Hutton, Thomas A. *The Transformation of Canada's Pacific Metropolis: A Study of Vancouver*. Montreal: Institute for Research in Public Policy, 1998.

James, Harold. *The End of Globalization: Lessons from the Great Depression*. Cambridge: Harvard Univ. Press, 2001.

Johnston, R. J., Peter J. Taylor, Michael J. Watts, eds. *Geographies of Global Change: Remapping the World in the Late Twentieth Century*. Oxford: Blackwell, 1995.

Kaplan, David H. "Two Nations in Search of a State: Canada's Ambivalent Spatial Identities." *Annals of the Association of American Geographers* 84 (December 1994): 585–606.

Karolle, Bruce G. *Atlas of Micronesia*. 2d ed. Honolulu: Bess Press, n.d. [c. 1991].

Kazin, Alfred. "In Washington." *New York Review of Books*, May 29, 1986, 11–18.

Langley, Lester D. *The United States and the Caribbean in the Twentieth Century*. Athens: Univ. of Georgia Press, 1989.

Latouche, Serge. *The Westernization of the World: The Significance, Scope and Limits of the Drive towards Global Uniformity*. Oxford: Blackwell, 1996.

Lecker, Robert, coordinating ed. *Borderlands: Essays in Canadian-American Relations*. Toronto: ECW Press, 1991.

Leibowitz, Arnold T. *Defining Status: A Comprehensive Analysis of United States Territorial Relations*. Dordrecht: Martinus Nijhoff Publishers, 1989.

Lerner, Max. *America as a Civilization: Life and Thought in the United States Today*. New York: Simon and Schuster, 1957.

Lundestad, Geir, ed. *No End to Alliance: The United States and Western Europe: Past, Present and Future*. New York: St. Martin's Press, 1998.

McArthur, Tom. *The English Languages*. Cambridge: Cambridge Univ. Press, 1998.

McCann, L. D. *Heartland and Hinterland: A Geography of Canada*. 2d ed. Scarborough, Ont.: Prentice-Hall Canada, 1987.

McPherson, James. "Quebec Whistles Dixie." *Saturday Night*, March 1998, 13–24, 72.

Matthews, Geoffrey J., and Robert Morrow, Jr. *Canada and the World: An Atlas Resource*. Scarborough, Ont.: Prentice-Hall Canada, 1985.

Meinig, Donald W. "Culture Blocs and Political Blocs: Emergent Patterns in World Affairs." *Western Humanities Review* 10 (Summer 1956): 203–22.

Mulcahy, Kevin V. "Cultural Imperialism and Cultural Sovereignty: U.S.-Canadian Cultural Relations." *American Review of Canadian Studies* 30 (Summer 2000): 181–206.

Mumford, Lewis. *The City in History: Its Origins, Its Transformations, and Its Prospects*. New York: Harcourt, Brace & World, 1961.

———. *The Myth of the Machine: The Pentagon of Power*. New York: Harcourt, Brace Jovanovich, 1964, 1970.

O'Rourke, Kevin H., and Jeffrey G. Williamson. *Globalization and History: The Evolution of a Nineteenth-Century Economy*. Cambridge: MIT Press, 1999.

O'Tuathail, Gearóid. "The Postmodern Geopolitical Condition: States, Statecraft, and Security at the Millennium." *Annals of the Association of American Geographers* 90 (March 2000): 166–78.

Paz, Octavio. *One Earth, Four or Five Worlds: Reflections on Contemporary History*. San Diego: Harcourt Brace Jovanovich, 1985.

Pérez, Louis A., Jr. *Cuba and the United States: Ties of Singular Intimacy*. Athens: Univ. of Georgia Press, 1990.

———. *On Becoming Cuban: Identity, Nationality, and Culture*. Chapel Hill: Univ. of North Carolina Press, 1999.

Porter, Philip W., and Eric S. Sheppard. *A World of Difference: Society, Nature, Development*. New York: Guilford Press, 1998.

Quigley, Carroll. *The Evolution of Civilizations: An Introduction to Historical Analysis*. New York: Macmillan, 1961.

Randall, Stephen J., and Graeme S. Mount. *The Caribbean Basin: An International History*. London: Routledge, 1998.

Samuels, Marwyn. "To Rescue Place." *Progress in Human Geography* 16, no. 4 (1992): 597–604.

Schell, Paul, and John Hamer. "Cascadia: The New Binationalism of Western Canada and the Pacific Northwest." In *Identities in North America*, ed. Robert L. Earle and John D. Wirth, 140–56. Stanford: Stanford Univ. Press, 1995.

Smith, Alan. *Doing the Continental: Conceptualizations of the Canadian-American Relationship in the Long Twentieth Century*. Canadian-American Public Policy No. 44. Orono, Maine: Canadian-American Center, 2000.

Smith, Merritt Roe, and Leo Marx, eds. *Does Technology Drive History? The Dilemma of Technological Determinism*. Cambridge: MIT Press, 1994.

Smith, Michael. *Western Europe and the United States: The Uncertain Alliance*. London: George Allen & Unwin, 1984.

Spengler, Oswald. *The Decline of the West*. 2 vols. New York: Alfred A. Knopf, 1926, 1928.

Stille, Alexander. "Globalization Now, a Sequel of Sorts." *New York Times*, August 11, 2001.

Stuart, Reginald. "Review Essay: Anti-Americanism in Canadian History." *American Review of Canadian Studies* 27 (Summer 1997): 293–310.

Toynbee, Arnold J. *A Study of History*. Abridgement of vols. 1–4 by D. C. Somervell. New York: Oxford Univ. Press, 1947.

Toynbee, Arnold J., and Edward D. Myers. *Historical Atlas and Gazetteer: A Study of History*. Vol. 11. London: Oxford Univ. Press, 1959.

The United Nations. Photographs by Ezra Stoller; Introduction by Jane C. Loeffler. New York: Princeton Architectural Press, 1999.

Verhovek, Sam Howe. "Torn between Nations, Mexican Americans Can Have Both." *New York Times*, April 14, 1998.

Von Laue, Theodore H. *The World Revolution of Westernization: The Twentieth Century in Global Perspective*. New York: Oxford Univ. Press, 1987.

Widdis, Randy William. "Borders, Borderlands and Canadian Identity: A Canadian Perspective." *International Journal of Canadian Studies* 15 (Spring 1997): 49–66.

Zaide, Sonia M. *The Philippines: A Unique Nation*. 2d ed. Quezon City: All-Nations Publishing, 1999.

INDEX